MW01630540

HELL
BY THE
ACRE

A Narrative History of the
Stones River Campaign,
November 1862–January 1863

Daniel A. Masters

Savas Beatie

California

Names: Masters, Daniel A., author.
Title: Hell by the Acre: A Narrative History of the Stones River Campaign, November 1862–January 1863 / Daniel A. Masters.
Other titles: Narrative History of the Stones River Campaign, November 1862–January 1863
Description: El Dorado Hills, CA: Savas Beatie, [2025] | Includes bibliographical references and index. | Summary: "After major defeats at Fredericksburg in Virginia and Chickasaw Bayou in Mississippi, it fell to Maj. Gen. William S. Rosecrans and his Army of the Cumberland to secure a victory that would give military teeth to the Emancipation Proclamation set to take effect on January 1, 1863. The full campaign was one of the largest and bloodiest battles of the war. This is an unparalleled soldier's view of Civil War combat and tactical command. Stones River marked a turning point for Federal fortunes in the Western Theater" —Provided by publisher.
Identifiers: LCCN 2024016440 | ISBN 9781611217124 (hardcover) | ISBN 9781611217131 (ebook)
Subjects: LCSH: Stones River, Battle of, Murfreesboro, Tenn., 1862-1863.
Classification: LCC E474.77 .M28 2024 | DDC 973.7/33—dc23/eng/20240418
LC record available at https://lccn.loc.gov/2024016440

First Savas Beatie Edition, Second Printing

SB

Savas Beatie
989 Governor Drive, Suite 102
El Dorado Hills, CA 95762
916-941-6896
www.savasbeatie.com
sales@savasbeatie.com

All Savas Beatie titles are available for bulk purchase discounts. Contact us for details.

Printed and bound in the United Kingdom

Dedicated to my ancestor James A. McLargin,
who gave his life at Stones River, and to all the men, blue and gray,
who consecrated that field so long ago.

Andy Thomas

Contents

Contents (continued)

Acknowledgments and a biography of the author follow the index

List of Maps

Photos have been placed throughout the book for the benefit of the reader.

Foreword

MAJOR GENERAL WILLIAM Starke Rosecrans took command of the newly designated Army of the Cumberland—formerly the Army of the Ohio—on October 30, 1862, three weeks after the Battle of Perryville. He replaced Maj. Gen. Don Carlos Buell, who the Lincoln administration found wanting after the Kentucky Campaign. Rosecrans's tenure would run 11 days short of one year until October 19, 1863, when Ulysses S. Grant replaced him with George H. Thomas. Under Rosecrans, the Army of the Cumberland grew and transformed into one of the three great armies of the Republic, destined to play a crucial role in winning the war and suppressing the rebellion.

As noted by the change in designation, Rosecrans inherited a force in transition. It was also in the middle of a supply crisis, as Confederate raids and the invasion of Kentucky disrupted the rail line between Louisville and Nashville, the army's two most important bases. It was also absorbing tens of thousands of new recruits in dozens of new regiments, rushed into service to meet the threat of Confederate invasion. Many of those new men saw their first combat at Perryville, that strange, lopsided battle for control of Kentucky. Prior to his promotion, Rosecrans had fought and won his own battle at Corinth, Mississippi, just a fortnight before. There, he led a force one-third his new command's size. Preparing the Army of the Cumberland to secure its rear and for future offensive missions was a huge task.

Confederate General Braxton Bragg, Buell's opponent in Kentucky and now Rosecrans's adversary in Tennessee, rose to command the Army of Mississippi in

June 1862, whose name would change to the Army of Tennessee that November. He would be this Western army's longest-tenured commander, holding the position for 17 months until President Jefferson Davis accepted Bragg's letter of resignation on December 3, 1863, after a damaging defeat at Chattanooga. During that time the army experienced great internal turmoil, at times nearing outright mutiny, despite Davis's largely ineffectual efforts to instill peace within the high command. Simply put, Bragg's querulous personality did not inspire harmony, but he was also saddled with equally quarrelsome and headstrong subordinates who, over time, increasingly found him wanting as a general.

The Battle of Stones River (Murfreesboro, to the Confederates) marked a significant milestone in the development of both armies. It was the first of three critical campaigns between these two forces and these commanders. The others were Tullahoma in the summer of 1863, and Chickamauga later that fall. Each campaign saw an increase in geographic scope. Although Tullahoma did not result in a major battle, Rosecrans forced Bragg out of Middle Tennessee via maneuver; the collision at Chickamauga in North Georgia resulted in the second bloodiest battle of the entire war.

Unlike in the Eastern Theater, where the Army of the Potomac often outnumbered Robert E. Lee's Army of Northern Virginia, the contest between Bragg and Rosecrans was about even. In early December, Bragg's army numbered 49,500 men, while Rosecrans could count about 55,000, some of whom would have to remain to guard Nashville during any offensive operations. Rosecrans carried about 41,500 to the field at Stones River, while Rebel estimates vary between 35,000–37,000. That number would have been larger had Bragg not been forced to detach Carter Stevenson's entire division to Mississippi on the eve of battle. In a similar vein, at Chickamauga in September 1863, Rosecrans engaged just fewer than 61,000 officers and men, while Bragg's command numbered nearly 65,000. In each case the strength advantage for the larger force was minimal and was not the decisive factor in success.

In many ways, Stones River was a curious battle. Although Rosecrans was on the offensive in the campaign, the battle saw a role reversal with Bragg's army doing most of the attacking. Each general adopted a similar battle plan, attacking with their respective left wings while holding on the right. Bragg threw the first punch, derailing Rosecrans's plans before they fully developed. As happened at Perryville (and foreshadowing Chickamauga) Union Maj. Gen. Alexander McCook's "Right Wing" was surprised and all but routed by the early attack, a fact that produced considerable finger-pointing and blame-laying after the battle was over.

The Union rout that followed did not produce a complete victory for Bragg. Instead, Rosecrans's men grimly clung to their final positions on the night of December 31 and, to the Confederates' shock and dismay, refused to retreat to Nashville. A second Rebel assault delivered two days later on January 2 failed utterly. On January 3, Bragg concluded that he had no choice but to fall back. This marked the second time in two battles that the Army of Tennessee had achieved tactical success but conducted an operational retreat. Bragg's decision astounded civilians, the Confederate government, and the army itself. The rift between Bragg and some of his generals, unhealed by the failure in Kentucky, widened. Long months of discontent ensued.

Though far from the largest battle of the war either by size of the force engaged or by overall casualty count, it was nonetheless an intense engagement. Total casualties were 24,645—more than 13,000 Federals and 11,000 Confederates, or 32.2 percent of the total forces involved. By contrast, Maj. Gen. George Gordon Meade's Federals at Gettysburg suffered a 24.7 percent loss and Lee's army 31.6 percent. The severity of the combat on December 31 and January 2 cannot be understated. Both armies went toe-to-toe and paid the price for doing so. Federal resilience matched Confederate tenacity—characteristics that would become hallmarks of both the Army of the Cumberland and the Army of Tennessee in the more than two years of fighting yet to come.

Many students of the war first come to appreciate a battle or campaign thanks to a visit to a national park. While Stones River National Battlefield serves as that gateway today, the limited nature of the modern park makes much of the action hard to grasp. In 1896, a veterans' association placed an option on thousands of more acres, intending to create a park similar to Chickamauga & Chattanooga National Military Park in Georgia and Tennessee. The United States Congress failed to pass the needed legislation. A much smaller park came into being in 1927 with just 570 acres—a fraction of the estimated 3,000 acres over which the main engagements unfolded.

Even today, with additional acquisitions and donations, only 709 acres are protected. While much of the battle has been lost to development (including key sites of the opening action on December 31), what remains still allows students to interpret many of the most crucial fights. Despite the current urban sprawl, acquisition opportunities still exist. Hopefully, over time, more land will be preserved. The park we have now should not be overlooked because of past lapses; this magnificent ground can still teach a dedicated scholar much about the battle.

Although the literature of the Civil War's Western Theater has not entirely neglected the battle, no single extant work can be considered definitive. In addition to some broad overview and specialty titles, there are just three modern studies of Stones River: James McDonough's *Stones River—Bloody Winter in Tennessee* (1980), Peter Cozzens's *No Better Place to Die: The Battle of Stones River* (1987), and Larry J. Daniel's *Battle of Stones River: The Forgotten Conflict between the Confederate Army of Tennessee and the Union Army of the Cumberland* (2012). All three have their merits and remain valuable contributions, and all three are largely top-down military and political studies. This new volume takes a much deeper dive into the campaign and battle.

Since both armies remained inactive in the six months following Stones River, there was ample time for commanders to draft reports, for civilian reporters and soldier-correspondents to write epistles to their hometown broadsheets, and for thousands of participants to digest and record their impressions of the struggle—all of which provides modern scholars a treasure trove of primary sources upon which to draw. Although Stones River is arguably one of the best documented battles of the war, there are still important untapped sources available. The most significant of these are the approximately 30 Confederate official reports of the battle that did not find their way into Volume 20 of the *Official Records* but are included in the Braxton Bragg Papers at the Western Reserve Historical Society. Equally crucial in importance are the many detailed soldier letters in period newspapers that put flesh on the bones and personalities to the statistics found in the official reports.

We are in a new era of Civil War scholarship. While this golden age is in part driven by the unprecedented ease of access to new source material thanks to the benefits of search engines and archival digital access, it is not solely due to a wealth of previously underused accounts. We are also benefitting from a new approach to military history that includes a broader spectrum of viewpoints, from a reappraisal of battle tactics to an exploration of environmental factors—without neglecting the work that has come before.

Hell by the Acre is a fine example of this new synthesis. Dan Masters has mined all these resources to produce both an unparalleled soldier's view of the battle and a superb command study.

David A. Powell

Introduction

"THE HISTORIES OF the Lost Cause are all written out by big bugs, generals and renowned historians," declared Sam Watkins in his landmark Civil War memoir *"1861 vs 1882. "Co. Aytch," Maury Grays, First Tennessee Regiment. or, A Side Show of the Big Show*, better known today as simply *Company Aytch*. As far as Sam was concerned, he had as much right to pen a history of his experiences as anyone. As he explained it, "I propose to tell of the fellows who did the shooting and the killing, the fortifying and ditching, the sweeping of the streets, the drilling, the standing guard, and who drew the ramrod and tore the cartridge."

Those few simple words perfectly describe why I wrote *Hell by the Acre*: to ensure that the men who did the actual fighting get their just due in the history of the Stones River campaign.

*　　*　　*

The Battle of Stones River provided the United States with a much-needed victory at a time when the fortunes of the Union had seemingly reached their nadir. Stymied at Fredericksburg, Virginia, and Chickasaw Bayou near Vicksburg, President Abraham Lincoln pinned his hopes for a victory on Maj. Gen. William S. Rosecrans and his Army of the Cumberland.

Marching from Nashville the day after Christmas 1862, Rosecrans's 41,500-man army took four days to arrive just northwest of Murfreesboro, where General Braxton Bragg and his 37,000-man Army of Tennessee awaited. On the last day of the year the two armies clashed in some of the war's most brutal fighting to date. By the time it ended, the casualty list approached 25,000, making it the sixth bloodiest battle of the entire war and the second bloodiest in the Western Theater.

The majority of these casualties occurred during a 10-hour slugfest on December 31 and roughly two hours on January 2, with nearly one in three men (32 percent) killed, wounded, or captured. Stones River rivals Antietam as the bloodiest 12 hours in American military history and was fought with 40,000 fewer men.

For more than a century after the war, the story of this campaign received scant scholarly attention. The only book-length studies were William D. Bickham's hagiographic 1863 tome *Rosecrans' Campaign with the Fourteenth Army Corps* and Alexander F. Stevenson's *The Battle of Stone's River Near Murfreesboro, Tenn.* in 1884.

The first modern historian to deliver a balanced treatment of the campaign was James Lee McDonough's *Stones River—Bloody Winter in Tennessee* (1980). A decade later Peter Cozzens released the first in a trilogy of the war in Tennessee with *No Better Place to Die: The Battle of Stones River* (1991), which remains the standard work on the battle. Lanny Smith released his privately printed two-volume campaign study *The Stone's River Campaign 26 December 1862 — 5 January 1863* in 2008 and 2010, a mammoth and detailed study that incorporated numerous heretofore undiscovered Confederate brigade and regimental after-action reports. Shortly thereafter, Larry J. Daniel weighed in with *Battle of Stones River: The Forgotten Conflict Between the Confederate Army of Tennessee and Union Army of the Cumberland* (2012), a fine overall history with a deeper examination of the political context of the campaign. All of these contribute mightily to the historiography of the campaign, adopting a mostly top-down view of the action with the narrative driven by accounts of the political and military leaders who set the events in motion.

To understand the battle from a different perspective, we need to shift our point of view to that shared by most of the men who lived through those events: the ground-level view experienced by the men in the ranks. As Sam Watkins might have asked, "What about what I saw and experienced?" *Hell by the* Acre is intended to fill that niche.

I approached the task of attempting to describe this Civil War battle with no little trepidation. Battle at its core is bloody terrifying chaos, which in turn makes soldier accounts little more than snapshots touching faintly upon the reality of the action being described. For the participants, the war was little more than the narrow slice of what they individually saw and did. Many correspondents frankly admitted their pens and command of language were inadequate to describe what they experienced. They could speak to its horrors in snippets and vignettes, but none could contemplate the whole, let alone command the language necessary to impart its reality to others.

Depicting Stones River as viewed from the ranks with a heavy emphasis on the accounts of company-level officers and enlisted men is the primary focus of this work. In the process of reading, reviewing, and processing thousands of documents about this campaign, I drew from the strongest sources to provide the best "you are there" feel and experience without overwhelming readers with minutiae. It is admittedly a messy process at best, but I hope readers will find this detailed ground-level view of combat at Stones River both fresh and enlightening—complimenting prior studies rather than competing with them.

To accomplish this, I assembled more than 20,000 pages of source material on the campaign and have walked nearly every inch of the battlefield, whether it is grass, trees, and limestone, or parking lots, buildings, and golfing greens. During the last seven years I used my research to publish more than 100 articles about varying aspects of Stones River on my blog Dan Masters' Civil War Chronicles. My work on this topic includes several articles in nationally recognized publications, including *America's Civil War* and *North & South*. I believe I understand the strategy, tactics, operational aspects, and terrain of this campaign as well as anyone.

But for me, there is more to this project than just an academic fascination with this battle. In September 2021, I toured several Tennessee battlefields with a group of fellow Civil War buffs. One of our most poignant stops was a visit to the grave of the aforementioned Confederate soldier and writer Sam Watkins. As a member of the 1st Tennessee, Watkins took part in the ferocious fighting at Stones River and was badly wounded charging the Wilkinson Pike. A cedar tree just a few yards from his grave beckoned my family's deep connection to Stones River.

Three of my forebears fought at Stones River in Rosecrans's army. Statistically speaking, we were like just about everyone else, losing one of the three. My fourth great-uncle James McLargin, a private in the 21st Ohio, was mortally wounded in the head on December 31, 1862. He was hit in the so-called "Slaughter Pen" amid cedar trees like the one growing over Sam Watkins' grave. Uncle Jim died of his wounds a few weeks later in Nashville and is buried at the national cemetery beneath a gravestone bearing the wrong name: Joseph McLargin.

My fascination with the campaign was triggered when I learned Uncle Jim's story in the late 1990s. A few pieces of bark and a sprig from the cedar tree growing over Sam Watkins's grave in Columbia, Tennessee, occupied an honored space on my desk throughout the writing process. They served as a constant reminder that I was writing this book for the ordinary men in the ranks like Sam and Uncle Jim, who shouldered their muskets, did their duty, and offered their lives in our country's greatest hour of peril.

This is their story.

A Study in Contrasts

ON THE MORNING of March 16, 1898, thousands of citizens lined the bustling streets of Los Angeles waving flags. Most were draped in black to mourn the death of one of the nation's few remaining Civil War generals. Some wore badges denoting membership in the Grand Army of the Republic or the United Confederate Veterans. "It was a soldier's funeral in the truest and tenderest sense of the word," reported the Los Angeles Herald. "There have been pageants more extensive and imposing when the other great Union generals were laid to rest, but never was there one more simply beautiful, more tender, and sympathetic than was that of Major General William S. Rosecrans."[1]

Such outpourings of emotion for Civil War veterans had become commonplace as the 20th Century approached, and now, more than 30 years since the guns had gone silent, the nation was on the precipice of war with Spain and a rising wave of nationalism had further inspired combatants of that earlier conflict to heal their wounds. Rosecrans's final letter, written mere weeks before his death on March 11, 1898, had focused on reconciliation with Confederate veterans. "My heart goes out in greeting to our brothers of the South, knowing well their dash and gallantry in the face of the leaden hail, their indomitable courage in the face of overwhelming obstacles," he wrote. "Happily, reunited and bound to us in the

---

1 "A Nation's Hero Honored: Stately Funeral of General William S. Rosecrans," *Los Angeles Herald*, Mar. 17, 1898, 7.

Major General William S. Rosecrans

Author's Collection

bonds of closest sympathy, should grim war again assail us, there will be none more ready with arms to strike as those gray-clad heroes and their descendants."[2]

The Army of the Cumberland's former commander valued this theme of reconciliation so much that he requested to have his casket borne to the grave by eight Civil War veterans: four Federals and four Confederates.[3] Rosecrans had outlived a number of prominent Union commanders: George Thomas, perhaps his closest friend during the war, passed in 1870, George Gordon Meade in 1872, and Ambrose Burnside in 1881, followed by Ulysses Grant, his wartime nemesis, and George McClellan, an old friend, in 1885. Rosecrans's protégé Phil Sheridan, a fellow Ohio Buckeye, died in 1888; William T. Sherman in 1891.

Moving to California after the war, Rosecrans entered politics. He would serve two terms in Congress, and one of his key actions was opposition to a bill providing a pension to Grant and his wife, Julia. Rosecrans was supposedly unaware of the precarious condition of Grant's family finances following his two presidential terms, but he had no doubt that Grant had destroyed his army career during the Civil War by making malicious false statements against him, particularly in the wake of the September 1863 Union travesty at Chickamauga. An unforgiveable sin for the devout Catholic.

Although bitter passions for some of his former commanders certainly died hard for Rosecrans, that did not extend to the men of the Army of the Cumberland. Almost to a man, those who served under "Rosey" adored him; he, in turn, had reciprocated. This esteem and respect were evident as the general's body lay in state at Los Angeles City Hall. More than 1,500 waited in line for a chance to pay their respects before the doors opened, and by the end of the day an estimated 15,000 mourners would pass through, among them veterans of Rosecrans's old commands.

"There were old men to whom the Civil War had been a stern reality, and young ones to whom it was but a fascinating tale of battles and heroes," the Herald declared. "There were aged women, plainly dressed, whose pained faces told of someone left on a Southern battlefield. A tall, square-shouldered veteran and a comrade with him leaned over the casket to see the face and burst into tears. Their

2 "A Nation's Hero Honored," 7.

3 Ibid., 7.

hands touched tenderly the shot riddled, tattered silk flag that lay on top. 'He was our commander,' they said as they slowly passed out.[4]

Praise came even from former enemies. Confederate veteran Spencer Thorpe, who fought Rosecrans's army in Tennessee with the legendary John Hunt Morgan's cavalry, was among those asked to serve as a pallbearer and would write that "in ability, in courage and magnanimity, [Rosecrans] had no superior among the military chieftains of the North. His chivalry was superb. When the sword was sheathed, he stood for a complete rehabilitation of the Union, a perfect reconciliation of the sections."[5]

The soldiers' fealty for Rosecrans began shortly after he assumed command of the army in October 1862. The new commander made it a point to see and be seen by his troops, his energy and constant drive immediately evident to all. That stood in stark contrast to his predecessor, Maj. Gen. Don Carlos Buell, rarely seen by his men and considered haughty, stiff, aloof, and unpopular. To help rebuild the army's morale, Rosecrans made sure to stage several reviews.

Veteran Lt. Marcus Woodcock of the 9th Kentucky (US) recalled the impression Rosecrans had on the men of his division, writing: "The smiling face of the commanding general was seen coming up the lines between the ranks, saying a word of kindness or instruction to almost every soldier he passed; asking one why he had no canteen, another 'where is your haversack?' and still another 'have you no blanket?' Thus, he proceeded along the lines creating a good opinion among the troops of his magnanimity and careful consideration for those under his control."[6]

"As the soldiers broke ranks, they appeared to be overcharged with enthusiasm, and there was loud cheering from one end of the camp to the other," echoed Wilbur F. Hinman, orderly sergeant of the 65th Ohio. "The boys had 'inspected' General Rosecrans and from the very outset he commanded their fullest confidence. 'Ain't he a daisy!' they shouted in the free and easy army vernacular, this expressing the highest compliments. Although General Rosecrans passed into the shadow of an eclipse at Chickamauga, he never forfeited the affection, esteem, and confidence of his soldiers."[7]

---

4 Ibid., 7.

5 "Last View of the Old Commander," *Los Angeles Herald*, Mar. 16, 1898, 6.

6 Kenneth W. Noe, *A Southern Boy in Blue: The Memoir of Marcus Woodcock, 9th Kentucky Infantry, U.S.A.* (Knoxville, 1996), 115.

7 Wilbur F. Hinman, *The Story of the Sherman Brigade* (Alliance, 1897), 326-27.

Fittingly, Army of the Cumberland veteran Austin Shafer of the 92nd Ohio delivered the eulogy at Rosecrans's funeral mass at the Los Angeles Cathedral. In describing the general's character, Shafer turned his thoughts to the battle of Stones River, Tennessee, on the morning of December 31, 1862, when the fortunes of Rosecrans's command were at perhaps their nadir.

"A scene rises in vision before me; it is at Stones River," the Yankee veteran recalled. "[Union Maj. Gen. Alexander M.] McCook is broken. The exultant foe, sweeping on in its taunting challenge, emerges from the cedars. As far as the eye can see, all is lost. A cannon ball sweeping on in its deadly mission missed [Rosecrans] by a hair's breadth but carried with it the head of Lt. Col. Julius Garesche, his chief of staff. His courage is undaunted, his spirit unconquered. He breathes upon the soldiers the inspiration of his own magnetic personality."[8]

*   *   *

A magnetic personality was a trait few used to describe General Braxton Bragg, Rosecrans's opponent at Stones River. Although the North Carolina native was industrious, brave, competent, and exhibited both a stern sense of duty and devotion to the Confederate cause, he made quick enemies with his autocratic, petulant, indecisive, and argumentative demeanor. His troops often laid the onus for their army's misfortunes upon his shoulders. Though accounts of Rosecrans's deep interest in his men made the rounds throughout the camps of the Army of the Cumberland, any stories told about Bragg centered on his harsh disciplinary measures.

"None of [his] soldiers ever loved him," insisted Private Sam R. Watkins of the 1st Tennessee, a Bragg veteran. "He was looked upon as a merciless tyrant. He loved to crush the spirit of his men. The more of a hang-dog look they had about them, the better."

Lieutenant General Alexander P. Stewart, a top subordinate, wrote that while Bragg was "an able officer, his greatest defect was that he did not win the love and confidence of either the officers or the men." Added Colonel William Preston Johnston, General Albert Sidney Johnston's son and a longtime aide to Confederate President Jefferson Davis: Bragg was "an able man, but he was too rigid and narrow to be a great one. He was very harsh and intolerant and was always

8 "A Nation's Hero Honored," 7.

a partisan and merciless towards those who resisted him. He did not inspire love or reverence, but he commanded respect and fear."[9]

Bragg's unpopularity and lack of success eventually led to his removal from command, and his postwar life mirrored his wartime personal struggles. The general bounced from job to job, his penchant for argument and dispute following him to each employer. At the end, he was working as a railroad inspector in Galveston, Texas, where he died of heart disease on the morning of September 27, 1876. Bragg's funeral lacked the pomp and circumstance that marked Rosecrans's 22 years later. Local army veterans did not issue proclamations praising his magnanimity, courage, or skill; surviving accounts indicate little public mourning at his demise. Bragg's body was briefly placed on display in Artillery Hall of the armory in Galveston for three and half hours of public viewing. Then, accompanied by 16 veterans of his army, his remains were delivered to an awaiting steamer headed to Mobile, Alabama. There, the general was buried with military honors a few days later, with mourners resorting mainly to memories of his "stern but noble qualities."[10]

The *Austin* (Texas) *American-Statesman* opined that "whatever opinions may be entertained of [Bragg] as a soldier, there are no differences in estimates of his sterling personal worth and stainless purity of conduct and character. Never knowing an emotion of fear, he was the very personification of truth and guileless simplicity. He was surely the most successful organizer of armies the country has produced."

The *Nashville Tennessean* praised Bragg as "crafty on the defense and a thunderbolt on the attack," but conceded, "Though a strict disciplinarian, even to the point of severity, and regarded as a good commander of a division and a brave man personally, [he] was not regarded as one of our first generals. It may have been unavoidable fatality, but as a commander he was invariably unsuccessful." The old army sentiments expressed by men like Sam Watkins still rang true for many, and

---

9 Sam R. Watkins, *Company Aytch, or a Sideshow of the Big Show: A Memoir of the Civil War* (Nashville, 2011), 45-46; Sam Davis Elliott, *Soldier of Tennessee: General Alexander P. Stewart and the Civil War in the West* (Baton Rouge, 1999), 48; William Preston Johnston, *The Life of Gen. Albert Sidney Johnston* (New York, 1879), 547-48.

10 "Death of Gen. Bragg," *Galveston Daily News*, Sept. 28, 1876, 4; *Mobile Daily Register*, Oct. 1, 1876, 2.

General Braxton Bragg

Rick Baumgartner Collection

the *St. Louis Globe-Democrat* simply used "The King of Terrors" as the headline for his obituary.[11]

Few would have predicted such an ignoble end for the general, who as a young captain rose to prominence for his exploits during the Mexican War. Bragg's start in life was inauspicious, however. He was born March 21, 1817, in Warrenton, North Carolina, with local lore maintaining that his mother Margaret—under detention for murdering a free African American who had been "impertinent"—was released from jail to give birth to him. Although Bragg's father ran a thriving local business, and Margaret Bragg never stood trial, the neighbors chose to keep their distance thereafter. Socially, the planter society considered Braggs "plebians" and "unfit associates."

Braxton, however, burned with ambition and proved to be a superb student. That studiousness led to an appointment to the U.S Military Academy in West Point, New York, which introduced Bragg to the strict discipline emblematic of his military career. Known for his integrity, he proved to be a good cadet who excelled in his studies. Outspoken and brusque, he refused to compromise and was both quick to argue and not afraid to take to his fists. The emphasis on direct offensive operations, as taught by famed military theorist Dennis Hart Mahan, appealed especially to his nature. Graduating fifth in West Point's Class of 1837, Bragg would be commissioned a second lieutenant in the 3rd Light Artillery and assigned to Florida. Army life proved a good fit for Bragg—with one exception. Realizing he was prone to illness, he struggled with recurring health issues for the rest of his life.

It was in those pre-Mexican War years that Bragg developed his irascible reputation, engaging in quarrels seemingly with anyone who crossed his path— typically prickly and quick to take offense at any perceived slight. "As a subordinate," noted one comrade, "he was always on the lookout to catch his commanding officer infringing his prerogatives . . . and was equally vigilant to detect the slightest neglect even of the most trivial order." Another comrade focused on Bragg's "morbid temperament, intolerant sectionalism, and dictatorial utterances," labeling him the "most cantankerous man in the army."

By the start of the Mexican War in 1846, Bragg had cultivated some high-ranking enemies, including his regimental commander William Gates, his

---

11 "The Death of Gen. Braxton Bragg," *Austin American-Statesman*, Sept. 28, 1876, 2; "The Late Gen. Braxton Bragg," *The Tennessean*, Sept. 29, 1876, 2; "The King of Terrors: Gen. Braxton Bragg Drops Dead in the Street," *St. Louis-Globe Democrat*, Sept. 28, 1876, 5.

division commander John Wool, Adjutant General Roger Jones, commanding General of the Army Winfield Scott, and Secretary of War William Wilkins.

Despite this appalling record in personal relations, Bragg's stern character and harsh discipline found a true calling on the battlefields of Mexico. His battery in the 3rd Light Artillery departed for Texas in July 1845 to join General Zachary Taylor's army, preparing for war. Bragg drilled his men constantly, impressing others with his "industry, attention to duty, and strict regard for discipline." His effort in the defense of Fort Texas in May 1846 earned him a brevet promotion to captain; he also fought at the battle of Monterey that September, securing a second brevet promotion to major.

The success in turn landed him command of Battery C of the 3rd Light Artillery, igniting his rise as a national hero. During the seesaw battle of Buena Vista on February 23, 1847, Bragg's battery held a critical position in the army's center and held off a determined charge of the Mexican army virtually unsupported, delivering three point-blank volleys of canister that gutted the Mexican attack. "Captain Bragg saved the day," General Taylor reported. A third brevet promotion would follow.

Returning to the United States after the war, Colonel Bragg was feted in town after town for his heroism. The planter society that had scorned Bragg and his family years before now sang his praises. Life in the peacetime army proved dull for Bragg, however, but he would be recognized for his continued push for army reforms. And while stationed in Louisiana in the late 1840s, he met an engaging young woman named Elizabeth Brooks "Eliza" Ellis, the orphaned daughter of a wealthy planter whom he found "intelligent, poised, and witty." The two married on June 7, 1849, beginning a 27-year marriage that ended only with Braxton's death in September 1876.

Frustrated with army politics, Bragg finally resigned his commission on December 31, 1855. In the spring of 1856, using his wife's wealth as a down payment, he purchased a 1,600-acre plantation near Thibodeaux, Louisiana, for more than $150,000 and soon began making a fortune cultivating sugar. Naming the plantation "Bivouac," Bragg drove himself and his 110 slaves relentlessly, eager to pay off his large debt.

By 1860, he was clearing $30,000 a year in profits, which landed him firmly in the wealthy planter class that dominated Southern politics before the war.[12] He also

---

12 The 1860 US census shows Braxton Bragg as a 43-year-old farmer with real estate holdings worth $93,000 and personal property worth $120,000; a large portion of that personal property

became involved in the state militia and advocated for the establishment of a state military school, helping secure the job for an old friend from his army days, William T. Sherman, in 1859.

Bragg, however, foresaw difficulties on the horizon as tensions with the Northern states increased during the presidential election of 1860. He regarded Abraham Lincoln's election as the virtual dissolution of the Union, and though he was not an advocate of secession, he worried whether "we can reconstruct the government without bloodshed." After Louisiana seceded on January 26, 1861, Governor Thomas Moore commissioned Bragg as major general in command of the Louisiana State Militia. A month later, he was commissioned at that rank in the Confederate army and took command of the seacoast defenses between Pensacola, Florida, and Mobile, Alabama. Not only did Bragg make it a point to personally inspect the quarters of his men, but he also took a great interest in sanitary matters and looked to bring some light into their otherwise dull encampment.

The men whom Bragg helped shape at the war's outset remained loyal to him throughout the hard days ahead. One of them wrote Bragg in December 1863 that "many of us have followed you with gladness from Mobile up to the present and we always felt sure that while General Bragg commanded no evil would ever befall us."[13]

When Bragg's Corps joined the Army of Mississippi at Corinth, Mississippi, in March 1862, the men's discipline and professionalism contrasted starkly with the unruly behavior of many of their fellow troops in Albert Sidney Johnston's command. Despite the Confederate defeat at Shiloh on April 6-7, 1862, Bragg's star rose because of his aggressiveness on the battle's opening day. Although that earned him praise from politicians and newspapers alike, historian Kenneth W. Noe acknowledged, "He had fought foolishly and wasted lives as bitter men in the ranks well knew." In a letter to his wife, Bragg lamented that "our failure [at Shiloh] is due entirely to the want of discipline and a want of officers. Universal suffrage, furloughs, and whiskey have ruined us. If we fail, it is our own fault."[14]

A cascade of Southern defeats in the first six months of 1862 created a perilous military situation in the Western Theater. The Confederacy—having lost its

---

was the 110 slaves he owned, as is shown in the 1860 slave schedule. In contrast, William S. Rosecrans reported personal property worth $600 and no real estate in the same census.

13 Grady McWhiney, *Braxton Bragg and Confederate Defeat,* Vol. 1 (Tuscaloosa, 1969), 1-186.

14 Kenneth W. Noe, *Perryville: This Grand Havoc of Battle* (Lexington, 2001), 20; Don C. Seitz, *Braxton Bragg: General of the Confederacy* (Columbia, 1924), 113.

foothold in Kentucky and control of the Tennessee and Cumberland rivers, as well as most of Tennessee and large swathes of northern Mississippi and Alabama—was in danger of being severed in two once portions of the Mississippi River fell under Federal control. General P. G. T. Beauregard, who assumed command of the Army of Mississippi when Johnston was mortally wounded on Shiloh's opening day, ham-handedly attempted to paint Shiloh as a Confederate victory, but with the deception his star lost much of the early-war luster it had enjoyed. The Southern populace reeled from mourning that hefty casualty lists brought to the doorsteps every day in just about every community.

After the setback at Shiloh, Beauregard retreated to Corinth, and for nearly two months held off Maj. Gen. Henry Halleck's vastly larger force aligned outside the key crossroads town. The effort, though, had wrecked the army's health, and Beauregard's. Seeing the handwriting on the wall, the Creole commander determined that, in the face of 125,000 Federals, there was no prospect of victory for him at Corinth. On the night of May 29-30, he decided to use clever subterfuge to slip away. "Troops were left behind to keep the campfires burning," noted one historian. "Drummers from each brigade stayed to beat reveille at the usual hour. Dummy guns and sentinels were placed where the Federals would be certain to see them. All night, an empty train of cars ran back and forth through the town. At frequent intervals it stopped with a loud whistle and specially detailed troops rushed forth to cheer the arrival of heavy reinforcements."

Convinced by the ruckus that they would be attacked in the morning, several Federal officers went on high alert, but the morning's light merely revealed Beauregard had pulled a fast one. Halleck's siege of Corinth was essentially complete, but the Confederates had gotten away and would fight again.[15]

*   *   *

General Beauregard's unwillingness to apprise the government in Richmond of his plans opened a long-running feud with President Davis. Initial reports from Corinth grossly inflated the magnitude of the Federal victory. Halleck, for one, claimed in a June 4, 1862, dispatch that 10,000 prisoners had been taken along with 15,000 weapons. It was here Beauregard's communication reticence hit him the hardest. Five days before the evacuation of Corinth, he had ordered all newspaper correspondents to depart, leaving those reporters "understandably indignant,"

---

15 T. Harry Williams, *P. G. T. Beauregard: Napoleon in Gray* (Baton Rouge, 1954), 154.

according to one historian. "Beauregard's order effectively eliminated on-the-spot press coverage of the evacuation of Corinth."

Beauregard sent a message to Richmond on June 3 providing the barest of details of the movement, but he did not follow with a more comprehensive account until some days later. By then, Halleck's dispatch had been published, stunning members of the Confederate government. Lacking information from Beauregard, they suspected there was truth in Halleck's claims.[16]

Caught off-guard, Davis was furious upon learning the truth. Beauregard's previous letter had indicated he intended to hold Corinth "to the last extremity," and now this report indicated the commander had evacuated without a fight. Although Beauregard would claim in a letter to the Mobile Evening News that the "retreat was conducted with great order and precision and must be looked on in every respect by the country as equivalent to a brilliant victory," the affair cemented Davis's belief that Beauregard lacked the ability to command the Confederacy's second largest field army. "There are those who can only walk on a log when it is near to the ground," he confided to his wife, "and I fear Beauregard has been placed too high for his mental strength as he does not exhibit the ability manifested on smaller fields."[17]

On June 12, 1862, Adj. Gen. Samuel Cooper chided Beauregard for not providing a detailed statement on his actions at Corinth, receiving a breezy reply from the Creole that he was too busy organizing the army, adding that the retreat had been "most brilliant and successful." Put off by the double talk, Davis dispatched his personal aide, William Preston Johnston, to Tupelo, Mississippi, to assess the overall condition of the army and question Beauregard about the evacuation of Corinth. Events had already raced ahead before Colonel Johnston arrived in Mississippi, however.

Because he faced numerous command problems in both the Western and Trans-Mississippi theaters, Davis was seeking to replace Maj. Gen. Mansfield Lovell in Louisiana with Bragg, only to hear from Beauregard that he needed him in Tupelo. Davis soon learned why. "After delaying as long as possible to obey the oft-repeated recommendations of my physicians to take some rest for the restoration of my health," Beauregard informed Cooper on June 15, "I have concluded to take advantage of the present lull in operations of this army . . . for

16 J. Cutler Andrews, *South Reports the Civil War* (Princeton, 1970), 156-57.

17 *Mobile Evening News*, Jun. 19, 1862, 1; Steven E. Woodworth, *Jefferson Davis and His Generals: The Failure of Confederate Command in the West* (Lawrence, 1990), 105.

absenting myself a short while from here. I will transfer the command of the forces of this department to the next officer in rank General Braxton Bragg."[18]

Meanwhile, Davis worked the wires to find a new assignment for Beauregard, who left clandestinely for Bladon Springs, Alabama, after contacting Cooper. Governor Francis Pickens of South Carolina had complained of Maj. Gen. John Pemberton's services in his state and requested that Beauregard replace Pemberton. Davis was only too happy to oblige.

Beauregard biographer T. Harry Williams maintained in his 1954 book Napoleon in Gray that the Creole commander's manner of communicating his temporary absence to Bladon Springs was "strange and ill-advised" and "should not have been taken until after the fullest conference with Richmond," playing "directly into the president's hands." When Davis learned from Bragg that Beauregard had indeed left the army, he seized the chance to supplant him, telegraphing Bragg on June 20 that "you are hereby assigned permanently to the command of the department." John Beauchamp Jones, a clerk in the war department in Richmond, stated in his diary entry of June 21 that the rumors in the office were that Beauregard was really being relieved for blundering at Shiloh, writing, "It is said the Yankee army might have been annihilated at Shiloh if Beauregard had fought a little longer."[19]

Army command proved no sinecure for Bragg, as his new army was in shambles—one historian commenting that he inherited "one great tangle of difficulties." Bragg himself recognized this and telegraphed Beauregard that he was "in despair" upon assuming command. The men had shown they could fight at Shiloh, but they had known nothing but defeat, retreat, and suffering since the start of the year. Morale was low, sickness and desertion widespread, the men indifferently armed and poorly equipped. Wagon transportation was lacking, and inefficiency reigned in the commissary and quartermaster departments. The long siege in the unhealthy environs of Corinth had reduced the army's ranks so much that a muster taken upon arrival in Tupelo showed only 45,335 of the 94,756 men

18 Williams, *P. G. T. Beauregard*, 156; The War of the Rebellion: *A Compilation of the Official Records of the Union and Confederate Armies*, 128 vols. (Washington, DC, 1880–1901), Series 1, Vol. 17, Part 2, 601, 606, hereafter *OR.*

19 Williams, *P. G. T. Beauregard*, 158-59; *OR* 17/2:614; John B. Jones with Earl Schenk Miers, ed., *A Rebel War Clerk's Diary* (New York, 1958), 83.

on the rolls were available for duty. It wasn't an army, Bragg complained, but a mob.[20]

Inadvertently, Halleck did Bragg the biggest favor: he handed the general the gift of time and left him alone. Having gathered a massive army at Corinth, Halleck chose to disperse it across the region, intent on guarding his railroad supply lines and pacifying the countryside instead of pursuing the Confederate army. "Old Brains" handed Grant command of the forces in western Tennessee and Mississippi and directed Buell to move his army east toward Chattanooga, following the Memphis and Charleston Railroad. With water levels dropping on the Tennessee and Cumberland rivers as they normally did during the summer, the Union army relied on the railroads and the region's rough country roads to supply their armies instead of steamboats. Consequently, Bragg deftly used the summer siesta he had been given to rebuild his command.

The Army of Mississippi was by no means a homogenous, harmonious unit, and Bragg's efforts to develop unit cohesion at first glance appeared daunting. When Albert Sidney Johnston assembled his army at Corinth in March 1862, its disparate character was unmistakable, as men arrived anywhere from towns straddling the Gulf Coast to the Western plains. Drawn together from every state in the Confederacy but Virginia, its ranks consisted of every type, from the rough-hewn mountaineers of eastern Tennessee and backwoodsmen of Missouri and Arkansas to the educated sons of wealthy planters from the Gulf states. The ranks included not only yeoman farmers from Tennessee, Kentucky, Alabama, Georgia, and Mississippi but also with cattle rustlers from Texas and Florida. It wasn't unusual to have a company of farm boys standing in rank next to a company of city-bred bluebloods or university students.

Immigrant Irish, Germans, and Frenchmen from New Orleans and Memphis added their own flavor to the army. The 2nd and 10th Tennessee styled themselves Irish regiments and were predominantly Catholic, a rarity in the largely Protestant South. "It was said that the regimental chaplain served mass in the afternoon and settled drunken brawls at night," recalled one historian. One of its lieutenants remembered that the 13th Louisiana from cosmopolitan New Orleans consisted of "Frenchmen, Spaniards, Mexicans, Dagoes, Chinese, Irishmen, and in fact, persons of every clime known to geographers or travelers of that day. If the enlisted

---

20 OR 17/1:792.

men were somewhat mixed, the officers were gentlemen in every sense of the word: by birth and prestige, education, and travel, by wealth and social standing."[21]

Local companies were assigned to regiments, meaning a large measure of a soldier's identity was immersed in his membership in that regiment. The "Pickens Rough and Readys" from Pickens County, Alabama, became Company A of the 19th Alabama; among their comrades in the 19th included the "Jake Curry Guards" and "Cherokee Mountaineers." The "Lake Swamp Volunteers" became Company C of the 10th South Carolina, which also contained its own company of "Rough and Readys" (Company G) along with the "Swamp Fox Guards" (Company I) of Marion County, named after one of the heroes of the Revolutionary War. The largely German 20th Louisiana from New Orleans included companies called the Turner Guards, the Reichard Rifles, and the Noel Rangers.

Few of them dressed alike, and how a soldier was clothed largely depended on his origin. Tennessee, for example, made thousands of "Tennessee-pattern" single-breasted frock coats with distinctive pointed cuffs issued to Maj. Gens. Leonidas Polk's and William Hardee's commands in Kentucky. Captain Charles Simonton of the 9th Tennessee recalled that due to a shortage of cloth "several hundred yards of dingy, slaty colored jeans" were chosen for their uniforms. "To say the boys who were expecting an elegant uniform were disappointed is putting it mildly," Simonton wrote, "but they came near rebelling still when they saw the calico of a sickly hospital yellow which was to make the stripes on the pants and adorn the collars of the coats." A Federal observer noted that "they looked as if the devil himself had manufactured and clothed them out of the hides of Jacob's cattle. There were no two of them of a size nor the same dress nor of the same color."[22]

Not all Confederates were dressed poorly. The flashy "Avegno Zouaves" of New Orleans went to war with the 13th Louisiana wearing red caps, dark blue jackets, and baggy red trousers. The "Orleans Guards" also wore dark blue coats; when they arrived at Shiloh, the regiment was fired upon by other Confederates who mistakenly thought they were Federals. The lack of uniformity extended to the army's battle flags, which ultimately encompassed eight designs, including the

21 Larry J. Daniel, *Soldiering in the Army of Tennessee* (Chapel Hill, 1991), 18; "In a Louisiana Regiment," by John McGrath, *New Orleans Daily Picayune*, Aug. 2, 1903.

22 Thomas M. Arlikas, *Cadet Gray and Butternut Brown* (Gettysburg, 2006), 36; James R. Fleming, *Band of Brothers: Company C, 9th Tennessee Infantry* (Shippensburg, 1996), 11-12; Jim, *Daily Pantagraph*, Feb. 21, 1862, 2.

This unidentified Confederate soldier is wearing the typical uniform and slouch hat preferred by the men of Bragg's Army of Tennessee. During the Stones River Campaign, most carried Model 1842 muskets (shown here) or older model smoothbores.

Library of Congress

original "Stars and Bars" national flag of seven stars that remained in service into 1863 despite incessant confusion with the U.S. flag.[23]

For all their differences, the soldiers shared much in common. A survey of the army showed that most of the troops were poor, non-slaveholding farmers "born in a small log cabin with limited public education." They didn't take well to discipline and were highly independent in thought and action. Discipline proved lax and respect for authority similarly lacking, with one civilian observer noting that the average Confederate soldier "was far more apt to talk back to his superior" and "there always seemed to be more ill-feeling for certain of their superiors and a lack of confidence, more of a disposition to saddle the responsibility of disaster upon the shoulders of their commanders." The ingrained distrust of centralized power and a fierce determination to defend their homes from Yankee invaders became the primary unifying forces that kept the army together through what would prove to be a hard war.[24]

As the Southern states were predominantly Protestant, religion seemed one potentially unifying element in the army. Early in the war, however, the men shed their usual forms of worship and embraced the relative freedom of military life.

---

23 Bell Irvin Wiley, *The Life of Johnny Reb: The Common Soldier of the Confederacy* (Baton Rouge, 1943), 109.

24 Daniels, *Soldiering in the Army of Tennessee*, 11-22; "Characteristics of the Armies," Horace V. E. Redfield, *The Annals of the War, Written by Leading Participants North and South* (Philadelphia, 1879), 367.

"Most of the soldiers were from the country and the transition from farm to camp assumed to a large extent the character of a visit of rural youths to a city," wrote historian Bell Irvin Wiley. "Soldering was regarded as a grand lark, and they wanted to derive the greatest possible pleasure from it while it lasted. They wanted to have a fling at gambling, drinking, and swearing and did not wish to be bothered with preachers."

Dozens of chaplains considered it a bad mission and would resign before the army saw any serious action. The great morale-building religious revivals throughout what became known as the Army of Tennessee in November 1862 occurred much later after the disappointments in Kentucky, at Stones River, and again at Chattanooga.[25]

The army's core was comprised of the hard-fighting regiments of the First Corps—the old Provisional Army of Tennessee led by Maj. Gen. Leonidas Polk, the former bishop of Louisiana. Given Polk's West Point pedigree and status as a religious leader, Bragg was appalled at the poor state of discipline in Polk's "mob" and quickly discovered to his chagrin that the good bishop's military education had soured over time. Polk could talk a good game, but he often demonstrated great uncertainty when it came to actual command. The bombastic and hard-drinking fighter Benjamin F. Cheatham of Tennessee rode at the head of one of Polk's divisions and earned Bragg's intense dislike and distrust. Regardless of its hard-fighting nature, the "Polk bloc" of the army would be a thorn in Bragg's side throughout his tenure, with Polk the motivating spirit and de facto leader of the army's anti-Bragg elements.

Leading the Second Corps (Bragg's former command) was Maj. Gen. Samuel Jones, a fellow 1837 West Point graduate whose tenure with the army would prove short-lived. Bragg's former division was led by Maj. Gen. Jones Withers, an 1835 graduate of West Point who would eventually become one of Bragg's most dependable allies. The troops hailed mainly from Alabama, Mississippi, and Georgia, and included a single regiment from Louisiana and a pair of regiments from coastal South Carolina.

William J. Hardee led the Third Corps, becoming Bragg's top subordinate. A former West Point commandant and author of the 1855 manual Rifle and Light Infantry Tactics used by both sides' armies, Hardee exerted enormous influence on his fellow officers. At this time, Hardee's Corps was organized into five brigades (no divisions) with troops hailing from Alabama, Arkansas, Mississippi, and

25 Wiley, *The Life of Johnny Reb*, 175.

Tennessee. Hardee was lucky to number among his brigade commanders a relatively unknown Irish immigrant from Arkansas named Patrick Cleburne, whose remarkable war record eventually earned him the nickname "Stonewall of the West."

John C. Breckinridge, the former vice president of the United States whose enmity Bragg cultivated to his detriment, commanded the army's Reserve Corps. The Kentuckian exerted enormous political influence and was adored by his loyal troops. Breckinridge's four brigades contained five regiments of Kentuckians and a mix of other organizations from Alabama, Arkansas, Louisiana, and Tennessee. The heart and soul of Breckinridge's Corps were the Kentucky troops he held dearest—the celebrated "Orphan Brigade" from the old Kentucky State Guard. Its commander, Brig. Gen. Benjamin Helm, was President Abraham Lincoln's brother-in-law.

In addition to the Army of Mississippi, the three divisions of Maj. Gen. Earl Van Dorn's Army of the West also fell under Bragg's command, but only Maj. Gen. John P. McCown's Division remained with him for long. McCown was another commander whom Bragg mistrusted, blamed for bungling his defensive assignment during the Confederate defeat at Island No. 10 in April 1862. McCown's two brigades consisted of dismounted Texan cavalrymen under Brig. Gen. William L. Cabell and a brigade of Arkansans under Brig. Gen. Thomas J. Churchill.

*   *   *

As the Confederate Army of Mississippi settled into camp around Tupelo, urgent attention was expended to improve the men's overall physical condition. Time spent around Corinth had left nearly a quarter of the army with some form of illness. Tupelo's location along the single-track Mobile and Ohio Railroad and significantly more healthy environment offered the promise of a chance to recover quickly. "The army," observed Colonel Johnston, "is at presently encamped on both sides of the Tupelo swamp on a series of sandy ridges covered with a growth of oak, black-jack, and hickory."

Beside ample rations, the soldiers discovered an undesirable surfeit of lice, or what the men called "graybacks." According to Sam Watkins, "Every soldier had a brigade of lice on him, and I have seen fellows so busily engaged in cracking them that it reminded me of an old woman knitting. At first, the boys would go off in the woods and hide to louse themselves," he added, "but it was unnecessary as the ground fairly crawled with lice."[26]

After appraising his force and getting the men on the road to physical recovery, Bragg's next priority was to instill his own brand of discipline on the "mob," which meant a thorough overhaul. Bragg insisted on strict observance of military law and customs, punished deserters with public executions, and groomed his troops on learning to be soldiers. An army veteran noted that before Bragg took command, "the din of firearms could be heard at all hours of the day. Now a gun is never fired without orders from the brigade commander. Bragg had one man shot for discharging his gun without orders, and since that time the discipline of the troops was improved very much. Men are not apt to disobey orders when they know that death is the punishment."

"[T]hese strong measures are the only ones that will do our army any good and from this time on, all cases of desertion, lawlessness, disobedience, and unmilitary conduct is going to meet with speedy and severe punishment," opined one of Bragg's staff officers. "We are going to have no more playing soldier in General Bragg's army."[27]

Drill became a constant feature of the camp at Tupelo, discipline the watchword of the day. Five hours a day six days a week, the veterans and the neophytes went through the exercise of the manual of arms and drilling at both the company and battalion level. It was tedious work and quickly grew monotonous. "Our battalion drill at 2 p.m. was hot work," remembered Private John S. Jackman of the 9th Kentucky. "All the time while encamped at Tupelo we had regular drills and the weather could not have been hotter. There was only one small spring to water the brigade which was guarded and no one could get water save at regular water calls."

Surprisingly little time was spent on weapons drills. According to Brig. Gen. Arthur M. Manigault, who would go on to pen a detailed and insightful postwar memoir, his brigade made no concerted effort at weapons training until January 1864. "They learned much more of their weapons, their capability, and how to

---

26 *OR* 17/2:607; *OR* 17/1:783; Watkins, *Company Aytch*, 55.

27 Stanley F. Horn, *The Army of Tennessee* (Wilmington, 1987), 156-57; Samuel Henry Lockett Papers, Southern Historical Collection, Wilson Library, University of North Carolina; John Buie Papers, David M. Rubenstein Rare Book & Manuscript Library, Duke University.

handle and direct them in those two weeks than in the previous two and a half years," Manigault would write.[28]

Earlier that spring, the Confederate Congress added to Bragg's woes by passing the Conscription Act. The act was wildly unpopular with the troops because it extended the term of service of every soldier for the duration of the war, and held that every man ages 18-45 could be conscripted into service. General Beauregard issued General Orders No. 39 on May 6 directing a mass reorganization of the army that included the election of new regimental and company officers. In many cases, though, the men had arranged to be away from their homes only for a year and wanted to return to them, even if only on a short furlough, and promised to return.

"Bragg would not grant a furlough to anyone, even if it were to transact business for others," remembered William Watson of the 3rd Louisiana. "A whole regiment then laid down their arms and refused duty. Bragg then brought up a strong force and surrounded them, and then directed a battery of artillery against them and gave them five minutes to take up their arms. The men sullenly obeyed, each muttering to himself that it would be but little service he would ever get out of them."[29]

Thus, under protest, the troops elected new regimental and company officers to conform to the order, though the net results pleased no one. Bragg complained to the war department about the effects of the act upon his army, noting that "the elective feature of the conscript law has driven from the service the best who remained and to a great extent has demoralized the troops." Colonel Johnston agreed, informing President Davis that the act "worked most disastrously in this army. A right to reorganize at will might have satisfied all whom a necessity did not call to their homes, but to be drafted for the war … engendered a spirit of bitter discontent which in many instances was fanned by designing men."[30]

Boards of examination cleared out the least qualified of the newly elected officers, but the imbroglio left a bitter taste with the rank and file. Sam Watkins felt the act conformed volunteers to "contemptible conscripts. From that time on till the end of the war, a soldier was simply a machine, a conscript. We cursed the war;

---

28 William C. Davis, editor. *Diary of a Confederate Soldier: John S. Jackman of the Orphan Brigade* (Columbia, 1990), 45; Daniels, *Soldiering in the Army of Tennessee*, 27.

29 William Watson, *Life in the Confederate Army: Being the Observations and Experiences of an Alien in the South During the American Civil War* (New York, 1885), 368.

30 Horn, *The Army of Tennessee*, 158; Johnston Report, 780-81.

we cursed Bragg and cursed the Southern Confederacy. All our pride and valor were gone, and we were sick of war."

Joshua Callaway of the 28th Alabama complained to his wife that "we are all nothing more than the subjects of a military despotism now and have no right to think and are hardly allowed to sigh at the fall of our friends and relatives." Watson added that "if such strong measures were necessary as was asserted by some, the evil effects of them were clearly shown before many days were past." Another Tennessee veteran contended that "unless the Conscription Act was enforced the Confederacy would be forced to surrender the cause."[31]

Capital punishments began while the army was encamped at Tupelo. One soldier of the 7th Arkansas was executed on June 17, 1862, for refusing "to do duty of any kind in defiance of military power." Lieutenant Frank Denton of the 8th Arkansas said "a young fellow was shot by a general court martial for mutiny and was made an example for the regiment and brigade. Our whole brigade was ordered out to see the execution. The men were very clamorous about going home when their time is out, until this youth was shot. Now they are taking it easy."

Desertions increased in the wake of the Conscription Act and the retreat from Shiloh, an evil Bragg intended to stop. Previous infractions had been handled by branding the offender with a "D" or shaving his head, among other humiliating punishments. Bragg decided to make an example of two deserters from the 21st Tennessee on June 30. The executions were conducted in public with the soldiers from the prisoner's regiment, brigade, or division as a captive audience. This served the twofold purpose of dispensing military justice, but it also was a stark warning to any observers.[32]

Lieutenant Colonel Camille de Polignac, serving as an inspector on Bragg's staff, wrote that "the men have been accustomed for years to have no check put on their proclivities. The system under which they are mustered in and kept together tends to keep up their former independent ways for want of impressing them with a sense of deference for their officers and making them sensible to the necessity for themselves of enforcing discipline. Evils in this army have to be corrected partly by persuasion, partly by compulsion." Historian Stanley Horn argued that "Bragg

---

31 Watkins, *Company Aytch*, 42; Judith Lee Hallock, editor. *The Civil War Letters of Joshua K. Callaway* (Athens, 1997), 44-45; Thomas A. Head, *Campaigns and Battles of the Sixteenth Regiment, Tennessee Volunteers in the War Between the States* (Nashville, 1885), 87; Watson, *Life in the Confederate Army*, 369.

32 Daniels, *Soldiering in the Army of Tennessee*, 110; Lieutenant Frank Desha Denton, Co. H, 8th Arkansas, Lyon College Library Special Collections.

would have attained better results by exercising tact and diplomacy. His stern application of discipline verged on brutality. His severity gained for him the name of tyrant throughout the army."[33]

*   *   *

Acquiring modern arms, ammunition, and equipment remained a struggle for the Confederates. Southern arsenals had thousands of outmoded flintlocks and smoothbores at the outset of the conflict, but demand quickly outstripped supply; and it was common for a Confederate regiment to have guns for fewer than half its troops in early 1862. Significant portions of the army still carried shotguns and flintlocks into action at Shiloh, and though captures from the Federal army at Shiloh had helped somewhat, the army remained unevenly and indifferently armed well into the summer of 1862. The 36th Mississippi, for example, joined Beauregard's army after Shiloh armed with 37 rifled muskets, 360 altered percussion muskets, and 270 double-barreled shotguns and rifles. "The altered rifles I find almost wholly worthless as they are badly bored out and locks of the most indifferent kind," reported one officer. "The main spring is also entirely too weak to explode our army caps." The shotguns were hardly in better shape as some of them were missing tubes and hammers.[34]

The supply of locally produced weapons also proved inadequate. Cook & Brother in New Orleans produced Enfield copies until late April 1862 when Federal capture of the Crescent City forced the firm to relocate to Georgia. The Marshall County Manufacturing Company in nearby Holly Springs, Mississippi, was under contract to manufacture 30,000 .54-caliber Mississippi rifles but managed to deliver only a few before the Federal army's approach. The lack of small arms was further exacerbated by the propensity of sick or discouraged men to abandon their guns, hundreds leaving their guns along the march route to Tupelo. "In the vast number of stragglers who deserted the line of retreat, many abandoned their firearms. It was melancholy to see so many soldiers returning without their

33 Jeff Kinard, *Lafayette of the South: Prince Camille de Polignac and the American Civil War* (College Station, 2001), 45; Horn, *The Army of Tennessee*, 157.

34 Inspection Report of the 36th Mississippi dated April 21, 1862, at Rienzi, Mississippi, from an article by Jim Pitts. www.westerntheatercivilwar.com/post/inspection-report-36th-mississippi-infantry-regiment-1862.

guns," noted Colonel Johnston. "The loss of small arms from this cause was large."[35]

What the troops wanted most were English-made .577-caliber Enfield rifle-muskets, which could be acquired only by ships willing to run the Union blockade or if captured from enemy soldiers. The Confederate government controlled imported arms issues and gave the Army of Northern Virginia first priority on most shipments, but a few thousand Enfields made their way west before Shiloh. Regimental commanders tried to compensate for the odd mixture of arms by giving the best weapons to the flank companies, those called upon more often for skirmish duty where the best advantage could be taken of their rifles' long-range capabilities. According to Adjutant Cornelius Irvine Walker of the 10th South Carolina, his regiment's colonel gave the regiment's allotment of Enfields to Company A, his Mississippi rifles to Company B, the Harpers Ferry muskets to Company E, while the balance of the regiment received smoothbores.[36]

In lieu of Enfields, Confederate agents in Europe procured other foreign imports such as the .54-caliber Austrian Lorenz rifle, which one veteran complained "was the most ungainly rifle mortals ever used being furnished with a heavy oak stock and trappings of iron and brass sufficient to decorate a howitzer." Larger-caliber Belgian imports, some larger than .70-caliber, were equally unpopular due to their fragility and propensity to kick like a mule when fired. The surfeit of arms meant that the average Army of Mississippi soldier in 1862 carried a .69-caliber smoothbore musket which, firing either a single cartridge or round ball with three buckshot (buck & ball), had an effective range of roughly 75 yards. This is key to understanding the battle tactics later used at Perryville and Stones River, where Confederates were forced to get dangerously close to their opponents for effective firing.[37]

In Bragg's opinion, the greatest deficiency in the army wasn't the disparity of numbers or equipment but the disparity of skill and talent in the officer corps. He felt most of his senior general officers, with the exception of General Hardee, had no business leading men in battle. That started with Leonidas Polk, whom Bragg consequently shuffled into the role of second in command to get him out of direct

---

35 William B. Edwards, *Civil War Guns: The Complete Story of Federal and Confederate Small Arms* (Secaucus, 1962), 382-83; Daniel, *Soldiering in the Army of Tennessee*, 39-43; Wiley, *The Life of Johnny Reb*, 287; Johnston report, 785.

36 Wiley, *The Life of Johnny Reb*, 292.

37 Wiley, *The Life of Johnny Reb*, 290-91.

corps command. Bragg didn't see much potential either in divisional commanders Cheatham or McCown, and he tagged several other brigadiers as "undesirables" whom he wanted out of his army.

Bragg saw some rising talent, and he was eager to promote those worthies to higher command, but with the current crop in command he foresaw only difficulties. He suggested rather indelicately to General Cooper that if the war department would "relieve this army from a part of this dead weight it would surely give confidence to the troops and add much to our efficiency."[38]

However unpopular, Bragg's reform measures made an immediate impact, the condition of the army rebounding in what could be called the "Tupelo Revival." Thomas Head of the 16th Tennessee noted that at Tupelo "everything was plentiful, and the men were all in good spirits. Clearing off the timber for their encampment, they pitched their tents and enjoyed the benefits of rest and quiet." One Tennessee soldier wrote that the army "is in better condition than has been since the battle of Shiloh. The health of the army is excellent, and the men are in good spirits and anxious to be led back to Tennessee." Corporal Benjamin Butt, a cannoneer, reveled that "there has been a great improvement in regard to discipline and drill. But of all the changes for the better, the greatest has taken place in the health of the army. Instead of a pale face, feeble gait, and dejected appearances of the invalid, I met with the clear complexion, the elastic step, and cheerful countenance that betokens health and vigor. Our army is recruiting so fast that it will not long remain inactive."[39]

Bragg formally communicated his assumption of command to the army on June 27 and provided his reasoning for the harsh measures he had adopted. "Relying . . . on the justice of the cause of an invaded people, in the zeal and skill of subordinate officers of all ranks and confidently depending on the bravery," he began, "devotion and individual intelligence of a soldiery fighting on their own soil in defense of all worth living for, I enter hopefully on my duties. But," he continued,

> soldiers, to secure the legitimate results of all your heavy sacrifices which have brought this army together, be assured of discipline at all times and obedience to the orders of your

38 McWhiney, *Braxton Bragg and Confederate Defeat*, 262-63.

39 Head, *Campaigns and Battles of the Sixteenth Regiment, Tennessee Volunteers*, 83-84; Fleming, *Band of Brothers: Company C, 9th Tennessee Infantry*, 99; Corporal Benjamin Butt, Stanford's Mississippi Battery, *Memphis Daily Appeal*, Jul. 11, 1862, 2.

officers on all points as a sacred duty, an act of patriotism. *Without this spirit, the bravest army must sink into an armed rabble as impotent for defense as of offense. Great events are impending; a few more days of needful preparation and organization and I shall give your banners to the breeze. But be prepared to undergo privation and labor with cheerfulness and alacrity.*[40]

When Bragg began moving the army in late July, it hardly resembled the ragtag force that had marched into Tupelo in early June. The Bragg touch—rough-hewn, severe, and harsh as it was—turned the Army of Mississippi into a well-crafted instrument of war. More important, the army grew to believe in itself again. One officer observed that "there has been a marvelous change for the better in the condition, health, discipline, and drill of the troops of this army since it left Corinth. It was a perfect rabble that there would have done much more running than fighting if they had been put to the scratch."

Another soldier commented that "the troops are all in fine spirits and seemed perfectly willing to fight on till the last invader is driven from the Southern soil. When our brave boys breathe the fresh mountain air of Tennessee, they will be soon prepared to ensure every toil and danger incident to the long and fatiguing marches they will be called on to make in the campaign before them."[41]

Despite the grumbling in the ranks and the other problems he had assumed on taking command, Bragg accomplished much in a brief period. Now that he had organized his army, it was time to put it to work. The question was where? The Army of Mississippi had no sooner settled into camp at Tupelo before the telegraph lines buzzed with calls for them to return to fighting. "General Buell seems to be directing the movement against this department," warned Maj. Gen. Edmund Kirby Smith, District of Eastern Tennessee commander, from his headquarters in Knoxville on June 15. "Since the withdrawal of the army from Corinth, they have been largely reinforced and the enemy in overwhelming numbers are systematically moving to the occupation of East Tennessee."[42]

A few days earlier, Smith implored Beauregard to send him reinforcements, only to be rebuffed, as the Creole reported he had enough problems of his own. Smith's requests found a more welcome reception with Bragg, and as the Seven

---

40 *OR* 17/2:626.

41 McWhiney, *Braxton Bragg and Confederate Defeat*, 265; Juvinis, *Memphis Daily Appeal*, Aug. 4, 1862, 2.

42 *OR* 16/2:685.

Days' Battles raged around Richmond in June and July, Secretary of War George W. Randolph encouraged Bragg to "strike the moment opportunity offers."[43]

Soon, Lincoln pulled Halleck from the theater. Riding high after his "victory" at Corinth, Halleck packed his bags for Washington, DC, to become the Union army's general chief in mid-July, a position he held until March 1864. Grant took his army west to Memphis, and Buell marched east to take Chattanooga. With Grant seemingly idle and Buell proceeding at a snail's pace in his mission, the initiative landed squarely in Braxton Bragg's lap.

Retaking Corinth and driving north seemed viable options, but that would expose his army to attack on both flanks, leaving the army's supply line equally vulnerable; it would ultimately do little to protect the Deep South. What was required was a bold stroke. By mid-July, Bragg decided it was time for the Army of Mississippi to move north. He had caught "Kentucky fever," and it would prove to be one of the turning points of the war.

43 Ibid., 17/2:627.

The Rise of Rosecrans

OPPORTUNITY HAD INDEED knocked for Don Carlos Buell in the West in June 1862, and it is telling that the general struggled as he did to grasp it. Admittedly, his was not an easy task. As commander of the Army of Ohio, he was ordered to march his force 200 miles east along the Memphis and Charleston Railroad through northern Alabama and capture the important railroad junction of Chattanooga, Tennessee.

Federal troops under Brig. Gen. Ormsby M. Mitchel provided needed help in the spring by securing control of the Memphis & Charleston at Huntsville, Alabama, on April 11, 1862, but as the summer drought conditions began lowering the level of the Tennessee River, it left Buell's army dependent primarily on the railroads for resources and meant the commander was further tasked with maintaining his own supply line as he progressed. As he marched, Buell also left behind small detachments to guard bridges and towns, reducing the size of his force as he approached Chattanooga. The nature of the work did not lend itself to rapid completion, much to the chagrin of the war department, which continually pestered Buell to pick up the pace.

Buell, a West Point graduate and career army officer, was decidedly conservative in his outlook, manners, and generalship. A relentless, talented organizer, he strove to instill the standards of regular army discipline into his freewheeling Western volunteer army, and at Shiloh those efforts bore fruit. Arriving overnight on April 6-7, the Army of the Ohio spearheaded the Federal counterattack that procured victory on April 7.

Buell took understandable pride in the achievement, and perhaps accorded himself and his army a bit too much credit in claiming they "saved" Ulysses Grant's Army of the Tennessee from defeat. But Buell's troops, by and large, did not like him, and as time progressed, he became widely unpopular. "Buell failed to recognize the distinction between the regular soldier in garrison during times of peace and the thinking volunteer during the active campaigns of the rebellion," wrote historian Henry M. Cist. "The latter could not and would not be made the mere machine the former becomes and Buell's failure to appreciate this caused great ill-feeling against him at the time in his army."[1]

By mid-July 1862, Buell's crawl toward Chattanooga had ground to a halt, thwarted by a lack of supplies. An army is a juggernaut of consumption, and in the summer of 1862 Buell's army of approximately 50,000 soldiers required monthly transportation to haul 1,125,000 pounds of pork; more than 1,875,000 pounds of beef; more than 10,000 barrels of flour; 3,365 bushels of beans; 150,000 pounds of rice; 150,000 pounds of coffee; more than 200,000 pounds of sugar; 15,000 gallons of vinegar; 942 bushels of salt; more than 660,000 pounds of potatoes; 22,500 pounds of candles; and more than 60,000 pounds of soap. Besides feeding the army, the soldiers needed clothing, shoes, tents, replacement camp equipment, weapons, and ammunition, and provisions, equipment, and replacement animals were likewise required for the thousands of horses and mules.

For a Civil War army to conduct offensive operations, it was necessary to stockpile supplies beyond the daily demands; transportation to the front by wagon or horses and mules was essential for these stockpiles; and troop detachments were vital for guarding the army's lengthened supply lines. The daunting logistical task Buell's quartermasters faced was exacerbated by the aforementioned drought that forced the army to rely almost entirely on the railroads and rudimentary Southern road network.[2]

The Western Theater's expansive geography compounded the problem. Buell's primary supply depot at Louisville, Kentucky, was 300 miles north of his army in northern Alabama, with the lightly guarded single-track Louisville and Nashville Railroad the lone line capable of carrying the tonnage first to the

---

1 Henry M. Cist, *The Army of the Cumberland* (Edison, 2002), 76.

2 The basic monthly ration for an army this size weighed roughly 7 million pounds which meant Buell's army required 24 fully loaded 10-car trains or 3,500 wagons a month to feed the army. Clothing, equipment, ammunition, and the need to transport men to and from the army easily doubled this freight requirement.

Tennessee capital. Although a secondary depot on the Cumberland River at Nashville offered Buell another supply option, once that river level fell during the summer, too, this vulnerable rail line became his army's principal lifeline.

Two railroads from Nashville were used to carry supplies to Buell's force. The Nashville and Decatur ran directly south but, because of a bridge burned in the spring, it terminated at the Tennessee River north of Decatur. A second line, the Nashville and Chattanooga, ran to the southeast through Murfreesboro, Tennessee, and terminated at the Memphis & Charleston in Stevenson, Alabama. Neither route was in a favorable state when the Federals occupied the area that spring, and since both lines crossed numerous rivers and creeks over bridges and trestles, they were ripe targets for bushwhackers and roving enemy cavalry.

By mid-July, Confederate horsemen attacked these susceptible supply lines with frightening rapidity. Colonel John Hunt Morgan's raiders rode roughshod through Kentucky in early July, and Colonel Nathan Bedford Forrest followed with a raid on Murfreesboro on July 13. In early August, Morgan struck again at Big South Tunnel near Gallatin, Tennessee. "The roof of the tunnel was of a peculiar rock which was liable at all times to disintegrate and tumble down," remembered Colonel Basil W. Duke, one of Morgan's top subordinates. "Some freight cars were run into the tunnel and set on fire and this woodwork was ignited." The supporting timbers buckled in the inferno, and the entire roof of the tunnel collapsed with a thunderous crash. "[T]he fire smoldered on after it had ceased to burn fiercely for a long time," Duke crowed, "and it was weeks before any repairs could be attempted on account of the intense heat and huge masses of rock which were constantly falling."

Morgan's sabotage severed Buell's primary supply line from Louisville for the next 98 days, halting the advance toward Chattanooga. Buell responded by placing portions of his army on half-rations or less, and unhappy authorities in Washington threatened to remove him from command.[3]

The Union supply woes had handed Bragg the initiative. "The Confederate problem was to devise some plan to turn the tide of disaster and recover at least a portion of our lost territory," remembered Brig. Gen. Joseph Wheeler, one of Bragg's cavalry commanders. Logistics determined Bragg's axis of advance as a move into West or Middle Tennessee would pin him between two Federal armies with vulnerable supply lines. "But there was another line for aggressive

---

3 Cist, *The Army of the Cumberland*, 76; Basil W. Duke, *Morgan's Cavalry* (New York, 1906), 141-42.

movement," Wheeler would write. "[A] rapid march through Alabama to Chattanooga would save that city, protect Georgia from invasion, and open the way into Tennessee and Kentucky. This movement was determined upon and resulted in what is called the Kentucky Campaign of 1862."[4]

The first breath of this "Kentucky fever" arrived via a dispatch from Morgan during his first raid of the commonwealth, the colonel reporting that Kentucky was bereft of serious defenders and ripe for Confederate recruiting. "The whole country can be secured, and 25,000–30,000 men will join you at once," Morgan claimed. General Edmund Kirby Smith quickly forwarded the raider's news to Bragg in Tupelo and to Richmond. The plan was clear: move to Chattanooga to flank Buell out of his position in northern Alabama and strike for Middle Tennessee; then after crushing Buell's supply lines, move into Kentucky, where eager recruits would double the size of his army, allowing Bragg to meet Buell on equal terms. This first blush of Kentucky fever proved heady stuff, indeed.[5]

With Morgan's intelligence and Smith's assurance of support, Bragg needed no further encouragement to begin moving his 35,000-man army by rail to Chattanooga. On paper, it was not an easy task, as the Southern railroad network combined with the Federal occupation of the Memphis and Charleston Railroad left few options for rapid transit to Chattanooga. After all, the route covered 776 miles on six separate railroads.

Once the deployment began, however, the advance elements of Bragg's army reached Chattanooga in only four days. Then, in late August, Smith's army entered Kentucky and overwhelmed a small army of inexperienced Federals at the battle of Richmond, a prime opportunity for Kentuckians to begin joining the Confederacy. A few weeks later, Bragg followed Smith, spurring Buell to send his army racing toward Louisville.[6]

Buell won the "race," as advance elements of his army reached the city on September 25, but the prize came at a high cost: nearly all the fruits of a year's campaigning were erased within a month. By the time Buell reached Louisville, the grumbling inside the ranks about the general's leadership began to rival that of the

---

4 Robert U. Johnston et al., editors. "Bragg's Invasion of Kentucky," Lieutenant General Joseph Wheeler, *Battles and Leaders of the Civil War Volume III: The Tide Shifts* (Secaucus, 1980), 2.

5 OR 16/2:733-734.

6 The Montgomery and West Point had 4-foot-8-inch gauge rail while the other railroads mentioned had 5-foot gauge rails, which meant that the troops had to change cars when the gauge changed.

government in Washington. Journalist and politician Whitelaw Reid described Buell's army as it marched into Louisville as "much dissatisfied, full of unsoldierly clamor, noisy in denunciation of its commander." First Lieutenant James Bragg of the 40th Indiana wrote that "we are now the tiredest, dirtiest, sore-footed, sleepy, hungry-looking set of men ever come into Louisville. We were the worst wore-out set of men I ever saw. The way they treat us, if things do not get better soon, we will throw down our arms and go home."[7]

Arrival of the bedraggled army at the army's base of supplies, however, breathed life into both Buell and his men. "The entrance … was the occasion of the most inspiriting scenes," noted William S. Dodge of the 75th Illinois. "The streets were filled with the populace and from doors, balconies, and windows beautiful ladies and children waved handkerchiefs and tiny Union flags and hailed our soldiers as deliverers and defenders of the city! Although ragged and barefoot, it was deemed no disgrace but the most honorable proof of devotion to the great cause. The ladies' smiles and cheers and their kindly words of welcome gladdened their hearts and they felt that with so much beauty and sympathy on their side, they could not fail of success."[8]

Buell began to reorganize his command, incorporating nearly 25,000 new troops into the ranks and appointing Maj. Gens. Alexander M. McCook, Thomas Leonidas Crittenden, and William "Bull" Nelson as corps commanders. That final assignment did not last long, as Nelson was gunned down during a dispute with Brig. Gen. Jefferson C. Davis on September 29, forcing Buell to appoint newly promoted Brig. Gen. Charles Gilbert to corps command. And in the middle of the reorganization, as Buell was also dealing with the Nelson murder and concerns about Bragg's threats, the hammer from the government in Washington struck.

In late September, General-in-Chief Halleck dispatched Colonel Joseph McKibbin to Louisville with orders to relieve Buell and hand his command over to Maj. Gen. George H. Thomas. After McKibbin departed, information about Buell's rapid march to Louisville and his preparations to attack Bragg arrived in the US capital. The news produced a change of heart for Lincoln, who directed Halleck to recall McKibbin. The colonel, however, did not receive Halleck's recall in time,

---

7 Whitelaw Reid, *Ohio in the War: Her Statemen, Generals, and Soldiers. Volume 1* (Cincinnati, 1895), 718; Diary of 1st Lt. James Bragg, 40th Indiana, Sept. 24-27, 1862, entries, Spared & Shared, https://sparedshared22.wordpress.com/2021/05/26/an-awful-neglected-army-the-partial-1862-diary-of-lt-james-bragg-co-f-40th-indiana-infantry/, retrieved Nov. 18, 2021.

8 William S. Dodge, *History of the Old Second Division, Army of the Cumberland* (Chicago, 1864), 332.

and on the morning of September 29, he delivered the dispatch to Buell, who accordingly contacted Thomas and relinquished command of the army.[9]

This put Thomas in a thorny position. His relationship with Buell had always been more proper than warm, and even with the current campaign upon them, Buell had not devised his plans in concert with his senior subordinate. Nevertheless, Thomas felt a mistake had been made. "[A]lthough he did not approve of his commander's judgment of the late campaign, [he] saw that the error of judgment did not sanction the cruel injustice," wrote Donn Piatt, Thomas's biographer.

Meeting with Buell at the Galt House in downtown Louisville, Thomas informed Buell he would refuse to take command and would telegraph Halleck to request the order be suspended. "General Buell's preparations have been completed to move against the enemy, and I therefore respectfully ask that he may be retained in command," Thomas alerted Halleck. "My position is very embarrassing, not being as well informed as I should be as the command of this army and on the assumption of such responsibility."[10]

With word out about Buell's imminent removal, four Kentucky political leaders sent Lincoln a message informing him of General Nelson's death and asking that Buell be retained. "These two events have caused great regret and something of dismay," the message stated. "General Buell has, in a very high degree, the confidence of this state and of the army. His removal, especially at this critical moment, will be dispiriting to the people and to the army. In our judgment, the removal of General Buell will do great injury to the service in Kentucky."

The uproar from Kentucky's power structure and Thomas's reluctance to assume command now had the United States government embarrassed and on the defensive. Halleck promptly sent a dispatch suspending Buell's removal. Still, Thomas's action was not taken well by many in the administration. "Whether consciously or not," Piatt would write, "Thomas was siding with a West Pointer

---

9 OR 16/2:554. McKibbin messaged Halleck at 12:45 p.m. stating that he had delivered the dispatches and reported it was "fortunate that I obeyed instructions. Much dissatisfaction with General Buell."

10 Donn Piatt, *General George H. Thomas: A Critical Biography* (Cincinnati, 1893), 170-72; James B. Fry, *Operations of the Army Under Buell From June 10 to October 30, 1862, and the "Buell Commission."* (New York, 1884), 49-50.

and regular army officer against what might be construed as uncalled-for civilian interference."[11]

*   *   *

In early October, Buell led his army out of Louisville in Bragg's direction and skirmished with Confederate videttes for nearly a week as they headed toward Perryville, roughly 75 miles to the southeast. "We overtook Bragg's rearguard near Springfield on the morning of the 6th," recalled Judson Bishop of the 2nd Minnesota. "Both armies moved about 17 miles towards Perryville where there was a small stream known as the Chaplin River. The country we had covered during the past week was almost destitute of water and probably its supposed presence in the vicinity had something to do with locating the collision of the armies at that place.

"On the 7th we halted in the valley of Doctor's Creek, a branch of the Chaplin River in sight of and about three miles east of the village. The creek was nearly dry, only small pools here and there to be found in the bed, and guards were placed over them to prevent the watering of horses and mules in any except those reserved for that purpose."[12]

The two armies finally clashed outright at Perryville on October 8. Generals Bragg and Smith were convinced the Union drive against Perryville was merely a feint and that a coordinated push for Frankfort by forces under Maj. Gen. Joshua Sill represented Buell's main line of advance. Only 16,000 of Bragg's men were on the field, while Buell had 55,000 in the vicinity, though only a small portion of Buell's contingent would actually see action. Most of the subsequent fighting was waged by the 13,000 men of General McCook's I Corps, consisting of two divisions under Brig. Gens. Lovell Harrison Rousseau and James Streshly Jackson. What developed when these forces finally came to grips was a confused, murderous, brutal, and remarkably brief bloodbath.

Although the two armies fought for roughly five hours at Perryville, the butcher's bill was horrendous. Buell had 894 killed, 2,911 wounded, and 471 captured or missing for a total of 4,276 casualties. McCook's corps bore the brunt of these losses and its leadership was gutted: General Jackson was killed, as were

---

11 OR 16/2:557-558; Freeman Cleaves, *Rock of Chickamauga: The Life of General George H. Thomas* (Norman, 1948), 112.

12 Judson W. Bishop, *The Story of a Regiment, Being a Narrative of the Service of the Second Regiment, Minnesota Veteran Volunteer Infantry in the Civil War of 1861–65* (St Paul, 1890), 71.

both of his brigade commanders, Brig. Gen. William Terrill and Colonel George Webster. General Rousseau's three brigades suffered nearly half of the total Union casualties, and one of his brigade commanders, Colonel William H. Lytle, was wounded and captured.

In contrast, Crittenden's II Corps suffered only 12 casualties, and the majority of the 944 casualties in Gilbert's III Corps were in Brig. Gen. Phil Sheridan's 11th Division and Colonel Michael Gooding's 30th Brigade in the 9th Division. Though in the fight, thousands of Union soldiers did not fire a bullet, and because of an "acoustic shadow" Buell—stationed only three miles behind the lines—never heard the fighting until a courier arrived in the evening, too late to do anything about McCook's plight.

In what proved a Confederate tactical victory, Bragg's army was badly bloodied as well: 532 killed, 2,641 wounded, and 228 captured or missing for a total of 3,401 casualties. About half of those were in Maj. Gen. Benjamin Cheatham's Division in Leonidas Polk's Right Wing, but Brig. Gen. James Patton Anderson's and Simon Bolivar Buckner's divisions in William Hardee's Left Wing suffered heavily, too.

Bragg could not afford the hefty losses. Shortly after sunset, he learned the Army of the Ohio's other two corps were on the field and conceded that his army could not stay where it was and survive. "The battle of Perryville, a hard-fought fight against many odds, was merely a favorable incident which decided nothing," recalled Colonel David Urquhart, one of Bragg's officers. "Our army, however, was elated and did not dream of a retreat as we had held the field and bivouacked on it. But the commanding general, full of care, summoned his generals [Polk and Hardee] to a council in which both advised retreat."[13]

The fight at Perryville convinced Bragg it was time for his army to forsake Kentucky. Only a few thousand recruits had joined the Confederate ranks, hardly matching Morgan's eager forecast in July. "If they would help us with 50,000 men, their freedom would be secured," observed one journalist. "If they do not help, there is no propriety in keeping a Southern army here to fight for the liberty of a people who will not strike a blow themselves. This army must retire and leave them to their fate with the Yankees. General Bragg found the keystone of his entire plan of campaign dropped out."

Bragg, as Urquhardt would write, had accepted by early October "that the reported desire of Kentucky to cast her lot with the South had passed away, if such a disposition ever existed, for not only was Kentucky unprepared to enter the

---

13 "Bragg's Advance and Retreat," David Urquhart, Johnston, *Battles & Leaders*, Vol. 3, 603.

Confederacy but her people looked with dread at the prospect of the state being made a battlefield. He remarked to me again and again 'the people here have too many fat cattle and are too well off to fight.'"[14]

Buell's pursuit of Bragg's army after Perryville has been fairly described as "vigorous but by no means vehement." In the afterglow of the "victory" at Perryville, however, the Lincoln administration was, according to Reid, "elated with the vision of the army rushing pell-mell after the fragments of the Rebel rout through the mountains and relieving east Tennessee. Nothing less than the speedy occupation of Knoxville and Chattanooga was confidently expected."

Buell evidently viewed things differently, and a week after the battle he informed Halleck that pursuing Bragg into the East Tennessee mountains was "useless and inexpedient. The country between Crab Orchard and Cumberland Gap is almost a desert. The enemy has been driven into the heart of this desert and must go on for he cannot exist in it. For the same reason, we cannot pursue in it with any hope of overtaking him."

Citing the poor condition of the single available road and the necessity of his army to transport all its supplies along that road, Buell suggested it was preferential he turn toward Nashville, finish repairs on the Louisville & Nashville, and then prepare for the next campaign.

The results thus far, Buell confessed, were "not all that I had hoped, or all that faction might demand, yet composed as the army is, one half of perfectly new troops, it has defeated a powerful and thoroughly disciplined army in one battle and has driven it away, baffled and dispirited at least, and as much demoralized as an army can be under such discipline as Bragg maintains over all troops that he commands. I should say that the present time is perhaps as convenient as any for making a change that may be thought proper in the command of this army."[15]

It was what no one in Washington hoped to hear. Halleck and Lincoln, among others, desired a move into eastern Tennessee—the sooner the better. "The capture of east Tennessee should be the main object of your campaign," Halleck stressed to Buell on October 19. "I am directed by the President to say … your army must enter east Tennessee this fall and that it ought to move there while the

---

14 John Forsyth, *Mobile Register & Advertiser*, Oct. 14, 1862, 1; Johnston, *Battles & Leaders*, Vol. 3, 602. Bragg's seeming harsh comment simply recognized reality—Kentucky's agricultural economy was booming thanks in part to large purchases of mules, cattle, hogs, wool, and foodstuffs by the Union army. The hearts of the Kentuckians may have been with the South, but their pocketbooks were firmly tied to the North.

15 Reid, *Ohio in the War*, 721.

roads are passable. He does not understand why we cannot march as the enemy marches, live as he lives, and fight as he fights unless we admit the inferiority of our troops and our generals."

Even realizing the handwriting of his removal was on the wall, Buell remained as stiff-necked as ever. He continued to argue his point in a lengthy message the following day, all boiling down to one key argument: Bragg's army could outperform Buell's because Bragg operated under stricter discipline than Buell could get his volunteers to accept. "I can give good reasons why we cannot do all that the enemy has attempted to do," the Ohioan wrote, "such as operating without a base, etc. without ascribing the difference to the inferiority of our generals, though that may be true. The spirit of rebellion enforces a subordination to privations and want which public sentiment renders absolutely impossible among our troops. The discipline of the Rebel army is superior to ours."[16]

Lincoln had already decided Buell needed to go, and he set the wheels in motion by instructing Halleck to bring Buell's replacement to Kentucky. Two names stood out during discussions among the Cabinet. Some favored promoting McCook; others favored Rosecrans. Reconsideration of Thomas was entertained, but Lincoln ended the debate by stating he would let Thomas wait and go with Rosecrans.

Rosecrans was in Corinth finishing his after-action report of the recent fighting there when he received an order to report to Cincinnati, Ohio. It took several days to make the trip via rail, and when Rosecrans arrived in what was his hometown on October 28, he received a packet of papers from Halleck. "I found an autograph note from General Halleck directing me to proceed to the headquarters of General Buell and assume command of the army," he recalled. The autograph note, addressed to Buell and dated October 24, 1862, stated that "the President directs that on the presentation of this order, you will turn over your command to Major General W.S. Rosecrans and repair to Indianapolis, Indiana, reporting from that place to the adjutant general of the army for further orders."[17]

The packet of papers also included a cover letter from Halleck that "ordered Rosecrans to drive the enemy from Kentucky and middle Tennessee and to take and hold east Tennessee, cutting the railroad so as to sever Virginia, Georgia, and the Carolinas from the rest of the Confederacy. I need not urge upon you the

16 Reid, *Ohio in the War*, 722-23.

17 Ibid., 723; Speech of General William S. Rosecrans, *Third Reunion of the Society of the Army of the Cumberland at Indianapolis, Indiana, December 15–16, 1869* (Cincinnati, 1870), 73.

necessity of giving active employment to your forces. Neither the country nor the government will much longer put up with the inactivity of some of our armies and generals."

Colonel Gilbert C. Kniffen, on Crittenden's staff, noted that the usual method of relieving an officer "had always been to issue simultaneous orders to both officers, thus affording time to the officer to be relieved in which to arrange the details of his office, but Halleck was a law unto himself and in relieving an army officer usually did it in a way to render it equivalent to dismissal from the service." Rosecrans later wrote that he "felt more like a constable bearing a writ for the ejection of a tenant than like a general on his way to relieve a brother officer."[18]

Rosecrans sent two messages. The first was to Halleck acknowledging the orders, the second was to his former commander, Ulysses Grant, in Tennessee. "My orders are to relieve General Buell and assume command of the Department of the Cumberland, and we are to cooperate so far as possible to support each other's operations," he stated. After waiting for the arrival of his horses and briefly visiting his family, Rosecrans and eight members of his staff traveled the following morning by train to Louisville. In Louisville, where he was nursing an injured leg, Buell learned through a newspaper article on October 29 that Rosecrans was replacing him. At 11:30 a.m., he messaged Halleck, "[I]f, as the papers report, my successor has been appointed, it is important that I should know it and that he should enter on the command immediately as the troops are already in motion." There is no record whether Halleck replied.[19]

Rosecrans arrived in Louisville that night and checked into the Galt House, the site of "Bull" Nelson's murder a month earlier. Rosecrans was a notorious night owl, and early in the morning on October 30, he composed a personal letter to Buell that included Halleck's command transfer directive. "I know the bearer of unwelcome news has a 'losing office' but feel assured that you are too high a gentleman and too true a soldier to permit this to introduce any personal unkindness between us," he wrote suavely. "I, like yourself, am neither an intriguer nor newspaper soldier. I go where I am ordered, but propriety will permit me to say that I have often felt indignant at the petty attacks on you by a portion of the press during the past summer and that you had my high respect for ability as a soldier. I

---

18 Gilbert C. Kniffen, "Army of the Cumberland and the Battle of Stones River." MOLLUS, District of Columbia, Vol. 3, 412; William M. Lamers, *The Edge of Glory: A Biography of General William S. Rosecrans, U.S.A.* (Baton Rouge, 1961), 181-82.

19 OR 16/2:650-651.

beg you to give me all the aid you can for the performance of duties of which no one better than yourself knows the difficulties."[20]

Buell accepted his removal with the stoicism and professionalism that had marked his career, and the formal change of command took place the following morning at Buell's headquarters. No doubt relieved that the hammer had finally dropped, Buell wrote a laconic farewell message to the army, stating that "it is impossible for the general, without feelings of regard and warm interest in their future success, to part with the troops whom he has been the instrument of converting from raw levies into a powerful army. He will pray that it may be the instrument of speedily restoring the Union to its integrity, and there is no individual in its ranks in whose honor and welfare he will not feel a special interest."[21]

The *Louisville Daily Journal* defended Buell to the last but finally conceded that Buell's "removal from the command, unjust and injudicious as we believe it to be, indicates at least a vigorous determination in a quarter where vigorous determination is much needed by the country. Vigorous blows are no doubt to be struck at once wherever there is a foe to be met."[22]

In Indianapolis, Indiana Governor Oliver Morton had organized a conference of governors demanding that Lincoln remove Buell. Learning that had occurred, however, the relieved governor rushed his thanks to the president and pointed out that "the removal of General Buell could not have been delayed an hour with safety to the army or the cause." The men of the army, too, were relieved and elated at the change. "It is said that the army in Flanders swore terribly," noted David Lathrop of the 59th Illinois. "But if anyone had been fond of profanity and wished to hear vigorous denunciations in unmistakable Saxon, they should have heard the Army of the Ohio on the merits of the arch traitor Don Carlos Buell."[23]

*   *   *

In late October 1862, disappointment was the feeling in Richmond, Virginia, but it was at least tempered with optimism that better days lay ahead for the Confederacy. Hopes that soared in September when Robert E. Lee marched into

---

20 Ibid., 653.

21 Ibid., 654.

22 "The report that Gen. Buell…," *Louisville Daily Journal,* Oct. 31, 1862, 2.

23 Stephen D. Engle, *Don Carlos Buell: The Most Promising of All,* (Chapel Hill, 1999), 319-20; David Lathrop, *The History of the Fifty-Ninth Regiment Illinois Volunteers* (Indianapolis, 1865), 172.

Maryland, Bragg into Kentucky, and Maj. Gens. Sterling Price and Earl Van Dorn into West Tennessee had been dashed, respectively, by bitter and bloody reverses at Antietam, Iuka, Corinth, and Perryville—all occurring in a matter of weeks. Daily newspapers devoted column after column to the casualty lists, underscoring the hefty price in lives the South would have to pay to obtain its independence. Already thousands of graves pockmarked the land, and the war appeared to have no end in sight. Foreign intervention that seemed so close in the heady days before Antietam slipped away in the wake of the failures east and west.

"It can no longer be concealed that the campaign in the west has proved a failure," grieved the Richmond Examiner. "Expectation was on tiptoe all the summer for a brilliant and successful campaign of our armies. But the season has passed, winter is coming on, and the enemy, without losing any ground, is already acting on the offensive. Tennessee, instead of being cleared of the enemy, is still overrun and under his heel. Kentucky, instead of being relieved, is abandoned to his mercy. The Mississippi is in his possession and in fact, everything is in a worse condition than it was in the spring.

"That this disappointment of Southern expectations is due to the want of generalship is perfectly clear and is the universal conviction. The loss of the campaign in the West is a most serious affair to the Confederacy."[24]

Lambasting Bragg's competence was a familiar theme for the Southern press. "With an iron heart, an iron hand, and a wooden head, his failure in a position where the highest intellectual facilities were demanded was predestined," howled editor John M. Daniel of the Richmond Examiner. "As commander-in-chief, he is worse than inexperienced for he has grown old and hardened in a subaltern position of a regular army." The editor of the Columbus (Ga.) Sun complained that Bragg's "late campaign in Kentucky speaks for itself-speaks in language which all cannot fail to understand. After three months of tramping, he has returned to east Tennessee having nothing to show for his campaign but a train of supplies or spoils, most of which were purchased with Confederate notes."[25]

The anti-Davis faction pointed to the failure in Kentucky as evidence of the president's faltering leadership. In their view, the collapse of the fortunes in the West began with Beauregard's removal the previous summer—chickens that had now come home to roost. "Many severe things are alleged against the President for depriving Beauregard of the command of the western army," noted John

24 "Generals Bragg and Van Dorn," *Memphis Daily Appeal,* Oct. 30, 1862, 2.

25 Andrews, *South Reports the Civil War,* 253.

Beauchamp Jones on October 25, 1862. "It is alleged that Bragg reported that the enemy would have been annihilated at Shiloh if Beauregard had fought an hour longer. Now it appears that Bragg would have annihilated the enemy at Perryville if he had fought an hour longer!"[26]

The burden for those failures fell foremost on Davis's shoulders, and no one understood this better than Bragg, which is why he paid a quick visit to his commander in chief in Richmond. Summoned to personally debrief the president on the Kentucky Campaign, Bragg left the army under his subordinate, Leonidas Polk, and arrived in Richmond "as unpopular with the citizens as a Union general." Having crowed for his head, the Richmond press "decided I was removed from command," Bragg wrote his wife, Eliza. If, however, the general feared for his job, Bragg biographer Grady McWhiney observed that Davis quickly put him at ease by dismissing "most of the complaints against [him] as the anticipated grumblings of administration critics; unpleasant, certainly, but nothing to worry about."[27]

No doubt relieved that his own neck was spared, Bragg used the meeting with Davis to explain the difficulties of the campaign and insisted he still had his peers' respect. The true cause of the reverse in Kentucky, Bragg averred, had nothing to do with strategy. Errors might have been made, but the fact was that the Kentuckians had refused to flock to the Confederate standard. Their failure to do so, he stressed, doomed the campaign. "Bragg's modesty and candor," McWhiney wrote, "obviously impressed Davis."

Bragg's version of the Kentucky Campaign quickly made the rounds and by October 28, Jones reported that "Bragg will not probably be deprived of his command. He was opposed by vastly superior numbers and succeeded in getting away with the largest number of provisions, clothing, etc. ever obtained by an army. He brought out 15,000 horses and mules, 8,000 beeves [cattle], 50,000 barrels of pork, a great number of hogs, and a million yards of Kentucky cloth. It is said Bragg's wagon train was 40 miles long! A western tale, I fear…"[28]

Richard Hawes, Kentucky's Confederate governor, complained loudly that Bragg's campaign had been riddled with strategic errors, chief among them that the general had not stayed long enough for Kentuckians to make their allegiance

---

26 Jones, *A Rebel War Clerk's Diary*, 110.

27 McWhiney, *Braxton Bragg and Confederate Defeat*, 326-28.

28 Jones, *A Rebel War Clerk's Diary*, 111. One Southern reporter investigated this and found that the 40-mile train of supplies "have their existence for the most part only in the imagination."

known. Long Federal occupation had terrified the populace into subservience, argued Hawes. "It was natural that our people should be slow in believing our power to hold the state," he explained. "Our rich men of Southern affinities loved their estates more than their liberties, but there were many, very many shining exceptions."[29]

The campaign's failure, however, had eroded the confidence in Bragg of many within the army. According to Dr. D.W. Yandell, "I concur in the judgment already rendered by the people and the army that as a military commander he [Bragg] is utterly incompetent." John Buie complained in a letter than "everybody seems to have lost all confidence in him since his Kentucky raid."

Resting in camp outside Knoxville, Joshua Callaway of the 28th Alabama reported that "we finally have had to evacuate Kentucky. We are now naked, bare-footed, dirty, filthy, and lousy. We have never been paid off yet. My little old blanket has long since failed but for the kindness of my messmates who let me sleep with them I should long since have gone under. It all feels really like we are naked, poor, despised, and forsaken."

Callaway became sick during the march from Perryville and had spent recent days bouncing along in an army wagon, where he "wept, cried, prayed, thought of home, wife, and children, blessed and cursed the teamsters, the wagon masters, the quartermasters, the generals, the Yankees, and the war generally."[30]

The roots of the dissension grew deepest in the officer corps. Brigadier General St. John Richardson Liddell recalled an incident on the march to Cumberland Gap that he believed proved "Bragg was not well supported by his generals." "In the presence of General Hardee, I was censuring Bragg severely for throwing away his chances," began the general, who continued:

Hardee said, 'You speak very plainly. I am half inclined to arrest you.' I answered, 'Very well, do so. I speak the truth at all events.' Hardee was jesting, but at the moment I was nettled and did not perceive his humor. Hardee remarked further that when all the facts were known, General Polk would be credited for saving Bragg's army in causing its timely retreat from Kentucky. Our chances were better in Kentucky than elsewhere but, alas, Bragg's failure here now deferred the whole thing. This was the last, aye the very last,

---

29 McWhiney, *Braxton Bragg and Confederate Defeat*, 332-33.

30 Ibid., 326-30; Hallock, *The Civil War Letters of Joshua K. Callaway*, 62-63.

chance to accomplish anything by strategy. The plainest man could see the fates were against us.[31]

Bragg nevertheless had his supporters, primarily troops from his old command who refused to join in the clamor against him. "I still think he is as good a general as we have in the Confederacy," wrote Brig. Gen. John K. Jackson. "It is certainly true that the army was disappointed when we were ordered to fall back, but every officer and man is now satisfied that it was the very best thing that could have been done. The opinion of the army sustains General Bragg … notwithstanding the censure of the newspapers."

One officer complained that Lee's invasion of Maryland had produced little except a horrific casualty list, yet Lee's campaign was being praised and Bragg's campaign, which had driven the Federals out of Alabama and a large portion of Middle Tennessee, was called a failure. "General Bragg, instead of hearing on his return the universal thanks of his countrymen for relieving them, is greeted with the upbraidings of an almost unanimous press and reproaches of an ungrateful people for not accomplishing an impossibility," the officer observed. "Which campaign of the two had been profitable to the country? The victories of General Lee with the spilling of oceans of blood, or the successes of General Bragg?"[32]

Davis remained concerned, however, about rumors of command dysfunction pervading Bragg's army, so he also summoned Smith and Polk to obtain their frank assessments of the Kentucky Campaign. Smith, already spouting off about how Bragg's indecision had cost the campaign that he had so brilliantly started, saw Davis immediately after Bragg's visit. He requested Bragg be replaced by General Joseph E. Johnston. Davis demurred, appealing to Smith's patriotism to persuade the Floridian to knock off his public criticisms of Bragg.

Smith followed Davis's injunction to keep quiet on that subject, but his distaste for any further service with the commander was abundantly clear. On his way out of Richmond, Smith and Bragg met on a train. Smith expected a stormy meeting, but, as he wrote his wife, Bragg was apparently unaware of Smith's dissatisfaction with his leadership and "spoke kindly to me and in the highest terms of praise and admiration of my personal character and soldierly qualities. I was astonished."[33]

---

31 Nathaniel C. Hughes, ed., *Liddell's Record* (Baton Rouge, 1985), 98.

32 Brigadier General John K. Jackson letter, Charles Colcock Jones Papers, Duke University; McWhiney, *Braxton Bragg and Confederate Defeat*, 331, 335.

33 Woodworth, *Jefferson Davis and His Generals*, 167.

Lieutenant General Leonidas Polk

Alabama Department of Archives and History

Leonidas Polk visited Davis in mid-November. His assessment was blunt and unequivocal: Regardless of Bragg's abilities as an organizer of an army, "he had been wanting in the higher elements of generalship in the conduct of the campaign. In view of the admitted possibilities of the campaign, he considered it a failure, an opinion he said he believed Generals Kirby Smith and Hardee shared with him. He further said that General Bragg had lost the confidence of his generals and in answer to a suggestion from the President of a change of commanders, requested that General Joseph E. Johnston should be assigned to the command."

The evidence is reliable that the "Fighting Bishop" orchestrated a behind-the-scenes campaign within the ranks to undermine Braxton Bragg and perhaps secure command of the army for himself, co-opting Hardee to use his considerable prestige "to turn the army's officer corps against Bragg. At this Hardee proved highly efficient." According to historian Steven Woodworth, Hardee conducted a series of classes of instruction, much like a course at West Point, for his volunteer officers and used the classes to mix "lessons with innuendo against and outright criticism of Bragg. Hardee soon had his subordinates believing that their commander was a blundering incompetent whose judgements could never be trusted."

For his part, Polk used his charming and ingratiating manners, combined with a facile pen, to reach out to prominent politicians to spread the anti-Bragg gospel throughout the Confederacy. Bragg's poor contemporary reputation underscores how successful this campaign ultimately proved.[34]

Davis faced a conundrum. Because he highly respected the opinions and service of both Bragg and Smith, the last he wanted to hear was that the Army of Mississippi needed a new commander, especially if that new commander would be Joe Johnston, with whom Davis had already had his troubles while Johnston commanded in Virginia. But Davis also had a blind spot for Polk. Despite Polk's insubordinate actions in bitterly denouncing his commander, Davis could not bring himself to remove a man he considered a personal friend. Davis wanted both to support Bragg and keep Polk. Demoting Bragg would feed fresh ammunition to the administration's critics and invalidate the official line that the Kentucky Campaign had been successful, so that was not an option.

Also, now that Johnston had recovered from his serious wounding at Seven Pines, Virginia, on May 31, 1862, he needed an appropriate command. Given Lee's recent successes with the Army of Northern Virginia, Davis had no plan to return Johnston to his former role. He instead compromised, recommending that Polk, Hardee, and Smith all be promoted to lieutenant general in recognition of their "distinguished" service in Kentucky (effectively glossing over any difficulties arising from their flawed performances during that campaign). He also retained Bragg in command of what would be renamed the Army of Tennessee, and on November 24 he appointed Johnston to command a new department that encompassed Bragg's, Smith's, and Pemberton's armies covering the Western Confederacy between the Appalachian Mountains and the Mississippi River.[35]

Davis and Johnston had been fellow cadets at West Point, but they were never friendly at the academy, and that tension set the tone for their fraught relationship during the Civil War. Few doubted the martial abilities of Johnston, one of the Confederacy's highest-ranking soldiers, and the courtly Virginian's gracious manners and gravitas made him a natural leader in the army's officer corps. Johnston, though, complained frequently about his rank as the fourth senior general in the army, feeling that his antebellum stint as the US Army's quartermaster general should have placed him at the top of the list.

He also became known as a risk-averse perfectionist who would not engage in battle unless the conditions were exactly right, and in Johnston's mind, conditions

---

34 Joseph H. Parks, *General Leonidas Polk, C.S.A. The Fighting Bishop* (Baton Rouge, 1962), 279-80; Woodworth, *Jefferson Davis and His Generals*, 165-66.

35 Woodworth, *Jefferson Davis and His Generals*, 165-73.

were never right. As such, he showed a preference to retreat rather than give battle and challenge the odds. Johnston's assignment to the overall command of the Western armies would prove to be his most challenging of the war. It would require all of his persuasive powers to cajole the three army commanders below him into unified action.

*   *   *

Rosecrans likewise grappled with multiple first-class personnel crises upon assuming command of the Army of the Ohio, the first order of business being appointment of a cavalry chief. Rosecrans assumed that an army the size of Buell's would possess between 12,000 and 15,000 cavalrymen; he learned upon taking command that Buell's army had less than half that, most of the troopers scattered in small detachments across the country and indifferently led. "A portion of these were chiefly valuable for their capacity to evade danger and good service," journalist and politician William D. Bickham noted acidly. "A troop of jockeys with riding whips were quite as effective as some of the squadrons."

Rosecrans telegraphed Halleck upon assuming command on October 30 requesting that his best divisional commander from Corinth, Maj. Gen. David S. Stanley, be sent to him. "Besides being an able and indefatigable soldier, he is a thorough cavalry officer, and he can do more good to the service commanding cavalry than an infantry division," Rosecrans insisted. "Stanley will double our forces without expense."[36]

The second personnel crisis arose after Rosecrans's arrival: his senior commander, George Thomas, now desired reassignment. Thomas—already a legend with the enlisted men, who freely bestowed upon the dignified (and subsequently embarrassed) Virginian nicknames such as Old Pap, Old Slow Trot, and Uncle George—was looked upon by many as the heir apparent to Buell. He was known throughout the army as a thorough soldier who had been in uniform since the beginning and intimately understood its strengths and problems.

For Thomas, Rosecrans's appointment came as a rude shock. He was offered command of the army a month before and had refused it for what he considered legitimate professional reasons, and he naturally felt now that Buell's removal set him up to be the army's next commander. "Today, I am officially informed that

---

36 William D. Bickham, *Rosecrans' Campaign With the Fourteenth Army Corps of the Army of the Cumberland* (Cincinnati, 1863), 24; OR 16/2:653.

Major General George Thomas

Author's Collection

Buell is relieved by General Rosecrans, my junior," Thomas messaged Halleck with thinly disguised disgust. "Although I do not claim for myself any superior ability yet feeling conscious that no just cause exists for overslaughing me by placing me under my junior, I feel deeply mortified and aggrieved at the action taken in this matter."[37]

The issue of seniority generally proved touchy to Regular Army officers such as Thomas. When he was informed that Rosecrans's commission as a major general was dated August 21, 1862, it meant he was not only Thomas's junior, but junior also to Army of the Ohio corps commanders McCook and Crittenden. What Thomas did not know was that upon appointing Rosecrans to command of the army. Lincoln had backdated his commission to March 21, 1862.

It was two weeks before Halleck replied to Thomas's note, and in doing so he blamed Old Pap for the situation. "When it was determined to relieve General Buell, another person was spoken of as his successor, and it was through my repeated solicitation that you were appointed. You having virtually declined the command at that time it was necessary to appoint another, and General Rosecrans was selected," Halleck wrote. "You are mistaken about General Rosecrans being your junior. His commission dates prior to yours. It was not possible to give you the command in Tennessee after you had once declined it."

Thomas took Halleck at his word and messaged back that had he known Rosecrans was his senior, he would not have objected. "I have no objection

37 OR 16/2:657.

whatever to serving under General Rosecrans now that I know his commission dates prior to mine."[38]

The anger Thomas felt at being passed over was considerably mollified upon his first meeting with his new commander at Bowling Green, Kentucky, on November 2. Rosecrans graciously offered to divide the army in any way required to get Thomas to stay. "I have been assigned to the command of this army," Rosecrans told the Virginian. "You are my senior in service, in years, and in merit; I do not come to take command without a great deal of diffidence, but as it has been so ordered by the government. I want a perfect understanding with you. You know well my friendship for you and I wish to know what you think about it."

Thomas, Rosecrans would write, "replied that he had the most perfect confidence and highest regard and friendship for me. He said that he had always placed entire confidence in me and that he had always a dislike for a violation of the regular system of promotion by seniority in the army. He thought of asking for service in Texas." When Thomas inquired about Rosecrans's date of rank, the commander confirmed it was March 21, 1862. "Well, that is older than mine and removes the last objection I have," Thomas replied.[39]

The ice finally broken, the two men talked for hours about how best to reorganize the army. The staff officers of both generals noticed how well the two worked together. It proved a superb pairing of command styles and personalities and laid the groundwork for Rosecrans's future successes with his new command. The quiet and reserved Virginian quickly warmed to the brilliant and rapid-tongued Buckeye commander. "The two were a contrast in temperament," observed historian Freeman Cleaves. "Thomas was careful, cautious, watchful, and deliberate, while Rosecrans was ebullient, pugnacious, impulsive, and subject to alternate moods of elation and depression." Thomas spoke slowly and was a close observer; Rosecrans spoke at a breakneck pace, quickly rendered judgments, and took in all manner of details with just a glance.

Thomas began making frequent visits to Rosecrans's headquarters, and members of their staffs recognized that Thomas was serving as Rosecrans's de facto chief of staff. "It had been observed that General Rosecrans did not 'consult' habitually upon the principles and policy of the campaign with other commanding officers. It soon got to be understood in the camps that Pap Thomas was chief

---

38 Ibid., 663. Thomas would be understandably angry after Rosecrans revealed that his commission had been backdated.

39 *Third Reunion of the Society of the Army of the Cumberland,* 74-75.

counsellor at headquarters and confidence in Rosey grew apace," remembered one staff officer.[40]

Rosecrans offered Thomas the position as second in command, the same position he held under Buell, but Thomas deferred, remembering that he felt like a "nobody" in that role and instead accepted command of five divisions of what would become the Center Corps. Rosecrans reorganized the army into three "wings," a lofty name for what were essentially corps-sized units. General Gilbert was demoted and sent back to Kentucky and his old III Corps was disassembled, with two of his divisions going to McCook and another to Thomas. McCook's own I Corps was likewise altered, and he was given command of the Right Wing, consisting of the divisions of Colonel William E. Woodruff and Generals Sill and Sheridan. Crittenden retained command of his II Corps, now called the Left Wing and consisting of the divisions of Brig. Gens. Thomas J. Wood, William Sooy Smith, and Horatio P. Van Cleve.[41] Thomas's new command consisted of the divisions of Brig. Gens. Ebenezer Dumont, Speed S. Fry, James S. Negley, John M. Palmer, and Lovell Rousseau.

*   *   *

William Starke Rosecrans was born September 6, 1819, in log cabin along Little Taylor Run near Berkshire in Delaware County, Ohio, to Crandall and Jemima (Hopkins) Rosecrans. Rosecrans's father was of Dutch lineage; the family's original name was Rosenkrantz but was changed to Rosecrans during the Revolutionary War so they would not be mistaken for Hessians. Crandall moved to the Ohio wilderness from Pennsylvania with his parents in 1808 and soon cleared a 160-acre farm next to his father's farm and started a family.

Prior to marrying Jemima in 1816, Crandall distinguished himself by serving as General William Henry Harrison's adjutant for two years during the War of 1812. Patriotism ran in the family; Rosecrans's grandfather on his mother's side fought as a lieutenant in the Connecticut militia during the Revolution and was related to Stephen Hopkins, a signer of the Declaration of Independence. "The Rosecrans

---

40 Cleaves, *Rock of Chickamauga*, 120; Bickham, *Rosecrans' Campaign*, 31.

41 In December 1862, Smith would be replaced by John Palmer and named a major general on November 29—likely an army seniority decision, as Smith remained a brigadier. Smith was transferred to division command in the 16th Corps with Grant and later led the Army of the Tennessee's cavalry.

family converted a militant patriotism into a tradition of soldiering and adventure," observed biographer William Lamers. "The family was deeply religious with religion expressing itself in a stern moral code."[42]

Most of Rosecrans's youth was spent helping his father operate a tavern and store near Homer in Licking County. Rosecrans attended the country schools but was primarily self-taught. A voracious reader with a deep love of history, William (he "would not permit" anyone to call him anything else) memorized a copy of the Declaration of Independence that hung in the family home and would recite it for neighbors. His parents taught him the values of integrity, charity, honesty, and devotion to study, but William also proved quick-tempered, strong-willed, and not above getting into scraps with other children of the neighborhood. His skill at arithmetic led to several clerkships with shopkeepers in town. The Rosecrans penchant for adventure also led to William making a river trip down the Mississippi River in 1835 at age 16, only to become ill at Vicksburg, Mississippi, and return home.

The boy's scholarly talents clearly called for further education to reach his full potential, but as college was not something Crandall Rosecrans could afford, William embarked on a 50-mile trek to be interviewed by Congressman Alexander Harper in hopes of securing an appointment to West Point. Harper elected to nominate William, but after waiting for three months with no reply from the academy, Rosecrans took matters in his own hands and wrote directly to Secretary of War Joel Poinsett. By June 1838, he was traveling east to join the 112 members of West Point's Class of 1842.

Along with classmates Don Carlos Buell, Earl Van Dorn, and James Longstreet, Rosecrans proved to be a fine student, graduating fifth in his class and earning assignment to the army's elite engineering corps. At West Point, he also met his future wife, Anna Hegeman.

Rosecrans's first assignment was at Fort Monroe near Norfolk, Virginia, but he returned to West Point the following year as an assistant professor of engineering with a promotion to the rank of first lieutenant. It proved to be his only promotion during his pre-war army career. Rosecrans missed action in the Mexican War, working domestic assignments that included a five-year stint supervising the construction of fortifications at Newport, Rhode Island.

---

42 General Rosecrans insisted his name be pronounced "ro-sa-krontz" in honor of his Dutch ancestors.

In 1845, Rosecrans discovered Catholicism, having been introduced to John Milner's The End of Religious Controversy by a book peddler. He was soon thoroughly converted, with fellow army officer Milo S. Hascall referring to Rosecrans as a "crank on the subject." Rosecrans's faith became the centerpiece of his life, and he enjoyed few things more than religious discourse, often keeping his staff awake at all hours discussing this topic.

Raising a family on a lieutenant's salary proved increasingly difficult, and in March 1854 Rosecrans resigned from the army to enter civil life. Restlessness and tireless energy marked his return to Cincinnati. He set up shop as a contract architect and engineer, but by June 1855 he and his family had moved to Wheeling, Virginia, where he took charge of the Cannel River Coal Company's mines up the Kanawha River.

Rosecrans soon devised a series of locks to speed the transport of coal down the Kanawha known as the Coal River Slack Water Navigation Company, but floods wiped out his locks and by 1857 Rosecrans was experimenting with what was then known as coal oil, now called kerosene. He returned to Cincinnati and founded the Preston Coal Company but suffered severe burns on the right side of his face when a flask exploded, taking 18 months to recover.[43]

Before the war, Rosecrans and his family still lived modestly, the 1860 census showing his personal property valued at only $600. The outbreak of hostilities found Rosecrans busily drilling the Marion Rifles, a militia company in Cincinnati, but the tireless inventor turned over operations to his business partners and offered his services to Governor William Dennison on April 19, 1861. Dennison promptly put Rosecrans on Maj. Gen. George B. McClellan's staff, and McClellan set him to work laying out Camp Dennison near Cincinnati. In May, Rosecrans was commissioned colonel of the 23rd Ohio, serving briefly with Eliakim Scammon and future US presidents Rutherford B. Hayes and William McKinley. That would lead to a brigadier general's commission, and he soon returned to his old stomping grounds in western Virginia to combat the Confederacy.[44]

McClellan commanded roughly 30,000 Federal troops in western Virginia, and after gaining a quick and relatively bloodless victory at Philippi in early June 1861, "Little Mac" pushed farther into the state along the Kanawha Valley. A

---

43 Rosecrans grew a beard that covered the worst of the scars, and most images of the general depict him with the right side of his face shielded or minimized. As he was sensitive about the scars, few images exist showing them.

44 Lamers, *The Edge of Glory*, 1-31.

Confederate force perched atop Rich Mountain was McClellan's next target, and he devised a plan to split his force, entrusting Rosecrans to lead a flanking maneuver along a little-traveled mountain road to land squarely in the Confederate rear. Once Rosecrans was heavily engaged, McClellan would attack from the other side of the camp. It was a solid plan, but communications between the two Ohioans lagged and Rosecrans ended attacking the Confederate force with only his own troops.

In the wild melee that followed, Rosecrans ordered his three regiments of Indiana troops to fix bayonets and charge, but regimental order fell apart as the men took to cover behind the trees and fought independently. Rosecrans was appalled seeing one captain "going around with a cane over his shoulder, no sword at all, haw-bucking his soldiers about with his finger. There was not a captain who knew how to manage his men."

Rosecrans turned to the 19th Ohio, a unit he had dismissively called "a bandbox regiment," and ordered the Buckeye boys to advance and open fire. "We then halted and fired a volley in good style," remembered Lieutenant Henry Wolcott. "Our first fire silenced the enemy's battery and the second was terribly destructive. Just as we fired the Rebels were forming in line in the woods behind their breastworks on the hill across the road from us, our shot struck right in their ranks and mowed them down in heaps literally." The 19th Ohio's volleys broke the Confederate line, and Rosecrans never called those Buckeyes "a bandbox regiment" again.

Even though McClellan praised Rosecrans in his reports, he garnered the lion's share of the press's adulation and soon departed to head the Army of the Potomac. Rosecrans felt betrayed; McClellan had failed to play his part in the battle, then shrewdly blamed Rosecrans's failure to communicate, yet he walked away with the credit and a promotion to boot![45]

Whitelaw Reid assessed Rosecrans performance at Rich Mountain, his first commanding troops in battle, and noted that it formed a perfect synopsis of Rosecrans's future generalship. Rosey's personal bravery, strategic sense, intelligence, energy, and industry were evident. "His conduct," Reid wrote, "showed a thorough comprehension of the true method of handling raw volunteer troops, that disposition to go wherever he asked his soldiers to go which always made him a favorite with the men in the ranks. But he already exhibited symptoms of the personal imprudence which was to form so signal a feature of his character by casual hints as to his dissatisfaction with the conduct of his superior officer."

---

45 Ibid., 36; Lt. Henry G. Wolcott, Co. C, 19th Ohio, *Western Reserve Chronicle*, Jul. 24, 1861, 2.

Rosecrans, it seemed, never knew when to quit; he developed a penchant for pushing himself to the point of exhaustion, and rather than rely on his subordinates, he felt he had to bear the whole load on his own shoulders. It would eventually prove to be his undoing.[46]

McClellan's departure dropped the command of the western Virginia army into Rosecrans's lap, but the 90-day volunteers in its ranks were returning home to be mustered out and longer-service volunteers were slowly arriving in theater to replace them. These new troops were just as green as the 90-day ones they replaced. Worse yet, Robert E. Lee's arrival in the theater to command the state's bickering brigadiers Henry Wise and former Secretary of War John B. Floyd promised a vigorous resumption of the fight for western Virginia. One of Rosecrans's recently arrived regiments, the 7th Ohio under Colonel Erastus B. Tyler, was handled roughly at Kessler's Cross Lanes on August 26, 1861, prompting Rosey to march three brigades of his "monstrously green" army south from Clarksburg to confront the Confederates at Carnifex Ferry along the Gauley River. Scouts and civilians exaggerated the size of the Confederate force, but Rosecrans would not consider turning back. "We cannot stop to count numbers," he growled. "We must fight and whip him or pass him."[47]

The resulting battle of Carnifex Ferry on September 10, 1861, was a sloppy affair; Rosecrans's lead brigade under an inebriated Brig. Gen. Henry W. Benham overran an abandoned Confederate camp before stumbling on Floyd's entrenched force, which left both forces blasting away at each other. Rosey did not have much choice but to order up additional reinforcements to support Benham; had he ordered a withdrawal, he feared his newcomers would unravel. Rosecrans considered staging a nighttime flanking assault with the 9th and 13th Ohio regiments but relented when he realized his men's exhaustion.

The piecemeal Federal assaults failed to budge the Virginians. As night closed and Rosecrans pulled his forces back, two of his regiments mistakenly opened fire on each other. Regardless of the confusion in the Federal ranks, Floyd literally had his back to the wall and in the darkness ordered his troops to retreat. It was a nominal Union victory that cost Rosey about 150 casualties and reflected little

---

46 Lamers, *The Edge of Glory*, 38.

47 Reid, *Ohio in the War*, 317-18.

credit on anyone involved, but this reaffirmation of Union power solidified Federal control of the Kanawha Valley.[48]

Through deft maneuvering, Rosecrans managed to hold his ground in western Virginia, and by November the army went into winter quarters to train and recuperate. Rosecrans hoped to march his troops into the Shenandoah Valley, but the administration, suddenly needing to find a home for Maj. Gen. John C. Fremont, ordered Rosecrans to Washington and gave command of the newly named Mountain Department to "The Pathfinder."

Before reporting to the capital, however, Rosecrans spent much of April 1862 hunting for Brig. Gen. Louis Blenker's division, which had gotten lost in the mountains while campaigning. But by mid-May, he received a new assignment in Corinth, Mississippi, under his old West Point classmate John Pope. In the command shuffling that occurred after Henry Halleck was transferred to Washington to serve as general in chief, Rosecrans found himself under Ulysses S. Grant's command. Grant's "subsequent ill-will was to prove so baleful," Whitelaw Reid would later note.[49]

*　*　*

When Braxton Bragg marched into Kentucky in August 1862, Confederate armies under Sterling Price and Earl Van Dorn marched into northern Mississippi to confront Grant's army, intent on preventing the dispatch of reinforcements to assist Buell. Grant tried to trap Price's army at Iuka before Price could join Van Dorn. He planned to use two converging columns, one under Rosecrans and the second under Maj. Gen. Edward O. C. Ord, to approach Price from the south and the west, a simultaneous strike that would overwhelm the Confederates. The plan, which called for close coordination and timing, stipulated that Rosecrans was to strike first, and once Ord heard that Rosecrans was engaged, he would attack as well. Coordination in the dense Mississippi woods, however, broke down.

Rosecrans arrived at Iuka later than planned on September 19, with about 9,000 men, and the head of his column marched directly into a waiting force of Confederates. Price jumped at the opportunity to take advantage of his numbers and struck while Rosecrans's force was deploying from column along the narrow

---

48 Ibid., 40-51.

49 Reid, *Ohio in the War*, 319-21.

road. The fighting was ferocious, but by nightfall Rosecrans had managed to hold his ground.

It came at a high cost. Grant, who was with Ord's column, reportedly could not hear the sound of the fighting and, figuring Rosecrans must have been delayed on his march, went into bivouac for the night—leaving Rosecrans to fight it out alone. Price, finally learning how close Grant's second column was to his rear, decided overnight to pull out. When Ord and Rosecrans met the next morning, Rosey learned that Ord had "left him in the lurch" on Grant's orders to halt the column. And while Rosecrans drew praise from Grant for his energy and skill at Iuka, he mistakenly slammed Ord's failure to support his attack in his official report. Grant took umbrage to that, believing it was a backhanded critique of his own generalship.[50]

Rosecrans led his force back into the fortifications of Corinth, and two weeks later the united armies of Price and Van Dorn launched an assault. On October 3, the Confederates struck the Federal outposts, and by dawn the following day they had moved strikingly close to Rosecrans's lines. In bitter fighting, Van Dorn's assault on October 4 came within a hair's breadth of cracking the Union position. Horrified that his army seemed to be falling apart, Reid would write, Rosecrans "plunged into the thickest of the conflict, fought like a private soldier, dealt sturdy blows with the flat of his saber on runaways, and fairly drove them to stand."

Modern scholars take a less generous view of Rosey's performance. "Rosecrans was in the thick of the battle, but his presence was hardly inspiring," offered historian Peter Cozzens. "The Ohioan lost all control of his infamous temper and he cursed as cowards everyone who pushed past him until he, too, lost hope. Rosecrans' histrionics nearly cost him his life." Regardless, Rosecrans's line succeeded in stopping the Confederate assaults, and by afternoon Van Dorn was heading back to Mississippi, leaving thousands of dead and wounded behind.[51]

At first glance, Rosecrans's record was one of unending victories: Rich Mountain, Carnifex Ferry, Iuka, and Corinth. In appreciation, the administration rewarded him to command of the Army of the Ohio. But a deeper examination of each of those victories shows that Rosecrans's impulsive nature and penchant for direct action led him to plunge hip-deep into the maelstrom of battle with his men,

---

50 Peter Cozzens, *The Darkest Days of the War: The Battles of Iuka and Corinth* (Chapel Hill, 1997), 78-126.

51 Reid, *Ohio in the War*, 325; Cozzens, *Darkest Days of the War*, 251-52.

and by doing so he lost the ability to see the broader picture and manage the battle accordingly.

On smaller fields, this method usually worked, but as Rosecrans's commands grew larger, he did not adjust the technique to fit the situation. What happened at Corinth shows that Rosecrans's emotional instability in times of extreme duress could render him unable to command. He never learned that it is a far different thing to motivate and inspire an army of 40,000 men than it was with a few thousand troops in western Virginia, and accordingly this personal touch that served him well and made him such a beloved figure in the army would be sorely tested at Stones River and ultimately fail at Chickamauga.

One of Rosecrans's first tasks upon assuming command—like that of his Confederate counterpart Bragg a few months earlier—was to instill proper discipline in his troops. Whereas Bragg focused his attention on getting the enlisted men to act like soldiers, Rosecrans focused on weeding out the deadweight in the officer corps. A quarter of the army was absent with or without authority. The slew of resignations tendered in the closing days of the Buell regime swamped the adjutant general's office and required a regiment's worth of clerks just to process the paperwork.

Rosecrans instituted a new rule: if an officer was physically well and deemed competent, his request to resign was denied outright, and the Ohioan refused to listen to personal appeals. "I don't care for any individual," he said. "Everything for the service, nothing to individuals." He was equally quick to dispense with incompetent officers who bogged down the army. A subsequent general order was published stating that officers "disgracefully dismissed should be divested of the insignia of rank in the presence of their respective commands and be escorted by the soldiers outside of the camps." William Bickham noted that the order was "severe but it had a most salutary influence."[52]

The energy with which Rosecrans worked proved a wonder to soldiers who had become used to the more methodical pace Buell set. Rosecrans's office hours ran from 10:00 a.m. until 2:00 the following morning, usually later, allowing him to transact an immense amount of routine army business. "Labor was a constitutional necessity for him," Bickham wrote. "He neither spared himself nor his subordinates. When in the field, General Rosecrans was apt to be the first officer in camp to spring from his blankets and the last to dismount at night. No member of the staff found an idle hour."

52 Bickham, *Rosecrans' Campaign*, 23-27.

"Lines of couriers connecting Nashville and the various camps were immediately established. Military maps were collected from every source; friendly people were required to furnish all possible information concerning the topography and geography of the country, and business of every character affecting the campaign was rapidly systematized and dispatched."[53]

By and large, the soldiers welcomed the change. "The frigid dignity which hedged … Buell, enclosing department headquarters as within a wall of ice behind which silence reigned and through the guarded portals of which none ventured unbidden," offered Colonel Kniffen, "was swept away by General Rosecrans who transformed its solemn precincts unto a busy workhouse, placing the new commander en rapport with the most minute details of his army." Noted Sergeant David Cummins of the 64th Ohio; "We have another general and I hope he will do better than that rascally old Buell who has cost the people so many precious lives by marching his men to death and all for nothing."[54]

Corporal Charles Hills of the 41st Ohio commented that "a change has taken place and the standard of discipline has been materially elevated. Courts martial are a terror to evil doers as cases are disposed of in a startingly summary manner and the proceedings are calculated to vindicate the majesty of military law." Hills confessed a liking for Buell but admitted Rosey had won over most of the troops, noting, "I was disappointed in his genial and familiar manner which was calculated to excite anything but awe and apprehension." The general, Hills wrote, reported to his regiment that "Fighting is a trade. Three things must be learned by all who would practice it with success. First, the soldier must learn to eat well. Second, he must learn to sleep well. And third, to fight well. Failing the first two things, he gives out and soon falls to pieces like an old shackly wagon."

Not all of the soldiers took to Rosecrans's populist command approach. "It was the general's manner rather than his command which had the greatest effect. But he failed to produce an impression as one who grasped the whole momentous situation with the hand of a master," the regimental historians of the 41st Ohio noted.[55]

---

53 Ibid., 22-23, 28-29.

54 Kniffen, *MOLLUS*, District of Columbia, 417; 1st Sgt. David T. Cummins, Co. H, 64th Ohio, *Bucyrus Journal,* Nov. 21, 1862, 3.

55 Corporal Charles W. Hills, Co. A, 41st Ohio, *Cleveland Morning Leader,* Dec. 27, 1862, 1; Robert L. Kimberly and Ephraim S. Holloway, *The Forty-First Ohio Veteran Volunteer Infantry in the War of the Rebellion, 1861-1865* (Cleveland, 1897), 43.

The first reviews took place in early November at Bowling Green, where Rosecrans quickly set tongues wagging within the ranks by demonstrating his thorough interest in their welfare. "He examined the equipment of the men with exacting scrutiny," a staff member noted. "No trifling minutiae escaped him. Everything to which the soldier was entitled was important. A private without his canteen instantly evoked a volley of inquiries. "Where is your canteen? How did you lose it? When? Where? Why don't you get another?" Soldiers thus addressed were apt to reply frankly, sometimes a whole company laughing at the novelty of such keen inquisition. "Can't get shoes," said one, while another "required a canteen and couldn't get it." Rosecrans told the men to go to their captains and demand to be supplied. "Go to him every day until you get it. Bore him for it! Bore him in his quarters! Bore him at mealtime! Bore him in bed! Bore him, bore him, bore him!"

Besides Rosey's evident concern for the small details, one courtesy won the men over in droves. "He was careful to acknowledge a private's salute, a trifling act of good breeding and military etiquette, costing nothing, but too frequently neglected by officers who have much rank and little generous sympathy with the soldiers who win them glory," Bickham wrote. Ira Owens of the 74th Ohio noted that the purpose of the reviews was to give Rosecrans a chance to see what his men needed and to be seen. Walking up to an Irishman in Owens's company, Rosecrans asked "Well, what do you want?" The Irishman replied, "If it's all the same to you, General, I want a furlough." Rosecrans burst out laughing and replied, "Well Pat, you'll do."[56]

As winter approached, Rosecrans's army lay concentrated at Bowling Green and nearby Glasgow, poised to continue its march to Nashville. Confederate cavalry detachments kept the capital under a state of virtual siege but lacked the force to drive James Negley's and John Palmer's divisions out of the city. It was abundantly clear to Rosecrans that Buell had been right: the Louisville & Nashville must first be repaired to put the army's logistics on a solid footing and to prepare for subsequent campaigning. He undoubtedly gave little serious thought to pursuing Bragg's retreating Confederates into the wilds of eastern Tennessee despite his instructions from Halleck. Logistics ruled out a campaign in East Tennessee, and once Rosecrans made that determination, he was unwavering in his judgment.

---

56 Bickham, *Rosecrans' Campaign*, 30; Ira S. Owens, *Greene County in the War, Being a History of the Seventy-Fourth Regiment, With Sketches…* (Xenia, 1872), 27-28.

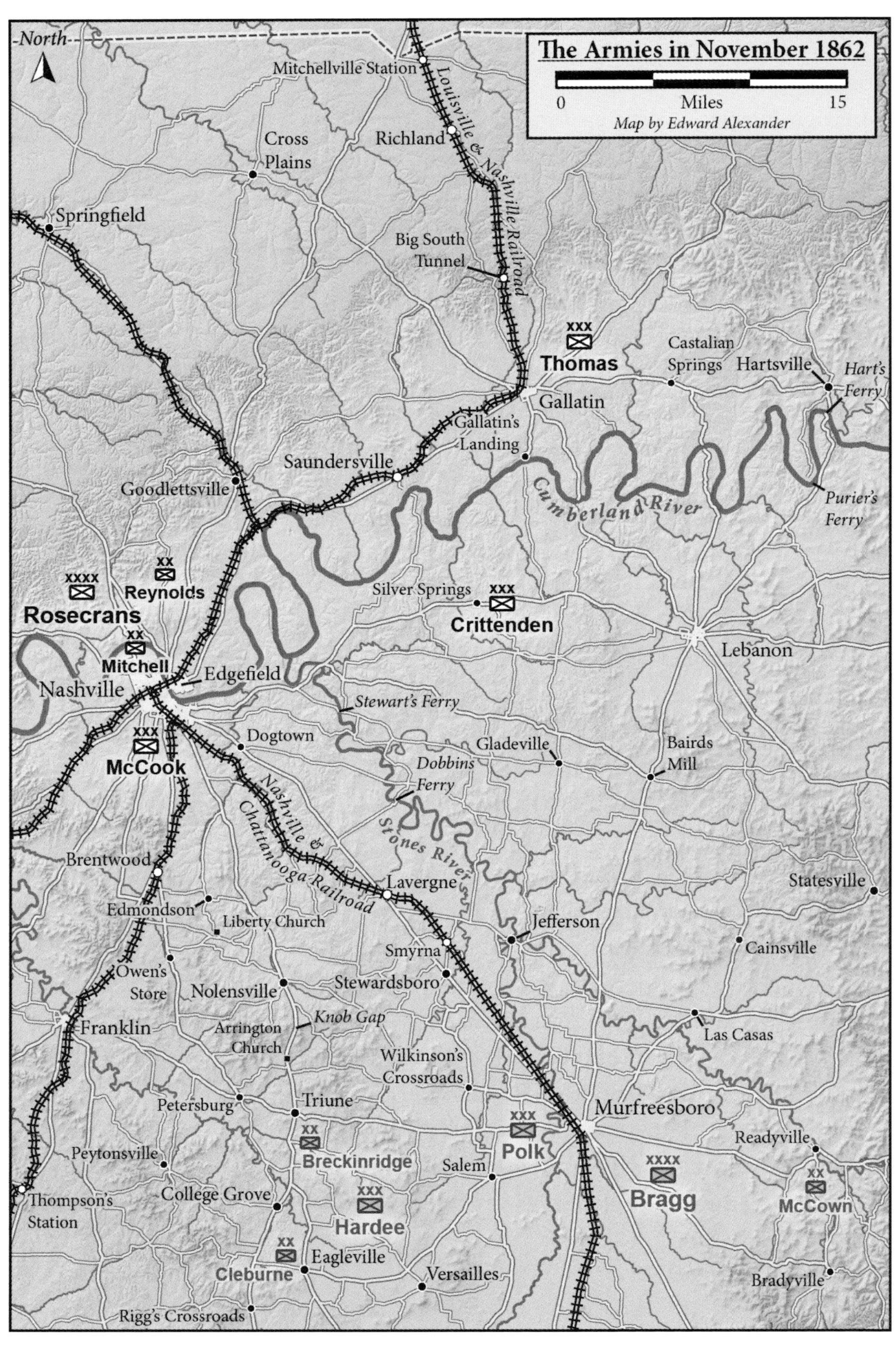
North
The Armies in November 1862
0   Miles   15
Map by Edward Alexander
Mitchellville Station
Louisville & Nashville Railroad
Cross Plains
Richland
Springfield
Big South Tunnel
Thomas
Castalian Springs
Hartsville
Hart's Ferry
Gallatin
Gallatin's Landing
Saundersville
Cumberland River
Purier's Ferry
Goodlettsville
Silver Springs
Crittenden
Lebanon
Reynolds
Rosecrans
Mitchell
Edgefield
Nashville
Stewart's Ferry
Dogtown
Gladeville
Bairds Mill
McCook
Dobbins Ferry
Stones River
Nashville & Chattanooga Railroad
Brentwood
Lavergne
Statesville
Edmondson
Liberty Church
Jefferson
Cainsville
Smyrna
Owen's Store
Nolensville
Stewardsboro
Franklin
Knob Gap
Las Casas
Arrington Church
Wilkinson's Crossroads
Petersburg
Triune
Murfreesboro
Readyville
Breckinridge
Salem
Polk
Peytonsville
College Grove
Bragg
McCown
Thompson's Station
Hardee
Cleburne
Eagleville
Versailles
Bradyville
Rigg's Crossroads

"Rosecrans concluded to go on in the same direction as had Buell," wrote staff officer Henry M. Kendall, "and the events showed clearly that Halleck's bureau-made plans, based upon theory alone and without an intimate knowledge of the real conditions, were the verist nonsense and that Buell and Rosecrans were quite right in ignoring them."[57]

By early November, it seemed probable that Bragg was concentrating his army in Middle Tennessee, as Buell had predicted he would, which made ensuring the security of Nashville as a base for future offensive operations an imperative. Roving Confederate cavalry again proved a catalyst to Federal movement, as they conducted coordinated attacks on both south and north Nashville on November 5. These vivid reminders of how vulnerable his railroad line was prompted Rosecrans to push forward McCook's corps to reinforce Nashville while giving the tough assignment of expediting railroad repairs to Thomas, who marched into Gallatin with Speed Fry's division and set to work.

Opening Big South Tunnel was crucial, as the Cumberland River's level remained too low to support significant steamboat traffic, forcing the army to continue relying on overland transportation. It took workmen three weeks to reopen the tunnel that Morgan destroyed in August. The combined efforts of Morgan's men and local guerrillas had ruined numerous trestles leading to and from the tunnels, all needing repair. Sawed lumber was in short supply, and the army even was without a force of men capable of cutting wood to run locomotives. In the meantime, Rosecrans ordered a large pack mule train to sustain the army and directed that those supplies be hauled along the Louisville and Nashville Pike between Mitchellville and Edgefield on the Cumberland River, where the supplies could be shipped across to Nashville.[58]

Meanwhile, Crittenden's corps crossed the Cumberland east of Nashville at Gallatin's Landing and camped near Silver Springs. McCook's corps marched 72 miles in three days, crossing into Tennessee on November 5 while singing "John Brown's Body." "We were marching back over the same ground we had marched over September 13 going north," recalled Alexis Cope of the 15th Ohio. "The chorus rose and swelled as regiment after regiment came to the line and took it up, and one felt the spirit of the old martyr to liberty was indeed pervading the hearts of the dusty men in blue and that they, willingly or unwillingly, were to be God's instruments to break the yoke of the oppressor and let the oppressed go free."

57 Henry M. Kendall, "The Battle of Stone River." MOLLUS, District of Columbia, Vol. 3, 4.

58 *OR* 20/2:141.

Lewis W. Day of the green 101st Ohio noted that "a stone had been set up on one side of which was the name Kentucky and on the other Tennessee. Each regiment and nearly every company passing this point raised a vociferous shout. We were at last in Tennessee. We entered the state in a drizzling mist and the hard rain which came on later in the evening failed to impress us with the far-famed beauty of Tennessee. The night was cold and wretched in every way and the boys decided the state was not worth fighting for."[59]

This portion of Tennessee may have been poor country, but it wasn't all drudgery, as the boys took every opportunity along the line of march to amuse themselves, usually at each other's expense. "Nearly every company had its funny man who was continually getting off some joke or making some odd expression to make the boys laugh," wrote Charles C. Briant of the 6th Indiana. "Then the boys will get a "rig" on some fellow in the company and they seem to take especially delight in whacking him over it until something else is sprung on some other fellow, and so it goes from day to day. This does a great deal toward driving away the blues or helping to while away the time."

After arriving in camp at Silver Springs, some soldiers of the 6th Ohio "hoisted Captain Driver's 'Old Glory' in front of Colonel Anderson's headquarters and perpetrated the joke of opening a 'recruiting office for the gunboat service' and in … three hours had examined and passed a large crowd of recruits made up from almost every regiment in the corps."[60]

Rosecrans left Bowling Green on November 10 to establish his headquarters in Nashville, and after taking a train to Mitchellville, he rode a horse the rest of the way, escorted by a detachment of the 4th US Cavalry. "The country was invested by roving bands of hostile guerrillas and the route was rather hazardous," Bickham recalled. "The first acre of Tennessee soil betrayed the ruthless track of war."

Nashville likewise revealed a war-worn appearance when the Federals arrived. "Most of our northern boys expressed themselves surprised and disappointed in regard to Nashville," wrote a 36th Illinois soldier. "It is not so large or so fine a city as we anticipated. Its buildings are old, dirty, and dilapidated. The streets are

---

59 Alexis Cope, *The Fifteenth Ohio Volunteers and Its Campaigns* (Columbus, 1916), 218; Lewis W. Day, *Story of the 101st Regiment, Ohio Volunteer Infantry* (Cleveland, 1894), 66.

60 Charles C. Briant *History of the Sixth Regiment Indiana Volunteer Infantry of Both the Three Months' and Three Years' Services* (Indianapolis, 1891), 162-63; Ebenezer Hannaford, *The Story of a Regiment: A History of the Campaigns and Associations in the Field of the Sixth Regiment, Ohio Volunteer Infantry* (Cincinnati: 1868), 380.

narrow, rough, and decidedly filthy. The statehouse grounds were bristling with 32-pounders protected by bales of cotton and guarded by soldiers."[61]

While waiting for the railroad repairs to be completed, the army foraged off the countryside. Both armies had moved out of Middle Tennessee during the fall harvest, leaving the area farmers free to collect their crops unhindered, and now those crops proved a rich prize from which both armies drew heavily. "Large trains have been sent out almost daily, bringing home large quantities of forage and cattle," noted a Minnesota soldier. "The guards accompanying the train usually arrive in camp with a pumpkin or squash on the ends of their bayonets, or maybe a sheep, turkey, goose, of chicken finds its way to their mess through the medium of the forage train."[62]

Lieutenant Colonel John E. Cummins of the 99th Ohio wrote: "[T]his is a fine country near Nashville. The citizens are principally Rebels and avow it, especially the ladies. They were regular spitfires, told me they wished they could poison all of us. We take what we need to feed the army horses and also whatever cattle we need. The government pays for anything taken from a man who shows himself to be loyal, but not a cent to the disloyal."

Captain Simon Perkins Jr., a divisional quartermaster in one of Crittenden's divisions, alone purchased nearly 135,000 pounds of forage from local farmers in November, but it wasn't enough to keep up with the growing army. "Many animals were underfed," he wrote. "Livestock in the division train received only half rations of hay, sometimes mixed with fodder, for twelve days and no hay for the remainder of November."[63]

Morgan's cavalry proved a constant nuisance to Rosecrans's army even as it lay in camp. "The enemy has become so emboldened by the success of their numerous raids that every foot of railroad south of the Cumberland must be well guarded or we can feel no security," recalled surgeon Alfred J. Phelps. "Only the other day, Morgan's troop hovered within a mile and half of our camp at Silver Spring [sic] and captured 130 stragglers besides an officer or two. They pride themselves on boldness and disperse or rendezvous according to the feats they wish to perform.

61 Bickham, *Rosecrans' Campaign*, 50-51; L. G. Bennett and William Haigh, *History of the Thirty-Sixth Regiment, Illinois Volunteers During the War of the Rebellion* (Aurora, 1876), 305-06.

62 E. B. M., *Weekly Pioneer and Democrat*, Nov. 28, 1862, 2.

63 Kevin B. McCray, *A Shouting of Orders: A History of the 99th Ohio Volunteer Infantry Regiment* (2003), 58; Lenette S. Taylor, *The Supply for Tomorrow Must Not Fail: The Civil War of Captain Simon Perkins, Jr., a Union Quartermaster* (Kent, 2004), 93.

Accordingly, it is hard to keep trace of them and makes it necessary to be on the lookout at every point."

Rosecrans worried that some of his soldiers were allowing "themselves to be captured and paroled by the enemy to escape from further military duty and in order to be sent home," so in mid-November he issued general orders placing all such soldiers under arrest.[64]

Once the army established its camps around Nashville, Rosecrans instituted a regime of frequent roll calls, daily company, and battalion drill and soon the redemptive effects of Rosecrans's efforts to improve discipline bore fruit. "General Rosecrans' assignment to this army has given it new life, brightened each countenance, and restored full confidence that something will be done, not to prolong this war, but to greatly aid in its speedy termination," commented Lieutenant Elias Ford of the 41st Ohio. "Without faltering or mercy, he is mustering out incompetent officers, shaving the heads of deserters, and drumming them out of camp, and in fact is reorganizing and re-disciplining this army."[65]

Various punishments were used by the officers of the 59th Illinois. "One young man was paraded through camp one day with both hands tied fast to a singletree hitched behind a mule," recalled veteran David Lathrop. "A man was riding the mule, two guards with fixed bayonets marching beside the captive, and the fife and drum beating the Rogue's March behind. Sometimes the punishment consisted in having a board strapped to the back with large letters in chalk stating the offense and being marched around through camp. Some are tied up, either with their arms encircling the trunk of a large tree or with their hands high above their heads. Some are made to pack rails on their shoulder with a guard following them for two or three hours at a time.[66]

The emphasis on daily drill apparently caused problems for one officer. "Our captain never could drill very well but this did not excuse him," recalled Charles Briant. "One day he took us out and began to drill us in a large meadow. Our captain thought he would show the colonel what an expert he was in drilling, so he started his company across the meadow toward a gap in a stone wall. All went well until he got to the gap and he could not think of the proper command to get them through the gap. They kept on going until they were about to run into the fence

<hr>

64 Surgeon Alfred J. Phelps, *Portsmouth Daily Times*, Nov. 29, 1862, 2; OR 20/2:49.

65 1st Lt. Elias A. Ford, Co. B, 41st Ohio, *Jeffersonian Democrat*, Dec. 5, 1862, 2.

66 Lathrop, *History of the 59th Illinois*, 187.

when the captain yelled out "halt!" Waiting awhile, he gave the command, "break ranks and form on the other side."[67]

Another Indiana soldier recalled his observations of a colonel of a newly raised East Tennessee regiment trying to maneuver his regiment on the march. "A Tennessee colonel was ordered to move his regiment to one side of the road to let the Second Division pass," he recalled. "The fellow spurred up to his men and almost out of breath ordered them to 'Fall in in two rows and march endways as you did yesterday!' His men hurried in all shapes and he shouted to them 'Two into four, get! Tote arms! Right whirl, and come on, the Regulars are looking at you!'"[68]

As the weather turned colder, the men settled in for what they hoped would be their winter encampment. The truth was that the men were physically exhausted. That was evident with the 44th Indiana, which after leaving its camp at Battle Creek, Tennessee, on August 20 marched nearly 700 miles with only six days' rest. "All this time the men were without shelter of any kind, carried but one blanket apiece, were nearly all the time on half rations, and very poorly shod," the regimental historian noted. A few quiet days in camp allowed the men time to build winter quarters, and they worked assiduously to improve their humble domiciles.

"Troops were furnished with tents of the old patterns, both wall tents and A-style tents but some Sibley tents were used, too," remembered Stanley. "The men, by their ingenuity, soon devised means for making themselves comfortable. Some dug a sort of cellar with the tent set over it for shelter with a rear chimney up from the fireplace. Others built a wall of logs or sod and topped this with the tent. The chimney building was destructive to all brick houses in the vicinity of a camp, for if a brick mansion was left unguarded, the men would throw off the roof and carry away every brick in the walls as ants carry away sweet cake."[69]

In early December, the newly designed shelter half was introduced to the troops as a replacement for their bulkier Sibley and A-style tents. The initial reception was decidedly negative. Soldiers in the 36th Illinois rejected the tents outright, calling them "miserable, coarse, muslin things" and "refused to take them, declaring that if they had to, they would burn them." Dodge recalled that "when

---

67 Briant, *History of the 6th Indiana*, 164, 169.

68 1st Lt. Richard W. Melendy, Co. A, 29th Indiana Volunteer Infantry, *Steuben Republican*, Dec. 27, 1862, 1.

69 John H. Rerick, *The Forty-Fourth Indiana Volunteer Infantry: A History of Its Services in the War of the Rebellion* (Lagrange, 1890), 74; David S. Stanley, *Personal Memoirs of Major-General D. S. Stanley, U.S.A.* (Cambridge, 1917), 119-20.

these tents arrived and were issued, everywhere were heard denunciations of the 'rags' and maledictions upon officers in general and quartermasters in particular were loud and deep."

A 49th Ohio soldier thought it better if the army waited until summer to issue the new tents, writing "no doubt General Halleck means a benefit, but if he had a gun, cartridge box, and all his clothing and effects strapped on his back, he would not like the addition of a shelter tent. It may be a good thing, but the soldier doesn't see it."[70]

The men of the 31st Ohio decided to have some fun when they received their allotment of shelter halves, observing that if the government was going to house them like dogs, they may as well act like dogs. "It wasn't long before they got into them when some fellow got to barking, then others commenced, and about dark the whole regiment commenced barking and playing dog," remembered Captain Henry C. Greiner. "If some fellow would come through another fellow's company street, some of them would run out on all fours and drive him away. If they would happen to meet, they would extend the usual courtesies dogs do, but maybe it would end in a fight, especially if one dog tried to get a little too familiar with the other. If they got into a fight, the other dogs would run out and get mixed in until sometimes eight or ten would be in a pile barking, biting, and howling."

Greiner's colonel was incensed, but the "dogs" had all returned quietly to their tents before the authorities could arrive to take them to the pound.[71]

---

70 Bennett, *History of the 36th Illinois*, 314-15; Dodge, *History of the Old Second Division*, 383; unknown soldier, 49th Ohio, *Fremont Journal*, Dec. 19, 1862, 1.

71 Henry C. Greiner, *General Sheridan as I Knew Him: Playmate, Comrade, Friend* (Chicago, 1908), 226-27.

The Coming Storm

NASHVILLE WAS AN epicenter of graft, theft, and smuggling in December 1862. One of Rosecrans's first appointments, in fact, was to put Colonel William Truesdail in charge of the army's police department, tasked with curtailing such guile. "Boots, shoes, uniforms, camp equipage, ammunition, and supplies of every kind serviceable to the Rebel army were daily sent beyond our lines in every possible way that the ingenuity of bad men and women could devise," grumbled John Fitch, provost judge of the Army of the Cumberland. "The city was full of violent and confessed Rebels, most of whom were both smugglers and spies as the opportunity offered. The entire community was rotten, morally, and socially."[1]

Begrimed and seedy as it was already, the city devolved further into a festering warren of drinking holes, tawdry theaters, gambling halls, and roaring bordellos. Nashville was known for its strong vice trade before the war, home to more than 200 prostitutes, some as young as 15 or as old as 59. Most of these women lived one step above grinding poverty, but a few were relatively fortunate, as the wealthier madams hosted more elite clientele. Ironically, the center of the skin trade could be found on a four-block long strip of brothels along Church Street known as "Smoky Row."

The Union occupation of Nashville that began in February 1862 would be merely a hiccup for the trade, as the Federals proved just as willing as their Confederate predecessors to support it. The rapid concentration of Rosecrans's

---

1 John Fitch, *Annals of the Army of the Cumberland* (Mechanicsburg, 2003), 349-50.

army around Nashville in November ramped up the market in sin, and by the end of the year, more than 1,500 prostitutes made a living there. "Freed of home restraints and facing an uncertain future, men often felt bound to taste the sweets of sin," wrote historian Bell Irvin Wiley. As one Indiana soldier bragged in a letter to a cousin: "I just run them little whores all the time. I have to go down and tend to them once and awhile to keep alright."[2]

Venereal diseases such as gonorrhea and syphilis became a major problem within Rosecrans's army. "During the winter of 1862-1863, the army had a social enemy to contend with which seriously threatened its very existence," one Federal captain admitted. Doctors had little knowledge of how to successfully treat venereal diseases, the commonly prescribed cure being salts of mercury leading to the phrase, "A night with Venus, a lifetime with Mercury." Eventually, Federal officials would adopt the expedient of licensing and inspecting the Nashville prostitutes, which successfully cut down the rate of venereal disease in the army. (Lest one conclude this was simply a Federal army problem, Braxton Bragg's forces suffered the highest rate of venereal disease in the entire Confederate army.)[3]

On the other end of the moral spectrum, the settling of the army into camp allowed regimental chaplains to attend to the soldiers' physical and spiritual needs. Chaplain William M. Haigh of the 36th Illinois organized regular weekly worship services that attracted a "large and solemn congregation. I found every Sabbath an increasing eagerness to receive what I brought. The accumulated influence of religious services for weeks had produced in the minds of men an unusual tenderness, and when our services closed it was with such a subdued and solemn feeling that the vast crowd seemed to disperse in almost entire silence. It was the last sermon that many a man heard."[4]

Rosecrans's energy in reorganizing and re-equipping his command might have delighted the army, but it did not impress Lincoln, and by the end of November he had already asked Halleck about a new commander in Tennessee. "The President is very impatient at your long stay in Nashville," Halleck warned on December 4.

---

2 Thomas P. Lowry, *The Story the Soldiers Wouldn't Tell: Sex in the Civil War* (Mechanicsburg, 1994), 76-79; Letters of George Waterman Jackson, 4th Indiana Battery, Spared & Shared website: https://sparedcreative21.art.blog/2020/02/08/1863-george-waterman-jackson-to-james-hall-smith/. Retrieved May 4, 2022.

3 Lowry, *The Story the Soldiers Wouldn't Tell*, 78; Daniel, *Soldiering in the Army of Tennessee*, 98-99. The Army of Tennessee averaged 1,700 cases of venereal disease per month Jan.–May 1863.

4 Bennett, *History of the 36th Illinois*, 308, 315-16.

"The favorable season for your campaign will soon be over. Twice I have been asked to designate someone else to command. As I wrote when you took command, the Government demands action and if you cannot respond to that demand, someone else will be tried. If you remain one more week in Nashville, I cannot prevent your removal."

With fresh memories of the treatment Buell received in his final days, Rosecrans called Halleck's bluff that evening in "few but earnest words. Everything I have done was necessary and has been done as rapidly as possible. If the government which ordered me here confides in my judgment, it may rely on my continuing to do what I have been trying to my whole duty. If my superiors have lost confidence in me, they had better at once put someone in my place and let the future test the propriety of the change. To threats of removal or the like I must be permitted to say that I am insensible."[5]

Halleck responded with a lengthy explanation that Lincoln feared that the British Parliament, about to go into session in January 1863, would join with France to intervene in stopping the war. "If the enemy be left in possession of middle Tennessee, which we held last July, it will be said that they have gained on us," Halleck advised. After pointing out that Union forces had regained all the territory they had lost over the summer, the general in chief noted that "Tennessee is the only state which can be used as an argument in favor of intervention by England. You will thus perceive that your movements have an importance beyond mere military success. It may be and perhaps is the turning point in our foreign relations. A victory or the retreat of the enemy before the 10th of this month would have been of more value to us than ten times the success at a later date."[6]

What troubled the president most was the need for a victory to coincide with the effective date of his Emancipation Proclamation: January 1, 1863. Lincoln had wrestled with the question of emancipation for months. According to historian William C. Davis, it was an issue that "haunted the entire Union, military and civilian alike." Emancipation would provoke a gamut of responses from Union soldiers, Davis noted, ranging from soldiers lauding Lincoln's genius to one saying, "I hope to sink in hell if I ever draw my sword to fight for the Negroes."

Indeed, the changing direction of the war had Northerners torn. Democrats already were sharpening their knives with the 1864 presidential election in mind, and whispers made the rounds in Washington that George McClellan, the darling

---

5 *OR* 20/2:118.

6 Ibid., 123.

of the Democratic press, would be Lincoln's opponent. Without a victory in battle, Lincoln feared he would lose the country, and with it the cause itself.[7]

* * *

Other sections of Nashville and the surrounding environs were abuzz as Bragg's army occupied its winter quarters across Middle Tennessee. Logistics ruled Bragg's selection of Murfreesboro, 30 or so miles south of Nashville, as his headquarters. The Nashville and Chattanooga Railroad, which was repaired after Buell's army left the area in September, offered an uncertain, though relatively secure, supply line from the army's main depot in Chattanooga, and the town's roads radiated like spokes in a wagon wheel. The extensive road network allowed Bragg to concentrate his army quickly upon any threatened point.

The shaky condition of the railroad and a shortage of rolling stock, however, compelled Bragg's men to forage heavily from the local farms, now flush with harvested crops and produce. The foraging quotient also necessitated that the army encamp in a 30-mile-wide semicircle, with Hardee's Corps occupying the left near Triune and Eagleville, Polk's Corps camped around Murfreesboro, and McCown's Division at Readyville a dozen miles west of town.

As the army settled into its camps, Bragg decided a reorganization was in order. One of his first moves in November was to rename the Army of Mississippi as the Army of Tennessee, a name it would carry with pride for the remainder of its existence. The government in Richmond also corrected one of his primary obstacles during October's Kentucky Campaign with Special Orders No. 255, which gave Bragg permission to pull troops from General Edmund Kirby Smith's department to assist in a combined operation in Middle Tennessee. Whether Smith would accompany those troops was left to his discretion, but it was a prudent measure and should have been adopted months before.

Bragg now had three corps: Smith's, Polk's, and Hardee's. He also reorganized his cavalry, placing Morgan's and Forrest's commands on detached duty as partisan raiders and promoting Joe Wheeler to chief of the "regular" cavalry. "With the remembrance of Richmond, Munfordville, and Perryville so fresh in our minds,"

---

7 William C. Davis, *Lincoln's Men: How President Lincoln Became Father to an Army and a Nation* (New York, 1999), 88-89, 101.

Bragg noted, "let us make a name for the new Army of Tennessee as enviable as those enjoyed by the armies of Kentucky and the Mississippi."[8]

Regardless of the name, the army desperately needed rest after extended campaigning. One Arkansan soldier complained that his shoes had been "marched to shreds" and that he carried only a single change of clothing and that "every man in the army is lousy." An inspection of the army's artillery branch revealed that "the greater portion of the men were very poorly and thinly clad and much in need of blankets." In addition, the impact of the hard marches was evident on the army's horses, with many of them condemned. "The trouble was that many of the animals counted on paper were in an unserviceable condition," observed historian Larry J. Daniel. "Disease and strenuous overuse, especially after the long overland trip from Knoxville, were taking an increasing toll. Captain Henry C. Semple reported that so many of his animals were run down that his caissons were being drawn by two rather than three teams."[9]

A return of the army from the beginning of November showed 33,416 men present, with another 24,000 absent with or without authority, as desertions had increased significantly. The longstanding problem of absenteeism with which Bragg had grappled since assuming command grew worse after Kentucky, with many of the regiments reduced to roughly 100 men. "Our armies here are gradually but certainly melting away," Bragg wrote on November 3. "We are getting no reinforcements, no recruits, and cannot see a source from which they are to come. For seven months the conscript act has been the law, but as yet I have to receive the first man in this army. Next spring, the enemy will be able to bring against us an army vastly superior to any he had yet operated with. We shall be less able to meet him than ever before unless active measures are immediately put in operation to collect our men and put them in shape."[10]

With the manpower situation dire and worsening, Bragg instituted a series of measures. First, he ordered, when possible, his army to hire civilians as substitutes for detailed soldiers. Second, he ordered lists compiled noting all absentees (including their residences) so these fugitives could be arrested by local officials. And, third, he arranged for a parole camp in Chattanooga as a clearing house for

---

8 *OR* 20/2:384-385, 411-412.

9 James Willis, *Arkansas Confederates in the Western Theater* (Dayton, 1998), 315; *OR* 20/2:399; Larry J. Daniel, *Cannoneers in Gray: The Field Artillery of the Army of Tennessee, 1861-1865* (Tuscaloosa, 1984), 56.

10 *OR* 20/2:386.

paroled prisoners. He next issued a full general pardon for enlisted men on November 29, urging them to "avail themselves of this privilege before the inauguration of the new system of military courts established by the law as a vigorous and prompt administration of justice to all delinquents. Hereafter, no excuse will be allowed those who abandon their colors and leave their comrades to perform their duties and defend their homes."[11]

In a final effort to improve the army's efficiency, Bragg reluctantly ordered consolidation of companies and regiments. "[They] will be consolidated so as reduce them as far as possible to half their present number," he ordered. "The battalions so formed will maintain their separate organizations for all purposes except for drill and field service, and each battalion will retain its own colors." Bragg recognized that his volunteers possessed great unit pride, so his stipulations that the consolidated units could retain their battle-scarred flags and essentially maintain separate organizations went far toward smoothing any ruffled feathers. This effort, limited only to the infantry, impacted 24 regiments in the army and led to the creation of the following 12 consolidated regiments:

Polk's Corps: 4th/5th Tennessee, 31st/33rd Tennessee, 1st/27th Tennessee, 6th/9th Tennessee, 12th/47th Tennessee, 9th/10th Mississippi, 10th/19th South Carolina

Hardee's Corps: 13th/20th Louisiana, 16th/25th Louisiana, 1st/3rd Florida, 13th/15th Arkansas, 6th/7th Arkansas.[12]

Bragg advocated promotions of officers who had demonstrated merit in the recent campaign. Heading up the list for major generals was Daniel S. Donelson, whom Bragg noted "was ever devoted to duty and conspicuously gallant," and the twice-wounded Patrick Cleburne—"young, ardent, and exceedingly gallant but sufficiently prudent, a fine drill officer, and the admiration of his command." Bragg also recommended six new infantry brigadiers: Roger W. Hanson, Edward C. Walthall, Zachariah C. Deas, Arthur M. Manigault, Thomas H. Hunt, and Lucius E. Polk, and that Richmond commission John A. Wharton and John H. Morgan as brigadiers of cavalry.[13]

11 *OR* 20/2:392, 429.

12 Ibid., 454.

13 Ibid., 508-509.

The commander struggled, however, in developing his personal staff—a quandary that would continue throughout the war with the Army of Tennessee. With any enormous army, a well-trained and appropriately sized staff is almost always absolutely necessary in maintaining control, and Bragg's lack of a strong chief of staff proved a barrier in the coming campaign. Bragg appointed Johnson K. Duncan from brigade command as his chief of staff, but Duncan contracted malarial fever and died on December 18, which thrust those duties on Lt. Col. George W. Brent, a volunteer officer who was overwhelmed by the job and did not perform to Bragg's satisfaction. Bragg requested Colonel William Mackall for the job, but because the war department took several months following through, that left Brent in over his head.

Bragg's legendary temper exacerbated the problem of securing competent staff officers, as few could tolerate for long the commander's acidity. Bragg wanted to replace his chief quartermaster, Lt. Col. Laurence W. O'Bannon. Unable to find a suitable alternate, he kept O'Bannon in place—and continued to heckle him. "Your best friends admit that your temper is irritable, that under excitement you are sometimes harsh when there is no necessity for it," a staff officer would write in protest, "and even wound an innocent man as I think you did O'Bannon."[14]

*   *   *

By late November, Bragg's men began to reap the benefits of their home in Murfreesboro. A field return from December 1, 1862, showed that Bragg's army (excluding Smith's Corps) fielded 39, 931 effectives, an improvement of more than 6,000 men in a month. "We are drawing immense supplies of subsistence with considerable amounts of clothing, leather, etc. from the region just vacated by the enemy," Bragg informed Richmond on November 22. "The people with few exceptions are loyal and true, having once felt the yoke of Abolition despotism, and are joining our ranks in large numbers."

Exchanged prisoners from Fort Donelson and other setbacks of the spring fighting began to rejoin their commands in late November, a significant boost. "The health and general tone of my old Army of the Mississippi were never better," Bragg informed Davis. "The Tennesseans especially are in fine condition having been fitted out by their friends. The ranks of those from this section, too, are

---

14 McWhiney, *Braxton Bragg and Confederate Defeat*, 342.

rapidly filling for having felt the heel of the tyrant, the people of this region are determined to resist and nobly furnishing men and means."[15]

Such was the situation in Middle Tennessee on November 24 when General Joseph E. Johnston was assigned command of the new geographical department embracing the Confederacy between the Appalachian Mountains and the Mississippi River. It was an odd command arrangement; each of the three departments still received orders directly from Richmond, and Johnston's authority was limited to matters of strategy and cooperation. In truth, Johnston cared little for the assignment, complaining to Senator Louis T. Wigfall of Texas that "a great mistake has been made in the arrangement of my command. Mississippi and Arkansas should have united to form it, not Tennessee and Mississippi which are divided by an impassable river and impracticable country. The troops of middle Tennessee could reach Fredericksburg, Virginia, sooner than Mississippi."

Johnston realized that the balance of forces he had been given was inadequate to the task at hand and requested the Army of the Trans-Mississippi be moved east across the Mississippi River to confront and drive away Ulysses Grant's army threatening in northwestern Mississippi. "Our two armies this side of the Mississippi have the further disadvantage of being separated by the Tennessee River and a Federal army larger than either of them," he messaged Cooper. "Under such circumstances, it seems to me that our best course would be to fall upon General Grant with the troops of General [Theophilus] Holmes and Pemberton united for the purpose, those of General Bragg cooperating if practicable."[16]

Johnston may have been deliberately tweaking Davis and the war department in making that call for Holmes to cross the Mississippi. On November 12, Johnston met with outgoing Secretary of War George Randolph in the aftermath of a particularly unpleasant recent episode between Randolph and Davis in which the president directed the secretary to rescind an order to do exactly that: have Holmes cross the river and support Pemberton. It wasn't that Davis disagreed with the directive, as he had approved of it when it was proposed. Rather, he was piqued Randolph had felt compelled to clarify one of Davis's orders in the first place, and he was doubly irked that Randolph did not secure his approval before sending that clarification.

15 *OR* 20/2:416-417, 421, 433.

16 McWhiney, *Braxton Bragg and Confederate Defeat*, 339; *OR* 20/2:424.

Unaware this had happened, Johnston on November 12 was explaining to Randolph how such a move would prove beneficial when Randolph showed him Davis's rebuke. Johnston was astonished Davis's touchy pride would prevent execution of what was obviously a sound military order. Regardless, the episode ended Randolph's tenure as secretary of war (he resigned November 15) and, as Steven Woodworth argued, "Davis was now bound by his pride not to allow the trans-Mississippi forces to cross the river and join in a unified command. To do so would be to admit that Randolph was right."[17]

By the time Johnston reached his headquarters in Chattanooga on December 4, the situation in Mississippi had grown worse and Richmond was requesting immediate reinforcements from Bragg. New to the department and unfamiliar with the railroad network, Johnston looked at a map and continued to argue that the wiser course was to send Pemberton men from the Army of the Trans-Mississippi. "It seems to me that the aid of General Holmes can be better relied on than that of General Bragg," Johnston reiterated to Richmond. "I therefore respectfully suggest that that officer be urged to the utmost expedition."

Johnston then boarded a train to visit Bragg in Murfreesboro and assess conditions at the front. Interestingly, Davis had already changed his mind and messaged Holmes to send Pemberton those reinforcements, but the president, for some reason, also allowed Holmes discretion to follow the orders or not. Holmes responded that if he sent these reinforcements, he would lose Arkansas, not realizing perhaps that if Vicksburg were lost to Grant, Arkansas would inevitably be lost, too. That said, Holmes chose to stay in place, Davis again decided he wasn't willing to force the issue.[18]

Pemberton also splashed cold water on Johnston's argument the next day in a lengthy communication that explained the condition of his army and the strategy he hoped to pursue. "I have no hope of any assistance from General Holmes and have telegraphed fully on that subject to Richmond," the Pennsylvanian explained. Johnston continued to stall any efforts of sending troops to Mississippi from Bragg's army. Noting that Rosecrans's army outnumbered Bragg's 65,000–42,000, Johnston observed that "we can cross the Tennessee only by ferrying, a very slow process which Rosecrans would certainly interrupt. The movement to join General Pemberton would by any route require at least a month. I believe the country between the Tennessee and General Pemberton could not support the trains our

17 Woodworth, *Jefferson Davis and His Generals*, 179-81.

18 *OR* 20/2:436; Woodworth, *Jefferson Davis and His Generals*, 182.

troops would require for a march through it. If I am right in the estimate, the President's object of a speedy reinforcement of the army in Mississippi cannot be accomplished by sending troops from Tennessee. To send a strong force would be to give up Tennessee and, the principal officers think here, disorganize the army."

As an alternative, Johnston approved Bragg's plan to let Nathan Bedford Forrest loose in West Tennessee to break up the railroads that Grant depended on to fuel his offensive and have John Hunt Morgan again ride north to disrupt the newly repaired Louisville and Nashville Railroad that supplied Rosecrans's army.[19]

Events in the West had assuredly reached a crisis point. Less than two weeks into his new assignment, Johnston was unwilling to exercise his responsibility as theater commander by ordering troops within his command to fend off Grant's offensive in Mississippi, and Davis was unwilling to grant another request by Johnston for Holmes's troops, leaving matters at a stalemate. If nothing were done, the likelihood of losing Vicksburg and control of the Mississippi seemed a certainty.

Also reaching a crisis point were events in the Eastern Theater, as Ambrose Burnside's massive Army of the Potomac lumbered up to the Rappahannock River and prepared to assault Robert E. Lee's army at Fredericksburg. A sickly Davis elected to visit the West personally to see his new theater commander and assess the propriety of moving troops from Tennessee to Mississippi. The president left Richmond incognito with only his personal aide Custis Lee on December 10, traveling by rail to Chattanooga.

*   *   *

As Rosecrans continued to review the divisions of his steadily growing army that December, he grew familiar with the men and with their commanders. The heart and soul of the army were the five divisions of the Center Corps (later designated the 14th Army Corps) led by George Thomas.

The Virginian was a legend in the making: "tall, heavy, sedate gentlemanly, modest, and a reliable soldier," recalled Colonel John Beatty, one of Thomas's brigade commanders. The 46-year-old graduate of West Point's Class of 1840 was already graying, and his deliberate nature and fatherly concern for his troops led his men to call him "Old Pap." Thomas saw action in Mexico, where he earned two

19 *OR* 20/2:440-441.

brevets for gallantry, and he was commissioned major of the 2nd Cavalry under then-Colonel Robert E. Lee in the 1850s.

The Civil War would cost Thomas his family; when he decided to remain loyal to the Union, his Virginia sisters, as well as other kin, disowned him entirely. He was a brigade commander in the early days of the 1861 Shenandoah Valley Campaign in Virginia before being transferred to Kentucky that fall, where he led a small Union army to victory at Mill Springs in January 1862. As Rosecrans's foremost counselor and the conscience of the army's officer corps, Thomas's importance to the commander and to the army in the coming campaign was crucial.[20]

Thomas would take only two of his five divisions to Murfreesboro, both led by veterans of the Mexican War, with the 1st Division under General Lovell H. Rousseau. Rousseau—like Thomas, a well-known and beloved figure in the army—was a man of fine and commanding appearance, a booming battlefield voice, and the knack for being able to say the right thing at the right time to his volunteer soldiers. To be sure, the men of the army adored him. The hard-fighting Kentuckian also liked to drink, and he kept a newspaper reporter on staff to ensure that the folks in Louisville knew about his successes in the field. Rousseau's division of four brigades was the largest in the army and featured a special project initiated by Rosecrans: the Regular Brigade, which consisted of all the regular infantry units of the army under Lt. Col. Oliver L. Shepherd's command. Colonel Benjamin F. Scribner led Rousseau's 1st Brigade, the redoubtable Colonel Beatty the 2nd, and hard-fighting Colonel John C. Starkweather the 3rd.[21]

Commanding Thomas's 2nd Division was former Pennsylvania horticulturist-turned-soldier James Negley. Although General Negley lacked Rousseau's flair, he was a competent officer, strict disciplinarian, and man of firm decision and bravery. When fighting broke out at Stones River on December 31, 1862, Negley's was the smallest Federal division on the field, with just two brigades. His first brigade had remained in Nashville, but the 2nd Brigade under Colonel John F. Miller and the 3rd Brigade of Colonel Timothy R. Stanley both made the march to Murfreesboro. Colonel Moses B. Walker's brigade of the 3rd Division

---

20 John Beatty, *The Citizen-Soldier: Memoirs of a Civil War Volunteer* (Cincinnati, 1879), 235-36; Ezra J. Warner, *Generals in Blue: Lives of the Union Commanders* (Baton Rouge, 1964), 500-01.

21 Rousseau's popularity was so pronounced that a frequently told story was that whenever cheering broke out without explanation, it was because of "Rousseau or a rabbit." "Rousseau or a Rabbit," *The United Service: A Monthly Review of Military and Naval Affairs*. Vol. VI (Philadelphia: L.R. Hamersly & Co., 1891), 92.

Major General Alexander M. McCook

Author's Collection

joined the corps on the march, while two provisional brigades under Brig. Gen. James G. Spears and Colonel Dan McCook (Maj. Gen. Alexander McCook's younger brother) joined later in the battle.

General McCook led the Right Wing, later designated the 20th Army Corps. It was a newly formed corps composed of three veteran divisions. McCook, the most prominent of the family of "Fighting McCooks" that served the Union Army during the war, had graduated from West Point in 1852 and served on the Plains with the 3rd Infantry. The Ohioan was serving as an instructor of tactics at West Point at the beginning of the war but soon found himself commissioned colonel of the 1st Ohio and sent to Washington, D.C. Only 31, McCook led his regiment at First Bull Run and, after reenlisting for three years, he took the 1st Ohio into the Western Theater, where Buell turned him into a brigade, then division commander. He led that division under Buell at Shiloh, successfully leading an attack on the Confederate center. Promotion to corps command would follow.

A hard and courageous fighter lacking in both years and prudence, the affable McCook swore "like a pirate and affected a rough and ready style" and was considered a command liability by some of his subordinates. McCook's headquarters was the most popular social spot in the army, and the rotund and laughing Ohioan struck some observers as lacking dignity and seriousness and appeared to be a man in over his head. "McCook has a grin which excites the suspicion that he is either still very green or deficient in the upper story," Colonel Beatty said with scorn.

Journalist William F. G. Shanks dismissed McCook as a well-meaning "overgrown schoolboy," while another brigadier complained that McCook "looks more like a blockhead than ever and it is astonishing to me that he should be permitted to retain command of a corps for a single hour."[22]

Whatever criticism was leveled at McCook for being a lightweight, the caliber of his division and brigade commanders more than compensated. General Jefferson Davis, who was never formally charged in the September "Bull" Nelson murder, returned to the army in early November (at Rosecrans's request) and commanded the 1st Division. His brigadiers included well-respected Colonel Philip Sidney Post, commanding the 1st Brigade; the prickly though competent regular army Colonel William Passmore Carlin commanding the 2nd; and Colonel William Woodruff commanding the 3rd.

Brigadier General Richard W. Johnson, captured in August by John Hunt Morgan's troopers near Gallatin, Tennessee, was exchanged that fall and rejoined the army, assigned command of McCook's 2nd Division (displacing the popular Joshua Sill). Brigadier General Edward N. Kirk, a Shiloh veteran, led Johnson's 1st Brigade; Brig. Gen. August Willich, the former German revolutionary, led the 2nd; and Colonel Philemon P. Baldwin the 3rd. Phil Sheridan, marked as a rising man in the army and a particular favorite of Rosey's, commanded the 3rd Division, with Sill commanding his 1st Brigade, Colonel Frederick Schaefer the 2nd, and Colonel George W. Roberts the 3rd.

The Left Wing (later designated the 21st Army Corps) was commanded by the steady, if unspectacular, Thomas Crittenden, the 43-year-old son of Kentucky Senator John J. Crittenden. Though not a West Pointer, Crittenden had served admirably in the Mexican War as an aide to General Zachary Taylor and then with the 3rd Regiment, Kentucky Foot Volunteers. He returned from Mexico to his law practice in Frankfort, and when the Civil War came, he chose to side with the Union, as did his father. Crittenden was a sensible charmer who wasn't afraid to fight, but he also was described as a non-entity on the battlefield. Given a brigadier's star in September 1861, he led one of Buell's divisions at Shiloh; promotion to corps command came that summer.

Crittenden led that corps during in Kentucky and gained a solid reputation with his troops for his steadiness under fire and superlative command of profanity. The lank and spare general enjoyed perhaps a little too much good Kentucky bourbon and displayed the refined manners expected of the scion of a politically prominent Kentucky family. But as Shanks noted, Crittenden did not have any

---

22 Beatty, *The Citizen-Soldier*, 235-36; Richard A. Baumgartner and Larry M. Strayer, *Echoes of Battle: The Struggle for Chattanooga* (Huntingdon, 1996), 22; Warner, *Generals in Blue*, 294.

"iron in his nature" and "never on the battlefield had an opinion of his own or ever assumed any responsibility he could possibly avoid." If he did not add much to the command equation, it could also be said he did not subtract much, either.[23]

Like McCook, Crittenden's liabilities as a field commander were offset by the generally high quality of his direct subordinates. In command of Crittenden's 1st Division was Thomas Wood, a fiery, profane former regular whose bravery was so pronounced that one observer said it was worth 20,000 men. Brigadier General Milo S. Hascall, another West Pointer, led Wood's 1st brigade, Colonel George D. Wagner the 2nd, and promising Colonel Charles G. Harker the 3rd.

Commanding the 2nd Division was John Palmer, with Brig. Gen. Charles Cruft in charge of the 1st Brigade. The 2nd Brigade was led by the stern Colonel William B. Hazen, and the 3rd by the steady Colonel William Grose. Leading Crittenden's 3rd Division was the bookish Horatio Van Cleve, at 53 the oldest general officer in Rosecrans's army. Van Cleve's 1st Brigade was commanded by Colonel Samuel Beatty (no relation to John Beatty), the 2nd by Colonel James P. Fyffe, and the 3rd by Colonel Samuel W. Price.

Overall, Rosecrans's reorganization of the army left it, as Sheridan remembered, "compact and cohesive, undisturbed by discord and unencumbered by jealousies of any moment." Rosecrans was a commander whom "we believed had the energy and skill to direct us to success, a national confidence in our invincibility made us all keen for a test of strength with the Confederates."[24]

Rosecrans put much stock in bringing in General Stanley to resuscitate the army's moribund cavalry. Though Stanley worked diligently, he could not work miracles, as the cavalry's subsequent performance during the campaign would demonstrate. "The cavalry had been badly neglected," Stanley admitted. "It was weak, undisciplined, and scattered around a regiment to a division of infantry. To break up this foolish disposal of cavalry," he added,

> and to form brigades was my first and difficult work. Generals commanding divisions declared they would not give up their cavalry regiments, but I insisted they should do so

---

23 The journalist Shanks also noted that the whatever competence Crittenden demonstrated came courtesy of his senior division commander Thomas J. Wood, as "Wood was ever at his right hand and as his right hand furnished him with all the military brains and formed for him all the military character he ever had." Shanks, William F. G., *Personal Recollections of Distinguished Generals* (New York, 1866), 295.

24 Philip H. Sheridan, *Personal Memoirs of P. H. Sheridan, General, United States Army* (New York, 1992), 115.

and General Rosecrans sustained me. Our cavalry had been poorly instructed and depended upon their carbines instead of the saber. I insisted on the latter and sent for grindstones and had all the sabers sharpened, each squadron being provided with the means for this work.[25]

Recalled William L. Curry of the 1st Ohio Cavalry: "[R]equisitions were made for horses, many jaded and worn-out horses were condemned and turned into the post quartermaster, and a general reorganization was commenced. Colonel Minor Millikin at once inaugurated strict discipline and resumed both mounted and dismounted drill which was very much needed as there had been little if any drilling since the evacuation of Corinth. General Rosecrans believed in the old maxim that 'the cavalry was the eyes of the army' and he proposed to use his cavalry for the purpose of observation as to the movements of the enemy."

Stanley's energy and enthusiasm soon resuscitated the cavalry arm, and he organized a "cavalry division" under Colonel John Kennett that consisted of only two brigades: the first under Colonel Robert H. G. Minty, the second under Colonel Lewis Zahm. Curry remembered Stanley as a "very active and aggressive" commander, "always on the alert for any duty required of his command and he did not propose to settle down and wait for the enemy to come to him."[26]

Tasked with building bridges, repairing railroads, and cutting roads through thick Tennessee forests was Rosecrans's Pioneer Brigade. In one of his first general orders, Rosecrans ordered the formation of this brigade by drawing 20 men from each regiment. "The 20 men will be selected with great care: half laborers and half mechanics," he ordered. "The most intelligent and energetic lieutenant in the regiment with the best knowledge of civil engineering will . . . command . . . . Under certain circumstances, it may be necessary to mass this force. The wagons attached to the corps shall carry all the tools and the men's camp equipage. The men shall carry their arms, ammunition, and clothing."

The Pioneers wore a distinctive patch of two crossed hatchets upon their sleeves and were exempted from picket and guard duty. One veteran recalled that the brigade's insignia was "the same as a pass. We can go anywhere and the guards don't bother us any." To command the brigade, Rosecrans selected one of his army's top engineers, Captain James St. Clair Morton, and accompanied the

---

25 Stanley, *Personal Memoirs*, 120-21.

26 Ibid.; William L. Curry, *Four Years in the Saddle: History of the First Regiment Ohio Volunteer Cavalry* (Columbus, 1898), 81-82.

assignment with a brigadier's star; by mid-December, the independent Chicago Board of Trade Battery, Illinois Light Artillery was attached to the brigade. The men were trained to operate independently as companies, but they would be consolidated into battalions during the forthcoming campaign.[27]

Rosecrans's army proved in many ways more cohesive than Bragg's. The men all marched under a common flag, and more or less wore the same uniform, but they, too, were stubborn individualists like their Confederate counterparts. The ranks consisted largely of farmers from the Midwest, hardy pioneering men inured to the hard task of harvesting an existence from their region's primeval forests. But the ranks featured men from all walks of life, and at least a dozen nationalities. It was common to find educated men such as schoolteachers and lawyers serving alongside common laborers and mere farm boys barely old enough to enlist.

Rivermen from Illinois and lumberjacks from Michigan fought alongside blacksmiths from Pennsylvania, while the prairie farmers of Missouri, Wisconsin, and Minnesota exchanged laughs with comrades from Kentucky, Indiana, and Ohio. The army even featured loyal Tennessee regiments raised in the eastern part of the state who had their own intensely personal reasons for waging war. German-born brewers of Cincinnati, who had fought for liberty in the Old Country during the 1848 Revolution, served alongside Welsh-born coal miners who had their own history of struggling for freedom in Europe.

The regiments they joined typically were led by prominent local attorneys or other notables with either prior military experience or the oratorical powers to convince others they could lead them in battle. Antebellum militia and Zouave organizations ensured that the men went to war under an assortment of colorful names: the men of the all-Cincinnati 6th Ohio called themselves the "Guthrie Grays," and two companies of Chicago Zouaves who had learned their trade under famed Colonel Elmer Ellsworth joined the 19th Illinois. Ripley County in southeastern Indiana sent two companies into the 37th Indiana—the "Ripley Rovers" and the "Ripley Rangers," while the 49th Ohio went to war with companies known as the "Senecas and Wyandots" and the "Fostoria Invincibles."

A heavier dose of foreign-born soldiers was found in this army than in the Confederate—German the most common nationality. Several all-German or mostly German regiments would fight, such as the 24th Illinois, the 9th Ohio,

---

27 OR 20/2:6-7; Cody J. Harding, "Crossed Hatchets and Detached Service: The Creation of the Pioneer Brigade", here: https://www.libertyrifles.org/research/regiments/ pioneer-brigade. Retrieved May 11, 2022.

August Willich's own 32nd Indiana, and the St. Louis-raised 2nd and 15th Missouri regiments. There were also a few predominantly Irish units, such as the 35th Indiana and 10th Ohio, along with the unique Scandinavian 15th Wisconsin featuring companies such as the "St. Olaf's Rifles" and the "Norway Bear Hunters."

These citizen-soldiers were drawn into the army to perform a messy job, and the sooner they could finish and return to their homes and farms, the better. Unlike the Army of the Potomac, which in its early years had a centralizing and beloved figure in George McClellan, Rosecrans's men learned the art of war under the pedantic Buell, who had elicited no such love and devotion. That meant the men usually became fiercely devoted to their local companies and regiments, exhibiting little loyalty to the centralized power structures: brigades, divisions, and corps.

This would change noticeably after Rosecrans assumed command, but the central focus of the men's lives and the core of their army identity was found within their regiments, which proved to be both a tremendous asset and an impediment. Historian Gerald J. Prokopowicz argued that this "poorly organized, amateur-led army that consisted of many dozens of highly cohesive regiments was like a dinosaur, a killing machine with powerful muscles and a tiny brain. It resembled a strong and ponderous beast whose component units could absorb enormous punishment on the battlefield without breaking, but which lacked the agility to execute the maneuvers necessary to destroy its enemies."[28]

When it came to the means of destroying its enemies, the Federal army struggled, too, with arming its volunteer regiments in this early period. As in the Confederate army, what the troops wanted was the English-made Enfield rifle-musket, but the volunteers headed to war with whatever could be acquired quickly, which led to the issue of a wide variety of foreign and domestic arms.

Ohio provides a good case study of how these Western regiments were armed. The flank companies (A and B) of each regiment were typically equipped with Enfields while the balance of the line companies received .69-caliber smoothbores or rifled muskets, including thousands of weapons that had been converted by Miles Greenwood's Eagle Foundry in Cincinnati. When supplies of these primary weapons fell short, other foreign makes were substituted; for example, the 19th Ohio carried .69-caliber Belgian-made Pondir rifles, while the 74th Ohio was equipped with .69-caliber Prussian-made Potzdam muskets. The quality of these

28 Gerald J. Prokopowicz, *All for the Regiment: The Army of the Ohio, 1861-1862* (Chapel Hill, 2001), 4.

imported arms varied considerably, as some were considered equal in quality to the Enfield and others "the poorest excuse for shooting irons I ever saw."[29]

Other Midwestern states adopted similar arming practices, but it was not unusual for a Union regiment at Stones River to carry up to five long-arm variations. One feels for the poor ordnance sergeant of the 35th Illinois, as his regiment was equipped with seven makes of arms requiring three varieties of ammunition. A few regiments were fully equipped with Enfields (the 74th Illinois and 90th Ohio, among others) but as Enfields were highly desired battlefield pickups, many regiments had some of these well-regarded arms sprinkled within their ranks.

Outside the Enfield, the most common foreign-made weapon was the Austrian-produced .54-caliber Lorenz rifle-musket, a solid if unwieldy weapon used by regiments such as the 21st Michigan, 24th Wisconsin, and 69th Ohio. While the Federal government ramped up production of the improved .58-caliber US Model 1861 Springfield rifle-musket, few of those weapons had yet been shipped west, and the few regiments that had them (the 42nd Illinois and 101st Ohio, for example) counted themselves lucky indeed.

The army's ordnance department made strides in weapons standardization, but it would not come in this theater until the spring and summer of 1863. That meant the typical Federal soldier at Stones River was equipped with some type of rifled musket with a theoretical effective range of several hundred yards. This provided a marked advantage in range over their Confederate counterparts, especially on the defense.

Few soldiers on either side, though, received specialized training in how to use the gun's long-range capabilities. A bullet fired from such a weapon did not fly in a level line. Rather, it flew in a parabolic curve with an approximate 75-yard long "killing zone" near the shooter and a somewhat smaller one farther out. For example, a soldier setting his sights and firing on a target 300 yards away had a reasonable chance of hitting a man within the first 75 yards before the bullet's flight path curved upward, above the typical height of an enemy soldier. It would begin curving downward about 240 yards out, creating a second "killing zone" the subsequent 100 yards before hitting the ground.

29 Greenwood converted 27,000 older model US muskets in July–November 1861. The gamut ran from conversions of flintlocks to percussion muskets to rifling these weapons and adding rear sights.

What this meant in the field was that a long "safe zone" existed between the killing zones in which advancing troops could march unhindered by the barrage of flying bullets passing just over their heads. This safe zone increased in size the farther out a soldier aimed. "It was incredibly difficult for the average soldier to compensate for the unusual trajectory and make his shots count at ranges longer than about 100 yards," argued historian Earl Hess. "This greatly decreased the effect of the rifle musket precisely in the area were advocates thought it might have a revolutionary impact on warfare." The result was that rifled muskets were typically used just like their smoothbore predecessors, as their primary "killing zone" of the first 75 yards nearly matched that of the smoothbore musket.[30]

"God fights on the side with the best artillery," Napoleon once said, and if there was one area in which Rosecrans's army enjoyed a clear superiority, it was in the size, organization, and striking power of its artillery. Colonel James Barnett served as the army's chief of artillery; during the Stones River Campaign, he had under his nominal command 27 batteries totaling 139 guns. Most of the batteries were attached to individual infantry brigades and under direct control of the brigade commander, but in Crittenden's wing, the artillery batteries assigned to Palmer's and Van Cleve's divisions were organized under the command of the divisional chief of artillery. This was the initial step to embracing the concept of massing batteries, as had become standard practice in the Army of the Potomac, offering improved command-and-control on the field while promising an increased concentration of firepower.

Each battery of roughly 120 men was divided into three sections of two guns, with each section under the command of a lieutenant, and individual sergeants having command over a single piece. A team of six horses drew the cannon and a limber chest that carried the ammunition assigned to each gun. Additional ammunition was carried in the caissons and preferably kept well behind the gun line. The individual crew consisted of nine men, including the sergeant commanding the piece. The task of firing a piece proved an intricate dance in which each soldier had to perform a specific task in a specific order at a specific time, so heavy emphasis was placed on learning the drill. The men drilled with their pieces daily when not on campaign, and some even took target practice.

---

30 Earl J. Hess, *The Rifle Musket in Civil War Combat: Reality and Myth* (Lawrence, 2008), 1-8 and 92-93. The level of marksmanship varied widely for the average Civil War soldier and is clouded with myth. Hess argued that less than a quarter of the men in either army could be considered proficient with their weapons, even by the end of the war.

"Three of our guns fired 20 shots, solid and shell, four of which hit the target," noted a cannoneer of Battery A of the 1st Ohio Light Artillery. "The distance was about three-quarters of a mile, and the size of the target was about 12 feet square. General McCook was present and seemed highly pleased with the result of the experiments. He said if we would do as well as that in an engagement, he would take care of the rest of the battle."[31]

Like their comrades in the infantry, Rosecrans's gunners used various cannons. The cast-iron 10-pounder Parrott rifle, black with a distinctive thick reinforcing band of wrought iron around the breech, was the most common artillery piece in the army at 36 guns. Produced by the West Point Foundry in New York, a 10-pounder Parrott rifle fired a 9.5-pound shell more than a mile, though problems with barrel bursts tended to make them unpopular with some gunners. The old cast-bronze M1841 6-pounder smoothbore field gun, an obsolete veteran of the Mexican War with limited range, was the second most common with 32 guns employed. The cast-bronze 6-pounder James rifle was third most common at 27 guns. The heavier 12-pounder M1841 short-barreled howitzer was the fourth most common (24 guns), and despite its obsolescence was admirably suited for throwing hefty canister charges at short range to break up infantry assaults. The remainder of the army's batteries consisted of an oddball mix of 6- and 12-pounder Wiard rifles (two of each), ten 12-pounder Napoleons, and six 3-inch Ordnance rifles.[32]

*   *   *

The sense of power felt within Rosecrans's army suffered a rude shock in the early days of December courtesy of John Hunt Morgan. The Federal army lay stretched across a 40-mile front, with Nashville as its primary base. On the far left flank was a single brigade under the command of Colonel Absalom B. Moore of the 104th Illinois, guarding Purier's Ferry, an important Cumberland River crossing near Hartsville (spelled Puryears Ferry in some sources). An inexperienced political colonel only months removed from civilian life, Moore was placed in command of the 39th Brigade on December 2 when the previous commander returned to his regiment in Nashville. As Moore's obituary later read: "It was his misfortune to hold a command for which he was unfitted by reason of

---

31 Unknown soldier, Battery A, 1st Ohio Light Artillery, *Cleveland Morning Leader*, Nov. 21, 1861, 3.

32 Fitch, *Annals of the Army of the Cumberland*, 203-300.

inexperience, the want of confidence on the part of many of his officers, and the absence of those military instincts which soldiers recognize and trust."

Tasked by Bragg to cut Rosecrans's supply line and cause havoc, Morgan left Murfreesboro with a mixed force of cavalry and infantry the morning of December 6. Arriving overnight in the midst of a snowstorm, he deftly split his force into two columns and struck the Hartsville garrison at dawn. "The first intimation we had of any threatened attack was by someone crying out at the top of his voice at about 6:30 a.m., 'Fall in, they are coming!'" remembered Lt. Col. Gustavus Tafel of the 106th Ohio. The long roll was beaten in camp, and the men of Moore's three regiments climbed from their tents into the snow, forming to the barked orders of their officers and sergeants into line along the company pathways. In the swirling fight that followed, the green soldiers made a poor showing marked by command confusion, with Morgan's men compelling nearly the entire brigade to surrender during a quick retreat to the camps.[33]

Suffering only 139 casualties, Morgan was delighted, as the triumph at Hartsville was arguably the apex of his storied career. "The battle was now won and the result exceeded my expectation," he reported. "We took in all 1,800 prisoners, 1,800 stands of arms, a quantity of ammunition, clothing, quartermaster stores, and 16 wagons." Morgan's force also captured three stands of Federal colors and five cavalry guidons during the engagement before setting fire to the camp. "Men could not possibly behave better than our troops did in this one," crowed Basil Duke. "They had literally made up their minds not to be beaten."[34]

Hartsville stunned, embarrassed, and angered Rosecrans. "Do I understand that they have captured an entire brigade of our troops without our knowing it, or a good fight?" the incredulous general messaged Thomas. "It seems impossible to me that an entire brigade could have surrendered. Are there none left?"

Lincoln and Halleck also demanded answers, asking "why an isolated brigade was at Hartsville and by whose command and by whose fault it was surprised and captured." The affair put Rosecrans in a difficult spot with the war department, especially as it came on the heels of his testy correspondence with Halleck about being insensible to threats of removal. That said, Rosey at first suppressed his answer to Lincoln's inquiry, refusing to name names until he completed his investigation. Two weeks later, however, he placed the blame for the brigade's

---

33 OR 20/2:52-62.

34 Ibid., 1:66-67; Duke, *Morgan's Cavalry*, 226.

"feeble resistance" on Colonel Moore, as "the disaster seems to be attributable mainly to his ignorance or negligence."[35]

John Beatty reported that "the whole army feels deeply mortified over the loss of the brigade at Hartsville," but he also believed the defeat would awaken "the army into something like life," adding: "Before it was idly waiting the rise of the Cumberland, but this bold dash of the Rebels has made it bristle up like an angry boar and it today it starts out to show its tusks to the enemy."

Northern newspapers likewise were appalled, George Prentice of the Louisville Journal labeling it a "disgraceful affair" and a "most wretched business. It is enough to make an honest patriot sick at heart. The miserable poltroons in the Hartsville affair should be first marched in old women's nightcaps all through the Nashville streets to the music of fife and drum, then marched in their nightcaps all the way on foot to Camp Chase."[36]

Meanwhile in Murfreesboro, December proved to be a month of reviews for the Army of Tennessee. The first occurred on December 5, when Joe Johnston visited Bragg's troops and was impressed. "[They] are in fine condition," he wrote Senator Wigfall. "Healthy looking and well clothed, in fine spirits, too. I see no evidence of the want of confidence and dissatisfaction of which we heard so much in Richmond."

President Davis arrived in Chattanooga on December 11. Finding Johnston ill in bed, he delayed his conference with the Virginian and moved on to Murfreesboro to meet with Bragg and review his army on December 12. Davis's appearance belied his lofty status. "His dress was plain and assuming and his baggage limited to a single leather valise with the initials 'J.D.' marked upon the side," the Chattanooga Daily Rebel reported. "Attended by one body servant alone, his mode of travel was without ostentation or parade. His reception of his fellow citizens of Tennessee at the different way stations was exceedingly cordial and hearty, and crowds of soldiers and citizens gathered around the window of the carriage where he sat whenever the train stopped."[37]

On December 13, a grand review of Bragg's army took place in a large, open field along the Shelbyville Pike, about a mile south of Murfreesboro. "The sun rose gorgeously above the spires of the city and sabers and bayonets glittered in every

---

35 *OR* 20/1:42-45.

36 Beatty, *The Citizen-Soldier*, 191; "Disgraceful Affair at Hartsville," *Louisville Daily Journal*, Dec. 10, 1862, 2.

37 McWhiney, *Braxton Bragg and Confederate Defeat*, 344.

direction as the regiments of the first division for review filed into the open area selected for the ceremony," reported the Daily Rebel. "An immense concourse of people assembled to witness it; the outskirts of the plain were bordered with people of all ages and costume, horses and vehicles of every description presenting a scene of bustle and excitement while the lines of infantry with waving banners and gleaming bayonets suggested vivid pictures of the glorious time of Napoleon."[38]

Breckinridge's Division marched first, the general seated atop a charger dressed in his finest uniform. Hanson's Kentucky "Orphans" marched at the head of the line. "Jeff was well pleased with the orphans," remembered the 9th Kentucky's John Jackman. "They conducted themselves every inch the soldier. They passed in review, marching perfectly. Hanson was made a brigadier general on the spot."

Davis, the *Daily Rebel* gloated, "followed [as] the corps, division, and brigadier generals of the command and their staff officers rode down the line at a full gallop." The general of each division rode on the right of the president "as their respective divisions were drawn up for review. The men in open ranks stood with arms presented, the officers saluting and the regimental bands playing, each band taking it up in succession as the cortege passed. The regiments, continued the paper, "were then wheeled into column and passed in review before the President."

"The men never looked in better condition and seemed never before to have marched with lighter step or more soldierly carriage. With few exceptions they were comfortably although not altogether uniformly clad. Their arms and accoutrements were in unexceptionable condition and their maneuvers executed with the skills almost of regulars."[39]

That evening, Davis was publicly feted at the gaily decorated Rutherford County Courthouse. The review impressed Davis, especially as the superb condition of Bragg's army flew counter to the reports he had received from Leonidas Polk. He noticed no evidence of poor morale, finding to the contrary the army in fine fighting trim and confident in its ability to defeat the Yankees. Davis reported that to Cooper in Richmond, noting that he felt the proposed cavalry expeditions under Forrest and Morgan in the Federal rear could cause considerable havoc.

All the same, Davis remained worried about the security of Mississippi and Vicksburg to the south. He and Bragg spoke at length about the situation in the

---

38 "President Davis at Murfreesboro," *Chattanooga Daily Rebel*, Dec. 17, 1862, 1.

39 Davis, *Diary of a Confederate Soldier*, 65; "President Davis," *Chattanooga Daily Rebel*.

West, with Davis arguing for the urgent need to send reinforcements to Mississippi. Bragg demurred, worried that a reduction of his army would leave him vulnerable to a move by Rosecrans but ultimately agreed to send a division. Conceding that defeat could not be ruled out, Davis instructed Bragg to "fight if you can and fall back beyond the Tennessee [River]." Rosecrans had yet to show any aggressive intent from his Nashville base, so Davis likely believed the Federal army was preparing to settle into its winter camps, delaying any offensive operations until the spring. With that in mind, Davis decided it was better at this juncture to risk losing Middle Tennessee than to allow the Confederacy to be cut in two.[40]

Upon his return to Chattanooga, Davis contacted James A. Seddon, his new secretary of war, that "General Johnston will go immediately to Mississippi and without delay reinforce Pemberton by sending a division of, say, 8,000 men from troops in this quarter." Johnston still opposed the transfer but knew he had little choice but to obey. Major General Carter L. Stevenson's Division was detached from Edmund Kirby Smith's Corps and promptly sent south via rail, following the reverse route that Bragg's army had taken from Tupelo to Chattanooga in July. Once Stevenson's Division was on the road, Smith returned to his departmental headquarters in Knoxville.[41]

Davis and Johnston left Chattanooga for Mobile by train on December 16, then headed west to Mississippi, arriving in Vicksburg on December 20. Continuing to argue his case that reinforcements for Mississippi should be drawn from Theophilus Holmes's command, Johnston finally persuaded Davis to agree. Strangely, Davis followed with a letter to Holmes encouraging him to cross the Mississippi, but he did not order him to do so. Without a positive order, Holmes would not budge, and Davis decided to let the matter rest.

On Christmas Day, Davis headed back to Richmond, confident about the morale and condition of the Western armies, though perhaps less confident in the ability of his senior commanders to cooperate for their mutual defense. The key decision he had made, however, would have a major impact on the upcoming battle at Stones River. The absence of a quarter of Bragg's infantry force that Davis had ordered to Mississippi would be sorely felt when the fighting broke out six days later in Middle Tennessee.

40 McWhiney, *Braxton Bragg and Confederate Defeat*, 345.

41 OR 20/2:449-450, 453.

The Confederates made no secrets of their intentions to have Forrest and Morgan commence raiding again, and numerous warnings that put Federal posts on notice were sent from Rosecrans's headquarters in the first weeks of December. Shortly after his arrival, Johnston was appalled to read in a Nashville newspaper a fairly accurate account of the plans for an upcoming raid of Morgan's into Kentucky. A December raid by Forrest was a particular masterpiece considering the Federals had received such ample warnings. Forrest's target was the network of railroads in West Tennessee that provided direct support to Grant's looming offensive into Mississippi. The Mobile and Ohio Railroad stretched from Columbus, Kentucky, to Corinth, and along its path two lesser lines led to Memphis, Tennessee, and Holly Springs, Mississippi, both important Federal depots. Two important railroad junctions, at the Tennessee towns of Humboldt and Jackson also were important targets for Forrest's raiders.

Forrest marched west from Columbia, Tennessee, on December 11 with 1,800 poorly armed troopers, accompanied by four cannons. After crossing the Tennessee River, he won a quick victory over a small and inexperienced Federal force of 700 men at Lexington on December 18, then pushed forward to strike the railroad at Jackson the next day. Arraying his troopers as though he intended to charge into town, Forrest kept the Federal garrison occupied while two smaller detachments rode north and south of town to cut the railroad.

Once their missions were complete, Forrest pulled back and struck north at Humboldt and Trenton along the Mobile & Ohio. Gathering prisoners and arms and ammunition along the way, he rode as far north as Union City near the Tennessee–Kentucky line before turning east with about 10,000 Federals in pursuit. An enemy force finally brought him to grips at Parker's Cross Roads on December 31. Forrest surrounded his opponents before being surrounded himself, but the intrepid trooper fought his way out and recrossed the Tennessee with a larger command than he started 20 days earlier. The raid was a complete success: more than 50 bridges destroyed, more than 2,500 total Federal casualties, but most important, the Mobile & Ohio had been reduced to a useless shamble.

Forrest was not the only Confederate cavalryman raising hell with Grant's command. Earl Van Dorn, humiliated at being superseded by John Pemberton after the disastrous attack at Second Corinth in October, sought redemption by taking command of Pemberton's cavalry and staging a daring raid on the Union supply depot at Holly Springs. Riding in at dawn on December 20, Van Dorn divided his 3,500 troopers into three columns and launched them into the Federal camps. The garrison commander—the inept Colonel Robert Murphy of the 8th Wisconsin, who had been run out of Iuka ingloriously in September—mounted a pitiful defense, and by 8 a.m. most of his 1,500-man garrison were prisoners. Van Dorn's troopers gleefully put the torch to the warehouses and three full trains crammed with $1.5 million worth of supplies and provisions, then turned north to wreck the rest of the Mississippi Central Railroad. By the end of the month, when Van Dorn returned to his camp in Grenada, Mississippi, the combined effects of both Forrest's raid and his own had undermined Grant's offensive. Grant's 40,000-man army retreated toward Memphis while a river-borne expedition to Vicksburg by William T. Sherman ended in defeat at Chickasaw Bayou, Mississippi, in the final days of December.

Bragg's orders for Morgan to raid in Rosecrans's rear assumed increased importance, as the need to derail Grant's offensive in Mississippi had prompted the dispatch of Stevenson's Division from the main army. Morgan's troopers left the morning of December 22, heading north to cross the Cumberland. "The men were never in higher spirits or more joyous humor," recalled Colonel William C. P. Breckinridge, a Morgan subordinate. "They were well-armed, well-mounted, in good discipline with perfect confidence in their commander and with their hearts longing for the hills and valleys, the bluegrass and woods of dear old Kentucky. The division had never operated together before since the brigades had been first organized, therefore every regiment was filled with the spirit of emulation and every man was determined to make his regiment the crack regiment of Morgan's cavalry. It was a magnificent body of men—the pick of the youth of Kentucky."[42]

Morgan's command was at peak strength and had colossal confidence in its leader, but much had changed since the first Kentucky raid in July. The Federal army had greatly increased in size, and substantial detachments of troops tangled Morgan's route into Kentucky. The defenses of the rebuilt Louisville & Nashville had been strengthened by the construction of blockhouses at important points, all manned by well-armed troops.

Rumors of Morgan's impending return to Kentucky had been daily fodder in the Nashville papers for weeks, so any element of surprise had been lost before the campaign even began. The Kentuckians had a tough slog ahead if they hoped to re-create their July success; they were also unaware that news of their departure was a key factor in Rosecrans's decision to march from Nashville and attack Bragg's army. One wonders how much more value Morgan's command might have been had it operated directly in Rosecrans's rear in Tennessee during the upcoming fight and had not galloped into the Kentucky wilds.

42 Duke, *Morgan's Cavalry*, 233.

The strict military discipline at the Confederate camps in and around Murfreesboro loosened a bit as the holidays approached. No doubt influenced by the pleadings of religious leaders such as Polk and Dr. Charles Quintard, Bragg issued general orders in mid-December cancelling all foraging expeditions on Sundays and encouraging the men to attend religious services. Performing services in the forests, the army's chaplains attracted sizable crowds of soldiers.

An observer noted the salutary effect of the order the following Sunday when "the hum and bustle of the camps was hushed and unmolested save by the distant booming of artillery as the young fellows who had strolled away from camps to the race paths were soon called away from them to listen to the enrapturing sounds of Jehovah and the counsel of the man of God." Bragg would not be baptized until the following spring, but the religious fervor that marked the latter days of the army's existence had its roots in this order.[43]

Murfreesboro resident John C. Spence lived among Bragg's army for two months. "The soldiers when they made a purchase of any article were disposed to pay and were liberal in doing so," he recalled. "The soldiers were very deficient in camp equipage, yet they appeared cheerful under these difficulties. Their clothing was warm and substantial, but not much uniformity in appearance—some gray, butternut, or brown, and others of rather a dirt color. Hats and caps of various forms, colors, and shapes."

George Turner of the 8th Texas Cavalry recalled that "the ladies here are our best friends. They slip into Nashville and bring us boots, clothing, etc. concealed about their persons. One of them smuggled out a pair of six-shooters hid in the collar of her buggy horse. They go out to the Yankee pickets and get the latest papers for us. The last they brought us was a *Harper's Weekly* full of pictures of Yankee camps and Yankee generals."[44]

The Christmas holiday proved routine for most in the army, as the men simply stayed in camp. Missing one's home and family became a common lament. Wrote Adjutant C. Irvine Walker of the 10th South Carolina:

Christmas has passed and we are still in the field. I spent it in the midst of camp and surrounded by camp friends. We, from the colonel down, ran races, wrestled, played prisoner's base, etc. We had a merry time although I might have found under other

---

43 OR 20/2:447; "Letter From Bird," *Knoxville Daily Register*, Jan. 2, 1863, 1.

44 John C. Spence, *A Diary of the Civil War* (Murfreesboro, 1993), 55; Helen J. H. Rugeley, ed., *Batchelor-Turner Letters, 1861-1864 Written by Two of Terry's Texas Rangers* (Austin, 1961), 40.

circumstances a pleasanter way of spending the day. All the visions of turkey, plum pudding, mince pies, and eggnog we realized in pork and rice, the latter being a delicacy. We are in luck, however, for neither the pork nor rice arrived until the day came. Not even a glass of wine to drink a Merry Christmas and a toast to absent friends. I had expected to dine in Cincinnati, but instead . . . the brave army of Mississippi reached Cumberland Gap and we were thus compelled to dine in Murfreesboro. Hard fate![45]

"Christmas has passed and gone, and how differently from that of 1861," wrote the 16th Tennessee's James J. Womack. "That I passed in Charleston and Fort Sumter, where I was delighted and pleased. This I have spent in my tent by the fire near Murfreesboro attending to the many daily duties of the soldier."

The men of the 12th Tennessee gathered their tin cups and frying pans and commenced banging on them while parading through camp to celebrate the holiday. "They serenaded quite a number in the brigade and they honored me with a visit to my quarters and called on me for a speech," said Captain Alfred T. Fielder. "I attempted to give them a short talk as did several others whom they called upon in the different regiments. All passed off finely."

Having just recovered from a smallpox outbreak that necessitated isolation and vaccination for the entire regiment, the men of the 13th Tennessee celebrated the holiday by getting drunk. "Eggnog was fashionable in camp and captains, lieutenants, and privates were drunk and very troublesome," remembered William J. Rodgers. "Two thirds of the Gaines Invincibles on a drunk."[46]

Souring the season, however, was a series of military executions on December 26 that laid bare simmering resentment still festering in the army from the Kentucky Campaign. The problem was the Conscription Act and Bragg's enforcement of it during that campaign. As mentioned earlier, the Conscription Act changed the term of service for the volunteer regiments from one year to three (or the duration of the war, whichever came first). Given Kentucky's status as a "neutral" state, the army's Kentuckians did not feel bound by the act's provisions. "No more independent men served the Confederacy than its Kentuckians," wrote historian William Davis. "However wild and reckless their conduct, they were men

---

45 Papers of Cornelius Irvine Walker, 10th South Carolina, SRNBP.

46 James J. Womack, *The Civil War Diary of Capt. J. J. Womack* (McMinnville, 1961), 76; Ann York Franklin, comp., *The Civil War Diaries of Captain Alfred Tyler Fielder, 12th Tennessee Regiment Infantry, Company B, 1861–1865* (1996), 96; William J. Rogers, "William J. Rogers Memorandum Book." *The West Tennessee Historical Society Papers*, No. IX, (McCowat-Mercer, 1955), 77.

who like their state guarded jealously every right, every prerogative. Not citizens of the Confederate States of America, they did not feel bound by its actions."

Members of the 5th and 6th Kentucky regiments had mutinied when compelled to serve beyond their one-year terms of enlistment that fall, and only a passionate appeal by General Breckinridge induced the men to return to duty.

The Kentuckians learned while in camp at Murfreesboro that Bragg had enforced the Conscription Act while in the Commonwealth, which in their eyes "amounted to slavery." It was the arrest and execution of the soldier Asa Lewis, however, that struck to the core. Lewis deserted from the 6th Kentucky in early December only to be quickly caught by a bounty hunter. In a court-martial on the 20th he was charged with desertion; Lewis's defense claimed he had enlisted to serve 12 months, had served out that term, and had returned home to provide for his widowed mother and siblings. Since his previous requests for a furlough had been denied, Lewis decided to take what was known as a "French leave" and would indeed return to the regiment once he had provided for his family.

The court didn't accept his explanation and sentenced him to execution. The officers of the Orphan Brigade campaigned earnestly to persuade Bragg to commute the sentence, delivering a petition on Christmas Day begging him to reconsider. A personal visit from Breckinridge pleading the case likewise did no good. Bragg, William Davis wrote, "was sick of the Kentuckians' grumbling and troublemaking. He would put a stop to it if he had to execute every Orphan in the brigade." Breckinridge lost his temper, telling Bragg that Kentuckians were not slaves and that shooting Lewis amounted to murder. Bragg was unmoved. He likewise rebuffed a final appeal the morning of December 26.

Lewis was not the only man slated for execution. First was a local named Gray, a convicted Federal spy, who would be hanged from the gallows near the railroad depot. Two other soldiers, one from Alabama and one from Tennessee, would join Lewis in front of the firing squad. "There may be an appearance of severity in these executions," noted one newspaper reporter, "but now is no time for the display of leniency on the part of our commanders. The good of the service demands that the articles of war be strictly enforced without regard to sympathetic feelings."

One of the condemned, Edward P. Norman of the 28th Alabama, had spent Christmas day and the morning of December 26 composing a final letter to his wife and children. The Alabamian, like Lewis, was caught taking "French leave" and had been sentenced to be shot. "I am listening every moment for when I will be called out for execution," he would write. "I see that I must die and I never on earth can meet you anymore but thank God I have faith to believe that I will meet you in a better world. I haven't language to tell you my feelings at this time when I think of leaving you and my little children. It don't seem like I can bear it, but I am condemned to die and no doubt this time tomorrow will be sleeping in the cold grave. I want you to raise my children right, treat them as well as you can and teach them to put their trust in God who is able to save them."[47]

Gray was the first to meet his end that day. The public hanging, according to a local newspaper, was witnessed by "an immense throng of soldiers and citizens. The gallows were erected near the railroad depot.… He appeared quite unconcerned and his forbidding features did not display any particular interest in the dread tragedy about to be enacted. Just after the noose had been adjusted around his neck and as the captain was reading the sentence, Gray leaped from the platform and thus landed himself into eternity. He struggled severely for five minutes and then expired."[48]

The military executions did not go smoothly. Lewis was carted into an open field surrounded on three sides by members of the Orphan Brigade. "I beg of you to aim to kill; it will be merciful for me," he told his executioners A witness wrote that "as the brigade was being formed, the clouds grew dark and heavy as if the very heavens frowned upon the bloody deed to be enacted. After bidding a few friends adieu, he, with a firm step and without kneeling or being blindfolded, faced the firing party composed of one lieutenant, one sergeant, and 15 men. Twelve of the guns were loaded with balls and three with blanks. At noon, the lieutenant gave the commands "ready, aim, fire," when the prisoner fell dead, pierced by eleven balls."

Breckinridge briefly spoke with Lewis prior to the execution, having received his personal effects the night before. The former vice president was crestfallen and barely made it through the proceedings, nearly falling from his horse in grief when the guns fired. The execution of Lewis "created a profound sensation and incensed Hanson's brigade beyond measure." The execution of Edward Norman of the 28th Alabama occurred in a separate field without a hitch, but the deserter from the 24th Tennessee received a last-minute reprieve from Bragg.[49]

And with that, Bragg's army concluded the Christmas season in Murfreesboro.

---

47 "Military Executions," *Montgomery Daily Mail*, Jan. 7, 1863, 2; Private Edward P. Norman, Co. C, 28th Alabama, SRNBP.

48 "Military Executions," *Weekly Pioneer and Democrat*, Jan. 30, 1863, 7. The Minnesota paper reprinted this account from the December 27 edition of the *Murfreesboro Rebel Banner*.

49 William C. Davis, *The Orphan Brigade: The Kentucky Confederates Who Couldn't Go Home* (Garden City, 1980), 130-50; Letter from "Volunteer," 2nd Kentucky, *Southern Confederacy*, Jan. 3, 1863, 2.

Knob Gap and La Vergne:
A Winter Offensive on the
Road to Murfreesboro

THE FIRST REPORTS of the Union travesty at Fredericksburg, Virginia, hit the Nashville newspapers on December 17. The sting of defeat "cast a shadow over [our] army," noted Colonel John Beatty, commanding one of Thomas's brigades. "We are in a deeper gloom now than ever. The repulse at Fredericksburg has disheartened if not demoralized a great army and given confidence and strength to the Rebels everywhere. It may be, however, that this defeat was necessary to bring us clearly to the point of extinguishing slavery in all the states. The mere reconstruction of the Union on the old basis would not pay humanity for all the blood shed since the war began. The extinction of slavery perhaps will."[1]

Sergeant Lyman Widney of the 34th Illinois recalled that "the first news we received of Fredericksburg promised a grand victory, but day after day our hopes were gradually dissipated by later scraps and fragments of news until at length we were brought to the knowledge of a great disaster. At the outset, we thought that our presence in the field would overawe the South; later we expected to finish the

1 Beatty, *The Citizen-Soldier*, 194.

war in one great battle, but after this last defeat of Burnside, we are forced to the conclusion that we must accomplish our work by the wearing out process."[2]

"There is a deep depression of spirit among the soldiers of this brigade which is a fair sample of the army here," Christopher Bowen of the 6th Ohio wrote on Christmas Eve. "They all believe that this is the darkest hour of our country's trial; when the non-combatants at home are quarreling among themselves, withdrawing their support from the Administration by word and deed; when the Grand Army making strategic movements which end in a tragedy, discord in the Cabinet, and a general division of sentiment in the whole North. This will break up with the recognition of the Southern Confederacy if something great is not done soon, then goodbye to the once proud and prosperous United States."[3]

The men ravenously consumed news about their Confederate foes, and the wedding of the renowned John Hunt Morgan on December 14 particularly resonated even in Federal-held Nashville. At 1:10 p.m. December 15, Rosecrans telegraphed Halleck, using details provided in a Murfreesboro Rebel Banner account, that "Jeff Davis attended John H. Morgan's wedding last night, was serenaded and made a speech in which he said Lincoln's proclamation put black and white on an equality. Urged them to fight until death and to hold middle Tennessee at all hazards until Grant could be whipped. Things will be ripe soon."

An hour later, one of Colonel Truesdail's spies delivered information about Confederate dispositions in the region. "The center composed of three divisions is at Murfreesboro [and] was reviewed by Jefferson Davis last Friday; the left wing under Buckner and Hardee moved from Shelbyville to Triune and Nolensville; the right under Kirby Smith is at Readyville. Morgan probably crossing the Cumberland [River] now near Hartsville; object a dash on the railroad. Rebel troops say they will fight us. Bragg to go to Mississippi, Johnston to stay."[4]

By December 20, Rosecrans's army critically had accumulated enough rations and supplies to keep it in the field until February 1, 1863—a remarkable logistical feat considering the department's entire force numbered roughly 90,000 men and,

---

2 Robert I. Girardi, editor. *Campaigning With Uncle Billy: The Civil War Memoirs of Sergeant Lyman S. Widney, 34th Illinois Volunteer Infantry* (Victoria, 2008), 124.

3 Private Christopher C. Bowen, Co. E, 6th Ohio, *Gallipolis Journal,* Jan. 15, 1863, 1.

4 OR 20/2:179-80. It appears Rosecrans conflated the public fete for Davis with the Morgan wedding, which took place the following day. Davis left for Chattanooga on the morning of December 14 and was not present for the wedding, which took place that evening in Murfreesboro.

with the Cumberland River not yet fully navigable, was still being supplied by a single-track railroad. The weather had remained fair and dry, making the region's dirt roads ideally still passable to the tens of thousands of feet ready to use them.

To Bragg, however, what seemed Federal inactivity indicated Rosecrans intended to spend the winter in Nashville, prompting him to send his men into winter quarters as well. Many in Rosecrans's force shared that conviction, though not Colonel Hans Heg of the 15th Wisconsin, who believed Rosey was enticing Bragg into an attack on his Nashville defenses, a move that offered the Federals an opportunity to deliver a "real threshing." Rosecrans indeed was planning to spring southward.[5] What finally triggered his decision to march from Nashville were the well-known departures of Forrest's and Morgan's cavalry commands from Bragg's army. "In the absence of these forces, and with adequate supplies in Nashville," he reiterated, "the moment was judged opportune for an advance on the rebels."

Thanks to Truesdail's extensive spy network, Rosecrans had a firm grasp of the Confederate dispositions. "Polk's and Kirby Smith's forces were at Murfreesboro," Truesdail revealed, "while Hardee's corps [is] on the Shelbyville and Nolensville pike between Triune and Eagleville, with an advance guard at Nolensville."

With Bragg's numerical superiority in cavalry reduced, Rosecrans was confident there was less risk to his army's supply wagons and supply lines.

For added security, the Union commander was guarding the trestles, bridges, and tunnels of the Louisville & Nashville entirely to Louisville with special detachments from Maj. Gen. Joseph Jones Reynolds's division in Thomas's Center Corps, based north of Nashville. Further, Maj. Gen. Robert B. Mitchell's division of Thomas's corps remained in Nashville, keeping the city secure and hopefully dissuading either Forrest or Morgan from doubling back and launching a surprise raid. With his line of supply therefore reasonably secure, Rosecrans turned his energies to his front. He never cited the absence of Carter Stevenson's Division, sent to reinforce Pemberton in Mississippi, as a factor in his decision to move when he did—but if anything, it cemented his determination.[6]

As it was Rosecrans's intent to turn Bragg's left while pinning him in place at Stewart's Creek along the Nashville Pike, thus allowing his flanking column to

---

5 Lamers, *Edge of Glory*, 198-99.

6 William Bickham, who accompanied Rosecrans's headquarters during the campaign, cited intelligence in his December 29, 1862, dispatch to the *Cincinnati Commercial* that "a division of Kirby Smith's army numbering 5,000" had been sent to reinforce Pemberton's army. If Bickham knew, it is virtually certain Rosecrans knew.

swoop in and threaten Bragg's rear, he arrayed his forces as follows: "McCook, with three divisions, to advance by the Nolensville pike to Triune. Thomas, with two divisions (Negley's and Rousseau's), was to advance on his right, by the Franklin and Wilson pikes, threatening Hardee's left, and then to fall in by the crossroads to Nolensville. Crittenden, with Wood's, Palmer's, and Van Cleve's divisions, to advance by the Murfreesboro pike to La Vergne. With Thomas's two divisions at Nolensville, McCook was to attack Hardee at Triune, and, if the enemy reinforced Hardee, Thomas was to support McCook. If McCook beat Hardee, or Hardee retreated, and the enemy met us at Stewart's Creek, five miles south of La Vergne, Crittenden was to attack him, Thomas was to come in on his left flank, and McCook, after detaching a division to pursue or observe Hardee, if retreating south, was to move with the remainder of his force on their rear."[7]

The plan was well-conceived, keeping the army's various corps within supporting distance of one another while taking advantage of the macadamized pikes to expedite movement. By massing five of his eight infantry divisions on his right, Rosecrans aimed to overwhelm Bragg's left and draw the remainder of the Rebel army toward a defensive position that Crittenden's wing would assume along Stewart's Creek. Once engaged there, Thomas could swing east and strike Bragg's left. McCook would march from Triune along the Franklin Pike toward Murfreesboro to sever Bragg's supply line. If Bragg took the bait and attacked at Stewart's Creek, Rosecrans could flank and pin his opponent against the west bank of Stones River, where few fords offered the opportunity of escape. The key to the plan's success was with McCook, who was tasked with driving back Bragg's left wing commanded by his old West Point commandant William Hardee and breaking into the Confederate rear to seize the railroad.

Preliminary orders on December 23 directed McCook's and Crittenden's wings to march at dawn the next day, though delays would dog their start. McCook's route south to Nolensville lay along the Edmonson Pike, and Crittenden would drive south along the Murfreesboro Pike as far as La Vergne, being sure to secure the road to Nolensville by which he would open communication with McCook's advance. Reveille sounded at 4:00 a.m., but the suddenness of the order to march led to confusion in the camps, and it wasn't until noon on December 24 that McCook was able to get his lead brigade marching.

The men didn't know their true objective, believing they were simply embarking on another foraging expedition. "This morning, we got orders to have

____

7 *OR* 20/1:189.

three days' rations in haversacks and that we were going after forage," recalled Lieutenant Fred Boyer of the 59th Illinois. "Laid around until noon then marched out southeast outside the picket lines, then returned to the old camp and stacked arms." General John Palmer's division in Crittenden's wing began moving on the Murfreesboro Pike before sunrise and marched a few miles before halting. Oscar Easley, serving with the Pioneer Brigade, remembered the only charging done by Crittenden's men that day was "on a pile of walnuts that the Negroes had piled up; we soon made them surrender but got no Butternuts except one and we took him prisoner."[8]

News of the offensive spread rapidly through the army and triggered a cacophony of activity. "The camps blazed with excitement," noted one observer. "The sturdy troops greeted the announcement with a shrill clamor. Thousands were cooking rations for the march. Muskets soon gleamed with a fateful luster. The horseman carefully brushed his equipment, adjusted his last strap, looked well to his holsters, and patted his faithful charger. The cannoneer burnished his trusty piece until it glistened, then poised it again and again, sighting it at imaginary foes so soon to assume stern substantial form."

The 57th Indiana's historian recalled that "all of our sick in the regimental hospital were taken to the city and the convalescents were sent to the barracks. But two wagons were to accompany the regiment and these were used for hauling rations. The men were ordered to carry besides their guns and equipment three days' rations in haversacks, one wool blanket, an oilcloth, and overcoat. All other baggage was loaded and sent to the rear."[9]

First Lieutenant Alfred Pirtle, commanding Rousseau's divisional ordnance train, described his preparations for the march. After consulting with the chief of artillery, he drew "fixed artillery ammunition for James's rifled cannon, ten-pounder Parrott, twelve-pounder smoothbore, and a small supply for six-pounder smoothbore, so that I had 22 wagons loaded with this branch of ammunition. I also drew small-arm ammunition for .69 caliber muskets, .58 Springfield rifles, .57 caliber for Enfield rifles, and .54 caliber for Austrian rifles, making 15 wagon loads of this branch of missiles. My train was fully equipped with

8 Diary of 2nd Lt. Frederick N. Boyer, Co. H, 59th Illinois, SRNBP; Private Oscar Easley, Co. F, 84th Illinois, Dec. 24, 1862, SRNBP.

9 Bickham, *Rosecrans' Campaign*, 132-33; *Annals of the Fifty-Seventh Regiment Indiana Volunteers: Marches, Battles, and Incidents of Army Life*. Dayton: W. J. Shuey, 1868, 145.

six-mule teams, and I had a citizen wagonmaster, his assistant, as well as white and black citizen drivers."

The 101st Ohio received early Christmas presents in brand-new Springfield rifle-muskets, one of the first regiments in Rosecrans's army to receive these well-regarded long arms. "We went wild over the exchange and acted much like little boys with new sleds," recalled Lewis Day. "At once we became anxious to try our new guns on the enemy, nor had we long to wait."[10]

By 1:20 that afternoon, McCook reported to Rosecrans that he could not reach Nolensville until dark and asked for a one-day delay. Crittenden likewise reported that even though his troops were ready to march by noon, he would not be able to reach La Vergne until nightfall and he would have no way of determining whether he had selected a good defensible position in the darkness. Both suggested a delay, and Rosecrans agreed. "I think the enemy is committed to stand at Murfreesboro to protect the raid into Kentucky," Rosecrans messaged Halleck at 5:30 p.m. on Christmas Eve, "and now having the essential ammunition and 20 days' rations in Nashville, I shall move on them tomorrow morning at daylight. If they meet us, we shall fight tomorrow; if they wait for us, next day. If we beat them, I shall try to drive them to the wall."[11]

Later that evening, Father Jeremiah Trecy, a Catholic priest who frequently accompanied Rosecrans, stopped at army headquarters to inquire about a rumor that the army was moving out the next morning. Rosecrans confirmed the rumor, to which Trecy replied, "General, tomorrow is the birthday of man's redeemer!" Rosecrans, having already agreed to delay the advance to Christmas Day because of the reports of difficulties from McCook and Crittenden, further considered Trecy's comment and conceded, "I did not think of it, Father." Turning to Garesche, he asked, "Colonel, can we countermand it?" Garesche nodded. "Send orders to the corps commanders and all will be right." And with that, the start of Rosecrans's ambitious campaign would be delayed until December 26.[12]

*   *   *

10 Alfred Pirtle "Stone River Sketches." MOLLUS Ohio, Vol. 6, (Cincinnati, 1908), 95-96; Day, *Story of the 101st Ohio*, 71.

11 *OR* 20/2:218-222.

12 David Power Coyngham, *The Soldiers of the Cross: Heroism of the Cross or Nuns and Priests on the Battlefield* (South Bend, 1870), 35.

It took time for the orders to make the rounds, and some regiments awoke Christmas morning girding for a fight. Lieutenant Colonel Daniel Griffin of the 38th Indiana noted that his regiment was up before dawn expecting to march. "Breakfast at daybreak, all packed and ready to move and ere the hour for the sounding of the 'general' at 7:10 arrived and the bugle notes had scarce died away when half of the tents were down, wagons in the quarters and everything and everybody on the move," Griffin wrote. "Just then orders countermanding the march arrived. The tents were again put up and now we await the arrival of tomorrow morning."

With orders delayed, the men tried to enjoy the holiday as best they could. Sergeant George Ridenour of the 6th Ohio noted that "we keep up a somewhat bleak form of 'ye merry Christmas' and everybody is garrulous with reminiscences and seasonable jokes. Many of the fellows have substantial remembrances from friends at home in the shape of express packages redolent of roast chicken and cake. The war is forgotten for one day as the soldier character is laid aside. Instead of the gathering of families around the hearthstone, we gather in tents around our monotonous beans and crackers."[13]

Captain Clement C. Webb of the 13th Michigan spent Christmas enjoying the contents of one of those express boxes. "All came safe but the brandy which had broken and all run out," he noted in his diary. "I was truly glad to get the box my wife sent me, just what I wanted. None but the best of wives could have thought of everything that a man wanted."

Christmas also introduced a commissary department concoction to the camps of the 21st Wisconsin near Nashville: squares of desiccated condensed vegetables. In honor of the holiday, one soldier called it "Hot Trinity"—with good reason. "It was queer looking stuff, pressed into cakes a foot square and two inches thick," remembered Lieutenant John H. Otto. "It consisted of all possible garden greens including cabbage, beets, rutabaga, turnip leaves, bean pods, onion vines, parsley, sage, celery, sliced turnips, kohlrabi, and last but not least, red pepper." The men threw the squares into their camp kettles, and upon soaking and boiling sampled the result. "Nobody could ever tell exactly how it tasted because there were so

---

13 Lt. Col. Daniel Griffin, 38th Indiana, SRNBP; 1st Sgt. George B. Ridenour, Co. G, 6th Ohio, *Sandusky Register*, Jan. 7, 1863, 2.

many tastes to it, but all agreed that it was hot, hot, hot, and when you were half through it was hotter and when you have done with it, it is just the hottest."[14]

Things were equally lively in the 18th Ohio's camp. "The boys had considerable fun…," noted Sergeant Launcelot Scott. "During the afternoon, some of the boys went over to the 31st Ohio where they got some commissary whiskey and returned to camp at night pretty drunk. After tattoo beat and all the camp got quiet, Charlie and Ed got their guns and commenced firing out of the tent. The guards were called out and marched to our quarters. They halted at tent No. 2 just as Charlie threw back the flap to fire again. 'Who are you,' asked the officer. 'Why I'm Christ's Sigarda,' says Charlie and bang went the gun in the officer's face. Charlie threw it down and ran, jumped into bed and soon was as sound asleep as apparently anyone. A light was procured, he was recognized and taken to the guardhouse. Ed escaped."

The imbibing of spirits led to fights in the 17th Ohio's camp. "The day seemed dull until noon when the ardent was quite generally distributed and quite a number of soldiers began to talk and act as though they felt merry," observed Captain John D. Inskeep. "Towards evening the steam got up a little too high and an altercation occurred between some of the boys resulting in two fights in which hatchets, axes, clubs, and spades were freely used. I used every argument I could to stop the riot and finally succeeded. Several were wounded but none seriously."[15]

Festivities proved more sedate in Colonel George W. Roberts's brigade in Sheridan's division. After gathering for a frugal dinner in Roberts's tent, "a toast was drunk to the success of our arms in the approaching battle," recalled Alexander Stevenson of the 42nd Illinois. "Roberts rose, speaking full of enthusiasm and eloquence of the great cause, thrilling his hearers as a man with a splendid voice only can. 'I will take all chances of Rebel bullets,' he stated. The other officers agreed and clinked their glasses."

Within a week, Roberts and several of the others who joined him in the toast would lie dead on the battlefield. It showed, Stevenson noted, "how ignorant and forgetful we are that the Angel of Death stands close to the soldier's side."

14 Diary of Captain Clement C. Webb, Co. E, 13th Michigan, SRNBP; David Gould and James B. Kennedy. *Memoirs of a Dutch Mudsill: The War Memories of John Henry Otto, Captain, Company D, 21st Regiment Wisconsin Volunteer Infantry* (Kent, 2004), 73-74.

15 Diary of Launcelot Scott, 18th Ohio, SRNBP.; Diary of Captain John D. Inskeep, Co. C, 17th Ohio, WRHS.

Chaplain Thomas Gunn of the 21st Kentucky recalled a discussion in which Major William Dowden said he wished there would be a battle and that "he would like to receive a slight wound, just enough to give him an honorable discharge. As he said this he pointed with his finger to the fleshy part of his thigh and said, 'just a slight flesh wound you know.'" After a lieutenant seconded the motion, Gunn replied, "Gentlemen, God sometimes answers even such prayers as that."[16]

Despite the holiday, three Federal brigades set out that morning to gather forage and ran afoul of General Wharton's alert cavalry videttes. Colonel P. Sidney Post's 1st Brigade in Davis's 1st Division, accompanied by the 15th Wisconsin, marched south with 200 wagons from Brentwood into the hilly wooded country along the Wilson Pike to gather corn, skirmishing constantly. They stumbled upon the 8th Texas Cavalry, about to enjoy its Christmas feast. "Some of the boys were preparing to have an eggnog for Christmas when suddenly our pickets were driven in and reported a large force of infantry and artillery moving upon us," recalled 1st Lt. James K. P. Blackburn of the 8th Texas. "The regiment was mounted at once to meet this advance. As soon as we come in full view of the enemy they opened fire with artillery, four guns throwing what seemed to be about six-pound shells. As we moved in columns of twos in front of the enemy their shells got our range pretty quickly. One shell burst in rear of my company doing slight damage, another one entered the body of a horse near my horse's head, bursting inside the horse and knocked my horse to his knees and covering him and me with blood and flesh from the other horse."[17]

The hard-riding Confederate cavalry made Post nervous as they probed along his flanks and rear searching for an opportunity to swoop in and wreck the wagon train. The colonel dispatched detachments to cover all quarters. "Foraging in such a country is attended with considerable risk," he noted in his report. "Our train could not be made to move in less space than four miles. It would not be difficult to suddenly attack so long a train and destroy some portion of it."

Wharton's troopers were also affected by the forested hills. "The country is very hilly and covered with cedar brakes which renders it totally unfit for cavalry," the general complained. "My force in camp has to be moved forward every day to

16 Alexander F. Stevenson, *The Battle of Stone's River Near Murfreesboro, Tenn. December 30, 1862, to January 3, 1863* (Boston, 1884), 7-8; Journal of Chaplain Thomas M. Gunn, 21st Kentucky, SRNBP.

17 James K. P. Blackburn, "Reminiscences of the Terry Rangers" *Southwestern Historical Quarterly*, Vol. 22, 1918-1919, 38.

sustain the pickets and never return until dark, so whether on picket or off, they have no rest. It will soon be unfit for service. I take great pride in the brigade and do not intend that it shall be used up."[18]

Colonel Harker's brigade, in Crittenden's wing, likewise marched along the Edmondson Pike to gather forage. The column reached Prim's blacksmith shop, where it found abundant corn, but it also clashed with roughly 600 Rebel cavalry. "The enemy's cavalry was found to be in considerable force on this road and retired only so far as they were compelled to," reported an officer of the 73rd Indiana. "The fire of the skirmishers was kept up vigorously but at too great a range to do much execution. Finally bringing up a piece of artillery, we advanced a strong line and succeeded in driving them." The 51st Indiana would suffer several casualties before the men finished loading their wagons with corn, marching back to Nashville as the Rebel cavalry nipped at their heels.

Orderly sergeant Thomas Prickett of the 9th Indiana, in Hazen's brigade, marched 12 miles along the Murfreesboro Pike to gather forage without encountering enemy soldiers. "It was a very pleasant day as it did not rain[;] neither was the mud knee deep," he wrote home. "On the contrary it was clear and the roads dusty. Our brigade was detailed as guards for a forage train, starting at sunrise and returned about 8 o'clock at night, pretty tired." Prickett enjoyed a simple Christmas dinner consisting of "hard crackers, cold meat, and water."[19]

Rosecrans's headquarters, located in George W. Cunningham's elegant two-story Renaissance Revival-style home on Nashville's High Street, buzzed with activity that Christmas night as well. The telegraph clacked throughout the evening as Rosecrans's senior commanders passed through to pay their holiday respects to the chief and discuss the next day's plans. Cigars and drinks helped take the chill out of the December air. "Ordinarily officers of all departments thronged the General's chamber during the day and every hour was absorbed in business," remembered William Bickham. "The nights were busy too, but there were pleasant episodes." Rosecrans loved to chat with his staff on assorted topics (particularly religion) and enjoyed drawing his commanders into this pleasant headquarters social circle. The Christmas season normally would have turned Rosey's mind and

---

18 *OR* 20/1:163-165.

19 Ibid.; Janet Hewitt, ed., *Supplement to the Official Records of the Union and Confederate Armies, 100 vols.* (Wilmington, 1994-2001), Vol. 18, 62; 1st Sgt. Thomas Prickett, Co. E, 9th Indiana, SRNBP.

tongue toward religion, but the focus this December evening was the forthcoming offensive.[20]

"There was consultation but no council of war," Bickham would write. Thomas and Rosecrans were found in frequent discussions as they looked over the topographical maps of the region, and McCook leaned on the fireplace mantel, chatting ebulliently about the condition of his wing. Crittenden, "stately and reticent," averred that "if the Rebels stood at all there would be damned hard fighting." Rosecrans's staff members cycled in and out of the house as the general's diligent chief of staff, the near-sighted, Cuban-born Julius Garesche, leaned close to the table in the dim candlelight, his quill pen in hand, firing off dispatch after dispatch. After downing a hot toddy, Rosecrans plunked the glass sharply on Garesche's desk and vowed, "We move tomorrow, gentlemen! We shall begin to skirmish, probably as soon as we pass the outposts. Press them hard! Drive them out of their nests! Make them fight or run! Strike hard and fast! Give them no rest! Fight them! Fight them! Fight, I say!"[21]

*   *   *

News of Rosecrans's planned advance reached the Confederates that evening courtesy of cunning Confederate spy Sarah Ann Carter of Franklin, Tennessee. The 36-year-old widowed mother of five, viewed as "young, handsome, and possessing extraordinary tact," had left her home a few days before to visit friends in Nashville. Picked up shortly after her arrival by Truesdail's detectives, Carter was interrogated at police headquarters and learned that "the Federals would start in a few hours." After obtaining her release and a pass to return home, "she hired a team and a young man to drive her and hurried on to Franklin," remembered Colonel Baxter Smith of the 4th Tennessee Cavalry. "She sent for me and told of

20 Bickham, *Rosecrans' Campaign*, 137-46. The George W. Cunningham home was located at what is now 221 Sixth Avenue North.

21 Bickham, *Rosecrans' Campaign*, 134-37. Rosecrans reported that he marched on Murfreesboro with 45,000 men as follows: McCook's wing 15,944, Thomas's corps 10,868, Crittenden's wing 13,288, the Pioneer Brigade 1,700, and the cavalry at 3,200. Rosecrans deducted 1,600 men from this total for train guards, leaving him 43,400 men for action.

the contemplated movements of the Federal army. I at once dispatched a courier apprising General Bragg of the contemplated advance on the next day."[22]

Rosecrans's army awoke December 26 to lowering skies and a chilly northerly breeze. "The day opened dark and gloomily," reported Ebenezer Hannaford of the 6th Ohio. "The soft southerly breezes of the day before had roughened into rude, spiteful gusts. The chill sweeping gusts that came freighted with the breath of coming storms and great heaving masses of clouds covered away out of sight every bit of blue sky beyond and robbed even the daylight of all its life and power and beauty." The men struck their camps early, formed into line, and fell into marching column, turning south to march along four parallel roads.[23]

McCook's men marched along two parallel roads, intent on reaching Nolensville by nightfall. General Davis's division followed on the Edmondson Pike, and Sheridan led the remainder of McCook's wing on the Nolensville Pike to the east. Thomas's two divisions, Negley in the van, covered McCook's right by marching to Brentwood on the Franklin Pike and then following the Wilson Pike south to Owen's Store at the intersection of the Old Liberty Road. With the three divisions of his wing, Crittenden advanced directly toward Murfreesboro along the Nashville Pike, as three regiments of Colonel John Kennett's cavalry screened John Palmer's 2nd Division in the van. Because Rosecrans hoped Bragg would choose to confront him at Stewart's Creek, he expected Crittenden's wing to arrive at the village of Stewardsboro by nightfall.

A long line of Confederate cavalry videttes and outposts stood in the way—three brigades under the overall command of General Wheeler, who was tasked with screening the army's front. On the left, Wharton's polyglot command of troopers held the line from Brentwood on the west to a point just northeast of Nolensville. Wheeler's own brigade of five regiments, two battalions, and a battery occupied the center of the line along Stewart's Creek, and Brig. Gen. John Pegram's small brigade (just two regiments) lay on the right, guarding the approach to Lebanon between Wheeler and Stones River.

Behind them, Bragg had aligned his army with Polk's Corps and three brigades of Breckinridge's Division (in Hardee's Corps) in Murfreesboro, and the balance of the corps in camps around Eagleville 24 miles to the southwest; John McCown's Division, formerly part of Edmund Kirby Smith's Corps, in camp at Readyville, 12

---

22 Colonel Baxter Smith, 4th Tennessee Cavalry, "Tribute to a Noted Southern Woman," *Confederate Veteran*, April 1910, 168.

23 Ebenezer Hannaford, "In the Ranks at Stones River," *Harper's Magazine*, Vol. 27, 1863, 809.

miles east of Murfreesboro; Brig. Gen. Abraham Buford's three regiments of cavalry in reserve at McMinnville; and John Jackson's infantry brigade spread out along the railroad line, performing guard duty between Murfreesboro and Bridgeport, Alabama.

By 10:00 a.m., the raindrops began to patter atop the wagons' white canvas covers and, as one Ohio soldier remembered, "a steady, persistent, pouring rain whose every component drop seemed to find a malicious delight in splashing in our faces and discovering every practicable breach in the rubber blankets" turned the road into a quagmire. "As the rain grew harder and the wind settled keen from the west, we halted by the roadside and squatting down in the mud or resting our dripping form against the picket fence and waited nearly an hour."

Major Anson McCook of the 2nd Ohio recalled that "as long as we remained on the turnpike, we made reasonable progress, but when we moved off it by cross-country dirt roads, it was simply dreadful, for even one division with its artillery, ammunition, and supply trains cut them up so badly that they were nearly impassable."[24]

"By the time we had gotten fully under headway, we encountered a General who, for the hour, was more enthusiastically received than 'Our Rosa,'" chaplain John H. Lozier of the 37th Indiana would joke. "It was General Rain, upon whom this army relies for supplies. The General was making for the Cumberland River but like a good many others, General Rain became less popular upon a more intimate acquaintance."

William Dodge of the 75th Illinois averred that "the prospect of meeting the foe cheered our men and their enthusiasm increased as the thermometer fell," but for many, the more it rained, the more miserable they became. Captain James J. Hanna of the 69th Ohio remembered that the men of his regiment "were all cheerful and frequent shouts of mirth would go forth from the ranks as we marched" but once the rain set in, spirits fell. One Illinois veteran later opined that the "cold soaking rain had reduced most of the men to a mood when they would have disputed the Ten Commandments and quarreled with their mothers. Everywhere one looked were drenched, depressed-looking men, melancholy steaming horses, sodden gloomy fields, yellow rushing streams, and boundless

24 Ebenezer Hannaford, *Story of a Regiment: A History of the Campaigns and Associations in the Field of the Sixth Regiment, Ohio Volunteer Infantry* (Cincinnati, 1868), 809; Richard A. Baumgartner, ed., *The Bully Boys: In Camp and Combat With the 2nd Ohio Volunteer Infantry Regiment, 1861-1864* (Huntingdon, 2011), 320-21.

mud that thousands of passing feet were churning into the consistency of building mortar."[25]

Colonel Zahm's 950-man all-Ohio cavalry brigade led Thomas's advance along the Franklin Road, or at least tried. By the time his men reached the road at 8:30 a.m., it was congested with hundreds of wagons following in the wake of Negley's and Rousseau's divisions. "I crossed over on the Franklin Pike beyond Brentwood," he reported, "then halted my command as I had not seen General Thomas yet." Leaving his command standing in the rain at Brentwood, Zahm galloped down the Wilson Creek Pike; failing to find the Virginian, he rejoined the command and led them toward Franklin on the Franklin Pike. Rosecrans believed there were 700 Confederates in Franklin and wanted them driven away to eliminate that threat to his flank. That left Thomas's column marching down the Wilson Pike without a cavalry screen.[26]

Rosecrans rode along the Murfreesboro Pike to check on Crittenden's advance and came across members of the 57th Indiana resting in the drizzle. "The men seated themselves on tufts of grass, rails, etc. and in a few moments, General Rosecrans came along accompanied by his staff and the 4th US Regular Cavalry as an escort," remembered one Hoosier. "Riding leisurely along, the general cast a quick glance, first at the men on one side and then on the other, stopping when he saw a soldier who had left his overcoat behind, to inquire the cause, and perhaps telling him cleverly to be careful and beware of such negligence in the future. He wore a large cavalry overcoat, smoked a cigar when not engaged in conversation, and beside him rode the noble Garesche."[27]

General Stanley intended to use the three regiments of the army's reserve cavalry to support McCook's advance on the Nolensville Pike. Events would hit a major snag that morning, however. Stanley's presence with the reserve was intentional, as the regiments were, in his words, "very weak" and, in one case, downright mutinous. The two Tennessee regiments, both composed of raw recruits from the state's eastern corridor, had just received horses a few weeks before the campaign. Meanwhile, the Anderson Troop, also known as the 15th

---

25 Chaplain John H. Lozier, 37th Indiana, *Cincinnati Daily Commercial,* Jan. 8, 1863, 1; William Sumner Dodge. *A Waif of the War, or a History of the 75th Illinois Infantry, Embracing the Entire Campaigns of the Army of the Cumberland* (Chicago, 1866), 56; Captain James J. Hanna, Co. K, 69th Ohio, *Cadiz Republican,* Jan. 21, 1863, 3; John McElroy, *Si Klegg: Thru the Stone River Campaign and in Winter Quarters at Murfreesboro.* (Washington, 1910), 15-17.

26 OR 20/1:632-633.

27 *Annals of the Fifty-Seventh Regiment Indiana Volunteers,* 146.

Pennsylvania Cavalry, was specifically raised to serve as headquarters guards and couriers but had mutinied that morning after learning they were to be used as regular cavalry. "The majority of the men in every company have stacked their arms and refused to move," stated one trooper. "In front of every tent is a pile of arms, sabers, pistols, and carbines."

"[T]hey were men of superior intelligence," Stanley recalled, "mostly clerks or young men of leisure and fortune. They were active, brave fellows, but had no discipline." The regimental officers eventually convinced about 300 of the recalcitrant Pennsylvanians to march, but they didn't leave Nashville until well after the rest of McCook's wing. When Stanley's cavalry failed to appear that morning, General Davis shook out his own headquarters escort (Company G of the 2nd Kentucky Cavalry and Company B of the 36th Illinois Cavalry), using them to clear the roads ahead of his marching column. The aggressive Davis often rode in the forefront, eager for any opportunity to mix it up with the Confederates.[28]

By noon, Stanley's cavalry caught the tail of McCook's infantry column on the Nolensville Pike. "The rain continued to fall and the mud to deepen," recalled John A. B. Williams of the Anderson Troop. "There were frequent halts to await the clearing away of Rebel skirmishers and other obstructions. Far away to the left we could hear occasionally the faint patter of musketry and the booming of heavier weapons proving that Crittenden was at work."

One trooper recalled that the command rode down the center of the pike singing, "We're All Bound for New York," but the late-arriving cavalrymen drew a fair share of barbs from McCook's foot-soaked sloggers. "Here comes these jockey-soldiers, riding over us," one infantryman complained loudly. "Soft thing they have of it!"

Another trooper recalled that the Pennsylvanians' bright new uniforms made them an object of derision. "In their eyes, we had an appearance of newness which they very naturally associated with inexperience," wrote C. Lewis Diehl of Company L. "The troopers, teamsters, and infantry soon singled us out as proper objects of sympathy. 'Sorry for that fine uniform you are wearing; it won't stay that

28 Suzanne Colton Wilson, *Column South with the Fifteenth Pennsylvania Cavalry* (Flagstaff, 1960), 38; Stanley, *Personal Memoirs*, 123.

way down here' said one, while another joked, 'Sonny, think of me tomorrow when you are out corn-shucking.'"29

Fifteen miles south of Nashville, McCook's advance ran into determined resistance near the outskirts of Nolensville. Wharton's cavalry videttes skirmished with McCook's men for most of the morning, but as the Federals drew closer to the Confederate general's headquarters in the early afternoon, increasing resistance forced Davis to redeploy his infantry regiments. Wharton's command consisted of troopers from Alabama, Georgia, Tennessee, and Texas, but it also had two Confederate-designated cavalry regiments featuring troopers raised largely from Alabama. The brigade totaled 1,950 horsemen, though Wharton had nowhere near that many in the vicinity of Nolensville, and the Texan could call on only four artillery pieces for support.

Wharton's men presented a motley appearance and carried a wide variety of arms, including shotguns, horse pistols, revolvers, flintlocks, and even Enfield rifles. Fortunately, they had gained valuable fighting experience on outpost duty in the past months and were ready for a clash. That would be vital. Wharton's mission, after all, was simply to delay Rosecrans's advance; he knew he did not have the firepower or numbers to do more than that against the array of Federal divisions marching on his position.

Colonel Post's brigade, leading Davis's advance, deployed to drive Wharton's cavalry from Nolensville. The hard-marching 59th Illinois—veterans of the March 1862 Battle of Pea Ridge and marching under the command of the strict and unpopular Captain Hendrick Paine, whom the men derisively called "Buck and Gag"—were deployed as skirmishers when Wharton's troopers, now dismounted, opened fire. Captain Oscar F. Pinney's 5th Wisconsin Battery followed Paine's men and unlimbered in a nearby field to open on the Confederate guns south of town. "As the regiment was advancing across an open common between the woods and town, a volley was fired at one of the companies from the windows of a large frame house in front of them," remembered David Lathrop of the 59th Illinois. "Captain Henry Pease [of Davis's staff] saw the shooting and being close to one of our guns ordered the cannoneer to plant a shell in the house. The first shell exploded in one of the upper rooms, doing wonderful execution among the

<hr>

29 John A. B. Williams, *Leaves from a Trooper's Diary* (Philadelphia, 1869), 35-36; Charles H. Kirk, *History of the Fifteenth Pennsylvania Volunteer Cavalry, Which Was Recruited and Known as the Anderson Cavalry in the Rebellion of 1861-1865* (Philadelphia, 1906), 130.

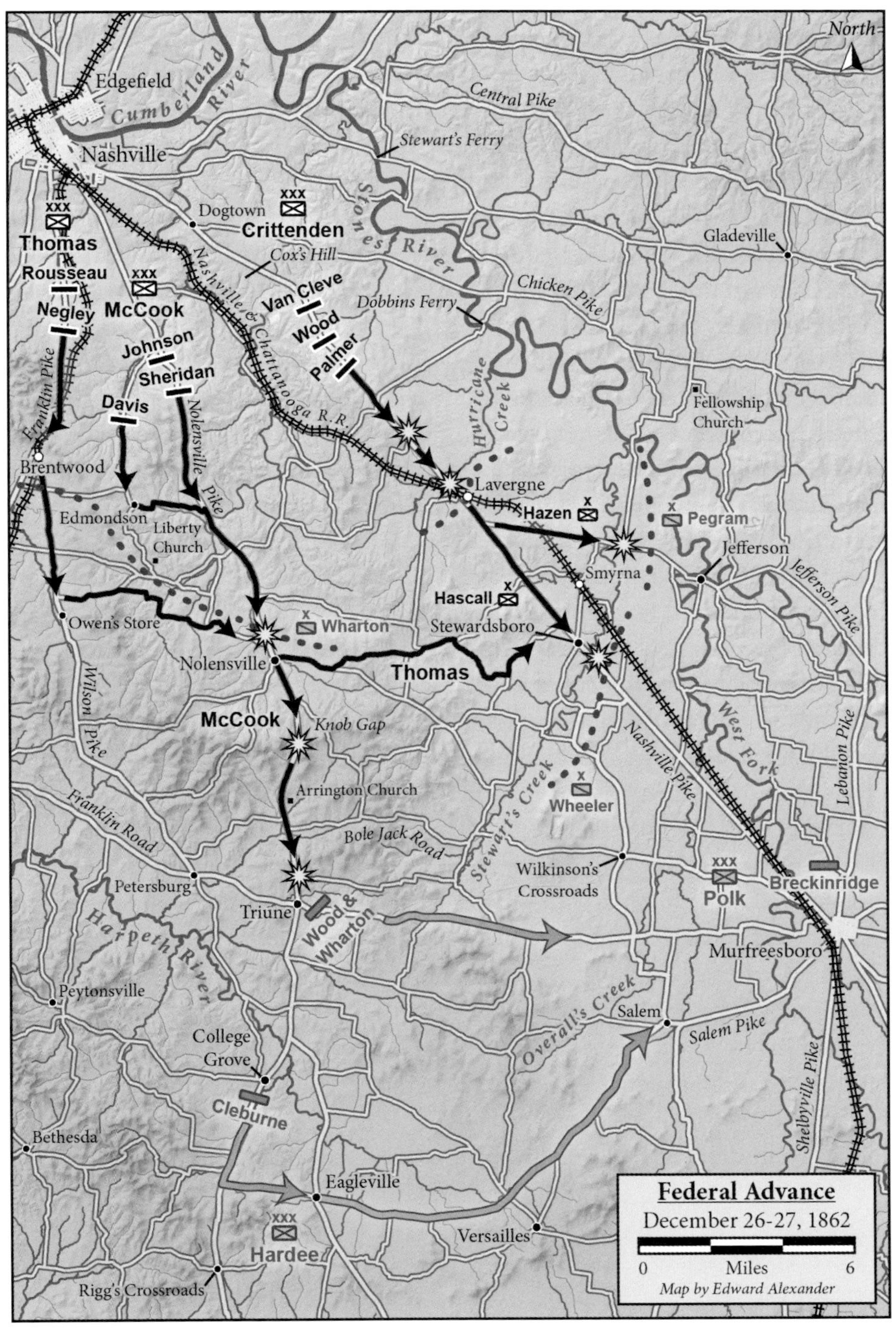
North
Edgefield
Cumberland River
Nashville
Central Pike
Stewart's Ferry
Dogtown
Crittenden
Cox's Hill
Stones River
Gladeville
Thomas
Rousseau
Negley
McCook
Van Cleve
Wood
Palmer
Dobbins Ferry
Chicken Pike
Johnson
Sheridan
Nashville & Chattanooga R.R.
Hurricane Creek
Fellowship Church
Davis
Franklin Pike
Nolensville Pike
Brentwood
Lavergne
Hazen
Pegram
Edmondson
Liberty Church
Jefferson
Jefferson Pike
Smyrna
Owen's Store
Wharton
Hascall
Stewardsboro
Nolensville
Wilson Pike
Thomas
McCook
Knob Gap
West Fork
Lebanon Pike
Arrington Church
Wheeler
Franklin Road
Bole Jack Road
Stewart's Creek
Wilkinson's Crossroads
Nashville Pike
Polk
Breckinridge
Petersburg
Triune
Wood & Wharton
Murfreesboro
Harpeth River
Peytonsville
Overall's Creek
Salem
Salem Pike
College Grove
Cleburne
Shelbyville Pike
Bethesda
Eagleville
Federal Advance
December 26-27, 1862
Hardee
Versailles
0   Miles   6
Map by Edward Alexander
Rigg's Crossroads

furniture and tearing the plaster into a thousand fragments. This brought the Rebs to light and a volley sent them howling to the woods."[30]

Wharton's resistance stiffened two miles south at Knob Gap, a natural defile through which the Nolensville Pike passed en route to Triune. The Confederates holding the position had four guns supported by dismounted troopers of the 8th Texas Cavalry, a colorful unit known better as Terry's Texas Rangers. Captain Benjamin F. White deployed two of his guns in the middle of the Nolensville Pike while Captain Elzaphon R. King deployed two of the 6-pounder field guns of his battery left of the pike.[31]

Post's brigade marched out of Nolensville with the 22nd Indiana and 74th Illinois on the right of the road, the 75th and 59th Illinois on the left, and Pinney's battery rolling along the pike itself. Meanwhile, Davis spied a column of Confederate cavalry moving toward his right. He ordered out skirmishers from the 22nd Indiana, then called up his next brigade under Colonel Carlin to deploy to the right to extend Post's line and protect the flank. The three regiments of Colonel Woodruff's brigade deployed on Carlin's right as Carlin's men marched toward the gap. Davis possibly feared the stout Confederate resistance had the power of Hardee's Corps behind it, so he was not shy asking for help from nearby units. He sent a dispatch to Sheridan to hurry his division forward and made a similar request to Negley, who was marching along the Wilson Pike a few miles west of Davis.

"Directly in our front and not more than a mile distant is a deep cut or gorge through the mountain through which the Nolensville and Triune turnpike passes," recalled Lt. Col. David McKee of the 15th Wisconsin. "This gap in the mountain is not more than 300 paces in width and is closed in by steep bluffy walls. Now an aide of General Davis rides up with orders: 'That battery must be taken at any risk.' Colonel Carlin turns around with his usual coolness and firmness and gives his orders: 'Lieutenant Colonel McKee, you will take command of the line of skirmishers and advance them rapidly.'"

McKee took a single company from each of the brigade's regiments and pushed into the muddy field. Carlin deployed the 21st Illinois on his brigade's right flank, the 15th Wisconsin at right center, the 101st Ohio at left center, and the 38th Illinois on the left flank. "All are pushed rapidly forward," McKee recalled. "Three

---

30 Lathrop, *History of the 59th Illinois*, 189.

31 King's Battery was also known as Co. D, 14th Georgia Artillery Battalion.

of the regiments are at times pretty well covered by the formation of the ground; the 38th Illinois was most terribly exposed."[32]

Carlin reported that "the ridge itself with the knobs forms as fine a military position to hold against an attack as I ever saw in an open country. It was my part to move directly over the open field in the face of a direct fire of artillery and of Wharton's cavalry dismounted and concealed behind trees. Hotchkiss's battery [2nd Minnesota] was brought into action in the road and threw a few shells into the gap. My brigade was formed into line parallel to the enemy's position and the command 'Forward!' was given. The field had been plowed late in the fall and the rains had converted the soil into sticky mud. Each man seemed to lift on his shoe a square foot of mud three inches deep at every step."[33]

"Our brigade formed in line of battle for a charge," recalled Charles Dennis of the 101st Ohio. "The men became uneasy as the bullets of the enemy were singing high and low and the shells of the Rebel battery were bursting overhead and plowing into the mud in front of the line. It was fortunate, even if uncomfortable, that the mud was everywhere two to six inches deep. This fact saved us the damage that ricocheting shots would have done had the ground been dry."

An officer of the 38th Illinois was struck down twice by the impact of Confederate shells, writing: "Once by the concussion of a shell and once by a dead soldier. He was dead when he hit me[,] for a cannon ball had passed through his right breast. How the devil it missed me I don't know and didn't attempt to stop to inquire."[34]

Colonel Heg wrote that "General [sic] Carlin's order to take the battery at all hazards stimulated the several regiments of the command to do their utmost. Keeping my regiment closely under the bluffs to the right and sheltered from view by the heavy timber, I succeeded in advancing to within 200 yards of one of the enemy's pieces before we were discovered by them." George S. Meyers of the 101st Ohio recalled that the charge turned into a "tedious walk. The fields had been in corn and the heavy rains had softened the ground so much that great loads of sticky

32 Lt. Col. David McKee, 15th Wisconsin, *Grant County Herald*, Jan. 13, 1863, 1.

33 Robert I. Girardi and Nathaniel Cheairs Hughes, eds., *The Memoirs of Brigadier General William Passmore Carlin, U.S.A.* (Lincoln, 1999), 72.

34 Memoir of Private Charles B. Dennis, Co. B, 101st Ohio, Rutherford B. Hayes Memorial Library; unknown officer 38th Illinois, *Evansville Daily Journal*, Jan. 26, 1863, 2.

clay clung to our feet. Shells came thick enough but away overhead they went; a few struck in front, splashing the line with mud but not exploding."[35]

Confederate artillerymen rammed shell after shell into their guns, the steady rain hissing as it struck the cannon's hot tubes. Firing shells and grape, White's guns in the road managed to pin down the 38th Illinois in the field for a period. "We were exposed for a distance of a mile to their fire which was concentrated on the left of the 38th Illinois, Companies H, I, and K suffering the most severely," observed William E. Patterson, also of the 38th Illinois. "The Rebel battery played on us full blast and our own battery in our rear (in an ineffectual attempt to cover our advance) exposed us to still more danger by their own shells bursting prematurely over our heads. The air resounded with the hideous noise of the shells whizzing and bursting before us, behind us, above us, and among us."

Sergeant George R. Bradshaw of the 74th Illinois, in Post's brigade, lay to the left of the 38th Illinois. "[T]his was the first time the regiment had been under fire and we felt uneasy as the shells came hissing along," he remembered. "Several came pretty close to me, nearer than I liked. I could see them coming through the air as plainly as one can see a ball thrown from a hand. One passed over my head knocking the top off a fence stake and striking the ground 20 feet behind me before it bounded again and burst in the woods behind."[36]

Although White's gunners had a clear view of their opponents, the undulations of the ground in front of the 400-foot-high knob, combined with the roiling smoke from their own guns, shielded Carlin's Federals from King's view until the bluecoats were almost atop his guns. Federal fire from Pinney's and Hotchkiss's artillery pieces took a hefty toll on the 8th Texas, as several horses were struck down and one lieutenant killed. Ole Streenland of the 15th Wisconsin wrote that "when we charged on the Rebels, they struck out as fast as they could and, in their hurry to retreat, they drove in between some trees and got stuck, and so we got on to them before they could get out of there. We did not have much fighting, but how we ran after the Rebels! Some of the boys were pretty near killed by running."

Heg recalled that "without firing, I ordered a charge. I charged with my regiment up to a battery and captured one brass cannon, seven horses, three

---

35 Report of Colonel Hans C. Heg, 15th Wisconsin, *Wisconsin State Journal*, Jan. 17, 1863, 1; "Costly Errors: Gen. Davis's Division and the Army of the Cumberland at Stone River," Private George S. Myers, Co. F, 101st Ohio, *National Tribune*, Jan. 3, 1895, 2.

36 Memoir of Private William E. Patterson, Co. K, 38th Illinois, Western Historical Manuscript Collection—Columbia, University of Missouri.; Sergeant George R. Bradshaw, Co. F, 74th Illinois, author's collection.

prisoners, and one caisson, and what is best of all, not one man wounded." Colonels Heg and McKee were the first officers to clamber over King's position and claimed capture of the single 6-pounder field piece that the Georgians couldn't limber up before they were overrun.[37]

The retreat of King's Battery convinced White and the remaining 8th Texas troopers it was time to abandon the position. L. B. Giles of Company D of the 8th Texas recalled that his regiment was in line and listening to the encouraging words of their captain "until we reached the top of a slight rise. Just over the crest was a solid line of infantry. Captain Kyle at once ordered a retreat; at least that's what he meant, though the words he actually used are not in the manual. "Get out of here, men! There's a whole brigade!" We understood him and so did the Yankees who sprang to their feet and delivered a volley." Patterson noted that "a gang of cattle got between the lines during the fight and ran wildly from line to line. One of them had its leg broken by a Rebel shell and was devoured by the heroes of the day."

Federal losses in the engagement were negligible, but the Confederates were hit hard. "Our good luck can be attributed to nothing else but the bad management of the gunners," McKee stated. "Had they fought with half the gallantry with which our men advanced upon them and stood their ground as soldiers should have done, the slaughter must have been frightful. The musketry fire from the dismounted cavalry lasted but a moment or two."[38]

One Texan commented that the Federals at Knob Gap were "as numerous as Egyptian locusts," and Chaplain Robert F. Bunting of the 8th Texas agreed with McKee's assessment, noting in a letter that "King's Georgia battery today abandoned a gun and it fell into the hands of the enemy. It was lost through pure cowardice." The Texans bolted over a crest and out of the gap, mounting their horses and heading south. Giles recalled having to clear a high fence "with bullets striking it like hail on a roof. I sprang up on it and just fell off on the other side. When I got up, the command was moving off rapidly. I had started to the rear as soon as the others, but they outran me. My saddle felt mighty good and restful."

37 "Knob Gap Once More," Streenland, Ole, *National Tribune*, May 27, 1886, 3; Heg Report. The single captured piece by the Federals was a 6-pounder brass gun purportedly captured at Shiloh by the Confederates.

38 L. B. Giles *Terry's Texas Rangers* (Austin, 1967), 49; Patterson Memoir; McKee Letter.

Wharton's weary troopers fell back a few miles to an old camp on the Page Farm on a ridge north of Triune, where the men rested and prepared themselves for the next day.[39]

*   *   *

Meanwhile, Crittenden's wing proceeded down the Nashville Pike on the Federal left. Light skirmishing commenced by 7:00 a.m. and steadily increased as the Federals pushed south. John Kennett commanded the cavalry advance. The colonel had the three regiments of Colonel Robert H. G. Minty's brigade screening the infantry column, with the 3rd Kentucky Cavalry under the command of 19-year-old Colonel Eli Murray on the left of the pike, the veteran 7th Pennsylvania Cavalry on the right, and the hard-riding 4th Michigan Cavalry moving along the center of the road with a heavy advance guard. The steady rain did little to slow Crittenden's men marching on the macadamized pike, but enemy cavalry opposition increased a few miles north of the tiny village of La Vergne.

Videttes from Wheeler's brigade patrolled this sector of the line with the outposts lying just 10 miles from Nashville. The brigade had five regiments, two battalions, and a four-gun battery of mobile horse artillery under Captain Jannedens H. Wiggins. Wheeler's command was spread out for a few miles west of the Nashville Pike, with the bulk of his troopers in camp along Stewart's Creek; however, one of the regiments and a battalion were away during the fighting at La Vergne. Troopers of Colonel William Wirt Allen's 1st Alabama Cavalry contested Minty's advance along the pike, setting up roadblocks at abandoned farms and thick cedar brakes just long enough to force the Federals to deploy before falling back to his next position.

Joe Wheeler suspected this wasn't just another foraging expedition. "The enemy are advancing [on] one front and we are engaging them," he messaged Bragg at 2:00 p.m. "They are also advancing on the Nolensville Pike and we are engaging them very warmly. There is very heavy firing on the Nolensville Pike."[40]

"Brisk skirmishing was kept until about 2 p.m.," recalled a 4th Michigan trooper, "when we were brought to a sudden standstill by Rebel shells thrown from

39 Confederate letters of Robert F. Bunting, 1861-1863, Tennessee State Library and Archives; Giles, *Terry's Texas Rangers*, 49-50.

40 Dispatch from General Joseph Wheeler, Dec. 26, 1862, Braxton Bragg Papers, William P. Palmer Collection, WRHS.

La Vergne, a rabid Secesh hole two miles in our front." After cresting a ridge overlooking the town, the head of the column spied groups of Confederate cavalrymen deploying ahead of them. Hurricane Creek protected the right side of La Vergne, and though the Nashville Pike did not pass directly through town, the Nashville & Chattanooga did, crossing the pike about a half-mile to the west.

Colonel Allen's command, along with two guns from Wiggins's Battery under Lieutenant J. Wylie Calloway, was joined by the 3rd Alabama north of La Vergne, determined to hold the town. "We discovered the enemy in some force in the town," noted Lieutenant Bernard Reilly of the 7th Pennsylvania Cavalry. "We commenced shelling them expecting them to skedaddle but were astonished not a little when upon firing the second shell to see a volume of smoke issue from their lines and the same instant a shell passed over our heads shrieking and hissing but did no further damage than demolishing the chimney of a house close by. We immediately deployed and an artillery duel commenced."[41]

As the cannon balls bounced down the turnpike—"clearing the road as fast as men's legs could carry them"—Colonel Minty ordered the Michiganders off the road to get out of range, then called for his own artillery to contest Wiggins. A two-gun section of black steel 3-inch Ordnance Rifles from Battery D, 1st Ohio Light Artillery under Lieutenant Nathaniel M. Newell took position while Minty placed two companies of the 4th Michigan Cavalry in ambush nearby for protection.

"We took position on the pike and opened fire on a section of Rebel artillery distant a mile," reported Lieutenant Newell. Though outnumbered, Newell's longer-range rifles proved their worth at La Vergne. "Every shot was well-planted and he nobly fought the four guns of the enemy for over half an hour," Minty recalled. "One of the gunners was killed by a shell from the enemy while serving his gun."[42]

Although their guns had inferior range, Wiggins's gunners made it hot for the Yankees. "Their shells came very near us," noted Private Leonard Beck of the 4th Michigan. "While in the road, the shots came howling directly over our heads causing considerable dodging and after getting over a fence, a shot passed directly in our rear between us and the fence. This shot was a good one, throwing up sand in every direction. With rifles in hand, we passed the battery and took position 15

---

41 Private Leonard Beck, Co. F, 4th Michigan Cavalry, *Adrian Daily Watchtower*, Jan. 29, 1863, 1; 2nd Lt. Bernard Reilly, Co. F, 7th Pennsylvania Cavalry, *Pottsville Miners' Journal*, Jan. 31, 1863, 2.

42 OR 20/1:623.

paces in advance lying flat on the ground under a fence, our rifles resting on the second rail and pointed towards the enemy battery. Occasionally some of us would raise our heads to see what was going on when an order would come from one of the battery officers, "Keep those heads down! Don't you see those shells?" Pretty good advice we thought."

Crittenden rode forward with his staff to observe the artillery engagement, drawing the attention of Wiggins' attentive gunners. "Quick as lightning a shell came hissing through the air and passed in the narrow space of a yard between our horses," remembered Captain Gilbert Kniffin. "It is needless to add that their curiosity being gratified, they lost no time seeking the friendly cover of a log house by the roadside."[43]

The shot that missed Crittenden nearly struck the lead elements of the general's infantry column (Charles Cruft's brigade) arriving on the scene. "We were marching between two thick groves of cedars when an enemy solid shot struck and shattered one of these trees," wrote Lieutenant Eben Sturges of Battery B, 1st Ohio Light Artillery. "Colonel [sic] Cruft sent a message to Lieutenant Baldwin to bring a rifled section to the front of the brigade."

The Ohioans deployed their guns in the middle of the road. "I saw the enemy trying to draw a section into battery about a half mile distant and I threw them a shell which passed just over their heads, scaring them out of the woods," Sturges wrote. "I had ordered the piece to be reloaded and was watching the movements ahead when the sudden report of the gun I just ordered loaded called my attention to it. The first thing I saw was my No. 1 man, who sponges and rams, lying on the ground face downward, to all appearances dead. A premature discharge had blown the rammer through his hands carrying off the thumb and two fingers of his right hand and had thrown him violently onto the hard pike, bruising him in several places. The powder had also scorched his arms, face, and breast."

Despite the Federal mishap, Wiggins's Arkansans—now outnumbered and armed with short range field guns and howitzers—did not last long against the six long-range Federal guns before being driven back closer to town.[44]

Captain George Knox Miller of the 8th Confederate Cavalry spent the morning in camp at Stewart's Creek, still feeling the effects of the Christmas

---

43 Beck letter; Gilbert C. Kniffen, "Army of the Cumberland and the Battle of Stone River," *National Tribune*, Jan. 7, 1882, 2.

44 Stanley Horn, *The Battle of Stones River* (1972), 14.; OR 20/1:622. The unfortunate soldier, Private John Blanchard, eventually lost his right hand but survived.

holiday, when he heard the first signs of the Yankee advance in the distance. "We had a drill in the morning, but about 12 o'clock heavy firing in the direction of LaVergne [sic] warned us that the enemy was not spending his holiday in festivities at Nashville," he wrote. "The cannonading gradually drew nearer and an order came for what was left of the brigade in camp to come up to LaVergne in all haste. We were soon in the saddle and a trot of five miles brought us to LaVergne and in front of that place we found the enemy. It was now 3 o'clock and as they did not retire, as when merely out foraging, we knew pretty well that something more stirring was in the wind."

The 51st Alabama Partisan Rangers rode into La Vergne with the 8th Confederate and went into position on the right of the railroad. After dismounting and sending the horses to cover, the Rangers skirmished with the Yankees. "This was kept up steadily on both sides until the orders were given to fall back and take a position nearer the turnpike to be in supporting distance of the artillery," reported Lt. Col. James D. Webb of the 51st Alabama. "They then formed a line of battle, the right resting on the turnpike and extending near to the railroad."[45]

As Wheeler reinforced his line with his two reserve regiments, Federal gunners continued to batter his outgunned Arkansans positioned on the left. "I moved to the left of the pike and took position near a small church from which position we fired until dark, silencing the enemy after a few rounds," recalled Lieutenant Newell of the 1st Ohio Light Artillery. "I fired 60 rounds, losing during the action one man killed and a horse disabled."

It was 3 o'clock and still raining when Cruft ordered two regiments of his brigade—the 1st Kentucky on the right and 31st Indiana on the left—to form a line left of the pike, drive the Confederate troopers from the woods, and take the town. The next Federal brigade in the column, Hazen's brigade temporarily under the command of Colonel Walter C. Whitaker of the 6th Kentucky, deployed to the right of the pike in a dense cedar brake to support Cruft. Eli Murray's 3rd Kentucky Cavalry rode out to cover Cruft's left flank, and the line squished forward through the muddy cornfields toward La Vergne.[46]

Sergeant William Buskey of the 1st Kentucky, in Cruft's brigade, observed that "we had forced our way to within about a mile of town when the word was given to charge, and we did with a yell that would have done credit to the wildest Indians.

---

45 George Knox Miller, *Monograph of the 8th Confederate Cavalry Regiment,* Alabama Department of Archives and History; *OR* 20/1:962.

46 *OR* 20/1:622. Wiggins reported three men and two horses Llost during the engagement.

We charged over fences and through cornfields pouring volley after volley into the Rebels who at length gave way."

The advance was not so tidy on the right. The 6th Kentucky and 9th Indiana (also of Hazen's brigade) advanced without a skirmish line into the cedar brake and soon found themselves engaged with Wheeler's troopers. "We marched in flank into the bush without skirmishers and without having loaded our rifles when all of a sudden 30-40 shots fell one after another on our right wing," remembered Sergeant John Daeuble of the 6th Kentucky. "The Rebels had hidden themselves and expected our arrival."

The barrage struck down four bluecoats, creating considerable confusion within the ranks, which gave Wheeler's intrepid troopers time to withdraw and redeploy before Whitaker could reorganize the line. By then it was nightfall, so the opponents settled uneasily into positions along Hurricane Creek.[47]

As the fight at La Vergne heated up, the 3rd Ohio Cavalry, the lead regiment of Colonel Zahm's column, clashed with Wharton's picket line a few miles north of Franklin on the Federal far right. It was a running fight that netted the Federals 10 prisoners and gradually pushed their opponents across the Harpeth River by sunset. "The enemy was taken by surprise and could not get their forces together before we were upon them," Zahm reported. "Therefore, it made it rather an easy task to drive them."

Zahm learned from the prisoners of the presence of significant Confederate infantry encamped at Petersburg and Triune, points along the Franklin Road leading to Murfreesboro. He knew his small unit would not stand much of a chance against infantry. Ordered to closely cover his army's right flank, Zahm had his troopers recross the Harpeth River and turn east. The brigade marched along the Old Liberty Road as darkness descended until it reached Rousseau's division camped near Owen's Store, intersecting the Wilson Pike, and encamped about 10:00 p.m.[48]

Alerted by the sound of Davis's fight for Knob Gap, Negley diverted from the Wilson Pike onto a badly rutted country road leading directly to Nolensville. Battery G of the 1st Ohio Light Artillery, equipped with long-range Wiard rifles, was instructed to hurry to Nolensville ahead of the infantry. "We were ordered to

---

47 OR 20/1:526; Sergeant William H. Buskey, Co. C, 1st Kentucky (US), *Springfield Republic*, Jan. 21, 1863, 2; Joseph R. Reinhart, *A History of the 6th Kentucky Volunteer Infantry U.S.: The Boys Who Feared No Noise* (Louisville, 2000), 146.

48 OR 20/1:635.

trot, but with our captain that order meant a run and we had used up all our spare wheels when we had reached the pike," said one gunner. At 5:00 p.m., the balance of Negley's unit halted for the day a few miles from town. The men had scarcely finished cooking their dinners, however, before they were ordered to fall back into column and continue through the rain to camp south of Nolensville, arriving about 8:00 p.m.[49]

Tailing the columns were the long wagon trains, heavily loaded with ammunition and rations. "There was some swearing done today in pulling up the steep hills," recalled Lieutenant Alfred Pirtle, managing the 37 wagons of Rousseau's ordnance train. "It was extremely amusing to me to watch the gestures and hear the cries of some of the drivers as they plied whip and spur, urging their long-eared steeds forward, making the woods ring again with cracking whips and loud calls to their teams. Every mule has his name which he seems to know, as well as to know the voice of his driver, obeying his commands when he seems deaf to anyone else, and minding the sound of the whip when a blow from a stick only makes him shake his head or give a switch with his tail. Managing a train on the march throws me in contact with the hardest cases in the service who are usually found in the trains and they commit almost all the depredations that are charged to the troops."[50]

McCook's men were not above prowling through Nolensville in search of eatables and shelter from the rain, but some soldiers took the opportunity to rob and pillage. "The boys just pitched in and opened the stores in the town and dwellings in the vicinity, completely sacking everything," remembered orderly sergeant George G. Sinclair of the 89th Illinois. "I confess as I badly as I hate the secesh, I had not the heart to destroy what I did not want as some did but took only what I wanted to eat. You would think it a hard sight to see the fine large mirrors broken, carpets torn up, pianos tuned by the soldiers, you can guess what a tuning they got. In fact, they played the devil in general with Nolensville, but I will say in our defense that the people deserved all that was put upon them."[51]

Davis's division camped directly on the Nolensville Pike at Knob Gap, in what was a cold and miserable experience. Sergeant Major Rudolphus Peake of the 74th Illinois spent the night sleeping on "a couple of rails and used my canteen for a

49 Account of Private John R. Woodworth, Battery G, 1st Ohio Light Artillery, James Barnett Papers, WRHS.

50 Alfred Pirtle Papers, Filson Historical Society.

51 Letters from George Gresham Sinclair, Co. C, 89th Illinois, Illinois State Historical Library.

pillow. It began to rain very hard about 11 o'clock and continued through the night. I was awakened every hour or two by the water running over my face when I would get up and walk around, poke the fire, and then lie down again."

Negley's wet and tired men tramped into Nolensville at nightfall and settled into an equally dreary camp. "It rained hard and long during the night," wrote Ira Gillaspie of the 11th Michigan. "Some of the 19th Illinois pressed a couple of barrels of whiskey. They had a jolly time of it I wager judging from the sound of them." David C. Shotts of the 18th Ohio noted that the brigade camped a mile south of Nolensville, and the poor condition of the roads proved too formidable an obstacle for their wagons, so the men slept in the rain without tents. "We had no blankets or overcoats," he wrote, "making it one of the most disagreeable nights we have experienced since in the service."[52]

"All night, orderlies clattered over the stony pike, detachments of troops were constantly on the move, swearing, shouting, and singing as they passed, and baggage wagons with discordant sounds went rumbling by," recalled William A. Beach of Battery E, 1st Ohio Light Artillery. "Occasionally a team would crowd too far to the right or left of the road and a pair of wheels would go down to their axles in the soft earth, and then the mild, patient mule driver's chant, floating in musical cadence upon the night air banished sleep from eyelids that were never so weary."

The soldiers of the 15th Ohio, part of Richard Johnson's division in McCook's wing, enjoyed a contented sleep in their newly issued shelter tents. "We were tucked safely away in them when it began to rain and we found them rainproof and comfortable," remembered Sergeant Alexis Cope. "From our regimental camp, we looked out on a great number of other camps which formed an irregular semi-circle overlooking a valley. The tents were lit with candles and they gave an impression of an almost innumerable host. It was an inspiring and comforting spectacle. At 9 o'clock, we were called to rest by the 'German Tattoo,' sounded by General August Willich's bugler. Never in all our lives had we heard anything sweeter than those

---

52 Letter from Sgt. Maj. Rudolphus W. Peake, 74th Illinois, *Rock River Democrat*, Jan. 28, 1863, 1; Daniel B. Weber, ed., *From Michigan to Murfreesboro: The Diary of Ira Gillaspie of the Eleventh Michigan Infantry* (Mount Pleasant, 1965), 41; Diary of Private David Christopher Shotts, Co. A, 18th Ohio, SRNBP.

long-drawn notes of that famous call as it was sounded that night on the hill near Nolensville."[53]

*   *   *

Rosecrans made his headquarters at a former tavern on the Nashville Pike, about 11 miles outside the capital city. At sunset, accompanied by a small escort and a few select staff officers, he rode about five miles west on a rutted country road toward Nolensville to meet with McCook. "Darkness, heavy clouds, and rain fell upon the cortege as it spurred briskly through the rugged narrow lanes and gloomy forests upon unknown paths which but an hour before had rattled under the hooves of Rebel horsemen," recalled William Bickham. Getting lost, the party secured the services of a civilian guide and continued at an intense gallop until one of the escort complained, "General, this way of going like hell over rocks will knock up the horses." Rosecrans concurred and ordered the men to walk the horses, but also barked, "[T]ell that young man that he must not be profane."

The group finally arrived at McCook's camp "in the heart of a grove just off the highway," Bickham wrote. "The flames of the roaring fire were soaring high and groups of officers were lounging about discussing the morrow. No tents were pitched but the General had established his quarters in a grove by the side of a rough moss-covered rock which served for lounges and fireplaces. A pair of roadmaster's cars, like ambulatory Daguerreian establishments, were drawn up in front and the quarters for the night provided within."[54] Rosecrans, McCook, and a few staff members conferred in the cars while Garesche wrote out orders for the December 27 advance.

The conference concluded just before 11:00 p.m. and Rosecrans and his party headed back to headquarters. McCook rode alongside for a short distance. Departing, he decreed, "Good night, General, with the blessing of God I will whip my friend General Hardee tomorrow!" With an appreciate nod, Rosecrans replied, "God bless you" before riding away.

"The darkness was now so dense," Bickham would write, "that horses and riders in front would have seemed phantoms but for the clattering hooves and clanging scabbards." Inevitably, the contingent became separated in the morass,

---

53 Private William A. Beach, Battery E, 1st Ohio Light Artillery, *Cleveland Daily Herald*, Mar. 12, 1863, 1; Cope, *The 15th Ohio Volunteers*, 229.

54 Bickham, *Rosecrans' Campaign*, 158-60.

and the men resorted to hollering to each other as they stumbled through the woods. Rosey finally arrived at his headquarters about 1:00 a.m., the rest over the next few hours. "The General," Bickham noted, "was in the saddle that day fourteen hours … riding 42 miles."[55]

Crittenden's column bivouacked along Hurricane Creek, near La Vergne. Orderly sergeant Wilbur Hinman of the 65th Ohio eloquently captured the essence of the campaign's first night, writing: "Night, dark and dripping, settled down upon the great bivouac. We could do nothing except spread our blankets upon the wet ground, choosing the spots where there was the least depth of mud. Rain drizzled down upon us during the whole night. We slept, however, but arose well-soaked and in a most forlorn condition."

It became evident that Crittenden's Federals had camped dangerously near Wheeler's skirmish line. "With the utmost quietness and carefulness, we took our places and stationed our lookouts [when] we discovered cavalry within a few steps of us," recalled William Buskey of the 1st Kentucky (US). "Each party challenged the other, each answered, and with playful sallies avoided questioning. It was impossible to tell friend from foe."

Word came from headquarters that there was no Federal cavalry on their front, which emboldened the Kentuckians. "The two parties had been conversing, each trying to outwit the other, and the cavalrymen were gently moving backwards when an emphatic challenge from our party rang out with emphatic earnestness, repeated three times, then the thunderous voice of Captain Hogan thundered 'fire' and both parties did. The flash of the guns, the gallop of the horses, and the rush of brave men to our rescue succeeded each other with lightning rapidity."[56]

Wheeler had reinforced his cavalry with Brig. Gen. George Maney's veteran infantry brigade, and once the fighting subsided at La Vergne, he rode back to Murfreesboro for a late-evening conference with Bragg. The diminutive Alabamian—barely 5-foot-5 and just 26 years old—hardly cut the image of a swashbuckling cavalryman. As one reporter noted, he was "polite and placid in manners and of a nervous sanguine temperament but is never satisfied unless there is a fight at hand. He loves the clash of sabers and roar of battle."

Wheeler's command soon found all the fighting it could handle, as it was clear this Federal thrust was more than a foraging expedition. Union prisoners taken at La Vergne convinced Wheeler that "Rosecrans entire army moved out today and it

55 Ibid., 160-63.

56 Hinman, *Story of the Sherman Brigade*, 335-36; Buskey letter.

is understood that there is to be a general movement. They were ordered to have three days' cooked rations and haversacks with rations were put in the wagons." The three Federal columns, Wheeler estimated, totaled 60,000 men.[57]

The offensive Bragg feared when he consented to Davis's demand to transfer Stevenson's Division to Mississippi had begun. Even then, the commander was caught flat-footed, his army spread across a 30-mile front and settled in winter quarters. With his army reduced by the cavalry raids underway by Forrest's and Morgan's commands and the departure of Stevenson's men, Bragg had roughly 38,000 effectives on hand. Only half of those troops, however, were in or near Murfreesboro on December 26, as the remainder were scattered throughout Middle Tennessee. Although Rosecrans expected Bragg to move forward from Murfreesboro to fight him at Stewart's Creek, Bragg had no intention of taking such a chance. As he indicated to President Davis, his strategy was to sit in Murfreesboro and let the Federals come to him, assuming a defensive posture to help negate the Federal superiority in numbers.[58]

What Bragg needed now was time to consolidate his army at Murfreesboro from its scattered outposts, as well as time to determine Rosecrans's tactical intentions. He at least had all of Polk's Corps and three of Breckinridge's four brigades already in camp near Murfreesboro. In Hardee's command, encamped to the southwest at Eagleville, were three of Cleburne's four brigades; they had the longest distance to march: 24 miles. At Triune, 17 miles west of Murfreesboro, were Brig. Gen. Daniel Adams's 1st Brigade, in Breckinridge's Division, and with Brig. Gen. Sterling Alexander Martin (S.A.M.) Wood's 4th Brigade in Cleburne's Division, positioned to support Wharton's cavalry.

McCook's advance posed a dire threat that these units would be cut off from the main army. General McCown's division lay a dozen miles east of Murfreesboro at Readyville, an easy day's march even in the drenching rain. Turning to his young cavalry chieftain, Bragg asked Wheeler how many days he could hold back

57 "Gen. Joseph Wheeler," *Jacksonville Republican*, Feb. 5, 1863, 1; Dispatch from General Joseph Wheeler, Dec. 26, 1862, 9:30 p.m., Braxton Bragg Papers, William P. Palmer Collection, WRHS.

58 Bragg's official report states that the total present for duty on morning of December 31 as follows: Polk's Corps, 14,118; Hardee's Corps, 14,069; McCown's Division, 4,414, and Jackson's Independent Brigade, 874, a total of 33,475 infantry and artillery. Wheeler's cavalry corps totaled 4,237 men, giving Bragg a total effective force of 37,712 men.

Rosecrans's army? Wheeler's reply has been variously given as anything from two to four days.[59]

Rosecrans could be pleased with the progress his army had made on the first day. Confederate opposition had been basically what he had predicted the night before, though a little stiffer than expected along the Nashville Pike. Meeting only cavalry opposition thus far, the Federals had suffered relatively light losses. Despite the heavy rains that day, the strategy of deploying infantry columns along the parallel roads expedited movement. Although the supply wagons had struggled to keep pace, the foot soldiers' ammunition supply was ample, and they had three-days' rations on hand.

Crittenden had not made it to Stewardsboro as planned, but his wing had marched half the distance to Murfreesboro and lay poised to cross Hurricane Creek at La Vergne on December 27. Likewise, McCook had covered half the distance to Murfreesboro and had taken Nolensville and Knob Gap—the capture of the gap raising morale particularly in the ranks. McCook's men would march on Triune the next morning, threatening to sever Hardee's men from Murfreesboro. Thomas's two divisions were in supporting distance of McCook. If there was any disappointment, it was the uncertainty whether Bragg was going to snap at Rosecrans's bait and engage him at Stewart's Creek, meaning the Federal army would have to continue marching south and confront Bragg at his main base of supply.

To borrow one of Rosey's favorite phrases, however, "things was workin'."

59 Edward G. Longacre, *A Soldier to the Last: Major General Joseph Wheeler in Blue and Gray* (Washington, 2007), 73.

La Vergne, Triune, and a Day of Rest

SATURDAY, DECEMBER 27, dawned gray, cool, and dank. The rain had ceased overnight, but heavy fog shrouded the rolling, saturated terrain—with visibility reduced to mere yards. Although Rosecrans had retired after 2:00 a.m., he managed at best four hours of sleep and was up early, as usual. "Not much progress today, I fear," he said to William Bickham, shaking his head as he studied the maps. "Obviously it was Bragg's true policy to draw Rosecrans as far as possible from his base," the journalist would write, "as every mile traveled diminished the effective force of the latter and opened his communications to dangerous attack." Rosecrans, he added, remained "uncertain whether Bragg would oppose his advance north of the Duck River."[1]

Bragg, of course, had decided to consolidate his extended army, and late on Friday ordered Hardee to march his corps from its camps around Triune back to Murfreesboro. Time would not be an ally, though, as Federal prisoners revealed that McCook's entire wing was nearby and was expected to push south in his direction from Knob Gap at dawn. One complication of Bragg's directive was that two of Hardee's core units were away from Triune: John McCown's 4,400-man division and Daniel Adams's Brigade in Breckinridge's Division—in Readyville and Eagleville, respectively.

---

1 Bickham, *Rosecrans' Campaign*, 164.

McCown, operating on the Army of Tennessee's far right flank, had the farthest to travel at this point, and orders for him to be in Murfreesboro by midnight would prove unrealistic. Wrote Captain John O'Brien of the 30th Arkansas: "After a while the troops were ordered to quarters again and told to be ready at a moment's notice. At about 2 a.m., [we] were again ordered to fall in and we took up our line of march for Murfreesboro distant about fourteen miles. The night was very dark and the recent heavy rains rendered the roads awfully muddy so that our march was very fatiguing."[2]

To their credit, the Arkansans marched effectually, swinging into eastern Murfreesboro by 9:00 a.m. Saturday. It would take the rest of Hardee's Corps longer to get packed and on the road, and to buy time the commander ordered John Wharton's cavalry to conduct a delaying mission. Wharton's troopers were positioned two miles north of Triune across the Nolensville Pike, atop a ridge on the Page Farm. The high ground covered the bridge over Wilson Branch, a small tributary of the Harpeth River. Videttes ranged a few miles farther north, busy watching the Federals in their camps near Knob Gap.

Wharton's tired troopers awoke Saturday "illy prepared for a renewal of the fight"—most of them, according to chaplain Robert Franklin Bunting of the 8th Texas, awake all night keeping watch on the nearby Federals. "As darkness came on it was found that the enemy was within a few hundred yards of the house occupied as headquarters by General Wharton," Bunting noted. "Our brigade bivouacked in his front was to be ready for work early in the morning."[3]

One bright spot in Wharton's gloomy morning was the arrival of S.A.M. Wood's 4th Brigade, in Cleburne's Division, and a fresh artillery battery to buttress his line. Roughed up the day before, and with detachments still scattered, Wharton's command was in no shape to handle its mission unaided. Hardee decided Wood's 950-man unit, composed mostly of Alabama and Mississippi troops, would be best for the challenge.

Wood, a native of Florence, Alabama, had his men awake by 4:00 a.m. December 27 and marched them forward to support Wharton. The brigade consisted of the 16th Alabama, 33rd Alabama, 45th Mississippi, and two companies of the 15th Battalion of Mississippi Sharpshooters. Two sections of Captain Semple's Alabama artillery battery, normally assigned to Wood's

---

2 Brian K. Robertson, *Things Grew Beautifully Worse: The Wartime Experiences of Captain John O'Brien, 30th Arkansas Infantry, C.S.A.* (Little Rock, 2001), 1.

3 Bunting Letters.

command, remained in Murfreesboro, leaving Wood just two bronze Napoleons under the command of Lieutenant Henry Goldthwaite.[4]

The additional artillery support would be the four guns of Captain Putnam Darden's "Jefferson Flying Artillery" in Brig. Gen. Bushrod Rust Johnson's Brigade. Wharton also had the two guns of Captain Benjamin White's Tennessee battery as well, as a surviving 6-pounder field gun from King's Georgia battery that had been slammed at Knob Gap on December 26, giving him a total of nine artillery pieces to contest McCook's advance.

Reaching Wharton, Wood deployed a section of Darden's battery, commanded by Lieutenant Frank W. Coleman, to the left of the Nolensville Pike, then placed the companies of the 45th Mississippi under Lt. Col. Richard Charlton across the pike, with three of those companies supporting the battery. A portion of the Mississippians supporting Darden's guns took position along a stone fence that stretched west from the pike. Darden took the other section of his guns and rode forward to support Wharton's forward lines closer to Knob Gap.

The 16th Alabama remained in reserve on a ridge in the rear of Triune, and the 33rd Alabama deployed about 300 yards east of town along the road to Murfreesboro. Wharton arrayed his troopers to the right of the 45th Mississippi but sent a sizable contingent up the road toward Nolensville to delay McCook's advance.[5]

*   *   *

As Wood's men took their positions across the Nolensville Pike, McCook was already headed toward Triune. Rosecrans directed him to march at dawn and attack Hardee's troops, supposedly camped at Triune. McCook's orders considered three contingencies: 1) if he battled Hardee and the Confederates retreated south toward Shelbyville, McCook would pursue Hardee with one division while directing the other two east along the Franklin Road toward Murfreesboro; 2) if Hardee went south without a fight, McCook was to pursue with two divisions and send the third toward Murfreesboro; and 3) if Hardee retreated east to Murfreesboro, McCook

---

4 Wood's Brigade was missing two regiments at Triune: the 3rd Confederate and the 32nd Mississippi (about 450 men in total) assigned to guard the railroad line south of Murfreesboro. The 150-man 3rd Confederate would rejoin the brigade in the fight at Murfreesboro, but the 300-man 32nd Mississippi would not.

5 OR 20/1:896.

would follow with his entire command. Rousseau's division of Thomas's corps, then camped at Owen's Store, would support McCook, while Negley's division, now camped at Nolensville, would march east to Stewardsboro to assist Crittenden in forcing a crossing of Stewart's Creek.[6]

The rolling topography and heavy fog had also delayed McCook's advance from Knob Gap, and the roads—reduced to a rust-red oozy paste by the heavy rainfall and thousands of trampling feet the day before—slowed the infantry to a crawl. "Any movement we might make was hazardous so it was deemed advisable to wait for [the fog] to rise[,] which it did about 8 or 9 o'clock," noted Union General Richard Johnson. Recalled William Dodge of the 75th Illinois: "The country here is a succession of ridges and bottoms, the former mostly covered with cedar thickets and the latter with open fields. A wintry fog covered the country so that only the most prominent points could be seen, making a successful movement of troops a difficult undertaking."[7]

Leading McCook's corps were the cavalry reserve regiments under Stanley's personal direction. Stanley was delighted to gain the services of four companies of the veteran 3rd Indiana Cavalry under Major Robert Klein that had seen more than a year's service with the Western armies. As Klein's troopers joined the column, Stanley remarked that he "had understood that the 3rd Indiana knew how to take these Rebels" and gave Klein the honor of leading the column south. The Hoosier sent out a company as advance guard, deployed two companies as flankers (Company I on the right, Company K on the left), then moved forward at a smart trot through the morning fog.[8]

The advance stumbled into Wharton's videttes just past Arrington Creek a mile south of camp, and Klein ordered a charge that forced the flank companies to flounder through the muddy fields to keep pace. "The column now moved on them at a gallop, receiving the whole of their fire into one company, the skirmishers on the flanks not being able to come up for some time on account of the soft nature of the ground and the intervening fences," Klein reported.

It was about 9:00 a.m. when the companies on the flanks finally caught up, allowing the whole force to drive Wharton's skirmishers across the cedar-covered ridge toward their supports. As Klein's troopers climbed the crest of the ridge, the

---

6 Ibid., 2:242.

7 Richard W. Johnson, *A Soldier's Reminiscences in Peace and War* (Philadelphia, 1886), 207-08; Dodge, *History of the Old Second Division*, 393.

8 Major Klein's battalion consisted of Companies G, H, I, and K of the 3rd Indiana Cavalry.

Brigadier General David S. Stanley

Library of Congress

fog had cleared enough to reveal the barrels of two Confederate artillery pieces on a nearby knob. Putnam's Jefferson Flying Artillery, out of Mississippi, had made a name for itself at Shiloh, where it fought alongside the Washington Light Artillery on the second day of the battle and brought off a captured 12-pounder howitzer it now took pleasure in firing at the Yankees. The guns promptly barked out a morning welcome to Klein's galloping troopers, who wheeled their mounts and fell back to escape the shellfire, as Wharton's skirmish line neatly ducked behind the cannons, dismounted, and opened fire.[9]

Colonel Joseph B. Dodge of the 30th Indiana, in Kirk's 2nd Brigade, led McCook's advance, and Kirk, Dodge, and Kirk's staff were among the Federals caught by the opening blasts of Darden's guns. "Whether they knew it or not, they landed every shot in the road along which our troops were advancing and owing to the creek on one side and a precipitous hill on the other, we could not get out of it," Dodge would write. Recalled Lyman Widney: "We could not see through the fog whence they came and naturally expected a few more of the same sort. Before the smoke of the shells had blown away, General Kirk gave us the order to deploy into line of battle in an open field to the left. We obeyed with unusual promptness, so glad we were to get out of the road before another discharge came."

Dodge pushed his men left of the road and across the fog-swept Arrington Creek toward Darden's guns. "We found in front of us a precipitous bank, probably 50 feet high with very soft, sticky clay and it was with the utmost difficulty that the men could climb up it," he wrote. "Thundering away right over our heads

9 OR 20/1:646-647.

was the battery not more than 30 yards from the edge of the bank. The enemy discovered us just in time to get away. Some of my men were within ten feet of one of the guns when it was taken off with the horses at a run."[10]

The scrambling Confederates took position on the next ridge back, where Darden's guns again thundered away at the advancing Federals. From the valley between the ridges, skirmishers of the 45th Mississippi opened fire on Federal cavalry. The Mississippians' appearance was particularly remarkable that morning, as they had recently received a shipment of red homemade shirts made "of fine Brussels carpet which made them look like British soldiers." The Anderson Troop, Pennsylvania Cavalry took over from Klein's Hoosiers and, upon seeing the Mississippians, charged headlong into the skirmish line.

When the inexperienced troopers fired their carbines, however, "the volley was more disastrous to us than to the enemy for with the whiz-bang-zip of the volley came a perfect hail of missiles flying in all directions," recorded Conrad Diehl after the projectiles hit several fellow troopers. During the night apparently, some of the Pennsylvanians allowed their carbines slip into the mud, which plugged the barrels with sediment, causing some muzzles to blow apart during discharge. "Some six or eight carbines were brought to this condition and it was lucky that in many cases the charge failed to explode," Diehl added.

Other troopers blazed away at what they believed were enemy sentinels, alarmed to realize their bullets had no effect. "Watts carefully poised his carbine and fired but the Rebel did not move," wrote John A. B. Williams. "The smoke cleared away but still stooped the supposed grayback. 'Thunder,' exclaimed my comrade in disgust, 'it's only a stump!' And so, we kept pegging away at stumps under the impression that it was the soldier's duty to burn as many cartridges as possible."[11]

Major Adolph Rosengarten of the Anderson Troop soon found himself in a life-or-death melee with a determined Mississippi corporal named Joel McBride who, like many in Wharton's command that day, seemed willing to defend every inch of ground. "When the crack of carbines and rifles got to be pretty lively, our colonel gave the command, 'Skirmishers retreat!'," recalled one Mississippi soldier.

---

10 Colonel Joseph B. Dodge, 30th Indiana, "What I Saw at Stone River." *Northern Indianian*, Feb. 25, 1875, 1; Girardi. *Memoirs of Lyman Widney*, 128.

11 David Williamson. *The Third Battalion Mississippi Infantry and the 45th Mississippi Regiment: A Civil War History* (Jefferson, 2004), 90; Memoirs of Lewis Conrad Diehl, Co. I, 15th Pennsylvania Cavalry, MSS CD, Filson Historical Society, 23-24; Williams, *Leaves from a Trooper's Diary*, 38.

"The entire company heard and obeyed except the captain and Corporal McBride who were too far away to hear and too busy at the time to heed."

As Rosengarten galloped at the head of a dozen troopers, McBride took a shot at him, only to have his musket misfire when he pulled the trigger. "The major dashed forward, almost standing in his stirrups, his saber raised to cleave his enemy's chest," the Confederate soldier continued, "when McBride clubbed his gun and before the major could strike, knocked him from his horse badly stunned."

McBride bolted for the rear but was caught trying to climb a slippery snake rail fence by a groggy and furious Rosengarten, who slashed at him with his saber and cut him across the chest. "This infuriated the corporal who sprang at the Major like a bulldog, caught him around the body, threw him down, straddled him, and nearly pounded the life out of him with his fists," claimed the Mississippian. "At this moment, the major's troops, a sergeant and eight or ten men, came up excitedly shouting, 'Shoot the Rebel! Shoot him! Kill him! No, don't shoot boys, you'll kill the major! Take him off! Jerk him off!'

The two were finally separated, but McBride, his dander up, struck and kicked ferociously at the sergeant and the men who had threatened to kill him. McBride's own captain finally commanded, "Surrender, Joe, surrender you fool!" which caused the corporal to submit, though reluctantly even then. Rosengarten, pummeled but still alive, was helped from the ground. He would, however, meet his end two days later during fighting at Wilkinson's Crossroads.[12]

Support for the Federal cavalrymen by Kirk was near, and upon arrival, Colonel Dodge noticed dead and wounded troopers scattered about. That was a surprising development, Dodge wrote, given that "our cavalry had up to this time never been very highly esteemed for its fighting qualities. I saw a dead Federal and a Rebel soldier lying dead by the side of each other, each with a revolver in his hand."

Kirk deployed four companies from both the 29th Indiana and 34th Illinois to cover his left flank, as the 30th Indiana stepped to the side of the pike to allow Captain Warren P. Edgarton and his six-gun Battery E, 1st Ohio Light Artillery, to engage the Confederate artillery. Adjutant Josiah Reiff of the Anderson Troop had already reconnoitered the Rebel position and provided the enemy dispositions to

---

12 Sergeant L. G. Williams, Co. A, 45th Mississippi, "Hand to Hand Fight in the Army," *Confederate Veteran*, Aug., 1894, 228. Adjutant Josiah Reiff of the 15th Pennsylvania Cavalry recalled that the fight grew so intense that McBride almost bit off Rosengarten's finger, this detail apparently gaining wide circulation within the brigade as multiple soldiers in different regiments mentioned it in their memories of the fight at Triune.

Edgarton's lieutenants. "Shortly afterwards, all of our guns opened fire and the range was splendid, forcing the enemy's infantry back," Reiff recalled.[13]

Edgarton reported that he fired only "a few rounds" before driving off Darden, the Confederates falling back to the next ridge and redeploying their guns. "The infantry skirmishers filed off the road to the left and our entire battery now moved rapidly after them," reported Lieutenant Albert Ransom. "Leaving the pike, the skirmishers moved to the top of another ridge and our battery was placed into position there from which point we opened with every gun, driving the Rebels out of range."

Their guns were double-charged with canister, recalled W. T. Charles of Lieutenant Richard W. Goldthwaite's section of Semple's Alabama Battery, to hold back the Federal infantry preparing to charge the guns. Charles described Goldthwaite as "white as a sheet but he was cool and not a bit scared. He gave the command to fire at last and just when it should have come. The infantry in the hollow between the two hills made it perfect for the Yankee battery to fire over their heads. Amid the smoke and din came the order 'Limber to the rear!'"[14]

"Our continued advance was of short duration as the enemy reformed their lines and turned to meet us at short intervals," explained William Doll of the 6th Indiana. "As the day advanced, they seemed to increase in numbers and grew more and more stubborn[,] and we were obliged to advance slowly and with great caution. They contested the ground hotly." Added Edgarton: "The duty of following the enemy on this day was very arduous as we were obliged to leave the traveled roads in order to gain position. We removed, dragged our pieces through the soft ground of the cultivated fields, through streams, and climbed hills where it became necessary to call for a detail from the infantry to help us."[15]

With more firepower than their counterparts, Edgarton's gunners had an edge. Confederate sharpshooters, however, proved quite dangerous. "We had just taken our position when they opened fire on us," recalled William H. Laughlin. "We returned this compliment as quickly as possible and while so doing,"

> our gunner noticed that every now and then a puff of smoke came from a tree standing just in front of the main line of timber and a ball came very uncomfortably near some of our boys. We decided a sharpshooter was trying his hand at us, so we trained our gun on the

---

13 Dodge, "What I Saw at Stone River"; Kirk, *History of the 15th Pennsylvania Cavalry*, 82.

14 *OR* 20/1:302; W. T. Charles, *Recollections of Christmas During the War* (1959), 8.

15 Memoir of Private William H. Doll, Co. C, 6th Indiana, SRNBP; *OR* 20/1:299-300.

tree and let him have it. The percussion shell struck the body of the tree about halfway from the ground to the top and exploded. I need hardly say that the Reb discontinued operations at once.[16]

As Confederate resistance stiffened, Kirk deployed his regiments en echelon behind the skirmish line, then moved the 29th Indiana and 34th Illinois to the right of the road, and the 79th Illinois, 30th Indiana, and 77th Pennsylvania to the left. The "smoke from the guns combined with the dense fog made it unsafe to move as it was impossible to discern anything at even a limited distance and a brief halt was made on that account," remembered one Federal. The fight through the afternoon waxed hot and cold. "At one time the musketry and artillery would be deafening, at another time it would entirely cease," wrote Assistant Surgeon Joseph Downey of the 77th Pennsylvania. "At intervals, the red flash of the cannon could be seen through the mist, and the loud hissing of shells could be heard close by, reminding us that the Rebels were still in position ahead of us. Once or twice during the day, we almost captured their battery, but they would move a little too quick for us and would be off whenever they found us approaching."[17]

Wharton's crafty ducking and dodging, aided immensely by the persistent fog and intermittent rain showers, burned plenty of daylight, and it was nearly sunset before Johnson's division came within sight of Wilson Branch and, beyond it, the village of Triune. A bridge carried the Nolensville Pike over the now-turbulent creek. As the Federals approached, a detachment of Confederate engineers busily prepared to burn the bridge. During the brief halt, Johnson ordered forward the four regiments of Colonel Philemon P. Baldwin's 3rd Brigade, aligning them right of the Nolensville Pike to extend Kirk's line, and added the six guns of Captain Peter Simonson's 5th Indiana Battery in hopes of driving Wharton and Wood out of Triune by brute force.

"A fine position on a hill overlooking Triune and within range of the Rebel cavalry in a line of battle facing our left was found here and four pieces opened from this eminence," wrote Lieutenant Ransom. "We threw shot and shell into and beyond the town and into the Rebels on the right and left. The road was filled with

---

16 Private William H. Laughlin, Battery E, 1st Ohio Light Artillery, James Barnett Papers, WRHS.

17 Edwin W. Payne, *History of the Thirty-Fourth Regiment of Illinois Volunteer Infantry* (Clinton, 1902), 37; Assistant Surgeon Joseph B. Downey, 77th Pennsylvania Volunteer Infantry, *Lancaster Inquirer*, Jan. 26, 1863, 2.

Rebel cavalry and one section, unlimbering in the road, made them its special mark. The town was soon made untenable."

When Charlton ordered the 45th Mississippi to retreat across the bridge into Triune, F. M. Martin of Company E decided not to leave behind his blanket and ran back to his original position to retrieve it. "Finding them wet and too heavy to carry, I dropped them and all of a sudden, bullets came hissing around my head," he remembered. "I thought I would be killed anyway so I wheeled around and deliberately fired at my pursuers. There were three cavalrymen all in a bunch so I fired and started on my run again. We halted in a skirt of woods out of a drenching rain when suddenly the Yankee cavalry commenced firing on us." The Mississippian bolted across the Wilson Branch bridge shortly before Captain J. W. Green's engineers torched it.[18]

*   *   *

After a long day of fighting, the Federal force finally had a commanding position but could not ignore the presence of Wharton's and Wood's commands across the creek ready to contest their advance further. "Here the enemy was in plain view in line of battle with the center in the town and the flanks extended to the right and left," General Johnson observed. It was clearly time, however, for Wharton to abandon Triune. "With their long-range guns, we were in their power," Bunting noted. "The cavalry of the enemy was becoming more daring, but the infantry was close by [in] support[,] for whenever his cavalry was pressed, they would fall back and draw us upon his infantry. It was a day of constant vigilance and fighting. Our last engagement was heavy and our losses increased."[19]

A member of Edgarton's battery recorded that the fight grew increasingly one-sided as the Confederates fell back to Triune. "We found the Johnnies who opened on us quite briskly," he wrote in his diary. "The battery was placed on a hill commanding their position to the left of the road and we soon returned their compliments and intimated that their presence was offensive to us. They seemed to take the hint, for they soon left the road unobstructed and we passed on towards Triune."

Nearly 200 Confederate troopers on the Confederate far left found themselves caught behind the surging Federals but boldly employed subterfuge to escape.

18 OR 20/1:302; Mamie Yeary, *Reminiscences of the Boys in Gray, 1861-65* (Dallas, 1912), 464-65.

19 Bunting Letters.

Wearing captured sky-blue Federal issue overcoats, many of the troopers walked brazenly through the enemy lines toward the creek. "They came out very coolly and were mistaken for our cavalry, nor was the mistake discovered until they passed through on a walk when they started on a full run," remembered Sergeant Will C. Robinson of the 34th Illinois. "Our boys, though a little late, brought down seven, killing two."[20]

The Federal pursuit bogged down in the muddy fields north of Wilson Branch. "[W]hen we again advanced, owing to the ground being very much softened by the rain and the men's clothes being so saturated with water that it was impossible to do so at the rate of speed desired," Dodge conceded. "The enemy destroyed a bridge across a stream that runs through the edge of the town, thus compelling the artillery to make a detour of nearly a mile to a ford and by this means the enemy gained time to collect his scattered forces and withdraw."

At the ford, the Federals jumped into the rushing waters. "The water was running very swiftly, was nearly waist deep, and was very cold, but we plunged in and waded through under a very disagreeable fire of musketry and artillery." Once Dodge's men crossed the creek, they stumbled through a muddy wheatfield toward the retreating Confederates. "It was astonishing to see the men, almost utterly exhausted as they were, form into line when ordered to charge the Rebel line as coolly as if they were on the drill ground," Dodge recalled.

Nevertheless, despite the colonel's best efforts to drive his men forward, Confederate shellfire would prove too great an obstacle, and they hunkered down obstinately, too drained to advance. "The Rebels gave us a heavy fire of grape and canister, but it had no effect at all, although we were within easy range," recalled orderly sergeant Kaufman Funk of the 30th Indiana. "Orders were sent immediately to advance and charge the battery, but it could not be done as the men were entirely fagged out."[21]

Wood and Wharton sent their batteries to various points along the teetering line to try to hold back the Federals, without much success. "We found the enemy to be advancing with a line of infantry extending a mile in length," Wood reported. "Our skirmishers fired quickly upon the line, but seeing the overwhelming forces against us, General Wharton and myself concluded at once to retire."

20 Elijah M. Strong, *Marches of Battery E, 1st O.V.L.A.* (Delta, 1892), 16-17; Sergeant Will C. Robinson, Co. A, 34th Illinois, *Sterling Republican Gazette,* Jan. 24, 1863, 1.

21 OR 20/1:319; Dodge, "What I Saw at Stone River"; Orderly Sergeant Kaufman Funk, Co. K, 30th Indiana, SRNBP.

The 34th Illinois, shelled throughout the afternoon, now sensed an opportunity to capture their tormentors, as Sergeant Robinson related. "Captain Van Tassel commanded the skirmishers, 'Boys, take those guns! Forward, double quick!' We rushed forward with a yell and were within 25 rods of the battery and could see the Rebels applying the brand," he wrote. "Down every man went on his face which saved us as the grape and canister went over us, tearing and rushing through the deserted houses in our rear like a hailstorm." By that time, Darden's gunners hitched up and were galloping east with Wharton's soaked and exhausted troopers covering the retreat.[22]

Wharton's rearguard soon stumbled into the 29th Indiana, which had crossed the creek and was now astride the Shelbyville Pike—the Confederate line of retreat from Triune. The Indianans' joy was short-lived, as the 1st Confederate Cavalry regiment appeared "on our left within 20 yards and moving leisurely to the front," reported Major Joseph P. Collins. "I ordered the reserve to wheel to the left and fire, which was heard by the Rebels who instantly quickened their pace to a gallop but were unable to pass in time to save their entire column. Several were seen to reel in their saddles, and all changed direction, making for the woods."

The 16th Alabama would become involved in the engagement, too. "As we were retreating, I discovered the enemy moving up on our right flank, but we were enabled to gain the turn in the road before they could cut us off," noted Colonel William B. Wood. "A piece of artillery opened on them at this point and checked their advance."[23]

The 77th Pennsylvania took the last shots as the Confederates exited Triune. "As soon as we neared the town, we were ordered to charge and charge we did with such yelling as I never heard before," recalled Captain William A. Robinson. "We did not get near enough to puncture them, but our unearthly yelling must have scared them thoroughly as they fled in the wildest confusion and through the worst mud I ever saw."[24]

At this dramatic juncture, Johnson marveled that "it seemed that the floodgates of Heaven were opened and the rain descended in blinding sheets, rendering pursuit out of the question." Recalled Colonel Dodge: "[I]t absolutely poured down and while it was doing its best, I was taken with [the] hardest ague

---

22 *OR* 20/1:897; Will C. Robinson Letter.

23 *OR* 20/1:328, 901.

24 Captain William A. Robinson, Co. E, 77th Pennsylvania, *Daily Pittsburgh Gazette*, Jan. 28, 1863, 4.

chill imaginable. I shook so that I could not sit on my horse, so I got off and plunged through the rain and mud on foot, then stood up against a fence and shook until it seemed to me that I was running a small earthquake on my own hook."[25]

Although the Federals now occupied Triune, the seven-mile march had taken all day, buying time for Hardee to march to Murfreesboro without Federal interference. Despite relinquishing Triune, Wharton's and Wood's men had fought superbly and accomplished their mission. The rain cleared about sunset, giving the men a chance to try to dry their soaked clothing. "Each soldier might now be seen carrying his fence rail and we soon had blazing fires to dry our dripping clothes and warm our chilling bones," wrote Corporal Uriah Young of the 93rd Ohio.

Members of the Anderson Troop, rattled but wiser for the experience, searched the battlefield in the falling rain for relics and mementos of their first battle. Doll and his comrades in the 6th Indiana also picked over the field, combing abandoned knapsacks and haversacks for something edible. "That evening, many a supper cooked for a Johnny was eaten by a Yankee," he said. Sergeant Robinson, meanwhile, picked up a saber from the battlefield and recorded that the Federal camps buzzed that night with the men talking about their many narrow escapes, showing off their battlefield souvenirs, and relishing the tale of Major Rosengarten's hand-to-hand fight with McBride.[26]

*　　*　　*

On the Federal left, the men in Crittenden's corps were awake early; as with the other commands, the heavy fog stymied any advance. Rosecrans directed the Kentuckian to slow-pedal it that morning, aiming to give McCook more time to gain the rear of Bragg's position, which Rosecrans hoped might still develop at Stewart's Creek. Minty had his cavalry out scouting shortly after dawn, but they had yet to report their findings when Crittenden sent Rosecrans a note requesting where to direct his troops. Should he focus on securing the bridge across Stewart's Creek and, if possible, push on toward Murfreesboro, or should he drive farther to the left along the Jefferson Pike and cross the creek there? "My column is so remote from General McCook that I cannot inform myself so as to conform to his

---

25 Johnson, *Memoirs of Service*, 208; Dodge, "What I Saw at Stone River."

26 Corporal Uriah Young, Co. H, 93rd Ohio, *Eaton Weekly Register*, Feb. 5, 1863, 3; Doll Memoir; Will C. Robinson Letter.

movements," Crittenden noted. "A small force of the enemy is reported in front, but I do not know certainly whether there is any or not."

Two hours later, Rosecrans replied, directing Crittenden to do both. "Go on driving them slowly before you until you reach Stewart's Creek," the commander directed. "Throw a brigade across the stream, if possible, and hold the bridge. Push another brigade along the Jefferson Pike with proper supports and try and seize the bridge on that road to cross Stewart's Creek. Take up a position there in order of battle along the front thus gained and await the arrival of Negley and Rousseau. That junction gained and provided things go well with McCook, we will advance on Murfreesboro."[27]

Along the Nashville Pike, General Thomas Wood's division assumed first position but sat until nearly noon waiting for the fog to abate before moving out. Hascall, commanding Wood's lead brigade, deployed as his front line the 26th Ohio on the left and 58th Indiana on the right, supported respectively by the 100th Illinois and 3rd Kentucky about 200 yards behind the front line. Crittenden reportedly rode up to Wood at 11:20 a.m. and asked, "Have you a regiment that can charge LaVergne?"

"I have," came his response.

"What regiment?"

"The 26th Ohio."

"Send it forward."[28]

As the Federals marched into the diminishing fog, they were not entirely sure the Confederates remained in the town. "Captain Edmund R. Kerstetter, the adjutant general, said we were not likely to find anyone [there], that it was barely possible we might have a little brush that afternoon," remembered Captain John James of the 26th Ohio. "The instructions the General gave me just before we started were to push ahead smartly and not allow ourselves to be stopped by any slight opposition, but if we met serious opposition which appeared too much for us to fall back or wait for the regiment to come to our support."[29]

Elements of George Maney's brigade of Tennessee infantrymen, along with Wheeler's cavalry, waited for them, hidden among the houses and barns. If Crittenden's mission was to slow-pedal his advance, Wheeler and Maney were happy to oblige, as their orders were to fall back slowly before the larger Federal

27 *OR* 20/2:243-44.

28 Colonel Edward P. Fyffe, 26th Ohio, *Madison County Democrat*, Feb. 19, 1863, 2.

29 Captain John A. James, Co. A, 26th Ohio, *Urbana Union*, Feb. 11, 1863, 1.

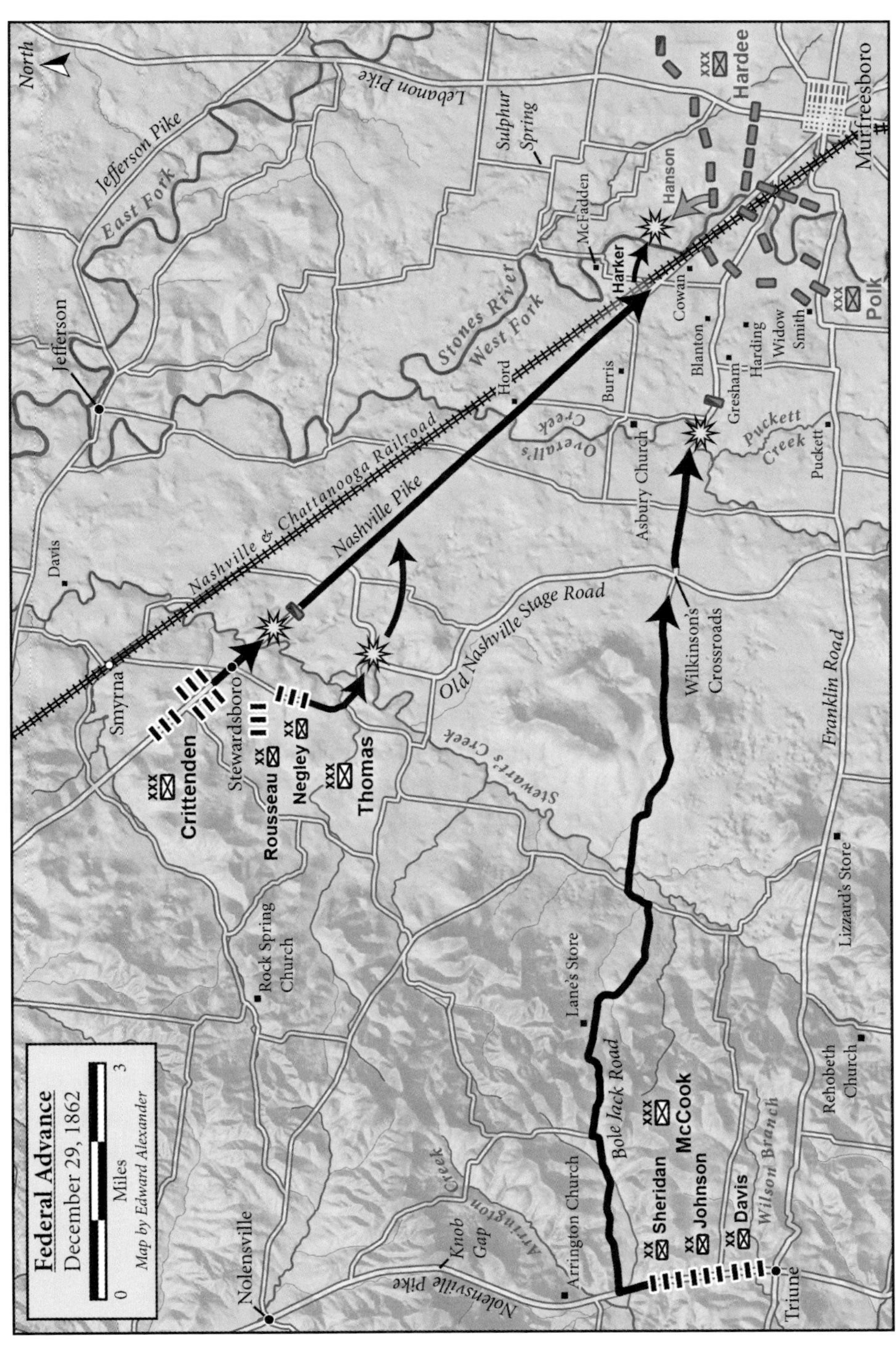
North
Jefferson Pike
East Fork
Jefferson
Lebanon Pike
Sulphur Spring
Stones River West Fork
McFadden
Hanson
Harker
Hardee
xxx
Murfreesboro
Cowan
Polk
xxx
Widow Smith
xxx
Harding
Blanton
Gresham
Burris
Puckett Creek
Puckett
Nashville & Chattanooga Railroad
Hord
Nashville Pike
Overall's Creek
Asbury Church
Wilkinson's Crossroads
Old Nashville Stage Road
Franklin Road
Davis
Smyrna
Stewardsboro
xxx
Crittenden
xx
Rousseau
xx
Negley
xxx
Thomas
Stewart's Creek
Rock Spring Church
Lane's Store
Bole Jack Road
Lizzard's Store
Rehobeth Church
Nolensville
Knob Gap
Arrington Creek
Nolensville Pike
Arrington Church
xxx
McCook
xx
Sheridan
xx
Johnson
xx
Davis
Wilson Branch
Triune
Federal Advance
December 29, 1862
Miles
0
3
Map by Edward Alexander

force. Wheeler and Maney decided to make their main defense along Stewart's Creek a few miles south of La Vergne. "With its precipitous banks and few fords and bridges presented a fine place for retarding the Federal advance," observed Samuel Seay of the 1st Tennessee, especially after the previous day's rains. Furthermore, the Tennesseans were contemptuous of their opponents, especially the cavalry. "Good-humored jokes about the 'buttermilk brigades' were studiously and unremittingly told," he wrote. "With all deference to the cavalry, the idea among the infantry was almost general that no number of cavalry could successfully cope with any approximate number of infantry of equal courage."[30]

"We started off and had hardly gone a hundred yards when the bullets began to whistle around us from the enemy posted in the houses of the village and the fields and woods on the left," James recalled, who continued:

> We advanced till we came out on an open space and we commenced firing. But not a man could we see though their bullets kept whistling past us thick and fast. I first told the men not to fire unless they saw something but finding that no one was to be seen and thinking a random fire better than none I told them to fire away. But our men were very much exposed in an open field and their advance was already checked and just then a piece of artillery (a good ways off but in easy range) opened on us.

Watching the action from behind the lines, Hascall realized the attack had stalled. "Not wishing to try and cope with the enemy under such unfavorable circumstances any longer than absolutely necessary, I ordered the skirmishers and the first line to charge at a double quick and get possession of the town at all hazards," he reported. "The front line was lying flat on their faces at the time of receiving the order, but in a twinkling of an eye, the entire line sprang to their feet, fixed their bayonets, and rushing forward with a yell had in five minutes time possession of the town and crest beyond."[31]

"I was getting a little doubtful as to what to do next, when the order came to 'double quick through the town' and we saw the regiment advancing in line close behind us," James added. "We kept a short distance ahead of the line and as the Rebs saw the advance, they evacuated the houses in time to escape; most of them that is, for some were killed and wounded."

---

30 Samuel Seay, 1st Tennessee Infantry, "A Private at Stone River," *Southern Bivouac,* Aug., 1885, 157.

31 John James Letter; *OR* 20/1:465.

For the 58th Indiana, it was a similar story. "As our skirmishers came in close range, a galling fire was opened upon our center and right from their infantry who were behind a strip of woods and the houses of the village, and as the line was about to recoil from it, Company F was thrown forward to support them and the battalion ordered to charge," wrote one Hoosier. "Quick as thought a bright flash of light shone along the front as the men struck the double quick and adjusted their Rebel bile pickers [bayonets] for the hot work before them." The clash abutted a picket fence, where the "enemy wavered, then deployed, then on the double quick quit for more peaceful quarters."[32]

Hascall's attack cost the brigade 27 casualties, but the Confederates were on the run. Delighted Federals marched into town to find it a shambles. "The houses were mostly burned down and the few that were still there were drilled through by cannon balls and had been ruined," recorded Sergeant John Daeuble of the 6th Kentucky (US). "The residents had all fled and the place was deserted and empty."

The Confederate line fell back right to left at La Vergne, leaving Wheeler's troopers on the left susceptible to capture as the Federals maneuvered around their flank. Lieutenant J. P. Bryant's section of Wiggins' Arkansas Battery took a support position on a hillock to the rear of the town and then fell back with the troopers. Captain George K. Miller of the 8th Confederate Cavalry wrote that "we fell back slowly, skirmishing all the way. Our forces on the right and between me and the pike having fallen back faster than I anticipated, threw me for a time in the rear of a large body of the enemy where I had a full view of the heavy column as it rolled down the pike—infantry, cavalry, and artillery. I was so close that I could distinctly hear the commands of the different officers."[33]

Hascall pushed beyond the town through cedar thickets and empty cornfields now churned into mud; a short distance from La Vergne, however, he could not overlook the unmistakable exhaustion of his frontline regiments. The general halted the line, brought his second line forward with the 3rd Kentucky on the right and the 100th Illinois on the left. It marked the first time the eager Illinoisans had been under fire. "During their advance through the cedar thickets, the boys encountered great numbers of rabbits, and somehow they could not resist the temptation to pop them over, and put them in their haversacks for future use," recalled George H. Woodruff of the 100th Illinois. "While they were advancing, much of the time on the double thick, and driving the Rebel cavalry before them, it

32 John James Letter; W.A.D., 58th Indiana, *The Clarion*, Jan. 10, 1863, 2.

33 Reinhart, *History of the 6th Kentucky*, 146-47; George Knox Miller Memoir.

was hard to tell whether they were popping at the Rebs or the rabbits, and it didn't seem to make much difference with the boys. General Hascall scolded them, telling them they would get caught with their muskets empty when they wanted to shoot a Reb, but he didn't say anything more about keeping them from running to the rear, the greatest difficulty he had now, was to hold them back."[34]

Lieutenant George Estep's 8th Indiana Battery rolled forward with Hascall's advance in a pouring rain, trading shots with the gunners of Wiggins' Battery as far as Stewart's Creek. The Confederate troopers continued their cat-and-mouse game, forcing Hascall to deploy his guns and infantry repeatedly, but they began to run out of space as they approached the raging creek. "The enemy were dislodged from not less than five or six of their hiding places and they frequently retained their fire until we had approached within less than 100 paces," noted Colonel Samuel McKee of the 3rd Kentucky. "They had the advantage of both short range and deliberate aim, yet we were so shielded by an overruling Providence that not a single casualty happened in my regiment."

The Confederate gunners took position on a hill overlooking the Stewart's Creek bridge and opened a sharp fire on Estep's guns as he appeared on the pike. "The fearful accuracy of their fire convinced us that this was a different battery from that with which we had been contending all day[,] as every shot from them either struck our pieces or came within close proximity," Hascall reported. "Having no long-range guns in Estep's battery, I sent to the rear for some other battery and as soon as they got into position, the enemy's fire was silenced."[35]

On reaching Stewart's Creek, the rearguard 8th Confederate Cavalry discovered to its horror that Wheeler's men had piled lumber and other combustibles on the bridge, and fired it, leaving them stranded on the north bank with the 7th Pennsylvania Cavalry closing in. "Stewart's Creek was a driving stream with very steep banks and our intention was to cross it at the bridge on the pike," Miller wrote. "But when we reached this point, we found that our artillery had already crossed over and General Wheeler had destroyed the bridge and the enemy's artillery was raking the pike. Fortunately, we found a narrow path leading

---

34 George H. Woodruff, *History of the One Hundredth; or Will County Regiment. Fifteen Years Ago: or the Patriotism of Will County, Designed to Preserve the names and memory of Will County Soldiers* (Joliet, 1876), 224-26.

35 *OR* 20/1:465, 488.

to a ford about a quarter of a mile above the burning bridge. Barely had we time to cross when the enemy came close upon our heels."[36]

The rain slowed the burn, though, allowing the 3rd Kentucky time to charge the structure in the fading daylight. "They rushed in and threw the combustibles from the bridge and saved it," Hascall reveled. "Great credit is due for this act as the loss of the bridge would have delayed the movements until another could be constructed, the stream not being fordable at this point." Hascall's men, however, had no sooner congratulated themselves on capturing the bridge when a detachment of the 51st Alabama Partisan Rangers barreled in on his left. "I ordered the 26th Ohio to change front forward on the left company to resist the attack in that direction and this repulsed the attack," reported Hascall.

Captain William Munger's 31-man Company G of the 100th Illinois was almost cut off by the charging cavalry but turned the tables by opening fire and demanding the Confederates' surrender, which Munger noted "they did, some with great reluctance. A number of prisoners, when they saw they must surrender, threw away their guns."[37]

George Woodruff recalled how one charging Confederate "kept on, and was shot in the abdomen, fatally." Apparently, the trooper had been unable to restrain his wounded horse, which would be killed after rambling past the 3rd Kentucky, its mortally wounded rider still in the saddle. "The boys carried him to an old shed," Woodruff said of the dying Confederate, "and took every care of him, greatly regretting that they had not understood his design to surrender."

The brigade's newcomers had done well. Munger's company, in fact, had wounded three troopers and accepted the surrender of a lieutenant and 24 enlisted men in this brief coda to the fight at Stewart's Creek "Since that time, it has been with much difficulty that we are able to stand up under our laurels," the captain proudly wrote home.[38]

Once Hascall's brigade cleared La Vergne, Hazen's brigade pushed out on the Jefferson Pike. Soon a 90-man battalion from the 4th Michigan Cavalry under Captain Frank Mix approached, directed by Hazen to move ahead and, if possible, take the bridge over Stewart's Creek. "As soon as the advance of the enemy was

---

36 George Knox Miller Memoir.

37 OR 20/1: 465-466, 482-483.

38 Woodruff, *History of the 100th Illinois*, 250; Captain William A. Munger, Co. G, 100th Illinois, on the Spared & Shared website, https://sparedshared22.wordpress.com/2021/07/28/1863-william-austin-munger-to-elisabeth-patrick-gookin/; retrieved May 29, 2022.

started, I directed him to put the spurs to his troop and not slack rein until the bridge was crossed," reported Hazen, whose men moved forward as quickly as possible to support Mix.

Deploying a company on each flank, Captain Mix moved down the pike with his remaining two companies and soon found Confederate pickets of the 51st Alabama Partisan Rangers contesting his passage. "I immediately started with companies B and L after them," he reported. "At every rod their number increased so that when we came to the bridge, we were chasing about 200 of them and we were so close to them that some of them were pushed off the side of the bridge and taken prisoners." Lieutenant Colonel James Webb of the 51st Alabama Partisan Rangers reported that "they commenced a heavy and brisk firing upon us as we were crossing Stewart's Creek. Their fire was returned with vigor and their advance checked until their artillery and infantry came up. Being heavily pressed by greatly superior numbers and opened on by their artillery with grape, canister, and shells, we retired in good order on the pike in the direction of Jefferson."[39]

The fight did not end with control of the span. "As soon as we got possession of the bridge, I sent couriers back to hurry up the infantry," Mix recalled. "While we were waiting, the enemy attacked us in strong force, but our boys nobly stood their ground and repulsed them." Hazen's infantry, though, was still too far off. When the Confederates reformed and charged again, Mix pulled his force back across the expanse. "I no sooner started them back when the enemy came down on us like bees, yelling as if they had us sure," he later wrote. "I had Co. B on each side of the road and Co. L came back to the bridge on the double quick with the enemy close at their heels. I ordered them to right-about, which they did handsomely, not a man flinching or wavering in the least. They immediately opened fire upon the enemy which soon made them leave for the woods."[40]

Mix then heard firing in his rear. Expecting further trouble, he placed Company B on the bridge in time to repulse the last attack as Hazen's force arrived. After rolling into a field adjacent to the pike, the six-gun Battery F of the 1st Ohio Light began firing away to speed up the Confederate retreat. That, along with a dash for the bridge by Union infantry, put an end to the clash. The Federals not

39 OR 20/1:543, 629, 963.

40 Ibid., 630.

only had their bridge across Stewart's Creek, but they also had 11 prisoners, leaving Captain Mix "perfectly satisfied with my trip."[41]

With the day's fighting all but over, Crittenden now had two secure bridges across Stewart's Creek, though it was now obvious that Bragg intended to fight Rosecrans not there but at Murfreesboro. Wheeler's and Maney's men, aided by the heavy fog and rain combined with Crittenden's orders to proceed slowly, held the Federal advance to merely four miles. Progress on the Federal right totaled about seven miles, also bedeviled by the persistent fog and the stubborn resistance from Wharton's troopers and S.A.M. Wood's infantrymen.

*　　*　　*

While McCook and Crittenden continued to push south, Thomas's two divisions turned east along the Jefferson Pike toward Stewardsboro. Because of the poor condition of the roads around Nolensville, teamsters resorted to tossing away baggage to lighten the loads. "On account of a heavy fog the next morning, the division started late," wrote Captain Silas Canfield of the 21st Ohio. "Being unacquainted with the country, General Negley pressed a citizen into the service as a guide, averring that his life depending on piloting us safely across." Negley's mud-bespattered division arrived at Stewardsboro about sunset and established connection with Wood's division near the Nashville Pike bridge across Stewart's Creek. Rousseau's division marched east from Owen's Store and likewise found the road a quagmire. A soldier from the 94th Ohio groaned that the road was "almost impassable in consequence of the heavy rain of the night before. Our brigades were scattered along with the trains and the 94th Ohio was kept in the rear and encamped that night near the road upon which the trains were moving. The troops and trains changed positions slowly and the head of the division did not reach Nolensville until night."[42]

Bragg paced nervously and impatiently at his headquarters in Murfreesboro, a day marked by great anxiety according to one staff officer. The sounds of combat at La Vergne were distinct, those at Triune much less so, and Bragg worried that his outposts would be driven into Murfreesboro before he had consolidated the army

41 Kimberly, *The 41st Ohio*, 39.

42 Silas S. Canfield, *History of the 21st Regiment Ohio Volunteer Infantry in the War of the Rebellion* (Toledo, 1893), 72; *Record of the 94th Regiment, Ohio Volunteer Infantry in the War of the Rebellion* (Cincinnati, 1895), 26.

and established a solid defensive alignment. As Wharton's and Wood's troops sparred with McCook's advance, Adams' Brigade, in Breckinridge's Division, left Triune around 10:00 a.m. and found the Franklin Road a bog because of the previous day's rain. According to a 5th Company gunner of the Washington Light Artillery, the brigade "had a hard time from beginning to end. We started off on a forced march in a cold rain with mud half a leg deep and the orders we were that we should be in line of battle in Murfreesboro by 10 o'clock the next morning. We made it, but in what condition! Every man in the brigade was saturated while the clothes froze stiff to our limbs."

As the battery rolled into Murfreesboro, Major Rice E. Graves, its new chief, rode out to meet them and was astonished to find the guns festooned with "all sorts of plunder in which figured extensively the denizens of barnyards and hen roosts in anticipation of an elaborate Christmas enjoyment." Graves was disgusted at the spectacle, and as the last section of guns rolled past him, he barked out "Is this how the Washington artillery travels?"[43]

Some of Hardee's troops, including three brigades in Cleburne's Division, had enjoyed comfortable winter quarters at College Grove near Eagleville for several weeks when Hardee sent orders directing Cleburne to get his brigades on the road to Murfreesboro at first light on December 27. They were to march east along the Salem Turnpike. "Our march today was a very hard one," recalled Robert Smith of the 2nd Tennessee. "I don't think I ever was out in as hard a rain. I got perfectly wet as it rained all day."

Captain Ezekiel John Ellis of the consolidated 16th/25th Louisiana, in Adams' Brigade, had likewise enjoyed a camp respite. "We had a fine camp in a hickory grove and the country around was full of eggs, chickens, fresh meat, milk, etc.," he wrote. "We had plenty of the best of good things. I do not desire to live on better fare that we had while we remained in Eagleville."

On Christmas, Ellis and his comrades celebrated the holiday with traditional rounds of eggnog. "[W]e all got merry and continued merry until the next evening when we were sobered by the long roll of the drum which, in a moment, called us from cups to arms."[44]

43 C. L., 5th Company, Washington Light Artillery, *Shreveport Weekly News*, Mar. 9, 1863, 1; Nathaniel C. Hughes, *The Pride of the Confederate Artillery: The Washington Artillery in the Army of Tennessee* (Baton Rouge, 1997), 79-80.

44 Memoir of Captain Ezekiel John Ellis, Co. F, 16th/25th Louisiana, SRNBP.

A few miles out of College Grove, members of the 23rd Tennessee, in Bushrod Johnson's Brigade, believed they saw Federals approaching the column's left flank and deployed into a line of battle along a ledge. "The Federals drew up on the ledge to the north facing us with artillery unlimbered, the intervening valley covered with timber," observed Captain William Harder. "After dressing the lines a minute or two I addressed my company, calling their attention to the situation of the lines and asking them and the regiment to follow me at the first fire of the artillery into the Federal line."

General Johnson rode up and, seeing the Federals, directed the men to prepare for action. Neither side made a move, however, and Johnson's column soon resumed its march "leaving the Federals looking after us but not pursuing or firing a gun." Other than this brush with what were possibly phantom Federals (none reportedly were within miles of Eagleville that day), Cleburne's Division marched undisturbed except by the rains and arrived within three miles of Murfreesboro by nightfall. A short march the following morning brought them safely within Bragg's lines.[45]

As Rosecrans feared, his army on December 27 could not duplicate the miles it marched the previous day, resorting to modest pushes of seven miles on the right and roughly four miles on the left. Negley's division linked up with Crittenden's wing that evening at the Nashville Pike bridge over Stewart's Creek, though Rousseau's division continued to flounder along the mud-caked Jefferson Pike and would not arrive until December 28.

What, however, were Bragg's intentions? Was he planning to fight at Stewart's Creek, Murfreesboro, or would he retreat farther south along the Duck River? Where, too, was Hardee headed? Apparently, that last question would expose Bragg's true intentions.

Late that evening, McCook informed Thomas of a report he received from one of Sheridan's scouts that Bragg's entire army was at Murfreesboro and "the impression was the Rebels, if they fought us at that place, would make a strong stand at Stewart's Creek and then fall back to Murfreesboro." The scout's report indicated that Bragg "is fully posted in regard to our movements."

Garesche accordingly informed McCook that Rosecrans desired more definitive intelligence on Hardee's movements "before moving on to

---

45 Jill K. Garrett, trans., *Confederate Diary of Robert D. Smith* (Columbia), 87; William Henry Harder Memoirs, 1861-1865, Tennessee State Library and Archives.

Murfreesboro with the left and center and trusts to your giving prompt information thereupon."[46]

At 9:00 that night, Bragg sent out a general communique to his senior subordinates reporting that he had directed the three cavalry commands (Wheeler's, Wharton's, and Pegram's) to fall back to Murfreesboro the next day and wanted the infantry divisions in line by 9:00 a.m. Noting "[t]he move of the enemy is evidently upon this place," Bragg ordered the troops to prepare two days' rations and be supplied with 40 rounds of ammunition, with another 100 rounds per man to be held in the ordnance wagons.[47]

With all of Bragg's scattered detachments concentrated at Murfreesboro on December 28, the commander called a council with Hardee and Polk to detail his plan of battle. His battle line would be positioned two miles northwest of Murfreesboro, the two corps separated by Stones River. Bragg believed he needed to defend against two potential axes of attack. Rosecrans would most likely advance in force along Nashville Pike, but Bragg also had to weigh the possibility that Rosecrans might try to flank the Confederates out of their defenses in Murfreesboro.

Hardee's retreat foiled Rosecrans' earlier flank attempt on Bragg's left, but a flank march on the right could not be ruled out. Federal possession of the Stones River crossings at Jefferson offered a direct march into Murfreesboro via the Lebanon Pike. Bragg's concern of that was behind his apparently flawed tactical deployment of Hardee east of Stones River and Polk to the west. For Hardee, the four brigades in Breckinridge's Division occupied the ground between the Lebanon Road on the far right and Stones River's eastern bank, opposite the junction of the Nashville Pike and the Nashville and Chattanooga Railroad. They were supplemented by General John Jackson's small brigade, which had just been pulled from railroad guard duty south of Murfreesboro, and Cleburne's Division was placed in reserve roughly 800 yards behind Breckinridge.

Stones River marked the boundary between Hardee and Polk. Cheatham held Polk's right between the river and the Wilkinson Pike. General Withers' Division occupied Polk's left, its left flank near the Franklin Road, and McCown's Division lay in reserve 1,000 yards behind Cheatham.

Polk ordered his division and brigade commanders to join him the morning of December 28 to reconnoiter their assignments. Because of the general's trademark

46 *OR* 20/2:246, 248.

47 Ibid., 464-465.

tardiness, however, his assembled subordinates made time for personal observations on an imminent battlefield. "The scene before and around us was very impressive," remembered Arthur Manigault, still a colonel in command of a brigade in Withers' Division. "Long lines of troops were moving in different directions as they filed towards their respective positions." The South Carolinian continued:

> Groups of cavalrymen constantly passed us consisting of sick or wounded troopers, also detailed men with led horses, many of them showing that they, too, had been in the fray. Then would come a train of heavily loaded wagons and interspersed among them here or there would appear the larger and more cumbrous machine of some unfortunate farmer, his household goods piled to an immense height, women and children occupying every available position. Horses, cows, sheep, hogs, and pigs formed an attendant drove in charge of the lads or Negroes belonging to the family.[48]

"The fog proved to be so thick as to prevent in a great measure a satisfactory reconnaissance," remembered another of Polk's brigadiers, J. Patton Anderson. "The line, however, was determined upon and the major general commanding the division designated the positions of the several brigades. They were immediately marched out from their encampments and drawn up in line of battle, and the troops remained under arms during the afternoon and night of the 28th."

That Polk's Corps was arrayed through a series of open fields and cedar brakes drew a complaint from Manigault. The overall impression of the ground was that it was "an unfortunate one for us," he wrote. "Commanders, whatsoever their rank or importance of their commands, are almost always dissatisfied with the positions assigned them in the line of battle, regarding that point entrusted to them as the weakest in the whole line, and I may be no exception to the rule."[49]

Rosecrans conceded that he had lost critical preparation time to Bragg, yet he kept the bulk of his army in camp on December 28. The weather had cleared overnight, and when the sun rose that chilly Sunday, some believed the Federals would push on to Murfreesboro. A recent war department directive, however, forbade military operations on Sunday, and, as the journalist Bickham noted, "General Rosecrans had frequently expressed his opposition to military operations

---

48 R. Lockwood Tower, editor. *A Carolinian Goes to War: The Civil War Narrative of Arthur Middleton Manigault* (Columbia, 1992), 54-55.

49 OR 20/1:762-763; Tower, *A Carolinian Goes to War*, 55.

upon the Sabbath unless they were indispensable. It was therefore a foregone conclusion that Sunday December 28th would be a day of comparative rest."

Determining Hardee's movements would be necessary, however. "If he had retired to Shelbyville, it indicated the withdrawal of Bragg's army from Murfreesboro," Bickham wrote. "If he had merely fallen back to Murfreesboro, it justified the conclusion that the enemy had determined to meet us in a general engagement in that vicinity." The Federals spent the day waiting for these answers, permitting Bragg an undisturbed 24 hours to prepare his troops and their defenses for the pending engagement.[50]

Scouting the location of the enemy would have been a perfect job for the cavalry, but the lack of Union troopers on hand reared its head. Lewis Zahm's three Ohio cavalry regiments continued to patrol the far right of the army toward Franklin, which left McCook the option of sending out only Stanley's battered troopers, accompanied at least by an infantry brigade. McCook dispatched General Willich's brigade at dawn on December 28 with orders to march south on the Nolensville Pike to Rigg's Crossroads to determine Hardee's whereabouts.

Captain Horace Fisher, McCook's topographical officer, accompanied the expedition. "My first move was to secure guides," he wrote. "I commandeered a dozen farmers and mounted them on spare horses. I then told them that there was 'just one thing that they all could agree upon—the truth. I gave them fair warning that if they led us into any trap, the orderly alongside of each one had orders to shoot him on the spot, but that if they did their duty, they would be taken back to their homes safe and sound. Otherwise, they would be left dead on the roadside.'"[51]

The brigade departed at 7:00 a.m., the green 2nd Tennessee Cavalry and 32nd Indiana leading the advance. After heading south for a few miles, the force turned east on a country road toward Salem. The road was lined with stragglers (41 were captured in all) who reported that the Confederates had marched to Murfreesboro the day before. Adjutant William Hall of the 2nd Tennessee reported that his cavalrymen had a sharp fight in which the Tennesseans lost four horses killed but captured a half-dozen members of the ubiquitous 51st Alabama Partisan Rangers, including a lieutenant. "A dense fog hovered over everything so that it was impossible to discern any object at a very great distance," reported Williamson Ward of the 39th Indiana. "We marched out about five miles when we returned to

---

50 Bickham, *Rosecrans' Campaign*, 172.

51 Horace Cecil Fisher, *A Staff Officer's Story: The Personal Experiences of Horace Newton Fisher in the Civil War* (Boston, 1960), 51.

camp again at Triune. We captured prisoners who straggled behind and were picked up by our cavalry. Some of them had on our uniform pants and seemed to be in destitution of proper clothing."[52]

Fisher offered a fascinating look into how he interrogated the captured Confederates:

My first question, notebook in hand, was their name, regiment, and brigade. My next step was to examine their haversacks to see how much food they had. When I found they had one day's cooked rations, I asked, 'When did you have orders for cooked rations for one day?' They substantially agreed that the order was issued about 9 o'clock Saturday night and that they marched at midnight. Of course, they did not know where they were going on that night march, but their haversacks told me. It was 26 miles from Triune to Shelbyville. Therefore, they were not going to Shelbyville as we generally thought up to that time. But it was only 15 miles to Murfreesboro and, therefore, only one day's march. I had found out for what I had been sent.[53]

General Willich sent a dispatch to McCook about noon that simply stated, "The enemy is no more here; all gone to Murfreesboro." Accordingly, the Ohioan passed the news to Rosecrans, who in turn sent a courier to Rousseau with orders to have his division on the road as early as practicable December 28. The courier, however, could not find the Kentuckian, whom Thomas, it was learned, had sent out to gather forage. Rousseau scrambled to get his command on the move upon learning Rosecrans' intentions, but that would not be until nearly sunset.

As the men got into column, they were appalled at the condition of the "road," which beggared description. "There was no regular road through the swamp, and as the night happened to be pretty dark, we had a sweet time of it," remembered Lieutenant Otto of the 21st Wisconsin. "The protruding roots of the mighty red cedar trunks were running in every direction. Boulders seem to have been thrown round in a reckless manner. Besides considerable brush was scattered between the trees. The front man would bend the brush aside, let it carelessly fly back and it usually would whack the next man in some tender spot where it was least wanted."

In an attempt to speed up the march, teams and baggage were ordered left behind. Colonel Beatty, commanding Rousseau's second brigade, noted in his diary that his men did not begin their march until nearly 4:00 p.m. and "night had set in

---

52 Diary of Private Williamson D. Ward, Co. D, 39th Indiana, Smith Memorial Library, Indiana Historical Society.

53 Fisher, *A Staff Officer's Story*, 52; OR 20/1:648; OR 20/2:254.

before the brigade was fairly underway. The road runs through a barren, hilly pine district and was exceedingly bad."[54]

Adjutant William McDowell of the 15th Kentucky (US) recalled that "we were only kept in the right direction by beacon fires which were kept burning the entire night." One veteran of the 42nd Indiana said that "the march of that night was terrible, hundreds of the men gave out and stopped by the wayside. Our route was through the woods and swamps lying between the Nolensville and Nashville pikes. We reached this latter road at Stewart's Creek about midnight and were glad to lie down on the cold ground supperless and without blankets for the night."

Alfred Pirtle, in command of Rousseau's ordnance train, rolled into camp early on December 29, exhausted after spending all day and night driving his wagons over "the most infernal mean road that ever a civilized country was cursed with."[55]

---

54 Gould, *Memoirs of a Dutch Mudsill*, 78; Beatty, *The Citizen-Soldier*, 198-99.

55 Memoir of Adjutant William P. McDowell, 15th Kentucky, *Southern Bivouac*, 1886–1887, 246; unknown member of Co. E, 42nd Indiana, *Princeton Clarion-Leader*, Jan. 31, 1863, 1; Pirtle, *Stones River Sketches*.

Saltpeter in the Breeze

WITH BRAGG'S INTENTIONS now clear, Rosecrans's immediate task was to consolidate his army and prepare for battle.

On the morning of December 29, he ordered each of his corps to converge on Murfreesboro. From their camps along Stewart's Creek, roughly 11 miles away, Crittenden's and Thomas's troops would proceed southeast along the Nashville Pike. Crittenden's corps would cross Stewart's Creek at the Smyrna Bridge (seized by the 3rd Kentucky on December 27) while Negley's division in Thomas's corps would ford the creek two miles upstream near Stewardsboro and advance to Crittenden's support. Rousseau's division, having just made its way to camp after a hellish night march from Nolensville, would remain there for the day, awaiting the arrival of the division's supply train.

McCook's men faced the longest haul. Retracing their steps on the Nolensville Pike, just north of Triune, they marched east along the Bole Jack Road to seize Wilkinson's Crossroads and the adjacent crossing of Overall's Creek about six miles northwest of Murfreesboro. This would keep McCook's men within three miles of Thomas and Crittenden as the army closed on Bragg's base. The three regiments of Colonel Zahm's cavalry brigade would cover the far right of the advance, moving toward Murfreesboro on the Franklin Road.

For Bragg, December 29 was wrought by anxious waiting and the shuffling of troops along the defensive positions he had selected the day before. Small troop detachments arrived by rail as part of his consolidation orders, and by the end of the day his army was as ready as it could be for the fight ahead. John Jackman of the 9th Kentucky spent the night resting by a campfire along the Manchester Pike after helping pack the regimental wagon. "The morning was beautiful, being the commencement of a lovely day, which reminded me of an Indian summer," he recalled. "Though the day was full of sunshine, we knew that a storm was brewing. There was a deep resonance of cannon rolling over the hills from the direction of Nashville, and we could already sniff the saltpeter in the breeze."[1]

George Wagner's 2nd Brigade, in Crittenden's wing, had to fight its way over Stewart's Creek that morning. "Two pieces of [Jerome B.] Cox's 10th Indiana Battery moved on the road with the front line and commenced shelling the enemy," observed a member of the 57th Indiana. "The enemy made a sharp fight at the creek but were driven off by our artillery. Captain Cox persisted in shelling a grove of timber which stood near the east side of the road south of the stream in which he thought the enemy must have a battery. 'Cox,' shouted Colonel Wagner, 'give that Rebel battery on the road hell! They're running, and the woods can't get away. You can tend to them after a while.'"

The colonel then ordered the 15th Indiana to cross the stream below the bridge and the 57th Indiana above it to prevent a dash by the enemy before the bridge's plank flooring, which had been removed by the Confederates, could be replaced. "Our regiment immediately forded the stream and hurried into line on the south bank," Wagner recalled, "but the plank was soon replaced and the artillery dashed forward, unlimbered as quickly as possible, and hurled their shells after the retreating forces of the enemy."[2]

Negley's division was to depart its Stewardsboro camp at dawn and strike for a ford at Stewart's Creek, two miles upstream from the main Nashville Pike bridge that Crittenden was using as a crossing. As the division set out, Captain Frederick Schultz's four-gun Battery M of the 1st Ohio Light Artillery swung into a position overlooking the ford and barked morning greetings to Wheeler's cavalrymen across the creek, supervised by Negley himself. Schultz's German gunners quickly cleared a passage for the infantry to cross unopposed. "As we unlimbered our guns, the General made his appearance and pointing toward the enemy ordered us to fire on a regiment of Rebel cavalry who were moving towards Murfreesboro," wrote Sergeant John Deis. "The second shell from our guns struck and exploded among the second company of the Rebel regiment and scattered them in all directions. The General being well pleased with the result ordered the battery to cease firing."

---

1   John S. Jackman, "Battle of Murfreesboro," *Southern Bivouac*, Mar. 1885, 296.

2   *Annals of the Fifty-Seventh Regiment Indiana Volunteers*, 149-50.

At 7:00 a.m., recalled Captain James Hanna of the 69th Ohio, "we started with a greater number of cartridges than hard crackers expecting to have an engagement at the creek. We soon came in sight of their pickets and they, having a natural aversion to shelling, made a hasty retreat."[3] Noted Sergeant Launcelot Scott of the 18th Ohio: "As the division marched out, we could see the Rebel cavalry fleeing for dear life. Our division crossed some distance above the pike bridge and fired a few times at the Rebel pickets."

Across Stewart's Creek, Stanley formed his brigade into line of battle, deploying a cloud of skirmishers in front, and embarked on a southeasterly cross-country march toward the Nashville Pike. "As we pushed over the fields and through the timber, one of our boys who could sing began to sing and had just got down to the chorus when the enemy sent us their compliments in the shape of a shell," related Samuel Linton of the 21st Ohio. "The shell went over us and exploded far in the rear, but our singer was made very sick and was sent to the rear by the captain. The Johnnies were soon on the run and we pushed on."[4]

The going was slow for Negley's skirmishers, forced to trade shots with Wheeler's troopers for the rest of the morning. They struck the Nashville Pike eight miles from Murfreesboro and fell in behind Van Cleve's division. The column then marched unfettered another five miles, arriving about three miles from Murfreesboro by sunset, and "we left the pike and went into an old field just at the right of the pike where we stacked arms by sticking our bayonets in the ground," said Ira Gillaspie of the 11th Michigan. "We did this to secure and keep dry the loads in our guns for it was raining. We made some coffee in our cups and ate some bacon and hardtack. We were gathered around our rail fires in the rain, some smoking and some trying to sleep." Noted Sergeant Scott: "[W]e thought that we would enter Murfreesboro the next day without serious trouble."[5]

Crittenden's lead brigades evidently felt that way, too. Shortly after crossing Overall's Creek near the pike's five-mile point, General Wood rode forward with his lead brigade under Wagner and demanded that Palmer clear Colonel William Grose's brigade off the road to let his troops pass. Wood was determined to be the first into Murfreesboro. "This order I refused to obey as General Crittenden was

3 Sergeant John Deis, Battery M, 1st Ohio Light Artillery; James Barnett Papers, WRHS; Hanna Letter.

4 Scott Memoir; Memoir of Private Samuel A. Linton, Co. I, 21st Ohio, Rutherford B. Hayes Library.

5 Weber, *From Michigan to Murfreesboro*, 41-42; Scott Memoir.

with the troops and controlled the movements of the column," Palmer claimed. "General Wood, however, brought up a brigade and he took the left of the pike and we marched pari-passu, as he said, until sundown when we came in sight of the enemy in line of battle between us and Murfreesboro."[6]

McCook's column moved out of Triune shortly after dawn, with the ubiquitous Anderson Troop again in the lead. After consulting with Brig. Gen. Jefferson C. Davis, commanding the infantry advance, McCook directed Major Rosengarten to push the Rebels across Overall's Creek, but not cross himself. The movement, recounted regimental bugler Charles Francis of the 88th Illinois, created confusion in the order of march. "Our regiment filed into the road,"

then marched and countermarched in the most admirable confusion, now forming in a field on the right hand in order to permit some other regiment to pass us or to allow some flying battery of artillery to take its proper position, and again advancing and retreating with no ascertainable object. Finally, after maneuvering for two or three hours in this manner, we were properly placed and upon reaching a point about a mile or a mile and half to the rear of our camping ground of the night before, we struck off from the road on the northeasterly side of it and plunged immediately into the midst of a dense growth of stunted cedars.

There was no road and as we went along like a band of stragglers, all our guidance was for each one to follow his leader. There was not the least sign of civilization to be seen in any direction, nothing within our view but the closely growing cedars. We were frequently compelled to stop in the wildest of places owing to the inability of the troops in front to move with expedition.[7]

The 15-mile march from Triune to Wilkinson's Crossroads proved uneventful for most of McCook's men. The country, though spectacular, was rough and untamed, and the muddy Bole Jack Road proved "awful," with Colonel Jason Marsh of the 74th Illinois among those complaining it was "almost impassable." Wrote Chaplain William Haigh of the 36th Illinois: "[W]e emerged from the timber on the brow of a hill from which there was an uninterrupted prospect of the country for many miles. Right beneath us was a belt of open farmland extending perhaps one or two miles across, then an extensive cedar grove while beyond it

6 John McAuley Palmer, *Personal Recollections of John M. Palmer—The Story of an Earnest Life* (Cincinnati, 1901), 143

7 Charles L. Francis, *Narrative of a Private Soldier in the Volunteer Army of the United States During the Period Covered by the Great War of the Rebellion of 1861* (Brooklyn, 1879), 100-01.

another belt of open country with timber still beyond that. Through the first open land was gliding like some anaconda a portion of our column while the advance could be detected winding through the first grove by the gleaming of arms as the light glanced upon them."

"We had many tedious halts caused in part by the difficulty of dragging artillery over such rough roads," Haigh added. "At one spot on the banks of a creek, we halted for a considerable time until other troops could form a junction with us, it not being considered safe to make the flank movement of today without the columns being within supporting distance of one another. We passed through several immense cedar groves. One peculiarity of these groves is that instead of soil there is very little besides immense rocks. In many places it was difficult to ride on horseback, the track very much resembling broken, slippery, uneven steps with winding passages between the rocks. By-and-by we came upon the fine rolling country, which is the glory of Tennessee. On our way, we began to feel that the air was heavy with rumors and premonitions of the coming conflict."

Once the men knew they were marching for Murfreesboro, Lewis Day of the 101st Ohio noted, "speculation ran high among the boys as to whether Bragg would wait for us. On the whole, we rather thought he would."[8]

During breaks, men would gather and consume juniper berries. "Many jokes passed around on account of the berries," Francis recalled. "'These are used to make gin, etc.' The atmosphere of the woods in some places was so impregnated with the aroma of cedar as almost to make it unbearable. Late in the afternoon, we met a detachment of our troops in charge of some prisoners who had been captured a short time before. The captives being anything but submissive or docile, we were assured that they had not been captured by their own connivance and from that we argued that we were not far removed from an active army. I noticed that the rank and file at once assumed solemn countenances. All hilarity ceased and the ranks were kept closer as was always the case when we were convinced of our proximity to danger and from that time the march was conducted in a more regular manner."[9]

Reaching Wilkinson's Crossroads, the 1st Ohio Cavalry of Zahm's brigade joined the column and moved right of the pike. "On arriving near where the enemy was known to be posted, the force was assigned to different positions from right to left, stretching over about a mile of ground," wrote Josiah Reiff of the Anderson

---

8 Bennett, *History of the 36th Illinois*, 323-25; Day, *Story of the 101st Ohio*, 78.

9 Francis, *Narrative of a Private Soldier*, 101-02.

Troop. "We were ordered to advance, throwing out skirmishers to carefully feel our way. After about an hour's movement on foot and mounted without finding the enemy, the troops on our right commenced firing which told us they had at last met those whom we were seeking."[10]

The Anderson Troop continued east toward Murfreesboro on the Wilkinson Pike, approaching Overall's Creek. "Co. K had the advance and the column moved at a rapid rate, and at about 2 p.m. we struck the Rebel pickets and started to drive them toward Murfreesboro," remembered A. D. Frankeberry, Rosengarten's orderly. "The column soon reached the bridge and halted. In a very short time the command was given by the Major, and we crossed over the bridge and moved about three-fourths of mile down the pike toward Murfreesboro, when the command halted. Major Rosengarten rode back to Major Frank Ward and had a few words with him. Major Ward's battalion turned into a field on the right, formed a line at right angle with the pike, advanced and soon opened fire on the enemy."[11]

Word reached the Pennsylvanians that two enemy regiments waited in ambush ahead. "We had forded Overall's Creek and were grouped around a large house," wrote Corporal Charles Kirk of Company E. "Major Ward was with us. There was a level stretch of country for a half mile to the front and then woods. Animated by a boyish spirit I waived my guidon, and immediately saw a puff of smoke from the woods, then the sound, and lastly, with a vicious thug, a bullet went into a tree at my back. 'Take care, Corporal!' said the Major. 'That was a close shot.'"

The skirmishers were called in and remounted, and the command inched cautiously forward before eyeing a line of Confederate cavalry 800 yards ahead. The Rebels fell back, perhaps tempting the Pennsylvanians to charge, but Rosengarten would not take the bait.

Ward's troopers, however, could not resist. "Instantly the boys took up the cry, 'There they go! Charge them! Go for them!'," remembered Kirk. "Major Ward who was close to me yelled, 'No, don't go! My orders are to go only this far.' Still the yells continued with some of the men advancing, so the major said, "Damn you! If you go, I'll go, too. Charge!' and then all started without semblance of formation, most of them down the road and others through a gate across a cornfield."

In moving off, the Confederate cavalry cleared a field of fire for two companies of the 10th South Carolina deployed behind a high fence as pickets for Manigault's Brigade. The charging Pennsylvanians leaped the fence and landed

10 Kirk, *History of the 15th Pennsylvania Volunteer Cavalry*, 84-85.

11 Ibid., 101.

Major Frank B. Ward, Anderson Troop, died of his wounds on January 4, 1863

Library of Congress

amid Company A. "It was a surprise from which the Rebels soon recovered and fired on the troopers, who escaped through a gap in the fence," Reiff recalled. "One was knocked off his horse by the butt of a musket." The Pennsylvanians, just as surprised, grabbed a few prisoners and galloped out of danger.[12]

"One … who had picked up a prisoner called out to a nearby officer, 'Come on, Lieutenant! There's plenty more in there' and then the whole detachment at a gallop went quickly up to the fence," Reiff added. "The first shots that had been fired had alarmed the Rebel infantry in the rear who reinforced their advance so that by the time Major Ward and his men reached the point, it was to meet a long line of infantry securely posted with a high stake-and-rider fence protecting them from being run over by our men."

Among those captured in this first charge was Lieutenant Charles White, commanding Company A of the 10th South Carolina. A small squad of Pennsylvanians led by a lieutenant guarded the prisoners, but when the fight renewed, reported C. Irvine Walker, adjutant of the 10th South Carolina, White bellowed in a "stentorian voice": "'Company A, rally on the right!' Rallying, they hesitated to shoot for fear of wounding their friends. 'Never mind us, fire!' White ordered and grappling their captors, the prisoners secured them, regained their arms, and rejoined their company. Co. A promptly changed front to meet the squadron, Co. B closed up, and the cavalry was driven off."[13]

---

12 Ibid., 86.

13 Ibid.; C. Irvine Walker, *Rolls and Historical Sketch of the Tenth Regiment So. Ca. Volunteers in the Army of the Confederate States* (Charleston, 1881), 89-90.

"So sudden had been our appearance that it confused them and although their musketry fire was heavy, it was not destructive, even when our men were up to the fence firing carbines and revolvers at the enemy not over ten feet away," Reiff noted. The South Carolinians' fire was destructive enough: Ward took a musket ball through his left breast near his heart and had his horse shot beneath him. Though mortally wounded, he gamely walked back down the pike supported by two troopers.

Kirk, carrying the company guidon, spied a group of four soldiers in the road. Thinking they were fellow Pennsylvanians, he galloped in, only to realize as he neared that they were enemy cavalrymen clothed in butternut brown jackets and armed with muskets. "I was too close to put a stop to my horse and doubt I could have done so anyhow, but in a flash came to me the drill with lances I had seen when I visited my brother Will in his regiment, Rush's Lancers [6th Pennsylvania Cavalry]." Lowering his guidon like a lance, Kirk plowed ahead. "My first adversary sat solidly on his horse fingering the trigger of his musket while his comrades were in the rear," he continued:

> But all my thoughts were on him and I think his were on the peculiar weapon I carried and his ignorance of its effectiveness magnified its power for when I got to within a dozen paces of him, he dropped his musket to the ground and raised his right hand in token of surrender. The others followed his example at one and for a few moments, I had four prisoners on my hands.[14]

The gunfire brought up the balance of the Anderson Troop to reinforce Ward, but this time the 10th South Carolina was prepared. White rallied his two companies, and now reinforced by Company C, aligned his command at a right angle of the fence, ordering the men to kneel behind it. Rosengarten soon approached with his battalion, the major conspicuous riding at the head of the column atop a large black charger named Zollicoffer. "We soon saw the Rebels in force, with barricades across the pike," Frankeberry noted. "They were also to the left of us, and we again halted opposite a heavy wood, on the right of the pike. The Major gave the command 'fours right!' which brought us in line facing the woods. Numbers one and three were then ordered to dismount and open the rail fence." Once this was done, the men remounted and Rosengarten gave the command "forward, gallop, march!" and, once the troops were partly through the woods, the

---

14 Kirk, *History of the 15th Pennsylvania Volunteer Cavalry*, 137-38.

command "charge!" Rang out and, "in a moment afterward we received a volley of musketry from the Rebels, who were behind a fence which ran parallel with the pike," recalled Frankeberry. The volley emptied several saddles and forced the Pennsylvanians to withdraw.

"[T]he Federal squadron [had] the greatest gallantry but little discretion, for it was futile for cavalry to attack infantry behind a high fence," recorded Irvine Walker of the 10th South Carolina. "The major rode up to the fence, shot a man in Co. A, but the company concentrated their fire upon him and the brave fellow fell, riddled. The squadron charged several times, but only to be repulsed."[15]

"I saw several of our men on the ground and horses rearing, one seemed to me to spin around on his hind feet," Kirk observed. "Near me were Lieutenant De Coursey and Will Kimber. 'This is pretty hot in here, let's get out,' De Coursey said. 'Just one more shot,' said Kimber and gave it, but got one in return square in the forehead. We were all getting out now and a little depression in the ground gave us cover and the chance to retreat in good order and all firing from the front ceased and was succeeded by some horrible agonizing cries from some of our wounded back on the field."

The Anderson Troop lost six killed and 10 wounded in the brief affair, including its commander, now crumpled on the ground alongside his dead horse. "Seven balls pierced Major Rosengarten and the horse was riddled with bullets," Reiff lamented. "The loss of both majors was a severe blow to the regiment."[16]

*　*　*

The noise from the Pennsylvanians' fight with the South Carolinians prompted Woodruff's three-regiment brigade, taking part in Davis's advance, to deploy at Overall's Creek. As it did so, the balance of McCook's column double-quicked to the front. As Woodruff's men took up their position, the battered survivors of the Anderson Troop stumbled back to the safety of the Union lines. The appearance of the cavalrymen surprised the foot soldiers, who had seen them trot by jauntily just a few hours before. "Some we met with saddles on their shoulders, their horses being shot, horses without drivers, ambulances filled with wounded men," observed

---

15 Kirk, *History of the 15th Pennsylvania Volunteer Cavalry*, 138. C. Irvine Walker, 10th South Carolina, "Promoted on the Field of Battle," *Confederate Veteran*, Vol. 34:46; C. Irvine Walker Papers, letter, Jan. 15, 1863.

16 Kirk, *History of the 15th Pennsylvania Volunteer Cavalry*, 86-87, 101-02, 138-39.

Captain Alvah Philbrook of the 24th Wisconsin. "The cavalrymen hailed our men and said, 'Boys, there is fun ahead for you.'" This was our first indication of a fight."[17]

The prospect of a fight spread like wildfire through McCook's column. "Forward came the order from our colonel," wrote Charles E. Belknap of the 21st Michigan. "There was no effort to hold us in order. The men with trailing guns, loaded as they were with equipment, could not make fast time. The weak ones soon fell behind and the strong-winded ones went to the front." Belknap continued:

> I could not suppress a feeling of horror at the sight that met my eyes. Scattered upon the ground were dead and dying troopers, their yellow-trimmed coats in strong contrast with the dead leaves upon the ground. Here and there about the woods were my ideal soldiers. I had seen dead men before, but these brave boys seemed to be of my flesh. They had come down the pike smiling, cheering, and without a thought that the moment was to be their last. I wiped the tears off my face with a coat sleeve and under my breath swore to avenge these boys.[18]

Woodruff's command, lining the banks of the creek, began a wary watch. Post's and Carlin's brigades soon arrived, stretching Davis's line south along one bank. Shortly, Sheridan's division marched into position north of the Wilkinson Pike, while Johnson's division, arriving last, supported Davis south of the pike. Charles C. Cunningham of the 5th Wisconsin Battery noted that "the army looked grand when marching in line of battle to take up their respective positions with the silken folds of the flags and banners of blue unfurled from regiment after regiment, while strains from the bands filled the air with melody and aroused my whole soul to a sentiment I cannot describe."[19]

Zahm's cavalrymen covered the right flank of McCook's march along the Wilkinson Pike in three parallel columns, each separated by a mile or more, with skirmishers and videttes providing connection between the regiments. The 1st Ohio held the left nearest the pike, the 3rd Ohio the center, and the 4th Ohio the right, advancing along and north of the Franklin Road. The 3rd made first contact

---

17 Captain Alvah Philbrook, Co. D, 24th Wisconsin, Philbrook Collection, State Historical Society of Wisconsin.

18 Charles E. Belknap, 21st Michigan, "My Recollections of Stone River," *National Tribune*, Mar. 7, 1893, 1-2.

19 Charles C. Cunningham, "A Cannoneer's Story: The Third Gun, 5th Wisconsin Battery," *National Tribune*, Sept. 27, 1888, 3.

and "shortly after both the right and left encountered pickets, driving them before them. After proceeding about one mile further, we came upon the enemy's cavalry and engaged them for three hours, sometimes the right wing, then the left, then the center, receiving several charges and drove the enemy some two miles," Zahm reported.

"The shots became more and more frequent and the excitement increased," wrote one trooper. "We quickened our pace, each regiment vying with the other for the first sight of our foes. Presently the 3rd Ohio … encountered Terry's Texas Rangers [8th Texas Cavalry] drawn up in line immediately in our front. 'Front into line, gallop, march!' and away we go, over fences and ditches. Our line is formed in a twinkling and the roar of our carbines is tremendous. They broke and ran down to our left and to their great surprise soon encountered the 1st Ohio. They give them a broadside, and the Rebels wheel, and run for camp closely followed by the 1st and 3rd Ohio."[20]

Suspecting an ambush, Zahm halted his Buckeyes and reformed the line. A larger line of Confederate cavalry soon appeared. The enemy offered "a splendid sight, just as the setting sun was throwing its golden rays from the neighboring treetops upon the glittering steel of those long and powerful lines," recalled the Ohio officer. Once within "easy range,"

the battle opened with terrible fury along the whole line. Finally, after about 20 minutes, the Rebels broke and fled in confusion and we pursued them a short distance when we were overtaken by General Stanley, our chief of cavalry, and were astonished to learn that we were almost within enemy lines being within three miles of Murfreesboro, and he ordered us to fall back about two miles and encamp.[21]

The 4th Ohio, however, would advance too far on the Franklin Road and found itself facing two Confederate artillery pieces with infantry support, as Wharton's troopers worked around the column's exposed flanks. The Rebels "opened a fire of grape on our advance," reported Major John Pugh. "In reconnoitering their position, we found a body of cavalry passing on our flank and soon discovered they were on our rear and flank. We attacked their whole force posted at the edge of the wood when a sharp skirmish ensued resulting in a loss on

20 OR 20/1:635.

21 Cavalry, 3rd Ohio Volunteer Cavalry, *Ohio State Journal*, Jan. 27, 1863.

our part of two killed, seven wounded, and nine prisoners. We captured seven prisoners from the enemy."[22]

As Crittenden's columns approached Murfreesboro, Bragg's engineers began to "prepare" the battlefield. It was decided that the outbuildings of the two-story brick home of Varner C. Cowan west of the Nashville Pike, about two miles out, obstructed the line of sight for the artillerists of Withers' Division, in Polk's Corps, and had to be removed. After unceremoniously booting the 66-year-old Cowan and his wife from their home, the soldiers, on Bragg's order, torched the outbuildings. Although the commander intended to preserve Cowan's residence, the wind "[u]nfortunately … was the wrong way and with the others it took fire and had the same fate," recalled John Spence, a Murfreesboro resident. Ed Porter Thompson of the Orphan Brigade's 4th Kentucky noted that "the flames had scarcely ceased to rage when the advance of the Federal army appeared along the front on each side of the turnpike and bivouacked in line of battle. As night drew on, the skies again became overclouded and the air exceedingly raw and disagreeable. Without tents, without fires, and on the Confederate side without adequate protection in the way of blankets and clothing, the troops prepared to sleep in line of battle."[23]

Three miles out on the Nashville Pike, Wagner's and Harker's brigades could see the spires of Murfreesboro in the distance. Wood ordered Harker to proceed toward town, which would lead him past Cowan's house. As they approached the pike's 2-mile marker, the entrenchments thrown up by Cheatham's Division became discernible through the lengthening shadows. "On arriving within two-and-a-half miles of Murfreesboro, the evidence was perfectly unmistakable that the enemy was in force immediately in our front prepared to resist seriously and determinedly our farther advance," Wood reported. "His troops, displayed in battle array, were plainly to be seen in our front. Up to this moment, the information received had indicated that the enemy would evacuate Murfreesboro, offering no serious opposition. But observations assured me that we should meet with a determined resistance."

Wood did not want to press his luck, as the rest of the army was not yet near Murfreesboro. Negley and Van Cleve were still a few miles in the rear, and Wood had no idea where McCook might be, though he heard firing to his right rear. "I did

22 *OR* 20/1:644.

23 Spence, *A Diary of the Civil War*, 57; Ed Porter Thompson, *History of the Orphan Brigade* (Dayton, 1991), 170.

not deem it proper to precipitate the force in advance on the entire force of the enemy with the remainder of our troops so far in the rear," he wrote. "Furthermore, the afternoon was well-nigh spent and an attempt to advance would have involved us in the obscurity of the night on unexamined ground in the presence of an unseen foe to whom our movements would have rendered us fearfully vulnerable"[24]

Anchoring the Confederate right on the eastern bank of Stones River, on Crittenden's front, were the four brigades of Breckinridge's Division, positioned at the edge of a forest between the Lebanon Road on the right and Stones River on the left. Daniel Adams held the far right, his right flank resting on the Lebanon Road; next in line to the west was Brig. Gen. William Preston's Brigade, then Colonel Joseph Palmer's command. Roger Hanson's Orphan Brigade covered the left flank, guarding an accessible ford over Stones River opposite the junction of the Nashville Pike and the Nashville and Chattanooga Railroad. "It was the strongest position the nature of the ground would allow," Breckinridge reported. "An open field of 800 yards in width extended along nearly the whole front of the line and was bounded on the opposite side by a line of forest similar to that occupied by us."[25]

General Hanson moved three of his regiments, along with Captain Robert H. Cobb's Kentucky battery—all under the command of Colonel Thomas Hunt of the 9th Kentucky—forward about 600 yards to Wayne's Hill, an eminence that commanded another good ford as well as the plains beyond extending to the Nashville Pike. Despite Breckinridge's strong position, Bragg remained concerned Rosecrans would cross Stones River at Jefferson and, by marching down the Lebanon Road, flank Breckinridge and take the town. That appeared to be a more likely scenario than the possibility Rosecrans would try to slog his way through the thick cedar brakes west of Stones River before attacking Bragg. To negate that alternative, General John Jackson's brigade, now attached to Breckinridge's Division, marched to the right of Adams's line along with Pegram's small cavalry brigade, which constituted the Army of Tennessee's extreme right flank.[26]

For the Federals, Generals Palmer and Wood found themselves in a quandary. "[We] halted our troops and rode some distance to the front to a point which we

24 *OR* 20/1:459. Wood does not mention Harker's reconnaissance in his official report, though he clearly ordered Harker to undertake it.

25 *OR* 20/1:782.

26 Ibid., 781.

Brigadier General Thomas J. Wood

Library of Congress

could see the enemy in strong force, evidently ready to receive us," Palmer would write. "While observing the enemy's forces and position, we were surprised to receive an order from General Rosecrans [passed along by Crittenden] in substance as follows: 'Stanley reports from Triune that the people say Bragg has abandoned Murfreesboro. You will therefore occupy the place with one division and camp your others near them.' Of course, General Wood and I knew the information which purported to come through General Stanley was erroneous."

Rosecrans claimed in his report that he had received a signal from Palmer claiming "he was in sight of Murfreesboro, and that the enemy were running," and hence gave the order to take the town—mistakenly believing Bragg had abandoned it. Both Wood and Palmer knew the order was folly, but until they could persuade Crittenden to call off Rosecrans's directive, they had to proceed. Wood ordered Harker to cross Stones River at a nearby ford and march into town. It would be a reconnaissance in force granting the possibility that Rosey's intelligence was correct. With a trained eye for topography, Wood realized that the commanding height of Wayne's Hill, looming over his line, was undoubtedly the key to the battlefield. If Harker's men could seize the hill, it would prove of great value if there were to be a fight.[27]

---

27 Palmer, *Personal Recollections*, 143-44. According to Palmer, "the fact that General Wood and I were actually observing the enemy when we received the order ought to afford conclusive evidence that General Rosecrans was wholly mistaken in his facts." Wood makes no mention in his official report of riding back with Palmer to protest his orders, but there is no doubt Crittenden countermanded the order on learning the true state of affairs at the front.

Night attacks were almost unheard of during the war, and Harker's men were about to demonstrate why. "Throwing a strong line of skirmishers over the stream," he reported, "orders were given to the 51st Indiana, 13th Michigan, and 73rd Indiana to cross simultaneously, form on the opposite bank, press forward, and seize the commanding heights beyond." It was almost dark before the skirmishers found the ford and splashed across the river, with Captain Milton Russell of the 51st Indiana in front.

"As we were fully aware that the enemy occupied the opposite bank and as none of our troops had up to that time crossed the river, it was necessary to proceed cautiously to avoid running into an ambuscade," noted William Hartpence of the 51st Indiana. "We moved down and crossed the river, wading it with the water in some places up to our hips. Talk about cold water or a cold bath, it was so cold that our teeth chattered!" recorded Captain Russell. "As the company was nearing the opposite shore, a terrific volley was fired from behind a rail fence not over 40 steps in our front. The enemy, being on higher ground than we, fired too high, their bullets taking effect in the regiment that was standing in line where we left them on the opposite side of the river."[28]

Russell continued:

> There was but two ways out of the trap: one was to recross the river; the other was to advance. It flashed through my mind that their guns were empty, ours loaded. I gave the command, 'On the right into line, double quick, charge!' And in less time that it takes to tell it, we were over that fence. The boys emptied their guns, fixed bayonets, and went at them. The Johnnies gave way and Co. A followed right on their heels.

Russell would receive the Medal of Honor in 1897 as "the first man to cross Stones River in the face of a galling fire from the concealed skirmishers of the enemy, leading his skirmishers up the hillside, and driving the opposing skirmishers before them." The captain later contended that, "had the charge proved a failure, I would have been court-martialed for exceeding my orders."[29]

Recalled Alfred Wade, adjutant of the 73rd Indiana: "[T]he order was given to our brigade alone 'Forward to Murfreesboro' which we received with a cheer and immediately advanced to the ford. The bed of the river is very rocky and full of

---

28 OR 20/1:501; W. F. Beyer and O. P. Keydel. "A Charge in Darkness and Water," *Deeds of Valor* (Detroit, 1907), 123-24.

29 Beyer, *Deeds of Valor*, 124.

holes so that the men went in at times waist deep. The enemy's skirmishers, of which they had a very strong line, opened fire upon us but we dashed across. The enemy continued their fire upon us until we formed the left wing which was first over and moving forward drove them back until we were near enough to the whole command of General Breckenridge to hear his officers rally their men and implore them to advance and drive us back."[30]

From atop Wayne's Hill, Colonel Hunt spied the advancing Federal line with grave concern. His men were scattered across the hill, having just finished their dinner of beef and cornmeal, and some already asleep when "bullets came whistling over and among them," noted Ed Porter Thompson. "It was a trying moment." Hunt could not determine the size of the force assailing his position, making "the situation critical in the extreme. Knowing their own weakness, being apprehensive of the strength of the attacking force, and conscious at first thought that their shots might be far more destructive to the retreating pickets than to the enemy, there was no alternative but for the Confederates to fall back under fire."

The Kentuckian gathered his wits, however, and ordered the 6th and 9th Kentucky into line in a cornfield, arraying the 9th on the left, Cobb's Battery supported by the 41st Alabama in the center, and the 6th on the right. In the increasing darkness, Colonel Abel D. Streight of the 51st Indiana saw a number of moving shadows he believed were Confederate reinforcements and ordered his regiment forward to sustain the skirmish line. "Before the regiment had entirely crossed the river, information came that the Rebels were advancing in line of battle just beyond the crest of the ridge about 400 yards to our front," Hartpence recalled. "It was at once determined to seize the crest before the Rebels could get there and we started on forward."[31]

"The enemy advanced and drove our skirmishers in," Jackman wrote. "They fired pretty briskly for a time, making the cornstalks rattle about us. In the darkness, the Federal skirmish line came right up among the battery which was unlimbered a little in advance of us. One of the Feds hallowed out, 'Boys, here is a cannon, let us get away from here," and they all skedaddled."

Added Johnny Green, also of the 9th Kentucky:

30 Diary of Adjutant Alfred B. Wade, 73rd Indiana, http://www.geocities.com/Athens/Pantheon/2106/excerpts.html, retrieved December 30, 2004.

31 Thompson, *History of the Orphan Brigade*, 171-72; William R. Hartpence, *History of the Fifty-First Indiana, Veteran Volunteer Infantry: A Narrative of its Organization, Marches, Battles, and Other Experiences in Camp and Prison From 1861 to* 1866 (Cincinnati, 1894), 106.

[T]he Yankees drove in our pickets and came with a rush at us in the dark. One volley from our lines drove them back, but our volley brought forth a volley of oaths from Mike McClarey who was out on the picket line when our boys were driven in. His comrade was wounded and to bring him home through a cornfield where the stalks had not been cut down and take care of his gun at the same time was a difficult task. But with his comrade on his back, Mike came swearing at us most vociferously, 'Sure, are you trying to kill your own men?' But his disgust was immense when upon laying his wounded friend down he discovered that a second ball had gone through his head and killed him, whereupon he remarked 'I thought you said it was your leg you were shot in.[32]

The 51st Indiana held the center of Harker's line, with the 73rd Indiana on the right and the 13th Michigan on the left. "The entire ridge seemed to issue forth a continuous flame of fire, yet not a man faltered, but seemed to strive to reach the desired point in advance of his comrades," Hartpence wrote. "The boldness of the movement and the alacrity with which it was executed with a well-directed fire struck terror to the Rebels who fell back in dire confusion. Orders came just then to advance no further but to hold our position."

It was at this point that the first Federal soldier was killed on the Stones River battlefield. The massive 6-ft, 7-in. frame of George Holbrook of Company F, 51st Indiana, offered an inviting target and he was struck down as he climbed the hill. "The Rebels had force enough within 800 yards of our position to have cut us all to pieces if they had the pluck to have attacked us," Wade noted. "Our position was perfectly untenable against a force even the same as ours and to have successfully retreated back across the river was an impossibility. The officers appeared to comprehend this at a glance, and yet all were determined if we must fight to win victory or die in the attempt. The skirmishers kept up a slow fire for an hour or two and as stray bullets were whistling through the ranks the men were ordered to lie down and remain in that position until the enemy should advance within ten paces."[33]

The 64th and 65th Ohio followed Harker's first line across Stones River. "Emerging from the river, we plunged into a thicket so dense that it seemed scarcely possible for even an unencumbered man to penetrate it," recounted Wilbur Hinman. "But we got through with torn clothes and scratched faces and

---

32 Davis, *The Orphan Brigade*, 66-67; A. D. Kirwan, editor. *Johnny Green of the Orphan Brigade: The Journal of a Confederate Soldier* (Lexington, 1956), 65-66.

33 James K. Bowers, Co. F, 51st Indiana, "First Man Killed at Stones River," *National Tribune*, Nov. 14, 1901, 2; Wade Diary.

entered a large cornfield in which the dry stalks were still standing. There was no firing until we had advanced a considerable distance into the cornfield[,] then the Rebels opened suddenly with a volley that made each particular hair stand on end. The bullets came as close as we cared to have them and quite close enough to appease our yearning desire for a fight."

Private Charles H. Nickerson, Hinman's comrade in the 65th Ohio, noted that "it was so dark that we could not see anyone over four or five rods [away] but the balls whistled and we could see the flash of the guns most plainly to suit me. We could hear the enemy give commands and were marching up to support their pickets. I heard them forward and halt one battalion and order them to lay down, they expecting us to come on. But we knew enough for that. They were not 20 rods from us."[34]

Colonel Streight moved among his 51st Indiana, cautioning them to lay low and conceal themselves among the tall weeds and cornstalks while the Confederates advanced on the isolated Federals. "They were allowed to come within 30 steps when we opened fire on them with such effect that they hardly waited for a reply, but broke and fled again," he wrote. The Confederates fired several volleys before retreating up the hill, one wounding Samuel Snyder, the 65th Ohio's commissary sergeant, as he rode behind the lines carrying dispatches. "When I had come to where Snyder was, I asked him where the regiment was and as he partly turned around on his horse, there came a Rebel bullet that struck him under the bridge of the nose," recalled John Body, Company A's orderly sergeant. "He fell off his horse and I caught him in my arms. He was knocked crazy; he didn't know anything."

Major Horatio Whitbeck ordered Body to transport Snyder back across the river to the regimental surgeons. "There was some very lively work between the skirmish lines and it seemed as if nearly every cornstalk was struck with bullets, the firing was so brisk," he wrote.[35]

*   *   *

---

34 Hinman, *Story of the Sherman Brigade*, 339; Diary of Private Charles H. Nickerson, Co. E, 65th Ohio, SRNBP.

35 Hartpence, *History of the 51st Indiana*, 106; "Wounded at Stones River," Orderly Sergeant John Body, Co. A, 65th Ohio, *National Tribune*, June 15, 1899, 3.

Harker's men grimly held their tenuous foothold on Wayne's Hill until about 10:00 p.m. Early in the fight, the colonel learned from a prisoner that "an entire division of the enemy was in my front. Movements along my entire front and flanks indicated that a strong force was near me." With the brigade in a perilous position, a river to the rear, and an aroused Confederate division on its front, he knew they needed to pull back or risk destruction in the morning. "I reported this to the general commanding the division at the same time indicating that I could hold the position until reinforced," Harker wrote. "I soon received orders to recross the stream which I did, nearly occupying the same ground as before crossing. This movement was so quickly executed as not to excite the suspicion of the enemy."[36]

It was also conducted so quietly it went undetected by some of Harker's own troops. Wade sent a company out to the skirmish line, only to find the regiment gone when he returned. "Somewhat puzzled at this I went along the line we had occupied to the center where I found the 51st Indiana still in position and learned that the brigade was being quietly withdrawn," he later wrote. "I forded the stream on foot and found the regiment evacuated for the night."

Although the withdrawal escaped the Confederates' notice, nervous members of the 13th Michigan pulling back off the hill spied moving shadows along their retreat and opened fire, believing what was actually the 65th Ohio were Breckinridge's men who had worked around their open left flank. Fortunately, none of the Buckeyes were hit and their identities were quickly established, but it underscored the danger of nighttime operations.[37]

"Our unquenchable zeal ought to have carried us right into Murfreesboro that night, but it didn't," Hinman confessed. "In fact, everybody was glad enough when the order to retire reached us. We did not know much about war yet, but it seemed to us that our advance was a mistake."

Granted, most Federal soldiers were relieved to be back on safer ground, but Colonel Michael Shoemaker of the 13th Michigan was convinced a golden opportunity was lost that night on Wayne's Hill. "If our advance had not been stopped by order of our own superior officers, we would have surprised the enemy before they could have formed their ranks and driven them from their position which would have left Murfreesboro open to us without further fighting. The Confederates evidently were not expecting us to cross Stones River so late in the

---

36 *OR* 20/1:501.

37 *History of the Seventy-Third Indiana Volunteers* (Washington, 1909), 117; Wade Diary; Nickerson Diary.

First Lieutenant Wilbur F. Hinman,
Co. E, 65th Ohio

Gary Milligan

day and were, in my opinion, not prepared to offer an effectual resistance to our advance had it continued."

Thompson agreed with Shoemaker's take. "[T]he loss of this important position would have thoroughly disconcerted all the plans of Bragg and changed the entire aspect of the battle," he later elaborated. "The Federals being once established upon it, the natural strength of Bragg's position would have been rendered nugatory."[38]

By the time Harker's men crossed the north bank of Stones River about 11:00 p.m., a cold rain was falling. Casualties had been light, a few killed and wounded in each regiment, but Harker's men survived the scrape relatively intact, though admittedly shaken. "What a horrible night to recall," wrote James Bowers of the 51st Indiana. "We were soaked to the skin because of twice wading the river and to add to their discomfort a cold, sleety rain fell the balance of the night. We lay all night on the cold wet ground without a fire to warm us or even dry our drenched clothes."

"I was very much fatigued, having been on the move since 3 o'clock in the morning," Shoemaker recalled. "Randall, my attendant, took my saddle from my horse, placed it on the ground as a pillow with a thin rubber blanket for a mattress, and on it I stretched myself with my cap on my head, booted, and spurred, my

---

38 Hinman, *History of the Sherman Brigade*, 339; "Narrative of Colonel Michael Shoemaker," 1878 Annual Meeting of the Pioneer Society of Michigan; Thompson, *History of the Orphan Brigade*, 172.

sword buckled to my side. My head was hardly on the saddle before I was sound asleep although the crack of the musket could be heard quite frequently."[39]

It was a melancholy night in the Anderson Troop's camp, the men disheartened by the heavy losses during their clash on the Wilkinson Pike. "Around the fires in low, sad voices, the calamity was discussed and the mysterious presentiments of some of the killed were made known," recalled John Williams. "Herring had written a line to his wife on the flyleaf of his pocket Bible to the effect that he was about to be killed. [Will] Kimber had, that morning, been unusually anxious to wash his face and upon being asked in a jocular way why he was so particular, replied with a sad smile that he would 'make a better-looking corpse.'"

"Rosengarten had expressed the belief that he would not come back alive while Ward had a noticeable depression of spirits, which even his natural gaiety could not conceal. The gloom created by the day's tragedy was forgotten in slumber, but even there it followed me. In a dream, I again opened the flap of my tent and saw a melancholy figure standing alone, listening to the voice of that fate which had now closed about him forever."[40]

McCook's corps camped in the woods along Overall's Creek. "This was the most uncomfortable place we ever bivouacked in, not only because the known proximity of the enemy irritated us and kept the men restless, but the field had been freshly ploughed and the rain that had fallen just before had made of the soil a nasty, pasty mud above ankle deep," wrote bugler Francis. The three-days' rations issued in Nashville started to run out Monday night. For those who had husbanded their rations, a cold meal of cold beans, hardtack, raw pork, and water sufficed.

"Our rations were exhausted and there were no means for supplying the want," complained 1st Lt. Otis Moody of the 51st Illinois. "By some mismanagement common at such times the commissary had brought along a lot of flour instead of hard bread. This would do very well in camp, but what could we do with flour on a march and especially on the battlefield. Nevertheless, some of the boys from pure necessity did mix up some of it with water, twist it around their ramrods, and bake it in the ashes. Others borrowed a few crackers from the boys of a neighboring brigade."[41]

---

39 Account of Private James K. Bowers, 51st Indiana, *Proceedings of the Eighth Annual Session of the Survivors of the Battle of Stones River*, Kokomo, Indiana, Jan. 2, 1908, 5; Shoemaker Narrative.

40 Williams, *Leaves from a Trooper's Diary*, 47-48.

41 Francis, *Narrative of a Private Soldier*, 102-03; Diary of 1st Lt. Otis Moody, Co. K, 51st Illinois, http://51stillinois.org/moody_st_river.html. Retrieved Dec. 13, 2015.

Opportunities for soldiers to cook or boil coffee that night proved limited once McCook—concerned the Confederates would shell the Federal camps—forbid fires after dark. The gloom of night had fairly set in when a cold drenching rain started again, making for a miserable night. Chaplain Haigh wrote that "we marched down the Wilkinson Pike and were ordered into a cornfield, the regiment preserving a line of battle behind a rail fence but forbidden to build fires, or pitch tents, or speak loudly, or do anything which could reveal our presence to the enemy's pickets. The only indulgence granted was to gather the cornstalks for bedding that we might not lie in pure mud."

The orders against erecting tents inspired novel alternatives for respite from the rain. Sergeant Major Rudolphus Peake of the 74th Illinois managed to spend a comfortable night in a cotton house. "I dug a hole in the cotton big enough to lay in and slept as easy as I ever did in a feather bed," he wrote, "but the rest of the regiment slept out of doors and they said it rained, but I knew nothing about it."[42]

Wilson Vance of the 21st Ohio slept soundly "on an old rubber blanket wrapped in a cavalry overcoat with a conveniently shaped stone for a pillow and a number of inconveniently-shaped pebbles ranging in size from a hickory nut to a goose egg lending variety to his couch." Vance slept "with the full knowledge that so far as we and the enemy in our immediate front were concerned, the issue was joined and the actual conflict might begin at any moment."

"[T]here was not much sleep all that night," recalled Francis of the 88th Illinois. He could observe the flickering light of the enemy campfires "not far to our front and we frequently heard the rustling noise of large bodies of troops moving from one place to another." The whistling of locomotives, which he described as "incessant," coupled with the rumbling of cars "denoted that we were not far from the town of Murfreesboro and that unusual activity prevailed there." Long before daylight he and his comrades "perceived that immediately in front of us there was a line of earthworks that had been evacuated by the enemy the day before, and apparently in some considerable haste because the Southerners had left behind them a number of articles such as cedar wood canteens, miniature lager beer kegs, wooden spoons, and empty meal bags."[43]

---

42 Bennett, *History of the 36th Illinois*, 325; Peake Letter.

43 Vance, Wilson. "A Man and a Boy at Stone River." *Blue and Gray*, Vol. 1 (1893), 348; Francis, *Narrative of a Private Soldier*, 102-03.

Almost a Battle: Moves and Thrusts on December 30

WITH GENERAL McCOOK now at Overall's Creek the afternoon of December 29, General Bragg transferred John McCown's Division from its reserve position east of Stones River to Leonidas Polk's Corps, extending Polk's line south of the Franklin Road. At this point, Bragg believed General Rosecrans's primary path of advance would be west of the river along the Nashville and Wilkinson turnpikes. He also fully expected an attack to come on Tuesday, though preliminary scouting reports from Wheeler indicated that Rosecrans had a column poised to march down the Lebanon Pike, in position to strike Bragg's right east of the river earlier. To verify the reports, Bragg ordered Joe Wheeler to head north along the pike to Jefferson, report on enemy dispositions, and if possible, attack Rosecrans's vulnerable supply wagons on the Nashville Pike.

Wheeler's 1,600 or so troopers had already put in a full day's work contesting Crittenden's advance on the Nashville Pike and had encamped north of Murfreesboro, on his army's right. The weary men had barely begun to rest when orderly sergeants rambled in to wake them. "At midnight, after a few hours rest, the word 'forward' was given, the little brigadier was in the saddle," recalled one of Wheeler's staff officers. "It was dark; a cold, drizzly rain fell, but nothing could dampen the ardor that beat in those valiant and trusty hearts. Then it was resolved to boldly attack the rear of that mighty Yankee host."

Tomorrow, as his lines move so vaingloriously forward," Wheeler reportedly said, "his heart shall shake with fear to hear that his trains are burning, his supplies cut off, and thousands of Southern cavalry hovering in his rear like birds of prey."[1]

Recalled Captain George Knox Miller of the 8th Confederate Cavalry: "In a few minutes we were following General Wheeler up the Lebanon Pike at a full gallop. The rain was falling and the darkness was so dense that a man could not see the comrade riding at his side. Two miles further on, we left the Lebanon Pike and took the one leading to the little village of Jefferson which was directly in the rear of the Yankee army. Daylight found us near that village where we halted and fed our horses."

At 4:00 a.m., Wheeler reported to Bragg that the Lebanon Pike was free of Federal troops, though he could see their campfires across Stones River. Finding the Sharps Spring Ford at Jefferson unguarded, the column crossed the river at nearby West Fork and soon could see the white canvas covers of Federal supply wagons—the train of Colonel John Starkweather's 3rd Brigade in Rousseau's division.[2]

Rousseau's men had spent the Monday in camp resting after their all-night march on Sunday, but by 8:30 a.m. December 30, his lead brigades were on the Nashville Pike heading toward Negley's division and Crittenden's corps, roughly eight miles ahead. Starkweather's brigade was camped about two miles northwest of Jefferson along the Lebanon Pike near Stewart's Creek, assigned as the division's rearguard. The 64 wagons constituting his train had rolled north from Nolensville the day before, heading along the Nashville Pike to join Rousseau.

Moving along the Jefferson Pike, the train was not quite 500 yards from Starkweather's camp when Wheeler's men hove into sight about 10:00 a.m. The Confederates stealthily approached the train from the adjacent woods. "Forward, but cautiously men, cautiously, close up quickly, but without noise," recalled one trooper. "A shot—a volley—a yell—and like the wolf on the fold, the men of the South hurled themselves on the invader."

"General Wheeler fell upon their rear with a charge and a whoop which spread consternation among the guards and teamsters," reported the Richmond Dispatch. "Quick as a thought,"

---

1 "General Wheeler's Operations," *Winchester Daily Bulletin*, Jan. 13, 1863, 2.

2 Miller Monograph.

An unknown Western Theater Confederate cavalryman armed with a revolver and D-handle Bowie knife.

Library of Congress

the traces were cut, linchpins removed, and the fore-wheels cut down and fire set to at least 50 wagons laden with the baggage of officers, company stores, ammunition, and clothing. Every soldier who wished provided himself with comfortable clothing, boots, hats, overcoats, overalls, pistols, revolvers, rifles, saddles, bridles, horses, mules, or what else might suit his fancy or comfort.[3]

One can credit Starkweather's men for their quick response to the attack. "The men were all near their stacks of arms in various positions and occupations in no expectation of immediate trouble," stated adjutant Michael Fitch of the 21st Wisconsin, positioned at the brigade's rear. "About 10 o'clock the camp was suddenly aroused by the rapid approach of the brigade wagon train, horses and mules running at full speed," recalled another Wisconsin soldier. "The shouts of the drivers and the firing of guns announced that the Rebels had attacked our wagons. Colonel Starkweather immediately appeared before his quarters and in a stentorian voice ordered the several regiments to 'fall in.' The 21st Wisconsin was encamped on the road nearest to the attack and were ordered out at the double quick to meet the enemy. This order was obeyed so promptly that Colonel Harrison Hobart formed his men into companies while they were upon the run."[4]

John Otto of the 21st Wisconsin remembered that the regiment was eating breakfast when the alarm sounded. "The contents of cups and pans flew in the fire

---

3 "The Dashing Operation of Our Cavalry in Rear of Rosecrans," *Richmond Dispatch*, Jan. 19, 1863, 1; "General Wheeler's Operations."

4 Michael H. Fitch, *Echoes of the Civil War as I Hear Them* (New York, 1905), 93; "The Old Flag," 21st Wisconsin, Vol. 10, Quiner Scrapbooks, Correspondence of the Wisconsin Volunteers, Wisconsin Historical Society.

and in two minutes we were flying along the road," he wrote. "About 40 rods back, Charles Warner who drove the regimental headquarters wagon team came dashing on, whipping the mules unmercifully; some ten rods further we saw the next wagon, the mules on the ground being shot while four Rebels busily chopped away at the spokes of the wheels. But seeing us coming, they jumped in the saddle and galloped away."[5]

The 21st Wisconsin double-quicked to close on the train. "On each side of the train, rapidly gaining on the head wagon, was a line of detached Confederate cavalry, pistols in hand, firing and hallooing at the drivers to stop," Fitch wrote. "Our regiment was in two ranks and when we reached the head wagon, we opened out, allowing the train to come between us but kept on the double quick until we came to the rear of the train, the Confederate cavalry falling back as we advanced. We then halted, formed across the road, and commenced firing at a lot of Confederate cavalrymen immediately in our front who were apparently preparing to charge our line. What was left of the train went into camp and we soon discovered that the woods a few hundred yards in front of us was full of Confederate cavalry, and that we would have our hands full to hold the advanced position we had taken."[6]

After moving to a nearby knoll, the 21st hunkered down to await the Confederate advance, while Starkweather's other three regiments quickly caught up and fell into line, assuming defensive positions blocking the pike. With no intention of charging into a line of Federal infantry, Wheeler broke off the attack, using the two guns of Wiggins' Battery to help cover his withdrawal.

*   *   *

The reconnaissance phase of Wheeler's mission had been successful and nearly bloodless. It was clear Rosecrans had no plan to advance down the Lebanon Pike for a strike on Bragg's right. Although Wheeler claimed 50 burned wagons and hundreds of Federal prisoners, Starkweather reported only 22 of 64 wagons lost and 122 men captured—about half from the 24th Illinois and half the 21st Wisconsin. "It was a bad piece of business for us," Otto recalled. "After we had

---

5 Otto, *Memoirs of a Dutch Mudsill*, 79.

6 Fitch, *Echoes of the Civil War*, 94.

driven off the Rebels, the other regiments came up to assist us but found nothing to do but to look at the ruins."[7]

From there, Wheeler headed north toward La Vergne and a potential crack at the traffic on the Nashville Pike. "To saddle and away before the roar of our pieces in the rear should bring up superior forces of the enemy," a Confederate recalled. "Over stock and rock, hills, fences, and ravines, burning wagons behind us, roaring artillery far to the right of us, hams strung to the saddle bow, mules with tattered traces coating the country around us. We came to with the sport of a Christmas holiday towards the village of LaVergne. The Yankee pickets had promised to give the 1st Alabama a Christmas ball; Bragg was giving them the music while we were dancing to Wheeler's quickstep."[8]

Arriving at La Vergne about 2:00 p.m., Wheeler would find a much larger prize than earlier in the day: hundreds of wagons comprising McCook's supply train. According to Sergeant John Gallagher of the 81st Indiana, the train had sat idle in camp all morning, expecting orders to move toward Murfreesboro at any moment. "As they were fixing to make themselves comfortable, they looked out back from the back of the wagons and beheld a sight that caused their hearts to beat quickly," recalled Gallagher, one of the train's guards, "for as far as they could see there was nothing but the enemy's cavalry galloping about, dressed in the well-known butternut clothing, whooping, yelling, and rushing around like madmen in every direction. The boys seized their guns and ran to the nearest house and breathlessly awaited further developments. No one seemed to have any command or authority over the men or train."

Gallagher would be among prisoners captured by the Confederate squad of cavalry. "All this took place in less time than it takes to write it," he recalled. "We were ordered, in no very polite manner, to march quickly up to a hill a few hundred yards in our front. Our men could be seen running in all directions, and we could see the enemy in every direction galloping about, showing plainly that we were surrounded before the charge was made upon us." Gallagher continued:

On arriving at the top of the hill we came upon a line of our men drawn up in two ranks. We were ordered to fall in with them, and a Rebel harangue was made to us by Colonel [William S.] Hawkins, C. S. A. The speech was made in a quick, excited manner and we were ordered to hold up our right hands and swear that we would not take up arms against

7 Otto, *Memoirs of a Dutch Mudsill*, 95.

8 "The Dashing Operation of Our Cavalry."

the Southern Confederacy until honorably exchanged. As soon as this was done the men broke ranks and scattered in every direction. Everything was done in the midst of excitement. Rebel horsemen kept yelling and riding in every direction. By this time all of our trains were fired and burning rapidly.[9]

Amid the clamor, some Confederate troopers reportedly separated and killed the Negro teamsters, tossing their bodies into a ditch along the road—a travesty Leonard Beck of the 4th Michigan Cavalry discovered days later. "A considerable force of Rebels got in our rear and committed many atrocious deeds," he wrote. "Negroes employed by the government as teamsters were ruthlessly murdered and their bodies thrown into the ditches bordering on the pike. Whole wagon trains were burned and the road strewn with dead mules, horses, Negroes."[10]

Wheeler considered it another almost bloodless triumph. "Scores of Yankees were seen flying about the streets while the teamsters forsook their wagons and endeavored to escape, but escape was impossible," wrote a Confederate trooper. "Five hundred prisoners surrendered, 150 richly laden wagons were consigned to the flames, while a thousand mules or horses were carried off or stampeded. The booty was rich and the men felt as though they had entered the den of the forty thieves. Every man had a prize: a horse, watch, Negro, rifle, sword, or flag."

George Knox Miller wrote that "the officers went quickly to work paroling prisoners, while the men set fire to the train. It was a scene that would have rejoiced all Rebeldom to behold, but we tarried only an hour at LaVergne and then turned in a westward direction. We had gone only a mile or two when we heard the Yankees in revenge shelling the innocent village of LaVergne, thinking no doubt that they were scattering death in the Rebel ranks." What Miller heard was the report of two guns of Battery D of the 1st Michigan Light Artillery, part of Thomas's corps.[11]

Moses Walker's 1st Brigade in Fry's 3rd Division, had just settled into camp at Stewardsboro after an all-night march from Nolensville when "the camp was alarmed and the 'fall in' sounded on all sides," recalled Captain John Inskeep of the 17th Ohio. "Colonel Walker came riding into camp with his hat off yelling at the top of his voice 'get ready my lads!' In five minutes, the brigade was in battle array

---

9 George W. Morris, *History of the 81st Regiment of Indiana Volunteer Infantry in the Great War of the Rebellion, 1861 to 1865...A Regimental Roster, Prison Life, Adventures, Etc.* (Louisville, 1901), 31-32.

10 Private Leonard Beck, Co. F, 4th Michigan Volunteer Cavalry, *Adrian Daily Watchtower*, Jan. 29, 1863, 1. Beck's account of this atrocity was corroborated by a *Harper's Weekly* correspondent in its Feb. 7, 1863, edition, who reported finding 21 bodies.

11 "The Dashing Operation of Our Cavalry"; Miller Monograph.

and quickly formed in line of battle across the road facing LaVergne. Colonel Walker was riding up and down the line with his hat off and flourishing his sword while every eye was straining to see the enemy."

Walker left the 82nd Indiana behind to guard the camp and marched double-quick with his three Ohio regiments toward La Vergne. "The distance from my camp to LaVergne was a little more than 2½ miles," he wrote, "and though the infantry moved with great rapidity, we were unable to reach LaVergne before nearly all the wagons and their contents had been destroyed. By pushing forward the artillery with all haste, I was able to get the two guns into position on this side of the town before the Rebels succeeded in paroling near all the men connected with the train. Many of the Rebel cavalry were engaged in trying to drive away the mules belonging to the train, but the timely administration of shells put an effectual stop to driving away the mules."

"[W]e arrived in town in time to see 132 wagons in flames which were loaded with camp equipage, quartermaster, and commissary stores belonging to General McCook's corps," Inskeep wrote. "Several hundred mules were running around loose in harness, which the Rebels could not drive fast enough to safety for themselves."[12]

To restore order and drive off the last of Wheeler's troopers, Walker split his command. A small detachment of the 1st Ohio Cavalry accompanied by the 31st Ohio vainly pursued Wheeler to the southwest on the Old Liberty Road. They scoured the country for about three miles, striking the pike near La Vergne "with nothing to contend with but briars, weeds, and cedar bushes. We didn't see a Rebel," grumbled Sergeant Thomas Talbott of the 31st Ohio. "The infantry couldn't get close enough to open on the train burners."

The cavalrymen had somewhat better luck and returned to camp later that evening with five prisoners. Walker also sent detachments from the 17th Ohio and 38th Ohio along the Nashville Pike to secure property that had not been burned or killed, which collected and transported it back to Nashville. "We got between 300–400 mules, 50 cattle, and a few wagons," Inskeep later recalled. About sunset, Walker ordered the Hoosiers of the 82nd Indiana north on the Nashville Pike to escort any wagons heading toward Rosecrans's position at Murfreesboro.

12 Inskeep Diary; *OR* 20/1:441.

With the loss of so many commissary wagons, replacement rations would be desperately needed.[13]

Joyously, Wheeler's command pounded cross-country to strike another target, reaching it in the waning afternoon hours. "A liberal application of the spur for two hours and down we swooped like a tornado upon quiet, little Nolensville," Miller remembered. Roughly 50 Federal prisoners captured between La Vergne and Nolensville would accompany the Confederate swarm, Sergeant Gallagher among them.

"Our companions told us to look through the timber and we would see something, as they were about to make a charge," Gallagher recalled. "We did so and could see a small town and near it were five or six United States army wagons. We could see the boys in blue walking about, and some of them appeared to be getting supper. Presently a long yell was given and a long line of Rebel cavalry charged down upon them and their wagons. They ran in every direction, but it was in vain, for what was a handful of men against thousands of the enemy. No doubt the enemy felt glorious over such a charge as that, and some of them did, too, because shortly afterward we saw several of them under the influence of whiskey taken from a sutler's wagon that was captured with the rest. These wagons were all burnt the same as were ours; and with a small addition of fresh prisoners, we took the road again."[14]

"It was scarcely more than LaVergne repeated," Miller offered. "We found scattered squads of Yankees here and there and 150 wagons, mostly loaded with ammunition and medicines. We found large numbers of their wagons filled with corn, bed clothing, house furniture, eggs, poultry, and butter just plundered from the farms. We mounted their guards bare back on their mules, burned their wagons, and rode on. The spoils of war were consigned to the flames and the Yankees sent on their way rejoicing with paroles in their pockets. You could not have made them happier by presenting them a Western homestead."[15]

As Wheeler's raid sowed mayhem in the Federal rear, it was fair to wonder why there was no Federal response. Patrolling an army's flanks and rear areas was, of course, the cavalry's job, but Rosecrans was impeded by his army's paucity of

---

13 Diary of Sergeant Thomas J. Talbott, Co. G, 31st Ohio, Spared & Shared website, https://sparedshared22.wordpress.com/2021/10/09/1861-64-the-civil-war-diaries-of-thom as-jefferson-talbot-co-g-31st-ovi/; retrieved June 15, 2022.; *OR* 20/1:441-442; Inskeep Diary.

14 Miller Monograph; Morris, *History of the 81st Indiana*, 34.

15 Miller Monograph.

Brigadier General Joseph Wheeler

Library of Congress

troopers, with Stanley operating on the army's far right, screening McCook's advance with Zahm's brigade and some reserve cavalry. Although Colonel Minty's brigade, screening Crittenden's wing during the march to Murfreesboro, was closest to La Vergne, on the afternoon of December 30 it was busily engaged as videttes just behind Crittenden's battle line "with orders to drive up stragglers." After news of Wheeler's attacks reached army headquarters, Minty led the 4th Michigan and a battalion of the 7th Pennsylvania Cavalry back up the Nashville Pike and skirmished with about 100 of Wheeler's rearguard between Stewardsboro and La Vergne, though that did little to slow Wheeler's path of destruction.[16]

*   *   *

As Wheeler's troopers surged north on the Lebanon Pike early that morning, Rosecrans summoned McCook to his headquarters on the Murfreesboro Pike. "I arrived there at 3:30 a.m.," McCook reported, "and received my instructions which were that the left of my line was to be thrown forward until it became parallel or nearly so with Stones River, the extreme right to rest on or near the Franklin road." The plan that day was for Crittenden and Thomas to maintain their positions waiting for a junction with McCook, advancing on the Wilkinson Pike.

Rosecrans's intentions for the balance of December 30 once that junction occurred were unclear. His official report fails to mention his plans, but Crittenden mentioned in his own report an afternoon request to Rosecrans permitting him to

16 OR 20/1:623-624.

open his attack across Stones River; Rosecrans apparently replied that McCook was not yet warmly engaged enough to merit an advance on the left. That ultimately was the battle plan for December 31, as detailed below.[17]

While the main body of the Army of the Cumberland slowly closed in on the Army of Tennessee, the front lines that separated the two began to take shape. Crittenden's wing held the Federal left, tucked into the bends of Stones River with Wood's division on the left and north of the Nashville Pike; Palmer's on the right and south of the pike; and Van Cleve's division in reserve along the pike. Negley's division, Thomas's only troops in the field at this point, formed on Palmer's right following a march through a dark cedar brake into the edge of woods near the Wilkinson Pike.

Rosecrans's plan was for McCook to push across Overall's Creek along the Wilkinson Pike. Sheridan's division would form on Negley's right. Davis's division would then come in on Sheridan's right later in the afternoon, followed by Johnson's division, which would take position on the army's right flank. All told, the Federal line would eventually stretch three miles flank to flank. The army would be dangerously extended, however, and the absence of connecting roads behind the lines would make the task of reinforcing one wing from other sectors difficult.

The Pioneer Brigade, commanded by Captain James St. Clair Morton, quickly proved an invaluable addition to the army. After spending the night of December 29 rebuilding two bridges over Stewart's Creek, the men marched out early the next day and were put to work behind the front lines. Captain Lyman Bridges' 1st Battalion aligned on the army's left flank and constructed a line of field fortifications; by nightfall, it was busily improving the fords over Stones River to support Rosecrans's planned cross-river assault. The 3rd Battalion under Captain Robert Clements used axes to cut some roads through the thick cedar forest that lay behind Palmer's and Negley's positions, providing access to the front for artillery and supplies. These roads, little noted at the time, were salvation for thousands of men the following day.

George Wagner's brigade held the center of Wood's division, covering the fords that Harker's brigade used during its crossing the night before. "Our line of battle was 600 yards from the lines of rifle pits established by the enemy," noted a 57th Indiana veteran. "The open ground to the left, front, and right was one vast field of cotton and the well-filled pods were hanging from the stalks when we took possession of the ground." Confederate sharpshooters kept up an annoying fire

17 Ibid., 254.

throughout the day. "Their balls now and then whistled by our heads or fell short in the cotton field," he added.

In anticipation of the coming fight, the ordnance sergeant of the 97th Ohio distributed an extra 20 rounds per man to supplement the standard 40 rounds in the cartridge boxes. "We were eager listeners to occasional heavy infantry and artillery skirmishes, mostly upon the right wing," reported one soldier in the regiment. "We felt the contending forces were whetting their steel for more desperate work." Joshua DeWees of the 97th, on picket duty in front of Wagner's brigade, reported that he was so close to the enemy lines that he "could hear the Rebels calling their regiment's rolls" and stated they had been "drove as far as they will go kindly."[18]

The 64th Ohio also maintained a line of picket posts along the river and at times came under a hot fire of both musketry and artillery. "About 8 a.m. the enemy's battery stationed on an eminence [Wayne's Hill] near the right bank of Stones River opened a severe fire of shot and shell upon my camp," Harker reported. The Confederates were Cobb's Battery of the Orphan Brigade who, now that they could see the Federal force that had threatened the battery the night before, opened fire with four smoothbores. Harker's men took cover, and Captain Cullen Bradley's 6th Ohio Battery rolled up and opened counterbattery fire with its two sections of 10-pounder Parrott rifles at a range of 1,500 yards. Cox's 10th Indiana Battery also opened fire on the Kentuckians.

It was a quick exchange that the Federal gunners won "after an engagement of 15 minutes, expending 72 rounds of shell and solid shot," Bradley claimed, "sustaining no damage except the loss of one sponge bucket struck by the enemy's shot"—a 6-pound solid shot, according to gunner Daniel Hoover, who wrote: "The enemy fired rapid and close and many had very narrow escapes. When an enemy is firing directly in front with solid shot, you can see the solid shot coming and almost every time they can be dodged. It was owing to this fact that none were hurt in the engagement."[19]

The artillery exchange might have been harmless to the primary combatants, but ricocheting shells have a nasty habit of showing up at the wrong place at the

---

18 *Annals of the 57th Indiana*, 152-53; Flip, 97th Ohio, *Morgan County Herald*, Feb. 13, 1862, 1; Joseph W. DeWees, ed., *Joshua DeWees: His Civil War* Diary (1991), 12.

19 *OR* 20/1:478, 502; Private Daniel Hoover, 6th Ohio Battery, *Summit County Beacon*, Jan. 22, 1863, 2.

"right" time. Battery H of the 4th US Light Artillery received several of Cobb's errant shots, with one man killed, one wounded, and one horse disabled.

Rosecrans's headquarters, located near the front, came under fire during the exchange. "The General commanding, not yet mounted, stood in front of his quarters watching the progress of affairs when the fire opened," recalled William Bickham. "The first compliment [sic] whizzed over a little crest and ricocheted in the road. The next cannon ball was in better range, striking nearer the general and the third whizzed almost in line with him and carried away the head of Daniel McDonald of the 4th U.S. Cavalry, one of the orderlies. It was deemed prudent to move and the General and staff rode up the slope to a less exposed position. It had begun to rain again and the prospect was dismal."[20]

For the bracing Confederates, it proved to be a miserable day of waiting with "much of the danger" but "without any of the excitement of a battle," as one soldier put it. Sergeant Dan Turney of the 2nd Kentucky noted in his diary that on December 30 "matters grow much warmer, the cloud lowers, and the storm will soon burst upon us in all its fury. Heavy cannonading all day; very active skirmishing with many casualties." Squire Helm Bush of the 6th Kentucky moaned that "I never suffered so from cold in any one day in all my life," and Ed Porter Thompson noted that "the weather had now set in windy, cloudy, and cold, and the situation of the men was trying beyond conception. Fires were forbidden and so, damp, cold and in much anxiety and suspense, they passed the time."[21]

"The day wore away but no attack was made," recorded one of Cobb's gunners,

> and the quick fire of the skirmishers or short artillery duels broke the silence which reigned over both armies. The Yankee sharpshooters resorted to all kinds of taunts to induce our skirmishers to disclose their positions. They would cry "Rebs, get off that wet ground, you will catch your death of cold," or "show your colors" and other expressions too low to repeat. A wag on our side remarked that this was a political difficulty and thought the Yankees were entirely too personal. Another when asked "Rebs, have you had your

20 Bickham, *Rosecrans' Campaign*, 182.

21 Diary of Sergeant Dan E. Turney, Co. G, 2nd Kentucky, C.S.A., SRNBP; Diary of Orderly Sergeant Squire Helm Bush, Co. B, 6th Kentucky, C.S.A., Filson Historical Society; Thompson, *History of the Orphan Brigade*, 173.

breakfast?" was rash enough to reply "yes, but the Hartsville braves didn't!" The next moment 50 balls whistled around his ears.[22]

Brigadier General James Chalmers's Mississippians spent the day lying behind their rifle pits a few hundred yards southeast of the Cowan House while skirmishers from the 9th Mississippi Sharpshooter Battalion traded shots with the 36th Indiana and 2nd Kentucky. "Although the troops were completely drenched with rain, their ardor and anxiety to meet the vandal foe was not a whit affected," noted Captain Simon Mayer of the 10th Mississippi. "Heavy skirmishing continued all along the lines, the enemy evidently wanting to feel our position, but our skirmishers held their ground."[23]

Ardor was no substitute for effective weaponry, and the men of Blythe's Mississippi regiment held their line with guns that their commander termed "worthless." A few days before, the regiment had been quarantined due to a smallpox outbreak. On December 26, while still in quarantine, the regiment was ordered to turn in its weapons, which were distributed to the other regiments of the brigade. Two days later, however, Blythe's men returned to active duty and were "furnished with refuse guns that had been turned over to the brigade ordnance officer," ranted Major John Thompson. "Some of the guns being bent, some without locks, some when cocked could not be pulled down, some whose hammers had to be carried in the men's pockets until time to commence firing, while others were so fouled as to render them impossible to ram home the cartridge."

Many of the guns lacked ramrods, and only one had a bayonet. "Even of these poor arms there was not a sufficiency," Thompson grumbled, "and after every exertion on my part to procure arms, only one half of the regiment moved out with no resemblance to a gun than such sticks as they could gather. Thus armed, this regiment was ordered to take its place in line for the bloody contest."[24]

The skirmishing adjacent to Nashville Pike was more desultory than not. Holding the Union line there was Colonel Grose's brigade with General Cruft's brigade to the right, on the edge of the cedar forest. Those positions had been established Monday evening, and neither side showed much interest in bringing on

22 Volunteer, Cobb's Kentucky Battery, *Southern Confederacy*, Jan. 13, 1863, 1.

23 Diary of Captain Simon Mayer, 10th Mississippi, SRNBP.

24 Lanny K. Smith *The Stones River Campaign: 26 December 1862–5 January 1863, Army of Tennessee* (2010), 28, 663.

a general engagement in this sector. "Ever since the peep of day, the skirmishers had been popping away from behind their rail fence with a harmless industry quite admirable and being popped away at in return," observed Ebenezer Hannaford of the 6th Ohio. "By and by the sport grew more dangerous and our regiment had two or three wounded during the day besides three or four more struck as we lay there in line by spent balls that came buzzing about our heads and buried themselves in the earth all around us."

The 36th Indiana had pickets out as far as the Cowan House, and Confederate sharpshooters so annoyed one captain that he sent a messenger to Grose asking for reinforcements to push the line even farther. The captain, Grose recalled, insisted "he would move on them fellows and clean them out. His officer reminded the captain the whole Rebel army was over there a little beyond him and he had best not advance too far in the cleaning out business for fear he might get cleaned out himself."[25]

Just after sunrise, Negley advanced with his two brigades from their reserve position on the Nashville Pike and aligned on Palmer's right—Colonel John F. Miller's 3rd Brigade on the left, Colonel Timothy R. Stanley's 2nd Brigade the right. Both brigades faced southeast, abutting the Wilkinson Pike. Miller deployed companies from two regiments as skirmishers: Companies D and E of the 37th Indiana on the left, linked with the 2nd Kentucky in Cruft's brigade, and Companies B and H of the 78th Pennsylvania on the right, connected to the 19th Illinois in Stanley's brigade. "The enemy had remained quiet on the open field in his entrenchments which were plainly visible and kept a battery of four pieces in position at his works all day without firing," Miller observed.

Battery G of the 1st Ohio Light and Battery B of the 1st Kentucky Light (known also as Hewitt's Battery) aimed their rifled pieces at Captain Overton Barret's four-gun Missouri battery, located on an eminence east of their position in the cedars. Barret, demonstrably outgunned and outranged, reported that he had been ordered to hold his fire "unless compelled or the infantry charged. In the first ten minutes after the enemy opened fire, I had one horse killed and two more wounded along with two men wounded at the limbers. I was obliged by the severity of the fire to send my limbers far to the rear. The fire of the enemy was very exact and severe, and but for my earthworks, my position would have been untenable."[26]

---

25 Hannaford, *In the Ranks at Stones River*, 811; William Grose, *The Story of the Marches, Battles, and Incidents of the 36th Regiment, Indiana Volunteer Infantry* (New Castle, 1891), 159.

26 OR 20/1:431, 768.

The quiet across the lines, however, prompted one of Thomas's staffers to broach with Negley the idea of marching out to capture the rifle pits about 1,000 yards in front of his lines. "General Negley said in reply, 'We can take them if you say so,' but a captain remarked in an undertone, 'He might add, 'But we would rather not.'" It turned out the Yankees were expending their ordnance on a wooden battery placed to lure the Federals into a trap. "Had we charged upon it," a Federal soldier later reported, "there was a masked battery in the orchard behind the house which would have cut us to pieces, but we only nibbled at the bait."[27]

The skirmishing in this sector tended to wax hotter the closer one approached the Wilkinson Pike: the 37th Indiana reported six casualties, and the 78th Pennsylvania, nearer the pike, lost 14. One of these dead Pennsylvania skirmishers served as 17-year-old Wilson Vance's introduction to the horrors of war. Serving as an orderly at Miller's brigade headquarters, Vance remembered seeing "a sad little procession bearing back to the rear the body of a Pennsylvania skirmisher who had been shot through the forehead. Then it was that I thought all the blood in my veins turned to water. The appearance of the awful shape borne on the rude litter was not calculated to tranquilize anybody's nerves. It was that of a stalwart young fellow with mud and blood over the poor fellow's face save where here and there the yellowish-blue pallor of death showed with dread suggestiveness."[28]

Stanley's men had a much hotter time. The Ohioan regulated the speed of his advance expecting McCook to march in on his right. "I directed Colonel Joseph Scott with his 19th Illinois as skirmishers to protect our right flank but not to bring on an engagement," he wrote. "It, however, became necessary to occupy some buildings in a field from which we were annoyed by the enemy; Colonel Scott drove them from the place and afterwards held it."

The morning skirmish was "decidedly spirited," wrote adjutant Leslie Bangs of the 19th Illinois. "We took advantage of trees and of all obstructions as skirmishers should ever do, but there was no scrambling, no hurrying, no excitement," he added. "Lines were maintained as closely as possible. The leaden messengers were buzzing around our heads like swarming bees. A bullet makes a peculiar noise as it goes whizzing by; frequently, one involuntarily dodges it—the action can't be

---

27 Joseph T. Gibson, *History of the Seventy-Eighth Pennsylvania Volunteer Infantry* (Pittsburgh, 1905), 51; Ordnance Sergeant Adoniram J. Hastings, 78th Pennsylvania, *Union County Star and Lewisburg Chronicle*, Jan. 27, 1863, 1.

28 Vance, *A Man and a Boy at Stones River*, 348. The dead man was Private James Myers of the 78th Pennsylvania, Co. H.

helped. The thought of saving oneself is very quick in its action, but the bullet that is coming is too swift in flight to dodge."[29]

The 19th Illinois engaged the skirmish line of J. Patton Anderson's brigade of Alabamians and Mississippians; the skirmishers ranged a few hundred yards in front of Anderson's main line, perched behind earthworks or temporary breastworks made of stone. Despite the protection, the incessant Federal shelling and skirmishing cost him 35 casualties that day. Lieutenant Colonel Junius Scales of the 30th Mississippi reported he lost one man killed and four wounded, feeling that at times the fight "appeared to grow into a general engagement. Some idea of the severity of this skirmish may be formed when it is known that although we were lying in a dense wood, the balls of the enemy frequently pattered and flattened against the stone breastworks which we had taken the precaution to throw up. This work was the means of saving several lives."[30]

The death of Sergeant Antonio Baptiste of the 27th Mississippi, killed by a shell as he lay behind breastworks south of the Wilkinson Pike, was perhaps the grisliest of Anderson's losses. "We had built slight breastworks, the first that army had ever built. We were not experts at the business then as we afterwards got to be," remembered fellow Mississippian John Simmons. "The Yankee sharp-shooters," he continued,

had climbed up in the timber beyond the old field and with their long-range guns were shooting every man that showed his head above the breastworks. Sergeant Baptiste was sitting with his back towards the enemy, leaning against the breastworks. He was struck in the middle of the back with a 10-pdr Parrott ball. The ball no doubt came from miles. It passed through the embankment, entered his body, and lodged with about one-half of the shell protruding from his chest. Death was instantaneous. He apparently never moaned; only his head dropped a little to one side as he remained in the same sitting position with the ball lodged in his breast.[31]

Ira Gillaspie of the 11th Michigan found that being in reserve had its own dangers. "The spent balls commenced to drop amongst our ranks but did not hurt

29 OR 20/1:420-421; John H. Haynie, *The Nineteenth Illinois: A Memoir of a Regiment of Volunteer Infantry Famous in the Civil War of Fifty Years Ago for Its Drill, Bravery, and Distinguished Services* (Chicago, 1912), 202-03.

30 Smith, *Stones River: Confederate Army*, 671.

31 John W. Simmons, Co. E, 27th Mississippi, "A Fatal Cannon Shot," *New Orleans Times-Picayune*, June 6, 1897, 16.

anyone," he recalled. "The bearers commenced carrying the dead and wounded which increased every hour. The 69th Ohio now took the front and there were four of their skirmishers picked off from one post by the Rebel sharpshooters. The sharpshooter finally got a ball from one of the 19th Illinois. About 3 p.m., our regiment took the front. Colonel Stoughton said we can try and see what the Michigan 11th can do. They did not shoot as much as the other regiments but they made sure every shot counted. Just as it began to get dark, the bearers came in with the corpse of Captain Joseph Wilson of Co. F, a much loved and respected officer."[32]

*   *   *

The three brigades of Rousseau's division made quick work of their morning march from Stewardsboro, crossing Stewart's Creek on bridges just built by the Pioneer Brigade, and by noon had arrived on the field, taking a supporting position to the left rear of Negley's division near what is today the Stones River National Cemetery.

"We came up to the line just a little before dark and filed off the road to the right, down into a deep wood and took our place in line," wrote Corporal Sophronius Landt of the 10th Wisconsin. "The sky was overcast and so full of moisture that great drops would fall down from the leaves which added much to the gloom in that trying moment. A cannon boomed in front and the bursting shells a few seconds later gave notice that the anticipated battle had begun. We were immediately ordered forward, an exercise that served to steady the nerves and warm the blood. After advancing a half mile or so, we came to a wooded ridge where in the earlier part of the day they had skirmishers with the cavalry: the dead were still lying on the ground. Here we halted, straightened up our lines, and slept on our arms through the night."[33]

Sheridan's division crossed Overall's Creek about 9:30 that morning and immediately clashed with Anderson's skirmishers on the left. Lieutenant Otis Moody of the 51st Illinois caught sight of McCook and Sheridan astride their horses as the men marched by, later writing, "McCook, burly and robust with a full red face indicative of plenty of good beef and brandy; Sheridan, with his small,

---

32 Weber, *From Michigan to Murfreesboro*, 42.

33 Memoir of Corporal Sophronius Stocking Landt, Co. D, 10th Wisconsin, SRNBP.

diminutive figure presenting a strong contrast to McCook and most emphatically a lightweight[,] though I presume he would not deny the brandy."[34]

With action imminent, Charles Francis noted, the regimental order of march was reversed. "As we usually marched, the band with its rub-a-dub-dub, was in the front, then followed by the colonel, solemn and alone; then came the staff and each company commander was at the head of his men. Now … the band was in the rear, then came the colonel and his staff, the company commanders were at the tail end of their respective companies and the regiment being left in front and Co. B being the left company and Tommy Corrigan being the smallest man in it, he had the honor of being the actual leader!"[35]

The advancing Federals discovered a country lane running south from the Wilkinson Pike that passed in front of the Gresham House and began to use it both to deploy their artillery and move infantry into position. Skirmishers from the 22nd Illinois of Colonel Roberts' 3rd Brigade linked with the 19th Illinois at about noon near the Blanton House on the Wilkinson Pike while men from the 42nd Illinois joined their fellow Illini near the Harding House, as the Confederates held the brick kiln just beyond.

According to Captain Alexander Stevenson of the 42nd Illinois,

> The 19th Illinois seemed sorely pressed as no one could show his head from behind the trees in that timber without being sure that a moment afterwards a bullet would pass very near it. When the 22nd Illinois came to their relief, a general shout arose and Colonel Roberts, but a few rods behind the skirmish line, gave this gallant regiment the order to drive the Rebels out. Having received no orders where to halt, he kept advancing until he had gone beyond Negley's line on his left. A few moments before this General Sheridan came in full speed down the Wilkinson Pike and halting the 42nd Illinois, which was immediately in the rear of the 22nd, he sent word to Roberts to come back and form a line on the immediately right of Negley, resting his own left on the Wilkinson Pike.[36]

"At this point the resistance was so strong as to require two regiments to drive them," recalled Sheridan, who ordered up his artillery and placed a dozen guns belonging to Henry Hescock's Battery G, 1st Missouri Light, and Charles

---

34 Moody Diary.

35 Francis, *Narrative of a Private Soldier*, 105.

36 Stevenson, *The Battle of Stone's River*, 15.

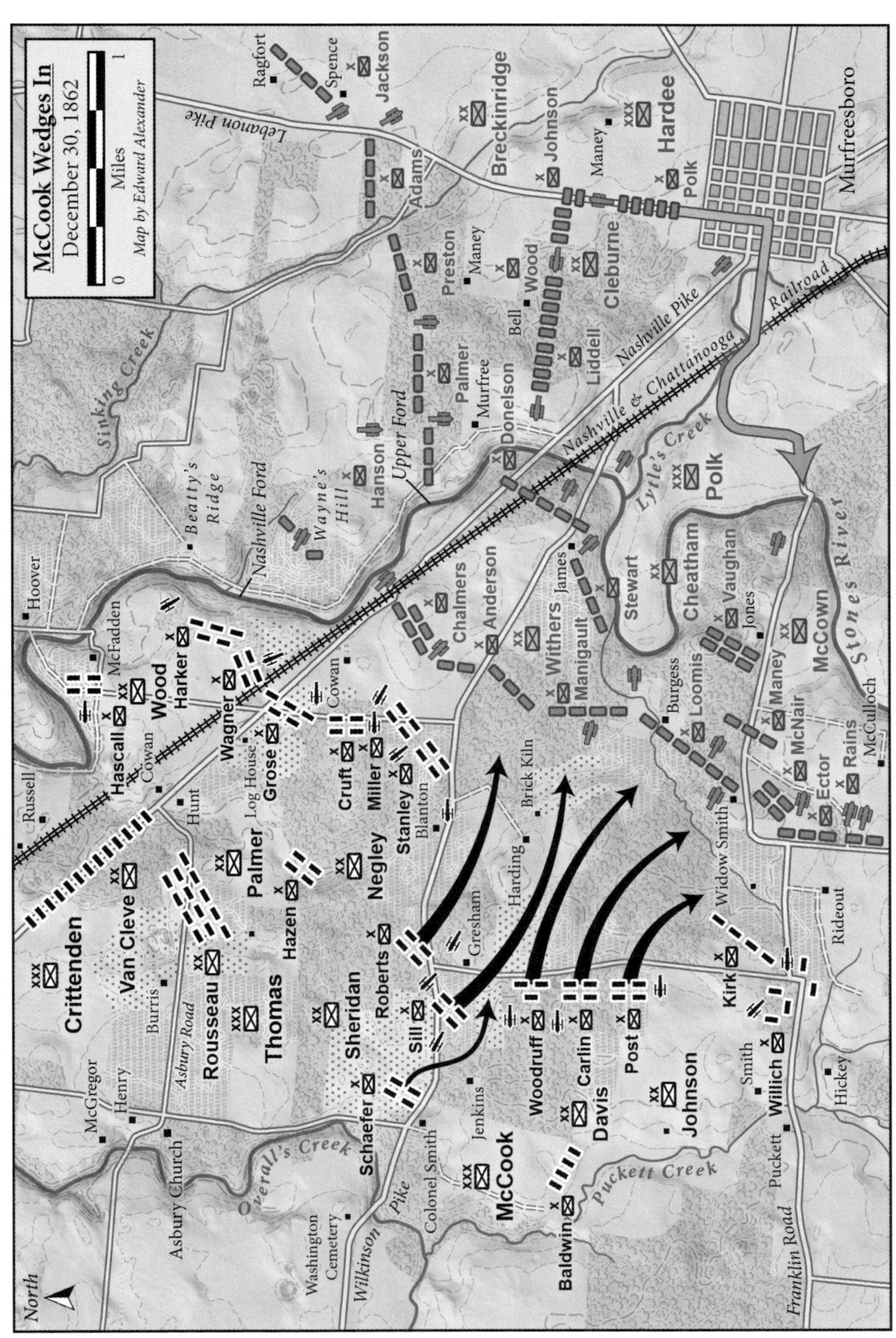
McCook Wedges In
December 30, 1862
Map by Edward Alexander
Miles
0   1
North
Ragfort
Spence
Jackson
Lebanon Pike
Breckinridge
Johnson
Maney
Hardee
Murfreesboro
Adams
Maney
Polk
Preston
Wood
Cleburne
Maney
Liddell
Nashville Pike
Railroad
Palmer
Murfree
Bell
Donelson
Nashville & Chattanooga
Lytle's Creek
Polk
Hanson
Upper Ford
Wayne's Hill
Beatty's Ridge
Nashville Ford
Chalmers
Anderson
James
Withers
Stewart
Cheatham
Vaughan
Jones
Sinking Creek
Hoover
McFadden
Manigault
Burgess
Loomis
McCown
Stones River
Russell
Wood
Harker
Hascall
Cowan
Wagner
Log House
Grose
Cowan
Hunt
Cruft
Miller
Stanley
Blanton
Brick Kiln
Maney
McNair
Ector
Rains
McCulloch
Crittenden
Van Cleve
Palmer
Hazen
Negley
Harding
Gresham
Widow Smith
Rideout
Burris
Rousseau
Thomas
Sheridan
Roberts
Sill
Kirk
McGregor
Henry
Asbury Road
Schaefer
Woodruff
Carlin
Post
Willich
Smith
Hickey
Asbury Church
Washington Cemetery
Overall's Creek
Jenkins
Colonel Smith
McCook
Baldwin
Davis
Johnson
Puckett Creek
Puckett
Franklin Road
Wilkinson Pike

Houghtaling's Battery C, 1st Illinois Light, on a slight ridge just south of the Wilkinson Pike to support the infantry's advance.

Early in the afternoon, Lieutenant Moody led his company in the 51st Illinois into the field to relieve the 42nd Illinois. "Men sought the cover of trees and fired when they could see an object," he wrote. "Sometimes it was pretty hot work. Charlie Hills said to me 'this is about as good fun as snowballing in Camp Douglas.' In less than five minutes his fun was brought to a sudden termination by a shot in the back of the head, knocking him down and flattening out the ball."[37]

Francis accompanied his company as bugler and soon found himself under heavy fire, too. "The musket balls from the enemy came thick and fast among us, but as we were protected by large trees, we suffered very little if any at all," he recalled. "Our men fired at the enemy near the end of the woods and then each man dashed forward to the cover of the most convenient tree when he reloaded and prepared for another dash. We continued to fire as rapidly as we could and always aimed in a general way in the direction of the battery, but I could not see whether our shots did any execution."[38]

McCook's biggest tactical concern was a nest of Confederates occupying the heavy timber on his right front. As Davis brought his division into line, McCook ordered the general to have Woodruff's and Sill's brigades conduct a wheeling movement to help clear those woods; once the woods were clear, he determined, the line would generally face east. The wheeling movement began about 2:30 p.m. Sill's command deployed with the 88th Illinois on the left, connected to the 42nd Illinois' skirmish line near the Harding House and the 36th Illinois on the right. The six guns of Captain Asahel Bush's 4th Indiana Battery rolled forward between the two infantry regiments at a trot.

"Sharp skirmishing was kept up until 3 p.m.," reported Colonel Nicholas Greusel, "when General Sill ordered an advance and the brigade moved forward, changing front to the left, the regiments keeping their relative positions across a cornfield and the battery was advanced into the woods beyond. Soon after the advance into the woods, a battery of the enemy opened on us from the low ground across a cotton field and in the edge of a strip of timber scarce 500 yards distant and then ensued a terrific artillery duel between our battery and the enemy."[39]

---

37 Moody Diary.

38 Francis, *Narrative of a Private Soldier*, 106-07.

39 *OR* 20/1:356.

Supplying the Confederates' heavy artillery fire was an Alabama battery of Manigault's Brigade commanded by Captain David Waters. "The enemy having forced in our skirmishers got possession of the [cotton] gin house and other outbuildings belonging to the farm of Mr. Harding in front of the line of our brigade about 700 yards distant from my position," recalled Waters, who noted that Manigault ordered him to "shell them out, which I did, firing 10-12 shells and four round shots at the house."[40]

With his advance stymied by Waters's guns, Sill galloped up to Captain Bush and ordered him to deploy and "silence that battery." Corporal Edgar Abbott, one of Bush's gunners, related that "we were surprised by an eight-gun masked battery which opened a deadly fire upon us. As we were only in line of march, we had to do some fast work in order to get into line of battle. The enemy had good range on us and were doing effective work. A piece of shell struck one of our lead horses at the root of the ear, took it completely off well down to the head which disabled him for further duty. But the horse did not go off his feet. A solid six-pound shot struck our No. 1 under the arm while he was in the act of loading and struck No. 3 just waist high and I believe they were both in heaven in less than two minutes."

"We moved our gun about six feet to the right and got a fine range on the gun that had been doing so much damage," Abbott continued. "The cedar brush had been shot away and we could see what we had on our hands; we soon got a good shot on the gun for we saw it topple over. That gun being out of the way, it gave us an oblique fire on the other seven guns which soon put them out of business."

According to Bush, "we killed about half of their horses, completely disabled one gun carriage, and lost one sergeant and three privates killed, five horses killed, two wheels disabled, and two limber chests damaged."[41] Bush's guns made Waters's position exceedingly hot. "A few minutes after I ceased firing, the enemy brought up a rifled gun battery and placed it in position about three-quarters of a mile from my position and opened on me with percussion shells," wrote Waters. "I immediately ordered my caissons to move to a position on my left under cover of a wood. Finding that my position was completely commanded by this battery and that my guns were not capable of doing them damage, I moved my battery to the left and took a position in the middle of the brigade covered by timber on my right."

<hr>

40 Ibid., 769.

41 Recollections of Corporal Edgar Abbott, 4th Indiana Battery, James C. Haddock Papers, Smith Memorial Library, Indiana Historical Society; *OR* 20/1:355.

Brigadier General Joshua Sill

Author's Collection

As the rest of Sill's line advanced, Waters opened fire from his new position, but Bush's gunners, unlimbered on a hill roughly 400 yards away, began to drop shells among his men and horses. They had help from the other batteries in Sheridan's command, located near the Wilkinson Pike. "He opened on me with shell and spherical case shot," Waters noted, "while at the same time a rifled battery posted to my right opened[,] assisted by two rifled guns posted in rear of Harding's dwelling; the battery on the right completely enfiladed my line but was firing over me, doing little damage except from falling limbs."[42]

Outranged by his Federal opponents, Waters called for help. Manigault eventually found two rifled guns belonging to Captain Thomas Stanford's Mississippi Battery, attached to A. P. Stewart's Brigade in reserve; Stewart agreed to send them forward. Corporal Benjamin W. L. Butt, one of Stanford's gunners, soon arrived with Lieutenant Ancil A. Hardin's rifled section and recorded the scene: "We came up immediately behind the battery which was engaged in a terrible conflict with a battery of the enemy only 400 yards distant. Here we remained a few minutes for orders while the shells were exploding among us every minute. There was scarcely a tree to be seen which was not shattered by these terrible missiles. Presently we were ordered into a cornfield to the left where we unlimbered and opened immediately on the enemy in front."[43]

Hardin's detachment quickly found itself the target of four Federal batteries. "As soon as we uncovered," Butts recalled, "our position exposed us to the view of

---

42 OR 20/1:769-770.

43 Corporal Ben Butt, Stanford's Mississippi Battery, *Memphis Daily Appeal*, Jan. 22, 1863, 2.

another Yankee battery on a hill to the right some 700 yards distant so situated as to give it a raking fire on us." He continued:

> For some reason or other, Waters' battery to our right ceased firing as soon as we opened, thus turning the whole of the enemy's fire upon us. In a moment, our ears were greeted with a perfect hurricane of shell and canister, the latter coming from the battery nearest us. The enemy had every advantage of us. It was a rash and unwise order that sent us into such a position. Whiz rattled the canister; bang exploded the balls around us, while the sharp crack of our two rifled pieces responded to the roar of the enemy's guns. The greatest portion of the enemy's shells was aimed too high and passed just over us. I suppose that at least a dozen shells passed within ten feet of my head. We maintained this unequal contest for half an hour and were ordered from the field having fired about 60 rounds. Up to this time, we had lost only two men wounded. We regarded our preservation as little less than a miracle.[44]

South of Sill's line, Woodruff double-quicked his brigade east from Gresham Lane to maintain its place in McCook's wheeling movement. Woodruff formed his small brigade into two lines behind a cloud of skirmishers: the 25th Illinois on the left, connected to Sill's 36th Illinois, and the 35th Illinois on the right with the inexperienced 81st Indiana in support. He also ordered Captain Stephen Carpenter's four-gun 8th Wisconsin battery to advance in the interval between his left-most regiment and Sill's right regiment and shoved off at 3:00 p.m. "The wood was so thick and bushy on my right that it was difficult to see farther than the left of [Carlin's] Second Brigade," Woodruff recalled, "but as I discovered it moving forward, we moved forward also to protect its flank. Sheridan's division halted 100 yards in rear of my brigade, his line of skirmishers joining my line of battle"[45]

Woodruff's skirmishers kicked up a hornet's nest of Confederates as they started crossing the cotton field on their front: sections of Manigault's and Colonel John Loomis's brigades. The severity of artillery and musketry halted Woodruff at the edge of the forest behind a rail fence, compelling him to order Carpenter's guns into action. "Our regiment advanced in splendid style until they reached the fence and when within 20 or 30 feet of it," recalled George Morris of the 81st Indiana. "Our boys opened fire on the enemy, but as they had retired with the exception of the skirmishers, it didn't amount to much." Wrote Lieutenant Hannibal St. Clair of

44 Butt Letter.

45 *OR* 20/1:287.

the 35th Illinois: "The shot and shell fell thick and fast in and about our line and it being the first music of the kind many of us ever heard, it made us feel rather peculiar."[46]

As McCook's men advanced under the cover of a barrage of Federal shells, they quickly learned Federal shells could be just as deadly as Confederate iron. "The 88th Illinois being on the skirmish line, a battery was posted on an eminence in their rear for their support, firing over them with solid shot and shell," observed one of McCook's men. "Major George Chandler, having occasion to ride out in front of the skirmish line to give some necessary order," he continued,

> a misdirected shot from the battery in the rear struck his horse in the side, passing entirely through him, cutting the Major's overcoat, pants, and saddle in its passage, and killing the horse instantly. The horse sank to the ground and Major Chandler, although partially stunned from the shock received, with the utmost coolness raised himself to his feet and turning to his men while swinging his sword above his head exclaimed, 'Give it to 'em, boys, I am not dead yet!" He had hardly spoken when a Minie ball passed through the fleshy part of his ear, making a slight wound, to which he paid no regard.[47]

Major Elisha T. Hibbard of the 24th Wisconsin was also struck while leading five companies of his regiment forward to support Bush. "I fought my regiment mounted until my horse was shot, the grape shot going through the sole of my boot and nearly throwing me from the saddle," he wrote. "The boys cried out, 'The Major is killed!' but I said, 'Not by a damned sight!'"

The Badgers of Adoniram J. Jones' 24th Wisconsin regiment had just taken up a position behind the guns when they were ordered to lie down. "So perfect was the range that the Rebels had on us that their shells, or most of them, went just over our heads. This was the first time I was under fire and to say I was scared is putting it mildly," he admitted in a postwar memoir. "Had we been up, loading and firing, it would not have been so trying on the nerves, but all we had to do was flatten ourselves to Mother Earth as best as we could and listen to the bursting shells over our heads."

Eugene E. Comstock, meanwhile, was an unfortunate spectator to the grisly death of Michael Pfaff of Company K, also part of the 24st Wisconsin. "A young

---

46 Morris, *History of the 81st Indiana*, 27; Gillett Family papers, Abraham Lincoln Presidential Library.

47 James Barnet, ed., *The Martyrs and Heroes of Illinois in the Great Rebellion* (Chicago, 1866), 149.

fellow in Co. K stood up and had hardly got to his feet before a shell from the enemy took his head away from him, spattering the brains all around," Comstock recalled. "A solid shot passed through the necks of two horses standing directly in front of me."[48]

Once Federal artillery dialed in Hardin's range, it proved just as lethal. "As we were leaving the field to avoid a company of sharpshooters who were flanking us with the intention of picking off our cannoneers, one of the enemy's pieces opened and about the third shot[,] Lieutenant Hardin was struck with a shell and instantly killed," Butt remembered. William A. Brown witnessed the fatal moment, recalling that "as he was riding on after his guns, a cannon ball passed entirely through his body, killing him instantly. Some of the boys saw him fall and turned back to help him, but they got there just in time to see his open his eyes and then close them forever, without a struggle or a gasp." Sheridan's artillerists won this first battle for possession of the Harding House and grounds, but the carnage would be even worse the next morning.[49]

*   *   *

The superiority in the Federal long arm tipped the balance in the fight for the Harding House, but the greater range of the Federal muskets was also an advantage. For example, the 10th South Carolina found itself badly outgunned against Colonel Roberts' brigade, as nearly 80 percent of Roberts' troops carried modern Springfield or Enfield rifle-muskets. "Our regiment was not armed all alike with the same caliber arms," noted C. Irvine Walker. "We were so poorly armed that more than half the companies of our regiment were armed with old flint and steel smoothbore muskets that had been altered to percussion. Their range was about 100 yards and at one time, the entire picket line of our regiment was armed thusly, and consequently the enemy showed themselves openly and rather laughed at us. Colonel Manigault slipped up to the picket lines some companies armed with rifles and then there was a general scamper of the enemy for cover as they opened fire. The picket fight amounted almost to a battle."

48 Major Elisha T. Hibbard, 24th Wisconsin, *Semi-Weekly Wisconsin*, Jan. 23, 1863, 4; Adoniram J. Jones, *A Private of the Cumberland*, 12-13; Corporal Eugene E. Comstock, Co. B, 24th Wisconsin, State Historical Society of Wisconsin.

49 Butt Letter; W. T. Dixon, *The Civil War Travels of William Alexander Brown*, Stanford's Mississippi Battery, http://www.geocities.com/Heartland/6519/travch10.html, accessed Aug. 29, 2003.

Manigault eventually brought forward roughly half of his brigade to support the skirmishers. Colonel John Reid of the 28th Alabama reported that "during the day nearly every company had borne some part in the hot and protracted skirmishes. Two men had been killed and several wounded but all seemed cheerful and to await with confidence and determination the events which the next day should bring forth."[50]

McCook's assault produced a clash between Woodruff's and Carlin's brigades and that of Colonel Loomis. Loomis's Brigade, five regiments of Alabamians along with the 1st Louisiana Regulars, occupied a position at the edge of woods near the Widow Smith House on Manigault's left. Unlike most of the Confederate line south of the Wilkinson Pike, Loomis was not alone. He had the close support of Colonel Alfred Vaughan's Brigade in Cheatham's Division, just a few hundred yards to his rear, and was covered on his left by McCown's 4,400-man division.

Two companies constituting the 17th Alabama Sharpshooter Battalion under the command of Captain Benjamin Yancey, the son of well-known secessionist William Lowndes Yancey, covered Loomis's front. The 1st Louisiana Regulars held the brigade's right, followed to the left by the 19th Alabama, 22nd Alabama, 25th Alabama, 39th Alabama, and 26th Alabama. The six-gun Florida battery commanded by Captain Felix Huston Robertson lay just beyond the 26th Alabama on the extreme left, north of the Franklin Road, and the 154th (Senior) Tennessee, detached from Vaughan's brigade as artillery support, covered the Franklin Road on Robertson's left rear.

The 23-year-old Robertson would prove himself a brave battery commander at Stones River, but unlike his beloved father Jerome Robertson, whom the soldiers branded "Aunt Polly" due to his unusual care for their welfare, his fearful gunners nicknamed him "Comanche." This sobriquet stemmed from both Felix's swarthy appearance (some soldiers whispered that he was a half-breed) and his savage brand of discipline. Strong-willed and prone to complaint, Robertson's unswerving support and admiration of Bragg served only to worsen his unpopularity with his men. Robertson was attending West Point when war broke out in 1861, but he resigned and offered his services to the Confederacy when his native Texas seceded. He was among the gunners who fired on Fort Sumter in April 1861, and after serving on the staff of then-Colonel Adley H. Gladden in Pensacola, he was

---

50 Walker Papers; Walker, *Rolls of the 10th South Carolina*, 90-91; Smith, *Stones River: Confederate Army*, 678.

Lieutenant Colonel David McKee
of the 15th Wisconsin

Author's Collection

given command of the Florida battery of six Napoleons that he now led into battle at Stones River.[51]

Colonel Carlin noted the stiffening Confederate resistance as his brigade pushed into the woods east of Gresham Lane. Assigning a contingent of skirmishers to Lt. Col. David McKee of the 15th Wisconsin, Carlin's men waded into the forest. "It was evident that we had at last come near the selected position of the enemy where he intended to give battle," Carlin wrote. "The enemy's pickets held their strong position with great obstinacy. No better fortifications for skirmishers could be had than this forest. The trees were large and close together; many felled trees lay on the ground and there were stumps; in addition to all these shelters, ledges of limestone cropped out at various places affording the best of ready-made breastworks."[52]

"We were ordered to drive the Rebel skirmishers out of the woods which we advanced to do and soon were engaged with them," wrote John Russell of the 21st Illinois. "We drew their fire and then advanced on a run. Soon we drove them from their hiding places and fired at them as they ran behind trees to load. As soon as loaded, we again advanced on the run in a zig-zag course so as to prevent the Rebels from taking aim. We kept it up till they were driven back to their lines."

51 Robertson's reputation was permanently sullied by his involvement in the massacre of black troops during the October 1864 battle of Saltville, Virginia. "Perjurer, sycophant, quite possibly a murderer, Felix Robertson was almost without a doubt the most reprehensible man in either army to wear the uniform of a general," opined historian William C. Davis. Robertson passed away in 1928—the last surviving Confederate general.

52 Girardi and Hughes, *Carlin Memoirs*, 74.

Recalled a soldier of the 101st Ohio: "[W]e had not gone far when we found what we were looking for and just about as much as we wanted, too. The enemy dealt out grape and shell and passed the small balls over from behind a fence in good style. We, the reserve, lay flat on the ground listening to the music of the balls over us. From my position, I could see every flash from the enemy's guns. You may guess how I felt there watching the explosions and thinking of each that it might send my death warrant."[53]

Carlin's advance into the woods outpaced Post's brigade, covering his right flank. Post had his own troubles beating back light cavalry thrusts with both his 22nd Indiana and the mounted men of General Davis's escort, Company B of the 36th Illinois. "The skirmishing in front grew brisker and late in the afternoon the enemy was found in force strongly posted and opened upon us with artillery from our front and right," Post reported. "This killed one man and wounded several while Captain Robert Hale of the 75th Illinois and Lieutenant Hall of my staff each had a horse killed under him."

Lieutenant Chesley Mosman of Post's 59th Illinois noted that "toward night we got into a cedar thicket so dense we could not see through. While we were marching, a cannon ball came near killing our regimental commander Captain Hendrick Paine while he was listening to the skirmishers firing. Some balls would come back to us and pieces of shell would come singing over us with a queer noise."[54]

"Colonel McKee and his line of skirmishers had a hard struggle indeed in driving the enemy out of these woods," Carlin continued. "It became necessary before the work had been entirely accomplished to relieve his line of skirmishers as they had exhausted their ammunition and were fatigued. The loss of men in the skirmish line was heavy as they were compelled to advance against an unseen foe. Colonel John W. S. Alexander of the 21st Illinois was detailed to relieve McKee, and a fresh line of skirmishers was detailed to relieve the first."

At this point, Carlin intended to have his men dig in and hold their ground. His brigade stuck out like a thumb from the rest of McCook's line, and with shadows lengthening, there was not time to organize a further advance. But Davis, his

---

53 Private John Russell, Co. G, 21st Illinois, Civil War Times Illustrated Collection, USAMHI; Sergeant John D. Blair, Co. D, 101st Ohio, *Norwalk Reflector*, Feb. 3, 1863, 2.

54 OR 20/1:270; Arnold Gates, ed., *The Rough Side of War: The Civil War Journal of Chesley A. Mosman, 1st Lieutenant, Company D, 59th Illinois Volunteer Infantry Regiment* (Garden City, 1987), 36.

ever-aggressive division commander, had other ideas.[55] Riding with his staff, he realized Felix Robertson's six bronze Napoleons sat without apparent infantry support; turning to Alexander, he directed the Illinoisan to get those guns.

"In moving forward, we came to a high cedar rail fence in a diagonal line to ours which divided the company," wrote 1st Lt. Abraham Songer of Company G. "The captain crossed the fence with the right of the company, and I followed with the left or advanced with the left along the fence until we reached a level timber land. The direction I had taken brought me in front of the 15th Wisconsin, but a line of Rebel infantry was waiting for us behind a fence hid by small brush. When we got right up near the skirmish line, the Rebels opened fire with a terrible fury."

Alexander's men returned fire and then charged. "I ordered my men to continue forward and fix bayonets with a view to charge the battery," the colonel reported, "and was upon the point of giving the necessary command when, the smoke lifting from the heavy volleys of musketry, I observed that the battery was further to the front than I had supposed and the space was obstructed by two heavy rail fences." Sergeant Nils Gilbert of the 15th Wisconsin noted that "our regiment and the 21st Illinois rushed on at double quick time to take the battery; we came within a rod of it when the enemy opened such a fire that you might think all Hell had been poured over us."[56]

Robertson's battery "proved to be bait thrown out for us," remembered Sergeant William Hensley of the 21st Illinois color guard. The guns, he continued, were

in a grove of large oak trees and it was a dark cloudy day and just in front of them was a lane and two high rail fences which they threw down to open the way of the artillery. It was so dark that we could not see where they were. We were in an open pasture on a small ridge and their artillery opened on us with grape and canister. Their second shot sent a ball about the size of a hen egg through the chest of the man to my left. Then we were ordered to lay down and fire. When one of their cannons would fire, the red blaze would show them in the dark and I would tuck my head to the ground till the balls would scatter all around us. About 50 feet in front of me was a pile of rails and I thought that if I could get there, the

55 Girardi and Hughes, *Carlin Memoirs*, 74. Davis does not mention ordering Alexander to make this charge; Carlin strongly suggests Davis did so. Colonel Alexander simply states the regiment was ordered to charge, but does not state who gave him the order.

56 Reminiscences of 1st Lt. Abraham W. Songer, Co. G, 21st Illinois, David T. Dixon Collection; Report of Colonel John W. S. Alexander, 21st Illinois, SRNBP; Waldemar Ager, *Colonel Heg and His Boys: A Norwegian Regiment in the American Civil War* (Northfield, 2000), 72.

rails would offer some protection. I quickly crawled to them and was firing and loading as fast as I could but once when I went to load my gun, I found I had no ramrod. In my haste, I had shot it away.

Hensley turned around thinking he could pick up a ramrod from a fallen comrade but was stunned to find himself alone. "I was there fighting the whole Rebel army by myself," he marveled.[57]

Robertson was in the fight of his life. He had two sections firing from near the Widow Smith's farmhouse while his third section, in position 250 yards to the north, opened a raking fire on the advancing Federal skirmish line. Two Federal batteries (the 2nd Minnesota of Carlin's brigade and the 8th Wisconsin of Woodruff's) were throwing shells into his midst, but four guns from Lieutenant William A. McDuffie's Eufala Light Artillery, in James Rains's Brigade in McCown's Division, dropped trail south of his position and started to exchange shots with their Federal counterparts in the woods. It was an equal fight at 10 guns per side: the 2nd Minnesota used four 6-pounder smoothbores and two 12-pounder howitzers, and the 8th Wisconsin had two 6-pounder field guns and two 10-pounder Parrott rifles. The Confederates used a mix of smoothbores and Napoleons.

It was the infantry, however, that posed the greatest danger to Robertson and his men. Despite firing round after round of canister, the gunners began to drop with frightening rapidity from Yankee long-range musketry. "Though the enemy was repulsed with great loss, canister shot being used freely and with fine effect, it was not without the loss of several brave men who were wounded by the sharpshooters who had affected a lodgment in easy range of the guns," Robertson reported.

Recognizing the peril, Lt. Col. Michael Magevney advanced his 154th Tennessee to combat Carlin's sharpshooters. "I drew up my command in the rear of the battery, extending the left wing of the battalion a little forward to take advantage of a dip in the ground," he reported. "At this time, the enemy came out of the woods in force, evidently intent on charging our battery. As our gunners were in a great measure disabled by the severe fire to which they were subjected, I moved forward the line in front of the guns, determined to meet them in a

---

57 Corporal William Wallace Hensley Autobiography, Co. C, 21st Illinois, MS2009-007, Special Collections, Virginia Polytechnic Institute and University.

countercharge, but they fell back under cover and I occupied my former position."[58]

Post's skirmish line had emerged from the cedar thicket and witnessed the 21st Illinois's impetuous charge, and though they admired its dash, they wanted no part of it. "This was the most gallant charge we ever saw, but it was one regiment contending against a brigade of the enemy and they could not sustain the charge and had to give back, which they then did in good order," recounted a soldier in the 75th Illinois. "We were then ordered back and retired without firing a gun amid the rattle of grape and canister. Recalled Sgt. Maj. Rudolphus Peake of the 74th Illinois: "We marched through the cedars without any opposition and as soon as we made our appearance, they opened on us with grape and canister. We fell back under the cover of the cedars on account of it being too dark to do any more. As soon as we commenced falling back, the Rebels opened on us with their cannon killing one man."[59]

In the early afternoon, as McCook was about to launch his attack, the general met with a local farmer, who described the Confederate positions. "The right of Cheatham's division rests on the Wilkinson Pike: Withers is on Cheatham's left, with his left resting on the Franklin road," McCook reported after the meeting. "Hardee's corps is entirely beyond that road and his left extending toward Salem pike." Although the information turned out to be erroneous, it convinced McCook that his right flank was opposite Bragg's center and "[it] made me anxious for my right." The general informed his division commanders of this and ordered two brigades of Johnson's division in reserve—those of Willich and Kirk, whom he called two of the army's "best and most experienced brigadiers"—to the right of my line for protection and "to guard against surprise there."[60]

Johnson's division had been waiting in reserve west of Gresham Lane until McCook's mid-afternoon thrust brought Davis's plea for reinforcements. General Kirk's brigade filed first into the lane and marched south, deploying on Post's right in the woods to the east. "Colonel Post informed me that his troops were much annoyed by a Rebel battery directly in his front," wrote Kirk, "and that the enemy

---

58 Smith, *Stones River: Confederate Army*, 654; OR 20/1:748.

59 Unknown, Co. D, 75th Illinois, *Sterling Republican Gazette*, Jan. 17, 1863, 1; Peake Letter.

60 OR 20/1:255. This section of McCook's self-serving report tries to make the case that McCook was alert to the danger on his right flank from the beginning; it appears that Kirk's and Willich's brigades were moved to Davis's right due to Davis's concern about his open flank and requests for reinforcements in the fight against Loomis's Brigade, not because McCook had the omniscience to perceive that Bragg would attack him on that flank the next morning.

Captain Warren Parker Edgarton,
Battery E, 1st Ohio Volunteer Light Artillery

Author's Collection

were now placing in position another battery opposite his right which would subject him to a crossfire and from the nature of the ground in his front he could not silence them. I found an excellent position for my battery just beyond my extreme right," he continued, "and directed Captain Warren Edgarton to open on the nearest one with the simultaneous fire of his six pieces."[61]

Edgarton, a 26-year-old law professor from Cleveland, had a reputation as one of the most "scientific" gunners in the army. Private William Laughlin described how that science played out when the battery went into action that afternoon:

Our captain drew us up behind a row of cedar trees which skirted a lane between us and the enemy. This lane led out into the open field we were to take. Captain Edgarton and his lieutenants then rode out on the ground and taking out their watches, they computed the distance to the Rebel battery by noting the time it took from the report of their guns to be heard after seeing the puff of smoke and then multiplying this by the number of yards that sound travels per second. They then took an average of the results of returned with it to the gunners.

While this was going on, I could not but note the different expressions on the countenances of my comrades, all evidently thinking fast or trying hard not to think at all. The compressed lips and nervous movements all showed that they were keenly alive to the danger which we were in a very few moments to face. We knew the battery we were to meet had rifled guns of the very best make; they were evidently well-trained in the use of these guns and had their guns unlimbered so that they were ready to turn as soon as we should

61 *ORS*, 3:625.

make our appearance. They could get our range almost instantly while we had to get on to the ground and unlimber before we could get in even one shot. In this time, they might send many of us to our long home.

Private Laughlin continued:

The gunners set their sights for the number of yards given by the captain. He looked over us to see that every man was in his place, no detail forgotten, then in a voice which inspired us all with courage, he gave the command "double quick, march!" Away we went, our drivers spurring and lashing our horses into the keen run while us gunners held on for dear life. We were in a moment in the open field and Edgarton gave the order "unlimber to the front and commence firing." Our range was accurate and every ball tore into their battery scattering death and destruction on every side. One of our percussion shells struck a wheel, destroying the gun while another struck just under the gun on the axle and exploded, throwing the gun end over end into the heavens.[62]

Elijah Strong of Battery E noted in his diary that "never were guns served with a better will. The long-suppressed excitement of the boys was worked off in a way that was extremely surprising to that Rebel battery." Edgarton's guns opened at less than 700 yards with their five 6-pounder James rifles, and the Confederate Robertson agreed with the Ohioans' descriptions of their deadly effectiveness. "The cannon firing at the battery was spherical shot and soon blew up a limber to a piece," he lamented. This single shot wounded four men. The battered Texan soon received orders to withdraw, as did McDuffie once he ran out of long-range ammunition.[63]

*   *   *

The late afternoon charge on the Confederate battle line near the Smith House was a bloody debacle that cost the 21st Illinois heavily. The regiment lost 135 men in less than an hour and limped back to Carlin's line in the woods sadder, if not wiser. Among the casualties was 1st Lt. Nineveh S. McKeen of Company H; wounded three times and conspicuous in leading his men during the charge, McKeen would miss the next day's battle but would return on January 1 after being

---

62 Private William H. Laughlin, James Barnett Papers, Western Reserve Historical Society.

63 Strong, *Marches of Battery E*, 17; Smith, *Stones River: Confederate Army*, 654.

briefly captured by the Confederates. In 1890, McKeen would receive the Medal of Honor not only for his actions at Stones River but also for capturing the battle flag of the 8th Arkansas during the battle of Liberty Gap in June 1863.

Loomis's casualty count during the fight for Robertson's guns proved the heaviest of any sustained by the Confederates on December 30: 51 killed or wounded, including 14 wounded in Robertson's Battery alone. But there was one more casualty to add. "Just at dark and whilst the last charge was being made," Loomis reported, "I approached the line to ascertain the results when I received a shot from a Minie ball that gave me great pain during the night." Hence, the colonel would be the first brigade commander of either army to be struck at Stones River, though he would not be the last.[64]

Kirk, the next brigade commander wounded during the battle, lauded Edgarton's performance in silencing the Confederate batteries. "It was the finest performance I ever saw," he wrote. "A number of men and horses were killed at the first and second discharge and the enemy was driven back in confusion, leaving some disabled carriages and pieces on the ground."

The sun was setting as the balance of Kirk's brigade filed into the woods north of Edgarton's battery and deployed. Willich followed and aligned perpendicular to Kirk, forming what looked like a croquet wicket. "We shortly found ourselves on the extreme right of our army and almost face to face with the enemy whose breastworks were in plain view across an open field," recounted Lyman Widney of the 34th Illinois. "Strict orders were issued that no fires should be allowed to disclose our position to the enemy. The air became quite cold after nightfall and we soon found it impossible to sleep. Some of my messmates concluded to build a rail pen and line it with long grass from the field. We found the exercise restored our warmth but it did not continue long after we lay down in the pen in vain hope of falling asleep, so I spent the most of my time pulling the long grass and carrying it in."[65]

---

64 Smith, *Stones River: Confederate Army*, 644.

65 Girardi, *Memoirs of Lyman Widney*, 130-31; Kirk report, *ORS*, 3:65

Positions and Plans:
The Night of December 30

THE CONCLUSION OF the artillery clash brought some measure of quiet to the battlefield, but the Confederate infantry remained vigilant. Yankee skirmishers from Kirk's and Willich's newly arrived brigades fanned into the fields south of the Franklin Pike, where they were confronted by their Confederate counterparts from McCown's brigades. A mere 300 yards behind the Confederate skirmishers, McCown's men rested behind hastily erected breastworks. Brigadier General Matthew D. Ector's dismounted Texans held their ground along a farm lane bordered on both sides by a cedar rail fence.

The presence of Edgarton's battery so close to the Confederate lines was a concern for Colonel Matthew Locke of the 10th Texas Cavalry, his regiment directly across the field from the deadly guns. "It was apparent that the fence which had obstructed the sight of the enemy would serve as an auxiliary in the enemy's hands if our position was discovered," Locke would note. "Knowing this, although the weather was very inclement and disagreeable, I did not allow any fire and the blankets having been left at camp, the men suffered very much and but for the fact that they had been lying on their arms without sleep for two nights previous, sleep would have been impossible."

The men tore down the section of fence closest to the enemy, recalled Private Lewis Jones of the 10th Texas, adding, "We spread the rails out over the ground next to the opposite string which was left for breastworks. On the rails, we passed the night without fires, most of the men sitting down watching the fires of the enemy some 400 yards away."[1]

Carlin's exhausted Federals, meanwhile, went into bivouac in some cases dangerously close to Loomis's line, and a routine rotation of skirmish lines at sunset cost the 15th Wisconsin dearly. "The other regiments were preparing to bivouac and to strengthen their position by placing fence rails, logs, and rocks in the form of breastworks," the colonel reported, noting that Loomis's' Alabamians, seeing the advancing Federal skirmish line, believed they were being attacked. "When thus engaged, the enemy just before dark raised up out of their sunken road and poured a volley into them as a parting salute for the day. Not expecting any attack at the time, the Scandinavians were taken by surprise and broke."

The 15th Wisconsin fell back a hundred yards before Colonel Heg and Lt. Col. David McKee restored order and marched the men sheepishly back to the line they had just abandoned. Farther behind the lines, some intrepid Federals lit fires to warm their evening coffee, but "no sooner had the fires been started when they were discovered and an order immediately followed, 'Put out those fires,'" wrote Corporal George Herr of the 59th Illinois in Post's 1st Brigade. "Many of the men, however, did not propose to miss their coffee, so they picked up burnt embers, held their cans over this, blowing the coal to keep it alive and succeeded in boiling their much-needed stimulant."[2]

As the trickle of casualties started to flow to the rear, both armies established field hospitals. The surgeons of Sill's brigade set up theirs on the Harding Farm and hung a yellow flag on the rooftop of the farmhouse to distinguish it as a hospital. "Dr. Coatsworth, our regimental surgeon, began his preparations for work," recalled Charles Francis. "He directed each of the drummers and fifers to place a piece of yellow rag around his arm."

William Haigh, chaplain of the 36th Illinois, noted that the field hospital was set up while they were still under fire. "Mr. Harding was at home with two or three Negroes and he looked with anything but complacency upon the Federal army," Haigh recalled. "Indeed, there was nothing particularly attractive in a body of men taking forcible possession of a man's house, covering his floors, carpets, beds, and bedding with bleeding men, and appropriating everything within reach that might

---

1 OR 20/1:930-931; Private Lewis P. Jones, Co. I, 10th Texas Cavalry, "Recollections of the Battle of Murfreesboro," *Confederate Veteran*, Vol. 31:341-42.

2 Girardi and Hughes, *Carlin Memoirs*, 75; George W. Herr, *Nine Campaigns in Nine States, et all.* (San Francisco, 1890), 124.

be made serviceable. We had no sooner attended to one wounded man when one and another began to arrive, some walking, and some carried upon stretchers, but all more or less dangerously wounded."

"There was work for all. I was assigned the duty of taking the names of the wounded, their regiment, and the location and character of their wounds," Haigh continued. "While all this was going on, the fight outside became fiercer as the forces came into closer contact; a battery planted near the house convulsed the ground at every explosion and threatening to dash in pieces every pane of glass."[3]

A second field hospital was erected for Richard Johnson's Federals farther in the rear at the Colonel Smith Plantation along the Wilkinson Pike, near Overall's Creek. "There was excellent water with plenty of hay and straw, as well as a large frame house with was surrounded by numerous log houses occupied as Negro quarters," related surgeon Solon Marks. "Having assigned to duty all the medical officers of the division, either at the hospital or on the field, I rode to the front as darkness was approaching for the purpose of selecting a route by which ambulances could reach our troops. I found that the lines had advanced much farther than I had expected, leading me to fear that the hospital was too far in the rear."[4]

Chaplain William Smith of the 75th Illinois reined up in front of a field hospital, encountering a captain from his regiment who was dejectedly leading a horse to the nearby woods. "I saw him borrow a rifle from one of the men, lead his horse to a clump of bushes in a little hollow and shoot him to put him out of his misery for a ball had penetrated in the rear of the saddle flap and he was evidently dying," Smith wrote. "I found one ambulance in the yard and that was my bedroom for the night, although it was well smeared with blood. Lying there, thinking of tomorrow, of home and loved ones, there came the fact of President Lincoln's proclamation in reference to the slave states; unless before 12 o'clock the next night something had been definitely proposed or arranged, every slave would be made free! The thought thrilled me and I rejoiced in my heart as I thought of it."[5]

During the afternoon fighting, Lieutenant Reuben Searcy of the 34th Alabama suffered a severe wound from two shell fragments and was rushed to a hospital in Murfreesboro. Sergeant James Maxwell found him that evening. "Nothing had

3 Francis, *Narrative of a Private Soldier*, 105; Bennett, *History of the 36th Illinois*, 330-31.

4 Solon Marks, "Experiences at the Battle of Stone River," MOLLUS Wisconsin, Vol. 2. (Milwaukee, 1896), 389.

5 William Hutchinson Smith, *Incidents and Reminiscence of the Civil War* (2002), 11.

been done for him except dosing him heavily with morphine under the effects of which he was lying in his torn uniform soaked with blood," Maxwell mourned. "The surgeons' hands were full giving aid to those whose lives might possibly be saved by prompt attention. Those impossible to save were kept dosed with morphine merely to ease their passage to the great beyond. The surgeons of our own brigade had worked all night and were still behind, so I found two other surgeons whose commands had not yet been in action who willingly came to do what could be done. At once they saw that there was no hope for my friend but to keep down mental and physical pain until the end."[6]

*   *   *

Many years after the war, a legend grew that at sunset on December 30 the bands of both armies played competing national airs until joining together in "Home, Sweet Home," a popular tune enjoyed by men on both sides. "The night before the battle, an incident took place such as history seldom records," remembered Samuel Seay of the 1st Tennessee Infantry. "The opposing lines of battle were very fully developed and were so near to each other as to be within easy bugle call. Just before 'tattoo,' the military bands on each side began playing their evening music. The still winter night carried their strains to a great distance. At every pause on our side, far away could be heard the military bands of the other. Finally, one of them struck up 'Home, Sweet Home,' and as if by common ascent, all other airs ceased and the bands of both armies as far as the ear could hear, joined in the refrain. Who knows how many hearts were bold next day by reason of that air."

Although Seay's story is certainly poignant and widely quoted, its historical basis is questionable, particularly the portion where the bands united to play 'Home Sweet Home.' Ed Porter Thompson of the 6th Kentucky recounted clearly hearing the drum and bugle corps of the Federal army taunting the Confederates that evening "by playing 'Dixie' for a long time and with uncommon pathos and following this with two airs which the Southerners were trying their best to forget—'Yankee Doodle' and 'Hail Columbia.'"[7]

---

6 James R. Maxwell, Co. G, 34th Alabama, "Service of Dr. James Thomas Searcy," *Confederate Veteran*, Jul. 1920, 250.

7 Seay, "A Private at Stones River"; Thompson, *History of the Orphan Brigade*, 173-74. In reviewing more than 25,000 pages of documents concerning this campaign, I found that Seay's

It was a beautiful sunset, legend or not. "The clouds which had been drenching us most of the day had begun to clear away in the west and the light of the setting sun shone full upon the blue uniforms and bright guns of the troops in line, and lighted up the winding marching of those still coming up from the rear," observed Sergeant Henry V. Freeman of the Pioneer Brigade. "Thousands of men looked that afternoon for the last time on earth at the setting of the sun when it sank beyond the trees."[8]

With the two armies again camped within shouting distance of each other that night, fires were forbidden on both sides. The bitter cold forced the men to find creative ways to stay warm, spooning the most common choice. For John Clark and John Snodgrass, two recently enlisted privates of the 22nd Indiana, this was their last night together. "We messed together and slept together all the time and when he was sick, I took the best care of him that I could," Snodgrass wrote Clark's sister a week later. "In fact, we were like brothers. We slept together the night before the battle on some cedar bushes that we gathered to keep us out of the mud. We were not allowed any fires at all and we had no blankets as they had been left behind with the wagons. It was very cold that night and we could not sleep hardly any, but he told me that if got killed he wanted me to write to you."[9]

The Chicago Board of Trade Battery found itself camped in a "pretty spot," remembered Silas Stevens. "The entire camp was situated in a quiet and pleasant nook," he wrote. "The boys built a booth of boughs, had our suppers, and sang songs until the order for taps was given. Orders came for us to lie near the gun that night, so gathering a lot of boughs from the limbs of the young trees, I laid them on the ground by the limber of the gun and spread our blankets."

Captain Lyman Parcher of Company F, 101st Ohio, spent a restless night on picket duty in the woods and fields among the carnage of the afternoon's fight for Robertson's Battery, recalling: "We went in front to our posts for the night, our anxious watch rendered melancholy by the presence of many dead around us. This I believe to be the most unpleasant night of my life. Extremely cold for this latitude, where we dare not trust our eyes to close lest we slept with nothing but the anxiety

account was the original source of this story. The event may have occurred as Seay described, but it is conspicuously absent from contemporaneous accounts.

8 Henry V. Freeman, "Some Battle Recollections of Stone's River," MOLLUS Illinois, Vol. 3 (Chicago: 1899), 227-228.

9 Private John A. Snodgrass, Co. H, 22nd Indiana, SRNBP.

and peril of our situation served to nerve us up and render our condition tolerable."[10]

William Dodge of the 75th Illinois recalled that "toward the night, the wind swept coldly from the north, and no bivouac fires were allowed on the real front; the aspect was truly cheerless. At midnight the stars faintly twinkled through the cloud-rifts which still hung heavily overhead, portentous of rain. Within a half mile of each other lay two mighty armies, in the most perfect silence, waiting for the morning's light, to rush together in the deadly rencontre."

A 30th Indiana soldier remembered how "the sentinels stood motionless, peering with anxious eyes into the curtain of night, watching the many maneuvers of the mighty force which was now taking position in front. Everything was still save the moaning of the forest winds through the branches of distant trees which breathed a low and plaintive wail and seemed a prelude to the deadly fury of the fast approaching light."[11]

While positioning his front-line regiments that evening, Sill and a group of officers came under fire and Sill's aide-de-camp, Lieutenant James Davidson, was struck in the thigh by a musket ball. Davidson was carried back to the nearby Harding House hospital. "After dark, General Sill came in to see him," relayed Haigh. "It was a great comfort to the wounded man to have his general take such an interest in him. Just before leaving, he [Sill] stood for a while, leaning on his sword, wrapped in deep thought, and I imagined a shade of sadness on his fine face. I wondered whether some sad presentiment of his fate was passing through his mind as he stood, gazing silently on his wounded aide."[12]

Gloom seemed to impede Sill's generally sunny disposition for the rest of the evening. "I returned at night and stayed with General Sill on the battlefield for we had considerable fighting on that day, especially in the evening," remembered one of his staff officers, Lieutenant Edwin DeBruin of the 33rd Ohio. "I helped him arrange his bed, but about 10½ o'clock I got up and found his bed on fire and assisted him in putting it out. I do not think that he slept much after that."

Sill wandered to a nearby campfire and sat with Captain Joseph Stearns until after midnight. "The General and I were sitting by the fire when the General made

---

10 Memoir of Private Silas C. Stevens, Chicago Board of Trade Battery, SRNBP; Captain Lyman Parcher, Co. E, 101st Ohio, *Bucyrus Journal*, Jan. 30, 1863, 3.

11 Dodge, *A Waif of the War*, 63; Private William A. Ogden, Co. B, 30th Indiana, *Dawson's Daily Times and Union*, Jan. 23, 1863, 2.

12 Bennett, *History of the 36th Illinois*, 332.

the remark that 'perhaps the next night, we will not be together here, Stearns.' I passed it off as lightly as I could but it seemed to me that from that time on, he was more sedate and melancholy than usual." After sitting a while longer, Sill called for an orderly to bring him his horse, which awoke the dutiful DeBruin. "No DeBruin, you lie down and take your rest. You will have plenty of work to do tomorrow."[13]

Sill was hardly alone in his forebodings, as the men of both armies later recounted. General Liddell wrote that the sound of McCook's Tuesday afternoon assault sounded "like the roar of a Southern tornado. There were but few of the bravest men who listened with any assurance that they would escape harm in the coming conflict. Before sunset tomorrow they knew that thousands would fall, but the excitement of troops moving in all directions preparatory to action obliterated the impulses of feeling save that of the fiendish desire of man. I was forcibly reminded of the expression war is the natural state of man."

Robert Smith, orderly sergeant of the 2nd Tennessee, noted that "the position the two armies hold tonight makes it necessary for one side or the other to draw off or have a battle tomorrow. We are now within 500 yards of the enemy. There is many a brave soldier that is now enjoying the full vigor of health that will not live to see the setting of another sun. For I have no doubt but that tomorrow will be one of the bloodiest days of the war."[14]

"Captain Joel Foster of Co. G took supper with us that night and during the meal had little to say and seemed quite despondent," related Edwin Nicar, adjutant of the 15th Indiana. "Pressed for the reason," continued Nicar,

he replied that he had an earnest conviction that he would be killed in tomorrow's battle. He said, however, that he should strive to do his whole duty let the consequences be what they might. The chaplain and I made light of his forebodings and tried our best to cheer him up, but it was no use and he bade us good night, as it proved, for the last time. As for myself, my nerves were wrought up to the highest tension in expectation of the battle which was before us and my sleep was not of the soundest. I removed the saddle from my

13 First Lieutenant Edwin M. DeBruin, 33rd Ohio, Sill Family Papers, Ross County Historical Society; Captain Joseph Edward Stearns, 21st Ohio, Sill Family Papers, Ross County Historical Society.

14 Hughes, *Liddell's Record*, 107; Garrett, *Confederate Diary*, 87.

horse, using it as a pillow, but the bridle I did not disturb. An occasional picket shot during the night would startle us, but for the most part the night passed quietly.[15]

Still shaken from the battering his regiment received in charging Robertson's battery that afternoon, McKee was also convinced his luck had run out. "[J]ust before the fight began on the 30th," remembered Lieutenant Joseph Rackerby of Company E. "Colonel McKee told me that if he and Colonel Heg were killed, to see that his remains were sent home and he then offered me his money and watch to keep for him. I advised him to give them to the surgeon which he did, keeping his watch to himself. On the night of the 30th I saw and conversed with him again and he said that if they went into the fight the next day, he would go on foot as there was more danger on horseback."

Heg laconically wrote to his wife, "[P]oor McKee, I believe he expected to be killed. He was very gloomy the day before and in the morning before the fight began, he asked his hostler to take his horse and wanted him to take his watch and also gave Dr. Himmoe most of his money."[16]

William Bickham found Rosecrans's chief of staff Julius Garesche, a devout Catholic like his chief, sitting alone under a tree carefully praying over a Missal "as stealthy as a woman with a sweet missive from a lover. He bowed meekly over his book, his lips uttered inaudibly, the index finger of his right hand described the imaginary cross which symbolized his faith. Garesche felt he was a doomed man. An old woman who fancied she had inspirations superior to mortal gifts dreamed that Garesche would be killed in his first battle. She warned him and he smiled with amiable contempt. He was at Washington and she on the Mississippi."

"A year later he was in front of Murfreesboro but a presentiment had possessed his mind," Bickham noted. "He left Washington fixed in the somber belief that he would fall in his first battle. This was confided to a near relative. He never spoke of it to others."[17]

Sergeant Gallagher spent his first night in Confederate captivity in a camp somewhere along the road near Petersburg. "The night was very cold and quite a

---

15 Adjutant Edwin Nicar, 15th Indiana, "A Reminiscence of Stone's River," *National Tribune*, June 13, 1895, 1.

16 First Lieutenant Joseph H. Rackerby, Co. E, 15th Wisconsin, *Grant County Herald*, Feb. 17, 1863, 2; Theodore Blegen, editor. *The Civil War Letters of Hans Christian Heg, 15th Wisconsin Infantry* (Northfield, 1936), 168.

17 Bickham, *Rosecrans' Campaign*, 184-85.

number of fires were burning in every direction," he later wrote. "In a few moments we were told to march up into a field a short distance and dismount and build fires." He continued:

This was certainly the most exciting day we had spent in the army so far; we felt so stiff and sore from riding that we could hardly move about. We had eaten nothing since dinner and our present surroundings did not give us any appetite. We did not have much for supper; a few crackers and a little piece of bacon, that was captured from us, was all we had. We laid down by the fire and tried to sleep, the night being very cold, and, having no blankets, we felt chilly. About the time we began to doze, an order came to jump up and be ready to march; so, we got up, feeling so stiff we could hardly move. It was about 2 o'clock in the morning, and the last day of the year 1862.[18]

*   *   *

President Lincoln needed a victory.

The mood in the national capital during the Christmas season reflected the overall mood of the country. "There was little gaiety in the Executive House during this time," recalled Lincoln's secretary John Hay. "It was an epoch, if not of gloom, at least of a seriousness too intense to leave room for much mirth. . . . Mr. Lincoln's life was almost devoid of recreation. Mr. Lincoln spent most of his evenings in his office, though occasionally he remained in the drawing room after dinner, conversing with visitors or listening to music."

"As time wore on and the war held its terrible course, upon no one of all those who lived through it was its effect more apparent than upon the president," Hay continued. "He bore the sorrows of the nation in his own heart; he suffered deeply not only from disappointments, from treachery, from hope deferred, from open assaults of enemies, and from the sincere anger of discontented friends, but also from the worldwide distress and affliction which flowed from the great conflict in which he was engaged and which he could not evade."[19]

Two weeks before Christmas, Maj. Gen. Ambrose Burnside led the Army of the Potomac across the Rappahannock River into Fredericksburg. Nearly three months had passed since the armies last met at Antietam, and now, under a new commander, Lincoln expected results. Robert E. Lee had a key portion of his Army

18 Morris, *History of the 81st Indiana*, 34-35.

19 John Hay, "Life in the White House in the Time of Lincoln," *Century Magazine,* Nov. 1890.

President Abraham Lincoln

Library of Congress

of Northern Virginia expertly positioned upon Marye's Heights, just outside the town, and waited for Burnside to attack. Burnside complied on December 13, dispatching brigade after brigade into the killing fields in Lee's well-protected front and accumulating thousands of casualties to no avail. Courage and valor there was in abundance, but by the time the Army of the Potomac retreated, approximately 12,500 men had been killed, wounded, or captured, with Confederate casualties less than half that total. It was arguably the Army of the Potomac's most discouraging defeat of the war.

Lincoln struggled with squabbling within the Union high command. In Fredericksburg's aftermath, Maj. Gen. Joseph Hooker testified to the Joint Congressional Committee on the Conduct of the War that Burnside knew the strength of the Confederate position at Fredericksburg but attacked anyway. Morale in the army cracked; desertions skyrocketed in the wake of the defeat, and the army struggled even to supply rations and pay to its soldiers. Crusty Maj. Gen. Edwin Sumner, who died in March 1863 at age 66 shortly after leaving his command in the Army of the Potomac, observed that the problem was "there is a great deal too much croaking—there is not sufficient confidence."

In late December 1862, Burnside decided to storm Fredericksburg a second time, but was forbidden to do so by Lincoln, who learned from some of Burnside's officers that "the army was in no condition to move." Within days, Burnside would offer to retire to private life and suggested that Lincoln rid himself of both his chief of staff Henry Halleck and secretary of war Edwin M. Stanton, as Burnside felt neither had the "confidence of the officers or the country."

The officers profoundly felt the discouragement and dismay rife in the ranks. Brigadier General Alpheus S. Williams, a division commander in the army's XII

Corps, observed that "the disaster at Fredericksburg affects us all deeply. From our standpoint, it seems a most unaccountable sacrifice of life with no results. I am as discouraged and blue as one well can be as I see in these operations much that astonishes and confounds me, and much that must discourage our troops and the people." As Brig. Gen. John Geary, Williams's fellow division commander in the XII Corps, wrote to his wife: "[T]he deplorable condition of our country at this moment in every respect awakens our liveliest sensibilities, and the future looks sometimes like a dark abyss."[20]

There was no disputing that Fredericksburg was a military disaster of the first magnitude, and according to modern historian Doris Kearns Goodwin, Radical Republicans in the Senate—fed up with Democrat-leaning generals such as McClellan and Burnside who led armies into slaughter without success—demanded that "unless a more vigorous prosecution of the war was adopted, conservative demands for a compromise peace would multiply and the Union would be restored with slavery intact." Deciding that the problem was within Lincoln's Cabinet, these Republicans focused principally on Secretary of State William H. Seward, Lincoln's most loyal Cabinet minister, as the author of the country's sorrows. Seward caught wind of the proceedings and tendered his resignation, which Lincoln refused to accept. A few days later, the president met with nine of the most vocal of his Republican critics and deftly defused the situation; the proceedings, however, quickly became public knowledge and weighed upon the populace as further evidence that the country was teetering on dissolution.[21]

Frustration, anger, and war-weariness gripped the North. Recruiting had come to a standstill, and more states were resorting to the draft to meet the US government's demands for new troops. Reviewing the carnage of the previous 12 months, the Rev. Francis Holland of North Carolina wrote that "in an unprecedented degree, this year has been a year of affliction and bereavement. The desolating tide of an obstinate and bloody war has continued to roll over our land. Upon a moderate estimate, it is computed that not less than 200,000 men on both sides have perished or been permanently disabled during this year. Were these

---

20 Walter H. Hebert, *Fighting Joe Hooker* (Lincoln, 1999), 161-162; Milo M. Quaife, *From the Cannon's Mouth: The Civil War Letters of Alpheus S. Williams* (Detroit, 1959), 154; William A. Blair, *A Politician Goes to War: The Civil War Letters of John White Geary* (University Park, 1995), 72.

21 Doris Kearns Goodwin, *Team of Rivals: The Political Genius of Abraham Lincoln* (New York, 2005), 486-495.

ghastly victims of war to march past us, two and two, in close ranks and at quick time, not less than two whole days from sunrise to sunset would be required for the dismal procession to sweep past a given point!"[22]

War-weariness found its most potent voice in Ohio Democratic Congressman Clement Laird Vallandigham, who argued that it was time for the federal government to face facts, admit defeat, and come to terms with an independent Confederacy. "Twenty months have elapsed, but the rebellion is not crushed out; its military power has not been broken; the insurgents have not dispersed," Vallandigham asserted during a speech. "The Union is not restored; nor the Constitution maintained; nor the laws enforced. Twenty, 60, 90, 300, 600 days have passed; a thousand millions have been expended; and 300,000 lives lost or bodies mangled; and today the Confederate flag is still near the Potomac and the Ohio, and the Confederate Government stronger, many times, than at the beginning." Vallandigham continued along the same line before ending, "War for the Union was abandoned; war for the Negro openly begun, and with stronger battalions than before. With what success? Let the dead at Fredericksburg and Vicksburg answer."[23]

Regardless, preparations continued to mark the pending Emancipation Proclamation, which Lincoln was set to sign on January 1, 1863. It had been 100 days since the president had issued his preliminary proclamation on September 22, and it was clear that the states of the Confederacy did not intend to return to the Union willingly. Lincoln entertained hopes that some states might choose laying down their arms rather than risk their slaves being freed, but that simply did not happen.

The Cabinet met on December 29 to review the first draft of the proclamation and proposed a number of changes. Any mention of colonizing the freed blacks was dropped; provision was made to accept blacks into the armed forces; and to combat the charge that the administration was stoking "servile insurrection," a proviso was added indicating, "I hereby enjoin the people so declared to be free to abstain from all violence unless necessary in self-defense." A second Cabinet meeting was set for 10:00 a.m. on December 31 to finalize the draft. "Nothing was left for anyone else to do but wait," noted historian Louis Masur. "Gather and

---

22 https://gastonlibrary.libguides.com/c.php?g=578800&p=4001413; retrieved Aug. 14, 2022.

23 Clement L Vallandigham, *Speeches, Arguments, and Letters* (New York, 1864), 429-430.

wait—for a sign, for the word, for freedom. Wait for midnight and for 100 days of waiting to come to an end."

The direction of the war had indeed changed, but Lincoln needed a victory on the battlefield to ensure that the proclamation was not the "last shriek on the retreat" as he had once warned. Stymied east and west, Lincoln's hopes rested with William Rosecrans and his army in Tennessee.[24]

* * *

The meaning of the Emancipation Proclamation was certainly foremost on Confederate President Jefferson Davis's mind at the end of the year. Davis recently had placed his signature on a general order dated December 23 combating Lincoln's commencement of "servile insurrection." General Orders No. 111 was primarily directed against Maj. Gen. Benjamin Butler and his command in Louisiana, whom Davis claimed had committed "repeated outrages and atrocities" and whose mode of warfare has "bore no resemblance to such warfare as is along permissible by the rules of international law or the usages of civilization. African slaves have not only been excited to insurrection by every license and encouragement but numbers of them have actually been armed for a servile war—a war in its nature far exceeding in horrors the most merciless atrocities of the savages."

Davis proclaimed that any commissioned officer captured from Butler's command would be "reserved for execution" while enlisted soldiers would be sent home on parole. "All negro slaves captured in arms be at once delivered over to the executive authorities of the respective States to which they belong to be dealt with according to the laws of said States." The Confederate Congress later passed a joint resolution "stating that all Negroes and mulattos who engaged in the war and were taken in arms against the Confederacy were to be turned over to the authorities of the states in which they were captured to be dealt with according to the laws of that state. A strict adherence to the state laws meant that Negroes would be put to death."[25]

---

24 Louis P. Masur, *Lincoln's Hundred Days: The Emancipation Proclamation and the War for the Union* (Cambridge, 2012), 197-201.

25 OR 5/2:795-797; Robert J. Zorick, *Study of the Union and Confederate Reactions to the Emancipation Proclamation* (1964), 154-55.

Confederate President Jefferson Davis

Library of Congress

Since the early days of the Confederacy, there had been high hopes of obtaining recognition from the governments of both England and France; however, the Emancipation Proclamation forced England in particular to view the war through different lenses. "The empire had freed its slaves years earlier and it would not do for the government to seem pro-slavery now," noted historian Richard Wheeler. A letter to the editor of the London Gazette proclaimed that "we English have to open our eyes to the fact that the war in America has resolved itself into a war between freedom and slavery. There is now no medium course: slavery or freedom must prevail."

The chances of international recognition slid as 1863 began, and without it, the odds of Confederate independence became increasingly remote. Southern morale remained high, however, buoyed by their repeated successes in Virginia and now emboldened by the change in US war aims. Varina Davis, first lady of the Confederacy, felt "the effect of the Emancipation Proclamation on the people of the South was unmistakable. It roused them to a determination to resist to the uttermost a power that respected neither the rights of property nor constitutional guarantees."[26]

The South bore its own fair share of difficulties as the war entered a new year. Inflation in the Southern economy steadily pushed prices higher and higher. At the end of 1862, corn in Richmond traded at $3 a bushel wholesale while trade in leaf

26 Richard Wheeler, *Lee's Terrible Swift Sword: From Antietam to Chancellorsville: An Eyewitness History* (Edison, 1992), 326-27.

tobacco had been suspended. Butter sold for $1.25–$1.50 a pound and flour roughly $25 a barrel. Potatoes ran from $3–$4 a bushel while onions commanded $8–$10 a bushel. Venison and country sausage sold for 75 cents a pound. Limitations on the supply of bacon drove prices up to 70 cents per pound if it could be found. Coffee sold for $3 a pound while apple brandy now commanded $20 a gallon. Whiskey sold at $25–$30 a gallon, though the same whiskey sold in Cincinnati for 35 cents a gallon.

Manufactured goods were scarce and incredibly expensive if they could be found. Bleached muslin sold at $1.30–$1.45 per pound, country jeans as much as $5 a yard, and ladies' gaiters sold at $14.50 a pair. The state of the Southern economy made war-weariness not just a Northern phenomenon; in North Carolina alone, 49 counties expressed growing dissatisfaction with the war and Governor Zebulon Vance wrote Davis asking him to negotiate with Lincoln to end hostilities.[27]

Hope remained that the Democratic victories in the North during the fall elections might mean a negotiated peace without foreign intervention. "The Democrats of the United States may be able to use the present desire for peace and the Cabinet imbroglio to effect the offer of a truce," opined the Richmond Enquirer, "and if that offer is accompanied with the withdrawal of all the United States forces both on land and in blockade from the soil and harbors of all the states of the Confederate States, such a truce might eventuate in permanent peace. No truce that is not accompanied with an entire evacuation of the Confederate States can be accepted. Another Confederate victory might aid the call of an extra session of Congress, and the prospects of an invasion of Ohio and Pennsylvania by Generals [Joe] Johnston and Lee would go very far towards increasing the desire for peace. We hope then that our generals will never weary in well doing but push on their columns towards the enemy's country."[28]

As exhilarating as the December victories at Fredericksburg and Chickasaw Bayou, Mississippi, may have been, neither battle changed the grand calculus of the war. The survival of the Confederacy depended on the continued success of its armies. "From the first battle of Manassas to that of Fredericksburg, the United States armies have met with disasters in the east. But in the West, they have done better and many reverses have befallen the Confederate arms," editorialized the

27 "Financial and Commercial," *Richmond Dispatch*, Dec. 31, 1862, 1; "Commercial Record," *Richmond Enquirer*, Dec. 30, 1862, 3.

28 "The Condition of Affairs," *Richmond Enquirer*, Dec. 30, 1862, 4.

Charleston Mercury on December 30, 1862. "The disasters of the West have been the result chiefly of inefficient preparations, bad engineering, and a dilatory deficiency of troops and arms. The West has hardly had a fair chance," continued the paper:

> It is well that a man of General Joseph Johnston's ability is there, however late, and however vast the field given him to supervise and direct. If General Bragg is no strategist, yet his capacity as a fighter and tactician may be considerable. He is likely to have a fair trial with Rosecrans near Murfreesboro. We trust that the army which fought as raw recruits at Shiloh will do their work upon the Yankees as effectually now as disciplined veterans.[29]

Bragg spent December 30 in the saddle, galloping along his line observing the advance of Rosecrans's forces. About midday, he held another council with Generals Polk and Hardee to decide his next move. Bragg initially wanted to strike the Federal left, but Polk "doubted the propriety of this line of attack and proposed to turn the enemy's right where we outflanked him," wrote Bragg's chief of staff, Colonel George Brent. Swayed, Bragg "adopted this suggestion and orders were accordingly given; General Hardee being ordered to assume command on the left." The assault would take place the following morning.

The Army of Tennessee's commander believed that only a bold stroke would allow him to hold his position at Murfreesboro. Wheeler's reports during the day removed any fears that Rosecrans intended to loop around the army's right flank on the Lebanon Road. That known, he was confident Breckinridge could repulse any cross-river assault that might take place on his front. "His advices convinced him that Rosecrans, under cover of the day's attack, had been massing his troops for a move on our left flank," remembered another of Bragg' staff officers, Colonel David Urquhart. Bragg understandably misread Rosecrans' intentions, as that was exactly the impression Rosecrans intended to make: to demonstrate with his right (McCook) to hold Bragg's attention while he launched an offensive on Bragg with his left.[30]

Typically offensive-minded, Bragg decided to stack McCown's and Cleburne's divisions on his army's far left, placing both under Hardee's direct command, and planned an attack on McCook's position at dawn. Most of the pieces to launch the

29 "Operations in the West," *Charleston Mercury*, Dec. 30, 1862, 1.

30 Urquhart, *Battles and Leaders*, Vol. 3, 606; Diary of Colonel George Brent, Braxton Bragg Papers, WRHS.

Lieutenant General William J. Hardee

Library of Congress

attack were already in place: Breckinridge's four brigades were well-entrenched atop Wayne's Hill, with several batteries holding commanding views of the river crossings. Withers' Division was entrenched in the center, and two brigades of Cheatham's Division (Maney's and Vaughan's) already had moved into supporting positions behind Withers' left flank earlier in the day. Donelson's and A. P. Stewart's brigades supported Withers's right and remained in position near the junction of the Nashville and Wilkinson pikes. All that remained was to move Cleburne's four brigades into position to support McCown.

"It was an admirable plan," Liddell contended. "By a sudden grand swing or right wheel of the whole line, the pivot flank touching Stones River, he would overlap and turn Rosecrans' right wing. This plan of attack would give Bragg the advantage of the initiative and at the same time force Rosecrans to take the hazard of changing position in the face of a vigorous attack. If everything went well, it would be only necessary to persist in this design and bring up the reserve to ensure complete success, neglecting his right wing which was protected by the precipitous bank of the river."[31]

Cleburne received his orders to move about 4:00 p.m. and had the 6,000 or so men of his division on the road before 6, though he had to wait at the ford until Hardee finished examining the ground. "It was dark when staff officers were sent to order me forward and show me my position," Cleburne reported. "The passage of the river in the night was attended with many difficulties, and my whole division was not in position before midnight. Soon after midnight I received an order from

31 Hughes, *Liddell's Record*, 107.

General Hardee, on which I based and issued the following circular, viz: 'Generals of brigades will have their respective commands in readiness to move upon the enemy at 4:30 this morning. The several commands will fall into line without signal of bugle or drum.'"[32]

Cleburne's Division promptly embarked on the five-mile march. "At twilight, the 5th Arkansas tramped down the Lebanon Pike through the darkened streets of Murfreesboro and out the Salem Pike," wrote one historian. "In order to come into position in darkness and remain unobserved, cavalry scouts led the corps to the right off the Salem Pike and forded the river in the rear of the McCullough farm. Cleburne's troops forded near waist-deep water to emerge dripping and shivering in the back fields of the McCullough farm."[33]

"We had the river to cross which made it so late going five miles as we had to cross it on rails and rocks," recalled Enoch Wall of the 2nd Arkansas. Added Captain Valentine McGehee of the 2nd Arkansas: "[A]bout 12 we were ordered to make no noise, all go to rest. The commissary came along and gave each man a small drink of whiskey."

General Lucius Polk's Brigade led Cleburne's column and crossed the river by 9:00 p.m., going into position with his right flank on the south side of the Franklin Road, followed by Bushrod Johnson's Brigade, which went into position on Polk's left. S.A.M. Wood's Brigade, now joined by the 3rd Confederate Infantry, followed but stepped out of the road to allow Liddell's command to assume position on the left of Johnson's line, forming as the division's left flank. Wood then assumed a reserve position astride the Franklin Road in support of Polk's Brigade. Hardee set up his headquarters in front of Liddell's Brigade a few hundred yards south of the road.[34]

*   *   *

Rosecrans was undoubtedly convinced he had Bragg where he wanted him the night of December 30. Although McCook's advance had been blunted, the damage had not been detrimental, and Rosecrans was positive Bragg would remain behind

---

32 OR 20/1:844.

33 Floyd R. Barnhill and Calvin L. Collier, *The Fighting Fifth: Pat Cleburne's Cutting Edge: The Fifth Arkansas Infantry Regiment, C.S.A.* (Jonesboro, 1990), 62.

34 Private Enoch J. Wall, Co. F, 2nd Arkansas, author's collection; Diary of Captain Valentine M. McGehee, Co. G, 2nd Arkansas, Arkansas Historical Association.

his entrenchments and wait for Rosecrans to move. The command was in good form; reports remained sketchy about the condition of the army's supply trains after Wheeler's raid, but plenty of ammunition was on hand to support the army in an engagement. Like Bragg, Rosecrans decided to strike against Bragg's right. The plan was to take Van Cleve's division, then in reserve, and move it east across McFadden's Ford. General Wood would follow Van Cleve across the river at the Upper Ford and join on Van Cleve's right. The two divisions would align on the broad plains east of the river and, under the cover of a Federal artillery barrage, strike at Breckinridge's isolated division.

"This would have given us two divisions against one," Rosecrans reported, "and, as soon as Breckinridge had been dislodged from his position, the batteries of Wood's division, taking position on the heights east of Stones River, in advance, would dislodge them, and enable Palmer's division to press them back, and drive them westward across the river or through the woods."

"Thomas, sustaining the movement on the center, would advance on the right of Palmer, crushing their right," he continued, "and Crittenden's corps, advancing, would take Murfreesboro, and then, moving westward on the Franklin road, get in their flank and rear and drive them into the country toward Salem, with the prospect of cutting off their retreat and probably destroying their army."

In the overall plan, McCook's force would be the anvil against which Crittenden and Thomas would hammer Bragg's retreating force. Once Bragg was cut off from his railhead at Murfreesboro, he would have no choice but to retreat south along the Salem Pike, where McCook ideally would be positioned to assail him.[35]

One point of controversy is Rosecrans's contention that there was a meeting with his corps commanders at his headquarters at 9:00 that night, where "the plan of battle was fully explained and that you all received verbally your orders for the next day's work." Rosecrans laid out his battle plan and stated that "it was explained to them that this combination, insuring us a vast superiority on our left, required for its success that General McCook should be able to hold his position for three hours; that, if necessary to recede at all, he should recede, as he had advanced on the preceding day, slowly and steadily, refusing his right, thereby rendering our success certain."

35 OR 20/1:192.

Having explained the plan, Rosecrans stressed to McCook: "You know the ground; you have fought over it; you know its difficulties. Can you hold your present position for three hours?"

McCook responded, "Yes, I think I can."

The commander followed with, "I don't like the facing so much to the east, but must confide that to you, who know the ground. If you don't think your present the best position, change it. It is only necessary for you to make things sure."

With that, Rosecrans reported, the officers returned to their commands.

None of the four corps commanders concurred that such a meeting took place. Crittenden declared he was unaware of it (the Kentuckian reportedly was asleep when the summons came, and Major Lyne Starling, his chief of staff, did not press the issue, cognizant of Crittenden's exhaustion) while Thomas recalled no meeting with the other corps commanders that night. Nevertheless, Thomas stated that he and Rosecrans talked at Thomas's headquarters, "during which time you explained to me in substance that McCook's corps was to engage the enemy's attention and hold him in his front the next day whilst our left was to attack and crush the enemy's right. I did not ride up to your tent that evening."

McCook likewise disputed Rosecrans's account. "I did not know that any such meeting had taken place until I saw it in General Rosecrans report," he asserted in March 1863. "No corps commander heard any conversation between General Rosecrans and myself on the night of the 30th as his report implies."

Bickham reported that about 6:00 that night Rosecrans dispatched orders written by Captain Robert S. Thoms to McCook for the following day: "Take a strong position. If the enemy attacks you, fall back slowly, refusing your right, contesting the ground inch by inch. If the enemy does not attack you, you will attack them not vigorously but warmly. The time of attack by you to be designated by the General commanding."

Later that night, McCook rode to Rosecrans's headquarters accompanied by Stanley and his aide-de-camp, Captain Beverly Williams. The party arrived about 9:30 p.m. "General Stanley was present during most of the conversation I had with General Rosecrans and Captain Williams was present during it all," reported McCook, who continued:

I did not understand General Rosecrans to say that I had the option of changing my line of battle, nor have I any recollection of "three hours" being mentioned in our conversation. General Rosecrans did ask if I could hold my line. I replied, "I think I can," meaning of course if I were assailed by the enemy that I had fought during the day, but most certainly not meaning against the combined army under General Bragg. The details of the plan of battle were never explained to me, nor did I know what they were until I saw the published report of General Rosecrans in the Cincinnati Commercial of February 28, 1863. I did receive a written order from Garesche which explained what I had to do on the 31st.[36]

There was a clearly a disconnect between what Rosecrans said transpired that night and what the witnesses remember, and the weight of evidence tends to support the corps commanders' contentions. It appears that Rosecrans's battle plan was delivered to the commanders piecemeal, but each seemed to understand its broad objectives. McCook received a written order around 6:30 that night and apparently discussed some portions of the plan with Rosecrans at 9:30 p.m. Thomas apparently covered his role with Rosecrans during an evening visit at Thomas's headquarters; Crittenden was asleep but had spent most of his day riding at Rosecrans's side and presumably the two men had discussed the next day's assault.

Stanley rode back with McCook after McCook's 9:30 meeting and agreed with McCook's version of events. "None of these instructions were addressed to me as I had just received instructions to collect a cavalry force and march to LaVergne for the purpose of protecting our trains," Stanley averred. About 1:00 a.m., Stanley's orderly woke him with a note from Garesche reporting that the one of the army's supply trains had been attacked the previous day and Rosecrans was worried that the roving Confederate cavalry would hit the army's largest train then parked along the Nashville Pike near Stewart's Creek. "I aroused our men and set out very soon for Stewart's Creek where our trains were supposed to be," Stanley wrote. "The night was cold, but before 5 in the morning I arrived at Stewart's Creek where I found Colonel Joe Burke of the 10th Ohio with two regiments, safe and secure. As day broke, my scouts came in and I was assured there was no danger to our trains."[37]

McCook passed along his understanding of Rosecrans's battle plan to his division commanders at some point during the night. "In the course of the evening, General Rosecrans furnished General McCook with an order to the effect that a great battle was to be fought on the following day," recalled General Johnson. "McCook called his division commanders together and explained to each one what was expected of him. On retiring from General McCook's headquarters, I called my brigade commanders around me and explained the order, and when they left, each understood thoroughly what was required of his command. General

36 Bickham, *Rosecrans' Campaign*, 199; OR 20/2:381-383.

37 Stanley, *Personal Memoirs*, 125.

Rosecrans desired to create the impression that he was massing his forces heavily on our right. Accordingly, he allowed no fires to be built by the troops in line but had immense log fires made away off to our right and Lieutenant Colonel Elisha B. Langdon of the 1st Ohio, who had an immensely heavy voice, was sent out to these fires to give commands locating imaginary divisions, brigades, and regiments. Now this plan would have succeeded with an unenterprising enemy, but Bragg knew as many of the tricks of war as Rosecrans."[38]

"The position of the right wing was mostly on a high cedar-covered ridge with open ground, corn and cotton fields in front," wrote William Dodge. "The center was on rolling and more commanding ground but covered by a dense cedar thicket to the rear and left. The left wing was posted on ground rather undulating, skirted with timber with open fields in front. All along this line of battle extended a valley, gradually narrowing from right to left and varying in width from 200-400 yards."

It was not a terrible position; Sheridan's front was a strong one, and Davis likewise had the advantage of a thick forest to shield his line. Kirk's and Willich's brigades, however, curled around Gresham Lane's intersection with the Franklin Pike, dangling like a worm on a hook. Kirk and Willich were Johnson's most experienced brigadiers and held this sector with battle-tested troops, but the position was the result of happenstance rather than choice. Neither Johnson nor his subordinates had much time to survey the ground before occupying it that afternoon. Their arrival just before sunset prevented more than a cursory survey.[39]

Robert Stewart of the 15th Ohio, in Willich's brigade, noted that "behind us was a large field of cornstalks, the ground gently sloping back for a mile or more to the creek. On the right were open fields as far as the eye could see and, on the left, a cedar thicket with large limestone rocks covering the ground. In front were heavy woods dark with cedar underbrush and full of we knew not what. But we had some reason for thinking that there was nothing there worse than the silent gloom."

A concern with Rosecrans's orders to Stanley to gather his cavalry and move north to La Vergne to protect the army's supply trains was that it pulled Zahm's brigade off the line, leaving the army's flank defended only by a thin skirmish line. There were no natural features on which to anchor the line, and actually Willich's right flank jutted out temptingly with nothing between it and Puckett Creek, several

---

38 Johnson, *A Soldier's Reminiscences*, 210.

39 Dodge, *History of the Old Second Division*, 400-401.

hundred yards west, other than a few scattered videttes who busied themselves lighting fires.[40]

Kirk deployed his pickets 150–200 yards in front of the brigade's main line on the edge of the woods just east of Gresham Lane. The 77th Pennsylvania held the brigade's left, linked with Post's brigade, followed by the 30th Indiana (with six of its 10 companies on the skirmish line), the 29th Indiana, and the 34th Illinois (holding the brigade's right). Edgarton, though pleased by his battery's inspired performance that afternoon, worried he was being placed in an exceedingly bad position if the contest were to continue in the morning. Only two of his guns faced southeast across the Franklin Road; the remaining four guns were parked along Gresham Lane. A superb artillery position lay a few hundred yards up the lane along the ridge, where Johnson had placed his headquarters and reserve brigade under Colonel Philemon Baldwin. As the divisional chief of artillery, Edgarton wanted all three batteries of the division placed on the ridge.

"I represented to General Kirk that my men were very weary, my horses almost famished, and my ammunition was short in the limber chests of the pieces and asked permission to withdraw long enough to prepare for the hard work on the following day," Edgarton reported. "General Kirk pointed out a spot about 100 yards in the rear of the position I then occupied, sheltered by a heavy growth of timber, and ordered me to bivouac there for the night. I reported to him that I could not place my guns into battery there or defend myself if assaulted. He replied that I should be protected and that ample notice should be given when I was expected to take a position in the line of battle. After I had brought my guns into park, the right of the brigade was thrown across the muzzles in front."

Edgarton was not shy expressing his displeasure about the battery's position. Recalled William Laughlin: "Our captain, seeing that we were in a very unfavorable position to meet an attack and feeling sure that the Rebels were preparing for such an attack, went to the General commanding our division and as ranking captain requested the privilege of moving our three batteries back to the brow of a hill some 40 or 50 rods back of the piece of woods we were in with an open cornfield between. His plan was to put the batteries in line and double charge them with canister and wait for the morning. The Rebs would need to cross this open field in getting to us, and he argued we could make their reception uncomfortably warm for them. As I have it, however, General Johnson told him to go back to his

40 Robert B. Stewart, 15th Ohio, "The Battle of Stone River, as Seen by One Who was There," *Blue and Gray*, Vol. 5 (1895), 12.

command saying, 'I guess I know my business,' so our captain came back in a rage and we stayed."[41]

Gunner George Stacey remembered Johnson's and Edgarton's conversation differently. "Our division general named Johnson gave orders for us to hold our ground right there and camp for the night," Stacey would write. "Our captain stepped up to him and said, 'General, I believe we will be attacked tonight. You had better let me come to an action front and load with double charges of canister so that if we should be attacked, we shall be ready to meet them.' The general replied, 'Never mind, you won't be attacked. You see there are eight more batteries to the left of us within a quarter of a mile.'"[42]

Reportedly Willich also had words with Johnson that evening regarding preparations for battle. "General Willich went to old Johnson and asked him if the brigade should load their pieces and the old fellow stopped him as short as he could," recalled David Wynn of the 49th Ohio. "He told our brigadier general that he was in command and that he should go to his quarters and he would send him word when he should load. We were ordered to lay on our arms and not one of them was loaded. Our major [Benjamin Porter] came up to our company and I asked him why we did not load and he said there was not a gun in the brigade that was loaded."

Edgarton, sick with a fever and now sick with worry, paced restlessly through his camp much of the night. "He walked through the park between 10 and 11 and admonished me to keep a sharp lookout," remembered William Beach of the 49th Ohio. "'Instruct your guard to be watchful and if anything suspicious occurs, notify me immediately for our situation is hazardous in the extreme. If we are suddenly attacked, we will be overwhelmed before our infantry can form.' … Generals Kirk and Willich were on the alert and both made the rounds frequently through the night to see that all was well."[43]

Willich's brigade formed on the right flank of the 34th Illinois. Holding Willich's left was the 39th Indiana, with five companies on the skirmish line, some as far out at 700 yards, and the other five forming a color line along a fence that paralleled the Franklin Road. The 32nd Indiana was aligned right of the 39th along the same fence, with three companies on picket 600 yards south of the position.

---

41 *OR* 20/1:300; Laughlin Letter.

42 Private George H. Stacey, Battery E, 1st Ohio Light Artillery, *Cleveland Plain Dealer*, Jan. 15, 1863, 2

43 Private David M. Wynn, Co. B, 49th Ohio, Lewis Leigh Collection, USAMHI; Beach Letter.

The 49th Ohio held the brigade's right on the Franklin Road, and the inexperienced 89th Illinois formed in double column in woods behind the Ohioans. Captain Goodspeed's Battery A of the 1st Ohio Light assumed an oblong square position west of the 49th Ohio while the 15th Ohio faced west just north of Battery A, completing the croquet wicket alignment.

Questions have been raised as to the mindset of the McCook and his generals on the night of December 30. Were they too confident or too oblivious to the danger? That sense of confidence eroded over the course of the night. Initially, McCook seemed confident that he could hold his ground. Before attending the 9:30 p.m. meeting with McCook and Rosecrans, Stanley rode beyond the army's right flank with an escort and "found the enemy extended in force far beyond McCook's right." Reporting that to McCook and Rosecrans, Stanley recounted acidly, "McCook seemly utterly indifferent and laughed, joked, and rolled around his rail pen, filled with fodder to make a soft bed, with the good nature and love of fun of a boy on his first picnic."[44]

However jocose and blithe McCook seemed, some of his brigadiers sensed danger and tried to nudge their commanders into taking action—Sill foremost among them. Detailed to duty with the army's provost marshal's office, James Woodard rode along the Federal lines that night and was startled by what he saw when he arrived at Sill's camp. "It was then probably about 10 o'clock and from General Sill's headquarters looking eastward and southward, we could clearly see large bodies of troops passing between us and the enemy's campfires, moving to their left which was our right," Woodard wrote. "I spoke to General Sill about this movement, and he informed me that it had been going on ever since dark and he was satisfied that the enemy was attempting a flank movement upon our right and suggested that I go on and ascertain how far the movement extended."

"I followed our line, keeping the movements of the enemy in sight, along in front of Davis's division and out to the Franklin Pike to Johnson's division," Woodard added. "When I reached Johnson's line, I found it lay in the shape of a hook. There was a body of cavalry lying in front of Johnson's extreme right with pickets for a considerable distance towards Overall's [Puckett] Creek. I attempted to follow this line further but was stopped by the pickets and after a good deal of difficulty found my way back to General Johnson's headquarters and was told by his staff officers that they had noticed the movements of the enemy and that the General had gone back to General McCook's headquarters which were said to be

---

44 Johnson, *A Soldier's Reminiscences*, 210-211; Stanley, *Personal Memoirs*, 124-125.

near the Gresham House. The officers of General Johnson's staff who were present seemed very uneasy about the movements of the enemy in front."[45]

Sill, unable to sleep and concerned with the continual tramp of Confederates a few hundred yards to the east, embarked on a ride along his lines. Alarmed that the Confederates might be aiming to strike the Federals' exposed right flank, he galloped back to apprise his dear friend Sheridan of the situation. "At 2 o'clock in the morning of the 31st," Sheridan remembered, "General Sill came back to me to report that on his front a continuous movement had been going on all night within the Confederate lines, and that he was convinced that Bragg was massing on our right with the purpose of making an attack from that direction early in the morning. After discussing the probabilities of such a course on the part of the enemy, I thought McCook should be made acquainted with what was going on, so Sill and I went back to see him at his headquarters not far from the Gresham House where we found him sleeping on some straw in the angle of a worm fence."[46]

Accompanying Sill and Sheridan, Woodward witnessed their predawn meeting with McCook. "General Sheridan woke him up and reported to him the general condition of the front of the line," he wrote. "General McCook said in substance: 'I have reported to General Rosecrans all the facts which you gave me. I have been advised by Johnson and Davis of the situation, but my orders from General Rosecrans are very definite. The plan of battle is for the attack to be made by our left wing. In fact, Crittenden and Thomas are expected to do most of the fighting. I am merely to hold my line if the enemy attacks me, and if he does not attack me, I am to attack him with sufficient force to hold his attention, but I am not to make an attack until further orders from department headquarters."[47]

Sill and Sheridan rode back to Sheridan's headquarters and discussed the matter further, Sill's anxiety finally convincing "Little Phil" to dispatch two regiments from the divisional reserve to bolster his right flank. "He then rejoined his brigade, better satisfied, but still adhering to the belief he had expressed when first making his report," Sheridan observed. Upon returning to his brigade, Sill visited Major Elisha Hibbard of the 24th Wisconsin, arriving about 3:00 a.m.

---

45 James H. Woodard, "General A. McD. McCook at Stones River." *Military Order of the Loyal Legion of the United States, California/Oregon, Volume 1* (Wilmington, 1995), 153. Puckett Creek lay just the west of Willich's position and is a tributary of Overall's Creek, the confluence of the two watercourses being before the Wilkinson Pike crosses Overall's Creek. Most period sources refer to the smaller watercourse as Overall's Creek.

46 Sheridan, *Personal Memoirs*, 119-120.

47 Woodard, MOLLUS, 154-155.

"General Sill came down to the regiment and said we would be supported from the reserve brigade," Hibbard recalled. "The men were then awake and ready for action."

While checking his lines before dawn, Sill met Colonel Woodruff, commanding the neighboring brigade of Davis's division. Woodruff shared his concerns about his position and indicated to Sill that he, too, had no support for his front line. "I pointed out to General Sill the weakness of the line at this point and requested him to order up some regiments of his brigade, held in reserve, to strengthen his right and protect my left, feeling certain that the enemy meditated an attack and that it would be made at that place," Woodruff wrote. "He agreed with me and immediately ordered up two regiments, which remained but a short time."[48]

Sheridan's orders arrived at Colonel Frederick Schaefer's headquarters just before daybreak, and the Missourian dispatched the 15th Missouri and 44th Illinois under the command of Lt. Col. John Weber to reinforce Sill. Nervously awaiting the arrival of his reinforcements, Sill called for Lieutenant DeBruin, telling him, "I wish you to report to General Sheridan again today for duty and tell him that the reserve has not arrived." As he left for Sheridan's headquarters, DeBruin came upon Weber's just-arriving reserves. Sill "gave me the directions as to which place I had to occupy," Weber reported, noting that he "formed his troops a few paces in the rear of the 24th Wisconsin, which also allowed the two regiments to keep watch on Sill's right flank."[49]

Woodard returned to Willich's camp before dawn. "I found General Willich about half past five in the morning sitting by a campfire, drinking some coffee, and he asked me to join him at breakfast which I did," recalled Woodard. "A few hours before all had been noise and confusion upon his front, but now everything was entirely quiet." The officers were eating when an orderly from General Johnson's headquarters arrived with a dispatch for Willich: "General McCook is apprehensive that an attack will be made upon your line at daybreak. See that your men are under arms and on the alert." According to Woodard, Willich laughed and said in his German way, 'They are so quiet out there I guess they are all no more here.'

48 Sheridan, *Personal Memoirs*, 120; *OR* 20/1:288, 364.

49 DeBruin Letter; Report of Lieutenant Colonel John Weber, 15th Missouri, *Daily St. Louis Republican*, Jan. 26, 1863, 1.

Nevertheless, he finished his breakfast and mounted his horse and rode along the line of his brigade."[50]

Before retiring in the early hours of December 31, Rosecrans dictated an address to be read to the troops before they went into battle that morning. "The General commanding desires to say to the soldiers of the Army of the Cumberland that he was well pleased with their conduct yesterday," it began. "It was all that he could have wished for. He neither saw nor heard of any skulking. They behaved with the coolness and gallantry of veterans." The address continued:

> He now feels perfectly confident, with God's grace and their help, of striking this day a blow for the country the most crushing, perhaps, which the rebellion has yet sustained. Soldiers! The nation may be said to hang on the issues of this day's battle. Be true then, to yourselves, true to your own manly character and soldierly reputation; true to the love of your dear ones at home whose prayers ascend this day to God for your success. Be cool. I need not ask you to be brave. Keep ranks. Do not throw away your fire. Fire slowly, deliberately—above all, fire low, and be always sure of your aim. Close readily in upon the enemy and when you get within charging distance, rush upon him with your bayonet. Do this, and victory will certainly be yours. Recollect that there are hardly any troops in the world that will stand a bayonet charge, and that those who make it, therefore, are sure to win.

"But four brigades of that splendid host had opportunity to hear it," Bickham later noted. "The shock of battle was felt before the ink with which it was penned was fairly dry."

Among those who never had that opportunity was Corporal Henry N. Rankin, of the 39th Indiana, farthest out on the picket line on the army's right flank. From his position at dawn, Rankin could hear "the Rebel pickets conversing in a low tone. I cautioned our reserve officers as to conditions in our front but they thought it would come out all right. I warned all of the pickets of a very early attack and told them at the first gun to give way and make for our reserve." Rankin had placed the last pickets on duty before daybreak and had barely reached his reserve and packed his knapsack "when the first gun was fired on my pickets."[51]

---

50 Woodard, MOLLUS, 155.

51 Bickham, *Rosecrans' Campaign*, 202; Corporal Henry N. Rankin, Co. D, 39th Indiana, "Midwinter Battle of Stones River," *National Tribune*, Jul. 22, 1926, 6.

Like a Thunderbolt

JOHN PORTER McCOWN was likely not Braxton Bragg's first choice to spearhead the Army of Tennessee's daring dawn assault on Wednesday, December 31. McCown, after all, commanded the last division of Edmund Kirby Smith's army still attached to Bragg's army and labored under a cloud of suspicion from the volatile commander—deemed one of Bragg's "undesirables" from the outset of their time together in June 1862.

This was unfortunate, as McCown certainly had the right pedigree. An 1840 graduate of West Point (ranking 10th in his class), the Tennessean served with distinction in the 4th Artillery during the Mexican War, earning a brevet for gallantry at Cerro Gordo. McCown resigned his commission in May 1861 as Tennessee prepared to leave the Union, and by March 1862 he wore the twin stars of major general, in command of the Confederate fortifications at New Madrid, Missouri, and Island No. 10.

The Southern press would skewer McCown for his hasty abandonment of New Madrid that March, and after being falsely accused of drunkenness for that decision and the subsequent setback at Island No. 10, he was reassigned to division command in Maj. Gen. Earl Van Dorn's Army of the West and then to the Army of Mississippi's Second Corps after Bragg took command in June 1862. Bragg went so far as to label McCown "his worst division commander."

Temporarily assigned to Hardee's Corps at Murfreesboro, McCown's 4,400-man independent three-brigade division may have been a third wheel organizationally in the Army of Tennessee, but the men in its ranks were undeniably first-rate fighters. Holding McCown's right was Brig. Gen. Evander

McNair's brigade of Arkansans; in the center was Ector, commanding a brigade of dismounted Texas cavalrymen; and on the left was 29-year-old James Rains of Nashville, a newly promoted brigadier like Ector. McNair's and Ector's units had played a key role in striking the Federal army's right flank during the August fighting at Richmond, Kentucky, and would reprise that role at Stones River.

Bragg later criticized McCown for his faulty deployment at the outset of the battle on December 31, claiming that in doing so he delayed the Confederate attack by an hour—charges that McCown heatedly (and rightfully) denied. The crux of the disagreement was an order from Hardee, shortly after sunset on December 30, directing McCown to move McNair's Brigade forward 200 yards from its position along the Franklin Road, which brought McNair in line with Loomis's position. McCown reiterated that when Hardee arrived on the left flank that Tuesday evening, he conferred with both McCown and Cheatham "to explain the location of our commands and the nature of the ground in our respective fronts. On the latter point General Cheatham and myself materially differed."

"General Hardee, as I understood, accepted [his] explanation of the ground, and ordered me to change the position of McNair's brigade. I told General Hardee that either he did not understand General Cheatham or I did not understand his order. I then requested General Hardee either to locate the brigade himself or to order General Cheatham to accurately point out the ground. General Cheatham was directed by [him] to comply with my request. I was thus particular because I felt satisfied that an attempt to locate the brigade as I understood General Hardee to direct, would bring on a night engagement, for which I would be held responsible."[1]

Hardee reported that McCown did not move McNair until early Wednesday morning, hence delaying the attack; the evidence, however, does not support either Hardee's or Bragg's contentions. McCown did not help his cause when he initially reported that "at the dawn of day, in obedience to orders from Lieutenant General Hardee, I moved my reserve brigade [McNair's] and placed it on my right, and moved upon the enemy in my front, about 600 or 800 yards distant." Cheatham, tasked with placing McNair's men in line, claimed it occurred "just before dark on Tuesday evening." McNair agreed with Cheatham, as did Ector, who reported that he had McNair moved into line with his brigade and wrote: "I am confident its movements could not have been concealed from the enemy and it would, in all probability, have brought on a fight during the night."

---

1 *OR* 20/1:917-918.

Captain C. B. Kilgore, Ector's assistant adjutant general, recalled seeing McNair's men marching into position on Ector's right about 8:00 p.m. Tuesday. Once in position, McNair's Brigade faced northwest, with its right flank on the Franklin Road and its left a hundred yards or so beside Ector's right flank. Federal pickets from Kirk's and Willich's brigades patrolled the cornfield less than 300 yards away.[2]

Ector's dismounted troopers took position facing west along a fence that paralleled the lane leading to the McCulloch Farm. The 10th Texas held the brigade's right flank, its own flank resting near the Franklin Road. To its left, in order, were the 14th Texas, the 15th Texas, and the 11th Texas. McNair was on Ector's right rear, facing northwest, with the 4th Arkansas Battalion on the brigade's left flank, placed to the right rear of the 10th Texas. The 30th Arkansas was next in line to the right, then the 4th Arkansas, and finally the 2nd Arkansas and the 1st Arkansas—regiments of dismounted riflemen holding the flank on the Franklin Road near the Widow Smith House. Having seen extended service together, McNair's and Ector's brigades concocted nicknames for one another: the Texans called McNair's Arkansans "Joshies," and the Arkansans labeled the Texans "Chubs"—both parties maintaining warm regard for the fighting abilities of their fellow Trans-Mississippi comrades-in-arms.

Rains's Brigade covered the division's left flank, with the 3rd Georgia Battalion on the right, adjacent to the 11th Texas, the 9th Georgia Battalion, the 11th Tennessee, and the 29th North Carolina.

Hardee summoned his division commanders to a 5:45 a.m. conference at Cleburne's headquarters, providing their final instructions for the assault. There was an important change, as Bragg had added Wharton's cavalry on the far left, straddling Rains's position. Wharton's mission was to ride out at dawn, launch a strike beyond the Federal army's flank, and then swoop into Rosecrans's rear to attack McCook's wagon trains along Gresham Lane and the Wilkinson Pike. Rosecrans's plan of having Stanley's cavalrymen light fires far outside the army's actual flank may have played a role in Wharton's deployment, in which case Rosey's attempted deception backfired badly. With the addition of Wharton's troopers, Hardee had roughly 14,000 men directly under his command for the assault, or more than one-third of Bragg's entire Army of Tennessee.[3]

2 Ibid., 922-924.

3 J. G. McCown, Co. K, 15th Texas Cavalry, "About Ector's and McNair's Brigade," *Confederate Veteran*, Mar. 1901, 113; OR 20/1:773.

All of McCown's men were awake by 5:00 a.m., though few had slept because of the bitter cold. In those frigid predawn hours, Captain John O'Brien of the 30th Arkansas recalled that "General McNair told us if we wished to run the risk, we could light fires. We did run the risk and kept warm all night and were not molested. A little before daylight, McNair sent to the brigade a barrel of whiskey and we all took a good drink of which we stood in much need and voted McNair the best of generals."

It had been a damp, bone-chilling night. "There was a drizzling rain falling which froze as it fell; we had only one blanket each and were not allowed to have any fire," recalled Benjamin S. King of the 15th Texas. "In the morning, the orderly gave us a gill of whiskey each and ordered us to charge. This was before daylight and it was so cold that water would freeze in our canteens." After moving into line that morning, the 11th Tennessee, in Rains's Brigade, kept warm, according to one soldier, by rebuilding "our defenses of rails three rails deep. As soon as we had completed them, we were ordered to load."[4]

"At last, the night wore away," recalled 4th Arkansas surgeon Washington L. Gammage, "and just as the gray dawn began to steal in upon the darkness an officer came silently and quietly along the lines on foot with the word—'be quiet, get your men in line, see that their guns are in order, let there be no talking or laughing.' The hour which decides the fate of the army is nigh at hand." Colonel Locke of the 10th Texas said it was "difficult to restrain the expression of joy and outburst of feeling manifested by the men at the opportunity being presented upon an open field of relieving ourselves from our unhappy condition and of deciding the fate of the Confederacy."

Remembered Captain O'Brien: "Adjutant General R. E. Foote came dashing along the line and said to us, 'Boys, load! You are in for it, Cleburne supports you!' This announcement was responded to with a suppressed cheer for the close proximity of the Yankees would not permit loud demonstrations as our object was to surprise them. As soon as the men got their guns loaded, we were ordered forward. We moved without any skirmishers and in five minutes we were on to them."

Meanwhile, Captain John Thomas of the 30th Arkansas pulled his orderly sergeant aside to make a confession. "I don't know how it is with you, but I have just had a strange dream about my wife and children and I feel this is my last fight,"

---

4 Robertson, *Things Grew Beautifully Worse*, 4; Yeary, *Reminiscences of the Boys in Gray*, 404; *ORS*, 66:612-613.

recalled William A. Garner. "He had not more than finished the remark when the order came, 'Forward march, charge bayonets!'"[5]

*   *   *

Most of the Federals in Johnson's division had also been awake since 5:00 a.m., but several in Willich's brigade later admitted they were permitted to sleep until daylight. Lieutenant Shepherd Green, Willich's acting assistant adjutant general,, was among those who arose about dawn. "We rose from our beds of blankets and corn blades and began eating our meal of hard bread and bacon," he wrote. "All seemed quiet; not even the firing of a single gun broke the ominous silence."

Sergeant Edwin Payne of the 34th Illinois noted that "there being no indications of the enemy advancing, the order was issued to prepare breakfast. The meal was frugal and soon ended. Meantime, a portion of the artillery horses (about one third of the whole number) were taken to water and the remainder standing ready to hitch to the pieces on the first indication of danger."[6]

"Captain Edgarton had been up for some hours awaiting orders, but none came," recounted William Beach of the 1st Ohio Light Artillery. "Our horses were suffering for water having thirsted 48 hours and at times their groans were almost like human wails. The Captain directed that the left half of the battery take their horses to a rivulet a few rods to the rear and the right half to hitch up." Edgarton dispatched his horses to what is now known as Puckett Creek. Camped nearby with his six-gun of the 1st Ohio Light, Battery A, Lieutenant Edmund Belding chose to do the same. "At daylight, a small stream was discovered 100 rods in my rear," Edgarton wrote. "It was quiet all along our lines. I could not hear a picket shot nor any indication that the enemy was in our vicinity. I ordered a half battery of my horses to go to water on a sharp trot and return at the slightest indication of danger."[7]

Willich checked in with his brigade's skirmish line before 6:00 a.m. "[He] ordered me, in case there should be any indication that the Rebels had placed a

<hr>

5 Washington L. Gammage, *The Camp, The Bivouac, and the Battlefield* (Little Rock, 1958), 63-64; *OR* 20/1:931; Robertson, *Things Grew Beautifully Worse*, 4; Orderly Sergeant William A. Garner, Co. C, 30th Arkansas, SRNBP.

6 1st Lt. Shepherd Green, Co. I, 49th Ohio, *Ottawa Telegram*, Feb. 7, 1863, 2; Payne, *History of the 34th Illinois*, 43.

7 Beach Letter; *OR* 20/1:300.

battery in our front, to move my picket line at once to the woods and hold it until the brigade could give me support." remembered Lt. Col. Fielder Jones of the 39th Indiana, who about 3:00 a.m. had dispatched a single company to patrol 600 yards out to search for any Confederates (they found none). After completing his morning investigation of the lines, Willich conversed briefly with his second in command, Colonel William Gibson of the 49th Ohio, instructing him, in the event of an enemy attack, to support the picket line with the balance of 32nd and 39th Indiana. Willich then rode to Johnson's headquarters, about a half-mile north on Gresham Lane.[8]

Ector's Brigade led McCown's assault, clashing first with skirmishers of the 39th Indiana and, from Kirk's brigade, Companies A and B of the 34th Illinois. As the sounds of more than 4,000 Confederates' feet moving through frozen muddy fields echoed across the damp stillness of dawn, the first shots of the battle were fired by the Indiana skirmishers. Roughly 300 yards from the main Federal line, Ector's men began advancing at the quick step, remaining silent; no Rebel yell at this stage.

The standing cornstalks helped hide the onslaught from the Federals' view. In the field behind his regiment's skirmish line, Lyman Widney encountered a man rushing back and recalled, "As he passed me, he exclaimed, 'They're coming' and continued on to the regiment to give the alarm. As all was so quiet, not a shot having been fired, I felt decidedly skeptical and walked still further out until the enemy's breastworks were in view and there, sure enough, a succession of long lines of gray were swarming over the breastworks and sweeping towards us but not yet within gunshot range. As there was no time to lose, I started back in a hurry to rejoin the regiment and met it advancing into the open field to meet the shock that soon must come."[9]

On McCown's left, Rains rode along his front lines atop a large black charger "splendidly dressed and full of ardor," in the words of one North Carolinian. "The command had just fairly got dressed when the word was given—forward! Not a gun was yet fired. About a hundred yards from where we had stood in line, we encountered a fence about 15 feet in height. While the fence was being laid down for the colonel to ride through and the men were climbing it, the sharp report of a

8 *OR* 20/1:313-314.

9 Sergeant Major Lyman Widney, 34th Illinois, "From Louisville to the Sea," *National Tribune*, Oct. 10, 1901, 7.

rifle broke the stillness. James Waldrep of Captain DeWese's Co. D was on top of the fence and the Minie balls from the hostile ranks killed him."

The sounds of those opening shots startled the drivers of the 1st Ohio Light's Battery A, who had just left the cornfield south of the Franklin Road toting shocks of corn for its horses. "It was placed before them and they had been eating but a few moments when a tremendous volley of musketry was heard, the bullets reaching the park, hitting two men and several horses," remembered gunner Henry M. Davidson.[10]

Having barely slept, Colonel Dodge of the 30th Indiana began inspecting his picket lines shortly after 5:00 a.m. "I found every man alert, on the lookout, and had part of them relieved and had them get their breakfast, which took them but a very short time, then they took their places and those who had stayed on the line got theirs," he later reported. The reserve was also got up, and after getting their breakfast were ordered to stand to their arms." The weather moderated some, and near daylight a heavy ground fog appeared "as perfectly concealing the movements of the enemy as if it had been a brick wall."

About 6:30 a.m., according to Dodge, Captain Henry Lawton heard some noise in front of his position and climbed a rail fence behind which Dodge's line was deployed. Lawton hailed Dodge and announced, "They're coming!" Dodge ran to the fence "from where we could see over the fog, it having settled down close to the ground, and there they were! It was a magnificent, but fearful sight. Their lines extended as far as we could see in the dim light, it must have been a quarter of a mile beyond our right and sweeping on so as to strike Davis and Sheridan towards the left."[11]

Wasting no time, Dodge left Colonel Hurd in command and ran along the line of Major Alexander Dysart's 34th Illinois to alert him the enemy approach because "from his position he had not been able to see them yet. His line was in splendid order." On his way back to his reserve, Dodge passed Edgarton's battery and was

10 Walter Clark, ed., *Histories of the Several Regiments and Battalions From North Carolina in the Great War 1861-65* (Goldsboro, 1901), 488; Henry M. Davidson, *History of Battery A, 1st Regiment Ohio Volunteer Light Artillery* (Milwaukee, 1865), 62.

11 Dodge, *Stones River*, pt. 1. The time the Confederate attack began has been variously reported. It is safe to say the Confederate line stepped off sometime between 6:00–6:15 a.m.; most Federal reports state initial contact occurred 6:20–6:30, with 6:22 most commonly reported as when the first shots were fired. Time references during the war were based on local time, not on the time zone references used in the 21st century. As such, any times referenced by participants in the battle are approximations at best.

surprised to find that at least half of the horses were nowhere to be seen and none of those near the guns were hitched up. When the surprised brigade commander shouted to Edgarton that the Confederates were attacking in force, the artillerist ordered his men to "fall in" and they began loading their guns. "All this had happened in less time than it takes to write it," Dodge would later report.

Charles Cope of the 77th Pennsylvania was on Kirk's skirmish line. "The Johnnies came out of the woods just at the peep of day," he recalled. "We could hardly distinguish them at first, but soon saw that they were alive and determined on mischief. They were in close column, battalion front, and a number of lines deep, marching by the left oblique directly towards where the bugle sounded. We opened fire but they ignored our marksmanship and moved along about their business." The skirmishers' bullets, Dodge recalled, "beyond killing and wounding a few had no more effect than if they had fired against a stone wall."[12]

*   *   *

Frightened skirmishers scurrying back into camp put Johnson's entire division on notice that the battle had begun. Edgarton had two of his six guns in position near Gresham Lane; the guns were quickly loaded and angled southeast, and then began firing over the heads of the retreating skirmishers. Dysart had assumed command of the 34th Illinois from Colonel Hiram Bristol only the day before, but he had the presence of mind to send Kirk a messenger informing him of the attack before getting his regiment in line and then riding to Willich's camp seeking support. "I failed to find Willich," he noted. "They told me that he had gone to see General Johnson. I informed some of the officers of the brigade that the enemy was advancing and hurried back to my regiment and then received an order to advance my regiment and try to hold the enemy in check."

Kirk reported that "we could see them advancing over the open country for about a half mile in front of our lines. They moved in heavy masses, apparently six ranks deep. Their left extended far beyond our right, so as to completely flank us. They moved up steadily and in good order without music or noise of any kind."[13]

---

12 Dodge, *Stones River Pt. 1*; Private Charles B. Cope, Co. H, 77th Pennsylvania, "The Fighting Line: A Veteran of Stone River Tells How His Regiment Did Not Break," *National Tribune*, Jan. 3, 1901, 3. Kirk's brigade reported 1,923 men available for duty on the morning of the attack along with about 120 from Edgarton's battery, giving a brigade strength of roughly 2,040 men.

13 OR 20/1:325; Official report of Brigadier General Edward N. Kirk, *ORS*, 3:624-630.

As daylight broke, Lieutenant Ransom recalled, "the pickets gave the alarm, and skirmishers were firing, but as yet we could see no enemy. The horses were quickly hitched, except a few, perhaps one-half of which were on their return from water and were brought up at once." Noted William Laughlin: "[W]e ran our guns forward by hand. We loaded and fired as rapidly as possible. Some of our first shots knocked down the guns of our infantry which were still in stack. It seemed to me as I worked the gun that the Rebel balls were trying to play the long roll on our gun as they sprinkled against the sides so rapidly."

"[S]ix rounds were poured into the moving mass with great effect," Ransom reported, "but attacked in front and flank, we soon saw our horses shot down, the work evidently of sharpshooters, who moved in the advance and on the right and left, until the whole column being now upon us, we had not enough horses to save our guns."[14]

Ector's men charged about 300 yards before stopping and unleashing a volley, aiming for the flash of Edgarton's guns, and then resumed their charge. "We poured a hot and deadly fire into them and continued the advance," Ector wrote. "Such determination and courage were perfectly irresistible. My brigade was within 30 yards of their cannon when their cannon fired the second round. Quite a number of my brigade were killed and wounded, but the gaps made by the canister and small arms were closed up in an instant. The infantry gave way about the time we reached their battery. We pressed them so rapidly they soon gave way a second time."

On Ector's right, Locke's 10th Texas bore the brunt of the canister blasts from Edgarton's guns and soon engaged the 34th Illinois in a hand-to-hand scuffle. In one of his final commands on the field that day, Kirk ordered the Illinoisans to charge into the field to buy time for the rest of the brigade to get into position. It was both incredibly brave and foolhardy: 354 men trying to stop 4,400. "After advancing into the open field about 15 rods [250 feet], the enemy opened on us, my men returning the fire," Dysart reported.

"When within some 30 yards of Kirk's line, the enemy partly changed front and moved at a left oblique on the right of our line and in double quick," noted Edwin Payne of the 34th. "Their yells were deafening, and they now moved so as to

14 OR 20/1:300, 302; Laughlin Letter. The number of rounds Edgarton's battery fired has been variously reported at 6–20.

completely flank Kirk's line and render the position entirely untenable. They came on like a huge tidal wave and terribly in earnest."[15]

The color-bearers of the two regiments caught sight of one another and a deadly struggle for possession of the flags commenced—the 10th Texas eventually triumphant. "The enemy's lines being formed immediately in our front, their standard bearer, directly in front of mine, was waving his flag, casting it forward, and by various motions urging the Federal column forward," Locke would write. "Sergeant Andrew Sims, flag bearer of this regiment, discovered him and pressed forward with incredible speed directly toward the enemy's banner and on reaching within a pace or less of his adversary, he planted the Confederate flag firmly upon the ground with one hand and with a manly grasp reached the other after the flagstaff of his enemy. But the other gave back, and in that movement they both fell in the agonies of death, waving their banners above their heads until their last expiring moments."

Sergeant Will C. Robinson of the 34th Illinois recalled that "the Rebel infantry had reached the fence with the lone star ensign of Texas in advance. A Rebel flag bearer planted his hateful colors and yelled out 'Run you damn Yankees!' at the same time climbing the fence." Payne reported that "five color bearers fell in quick succession[,] but as fast as they fell, the flag was raised aloft and flaunted in the face of the foe. The entire color guard being killed or wounded, the colors over which so much precious blood had been spilled were trailed in the mud and borne off the field by the hands of the enemy." Observed musician John Wingert of the 34th Illinois: "[W]e had no support and when the word was given to retreat, the boys broke and fled in all directions. It was a general stampede, a Bull Run race."[16]

The fight was short, sharp, and bloody—the 10th Texas losing 80 men, more than a quarter of its ranks, in the opening moments. For the Federals, Dysart reported that the 34th Illinois lost a dozen killed and roughly 60 wounded before retreating. "When we got to within about 100 yards of them," remarked Sergeant Henry Watson of the 10th Texas, "they was a-running and about the time they started to run the Minie balls came as thick as I ever saw hail fall in my life, but we soon routed them."

15 OR 20/1:927; Payne, *History of the 34th Illinois*, 44.

16 OR 20/1:931; Sergeant Will C. Robinson, Co. A, 34th Illinois, *Sterling Republican Gazette*, Jan. 24, 1863, 1; Payne, *History of the 34th Illinois*, 44. Musician John H. Wingert, Co. C, 34th Illinois, SRNBP. The first color-bearer of the 34th Illinois who was killed in this hand-to-hand struggle with Sergeant Sims was Private Charles Santee of Co. C.

Eldridge Littlejohn of the 10th Texas observed that "the order to charge came down the lines with electric speed and onward we went dashing with a furious yell against their well-formed lines. They stood but a moment, and then they fled in disorder. But as they were running, they did not forget to shoot." Littlejohn was among those Texans struck down early. "I had shot my gun once, loaded again, and was within a few steps of the spot where we took their flag when a Minie ball hit me on the right hip bone and scaled off a little piece of the bone. The ball passed out through the fleshy part of my thigh. It is not a serious wound, but I assure you it hurt very badly."[17]

Kirk was hit early in the contest. "Seeing the contest was so unequal and that it was physically impossible that I could long sustain it, I sought General Willich with a view of asking his immediate active support," he wrote. "But he had gone to division headquarters. His brigade had not yet learned that he was captured; no other officer had assumed command. I appealed personally to two of the regiments to come to my support, but they declined moving without orders from their commander." While rallying his line, Kirk was severely wounded in the hip by a Minié ball, though he managed to stay on his horse.[18]

Adjutant Samuel Davis of the 77th Pennsylvania witnessed the clash from his position on Kirk's left. The Rebel column moved directly on the 34th Illinois in what he described as "an overwhelming force." The Illini troops advanced at a steady pace into the open field, leveled their weapons, and commenced firing, "but its position was an especial mark for Rebel practice and they poured into it a murderous fire." Edgarton's battery, meanwhile, opened fire. The gunners could not immediately distinguish the enemy and satisfied themselves by lobbing several shells in the direction of their fire. That changed almost immediately, explained Davis, when the enemy "came in sight of and near the battery," which opened with canister. "The Rebel line replied and at the first fire killed or wounded 75 horses which entirely disabled the guns. At this time, the fight had not been raging five minutes yet it was terrific. The 34th Illinois poured volley after volley into the advancing hosts. The skirmishers of the 29th Indiana, 30th Indiana, and 77th

17 Sergeant Henry Watson, Co. H, 10th Texas Cavalry, Richard Baumgartner Collection; letter from Private Elbridge Littlejohn, Co. G, 10th Texas Cavalry, SRNBP.

18 *ORS* 3:624-630. Kirk escaped capture but never recovered from his wound, eventually succumbing at his home near Chicago in July 1863.

Pennsylvania, he continued, "directed an oblique fire on the advancing column, but it moved like an automaton and scores of our men were killed and wounded."[19]

The chaos in Kirk's camp gripped the attention of 34th Illinois Captain Amos Hostetter. "We tried to rally behind Edgarton's battery," he would write, "but the reserve, which should have been in readiness, was cooking breakfast and a great many did not even have their guns loaded so that when they found us in retreat, they made a rush for their guns, became bewildered, and then all was confusion. God knows I never want to see another like that. Horses running loose through the ranks, maddened by the pain of wounds, and men falling thick and fast while the bullets rained like hail among us. The men soon became mixed up with another brigade and then all was confusion, although a great many officers did all they could to rally the men, we all saw that nothing was to be done but retreat, and that soon."[20]

As the 34th Illinois streamed back over his position, Edgarton's worst fears became reality, with his guns out of position. "[T]he infantry gave way on the front and flank in disorder, almost with the first volley," he wrote. "The assault of the enemy was fierce and overwhelming. After the first fire, in which I had one man killed, a number of men wounded, and twelve horses killed, the enemy charged with an impetuosity which carried everything before him."

Private George Stacey recalled that "we opened on them with canister. They charged us four times and our men met them every time, but they were too strong for us and before we could get our horses on the guns, they commenced shooting our men. My howitzer had all the men shot down except myself, and my coat collar was cut off and my pantaloons cut all to pieces. I was shot in the hand and the leg but not very bad."[21]

Edgarton's resolve impressed Davis. "When within about 30 yards of our line, the Rebel column partially changed front and moved on our right at the left oblique and the double quick," the adjutant recalled. "Their yells were deafening. They moved so as to completely flank Kirk's line and render the position untenable." That would lead to a rush on Edgarton's guns. The captain implored his gunners to retreat. "'Save yourselves boys, and get out if you can!',' was Edgarton's desperate

19 Address of Adjutant Samuel T. Davis, 77th Pennsylvania, "Memorial Day: The Appropriate Observance in Chambersburg," *Valley Spirit*, May 31, 1887, 3.

20 Capt. Amos W. Hostetter, Co. I, 34th Illinois, *Weekly Carroll County Mirror*, Jan. 28, 1863, 1.

21 *OR* 20/1:300; Private George H. Stacey, Battery E, 1st Ohio Light Artillery, *Cleveland Plain Dealer*, Jan. 15, 1863, 2.

Private Julius Waite of Battery E of the 1st Ohio Light Artillery was killed during the opening moments of the Battle of Stones River.

Author's Collection

command, according to Sergeant Henry A. Vincent. "Everyone began to look out for himself and started on the dead run to get out of the way. The bullets came among us like a storm of hail battering among the dry leaves and rattling against the trees like a shower of stones."

Davis watched breathlessly as Edgarton "grimly stood by one of his pieces and assisted by Lieutenant Berwick, loaded, and discharged it into the living column as it closed upon him, mowing a huge road through it and in an instant after he was wounded. Many of his men refused to leave him and fought the foe with their swabs and were killed or captured." Struck in the groin by a spent ball, Edgarton stumbled around his guns and was then struck in the arm by two more bullets after falling across the trail of one of his pieces. Each of Battery E's guns was captured, as was Edgarton. "I lost my guns," the Ohioan stated grimly, "but I took the enemy's receipt in full in red ink."[22]

Edgarton's volleys of canister inflicted heavy casualties on Ector's men, particularly in the 10th and 14th Texas. Sergeant Zacheriah Bailey of the 14th Texas found remarkable the heroism of Captain James Howze, who held the company together under that withering fire. "The enemy commenced to shell us when a bomb exploded at the head of Captain Howze's company, killing Billy Melton who was at his side and the company was about to be thrown into confusion," Bailey

22 Davis Address; Sergeant Henry A. Vincent, Battery E, 1st Ohio Light Artillery, SRNBP; Beach Letter. Edgarton reported losing three men killed, 25 wounded, and 22 captured, or 50 of the 120 (42 percent) he took into the fight.

wrote. "The captain's face was pale, but his eyes flashed as he waved his sword and cried out to Company D, 'Stand steady!'"[23]

Colonel John C. Burks of the 11th Texas—a 37-year-old attorney from the Red River Valley considered "the idol of his regiment and a great favorite with the entire brigade"—suffered a mortal wound leading his men against Edgarton's battery. "Holding his hand on the wound to control the bleeding, he continued at the head of his command, urging his men forward, until he lost consciousness," it was reported. Thomas Colman of Company F remembered the "roaring of cannon, our colonel falling pierced through the lungs with a Minie ball in the very commencement, his last command being 'Forward my brave boys!' and after he was carried off the field his last dying words were inquiring about the regiment."[24]

*   *   *

With Kirk's line swept from the field, Ector's Texans barreled into the two Federal brigade camps among the scattered timber at the intersection of Gresham Lane and the Franklin Pike. "The boys drove the enemy back into their camps which were well-lit with fires around which they were cooking breakfast," related Lewis Jones of the 10th Texas. "The onslaught was so sudden and the slaughter so great that they retreated in great confusion, every fellow for himself and devil take the hindmost. They had abandoned everything to get away. One of their dead some 200 yards to their rear had been killed still holding firmly his pot of coffee."[25]

Lieutenant J. T. Tunnell of the 14th Texas recalled that "many of the Yanks were either killed or retreated in their nightclothes. We pursued them with a Rebel yell. In advancing, we found a caisson with the horses attached lodged against a tree and other evidence of their confusion. The Yanks tried to make a stand whenever

---

23 Sergeant Zacheriah W. Bailey, Co. D, 14th Texas Cavalry, "The Star Company of Ector's Texas Brigade," *Confederate Veteran*, Sept. 1914, 404.

24 John C. Burks, *The Handbook of Texas Online*, retrieved Aug. 20, 2003.; A. H. Heiner, 11th Texas Cavalry, "The Battle of Murfreesboro Again," *Confederate Veteran*, Mar. 1904, 118; Colman-Hayter Family Papers, Folder 6, Western Historical Manuscript Collection–Columbia, Missouri. Colonel Burks would die of his wound in Shelbyville on January 4, 1863.

25 Private Lewis Jones, Co. I, 10th Texas Cavalry "Recollections of the Battle of Murfreesboro," *Confederate Veteran*, Sept. 1923, 341-42.

they could find shelter of any kind. All along our route, we captured prisoners who would take refuge behind houses, fences, logs, cedar bushes, and in ravines."[26]

As the 34th Illinois fell back, Lt. Col. David Dunn of the 29th Indiana directed Company C to reinforce his skirmish line, while ordering the rest of the regiment to lie behind the fence and await the Confederates. That proved a mistake, as the company came tumbling back, in the process blocking Dunn's field of fire until McNair's Arkansans closed within 20 yards. "Our first fire delivered lying down, partially checked the advance and enabled the men to load and fire four or five times," wrote Major Joseph Collins. "But while engaged in front, the column which pressed on the 34th Illinois and the battery had moved so far forward as to uncover our line, giving them an opportunity to deliver a raking fire on us." Dunn's line buckled and retreated.[27]

McNair's men charged into the woods on the Texans' right, pursuing Kirk's disintegrating line. Orderly Sergeant Coke Witten of the 1st Arkansas Rifles wrote that "we were ordered to put our blankets and knapsacks in a pile together. As soon as I heard that, I knew what was coming. We were then told that we were to make the attack and as soon as it began to get light, we were ordered on." Colonel Henry Bunn of the 4th Arkansas explained that "the enemy was in position in a dense thicket of cedar, the entrance to which was obstructed by a parallel fence, rendering his position one of great advantage. His sharpshooters fired upon us at long range and continued to do so as we advanced."

"[O]rders were to advance with as little noise as possible and not to fire a gun until ordered," noted Captain John Lavender of the 4th Arkansas. "The idea was to get just as close to them as possible before they knew it. We were getting near the woods and saw a rail fence at the edge of the wood and were ordered to hold our fire until we got to the fence." Witten recalled that "we went about one quarter of a mile to the upper end of the field and I looked across another field and I saw two of the enemy's flags. They were in a cedar brake and we had to go about six hundred yards and cross four high fences to get to them. So, we started on and they commenced shooting at us but we raised the yell and soon routed them."[28]

26 J. T. Tunnell, 14th Texas Cavalry, "Texans in the Battle of Murfreesboro," *Confederate Veteran*, Nov. 1908, 574.

27 OR 20/1:329-330.

28 OR 20/1:951; Ted R. Worley, editor. *The War Memoirs of Captain John W. Lavender, C.S.A. They Never Came Back: The Story of Co. F, Fourth Arkansas Infantry, C.S.A.; originally known as the*

Skirmishers from the 77th Pennsylvania opened fire on the Arkansans. According to one Pennsylvanian, the Confederates "paid not the slightest attention to it, but kept steadily on singing as they came. Enough words could be distinguished that the song was something about Southern rights." The Confederates, recalled Captain William A. Robinson, charged past them with "their hats pulled over their eyes as though afraid to look at what was before them. The enemy swept past us by thousands."[29]

Washington Gammage of the 4th Arkansas concurred, writing, "here and there a Federal sentinel fired a stray shot, but we heeded it not. A fence is scaled, the Federal sharpshooters have opened upon us, a battery of the enemy is in front and with one wild, loud, simultaneous shout, the word goes forth from right to left and all along the line, 'Charge my brave boys! Charge the vandals!' Then with a yell like 10,000 demons turned loose from Hades, they rush like an avalanche upon the foe."

Lavender reported that "every company officer was in front of his men urging them to hold their fire. The last order I gave my company was keep cool and aim low. At that time, we struck the fence and fired a deadly volley at the enemy at not over 50 or 75 steps. The line seemed to strike the fence at the same time and knocked it flat to the ground, raised a yell, and charged the Feds like a storm."[30]

Kirk's men fought fiercely as they retreated. The 30th Arkansas lost several lieutenants and its color-bearer, and had seven company commanders struck down, including O'Brien, who noted that "the Yanks again broke cover but alas for the chances of war just at this moment an unlucky Minie ball struck me just below the right knee, ranging downward and to the rear coming out near the ankle. This of course stopped me effectively. For a moment I was undecided how to act, but I said not a word. The line continued to advance and I becoming faint could no longer stand and sank upon the field amongst the dead and the dying."[31]

Willich and Johnson were discussing the plan for the day when the sounds of rapid gunfire from the south reached their ears. "About 6 o'clock, General Willich

Montgomery Hunters, as told by their commanding officer (Pine Bluff, 1956), 39; Orderly Sergeant Coke Witten, Co. F, 1st Arkansas Mounted Rifles, Anthony Rushing Collection.

29 Pennsylvania Shiloh Battlefield Commission. *The Seventy-Seventh Pennsylvania at Shiloh, History of the* Regiment (Harrisburg, 1908), 139; Robinson Letter.

30 Gammage, *Camp, Bivouac, and Battlefield*, 64; Robertson, *Things Grew Beautifully Worse*, 7-9; Worley, *War Memoirs of Captain John Lavender*, 39-40.

31 *OR* 20/1:951, 953; Robertson, *Things Grew Beautifully Worse*, 7-9.

rode up to my headquarters and while talking with me a shot was fired," Johnson remembered. "I looked at my watch and noted that it was just 22 minutes after 6 o'clock. At once Willich started at full speed to join his command." Willich galloped back to his line with surgeon Gustavus Kunkler of the 32nd Indiana at his side. "Amid the smoke and confusion, Willich and Kunkler galloped directly into McNair's Arkansans who were mopping up what was left of Kirk's broken brigade," noted historian David Dixon. "James Stone, a volunteer aide to General McNair, confronted Willich and demanded his surrender, but Willich and Kunkler turned their horses and fled."

Gunfire killed Kunkler's horse and wounded the surgeon; Willich's horse had its hindleg shattered and crumpled to the ground, Willich escaping injury but quickly captured. Gammage reported that the flustered German "by way of apology" said "My God, I vast never so much surprise. I thinks te Teevil, and dens I puts te spur to mine horse and den I vash captured."

One of Willich's aides, Lieutenant Milton Miles, also stumbled into McNair's swarming ranks. "Having on [an] overcoat, [I] was mistaken for an aide of the one of the Confederate generals, and ordered to place an Arkansas regiment into position," Miles later wrote. "I saluted him as I would one of our own commanders, wheeled my horse and rode in the direction of their reserve until behind a cluster of bushes when I turned to the left and came out through Davis's lines."[32]

The chaos of the sudden attack spread quickly from Kirk's brigade to Willich's. "We had just got our coffee ready to drink when bang, bang went several guns on the picket line immediately in front of our brigade and the next second volley after volley and the bullets were whistling in too close proximity to our heads to be comfortable," remembered Lieutenant Samuel Pettit of the 15th Ohio. "The cry to arms came up to the regiment from Colonel William Wallace. We left our coffee, threw down our tents and blankets in a pile and sprang for our arms. By this time, we could distinctly hear Rebel cheering. They were charging our batteries. We were taken by surprise. The men became panic-stricken."

Robert Stewart, Pettit's comrade, agreed, stating that "there was no need nor time for any order to fall in. We just tumbled over each other to get in, dropping our

---

32 Johnson, *A Soldier's Reminiscences*, 212; David T. Dixon, *Radical Warrior: August Willich's Journey from German Revolutionary to Union General* (Knoxville, 2020), 161, Gammage, *Camp, Bivouac, and Battlefield*, 68; Cope, *15th Ohio Volunteers*, 234.

pots and pans, leaving our haversacks and blankets and snatching up our cartridge boxes and rushing for our guns."[33]

Willich's ranks quickly unraveled. The 39th Indiana companies on the skirmish line found themselves cut off from the rest of the brigade by the fast-moving Texans, and most of Company C would be captured. Corporal Henry Rankin of Company K managed to reach a fence paralleling the Franklin Road before the Confederates opened fire. "Several who jumped the fence were shot as they jumped over, and I had just alighted on the ground when a ball struck my head, knocking me to the ground," he wrote. "I was struck just right above my right ear, the ball going through the rim of my hatband and then cutting a gash on my scalp, then going out through my hatband again, thus making four holes in my hat. All of the pickets that were not shot down at the first volley were now scattered badly while Colonel Jones was on horseback trying to gather the boys under the 39th Indiana flag behind some rail fences from where he could make a stand."[34]

The 32nd Indiana, Willich's former command, was caught amid the 34th Illinois's retreat and Ector's rapid arrival and barely had time to fire a few rounds before being overwhelmed. "The position of the 32nd Indiana was a very difficult one," one veteran observed. "We barely had a split rail fence for protection and were nearly run over by fleeing men and by the runaway artillery horses." As Lt. Col. Frank Erdelmeyer attempted to draw in his picket line, the veteran noted, Kirk's rattled Federals "forced our men to give way and fall back. The confusion and panic then becoming general, I was unable to reassemble the regiment until we had retreated along the creek for nearly three-quarters of a mile."

Captain William G. Mank likened the panic to "a second and improved version" of First Bull Run. "Confusion arose, a terrible panic gripped the troops," he observed. "Artillery horses, cannon, ambulances, wagons, all mixed together with fragments of regiments. It was impossible to form up the regiment. One comrade after another fell dead or wounded there." In breaking for the rear, the regiment streamed west along the Franklin Road, where their numbers broke through the 39th Indiana's line, unraveled the formation of the 49th Ohio, and

33 2nd Lt. Samuel S. Pettit, Co. D, 15th Ohio, *Wyandot Pioneer,* Feb. 6, 1863, 1; Stewart, *Battle of Stone River*, 12.

34 Rankin article.

eventually became entangled with the retreating artillerymen of Battery A of the 1st Ohio Light.[35]

Second Lieutenant James Rea of the 39th Indiana relayed his experience on the line. "Our pickets wholly failed to check them and our reserves checked them but a moment," he wrote. "The enemy was within 20 yards of us and the air seemed thick with missiles when the order was given to fall back. We were literally driven back by overwhelming numbers, rolled back as it were by the superiority of numerical strength." Opening fire at point-blank range, the charging Confederates struck down the Hoosiers by the score, 30 of them falling at the fence along the Franklin Road. Enraged and in tears at the misfortune that had befallen his regiment, Colonel Jones succeeded in leading a remnant out of the jam, but the 39th Indiana would suffer more casualties (380) than any other regiment, Federal or Confederate, during the battle.[36]

The experience proved similarly terrifying for the rookie 89th Illinois. Raised among the railroad men of the Chicago area, Wednesday morning marked the regiment's first time under fire. "As my men were building fires for cooking," reported Lt. Col. Charles Hotchkiss, "rapid firing was heard on Kirk's front[,] which was almost instantly followed by the men of his brigade rushing in confusion and indiscriminately through our ranks and over our men." Alfred French was hunched over a fire cooking bacon when "we heard a terrific yell right close. My orderly sergeant said, 'That sounds like a charge.' We jumped up and here came the enemy on the double quick! I had my equipment on and my gun by my side. So, I got in a couple of quick shots, but all was confusion."

Orderly Sergeant George Sinclair saw "a little fellow from a company on our left come running toward me and away from the firing. Thinking he was getting scared rather early, I tried to stop him but he said he was shot in the bowels. Just at that moment another sings out 'I've got one' putting his hand to head, and even then, I would not believe that they were anything more than spent balls. But in a jiffy of time the balls were zipping past us from nearly all sides and the men were

35 OR 20/1:312; Joseph R. Reinhart, ed., *August Willich's Gallant Dutchmen: Civil War Letters from the 32nd Indiana Infantry* (Kent, 2006), 128-34.

36 2nd Lt. James S. Rea, Co. H, 39th Indiana, *Madison Daily Evening Courier*, Jan. 27, 1863, 2. Colonel Fielder Jones reported 31 men killed, 118 wounded, and 231 captured or missing.

tumbling pretty fast. Then we began to realize that there was an enemy firing at us."[37]

Facing west, the 15th Ohio found itself badly out of position—"our backs to the foe," Stewart recalled. Colonel Wallace formed the regiment in line and attempted a countermarch, even as bullets flew in, striking men down from behind. "Advancing to the open field in the edge of which we had lain, we received the order to countermarch by file left to bring us facing the enemy," a veteran recalled, "but before this movement could be executed, our men began to fall and after delivering one volley, we were ordered to fall back." Wallace's blundering movements "seemed only to tangle the men all the more. We were then ordered to lie down."

Wallace also would not command his men to fire, angering Lt. Col. Frank Askew, who roared, "Damn it, don't you see their Rebel flag? 'Fire!'" "And fire we did," recalled Sergeant Morris Cope. "But as they were close to our single line of battle we could not stand long before them." Panic ensued. "It soon became apparent that the enemy was rapidly closing in on our front and flank and threatening our rear in such numbers that our only hope of escape was in rapid retreat," recalled Alexis Cope of the 15th Ohio.[38]

With the retreating Federals coursing through the ranks, Hotchkiss could not form the 89th Illinois into line, and "to protect the men as much as possible from the enemy's fire, I ordered them to lie down." They remained in that position "until my left wing was uncovered of fugitives and with the enemy within 50 yards of my position, I ordered that wing to fire." According to Sergeant Sinclair,

> we lay there for a few moments like good fellows, our colonel waiting for some command from our brigadier general but not getting any command he let us lay there, he sitting on his horse, our adjutant being wounded and unhorsed, the major unhorsed and bullets whistling like hail by him. He was a brick; his actions gave a great deal of confidence to the men. Just then the adjutant general [Captain Carl Schmitt] said to the colonel, 'Order a retreat, Colonel! For God's sake, give your men a chance for their lives.' The order was given and as we rose up, the enemy was within 20 yards of us and as they caught sight of us, they fired a murderous fire into our ranks, completely riddling the regiment.[39]

---

37 OR 20/1:310; Memoirs of Private Alfred D. French, Co. A, 89th Illinois, Robert Grenier Collection; Sinclair Letter.

38 Stewart, *Battle of Stone River*, 12; Cope, *15th Ohio Volunteers*, 235-36, 246, 249.

39 OR 20/1:310; Sinclair Letter.

"When our colonel gave us the order to retreat, the bullets were falling very thick among us," remarked Private Joseph Buckley of the 89th Illinois. "We retreated until we got to a cotton field then the Colonel gave us the order to rally and give them a few of our bullets. We did so and checked them some there. Our Colonel's horse was shot from under him there and our captain was killed, too, shot in the head by a bullet just as he was turning around to face the enemy."

Sinclair reported that "we had an open field to cross of about 40 rods and it was impossible to keep a retreat in good order. We did the best we could to get to the first fence where there was a second growth of timber and underbrush. Here a part of us rallied about 50 men with our colonel. It was clear that the Rebels are in a steady column, their banners flying. I took a good deliberate aim at their banner carrier; the banner was a triangle supported by a round frame. It was the second time that I had covered him with my musket and failed to bring him down and at a good near shot at that, but I am satisfied that I could not shoot in that direction without hurting somebody."[40]

The 49th Ohio, facing south across the Franklin Road, was struck initially on its left flank and quickly rolled up. "We were ordered to fall in and take arms, the balls commenced flying all around us and as we took arms I saw the butt of a musket shot off," recalled Thomas Roughton. "We were ordered to lay down and just then I saw the first man fall at the battery in our front. The Rebels were within 100 steps of our lines when we got orders to get up, about face, and forward march. The balls flew like hail around our heads and the lines soon broke and run. Several fell before we left the ranks. Shrieks arose from every direction and the wild cheering of the Rebels and the whistling of the bullets all was fearful."

*　*　*

After ordering Lieutenant Belding to hitch up his guns, Colonel Gibson rode forward to determine how his regiment was faring and found himself surrounded by swarming Confederates, his men fleeing in desperation. According to one report: "The Colonel, who was in such close quarters that the Rebels had demanded his sword, put the spurs to his horse, broke away from them and rallied

40 Private Joseph Buckley, Co. H, 89th Illinois, SRNBP; Sinclair Letter.

five cavalrymen and with them returned to rescue Henry F. Arndt who succeeded with their help in escaping."[41]

Willich's retreating Federals did not hold their position at the fence in the cotton field long, as Rains's line swept beyond their right flank. "We went back in fairly good order until the picket fence," remembered Alexis Cope. "Many of our men tried to pull the pickets apart in order to get through. Some got over and many were either killed or wounded trying to do so." Seeing he could not get through, Cope ran to the end of the fence but was struck in the right arm by a Rebel bullet, his gun knocked from his hand. "I picked it up with my left hand and continued to retreat now knowing whether my arm was broken or only bruised," he recalled.

Five 15th Ohio officers were struck down at the fence, including Askew, and it was here that the regiment incurred its heaviest losses during the battle. John Rennard of Company K recalled that after getting over the fence, "I was trying to reload my gun as we ran. I had succeeded in getting the charge in the muzzle, took my place in line, and was in the act of trying to ram the charge home when I was shot in the right thigh by a Minie ball. I threw my gun in one direction and the ramrod in another, spread my arms, a black curtain came before my eyes, and I fell on my side." Meanwhile, two soldiers in Company E who "were disposed to be a little irritable when matters didn't suit them" and who "would quarrel at the drop of a hat" arrived at the same spot along the fence at the same time. "It was too narrow for both to pass at the same time and each was determined to go through first," Morris Cope recalled. "They quarreled about it until both came near being captured."[42]

Buckley noted that "our Colonel gave us the order to retreat as we could do nothing with them alone and at that time, the Rebels had got so far around us as to throw a flanking fire on us. Bullets were flying thick and fast and how it was so many escaped without being killed is a mystery to most everyone." Recalled Robert Stewart: "[T]the ground was frozen and rough and I could hear the bullets striking the stalks. I could hear them strike a comrade as he ran, there would be a groan, a stagger, and a fall. I could hear the wild yelling behind and the roar of the guns that

41 Richard F. Mann, *The Buckeye Vanguard: History of the 49th Ohio Veteran Volunteer Infantry, 1861-1865* (Milford, 2010), 60; "An Incident at the Battle of Murfreesboro," *Sandusky Register*, Feb. 3, 1863, 2.

42 Cope, *15th Ohio Volunteers*, 235-36, 246, 249. The 15th Ohio lost 17 killed, 68 wounded, and 127 missing during the battle.

were now getting into action. I felt like running. I felt as though I would like to be all legs with no other purpose in life but to run."

Lieutenant Rea reported that "at every fence, at every place where such a thing was possible, a stand was made, our voices were yelling defiance on the hosts trying to surmount us."[43]

As he did what he could to rally his broken regiment, Lt. Col. Levi Drake of the 49th Ohio yelled himself hoarse so he could be heard above the din of battle. "In riding rapidly along the lines, giving commands in a loud tone of voice, he became hoarse and when the fatal ball pierced him, he was waving his hat and cheering his men by an exhibition of courage," lamented Chaplain Eurotus Bush. "He dismounted from his horse and calmly said, 'I am killed' and sank to the earth. Two of his men supported him a few steps, but the Rebels were upon them and they were compelled to leave him."

During the clash, the 49th Ohio's command staff was decimated: Drake was killed, Major Benjamin Porter severely wounded in the shoulder, and several company commanders killed, wounded, or captured; Colonel Gibson narrowly escaped capture twice, and with Willich's capture, he assumed command of the brigade. Captain Samuel F. Gray, the senior surviving officer, would lead the regiment's battered remnants off the field.[44]

Rains's Brigade made easy progress on the left as the Federal skirmishers, after firing their first shots, raced back toward Willich's camps along the Franklin Road. The brigade, moving rapidly as the outer end of a grand right wheel, crossed nearly 600 yards of open field and took negligible losses as Willich's men focused their attention on blunting Ector's attack. "[W]e received the fire of the enemy's pickets who fled," noted Lt. Col. Marcus Stovall of the 3rd Georgia Battalion. "If there was any line of the enemy in front of the 3rd Georgia, they fled without firing and we swept entirely around that which was in front of Ector's and McNair's brigades."

Hugh Cummings of the 39th Indiana remembered that the Confederates overpowered his regiment "with that demonic yell and by the very force of numbers and the impetuosity of the charge they swept us off the field. I even now

---

43 Buckley Letter; Stewart, *Battle of Stone River*, 12-13; Rea Letter.

44 Chaplain Eurotus Bush, 49th Ohio, *Cleveland Morning Leader*, Feb. 23, 1863, 1.

can hear the balls as they go crashing through the bones of our comrades as they fell before that withering fire."[45]

The Indiana skirmishers fell back behind the gun line of Belding's battery. Only one section of his guns faced south; the other two sections faced west to protect the army's flank. "At the first fire, Lieutenant Belding ordered us to hitch our teams which we proceeded to do," wrote gunner Alpheus Bloomfield. "But before we were half hitched, we saw the Rebels advancing and driving our advance at the same time pouring in volley after volley."

Rains's lines closed to within a hundred yards of Belding's position before Gibson galloped up to the young lieutenant and, according to Corporal William Tomlinson, ordered him to "get our guns out of the way as quick as possible.… I was putting my blankets on one side of the caisson and the Rebs were on the other. We were all together Rebs and Yankees [and] I saw if I must get out alive, I must get out of that and out I started through a cornfield. I made good time and the balls made as good time as two men fell that were running with me."[46]

The advancing Confederates expertly targeted Belding's horses; dozens were shot in harness. Henry Davidson, a gunner with the 1st Ohio Battery, vividly recalled the event:

> Through the assistance of the cannoneers, the drivers succeeded in attaching their teams to the carriages and began to move to the open field to the rear. Lieutenant Charles Scovill, commanding a section, had his horse shot under him while No. 1 gun, upon attempting to leave the park, had a horse shot which fell upon the pole and broke it. With great effort, the horse was speedily extricated and the gun taken to the open field. The support for the battery was now rapidly crumbling to pieces under a murderous fire, leaving it to the mercy of the foe. Lieutenant Belding moved back with the guns but was so hotly pressed that he could not put them in position with safety. He had done nothing in his original position because the lines falling back in our front were between his guns and the enemy's lines.[47]

Unable to draw off their last gun and without a clear field of fire, the Ohioans stood helplessly by their remaining gun, a 6-pounder James rifle, as Rains's men

---

45 OR 20/1:941; Clark, *Histories of the Several Regiments*, 488; Address of Private Hugh A. Cummings, *Report of the Proceedings of the 15th Annual Re-Union of the Eighth Indiana Veteran Cavalry*, Noblesville, Indiana, 1898.

46 Private Alpheus S. Bloomfield and Corporal William Tomlinson, Battery A, 1st Ohio Light Artillery, SRNBP.

47 Davidson, *History of Battery A*, 62-63.

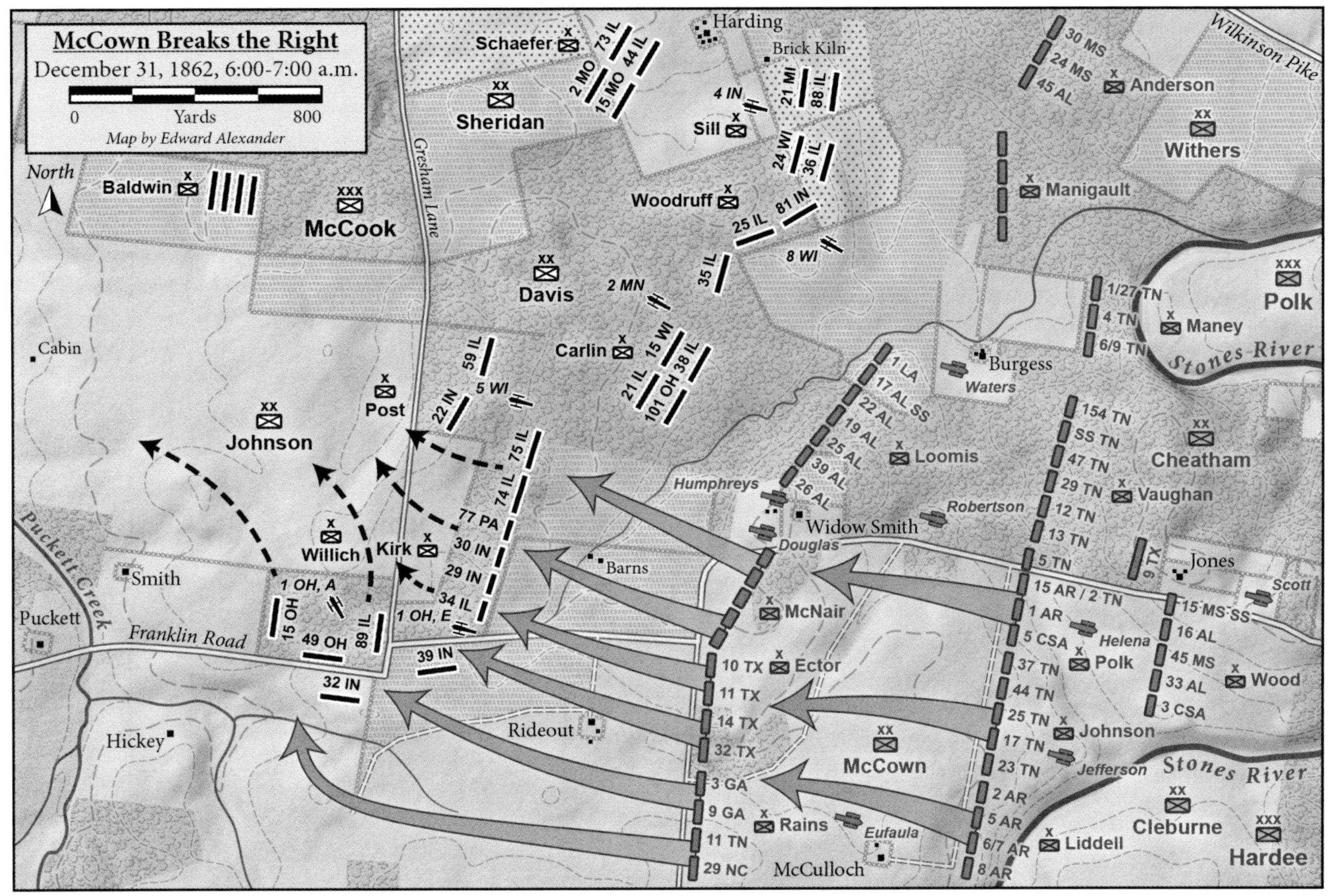

McCown Breaks the Right
December 31, 1862, 6:00-7:00 a.m.
0   Yards   800
Map by Edward Alexander
North
Baldwin
McCook
Schaefer
73 IL
44 IL
2 MO
15 MO
Harding
Brick Kiln
4 IN
21 MI
88 IL
Sill
24 WI
36 IL
Woodruff
81 IN
25 IL
8 WI
35 IL
30 MS
24 MS
45 AL
Anderson
Withers
Manigault
Sheridan
Gresham Lane
Davis
2 MN
Carlin
59 IL
5 WI
21 IL
15 WI
38 IL
101 OH
Cabin
Johnson
Post
22 IN
75 IL
74 IL
77 PA
30 IN
29 IN
34 IL
1 OH, E
Willich
Kirk
Smith
1 OH, A
15 OH
49 OH
89 IL
39 IN
32 IN
Puckett Creek
Puckett
Franklin Road
Hickey
Rideout
1 LA
17 AL SS
22 AL
19 AL
25 AL
39 AL
26 AL
Humphreys
Widow Smith
Douglas
Barns
McNair
10 TX
11 TX
14 TX
32 TX
3 GA
9 GA
11 TN
29 NC
McCulloch
Loomis
Robertson
Rains
Eufaula
McCown
Ector
Burgess
Waters
1/27 TN
4 TN
6/9 TN
Maney
154 TN
SS TN
47 TN
29 TN
12 TN
13 TN
5 TN
15 AR / 2 TN
1 AR
5 CSA
37 TN
44 TN
25 TN
17 TN
23 TN
2 AR
5 AR
6/7 AR
8 AR
Helena
Polk
Johnson
Jefferson
9 TX
Jones
Scott
15 MS SS
16 AL
45 MS
33 AL
3 CSA
Wilkinson Pike
Stones River
Polk
Cheatham
Vaughan
Wood
Cleburne
Liddell
Hardee
Stones River

overran them. "Ere long we sighted a section of artillery and the regiment charged," recalled one North Carolinian. "The guns were shotted but the gunners did not have time to fire and the officer in charge broke into a run. Captain John Teague soon overhauled him, however, put a hand on his shoulder and stopped him. The Federal officer said, 'You've got me,' to which Teague replied, 'Yes, but you gave us a mannerly race."

According to Colonel Robert Vance of the 29th North Carolina, "the pickets fell back behind the cover of a field battery which the men, sweeping on, took before it could be got into position to open fire. Four of the gunners were captured at their guns besides some other of the enemy's videttes who were run down by our men in the chase." Rains's men captured the piece, battery wagon, and forge and soon gathered up a 12-pounder howitzer that Belding's men abandoned in their hasty retreat along the Franklin Road.[48]

* * *

As Kirk's and Willich's fractured lines were driven northwest, the 77th Pennsylvania—screened by the cedar brake and the dim morning light—reformed at a right angle to its original position, in alignment with the 22nd Indiana. The Pennsylvanians poured flanking fire on Ector's and McNair's troops as they charged past them through the woods. "In our front, the column we had repulsed and driven across the brook but a few minutes before was reformed and again advancing," Davis recalled. "Directly in front of the 77th and about 400 yards distant was a Rebel battery."

After the regiment formed into line, Captain Robinson recalled, Post "ordered us to charge on the Rebel battery as he could do nothing until it was silenced. Expecting his support—we undertook the job." Davis explained that "a little to the right and in front of this battery were Edgarton's guns which the enemy had captured and turned against us. Colonel Peter Housum, deeming the moment opportune, ordered the regiment to charge these batteries which were across somewhat open ground. With a yell, the regiment pitched forward on a full run shoulder to shoulder amidst a storm of shot, shell, grape, and canister."[49]

---

48 *OR* 20/1:938; Clark, *Histories of the Several Regiments*, 488; Davidson, *History of Battery A*, 63. Battery A lost 73 horses killed and had 29 casualties.

49 Davis Address; Robinson Letter.

When Housum's charging Pennsylvanians appeared, the wounded O'Brien lay on the ground near the wreckage of Edgarton's battery waiting for the Confederate infirmary corps to transport him to a field hospital. "I [was] in a state of stupor and bewilderment and all this time the infirmary corps never made their appearance," he recalled. "Around me lay in all forms and attitudes the dead and wounded, the principal part of which were Yankees. I began to wonder how long I'd have to remain here when I thought I heard a bugle sound close behind me. I listened and heard a discharge of musketry. With the aid of my saber, I got up from the ground and strove to hobble off. I hopped a few steps when again the fire was repeated behind me and I could distinctly see the leaves on the ground pop all around me as the bullets struck them."[50]

Captain James Douglas's four-gun Texas battery, attached to Ector's Brigade and armed with two 6-pounder field guns and two 12-pounder howitzers, moved into a position south of the Gresham Lane intersection and became a target for the charging Pennsylvanians. "After riding to the point where the enemy's first battery was captured, I found that the brigade had driven the enemy and was advancing rapidly," Douglas reported. "I returned to the battery and put my horses to their best speed, to assist in holding the advanced position obtained. When I arrived within 150 yards of the captured battery, I discovered a large body of Federal infantry drawn up in line in front of the position occupied by the captured guns, and about 125 yards from my lead team."

Riding into action with the battery, Sergeant John Templeton was astonished by "a brigade of live Yankees. I thought we were going to be charged as they were in less than a hundred yards of us advancing and not a gun unlimbered." Douglas ordered the battery into line. "As no time was to be lost, I ordered the gunners to commence firing with canister," he wrote. "The enemy, doubtless hearing my command, opened a brisk fire, wounding one man and killing three horses and wounding three. They stood but a few discharges when they retreated in considerable disorder."[51]

"When we got about halfway, we came to a lane with fences on both sides," wrote Charles Cope. "The battery was all ready and threw a lot of tin cans on the ground in front of us and they broke open and scattered cast-iron balls and

---

50 Robertson, *Things Grew Beautifully Worse*, 10-11.

51 *OR* 20/1:936-937; Sergeant John Allen Templeton, Douglas's Battery, "War Time Letters of the Sixties," *Confederate Veteran*, Jan. 1904, 24.

knocked the fences down so [we] could come over without climbing. Very accommodating!"

The Pennsylvanians charged to within yards of Douglas's Texans. "On we rushed and when within a few yards our guns discharged a volley of leaden hail which almost completely annihilated the Rebels who were pouring missiles of death among us from our own guns," Davis noted. "Edgarton's battery was again in our possession and a deafening cheer went up from every throat which was loud enough to be heard above the din of battle. No attention was paid to the captured guns, but straight on to the other battery flushed with what proved to be only an apparent victory. We continued to advance under a raking fire of grape and canister until we were suddenly confronted by a largely superior force concealed in the edge of the woods."

It was Bushrod Johnson's and Lucius Polk's brigades. To be sure, the Pennsylvanians were surprised to find they were in the field alone. "We found ourselves suddenly faced by a heavy force of infantry close upon us and sure of capturing us," Robinson wrote. "Turning our eyes to the rear for the first time, we found we had no support at all and were nearly half a mile in advance of any of our forces!" The regimental bugler sounded retreat, and the Pennsylvanians scrambled back, pummeled by repeated rounds of canister.[52]

Douglas's canister blasts gutted the 77th's color guard. "Color Sergeant Scott Crawford was wounded in both legs during the attack," noted historian Richard Sauers. "As Crawford fell, 15-year-old James Rodgers of Co. E seized the flag but quickly fell wounded himself. Lieutenant John Shroad of Co. K then grabbed the colors and brought it from the field as the survivors withdrew." Recollected Captain Thomas Rose, "the old flag was literally torn to pieces with grape shot when we charged the battery." With the flag staff now broken, Captain Joseph Lawson of Company C gathered it, the tattered colors, and Lieutenant Shroad and bellowed, "Boys, we have got to get out of here or we will all be killed!"

The regiment rushed in the direction of Post's brigade. "Colonel Housum and myself dismounted and were in the rear of our line between them and the enemy encouraging our soldiers to fall back in good order," Davis recounted. "Here he received the fatal wound. I caught him as he staggered when he coolly remarked, 'Davis, I am wounded. Stay by the brave boys of the 77th.' The strong arms of four

<hr>

52 Cope Article; Davis Address; Robinson Letter.

of his regiment bore him tenderly amidst a shower of bullets from the bloody field of carnage."[53]

Cleburne's men were equally surprised to find they had marched into a nest of Yankees. "Though we had moved out on the second line to support General McCown's division, it became evident that there was here nothing before us but the enemy whose sharpshooters were posted at the fence and in the woods along the north side of the Triune Road," General Johnson observed. "We therefore prepared to take our place in the first line; I ordered out skirmishers in front of each regiment, halting and correcting the right of my line."

The Pennsylvanians targeted Johnson's two regiments on the right, the 37th and 44th Tennessee—wounding Colonel Moses White and Lt. Col. Robert Frayer of the 37th, both mounted, and several members of the 44th. Despite the success, the fight was out of the Pennsylvanians, who scrambled back north along Gresham Lane under covering fire provided by Captain Pinney's 5th Wisconsin Battery. At least one Pennsylvanian was grateful for the relief. "This at once drew the attention of the enemy's cannon on them and relieved us from the artillery fire," recalled McKinsey Houck. "Our battery could do but little as the enemy had the advantage of position."

Lieutenant Charles Humphrey made no mention in his report of engaging in counter-battery fire, simply stating: "[I]n a short time we took position in a cornfield supported by the 22nd Indiana on the right and the 59th Illinois on the left. The enemy could be seen in heavy force advancing upon us. We opened fire immediately from all of our guns."[54]

*　*　*

Although Captain O'Brien was pleased to be back in friendly hands, he was not out of danger. "At first, I was greatly relieved to see the scamps driven off, but the artillery continued to fire and they shot very low and every shot covered me with rotten branches that the shock knocked out of the tree," he wrote. "I thought every minute would be my last as the shells burst in rapid succession all around me. As

---

53 Richard A. Sauers, *Advance the Colors! Pennsylvania Civil War Battle Flags* (Harrisburg, 1987), 208; Davis Address; Cope Letter. Colonel Housum was severely wounded in the hip by canister and died of his wound in a Federal field hospital the following day.

54 Private McKinsey W. Houck, Co. F, 77th Pennsylvania, "The 77th Pa. A Sketch of Its Part in the Battle of Stones River," *National Tribune*, Dec. 30, 1886, 3; OR 20/1:267, 875.

they moved up, the artillery ceased and I saw two litter bearers coming. They kindly took me on their litter and carried me to where the wounded was kept."

Gammage walked among the detritus in Kirk's camps, alarmed by what he saw. "At one place I saw a kettle on the fire and a man sitting down at the root of an oak tree with a coffee mill overturned in front of him, his hands having fallen by his side, his head bowed down to his knees and at his feet a pool of clotted blood," he wrote. "He had evidently been shot while grinding his coffee. At another place lay a Yankee soldier stretched across the path with the handle of his little oaken bucket grasped in his hand; he had either been to the branch for water or was just on his way when the leaden messenger overtook him and closed forever his labors."[55]

As Johnson's division fell back in confusion, scattered pockets of Federal resistance vainly tried to stem the onslaught. Ohioan Robert Stewart took shelter behind the chimney of a house and "reloaded and fired and loaded again. I do not know that I hurt anybody and I am not sure that I shot at anybody in particular, but it was a good thing to do. It made me feel better. My fingers were so cold that I could hardly handle the cartridges but they very soon warmed up to the work."

Aurelius Willoughby of the 39th Indiana recalled seeing a large soldier of the 89th Illinois behind a large tree loading and firing "very coolly." Each time he fired, observed the Hoosier, "he would yell out to the advancing Rebs, 'Here's your mule!' and then load again. After firing several shots and yelling as usual after each shot, he caught an ounce ball in his shoulder as he stepped from behind the tree to fire. Yelling out that he was shot, he about faced, threw his gun away, and did some of the tallest running to the rear that was done, never stopping to look back for fear he would catch another one. The mule business was 'played out' with him."[56]

The fleeing mass of Federals was a ripe target for Wharton's cavalry. Wharton's directive from Hardee had been straightforward: "Reach the enemy's rear as soon as possible and do them all the damage I could." To accomplish this, Wharton divided his brigade into three commands. Colonel Thomas Harrison of the 8th Texas Cavalry led his regiment plus the 3rd Confederate and 2nd Georgia. Colonel John Cox of the 1st Confederate led his regiment along with Lt. Col. James C. Malone's (Alabama) Battalion, Major John R. Davis's (Tennessee) Battalion, and Murray's Tennessee Cavalry, under Major William S. Bledsoe. Wharton kept back the remaining four battalions of cavalry as support for White's Tennessee Battery

---

55 Robertson, *Things Grew Beautifully Worse*, 12-13; Gammage, *Camp, Bivouac, and Battlefield*, 69.

56 Stewart, *Battle of Stone River*, 13; Diary of Private Aurelius M. Willoughby, Co. H, 39th Indiana, SRNBP.

and as a general reserve. "I moved the command promptly at daylight proceeding first at a trot and then at a gallop," he reported.

According to Lieutenant William R. Friend of the 8th Texas, Wharton's cavalry could be mounted infantry: "With the exception of Terry's Texas Rangers, their only weapon was the Enfield rifle, a weapon wholly unfit for fighting on horseback for after the first volley they could not well be reloaded in the excitement of battle. The Rangers were armed from one to three six-shooters and breech-loading carbines, easily reloaded and readily slung to the horn of the saddle."[57]

Colonel Harrison's troopers made their first big capture near the Smith House field hospital. "As far as the eye could reach, fields and open places were covered by more men than I ever saw before at one time," Friend wrote. "The enemy was routed and retreating, some running apparently for dear life. There would be seen squads, companies, and fragments of regiments in measurably good order, doggedly falling back, and while doing so, wheeling and firing on the advancing Confederates who soon became a mixed mass of cavalry and infantry. The game was noble and the pursuit was so exciting that the verist coward on earth could not have skulked to the rear."

Joseph B. Downey, a surgeon in the 77th Pennsylvania, had just brought in eight wounded men of his regiment when Wharton's troopers galloped into view. "Seeing that there were plenty of surgeons willing to remain with the wounded and knowing that my services would be needed with the command, I dashed out and amid the howling of the Rebels in pursuit and the confusion of the troops, escaped and again joined the regiment," he wrote. "I am very fond of certain kinds of music but the music which the Rebel cavalry treated us to that morning made by bullets propelled with great velocity flying by us was, to my ear, very annoying."[58]

"We could now see the Yankees in the distance running for life," recalled Chaplain Bunting. "Soon squads were overtaken and hurried to the rear. Onward swept that outer wing and the horses seemed to catch the spirit and they dashed forward with fresh speed. To our right the Confederate flag was flying and the infantry was keeping pace with us, sweeping everything in their course. The farther we charged, the more inspiring." The 8th Texas captured most of the 39th Indiana, including (briefly) the regimental colors, but some of the plucky Federals continued

---

57 OR 20/1:966; William R. Friend, Co. E, 8th Texas Cavalry, "The Rout of Rosecrans," *Philadelphia Weekly Times*, Aug. 9, 1885.

58 Friend Article; Assistant Surgeon Joseph B. Downey, 77th Pennsylvania, *Lancaster Daily Inquirer*, Jan. 26, 1863.

to resist even after capture. "Captain Thomas Herring with several of his men were captured and the guard having charge of him ordered him to double quick," recalled Private Noah W. Downs, "but the captain told him in his peculiar way that he had 'quit doing that.' The guard, much enraged, drew a revolver and swore he would shoot him. 'Shoot and be damned,' yelled the captain, 'I'm tired.'"[59]

Federal gunner William Beach fell in with the fleeing 32nd Indiana but ran afoul of Wharton's troopers near the Smith House. "I passed through a gap in the fence where a stalwart lieutenant stood waving his sword, the tears coursing down his cheeks, and beseeching the fugitives to rally round the flag of the 32nd Indiana, and die by it," he wrote. "No one heeded his appeals." Beach was struck in the back by a shell fragment and "turned a double somersault like an acrobat over an elephant. The unpremeditated flip-flop completely knocked the wind out of me." Behind him he spotted several regiments of Rebel cavalry rapidly approaching.

Beach helped another man toward the field hospital, but the 8th Texas troopers surrounded the party, "yelling like demons and threatening to shoot everyone inside unless they surrendered immediately. I demanded protection for the inmates informing them that this was a hospital, but another officer, excited by success and busthead whiskey, cut me short, and brandishing a revolver in my face, motioned with his hand towards their lines and said, 'Yank, pint.' Well, I pinted."[60]

Hardee's original attack plan called for McCown's three brigades to execute a wheeling movement, turning from west/northwest to the north. In the excitement, that wheeling movement went astray. Ector's Texans, following up on their success after defeating the 34th Illinois and capturing Edgarton's guns, continuing driving west/northwest toward Puckett Creek, where they soon met Rains's Brigade and Wharton's troopers. McNair's Brigade chased the remnants of Willich's and Kirk's brigades into the fields north of the Franklin Road and west of Gresham Lane, with all semblance of divisional alignment lost.

To be sure, Ector's and McNair's success disorganized their brigades. Major Jesse Ross of the 4th Arkansas Battalion reported that after crossing several fences, "our line of battle became disordered in getting through the dense cedar thicket which intervened. Upon emerging from this thicket, I could only see a portion of the left wing of the battalion. With this I continued to push forward in the original

59 Bunting Letters; Private Noah W. Downs, Co. D, 39th Indiana, *Howard Tribune*, Feb. 12, 1863, 1.

60 Beach Letter.

direction of the line of battle [west] and united with General Ector's brigade, pursued the fleeing enemy."[61]

*   *   *

For hundreds of Federals, the battle was already over. John Rennard of the 15th Ohio regained consciousness while bleeding from a nasty leg wound. "I was dreadfully cold, my teeth were chattering, and I saw the hospital flag hoisted over the Smith house about 200 yards away," he wrote. "I thought I would try and drag myself to it as it did not seem very far off. My feet were towards it, and I found I must get around with my head towards it. I drew up my sound leg, anchored my heel in the horse track, and made the effort. But I might as well have tried to crawl away with my body chained to the rock of Gibraltar."

Gammage came across a private from his 4th Arkansas seated comfortably by a fire alongside three Federal prisoners devouring a captured breakfast. "I called out to know what he was doing," Gammage recalled. "'Oh, nothing much!' was his ready answer. 'I've got three pets here that I caught and we are going down to see General Bragg as soon as we eat this pork and coffee.'"

Private John Wilson of the 39th Indiana said he "was taken by the Texas Rangers and they were all about half drunk or a little more. After robbing me of everything they wanted, I along with a great many others was turned over to some Tennessee infantry to be taken into town and a half dozen Rangers also went with us; indeed, the Rebel soldiers were very anxious to guard prisoners and the corporal in charge had to send several back to their regiments. The Rebels were very kind and used us as best they could. I saw several of them dismount and help up wounded Union prisoners on their horses and walk themselves."[62]

"They entered into conversation with us very freely," Wilson continued. "Every one of them had plenty of tobacco, an article we were all sadly in want of. They gave us the weed very readily and liberally. The Rebel soldiers treated us far better than the citizens all throughout our trip through the South. When we got to Murfreesboro in going up the street to the courthouse, I saw four or five women standing on a portico. When we got opposite to them, an old Jezebel of iniquity who had no teeth mumbled out in the peculiar manner of toothless people, 'I

61 *OR* 20/1:955.

62 Cope, *15th Ohio Volunteers*, 246; Gammage, *Camp, Bivouac, and Battlefield*, 69; Private John Wilson, Co. D, 39th Indiana, *Howard Tribune*, Feb. 5, 1863, 1.

would sooner have seen them all left on the battlefield,' then the rest of them joined in the same cry. One of the Rebel soldiers riding alongside of me said, 'You would not say that you damned old bitch if you had to go and fight,' but not loud enough, of course, for her to hear."[63]

Much ink was spilled after the battle in assigning blame to Johnson's division for being unprepared and not holding its ground at dawn, but most of the comments were based on misinformation or campfire rumors. Rosecrans, eager to shield both himself and McCook from any possible criticism, seized on Edgarton's decision to send a portion of his horses on a water break as a major factor in the Union collapse and censured him in his official report.

Captain John Sherratt of the 74th Illinois demurred:

"[I]t has been charged that they were surprised, but that is a slander on those brave men. True, some of the artillery horses were away to water, but the guns were there ready for action. It is also true to some of the men were preparing breakfast, but a soldier's breakfast at such a time is not of such an elaborate character as to incapacitate him for instant service. The truth is the pickets were well out, and the men had been standing in line from 5 o'clock until daylight. The trouble was not with the men in front, but with the men who left them there without the shadow of a chance to do themselves justice."[64]

McCown's dawn attack cracked the Federal right flank, and for the remainder of the morning, brigade after brigade in McCook's corps scrambled into position to face the Confederate tsunami surging north from the Franklin Road. It was a bloody affair for all involved, but the spoils in this initial contest almost entirely fell to the Confederates: one general captured (Willich); one general wounded and out of action (Kirk, who would linger in agony before dying in July 1863), and eight cannons captured (Edgarton's battery and two of Belding's guns). In addition, hundreds of Federals had been killed or wounded and hundreds more taken prisoner. The Federal army was opening the battle on the run.

Thus far the fighting was nothing short of a spectacular success for the Confederates. It would take hard fighting and significant luck on the part of the Army of the Cumberland to recover from its early-morning misfortunes.

---

63 Wilson Letter.

64 [64]*Society of the Seventy-Fourth Illinois Volunteer Infantry: Reunion Proceedings and History of the Regiment* (Rockford, 1903), 71.

"All Was Chaos
in the Woods"

COLONEL POST SUSPECTED that the Federal right would be assailed early on the morning of the 31st and had his men awake by 4:00 a.m. "[A]s soon as it became light," he recalled, "the enemy was discovered moving in great numbers toward our right and nearly parallel with our line with the evident design of turning the right wing of the army." His skirmishers were watching Evander McNair's Brigade moving to attack General Kirk's position. Because of the dim light and uncertainty of who they were, the men were told to hold their fire.

"Captain Oscar Pinney stood by his guns in a perfect frenzy of impatience to open on the enemy as he passed in front of Davis' pickets," wrote William Dodge of the 75th Illinois. "It was a sad mistake for as the enemy moved their flank within rifle shot Pinney could have dealt death in his ranks, and aided by Post's brigade, all of whom were anxious for the fray, the tide of battle might have been turned." Corporal John Sheaffer of the 75th Illinois reported that "impatient soldiers in Post's brigade now and then stepped to the front with their guns at an aim and were compelled to desist from firing under threat of arrest."[1]

Post dispatched Lieutenant Samuel Jones on his staff to notify General Davis of the Confederate movement; however, the colonel already intended to shift his

---

1 Dodge, *Waif of the War*, 64; Corporal John W. Sheaffer, Co. D, 75th Illinois, "Stone River: A Terrible Blunder on Somebody's Part," *National Tribune*, Sept. 18, 1890, 3.

brigade's alignment. "The right of the brigade extended into a dense and impenetrable thicket of cedars, connecting there with the left of General Kirk's brigade [77th Pennsylvania] and in that direction nothing could be seen on account of the thicket," Post reported. Nevertheless, the crescendo of gunfire and the Rebel yells soon told him all he needed to know: "I accordingly changed front nearly perpendicularly to the rear to meet them."[2]

Cleburne's Division advanced at dawn in support for McCown's main assault, marching roughly 1,000 feet behind McCown. Cleburne deployed three of his brigades in line abreast: Lucius Polk's on the right, with S. A. M. Wood in direct support; Bushrod Johnson's command held the center; and Liddell's the left. Cleburne was directed to wheel his division as it proceeded, making Polk his pivot on the right. Although Polk was ordered to maintain a firm link with Colonel Alfred Vaughan's left flank, he lost contact as Liddell's and Johnson's brigades, marching to the northwest, advanced. Hardee, therefore, pulled Wood's Brigade out of its reserve position, placing it on Polk's right and making Cleburne's Division now a four-brigade front, totaling more than 6,000 men.[3]

To counteract Cleburne's wheeling movement, General Davis directed Post to shift his right flank back and anchor his position with the 74th Illinois on the left in the cedar brake and the 75th Illinois farther west—both regiments sheltering at the edge of the wood line along a fence that ran north of the cornfield. Post also deployed his two more experienced regiments on the right: the 59th Illinois to the right of the 75th Illinois, and five companies of the 22nd Indiana on the brigade's right flank, both occupying open ground west of Gresham Lane. The six guns of the 5th Wisconsin Battery rolled into the cornfield between the 22nd Indiana and 59th Illinois, blessed with a clear field of fire in front.

As detailed in the previous chapter, the 77th Pennsylvania rallied on Post's right, adjacent to the 22nd Indiana, after it had been repulsed charging Captain James Douglas's Texas Battery. All told, Post had 1,418 men in his brigade plus approximately 200 survivors from the 77th Pennsylvania to hold the line. Several hundred yards to the right rear of Post's right flank was General Johnson's reserve brigade under Philemon Baldwin, though Colonel Baldwin was too far away to provide active support and would shortly incur trouble of his own.

Repositioning the line occurred so hastily that Post's skirmishers—consisting of three companies of the 74th Illinois, two of the 75th Illinois, and five of the 22nd

2 OR 20/1:270.

3 Ibid., 844.

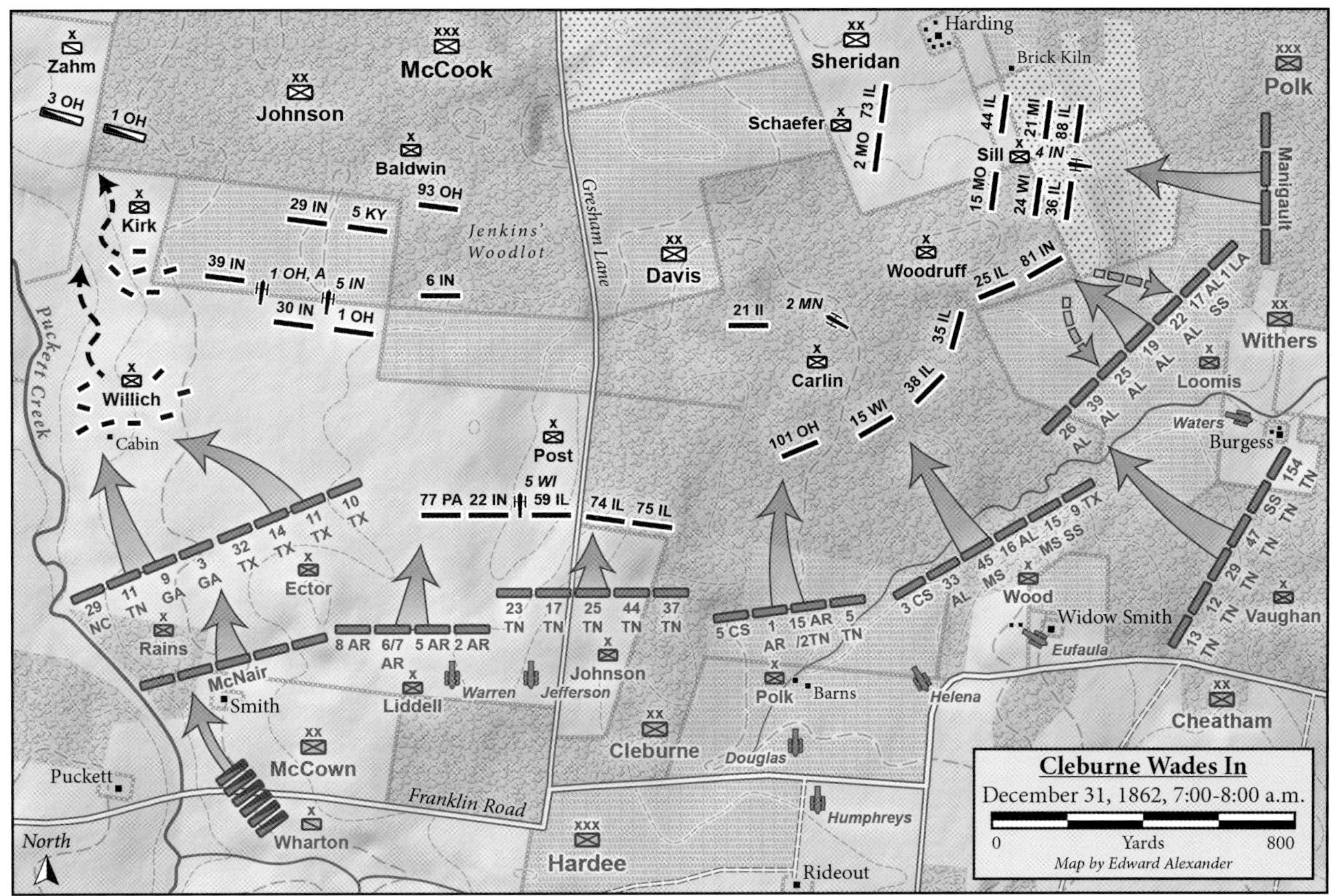
Zahm
3 OH
1 OH
McCook
Johnson
Kirk
Baldwin
93 OH
29 IN
5 KY
Jenkins' Woodlot
Gresham Lane
Davis
Sheridan
Harding
Brick Kiln
Schaefer
73 IL
2 MO
44 IL
21 MI
88 IL
Sill
4 IN
15 MO
24 WI
36 IL
Polk
Manigault
39 IN
1 OH, A
5 IN
30 IN
1 OH
6 IN
Woodruff
25 IL
81 IN
22 AL
17 AL
1 LA
SS
19 AL
25 AL
39 AL
26 AL
Withers
Loomis
Waters
Burgess
21 Il
2 MN
Carlin
35 IL
38 IL
15 WI
101 OH
154 TN
Willich
Cabin
Puckett Creek
Post
5 WI
77 PA
22 IN
59 IL
74 IL
75 IL
45 AL
16 AL
15 MS
9 TX
SS
3 CS
33 AL
MS
Wood
Widow Smith
Eufaula
47 TN
29 TN
12 TN
SS
13 TN
Vaughan
10 TX
11 TX
14 TX
32 TX
3 GA
9 GA
11 TN
29 NC
Ector
Rains
23 TN
17 TN
25 TN
44 TN
37 TN
5 CS
1 AR
15 AR
/2TN
5 TN
Polk
Barns
Helena
Cheatham
McNair
Smith
8 AR
6/7 AR
5 AR
2 AR
Liddell
Warren
Jefferson
Johnson
Cleburne
Douglas
Humphreys
McCown
Puckett
Wharton
Franklin Road
Hardee
Rideout
North
Cleburne Wades In
December 31, 1862, 7:00–8:00 a.m.
0   Yards   800
Map by Edward Alexander

Indiana—were soon stranded. Discovering that, the soldiers retreated north toward Colonel Carlin's line but were mistaken for Confederates. "The tide of battle pushed back so rapidly as to leave these companies so far in the advance that some of Carlin's brigade, already furiously engaged with another force of the enemy … mistook it for a Rebel force, dimly seen through the trees and bushes, and fired into it a terrible volley, fortunately doing but little damage," William Dodge noted.

These troops would not rejoin the brigade until after Post had been driven from this position. The loss of roughly 300 rifles would exacerbate the discrepancy in numbers between Post and Bushrod Johnson in the subsequent fight.[4]

"My whole division was now advancing in line of battle, gradually wheeling to the right as it advanced," Cleburne reported. "My left had not moved half a mile when heavy firing commenced near its front, supposed to be McCown's division engaging the enemy." As Cleburne moved forward, his men came under increasingly heavy fire, the general concluding he was now "the foremost line on this part of the field, and that McCown's line had unaccountably disappeared from my front. Skirmishers were immediately thrown forward, and I pressed on, continuing the difficult wheel under fire, through a country cut up with numerous fences and thickets. There was a great deal of crowding and improper opening in the center of my line. Polk's and Johnson's brigades had to be moved by the flank more than once to regain their true positions."[5]

Captain Irving Buck on Cleburne's staff noted that the ground and din of battle made coordination and communications increasingly difficult. "The ground fought was in many places limestone ridges and dense cedar thickets with farmhouses and clear fields interspersed," he wrote. "The cedars were so dense as frequently to form an impenetrable screen rendering it impossible to see but a short distance in front, and the continuous roar of musketry and artillery made it difficult to hear orders given by voice and the direction of movements were on both sides at times by the bugle."[6]

Cleburne's struggles in keeping his brigades aligned and dressed gave Post's men time to settle into their new position. Pinney pulled aside one of his officers and said, "Lieutenant, look well to your section for I am confident that this will be a day when our very souls will be tried." The delay also gave time for General Davis

---

4 Dodge, *Waif of the War*, 64.

5 *OR* 20/1:844.

6 Irving A. Buck, *Cleburne and His Command* (Wilmington, 1991), 120.

to make an appearance. "As soon as our men had been formed and while every nerve was tense and every sense expectant," one veteran noted, "our division general rode along in front and turning to the men with eyes that fairly blazed said in his unregenerate fashion, 'Give 'em hell, 74th! Keep cool and fire low!' and then trotted calmly past as if it had been a review."

Lieutenant Colonel Thomas Tanner of the 22nd Indiana rode forward 50 paces from the new line to observe the enemy movements. While dismounting his horse, he was struck twice by enemy bullets (one fracturing a hip bone) and crumpled to the ground. Because of the proximity of the advancing Confederates, his men were unable to retrieve him.[7]

"Almost immediately on the formation of this new line the enemy emerged from a wooded belt some 300 yards distant and across the open field in the immediate front of Post's brigade," wrote George Herr of the 59th Illinois. General Bushrod Johnson's all-Tennessee brigade of 2,016 men found itself squarely opposite Post's line, and though they were separated by a 300-yard-wide cornfield, with stalks still standing, both sides had adequate lines of sight.

Cleburne commended the strength of Post's position: "The left of this line opposite Wood's and Polk's brigades stretched through a large cedar brake; the right opposite Liddell's and Johnson's through open ground. In many parts of the brake the enemy found natural breastworks of limestone rock. In the open ground he covered most of his line behind a string of fence. Opposite my left, where the ground was open, a second line of the enemy, supported by artillery, could be seen a short distance in rear of his first." It is worth noting that Cleburne had three artillery batteries supporting his assault, and all were soon hotly engaged.[8]

*   *   *

Bushrod Rust Johnson was an odd duck among the commanders of the Army of Tennessee. An Ohio-born Quaker whose family harbored strong abolitionist sentiments, Johnson attended West Point and was a graduate of the Class of 1840 alongside McCown, ranking 23rd out of 42 cadets. Johnson saw action as a lieutenant with the 3rd Infantry during the war with Mexico but resigned his

---

7 Herr, *Nine Campaigns*, 410; *Society of the 74th Illinois*, 13; Randolph V. Marshall, *A Historical Sketch of the Twenty-Second Regiment Indiana Volunteers* (Madison, 1884), 25; "A letter from Mrs. Gordon Tanner," *Daily State Sentinel*, Jan.15, 1863, 3.

8 Herr, *Nine Campaigns*, 125; OR 20/1:844-845.

Brigadier General Bushrod Johnson

Library of Congress

commission in October 1847 to accept a professorship at the Western Military Institute in Georgetown, Kentucky. Casting his lot with the South in the Civil War, Johnson's West Point education and collegiate connections gained him a quick commission as a colonel, then a brigadier general. He saw service at Fort Donelson in February 1862, was wounded at Shiloh that April, and then led his current brigade through the Kentucky Campaign in August through October. Known as a "quiet, dignified, studious, and courteous gentleman," Johnson drew the decidedly uncourteous task of pummeling through Post's position that opening day at Stones River. He would deploy his five regiments in line abreast: the 23rd Tennessee on the left; the 17th Tennessee next, directly opposite Pinney's 5th Wisconsin Battery; the 25th Tennessee astride Gresham Lane; and the 44th Tennessee and 37th Tennessee tasked with marching through the small cornfield that separated them from the Yankee line.[9]

Post reported that "Captain Pinney opened upon the advancing line with all his guns and when they came within range of his canister and the fire of the supporting regiments, the execution was so great that the entire line recoiled before it, but after temporary confusion, [the Confederates] were rallied and lay down." Chesley Mosman of the 59th Illinois watched the approaching enemy so intently that he remembered to lie down only after the first volley was fired. "We fired like thunder and stopped the Rebel advance and made them lay down, too," he wrote. "The

<hr>

9 Charles M. Cummings, *Yankee Quaker, Confederate General: The Curious Career of Bushrod Rust Johnson* (Rutherford, 1971), 234; "Col. Tillman Pays Tribute to Gen. Bushrod R. Johnson," *Confederate Veteran*, Jan. 1906, 12.

Rebels on our left came, not stopping until within a hundred yards when they came to a halt."

According to a veteran of the 74th Illinois, "the enemy commenced firing at long range, but heedful of the good advice we were given, the regiment reserved its fire until they were close open us and then opened with volley after volley which made the solid lines recoil. With undaunted courage the Rebels came on and we could plainly hear the commands 'forward and close up' amid all the din of shot and shell."[10]

Colonel Gooding of the 22nd Indiana recalled that his men held their fire until the Tennesseans were merely 30 yards away. "I ordered my regiment to fire with deliberate aim," reported the Hoosier colonel, "and our fire was returned by a raking fire from their extended lines of infantry while their batteries played on us from the front and right." Captain Hendrick Paine of the 59th Illinois reported seeing "long lines of the enemy on the opposite side of the field moving directly to our front." When they approached within easy musket range, he gave the order to "fire, lie down, and load; at the same instant, the enemy's balls came whistling over us in awful proximity to our heads."

One of Paine's men, Alexander C. Pepper, soaked in the details that would stay with him for the rest of his life. "[W]e lay there on the ground loading and firing as fast as we could for loading a muzzle loader and keeping very low down is hard to do," he began. He continued:

> I looked up the corn row that I was on and saw the corn stalks clipped off with their bullets. I got down straight with my head down the corn row and thought to myself now, if you hit me, hit me in the head! It was not long until I discovered that I was hit, my hands and fingers were so cold I hardly knew when I was hit until I discovered the blood on both hands. I was hit twice and two bullets struck my gun in different places while it was in my hands. I still kept trying to shoot and the last shot I forgot to return my ramrod and sent that over to the Rebels.[11]

"As soon as the brigade entered upon the open ground it was exposed to a very heavy fire of grape, shells, and bullets," reported Johnson. It would be a standup fight with no maneuvering or elaborate tactics, and Johnson's men, fighting in an

---

10 *Society of the 74th Illinois*, 13, Gates, *The Rough Side of War*, 36.

11 OR 20/1:273, 278; Dean C. Anderson, editor, *Alexander Campbell Pepper: Memoirs of the Civil War* (1987).

open cornfield with little or no protection, suffered significantly more than their Federal opponents. The 17th Tennessee, Johnson's largest regiment at 598 men, marched to within 150 yards of Pinney's battery "under a galling fire from the artillery and infantry," according to Lt. Col. Watt Floyd. Detecting Pinney's guns, Colonel Albert S. Marks exclaimed, "Boys! Do you see that battery? It is ours, is it not?" Marks, however, fell quickly, ultimately losing a leg to a canister shot as the Tennesseans dropped to the ground and engaged in long-range fire with their muskets. T. C. Mitchell of the 17th Tennessee observed that "when we came within 150 or 200 yards, coming to a sag, we were ordered to lie down and kill the horses."

The 25th Tennessee, marching astride Gresham Lane, also halted when Colonel John M. Hughes was wounded. "No firing was done by the skirmishers or the regiment until the brigade was in full view of the enemy on top of the rise," recalled Lt. Col. Samuel Davis of the 25th. "The regiment then commenced firing and I never saw in any battle a more regular and constant fire which was kept up until the enemy gave back. Although a great many of our men were killed and wounded at this place, the line was not confused and the men continued to fire without noticing those killed or wounded."

The 23rd Tennessee, advancing on the 17th Tennessee's left, likewise was hit hard, receiving "a most terrific fire from the enemy of canister, grape, and small arms," noted Lt. Col. Richard Keeble. The volume of fire from the 5th Wisconsin Battery, 77th Pennsylvania, and 22nd Indiana convinced Keeble that a wider move to the left was needed to get around the Federal flank.[12]

The 509-man strong 44th Tennessee, under Colonel John Fulton, pushed across the cornfield directly in front of the 74th Illinois. "We had a severe engagement fighting some 20 minutes before the enemy gave away," Fulton reported. "Our color-bearer was struck down and Major Henry Ewin was shot from his horse [mortally wounded] while eight company officers fell." Fulton also received a painful wound in his left hand and was unable to control his horse. "He put his horse in charge of a groom, ordering that he be taken to the rear, but the horse became unmanageable, made his escape from the groom and ran into Federal lines," recorded Sergeant G. W. D. Porter of the 44th Tennessee. "We came upon a line of infantry strongly posted behind a rail fence and they were playing on the 44th. The order to advance was given and as soon as we passed from the timber, the Federals opened a terrific fire on us with fearful effect. Fulton pushed his column to within 50 yards of the enemy, but their fire was so terrible and lethal that

---

12 *OR* 20/1:876, 883, 889-890; Yeary, *Reminiscences*, 525.

his line wavered. At this crisis, Fulton rushed between the wavering lines, brandished his flashing sword in fiery circles above his head, and shouted in inspiring tones, 'Forward, my men, forward!' This evoked the familiar Rebel yell and with a rush we fell upon the enemy's lines."[13]

The 37th Tennessee arrived at the southern edge of the cornfield opposite the 74th and 75th Illinois. The Tennesseans were already rattled, as two of its officers were knocked out of action as the regiment marched into position, gunned down by riflemen from the 77th Pennsylvania. Major Joseph McReynolds took command and was in the process of sending out skirmishers, hoping to prevent a repeat of such a surprise, when orders arrived to advance. Holding the brigade's right flank, the 37th needed to march through the cedar thicket that had previously concealed Kirk's men. "The enemy retreated back to a cedar glade where they had several pieces of artillery planted," reported Captain Charles Jarnagin. "Owing to the advantageous position the enemy held, we did not pursue them immediately but moved by the left flank into a skirt of woods and there formed a line of battle and moved forward. We charged across to a cedar thicket and met with a warm reception."

As they approached the Federal line, the Tennesseans began taking fire on their right from the 75th Illinois, and McReynolds ordered the 37th to fall back before he was mortally wounded while retreating. Jarnagin took command, the regiment's fourth commander that morning alone.[14]

Captain Putnam Darden and his Jefferson Flying Artillery trotted behind Johnson's Brigade as it moved into position, and, with the infantry now fully engaged, he sought a spot to deploy his four guns. "I immediately moved by the left flank to an elevated position and came into battery to the right under a murderous fire of canister from one of the enemy's batteries, posted about 400 yards distant," he wrote. "We opened fire with shell, shrapnel, and solid shot; we could not use canister without injuring our own men."

The engagement, Bushrod Johnson opined, was "very severe, as much so as at any period during the day. More than one half the whole loss of this brigade occurred in this conflict. It is known that in killed and wounded the 44th lost here its major, eight officers, and its color-bearer; the 17th lost its colonel, adjutant, and

---

13 *OR* 20/1:893; Biography of Colonel John S. Fulton from notes of Sergeant G. W. D. Porter, Co. B, 44th Tennessee, http://www.tennessee-scv.org/4455/fulton.html, accessed Sept. 4, 2022.

14 *OR* 20/1:892-893.

twelve company officers; the 25th lost its colonel and six company officers; the 23rd lost two officers; the 37th lost its colonel and lieutenant colonel."[15]

*   *   *

Pinney's battery became the focal point of combat. "We commenced briskly firing shot and shell, until the enemy were advancing too close, then used canister," remembered Charles Cunningham, one of Pinney's gunners. "The volleys of musketry and booming of artillery, screeching and bursting shells with the movement of troops and the thundering of both armies, made us all know that the battle raged fiercely and that the approaching columns of Rebels were pressing us when we saw our infantry support falling back. Many of the horses of the battery were wounded, some dying, some killed; the riders were busy extricating such from the limbers and caissons. Amid this ordeal, the battery remained, firing canister at the advancing Rebel ranks."[16]

Prentiss Bannister of the 75th Illinois admired the bloody work that Pinney's men performed, but he was equally awestruck by the courage of Johnson's Tennesseans. "As the enemy advanced nearer, our battery opened with grape and canister," he would write. "We could see every shot from the cannon that would mow a road about 20 feet wide right through their ranks, but they halted not. They closed up their ranks and marched on right in the face of death, never flinching. The ground was piled with their dead. It was a sight I shall never forget." Pinney's guns, observed Lieutenant Addison Sawyer of the 22nd Indiana, "cut swathes three ranks deep through the Rebels and legs, arms, and fragments of bodies filled the air."[17]

Colonel Jason Marsh's 74th Illinois fired 10–15 rounds before receiving the order to fall back. One of his soldiers commented that "as we were behind a fence, we held our position longer than the one on our right and we did not fall back until the Rebels were on three sides of us. Everyone could see that further resistance would be folly and had we stopped longer we would all have been taken or killed."

When Colonel Gooding of the 22nd Indiana became separated from the regiment in the heat of battle, his subordinates had the delicate task of extricating

---

15 Ibid., 876-877, 894.

16 Cunningham article.

17 2nd Lt. Prentiss S. Bannister, Co. C, 75th Illinois, *Whiteside Sentinel*, Jan. 22, 1863, 2; 1st Lt. Addison D. Sawyer, Co. B, 22nd Indiana, *Western Reserve Chronicle*, Jan. 21, 1863, 3.

five of his companies from the action. "Captain William Snodgrass, Captain Powers, Adjutant William Adams, myself, and others, seeing the folly of attempting longer to remain in front of such an overwhelming force, held a brief consultation," wrote Lieutenant Randolph Marshall. "[We] determined to yield the ground, falling back in as good order as possible." Snodgrass personally took the colors and directed the regiment back. Unfortunately, four of Gooding's officers took opportunities to leave "the field in the early part of the engagement, taking with them quite a number of non-commissioned officers and privates, most of whom were taken prisoner and paroled at LaVergne," Gooding noted.[18]

Post's men managed to stymie Johnson's Tennesseans temporarily, but with Liddell's Brigade advancing past the Federal unit's right flank and Polk's and Wood's brigades moving through on its left, a retreat was the most prudent option. "Our position was so critical that it became ludicrous," Post noted. Lieutenant Charles Humphrey of the 5th Wisconsin Battery reported that "after firing on the enemy for about 30 minutes, the order was given to limber up and fall back. This was done in good order though we were obliged to leave one gun and two caissons on the field on account of the horses being killed."

One veteran recounted that "just before the order was given to fall back, Captain Pinney was wounded, a ball striking his thigh and crushing the bones. As he fell, he turned to the men and directed them to get off the field with their guns in as good order as possible and not to mind him as he would encumber their movements. The order was sorrowfully obeyed for it was then believed that he could survive but a few moments." They were correct.

Alexander Pepper noted that "Colonel Post saw the condition we were in and ordered one of his staff to go and tell us to fall back. But he was shot off his horse before he got near to us, and it was said that three commissioned officers lost their lives trying to get the order to us. Finally, there was a little fellow, a private soldier that the colonel had detailed for an orderly came in there and rode the full length of the troops When he passed us, he said, 'Company H, the Colonel thinks you had better fall back!'"[19]

"When the order was given to 'fall back to the rail fence at the edge of the timber,' this was not a very military-like order or in accordance with tactics," Herr

---

18 Corporal Josiah D. Austin, Co. G, 74th Illinois, SRNBP; Marshall, *Historical Sketch of the 22nd Indiana*, 25; OR 20/1:279. In February 1863, all four of the runaway officers would be dishonorably dismissed, charged with cowardice before the enemy.

19 OR 20/1:267; *Society of the 74th Illinois*, 14, 50; Anderson, *Alexander Campbell Pepper*.

pronounced. "While executing this order a shout was plainly heard above the din of battle coming from the direction of Pinney's battery and was accompanied by 'lay hold of the ropes.' The situation was taken in at a glance." With Pinney's horses down, the men of the 59th Illinois and 22nd Indiana "laid hold of the gun ropes with a firm determination that they should not be left abandoned on the field although [they were] compelled to leave one."

Cunningham remembered one man "urging his horses on until he reached the opening where there was a hill. The horses drew it halfway up and were completely tuckered out. [Private Bostick] Clark asked some of the boys of the 59th if they would help him run the gun a few rods up the hill so Curly [a fellow soldier] could get it off. They answered, 'Yes, the damn Rebels shouldn't have the gun anyway.' Some of the boys took hold with a will and helped run the gun to the top of the hill."[20]

By now, the 23rd Tennessee had completed its flanking move to the left and had begun a push against the 77th Pennsylvania. "Again, facing to the front, we marched through an open cornfield fighting the enemy during that time. The action continued for half an hour when the enemy fled into the cedar glade." Keeble immediately advanced his men "to his battery, which he had left when we received a heavy fire from them concealed in the midst of the glade. While they were firing upon us and we were unable to get to them or see them on account of the undergrowth, my attention was called to the fact that our right had fallen back." Thus exposed, Keeble ordered his command to call back, with the intent of reforming "at our old position at the fence which we found occupied by a portion of General Liddell's brigade."[21]

The men of the shaken 77th Pennsylvania, aware of Liddell's advance beyond its right flank and the subsequent sweep over the same ground by Keeble's Tennesseans, concluded that their best option was to retreat. "As soon as the battery was safely off, we retired to the fence on the opposite side of the field where we stood alone for some time contending with the Rebels until they commenced scaling the fence on our right and left," explained a Pennsylvania captain named Thomas Rose. "We then retired to the woods and again made a stand. We thus continued for some time, taking advantage of everything that came in our way,

20 Herr, *Nine Campaigns*, 126; Cunningham article.

21 *OR* 20/1:889.

moving slowly, but fighting every time could find a line to rest on or wherever we could gain a position in we could for a minute successfully make a stand."[22]

Pinney's departure spurred a surge forward by the left portion of Johnson's line, but, as Samuel Davis recalled, casualties were so heavy in the 25th Tennessee "it was impossible to keep a line any longer. The space between the 44th and 17th regiments was then too long for so few men, but the men took advantage of the good room they had and went forward like skirmishers." Watt Floyd saw Pinney's guns being drawn off and ordered his regiment to charge. Eighteen-year-old Adjutant Jimmy Fitzpatrick was the "first to reach the enemy's [battery] and took formal possession by throwing his sword across one of the guns, but he was immediately shot down, severely wounded in the thigh by a Minie ball," wrote a member of the 17th Tennessee. "The regiment immediately moved forward while the right of the brigade was held in check by a strong Federal force, such being the impetuosity of the boys, that Lieutenant Colonel Floyd felt safe in saying forward." The 74th and 75th Illinois were the last to leave the line and gave the 44th and 37th Tennessee a rough go for as long as possible. Davis realized those two regiments lagged behind the rest of the brigade and directed his men to fire into the 74th Illinois's right to speed its departure.[23]

*   *   *

As Post's men fought their delaying action along Gresham Lane, reinforcements were on the way to support the embattled right. The 79th Illinois was guarding Kirk's supply wagons along the Wilkinson Pike when the fighting commenced. Without formal orders, however, Colonel Sheridan Read ordered his men into column and marched to the sound of the guns. The Illinoisans proceeded into a field west of Colonel Baldwin's position adjoining Gresham Lane and received orders to rejoin Kirk's brigade, then rallying at a fence along its front, and arrived about 7:00 a.m. Kirk had managed to keep most of the 30th Indiana together with fragments of the 34th Illinois and 29th Indiana and now welcomed the pending arrival of the 79th Illinois. Having already had two horses shot from beneath him and bleeding profusely from the hip wound he received at the outset

22 Ibid., 335.

23 Ibid., 891; A., 17th Tennessee, *Chattanooga Daily Gazette*, Jan. 27, 1863, 1. Multiple Confederate accounts mention capturing a "4-gun battery" at this location, but the veterans of Post's brigade adamantly stated that only one cannon was left behind.

of the Confederate attack, Kirk turned command over to Colonel Dodge. For Dodge, it was déjà vu from Shiloh, when the 30th Indiana's colonel previously assumed command from a wounded Kirk.[24]

"Colonel Read requested that I should go forward and learn of Colonel Dodge what he should do," remembered Major Allen Buckner of the 79th. "Dodge directed me to hurry the regiment forward as soon as possible." The regiment double-quicked more than a mile to move within sight, drained but eager. "Before the 79th Illinois reached the fence and while it was at least 200 yards distant from it, the enemy made his appearance and instantly poured a terrible fire into their ranks," Dodge recalled. "Although a new regiment, they advanced with a firmness that would have done credit to veterans."

Read arrived on the field "guided only by the sound of the heaviest firing," Dodge would write. "I showed him the position that I wanted him to occupy on the right of the brigade. [He] had to cross an open field 150 yards across to get into position under a terrific fire." The colonel, however, advised Read to dismount, as "it was simply murder for him to go on horseback." Despite objecting briefly, the Illinoisan complied and led his inexperienced command into action, only to be slain by a single shot through the head almost instantly.[25]

Baldwin's four-regiment brigade constituted Richard Johnson's sole reserve and spent the night of December 30-31 camped in woods near the Jenkins' Farm, about a half mile north of Kirk's and Willich's encampments. Johnson had his headquarters nearby, and after the outbreak of fighting, the general attached himself to Baldwin's brigade. About 7:00 a.m., as the sun rose, Baldwin's men noticed a swarm of Federals running across the fields in their front. "I immediately ordered the brigade under arms," Baldwin reported, "and proceeded to form a line of battle in the edge of the timber facing the large open fields over which I knew the enemy must come to attack me."[26]

On his front line, Baldwin placed veteran regiments—the 6th Indiana, the 1st Ohio, and the 5th Kentucky (known as the "Louisville Legion")—that had fought together at Shiloh. He aligned the 6th on the left, facing south at the edge of a field of cornstalks; the 1st behind a rail fence at center, slightly behind the 6th; and intended to position the 5th on the right but decided instead to move the Kentuckians back 75 yards (in support of the Buckeyes and Hoosiers) as Colonel

24 *ORS* 3:628.

25 *OR* 20/1:320, 326.

26 Ibid., 337.

Dodge had already pieced together a line at that location. Baldwin also kept the 93rd Ohio, a rookie regiment under Colonel Charles Anderson, in reserve in the adjoining woods.

In addition, Baldwin deployed a section of two 12-pounder Napoleons under Lieutenant Henry Rankin, in Captain Peter Simonson's 5th Indiana Battery, between the 1st Ohio and 6th Indiana, and he placed the remaining four guns in an open field between the 1st Ohio and Dodge's line. Simonson's guns were inserted as such so they had a clear field of fire. Simonson found his battery perched atop the ground that Edgarton hoped to convince Johnson to occupy with his division's batteries the previous night (see Chapter Seven). Simonson would show why Edgarton's advice had been prudent and should have been heeded, as he turned the open ground on his front into a killing field.[27]

Baldwin soon spotted Liddell's 1,709-man force marching toward him. Liddell's Arkansans were part of Cleburne's Division but had assumed this role at McCown's request. Concerned about the disorganizing impact his dawn assault had made on his formations, McCown informed Liddell that "his men were considerably cut up." Recalled Liddell: "The arrangement was agreed to and I moved up on his right. I then told my men that we were about to 'go in' and that I did not wish them to stop to take charge of prisoners which would weaken our strength by escorting them to the rear, but that every man must stand to the front for we needed all. Then I gave the orders to advance to the attack."

As Liddell's men stepped into the fields to their front, Lieutenant Harvey Shannon trotted into position in an open field near Willich's old camp with his four guns, dropped trail, and commenced firing round shot and shrapnel shells at Simonson's guns 600 yards away.[28]

Just before 7:30 a.m., Liddell maneuvered his regiments in line and advanced. Skirmishers from Companies A and B of the 6th Indiana confronted the head of Liddell's advance, slowing it as they fell back to their main line. Once safely under cover, the Hoosiers opened fire to halt the oncoming Confederate skirmishers in the middle of the field. "A few shots from my line served to hold them in check," recalled Lt. Col. Hagerman Tripp of the 6th Indiana. "Their main line advanced and deployed column after column, making some four or five lines approaching our front. When within 100 yards, I ordered my men to fire and they went at it with a right good will, it having been difficult to restrain them so long." The Hoosier fire

27 Ibid.

28 Hughes, *Liddell's Record*, 108; OR 20/1: 871.

ripped into the enemy lines, checking their advance. "They were not idle but threw upon us their leaden hail which caused my men to hug closer to their frail defense," added Tripp, "delivering their fire with the steadiness of veterans."[29]

Liddell recorded his views from the opposing side of the field. "When we got within 75 yards of a fence on the edge of woodlands and partly hid by undergrowth, the enemy's line was developed in ambush behind this screen," wrote Liddell, who noted that throughout the engagement he turned to his bugler, Jake Schlosser, and bellowed, "Blow your horn, Jake! Forward! Forward!' Despite those repeated blares by Schlosser, the men refused to advance farther. "The fire was very trying," Liddell wrote. "My men, seeing the great advantage of the enemy and the certain destruction awaiting them, dropped down on their faces, almost as if by common consent, and commenced firing with great accuracy and precision through the interval between the rails and the brush. I tried to move them forward and ordered the charge sounded repeatedly—all to no purpose. They had deliberately set themselves to work to kill all they could. I had nothing to do but await the denouement which I knew could not long be deferred under the heavy firing then going on."[30]

"My infantry and artillery poured in a destructive fire into their dense masses, checking them in front," Baldwin remembered, "but their left continued to advance against my right. Here four pieces that Captain Simonson posted near the woods in the rear of my first line poured in a terrible fire." The 1st Ohio, kneeling behind the rail fence, faced off against the 6th/7th Arkansas and the 8th Arkansas. "As soon as they arrived within 150 yards of my line, I opened fire which checked their advance for 15 minutes" reported Major Joab Stafford. "Their line in front of me seemed to separate and I saw them marching by the flank to the right and left of us."[31]

"The air was full of the hiss, crack, and whine of Minie balls and canister," remembered one 6th Arkansas soldier. "Every few seconds a round shot roars through the files. The very air seems to burn." Wrote John Berry of the 8th Arkansas: "[W]e found ourselves in an open field face to face with the Federal force stationed behind a rail fence. I thought they would kill us all. We laid down and firing as best we could, would roll over on our backs and load, then turn back and fire. I remember shooting right over Dick Jones' head. He looked back at me and

---

29 *OR* 20/1:339.

30 Hughes, *Liddell's Record*, 109.

31 *OR* 20/1:337, 343.

said, 'John, you'll shoot me.' I said, 'No, I'll not. You keep your head down.' I loaded and bang went my gun again, right at his ear. It so deafened and alarmed him that he turned again, used some very rough words, and declared I would kill him yet."[32]

Liddell would take a pounding. Rankin's section of Napoleons poured round after round of canister through the Arkansans, in some cases double-shotting the canister as the fighting grew more desperate. Lieutenant Colonel George Baucum of the 8th Arkansas lamented that his regiment was pinned down for up to 15 minutes "suffering severely in killed and wounded. The firing was kept up in that exposed position at which time McNair's brigade moved up on our left and on the enemy's right and opened fire." Major William Douglass of the 6th Arkansas reported that "in the exposed condition occupied by our men, our loss just at this point was five times greater than during the rest of the day."

Nevertheless, the repeated blasts of canister proved only a temporary obstacle for Liddell's veterans, who reformed their lines and kept pushing ahead. "Our battery … cut them down by hundreds, but they could stand it," noted John Hook of the 6th Indiana. "They filled up the ranks again, checking not a moment. The Rebels charged yelling Bull Run."[33]

Confederate gunners in turn concentrated their fire on Rankin's gunners, which had particular effect on the nearby 6th Indiana. "The storm of shot and shell and the leaden hail of bullets which were raining in our midst was terrific," noted Private William Doll of the 6th Indiana. "The Rebel sharpshooters soon picked off all the battery horses belonging to the guns in front of us, thus rendering it impossible for them to be moved off the field. The firing continued to grow heavier every minute and to move down the right." Overshots fell into the Louisville Legion, killing and wounding many, but Major Douglass reported that Confederate artillery killed or wounded several of his men when its shots fell short.[34]

On McNair's front lay the scattered and reforming portions of Kirk's and Willich's brigades, as well as a single gun of Battery A of the 1st Ohio Light, now positioned to rake the open field. Belding, down so many gunners that he and

32 Calvin L. Collier, *First In-First Out: The Capitol Guards, Ark.* Brigade (Little Rock), 60; Sergeant Major John M. Berry, 8th Arkansas Infantry, "Reminiscences from Missouri," *Confederate Veteran*, Feb. 1900, 73.

33 Private John M. Hook, Co. G, 6th Indiana, SRNBP; *OR* 20/1: 327, 330, 333, 867, 870.

34 *OR* 20/1: 867; Doll Memoir.

another lieutenant assisted with loading, unlimbered his gun near the banks of Puckett Creek and "opened fire with the terrible effect upon the Rebel column. But the new line was but a cobweb to the enemy's forces for they opened with artillery and infantry, compelling an immediate falling back," reported gunner Henry Davidson. Colonel Fielder Jones of the 39th Indiana agreed. "At this time the panic was at the highest, and our men were swept away as by a whirlwind, leaving me but a handful of men and officers," Jones wrote. "I met Colonel William Gibson near this point, and we selected a ground on which to rally our two regiments; but ignorance of the topography of the country, and the operations of our cavalry, threw me so far over to the right as to separate me from Colonel Gibson and involve me in difficulty with the Rebel cavalry, which was swarming on our flank."[35]

McNair advanced his reorganized line, determined to drive the Yankees from the field. "The enemy had already engaged General Liddell's brigade, on my right, holding it in check and pouring a destructive fire into their ranks," he wrote. "Discovering his critical position, I immediately ordered a forward movement, and had to advance across an open field a distance of about 400 yards. Though the enemy poured a heavy fire upon my line from behind their cover, yet not a man faltered, but pushed forward with the stern determination of veterans." Captain Lavender of the 4th Arkansas wrote that "when we were about 300 yards from them, they turned the field guns on us and opened fire from a line of infantry behind the fence. We had a heavy body of men and were ordered to take the guns."

McNair ordered a charge "and, as before, officers and men seemed to vie with each other in performing acts of gallantry, and one simultaneous shout rent the air. The enemy, made bold by his front being protected by the fence, held his position with more tenacity than usual; but the terrific fire poured upon his ranks, and the velocity with which my men charged, drove him from his position in confusion, thus relieving General Liddell's brigade, which was already faltering under the heavy fire of the enemy. This was perhaps the hardest contested engagement of the day. Here my loss in killed and wounded was heavy, though small compared with that of the enemy."[36]

Colonel Robert Harper of the 1st Arkansas Mounted Rifles declared that for a few moments "the result seemed doubtful. Forward rushed our gallant men, with the wild yell of an infuriated soldiery. The enemy, almost securely posted,

---

35 Davidson, *History of Battery A*, 64; OR 20/1:314.

36 OR 20/1:345; Worley, *John Lavender Memoirs*, 40-41.

stubbornly held their ground, and it seemed as if our lines would clash in close combat. But again, the intrepidity of our troops prevailed, and when distant only 50 or 75 yards, his lines gave way, and were soon thrown into utter confusion and terribly cut to pieces by our fire as they retreated across an open field." Lavender noted that "they fought slow and fell back stubbornly. The gunners stood their ground until we were on them. It seemed to rain grape shot from those guns but we went on to them. Federal infantry contested every foot of ground with us."[37]

Dodge's scratch line held for roughly half an hour, performing admirably, but McNair's assault broke the Federal resolve to hold the position. Major Allen Buckner of the 79th Illinois saw that "the enemy was flanking us on our right. I ordered the men to fire right oblique but could not check them. The enemy rushed forward, opening on us a deadly crossfire and I saw that in a few moments we would be surrounded, and consequently ordered a retreat which was made across an open field to the woods."

The regiment lost its colors to the 4th Arkansas during the retreat. The 29th Indiana, to Dodge's right rear, soon took casualties from Confederate artillery fire aimed at Simonson. Likewise, once pressed, the 30th Indiana fell back toward the Wilkinson Pike, the men "becoming very much scattered" such that they took no active part in the fighting the rest of the day. The Hoosiers suffered mightily in the effort, with 210 casualties, and left the field with their colors perforated with 52 bullet holes.[38]

Simonson saw Dodge's line crumbling, and Dodge "hardly had time to inform me that a very large body of the enemy was in close pursuit when they appeared," recalled the Hoosier. "Three of my four guns opened upon them with canister and checked them in front and the right oblique, but more appearing almost directly on my right flank, the order was given to leave the field." McNair's infantry targeted Simonson's horses, and pulling out under a barrage of musketry, the Indiana battery lost 23 horses and 24 men in a matter of minutes.

*　　*　　*

Dodge's sudden collapse surprised the soldiers of the 1st Ohio. Sergeant Samuel Timmons was blasting away at the Confederates 50 yards in his front when "the first thing we knew, every regiment on our right had gone and the Rebels were

---

37 *OR* 20/1:948-949; Worley, *John Lavender Memoirs*, 41.

38 *OR* 20/1:327, 330, 333; "The Flag of the 30th Ind. Reg.," *Northern Indianan*, Feb. 19, 1863, 2.

pouring it in from both sides. We received orders to retreat and not till then did we realize what a pickle we were in. Column after column were pouring in on us and paid no more attention to the canister and grape that were ploughing their ranks than were they flies." Major Stafford reported that once Dodge's line crumbled, the Confederates pivoted their line toward his regiment's now-uncovered right flank. "Finding it impossible to hold my position without being annihilated," he wrote, "I ordered my regiment to fall back, intending to take a position in the rear of the Louisville Legion."[39]

Colonel William Berry of the Louisville Legion witnessed Dodge's retreat and saw the 1st Ohio waver as well. "Supposing that the 1st Ohio had exhausted their ammunition, I instantly prepared to take its place but just before it reached my lines, to my utter amazement, a mass of the enemy appeared moving obliquely upon my right flank," he recalled. "A change of front was imperative. While executing this movement, refusing my right to the enemy, the 1st Ohio passed through the right of my regiment and threw into great confusion my four right companies."

The clashing of the lines broke the 1st Ohio apart, one soldier terming it a "general stampede," and Lieutenant Alexander Varian averred that the regiment withdrew "in disorder, the enemy pouring a galling fire into us all the time and as it was all open country, we got the full benefit of it." While Berry's right was in disarray, his left six companies finished wheeling into line and, he noted, "poured its fire into the steadily advancing columns of the enemy, but the right of the division was completely crushed in, and I had no connection and consequently no protection there. It was soon manifest that I must fall back or be isolated."[40]

Liddell saw the Federals wavering and again ordered Jake Schlosser to sound the charge. "At last, it was answered with loud cheers and a rush," he wrote. "My horse carried me bravely forward with excitement in the interval between two Yankee regiments. The enemy's front line now gave way in great confusion; the panic carried to the second line which also quickly yielded to the pressure." Major Douglass noted that "the enemy gave way, our men rapidly following past two abandoned guns of the enemy's battery and scores of their dead across the field and into the woods beyond. After crossing the fence with my regiment and reaching the position occupied by the enemy's battery, it was observed that a line of the enemy

---

39 Orderly Sergeant Samuel Timmons, Co. A, 1st Ohio, *Scioto Gazette*, Jan. 27, 1863, 2; *OR* 20/1:298, 343.

40 *OR* 20/1:341; 1st Lt. Alexander Varian, Co. D, 1st Ohio, L. M. Strayer Collection.

Brigadier General St. John R. Liddell

Author's Collection

in front of the 5th and 2nd Arkansas had not given way, but still occupied their position behind the fence."[41]

It was the 6th Indiana stubbornly clinging to its position. Recognizing the danger, Douglass and Baucum deftly ordered their Arkansans to "face obliquely to the rear and deliver an enfilading fire." With yelling Confederates in front and on both flanks, the Hoosiers settled for retreat. "The enemy advancing on the 1st Ohio and [the] Louisville Legion on my right were already some 100 yards in my rear," Tripp recalled, "and being closely pressed in front, I gave the order, 'Fall back slowly and in good order,' which was done at the double quick." The 6th Indiana scooted out of danger but suffered 104 casualties during the brief engagement with the Arkansans.[42]

"At this time," Tripp added, "the artillery ceased on my right and in a few minutes the 1st Ohio gave way and fell back on the Louisville Legion, which in turn also fell back before an overwhelming force of the enemy which was passing my right flank in line of battle, their right passing within 50 yards of the right of my regiment." "This produced some unsteadiness in one or two companies on my right, they getting out of place for the purpose of firing into the enemy's flank as they passed. I promptly rallied them on the fence." Soon the troops on Bushrod Johnson's left, pursuing Post's men along Gresham Lane, pushed into the woods on Tripp's left. Retreating members of Post's brigade rushed back through the unsettled Indianans. "We were receiving a perfect hail of missiles but the 22nd Indiana lapped over our line and we had to hold our fire until they retreated

---

41 Hughes, *Liddell's Record*, 109; OR 20/1:867-868.

42 *OR* 20/1:339; Doll Memoir.

through our line to the rear," noted William Doll. Thousands of Confederates were right behind them.[43]

Colonel Charles Anderson grew increasingly impatient as his 93rd Ohio watched the fight from the woods, yet to contribute. Repeated requests for orders brought no response from Baldwin, so Anderson deployed his Buckeyes into line and waded into the fight on his own authority. He had no sooner deployed his regiment than Baldwin halted the move and directed the 93rd to form farther to the left toward Gresham Lane.

By now, the 1st Ohio and 6th Indiana were in midflight through the woods. "I ordered the skirmishers to rally on the right wing which had not yet begun its deployment and the colonel commanding [Baldwin] then gave me orders to retreat," Anderson recalled. "The regiment still being in line of battle, I ordered it to about face and to march in slow time. This order was executed for a little time in some regularity." But with Liddell's men pouring into the woods and bullets whizzing into the ranks with fearful regularity, Anderson noted, "our regiment of course much increased its speed so that by the time it passed out of the woods into the cottonfield to the northward the march had degenerated into a run."[44]

Simonson guns "were brought off successfully[,] though the enemy was 50 yards away yelling like maddened fiends," recalled gunner David Holm. Harry Comer of the 1st Ohio remembered that "we gave way and retreated at a slightly augmented double quick to the woods where we rallied in ones and twos behind the heavy cedar thickets and picked off the advancing columns of the enemy." All was chaos in the woods. Adjutant Joseph Siddall of the 6th Indiana agreed that the "retreat was quite disastrous, indeed partaking the nature of the panic. Colonel Baldwin did all in his power to rally the men, but it was impossible to rally them for a permanent stand."[45]

Lieutenant Jerome Holcomb of the 6th Indiana noted that "the word was given to fall back, but the men were so confused that they just ran in every direction while the enemy began to shoot them down as they retreated." It was in these woods that Simonson lost two guns, the Confederates targeting the horses and

---

43 *OR* 20/1:339; Doll Memoir.

44 OR 20/1:346; David T. Dixon, *The Lost Gettysburg Address: Charles Anderson's Civil War Odyssey* (Santa Barbara, 2015), 126.

45 David D. Holm, *History of the Fifth Indiana Battery*, 20; Letter from Private Henry H. Comer, Co. A, 1st Ohio, *Weekly Lancaster Gazette*, Jan. 22, 1863, 1; Adjutant Joseph J. Siddall, 6th Indiana, *Madison Daily Evening Courier*, Jan. 16, 1863, 2.

driver of one team pulling a Parrott rifle, which careened into a tree, and the crew of one of the 6-pounder James rifles had all its horses shot. An officer of the 1st Ohio blamed the bedlam on "panic-stricken stragglers from other commands and our line was broken by the overwhelming mass which surged through and carried off its parts."[46]

As Baldwin's shattered lines retreated through the Jenkins Farm woodlot, officers attempted a rally, but Stafford confessed that the retreat so scattered his 1st Ohio it was "impossible to get them into line until we had fallen back through the woods into a cotton field." Berry felt that in this new position "we could have successfully resisted the enemy but some general ordered the entire line to fall back further." That general was likely Richard Johnson, who rode among the flotsam of his division, bellowing for his soldiers to reform. "I saw one of our men standing behind a tree loading and firing as rapidly as possible," Johnson recalled. "I heard him say, 'I will not fall back another inch but die right here.' I admired his courage but not his discretion. It was not long before he abandoned his position, running as fast as his legs could carry him."[47]

Doll described this brief stand in the woods. "The Rebels were less than a hundred yards from us and they came steadily on with a yell that could be heard above the din of battle," he wrote. "Our flank was still unprotected and being in danger of being surrounded again, we were again forced to fall back and form a new line." Doll did not make it far before he was taken prisoner. "We were met with the taunting cry of 'Oh, you damned, blue-bellied Yankees, we are giving you hell this morning," he lamented.

Ohioan William Rockey grew so exasperated by the Confederate demand to surrender that he took his rifle and struck it against the side of a shed, "fracturing the lock and demolishing the stock. I then told the Rebel he might have it, upon which he demanded my cartridge box and equipment which I was compelled to give up and was then sent to the rear."[48]

Even in the midst of a bloody retreat, Federals saw things that triggered a laugh. "One of our captains complained of being quite lame from rheumatism, so

46 2nd Lt. Jerome P. Holcomb, Co. G, 6th Indiana, SRNBP; Unknown officer of 1st Ohio, *Dayton Journal,* Feb. 2, 1863, 2.

47 *OR* 20/1:341, 343; General Richard W. Johnson, "Contest of Skill: The Campaign and Battle of Stone River," *National Tribune,* Jan. 16, 1896, 2.

48 Doll Memoir; Private William H. Rockey, Co. A, 1st Ohio, *Weekly Lancaster Gazette,* Feb. 12, 1863, 3.

much so that he could scarcely get along even with the assistance of a large cane," recorded Charles Briant of the 6th Indiana. "In the scramble for life or death for the rear, it was for a few minutes 'every fellow for himself' and our rheumatic captain had been lost sight of for the time being. But just as we were getting out of the woods, one of his boys was heard to call out, 'My God, look at the captain going across that field! He is just touching the high places!'"[49]

49 Briant, *History of the 6th Indiana*, 194.

The Hottest Place You've Ever Struck

LUCIUS POLK'S 1,343-man brigade trudged through the thick cedar forest on Bushrod Johnson's right flank, somehow missing everything except Colonel Post's Union skirmish line during its advance.

Deep in the glade, the men were surprised to see assorted woodland animals seeking refuge with the troops. "The continuous din of battle from dawn so alarmed and dazed the denizens of the rocks and cedars that they lost all fear of men, their natural enemies," observed Captain Irving Buck, on Cleburne's staff. "The poor, frightened creatures, owls, hawks, partridges, and rabbits, sought refuge in the ranks of the troops, flying and running to their feet and so close and deadly was the fire that in cleared fields and near houses, dogs, horses, cattle, and other domestic animals were killed." As had Buck, S. H. Williams of Company I, 1st Arkansas, marveled at the cavalcade of creatures: "[I]n the first charge we made on the Yankees, we came upon a flock of turkeys," he recalled. "They were so badly frightened that they could not fly, but ran helter-skelter in every direction, not knowing where to go. Innumerable rabbits were hopping about, running hither and thither, the poor creatures frightened almost to death. Many of them were trampled to death in the melee."[1]

---

1 Buck, *Cleburne and His Command*, 121; John C. Hammock, *With Honor Untarnished: The Story of the First Arkansas Regiment, Confederate States Army* (Little Rock, 1961), 82.

Brigadier General Lucius Polk

Generals in Gray

On Polk's right, S.A.M. Wood's 1,150-man brigade marched through the open fields near the Smith House before it, too, waded into the thick cedar glade. The ground, according to one soldier, was "terrible cedar rough. Anyone who understands a cedar rough can understand what that means: limestone rocks, gnarly cedar trees, stub arms sticking out of the ground, make it almost impassable at best." Wood deployed the 15th Battalion of Mississippi Sharpshooters on his right near Colonel Vaughan's Brigade, followed from right to left by the 16th Alabama, 45th Mississippi, 33rd Alabama, and 3rd Confederate. He also shook loose skirmishers and, keeping close watch on Cheatham's line to his right, progressed in the direction of the abandoned skirmishers of Post's brigade.

"I ordered my regiment not to fire until the enemy could be plainly seen," noted Colonel Samuel Adams of the 33rd Alabama. "When I first saw the enemy, he was about 140 yards off and I immediately gave the command to my regiment to fire. In about ten minutes after the firing commenced, the enemy's line in front of my regiment commenced giving way. I immediately ordered the regiment forward[,] which order it promptly obeyed, running at a rapid pace and firing as it advanced." To further scope out the Federal position, Captain Aaron Hawkins deployed a company of sharpshooters, only to have the men tumble quickly back into line. "They were not long in finding them and were rallied on the reserve," he wrote.[2]

What Hawkins' men discovered was Colonel Carlin's brigade hidden among the limestone outcroppings and heavy underbrush of the cedar forest. Since dawn,

---

2 Daniel E. Sutherland, ed., *Reminiscences of a Private: William E. Bevens of the 1st Arkansas Infantry, C.S.A.* (Fayetteville, 1992), 115; OR 20/1:898, 903-904, 907.

Carlin's men had clashed with Loomis's skirmishers, and after seeing the Confederates' advance on Johnson's division, Carlin pulled his brigade back into the relative safety of the woods, ready for a fight. The 21st Illinois took position on his right rear—200 yards behind the 101st Ohio, which constituted the brigade's right flank;. the 2nd Minnesota Battery lay left of the Ohioans, with the 15th Wisconsin protecting the battery's left; and the 38th Illinois held Carlin's left flank. "The rapid volleys of musketry mingling with the roar of artillery, the screeching and bursting shells reverberating through the dark cedar forest, each volley sounding nearer, closer, and deadlier than before informed us that the tide of battle was rolling toward us and would soon be upon us," recalled William Patterson of the 38th Illinois.[3]

Colonel Leander Stem of the 101st Ohio called for volunteers to flush out Hawkins's sharpshooters, currently dropping soldiers in Stem's still-idle ranks. According to Charles Dennis, a volunteer, Stem directed the group to move forward a hundred yards, thus making it more visible to Wood's skirmishers. "When these Rebel skirmishers began shooting," Dennis wrote, "we were ordered into line, standing like a wall of human beings for them to pick off. Still the order came to us, 'Hold your fire, men! Give way to the right, give way to the left, steady, steady.' All this time we heard the thud of bullets as they found their way into some poor fellow's flesh and the falling men all along the line were easily seen as they pitched forward on their faces. Finally, their skirmishers came out of the bushes a little, keeping up a steady fusillade[,] but it was then that we could see what was behind that skirmish line."[4]

"Just as we were entering an open wood, the enemy's artillery opened on our lines," recounted Lt. Col. Richard Charlton of the 45th Mississippi, with the 2nd Minnesota Battery creating chaos well in excess of its numbers. According to one Confederate, the Yankee shelling actually proved too much for one of Charlton's men, who quipped, "Boys, we're whipped,' [and] dropped his gun and ran like General Gordon's cottontail rabbit." Charlton reported some command confusion within the brigade once it came under fire. "The command was given to halt and repeated by someone as forward; the men became confused and our lines were again formed," he noted. "We next charged the enemy in the open and were driven

3 *OR* 20/1:280; Patterson Memoir.

4 Dennis Memoir.

Colonel William P. Carlin

Library of Congress

back, the brigade on our left [Polk's] failing to move forward and thus leaving our flank exposed."[5]

"The enemy advanced and opened a vigorous attack all along my line but they were repulsed by the steady valor of my troops," Carlin applauded. "The firing was very heavy. In the woods just in the rear of the 38th Illinois, the clatter of bullets from the enemy's line against trees, rocks, and men was incessant. Many of these bullets seemed to explode; the effect may have been produced by striking muskets or trees."

"[A]t first, we were ordered to deliver volley firing," Dennis noted. "Then came the order 'fire at will and fire low, aim at their knees!' We could see their knees as they came on and we did aim at them, although I think the first shot I fired went very nearly straight up in the air." John Blair, Dennis's comrade, was among the first men struck. "I was at the head of the company dressing it when I was hit by a rifle ball and I thought seriously wounded," Blair recalled. "I could not speak or scarcely breathe at first. I gave my gun to Lieutenant Latimer and went back of the line and as soon as I was out of reach of the balls, I examined my wound and found that the ball struck me directly over the heart and as it was, the force of a ball inflicted a severe bruise and caused much pain, but as I soon as I learned of my condition, I returned to the field."[6]

Carlin repulsed Wood's first attack, but the Confederates duly rallied and pitched in a second time. It was now approximately 7:30 a.m. "The foe in our front was upon us again like demons and again we sent them back after a half hour's

5 OR 20/1:906; Yeary, *Reminiscences*, 465.

6 Girardi and Hughes, *Carlin Memoir*, 76; Dennis Memoir; Sergeant John D. Blair, Co. D, 101st Ohio, *Norwalk Reflector*, Feb. 3, 1863, 2.

contest," recalled Lewis Day. "The few minutes' lull that ensued revealed to us the fact that the fighting far to the right was still further to the rear and we realized that Johnson was giving way. We moved a short distance to our left and our new position brought the line of the regiment across a great flat rock as level as a floor almost and flush with the surface of the ground. Before we had fully reached our new position, the Rebel lines again advanced but were rather more respectful and they did not come so close. We opened a galling and to all appearances a very discouraging fire upon them. The affair was excessively hot, the firing being almost continuous for what seemed to be a long time."[7]

Although Carlin's right held firm, the 21st Illinois, positioned at the right rear of the line, wavered when flanked by Polk's Brigade, pursuing Post's now-retreating ranks. "Wishing to increase the fire on the enemy, I sent an order to Colonel [John W. S.] Alexander to advance and form on the right of the 101st Ohio and to Colonel [Hans] Heg to form on the left of the 38th Illinois, and for my battery to retire," Carlin reported. "To my surprise, I received a reply from Colonel Alexander that he was already so hotly engaged that he could not come forward. This startling intelligence was also at this moment communicated to me by one of my orderlies that all our forces on the right had left the ground." A heavy fire from his right rear "unmistakably announced that I was also attacked from that direction."[8]

By that time, the 21st Illinois was in serious trouble. Seeing the 101st Ohio retreating, recalled Private Alexander S. Freeland, the colonel "ordered a part of the regiment to front in that direction till they were nearly surrounded then gave the command to retreat in order, the enemy in masses closely following up. Suddenly a cry was raised: 'Our colors! Our colors!' Several rods to the rear lay our color sergeant and guards all shot down, but a score of resolute men sprang back for the rescue and they met the enemy face to face. The clash was dreadful but only lasted a few seconds as shots, clubbed muskets, and bayonets were used. Men on both sides were down but Sergeant William Hunter of Co. F bravely brought the colors safe to the regiment."

While retreating, Lieutenant Abraham Songer of the 21st Illinois caught sight of Post's and Baldwin's disjointed brigades scrambling along Gresham Lane. "To see our men along that field falling back in such confusion was enough to discourage us who were trying to keep our line in shape," he wrote. "The sight is

---

7 Day, *Story of the 101st Ohio*, 86.

8 OR 20/1:280.

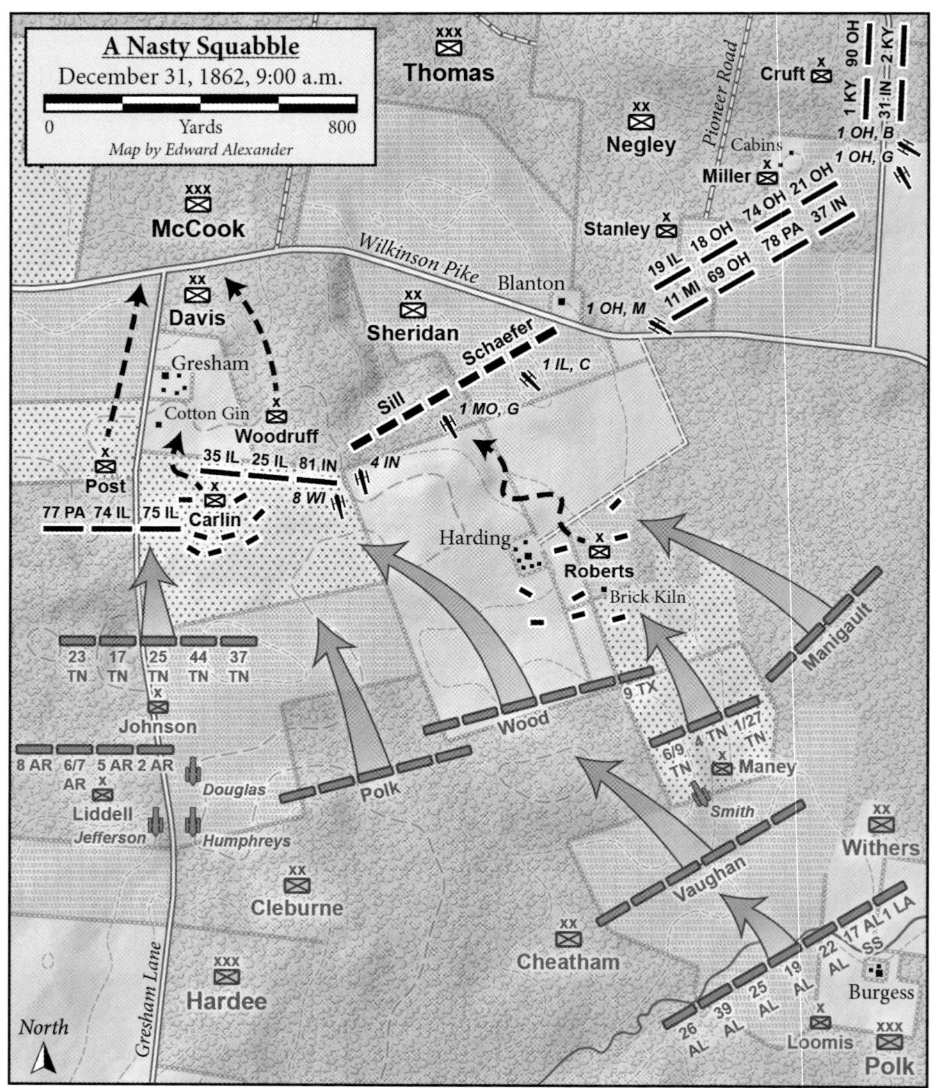

beyond description; in fact, it looked frightful but before we got across the field, I could see a line of blue marching along to support our broken lines."[9]

With Carlin's line in gradual disarray, it was time for Wood's Confederates to force the issue. Colonel William Wood of the 16th Alabama reported that "the

[9] Memoir of Private Alexander S. Freeman, Co. E, 21st Illinois, Civil War Misc. Collection, USAMHI; Songer Memoir; Private John Russell, Co. G, 21st Illinois, *Civil War Times Illustrated* Collection, USAMHI.

general gave the order to 'charge' and the men with a yell made a charge in gallant style, dislodging the enemy from their strong position and killing scores of them as they fled." The 33rd Alabama also surged forward. "The enemy's lines in front of my regiment commenced giving away," reported Colonel Adams. "We charged with a yell, firing as we ran, breaking their line and leaving their belongings such as breakfast by the fire, especially coffee, knapsacks, and blankets where they had been sleeping, shelter tents, guns, accouterments, and ambulances without the mules hooked up. We kept them going through the thickets on comparatively level ground where at times they would make short stands behind trees and rocks, and then again in line, but would soon break and fall back, leaving their wounded and dead."[10]

"Many Federal prisoners who were not wounded greeted us as [Simon Bolivar] Buckner, not knowing Cleburne then had command, saying they knew us by our blue and white flags," recalled W. E. Matthews Preston of the 33rd Alabama. Federal fire, however, had struck down dozens of charging Rebels, including Joseph McGowin of the 16th Alabama. "He was within a few steps of me...," wrote McGowin's brother, Alex. "I did not see him fall but was told that he was dead, and I went to him, but he could not move, for as soon learned, he was shot through the brain. The balls were then flying thick around me and the men falling fast. Soon after Joseph was killed three others fell immediately at my side, two of them dead. Although we lost many men, the enemy lost many more than me from what I saw. They lay thick."[11]

With Confederates surging around their right flank, time ran out for the 101st Ohio. The rock outcroppings that provided such good cover proved a deadly maze for the retreating bluecoats. Lieutenant Colonel Moses Wooster crumpled after being struck by seven bullets, both of his legs broken, and Stem soon fell also, shot in the kidneys. "Colonel Stem fell just as he called out, 'Stand by your colors, boys, for the honor of the good old state of Ohio,' " recalled Major Isaac Kirby. Lamented Day: "A heroic effort was made to bear him from the field, but he was too badly wounded and the almost unheard-of fierceness of the assault made this impossible. We held our ground, not yielding one inch until we were assailed on our right flank and until we were fired upon from the rear. It would be madness to remain longer and the order was given to fall back."

10 OR 20/1:901, 904.

11 W. E. Matthews Preston, Co. B, 33rd Alabama, Richard Baumgartner Collection; Private Alexander McGowin, Co. D, 16th Alabama, SRNBP.

An attempt was made by the men to carry both colonels back to a field hospital. As bullets zipped around the party, however, Wooster ordered, "Put me down, boys, and rally to the support of the flag." Both colonels would be captured, dying of their wounds over the next few days.[12]

The Buckeyes' retreat exposed the right flank of Heg's 15th Wisconsin, and the colonel ordered his men to take cover behind a snake rail fence and reserve their fire until the Confederates moved closer. "We were lying quietly and planned to let the enemy come close enough so we could make an effective volley," wrote Sergeant Niles Gilbert, "when suddenly one of our captains shouted, 'Fire away boys!' Immediately we blazed away with full force, but then the enemy covered us with a fierce barrage that I am unable to describe. We were caught in a terrific crossfire. After a half hour's stiff resistance, we received orders to retreat. As soon as we got up, some began to run. This threw us into confusion which was true of the whole division."[13]

Unhorsed during the clash, Heg vainly tried to rally his men but soon realized resistance was futile and joined the rest of the brigade's mad dash from the woods. "As we retreated, the Rebels came pouring along shouting like Indians," Heg would write. Lieutenant Joseph Rackerby, who was driving an ammunition-loaded wagon to the regiment in the woods, recalled that the Confederates were so close "we could almost see the whites of their eyes, and the shot, shell, canister, grape, and ball were flying thicker than I ever saw. I saw Lieutenant Colonel David McKee trying to rally his scattered men and as he passed me, he remarked, 'Joe, God bless you, you are yet safe! This beats Bull Run!'"[14]

With Carlin leveraged from his seemingly strong position in the cedar glade, the right flank of William Woodruff's brigade, on Davis's left, was exposed. A veteran of the Mexican War and former commanding officer of the 2nd Kentucky Infantry, Woodruff was new to brigade command—assigned to Davis's command in early December. His small brigade featured the 35th Illinois (under Lt. Col. William Chandler) on the right; the veteran 25th Illinois (under newly promoted Colonel Thomas Williams) on the left; and the inexperienced 81st Indiana (under Lt. Col. John Timberlake) as a reserve in the woods. The two Illinois regiments took position along a rail fence bordering a wide cotton field that provided both

---

12 OR 20/1:285; Day, *Story of the 101st Ohio*, 86.

13 Ager, *Colonel Heg and His Boys*, 72-73.

14 1st Lt. Joseph H. Rackerby, Co. E, 15th Wisconsin, *Grant County Herald*, Feb. 17, 1863, 2; Blegen, *Heg Letters*, 166.

cover and an expansive field of fire to their front; to their rear lay the northern extension of the same cedar glade that Carlin and Post defended to the south. Captain Stephen Carpenter's four-gun 8th Wisconsin Battery—after knocking down a section of fence to provide a clear field of fire—took position on the brigade's left between the 25th Illinois and General Sill's line to the north.[15]

Concerned about his left, Woodruff sent a message to Davis requesting support, receiving a quick reply that no support was available. "The general informed me that I must hold the position as best I could," Woodruff recalled. Carpenter detected movement beneath the trees across the field and ordered one of his sergeants to "drop a shot over in the timber there and see what is there," recalled one of his gunners, Sergeant Emerson Calkins. "He sent a solid shot at the point indicated and for a few minutes everything was as still as could be. When all of a sudden, a few puffs of smoke and the shot and shell from a battery came crashing through the timber. Limbs from the trees were torn off, shells bursting in every direction and as some of the boys expressed it, hell had been let loose." The Confederates, Woodruff recalled, "made their attack in five heavy lines and we were immediately engaged. Captain Carpenter's battery opened with terrific effect with grape and canister and they were mowed down as grass beneath the sickle. Sheltered by a rail fence, they were partially protected and fired with the coolness of veterans."[16]

Colonel Loomis, in temporary command of Brig. Gen. Zachariah C. Deas's Brigade, stepped off with 1,400 men to attack Woodruff. Loomis had only recently recovered from a wound received at Shiloh in April and was already smarting from the wound he suffered the night before while leading his brigade into action on horseback. From left to right, the brigade deployed the 39th Alabama, 26th Alabama, 25th Alabama, 22nd Alabama, 19th Alabama, and 1st Louisiana—with support from Yancey's two sharpshooter companies. The regiments attacked en echelon, with the 1st Louisiana farthest to the front; the plan was to make a grand right wheel to sweep through the cedars and drive away the Federals. "Colonel Loomis issued instructions to the men to watch the artillery and whenever smoke belched from the gun, to fall to the ground," noted historian Mark Owen. "Loomis' men split into two directions; the 26th, 39th, and 25th drifted to the left of the

---

15 OR 20/1:288.

16 Ibid., 1:288; Memoir of Corporal Emerson R. Calkins, 8th Wisconsin Battery, Civil War Times Illustrated Collection, USAMHI.

cannon ahead while the other half of the brigade attacked the Federals on the other side of the artillery pieces [Sill's brigade]."[17]

Sergeant Calkins reported seeing "the long lines filing out of the woods with the well-known Rebel yell advancing towards us. At every discharge of our guns great gaps were opened up in their ranks when it seemed as if not a man was left," he continued,

> yet closing up, on they came with fresh troops. They came across that bloody field in serried ranks only to be hurled back shattered and bleeding, but only to try again. We worked our guns just as fast as we could firing shell and spherical case shot until they sizzled like red-hot rain as we forced the sponges into the muzzles. Our sponge buckets were getting empty and water we must have to sponge the gun, so we emptied our canteens into the sponge buckets. It was hot work. The smoke was so thick that at times we could see nothing ten feet from us. The boys working the gun were as black as burnt powder and perspiration mixed together could make them.[18]

Loomis had not even cleared the Confederate wood line before one of Carpenter's shots blasted a limb from a tree, knocking the colonel off his horse. "He received a hurt from the falling of a limb cut from a tree by a cannon ball and had to retire from the field," reported Lieutenant Martin Smith of the 25th Alabama. "The command then devolved on Colonel John Coltart [26th Alabama] as senior officer of the brigade who led it forward through an open field for 300 yards under the most terrific and galling fire of musketry and artillery I have ever witnessed."[19]

The three left regiments of Loomis's line approached the Federal position at an angle. Colonel Williams redeployed the 25th Illinois to meet it "under a heavy fire of musketry," wrote Captain Wesford Taggart. "Our regiment then opened a murderous fire on the enemy, completely checking him and finally driving him back in some confusion." Remembered James Watson: "We waited until they got near enough and then gave them a sudden volley which staggered them and they had to stop. They tried it again and we were behind a fence, we had a little

---

17 Mark E. Owen, *A Narrative of the Campaigns of the 39th Alabama Volunteer Infantry, Deas' Brigade, Army of Tennessee, Confederate States Army* (1862-1865).

18 Emerson R. Calkins, 8th Wisconsin Battery, "Recollections of the Battle of Stones River,"8th Wisconsin Battery, *National Tribune Repository*, Vol. 1 No. 4 (1907), 53; Calkins Memoir.

19 1st Lt. Martin H. Smith, Co. I, 25th Alabama, *Daily Selma Reporter*, Jan. 10, 1863, 2.

advantage of them and held them off for several charges that they made. We were driven from the fence three times and twice took it again." After driving off the Rebels a second time, Sergeant James Weir noted, "I did not think they would bother us again, but we saw the brigade on the right [Carlin] falling back and the firing came nearer and directly it was one sheet of flame and smoke on our right."[20]

Henry Clayton's 39th Alabama marched into action for the first time that morning and received a harsh introduction to the horrors of war. "We were ordered to charge a battery which we immediately did and found ourselves in the tightest place I was ever in," wrote Captain Abner Flewellen. "We advanced through an open field, not knowing the enemy was posted in the cornfield until we were fired upon. At the same time, the battery was cross firing all the time and between the two fires we suffered heavily."

"I went into the charge with 22 men and had two killed and nine wounded," he added. "We reached the battery or very near it and captured one piece but were compelled to fall back under a heavy fire to where we had first started. We were thrown into confusion and when we were ordered to rally and charge again, I could not find two of my men. We passed through the same fire and just as we reached our first position near the battery; we were again repulsed, being greatly overpowered. As we retreated or fell back for reinforcements, a spent ball struck me in the back but I was not hurt."[21]

Chandler's 35th Illinois on the right had an easier time than the 25th Illinois. During the advance, Loomis's line presented its flank to the 35th, which unleashed a storm of musketry. "We opened a murderous fire on their flank which checked their advance," Chandler recalled. "Our loss in this first charge was light owing to the strong position we had. Soon, however, the enemy reformed his broken lines, appearing with fresh troops on our right, and made a second desperate charge on our lines, causing them to waver and fall back, but again they were repulsed with terrible slaughter and our original position regained."

"[O]ur battery of four pieces poured grape and canister into their ranks but it did not seem to affect them," remembered Lieutenant Hannibal St. Clair. "On they came like infuriated demons, not like human beings, until when within range of the infantry a few volleys checked them only for a moment. They rallied and rushed on

---

20 OR 20/1 291-292; *A Middletown Yank's Journey: Letters of Musician James C. Watson, Co. I, 25th Illinois Volunteer Infantry*, SRNBP; Sergeant James K. Weir, Co. B, 25th Illinois, SRNBP.

21 Captain Abner H. Flewellen, Co. F, 39th Alabama, *Montgomery Weekly Advertiser*, Jan. 14, 1863, 1.

to the conflict; they had a reserve that came in fresh and right flanked our forces and commenced a crossfire. Then the fighting became desperate."[22]

As the 25th Illinois reluctantly fell back from its position at the fence, it was fitting for Woodruff's reserve regiment—the 81st Indiana—to make its presence known. Corporal George Morris of the 81st was among those to witness the 25th's retreat and the gray wave that followed. "Like an avalanche they came on our boys pouring into us volley after volley until they had reached the fence when the order was given us to fall back," he wrote. "Reluctantly the order was obeyed, the boys firing all the while. As soon as the order was given to rally, the boys moved forward and with a cheer our brigade advanced on the enemy. The enemy was driven back into the fields. After a desperate resistance and being exposed to a crossfire on each flank, our brigade again fell back. We soon rallied and with a cheer threw ourselves forward upon the foe who were unable to stand the onset and again retreated and got back into the field. Our boys followed them up to the fence."[23]

"Our brave boys fell at every step, yet steadily onward moving they reached the woods, driving the abolitionists from their guns and position," wrote Lieutenant Daniel Monroe of the 25th Alabama. "At this moment, however, the Federals were reinforced by heavy columns of their infantry on the right, left and center and our brigade was compelled to fall back under the concentrated fire from these points. They rallied and charged again but with no better success."

Captain William Howell concurred, noting: "[O]ur loss was very heavy in going through the field. Four of my men were killed outright. Our line in the face of their concentrated fire got within 50 yards of their battery when our line gave way and stampeded back through the field, and we suffered worse than while advancing. It looked for a time that all was lost, and we had some difficulty in rallying the men and reforming the line of another attack."[24]

Matters were hardly better on Loomis's right. During its charge, the 22nd Alabama lost 95 of 265 men, nearly 36 percent. "[T]he officers and men generally behaved well advancing steadily under dreadful fires of grape and canister with heavy volleys of small arms," one veteran wrote. "The regiment suffered severely including Sergeant Albert Austin of Co. H bearing the colors of the regiment who fell mortally wounded while leading the charge on a battery." Charles Landrum of

---

22 OR 20/1:293; Lt. Hannibal C. St. Clair, Co. G, 35th Illinois, *Lincoln Herald*, Feb. 5, 1863, 1.

23 Morris, *History of the 81st Indiana*, 27.

24 1st Lt. Daniel Monroe, Co. K, 25th Alabama, *Troy Messenger*, Jan. 28, 1863, 2; Steven Driskell, *History of the 25th Alabama Infantry Regiment, 1861-65*.

Second Lieutenant William J. Rozzelle,
Co. B, 19th Alabama Infantry

Stan Hutson Collection

the 22nd Alabama went into action with "a very large canteen with several piles of thick red flannel between the tin and the leather. Before the battle, I had filled it with water. The Yankees shot a hole clear through my canteen and the ball pulled a fragment of the red cloth through with it. I could feel the trickling of the water down my leg and thought it was blood and saw the red string waving around and it looked like blood and I was sure half my hip had been shot away."

Major John Weedon reported that he was able to rally only 75–100 men of the 22nd after the initial repulse, retiring under a "heavy fire of grape and canister from which the regiment suffered severely." Sergeant Ambrose Doss of the 19th Alabama, a Shiloh veteran, wrote to his wife that "the Shiloh battle was not a comparison to this for I saw more dead men in one field than I saw in the whole Shiloh battle."[25]

The 19th Alabama and 1st Louisiana Regulars would attack the Federal line alone, as the brigade had lost its alignment, and the 1st Louisiana fell apart in colliding with Woodruff's line when an unknown staff officer issued conflicting orders that left the regiment in disarray. "We had to cross an open fire exposed to a galling fire, but we carried the point," noted Captain Taylor Beattie. "As we were pursuing the enemy, an order came for us to fall back and was repeated along the line. The men commenced to break while Captain Douglas West seized our colors and tried to stop it, but it was of no use as the troops on our right and left had already fallen back. The enemy had also rallied and were advancing to attack us. We

25 Letter from "T." of 22nd Alabama, *Mobile Advertiser & Register*, Feb. 14, 1863, 1; Smith, *Stones River: Confederate Army*, 647; Sergeant Ambrose Doss, Co. C, 19th Alabama, Richard Baumgartner Collection; Yeary, *Reminiscences*, 420.

fell back in some disorder to our original position and then I rallied the men. I saw Colonel [John A.] Jaquess and he seemed to be doing nothing."[26]

Indeed, the assault was a bloodbath, and for the first time that morning the Confederate drive had been truly repulsed. The rookies of the 39th Alabama had as many as 80 casualties, and only with difficulty could the regiment be reformed. In the 25th Alabama, the command staff was decimated: Lieutenant Colonel George Johnston was slightly wounded in the thigh by a shell fragment but remained in command; acting Major Pierre Costello was mortally wounded; and adjutant Jonathan Stout was wounded three times in the leg. Of the 19 officers who went into action, three were killed and 10 wounded, and the 280-man regiment had 117 total casualties (nearly 42 percent). The 26th Alabama also lost heavily, one veteran reporting that the regiment "melted away" under the fire of Woodruff's men. Even Yancey's sharpshooters lost 22 of 72 men while trying to break Woodruff's lines.

Reinforcements, however, were already at hand, ready to renew the attack. As Cheatham rode among the Alabamians, calling on them to rally and attack again, Vaughan aligned his five regiments and prepared an assault. As Loomis had done with Deas's Brigade, Vaughan was in temporary command of what was Brig. Gen. Preston Smith's veteran brigade, with Smith home attending to his sick wife. Few troops on the battlefield had more combat experience than this brigade, with Belmont, Mill Springs, Shiloh, and Richmond (Kentucky) already on its resume. From right to left, Vaughan deployed the 154th Tennessee, 13th Tennessee, 12th/47th Tennessee, and 29th Tennessee. Initially, the 9th Texas was squeezed from this alignment, engaged on the right flank of S.A.M. Wood's Brigade.

Vaughan's veterans witnessed the desolation of Loomis's command at close range. "The Alabamians had to go through an open field to attack," remembered William McDearman of the 12th/47th Tennessee. "The fighting was terrific for some time and our men had to fall back. They were cut to pieces terribly when we were ordered forward to the edge of the field to lie down by an old hedgerow. The enemy cheered like a lot of little schoolboys."

The Tennesseans chided the Alabamians as they fell back. "Our men would guy and jeer the Alabamians for taking the back track as they passed through our line," recalled A. H. Brown of the 13th Tennessee. "One tall fellow said in reply to

---

26 Diary of Captain Taylor Beattie, Co. A, 1st Louisiana Regulars, Taylor Beattie Papers #54, Southern Historical Collection, The Wilson Library, University of North Carolina at Chapel Hill.

one of our boys, 'Yes, and you'll find it the hottest place you've ever struck in a little while!' His remark was about right."[27]

Reports circulated after the battle that Cheatham was drunk during the fighting. Several Tennesseans in Vaughan's Brigade alluded as much, although Cheatham's supposedly tipsy condition did nothing to minimize the inspiration the men drew from his exhortations as he rode behind the lines. The general had no compunction when it came to matters of state pride. When a brigade ordered to the charge did not do so "with that alacrity which the General deemed proper in the emergency," reported a newspaper soon after the battle, Cheatham guided his horse up to the color bearer, seized the staff of the brigade's battle flag, and loudly addressed those within earshot: "The Tennessee boys are a mile ahead of you. Don't you hear their guns? Follow these colors or I will have every man shot that falters! You have insinuated that we won't fight. Look to it that you don't yourselves deserve the insinuation. Forward the brigade! Double quick, march![28]

Before going into action, Colonel William Young of the 9th Texas rode in front of his men and steeled their courage for the task ahead. "Men, we left our homes to meet the enemy," he wrote. "He is in our front. Do your duty. The safest place you can find is at your post. Steady, men, steady. Don't dodge. Never leave your place in the ranks to get behind shelter. Forward!" Orren Hearne, a private in Company F, 154th Tennessee, had missed Shiloh and Perryville because of illness, and after being assigned to months of "soft" hospital duty, he went into battle attired in "some rather fancy clothing." That, admitted the chastened Tennessean, raised the hackles of his veteran comrades, who derided him by saying, "'There goes your hospital rat, oh what a pretty shirt!' I could not talk back for they were begrimed and footsore from much fighting and marching."[29]

"Cheatham gave orders for every man to be ready and at the command 'Attention' for each to rise on his right knee and shoot under the smoke of the enemy's guns," McDearman noted. "Then we were to load and fire as we advanced. At the command, every man was in his place, we fired all at once, and rose yelling. Cheatham's and Pat Cleburne's men could beat the world on a yell.

---

27 Private William J. McDearman, Co. H, 12th Tennessee Infantry, "Private M'Dearman at Murfreesboro," *CV*, 9:306; Private A. H. Brown, Co. B, 13th Tennessee Infantry, "Reminiscences of a Private Soldier," *CV*, 17:449.

28 "An Incident of Major General Frank Cheatham," *Fayetteville Observer*, Jan. 15, 1863, 2.

29 E. Russell Tanner, *The Stephen Jennings Tanner Autobiography and Genealogy* (1970), 38; Yeary, *Reminiscences*, 322.

When we got to where they were when we fired on them, there was a blue line of dead Yanks across the field." Lieutenant James D. West of the 13th Tennessee asserted that "now came a scene of terror. The men sprang up with a yell and advanced through the open field while the enemy beyond disputed the advance with a perfect storm of deadly missiles. Our ranks were fearfully thinned at every step, but nothing could shake the determination of these hardy veterans of Tennessee. On they went, their shouts rising above the din of battle."[30]

The 29th Tennessee on the left flank took a beating. Charging into the angle between Carlin's and Woodruff's brigades, the Tennesseans were exposed to a "brisk fire of shot and shell" and "exposed to an enfilading fire on the left," with 112 casualties of the 220 who went into the fight (nearly 51 percent). The adjacent 12th/47th Tennessee found itself in a similar vortex of flying lead. "That was a squally time," McDearman remembered. "The Yanks' battery at our front in the woods opened on us with grape and canister and then their infantry too. Our officers hallooed, 'Charge! Charge! General Cheatham says that battery must be taken if it costs the life of every man!'"[31]

The 9th Texas suffered heavily as it closed on Woodruff's position. "I ordered my regiment to cross the fence for the purpose of charging the enemy's position which they did, but mistaking my intention, they advanced 50 paces and again halted and opened fire," reported Colonel Young. "While endeavoring to get them to hear my command 'forward,' my horse was shot as well as that of the lieutenant colonel and for five minutes the regiment received a most murderous fire which killed and wounded more than 100 of my men including nearly all the commissioned officers." According to Sergeant John Street, "they poured into our ranks a most deadly and destructive fire. Man after man fell either killed or wounded, but our onward course was not to be stayed."[32]

Young decided that he had to break the logjam. "Seeing that we were suffering from a crossfire, I resolved to charge and rout the enemy from his position," he reported. "Passing down the line, I notified each company of my intention and then, taking the colors, I ordered the regiment to move forward with a shout, both of which they did a la Texas. Charging through the cedar brake in our front, the

30 McDearman Article; Memoir of Lieutenant James Durham West, Co. L, 13th Tennessee, SRNBP.

31 McDearman Article.

32 OR 20/1:749; Sergeant John Kennedy Street, Co. A, 9th Texas, Street Papers, The Southern Historical Collection, Wilson Library, University of North Carolina at Chapel Hill.

enemy fled at our approach." Added Street: "[W]e charged up to the fence, the enemy slowly retiring, the fence was next thrown down and we crossed over but found ourselves without any support on the right. The color bearer was shot down and Colonel Young seized the colors and bore them almost within the abolitionists' ranks. The boys rushed forward yelling and shouting at the top of their voices and the enemy broke and fled in wild confusion, leaving the ground covered with their dead and wounded."[33]

Lieutenant Colonel Miles Dillard of the 9th Texas contended that "we would never have gotten through but General Cheatham ordered a brigade to our assistance. The brigade moved firmly and steadily but never reached the firing line. When they got to within 100 yards of the Federals, the enemy wavered and the boys ran them to the next line where they stood and fought until the brigade got up near them and the same thing occurred again. At this time, a rabbit jumped up when Joe Russell saluted it as it ran off and said, 'Go it, cottontail! If I had no more at stake than you, I'd be leaving, too![34]

John King of the 9th Texas recalled the horrors of close-quarters combat. "My cousin Doc King was the first man struck in the regiment," he wrote. "He fell by my side in the stalk field and hallooed for me and I told the infirmary corps to carry him to the hospital and I would come for him after the battle. He was shot through the hips with a Belgian musket ball as big as a man's thumb. His screams were in my ears all day."[35]

Vaughan's renewed assault broke Woodruff's position. According to Captain Wesford Taggart, "the enemy immediately made another advance and were received with a terrific fire of musketry and our regiment was forced back a short distance. Colonel Williams fell mortally wounded by a musket ball passing through his right breast while bravely rallying his men which by this time had fallen back a distance of 150 paces from the first position." Another 25th Illinois officer reported that three of the regiment's color-bearers had fallen when Williams seized the standard and bellowed, 'Here men, we will stand or fall by our flag!' Hardly had he uttered those words when he fell mortally wounded."

The Confederates also lost heavily in regimental commanders; in the 13th Tennessee, Lt. Col. William Morgan, his second-in-command Major Peter Cole, and ranking captain William Crook were all struck down during the charge, leaving

---

33 OR 20/1:749.

34 Street Papers; Yeary, *Reminiscences*, 187-88.

35 King Papers.

Captain R. F. Lanier in command. Despite the losses, Vaughan's line "rushed in with a shout and entered the woods, driving the enemy before them," Lanier reported. Corporal Morris of the 81st Indiana remembered that "as the enemy had overwhelming numbers flanking each wing, we were compelled to fall back which was done, many of the men firing sullenly as they went."[36]

As his infantry support melted away, Carpenter began to extricate his 8th Wisconsin Battery from the woods but would be killed almost immediately. "The captain was shot in the head as he was about to give the order to 'limber up' the pieces preparatory to going off the field," one gunner wrote. In a sudden command abyss, orderly sergeant Obadiah German, one of Carpenter's acting section leaders, took control of the battery. The Confederate infantry quickly closed in, trying to capture the guns.[37]

"We poured canister into them," Calkins reported. "Every time we discharged our gun it seemed to me that it made a gap 20 feet wide where every man went down." Woodruff's gunners iron rain of shot and shell stymied two Confederate charges and littered the field with broken men. There was still more bloody work to do. "[T]he third line came at us with a yell. They were within 20 yards of the muzzles of our guns when the command came, 'Limber to the rear,' and quicker than a flash the team swung around with the limber," recounted Calkins, whose eye for detail in combat was second to none. "We dropped the eye over the pin and stepped back, but a volley was fired into us. The wheel driver fell from his horse and the team swung round against a tree."

By this time the Rebels were almost upon them and screaming for the gunners to surrender. One of the Union artillerists, George Marsh, "quickly mounted the wheel horse; the piece was quickly unlimbered and got loose from the tree and as quickly limbered up again and the command given to forward. The Rebels were not ten feet from our guns and commanding us to surrender but they were too late." The battery had inflicted a terrible price upon the enemy, but left behind its captain, half a dozen men, a dozen horses, and a Parrott rifle.[38]

Carlin's retreat on the right also signaled the end for Woodruff. "I received orders to take a position to the rear some 300 yards in the belt of timber," he reported. "I informed the staff officer who brought the order that we could

---

36 OR 20/1:291-292, 746; Lt. Col. James S. McClelland, 25th Illinois, *Cincinnati Daily Commercial*, Jan. 19, 1863, 1; Morris, *History of the 81st Indiana*, 27.

37 Unknown member of 8th Wisconsin Battery, *The Wisconsin Pinery*, Jan. 30, 1863, 2.

38 Calkins Memoir; OR 20/1:268.

maintain our position if supported, but he said the order was peremptory, and I hastened to execute it."

By the time Woodruff's men began their retreat, the Confederates had already surged around both flanks, forcing the brigade to retreat through a blistering crossfire. It took several commands to convince the 35th Illinois to retreat. "The division on our right was badly whipped and gone back in disorder which allowed the enemy to attack on us two sides," St. Clair recalled. "Our men were out of cartridges. We were ordered to retire twice before we did, but this time we left the field under a galling fire of musketry, canister, and shells."[39]

To provide cover for the 8th Wisconsin Battery, Woodruff wheeled his two veteran Illinois regiments back into line and counterattacked. "We made a vigorous charge and drove the enemy back in our front and, strange to say, not only carried our point, but swung the enemy's line upon right and left with it," the colonel reported proudly. Taggart wrote that his regiment, bereft of ammunition, fixed bayonets and "charged on the enemy once more, driving him from the field and retaking one Parrott gun which had been taken by the enemy from the 8th Wisconsin Battery."

The men made it back to their old position at the fence but lacked the strength to hold it long and soon were again forced back through the woods. "Finding all of our supplies gone and flanked on the left, the enemy's lines having passed us on the right and being unable to communicate with Colonel Woodruff, I assumed the responsibility of withdrawing the regiment in good order," Taggart wrote. His men gamely dragged along the recaptured Parrott rifle for about 300 yards before they abandoned it in Harding's field and sprinted north for Davis's new defensive line near the Harding House.[40]

Wood's front line emerged from the forest to find Lucius Polk's men surging up Gresham Lane just ahead of Johnson's Brigade; it was a mass of gray uniforms yelling and hooting with a cloud of blue being driven before them. But Wood's success temporarily disorganized his lines, the general noting that order fell apart due to "the eagerness of the pursuit, the men of each regiment mixing together. As the enemy retired through a piece of woods extending forward between two fields, a battery directly in front of us was firing on us."

Vaughan's triumphant infantrymen also poured out of the woods to the east of Wood into a blizzard of Federal shells and bullets. "As we emerged from the timber

39 OR 20/1:288; St. Clair Letter.

40 OR 20/1:288, 291-292.

through an open field, they poured into us such a terrific fire that we were compelled to lie down," Hearne would write. "Near me was a dead Federal soldier and I took his lifeless body for breastworks, believing that under the same circumstances he would have acted the same way towards me."[41]

Carlin's brigade rallied at a fence east of Gresham Lane, several hundred yards northwest of its first position in the cedars. The 38th Illinois arrived first and delivered a lethal covering fire on Wood's pursuing Confederates. That gave the rest of Carlin's men a chance to rally, though they soon saw Woodruff's men streaming out of the woods to their left. "I did not know what the trouble was until we came into the cotton field," Weir wrote. "The whole line of battle was running for life and I thought everything was lost. It was a stampede and a Manassas affair."[42]

The night before, McKee confessed to Rackerby that he feared he would die in the engagement, and Rackerby would witness him struck down near the fence. "I started to go to him but I met Colonel Heg who told me he was dead and ordered us to get away from there as the enemy was pressing us very close," the lieutenant grieved. McKee, according to one account, "was shot through the head, the ball entering in a little back of his left eye and coming out near his right ear." The 15th Wisconsin took position behind the 38th Illinois and took control once the Illinoisians exhausted their ammunition. "My regiment opened fire on the enemy who was at that time about 200 yards from us and advancing towards us in a very solid column," Heg reported. "While holding this position, many of my men were killed and wounded. We held this position until I discovered a large force of the enemy on our right, leaving no alternative but to retire as best we could or have the regiment taken prisoner."[43]

"Back of us an eighth of a mile was an open cotton field extending westerly and northerly to the woods that bordered it on these two sides," recalled Lewis Day. "In the southern edge of this field, just back of a fence which separated it from the woods, we formed our second line. It proved, however, to be as untenable as our former position and for the same reason. The Confederates were squarely on our

41 Ibid., 898; Yeary, *Reminiscences*, 322.

42 Weir Letters.

43 Report from Colonel Hans C. Heg, 15th Wisconsin Volunteer Infantry, Quiner Scrapbooks: Correspondence of the Wisconsin Volunteers, Vol. 9. Wisconsin Historical Society; Rackerby Letter; "How Lt. Col. McKee of the Fifteenth was Killed," *Wisconsin State Journal*, Jan. 19, 1863, 1.

flank and were protected by the fence along Gresham Lane behind which they were sheltering themselves and from between the rails of which they were deliberately murdering us." Carlin had no choice but to continue falling back.[44]

Carlin's embattled infantrymen poured out of the woods only to collide with the retreating ranks of Post's and Baldwin's brigades along Gresham Lane, with the Confederates in hot pursuit. The men quickly mixed together, merely adding to the chaos and confusion. "[H]ow in the world any of us got away was a mystery," an officer in the 38th Illinois offered. "But a kind Providence, a good cedar tree, a good pair of legs, and an excellent disposition to use them saved me." Captain Hotchkiss of the 2nd Minnesota Battery struggled to pull his guns from the woods and asked for help from the 21st Illinois. "He called on us to save his guns, the trees being so that the men had to pull them loose from the trees which caused Captain Hotchkiss never to forget the peril he and his guns were in," noted Lieutenant Songer. With the Illinoisans' help, Hotchkiss managed to get out of the forest with his entire battery intact, the first battery commander on the right wing to manage the feat that morning.[45]

Hotchkiss's guns rolled into position on a knoll a few hundred yards north next to the six guns of Captain Charles Houghtaling's Battery C, 1st Illinois Light, in Sheridan's division. Soon, both batteries squared off with Confederate artillery, including the Helena Battery, which dropped trail near Gresham Lane and opened fire on the fleeing Federals. "One of their batteries was discovered firing upon General Polk's lines and immediately my battery rushed in advance of the brigade in open field and engaged the enemy," wrote Lieutenant Thomas J. Key. "So soon as we opened upon the enemy's artillery, it returned fire with deadly aim wounding one man and killing three horses. My artillery killed the abolition captain, a sergeant, two or three cannoneers, and cut down one of his caissons and a number of horses. The battery was silenced and made a hasty retreat. With all possible speed the harness was cut from my dead horses and I moved forward in pursuit of the enemy."[46]

Carlin's and Woodruff's brigades would rally under the Federal batteries near the Gresham House, but the men first had to cross the killing field. Lieutenant Jay Butler of the 101st Ohio claimed that "everything was perfect confusion, men and horses running in every direction, and the Rebels after us, firing upon us and yelling

---

44 Day, *Story of the 101st Ohio*, 88.

45 Unknown officer of 38th Illinois, *Evansville Daily Journal*, Jan. 26, 1863, 2; Songer Memoir.

46 OR 20/1:855.

like Indians." Sergeant Francis Allhands of the 35th Illinois noted that "most of our boys were very stubborn in giving way, returning the fire while retreating across the open field where the Rebels had a crossfire with artillery upon us. We made for the woods on the north of us as soon as convenient but in crossing this field we suffered more than in all the six days' fighting."[47]

As he crossed that field, Niles Gilbert was struck in the leg. "I did not have my gun loaded when we left the fence," he recalled, "so I snatched a cartridge, got the powder into the barrel and the bullet into the muzzle of the gun, but just then I was shot and had to jump along on one leg as best I could through a cornfield across which everyone was running. Soon I became so tired that I had to lie down. I could not see any way of escape from the firing as the loss of blood made me incapable of movement. After a while, however, I regained sufficient control of myself so I could get up and when I saw the Rebels coming, I set off again. Being between the two lines, I jumped on one foot towards my companions and as soon as they saw me, they came to my aid. I fainted and was soon put into an ambulance with others who were wounded."[48]

*   *   *

At army headquarters early that morning, Rosecrans attended mass with Father Peter Cooney of the 35th Indiana, assisted by Father Jeremiah Trecy. "[He] knelt humbly in the corner of his tent," Bickham recalled. "Garesche, no less devout, by his side; a trio of humble soldiers meekly knelt in front of the tent while groups of officers, booted and spurred for battle with heads reverentially uncovered, stood outside and mutely muttered their prayers."

In the midst of a hurried breakfast, Crittenden reported that the lead elements of Horatio Van Cleve's 3rd Division were crossing Stones River. Rosecrans directed Thomas Wood's 1st Division to follow, but as "officers of the staff were grouped about little fires in the avenue between the tents, suddenly all hearts were thrilled by a sound sweeping from the right like a strong wind soughing through a forest," Bickham wrote. "Now a deep reverberation like thunder rolling in a distant

47 Jay Caldwell Butler, *Letters Home: Jay Caldwell Butler, Captain, 101st Ohio Volunteer Infantry* (Binghamton, 1930), 52; Sergeant Francis M. Allhands, Co. E, 35th Illinois, Richard Baumgartner Collection.

48 Ager, *Colonel Heg and His Boys,* 73.

cloud. Directly a prolonged, fierce, crepitating noise like a canebrake on fire. The din of battle swelled rapidly."[49]

The ominous sounds from the south meant Major General Alexander McCook was engaged, but whether he was attacking or being attacked no one knew. Rosecrans dispatched a pair of staff officers to ride to the right and ascertain affairs. By 7:00 a.m., however, headquarters staff spied a stream of stragglers pouring north toward the Nashville Pike. "A tide of fugitives poured out of the thickets—Negroes, teamsters, and some soldiers," Bickham noted. "What is the matter? Why do you run? Many push on heedless of stern questioning. A cocked pistol brings a squad to a halt. 'We are beaten! The Right Wing is broken! The Rebel cavalry is charging the rear! The enemy are sweeping everything before them!'"

Rosecrans considered these initial reports the harbingers of doom usually spread by craven souls within the army, but in the absence of word from McCook, he was worried. Soon one of Rosecrans's staff officers galloped up. "The Right wing is broken and the enemy is driving it back," he announced, only to receive a cheerful response from Rosecrans, "All right, never mind it, we will rectify it."[50]

It took another hour before one of McCook's staff officers arrived with more definite news—"announcing to me that the right wing was heavily pressed and needed assistance," Rosecrans later reported, "but I was not advised of the rout of Willich's and Kirk's brigades, nor of the rapid withdrawal of Davis's division."

Rosecrans confessed he did not know how McCook had dispositioned his troops, "having supposed his wing posted more compactly, and his right more refused than it really was, the direction of the noise of battle did not indicate to me the true state of affairs. I consequently directed him to return and direct General McCook to dispose his troops to the best advantage, and to hold his ground obstinately. Soon after, a second officer from General McCook arrived, and stated that the right wing was being driven, a fact that was but too manifest by the rapid movement of the noise of battle toward the north." Bickham reported that Rosecrans' orders to McCook were "to contest every inch of ground. If he holds them, we will swing into Murfreesboro with our left and cut them off.' Then to his staff, he said, 'It is working right.' But alas, it was not working right."[51]

Alexander McCook made his first appearance in the battle atop the knoll near the Gresham House. It was too little and too late. Two of McCook's divisions had

49 Bickham, *Rosecrans' Campaign*, 206-07.

50 Ibid., 207-09.

51 OR 20/1:193; Bickham, *Rosecrans' Campaign*, 209.

already been broken by the ferocity of Hardee's morning assaults. His men had fought hard, and in some cases magnificently, but were driven from one line to the next because of the faulty deployment of Richard Johnson's division the previous night. All had gone wrong on this front, and with little in the way of immediate reinforcements, the situation seemed bleak. Still, Federal resistance appeared to be stiffening.

In the fields southeast of the Gresham House, meanwhile, awaited the troops of a diminutive Ohio brigadier, whose eventual illustrious reputation was about to receive its cornerstone.[52]

52 Day, *Story of the 101st Ohio,* 88.

Sheridan Rises
to the Occasion

TO THIS POINT in the war, 31-year-old Philip Henry Sheridan had done little to distinguish him from any of Rosecrans's other talented young division commanders. That was all about to change.

A West Pointer from the Class of 1853, Sheridan ranked 34 of 52 cadets and served with the 4th Infantry on the Pacific Coast before the war. When he joined the 13th Infantry in St. Louis, Missouri, after the outbreak of hostilities, he took on the thankless task of straightening out the financial mess left by controversial General John Frémont. His work impressed his boss, Henry Halleck, who secured Sheridan's services for his own command as a quartermaster and commissary general. Sheridan saw action at Pea Ridge in March 1862 but ran afoul of Maj. Gen. Samuel R. Curtis when he uncovered profiteering within Curtis's command. Halleck's intervention soon brought Sheridan to Halleck's army in Corinth, with Sheridan given command of the 2nd Michigan Cavalry. In Corinth, he met Rosecrans and so impressed his fellow Ohioan at the battle of Booneville, Mississippi, in July 1862 that Rosecrans requested President Lincoln make Sheridan a brigadier, as "he is worth his weight in gold." Lincoln agreed, and by October Sheridan was commanding a division in Buell's Army of the Ohio in Kentucky.

Lincoln later described Sheridan as a "brown chunky little chap with a long body, short legs, not enough neck to hang him, and such long arms that if his ankles itch, he can scratch them without stooping." What "Little Phil" lacked in physical

Brigadier General Philip T. Sheridan

Library of Congress

grace, however, he compensated for in zealous drive, fearlessness, professional competency, and a superlative command of profanity. The men might have chuckled at Sheridan's gangly appearance, but he was both highly respected and eminently approachable. Henry Castle of the 73rd Illinois recalled that "I afterwards found this accessibility and willingness to instruct on the part of Sheridan to be one of his prominent characteristics, and it was necessarily the means of greatly increasing the efficiency of his command." Judge John Fitch, later adjutant general of the Army of the Cumberland, praised him as "gentle and modest almost to a fault in ordinary discourse, [but] a very lion in daring when roused by the din of battle."

Indeed, it was in battle that Sheridan became a man transformed. "[W]ith the first smell of gunpowder he became a blazing meteor," opined journalist Sylvanus Cadwallader. "I think it no exaggeration to say that America never produced his equal for inspiring an army with courage and leading them into battle." The next three hours at Stones River would give Sheridan ample opportunity to demonstrate his leadership talents, so much that he was soon marked as "the rising man in the army."[1]

Sheridan deployed his 5,039-man division with two brigades in front, one in reserve. Colonel George Roberts's all-Illinois brigade of 1,520 men held the left, its regiments posted between the Wilkinson Pike and the Harding House. Roberts' front line consisted of his senior regiments: the 22nd Illinois on the left, with the 27th Illinois in support, and the junior regiments, the 51st Illinois supported by the 42nd Illinois, on the right. Two of the division's three batteries, 12 guns total, were

---

1 Fitch, *Annals*, 140-46.

arrayed behind Roberts's brigade on a slight ridge, supported by a battalion of the 73rd Illinois.

A sizable gap existed between Roberts and Sill that Sheridan covered with two regiments from Colonel Schaefer's 2nd Brigade. A more unlikely pairing could not be imagined: the German-speaking 2nd Missouri from St. Louis, veterans of Pea Ridge and Perryville, stood in line next to the 73rd Illinois, known as the "Preacher Regiment" for the large number of ministers within its ranks. The cantankerous Germans, their ranks sprinkled with freethinkers, atheists, and other radicals who had left their home country in the wake of the failed 1848 Revolution, delighted in swiping blankets and canteens from the camp of the pious 73rd while those men attended morning and evening prayer services.[2]

Sill's 1,839-man 1st Brigade occupied Sheridan's right, with the Chicagoans of the 88th Illinois on the left (supported by the 21st Michigan) and the 36th Illinois (supported by the 24th Wisconsin) anchoring the right. By dawn, the 44th Illinois of Schaefer's brigade slid into position behind the Michiganders while another St. Louis-raised German regiment, the 15th Missouri, supported the Badgers. Captain Asahel Bush's six-gun 4th Indiana Battery occupied the ground between the two front-line regiments. Sill's position was a strong one, as his regiments held the crest of a low ridge with an open valley on their front providing a wide-open field of fire, ideal for artillery.

For Sill, command of this brigade was new, as Richard Johnson had recently replaced him as the 2nd Division's commander. Graduating third in the same West Point class as Sheridan, Sill resigned his commission to become a professor in New York just before the war. After Fort Sumter, he returned to his native Ohio and was given command of the 33rd Ohio, which led shortly to brigade command. "In stature, [he] was rather below the medium height," remembered Sill's nephew Albert Douglas. "His figure was well nit and erect, his carriage and movements vigorous and somewhat nervous." One historian labeled the general "plain, simple, mild-mannered gentleman, very modest, never assertive, always kind and fair to his men."

Despite Sill's retiring nature, he proved an exceptional military leader. As Captain Joseph Stearns, Sill's adjutant general, proclaimed, "no officer in this entire

---

2 Schaefer's brigade went into the fight with 1,680 men. Henry A Castle, "Sheridan with the Army of the Cumberland." *Military Order of the Loyal Legion of the United States. Commandery of the District of Columbia* (1900), 34.

army was so much admired, beloved, and respected by both his inferiors and superiors as was General Sill."[3]

Sheridan's division was the only one in McCook's wing that had time to hear Rosecrans's general order read. It did not impress Lieutenant Otis Moody of the 51st Illinois, who likened it to "reading one's funeral oration in advance. The adjutant had scarcely finished reading when the Rebel lines were seen approaching and we found we had work on our hands." Sheridan's men saw their first action about 7:15 that morning as the 1st Louisiana and 19th Alabama on Loomis's left flank executed their assault on Woodruff's brigade in the cedar glade and on Sill's right. Sheridan's batteries opened fire as Loomis's troops maneuvered in Sheridan's view. "The enemy attacked me, advancing across an old cotton field in Sill's front in heavy masses, Little Phil recalled, "which were furiously opened upon by Bush's battery from Sill's line and by Hescock's and Houghtaling's batteries which had an oblique fire on the field from a commanding position in rear of my center. The effect of this fire on the advancing column was terrible, but it continued on until it reached the edge of the timber where Sill's right lay when my infantry opened at a range of not over 50 yards."[4]

Sergeant Chester Whitman of the 1st Illinois Light noted that his guns in Battery C received plenty of Confederate counterbattery fire early. "I was ordered to attend to the issuing of ammunition for our gun and to see that it was sent forward fast enough not to keep the gun silent for a moment and to see that the right time was given to the shell and case shot," he wrote. "I dismounted from my horse and went to obey the order and not more than a minute afterwards a cannonball struck the horse, nearly cutting him in two and killing him almost instantly. Sergeant George Cooper was near me cutting time fuses when a shell burst, smashing the gun limber and killing him and his horse at the same time. He fell with the fuse gauge in his hand by the side of his horse, a mangled corpse. Poor fellow, he never knew what hit him so sudden was his death."[5]

Colonel Francis T. Sherman of the 88th Illinois, on Sill's front line, recalled that Loomis's men advanced "with steady front and firm tread with colors flying as if on parade, their officers leading the advance of the column and cheering their

---

3 Albert Douglas, "General Joshua Woodrow Sill," *Ohio History Journal*, Vol. 31, No. 2 (April 1922); DeBruin Letter; Stearns Letter.

4 Moody Diary; Sheridan, *Personal Memoirs*, 121.

5 Sergeant Chester P. Whitman, Battery C, 1st Illinois Light Artillery, *Ottawa Republican*, Jan. 31, 1863, 1.

men. For a few moments, everything was still as death as that dark host moved toward our front." Captain Porter Olson of the neighboring 36th Illinois reported that "they came diagonally across the field. Upon reaching the foot of the hill, they made a left half-wheel and came up directly in front of us. When the enemy had advanced up the hill sufficiently to be in sight, Colonel Greusel ordered the regiment to fire, which was promptly obeyed. We engaged the enemy at short range, the lines being not over 10 rods [55 yards] apart." Wrote one veteran of the 88th Illinois: "[F]our regiments of the enemy marched directly on the position held by us. Colonel Sherman gave orders that not a gun of the 88th should be fired until he gave the word, and we obeyed. The regiment waited until the first line was within 75 yards of where it lay. With a yell, the enemy took the double quick for a charge and then our colonel gave the order to fire and fire low."[6]

Both Illinois regiments unleashed a fearsome barrage, the discharge of nearly 1,000 muskets at close range staggering the Confederate line. "As that volley went tearing through the Rebel ranks, it shook them as if an earthquake was rumbling beneath their feet," recalled one soldier. "So unexpected was the volley that the whole column came to a dead halt giving the 88th time to reload." Added another: "Again, the Rebel officers succeeded in getting the column to advance and again another volley, more terrible than the first, swept through their ranks. This they could not face and the remnant of the brigade sank to the ground to find shelter. The colonel now ordered file-firing upon them as they lay and soon drove them from our front in utter confusion."

Corporal William McGregor, also of the 88th Illinois, remembered that the Confederates "commenced firing but without much effect. We gave them the best we had. They made a right face and sought shelter in a piece of timber where they lay down but still in sight. We made it too hot for them there, so they made a second attack which fared no better."[7]

With the Confederates wavering, Sill ordered the 36th Illinois to affix bayonets and charge. Captain Olson of the 36th Illinois said that "the enemy fled in great confusion across the cotton-field into the woods opposite our left, leaving many of their dead and wounded upon the field. We poured a destructive fire upon them as

<hr>

6 C. Knight Aldrich, *Quest for a Star: The Civil War Letters and Diaries of Colonel Francis T. Sherman of the 88th Illinois* (Knoxville, 1999), 21-22; A. T. Andreas, *History of Chicago from the Earliest Period to the Present Time* (Chicago, 1885), 237; OR 20/1:358-359.

7 Aldrich, *Quest for a Star*, 22; William McGregor Papers, 1863, Pearce Civil War Collection, Navarro College.

they retreated until they were beyond range." Sill then sent a dispatch to Lt. Col. John Weber to bring the 44th Illinois and 15th Missouri forward to provide additional support for the charging 36th Illinois and to shore up his right flank, as Woodruff's brigade was reeling under the Confederate assault. Sherman wrote that "now I ordered the battalion to rise and give them hell. At the word, every man sprung to his feet and we poured in such a fire upon them that they were forced to leave the ground on the double quick and retire."[8]

The charge broke Loomis's Brigade, which retreated back to its original position 300 or so yards across the cotton field "in some confusion," having sustained heavy casualties. Overcome with enthusiasm, the 36th charged heedlessly after them. "They were ordered thrice by their officers to retreat but did not understand and kept on, dealing death all around until compelled by overwhelming numbers to fall back," an observer conceded. Vaughan's Brigade, already deployed in line and ready to launch its own attack, met the Illinoisans as they crossed the field with a crashing volley of musketry that halted the counterattack completely. "We had hardly commenced enjoying our little victory when a heavy flank line advanced on us and poured in a crossfire from our right front and rear," said Private Nathaniel B. McCutcheon. "We stood as long as we could then retreating leaving 200 of our poor fellows in their hands. This was the darkest hour of my life."[9]

With pending trouble on its own front—Manigault's Brigade—the 88th Illinois stayed put. Manigault arrayed his five regiments en echelon, with the 34th Alabama on the left in front. In order to the right were the 28th Alabama, 24th Alabama, 19th South Carolina, and 10th South Carolina (about 50 yards distance separated the front lines of each regiment). The ground in their front was daunting—an open field roughly 300 yards wide that gently sloped downward before making a sharp, slanted rise about 100 yards from the Federal position.

"Our instructions were to attack the troops in our front, defeat and drive them back, endeavoring to swing ourselves around so as to form a line continuous with the one to the right of our brigade," Manigault reported." Colonel Julius Mitchell of the 34th Alabama was to govern his advance on Loomis's progression to his left; once Loomis was engaged, Mitchell was to launch the assault. L. E. Huffman of

---

8 *OR* 20/1:358-359; Weber Report; Aldrich, *Quest for a Star*, 22.

9 Private Nathaniel B. McCutcheon, Co. B, 36th Illinois, American Civil War Documents, Manuscripts, Letters, and Diaries, Grand Army of the Republic Collections, Chicago Public Library.

Company K, 10th South Carolina, recalled that "General [Leonidas] Polk and General Cheatham rode down the front of our lines and made us a talk, telling us that we would soon be engaged in battle, that we must drive them back to Nashville. After talking to us, General Polk turned to General Cheatham and said, 'General, talk to them in your way.' General Cheatham straightened in his stirrups and said, 'Men, give them hell!' and rode on."[10]

The men advanced but soon found themselves pummeled by a blizzard of Federal iron and lead. The regiments on Manigault's left managed to get close to the Federals in the woods before the combined fire of Woodruff's survivors, the 36th Illinois, and Sill's two reserve regiments buttressed by the 4th Indiana Battery brought them to a halt. "When the regiment arrived in the woods, the crossfire became fierce and terrible," Mitchell recalled. After witnessing the general retreat of Loomis's Brigade, Mitchell was not long in following suit, with 50–60 casualties of his own. The 28th Alabama did not make it as far forward as the 34th, convincing Colonel John C. Reid they were attacking a line of US Regulars and "that [as] another brigade was seen moving up to the support of the enemy, we were forced to withdraw and resume our former position."[11]

Manigault's other three regiments would be caught in the open field. Lieutenant Colonel William B. Dennett of the 24th Alabama explained that his regiment was exposed "to a very heavy fire and not being properly supported on the right, we did not proceed more than 150 yards before we were checked in the advance." Colonel William Buck ordered the 24th to move to the right in tandem with the 19th South Carolina, but "the enemy's guns were playing upon us with such a terrible effect that the order was given by someone to march in retreat." Buck was soon lost to a painful hand wound—as was Dennett, concussed by an exploding Yankee shell—leaving the regiment under the command of the senior captain.

Captain David Waters brought up his battery on the South Carolinians' right to provide counterbattery fire on Sheridan's artillery. "I commenced firing on the enemy's infantry and was immediately opened on one of the enemy's batteries posted in the wood to the right of the Nolensville turnpike," Waters reported.

10 Tower, *A Carolinian Goes to War*, 56; Yeary, *Reminiscences*, 364.

11 Smith, *Stones River: Confederate Army*, 678 and 680.

"Our infantry having fallen back to the old line[,] I kept up a regular fire to cover their preparations for a fresh charge."[12]

In Manigault's opinion, the first assault's failure was twofold. Because expected support from Maney's Brigade never materialized, it allowed a response from both the Federal position under attack and uncontested troops and two batteries on Manigault's right. The Yankees could devote their attention to us," Manigault conceded, and "the formation of their lines corresponding to our own enabled them to pour into our flank a heavy fire in addition to that from the lines against which our movement was directed."

Colonel Augustus Lythgoe of the 19th South Carolina was mortally wounded in this charge, as was Major John Crowder. The 10th South Carolina also suffered heavily. "Our advance was continued under a most terrific fire of grape shot and musketry to within about 120 yards of the enemy's battery," reported Lt. Col. James Pressley of the 10th South Carolina. "His infantry force so largely outnumbered our own that we were compelled to retire. In this single charge, we suffered seriously, losing in killed and wounded 85 men."[13]

*   *   *

It was about this time that Rosecrans's army would suffer the loss of beloved commander Joshua Sill. Sergeant Charles Belknap of the 21st Michigan, on the second line of Sill's brigade, recorded the tragic moment. While observing the 36th Illinois returning "with a confused crowd of prisoners … General Sill came dashing by the right of our regiment, going to the front," Belknap wrote. "As I looked upon his handsome face, all aglow with fire, a jet of blood spurted from his forehead, his saber dropped from his hand, his form bent forward for an instant, then he fell from his horse. One foot caught in the stirrup and the unguided animal dragged the lifeless form a few rods before the foot became loosened." A musket ball had struck Sill through his upper lip and under his left eye, penetrating the brain, and blowing out the back of his head.

In the smoke and confusion of battle, Sill's staff had momentarily lost sight of him. Lieutenant John Mitchell came across Captain Joseph Stearns, who indicated he had just seen the general's riderless horse bolting for the rear. "In our search for Sill, we almost stumbled over his prostrate body," Mitchell recalled. "He lay

---

12 Smith, *Stones River: Confederate Army*, 677; OR 20/1:770.

13 Smith, *Stones River: Confederate Army*, 677-678; Tower, *A Carolinian Goes to War*, 56.

unconscious and alone, bubbling out his last breaths through the blood that thickly flowed over his fair face and silky beard." Stearns raised Sill's head and implored him to speak, "but he closed his eyes, rested back his head, and before we could get a stretcher, he was dead."[14]

Anxious the Confederates were reforming to renew the attack, Stearns removed Sill's sword, handed it to Mitchell, then galloped off to find Colonel Greusel to inform him he was now in command of the brigade. Left alone with Sill's remains, Mitchell acquired a blanket and, with the help of two stragglers "who were with difficulty persuaded to aid in taking his body," carried the general to the Harding House field hospital. Stearns found them minutes later. Alarmed at the brigade's imminent collapse, the captain accompanied Mitchell and the two stragglers in carrying Sill's body farther west to the perceived safety of the Gresham House field hospital. News of Sill's death spread quickly within the division. Lieutenant DeBruin was with Sheridan when an orderly brought the word. "Is that true? Is he dead?" Sheridan asked. "Yes," was the reply. "My God, so good and so pure a man," Sheridan grieved. The incensed general, DeBruin would write, then turned to Captain Hescock's battery and demanded, "'[N]ow give it to the scoundrels,' and from that time his whole aim seemed to be avenging the death of General Sill."[15]

The 24th Wisconsin, at the rear of Woodruff's line in support of the 36th Illinois, had its hands full. "Soon after, firing began, and the pickets were driven in by the enemy's skirmishers directly in my front their column of attack came close on the rear of their skirmishers, and I ordered the men to fire," wrote Major Elisha Hibbard. "At the same time my attention was directed to a column coming out of the wood on my right flank. They were in line and advancing very rapidly." Hibbard sent his adjutant, Arthur McArthur, to notify Sill that a sizable Confederate brigade was on his right flank; McArthur returned to report that Sill was dead and no one knew who had command.

The 24th Wisconsin stood for a short time, then broke in confusion for the rear. "I maintained my position, waiting for orders, until the enemy were in the woods in my rear, and had come on my flank and delivered a crossfire, doing me considerable damage," Hibbard recalled. McArthur noted that "the firing by this time seemed to be on all sides. It seemed as though the enemy had entirely

---

14 Belknap Article; "Murfreesboro," *Chattanooga Daily Rebel,* Jan. 6, 1863, 1; John L. Mitchell, *In Memoriam: John Lendrum Mitchell* (Milwaukee, 1906), 29.

15 DeBruin Letter; Bennett, *History of the 36th Illinois,* 342.

surrounded us. The shell and solid shot flew worse than at any time previous." According to Hibbard, "no orders having been received and thinking it improper to remain longer in this position, I ordered the regiment to break to the rear by companies. Some of the officers not hearing the order, the left did not move with the right, and the regiment came off in some disorder, but was quickly reformed in the open field to the right of the log-house used for a hospital."[16]

In the wake of Woodruff's and Hibbard's departures, Vaughan's infantrymen barreled into the cedar glade directly against Schaefer's two reserve regiments under Weber's overall command. "Weber found himself in front of the enemy, the artillery previously stationed there having retreated," reported Lt. Col. Bernard Laiboldt. "The two regiments kept up a strong firing and even when one regiment on their left broke and ran, they held their position until attacked from the flank and front at once." Vaughan's two right-most regiments, the 29th Tennessee and the 154th Tennessee, took the brunt of Weber's fire and shuddered to a halt.

Major John Johnson of the 29th Tennessee complained that "not being supported on the flank, the enemy came up with fresh troops and exposed to an enfilading fire on the left, the regiment and brigade were ordered to fall back." Weber noted that "showers of balls were poured in upon us, but my boys with undaunted courage stood firm in their appointed place so that the enemy was really forced to give way. Whilst we were moving forward on the double quick, the artillery endeavored to withdraw their two pieces which were lying before us and with great trouble, they succeeded in withdrawing one of them whilst they had to leave the other in the enemy's hands."[17]

With Manigault's advance blunted, C. Irvine Walker, adjutant general on Manigault's staff, galloped back to request support from Maney. Before that could be arranged, however, Roberts' Federals waded into the fray. "Colonel Roberts, furious that our troops had been driven, rode to General Sheridan and asked for leave to charge on the advancing Rebels," remembered Captain Alexander Stevenson of the 42nd Illinois. "General Sheridan responded with one of his enthusiastic orders for Roberts to try the bayonet." Roberts formed his brigade in the open field and faced south with the 51st Illinois on the left, the 42nd Illinois on the right, and the 22nd Illinois in support.

16 Stearns Letter; Mitchell, *In Memoriam*, 29-30; *OR* 20/1:364; Adjutant Arthur McArthur, 24th Wisconsin, *Daily Milwaukee News*, Jan. 28, 1863, 1.

17 *OR* 20/1:366, 747; Weber Report.

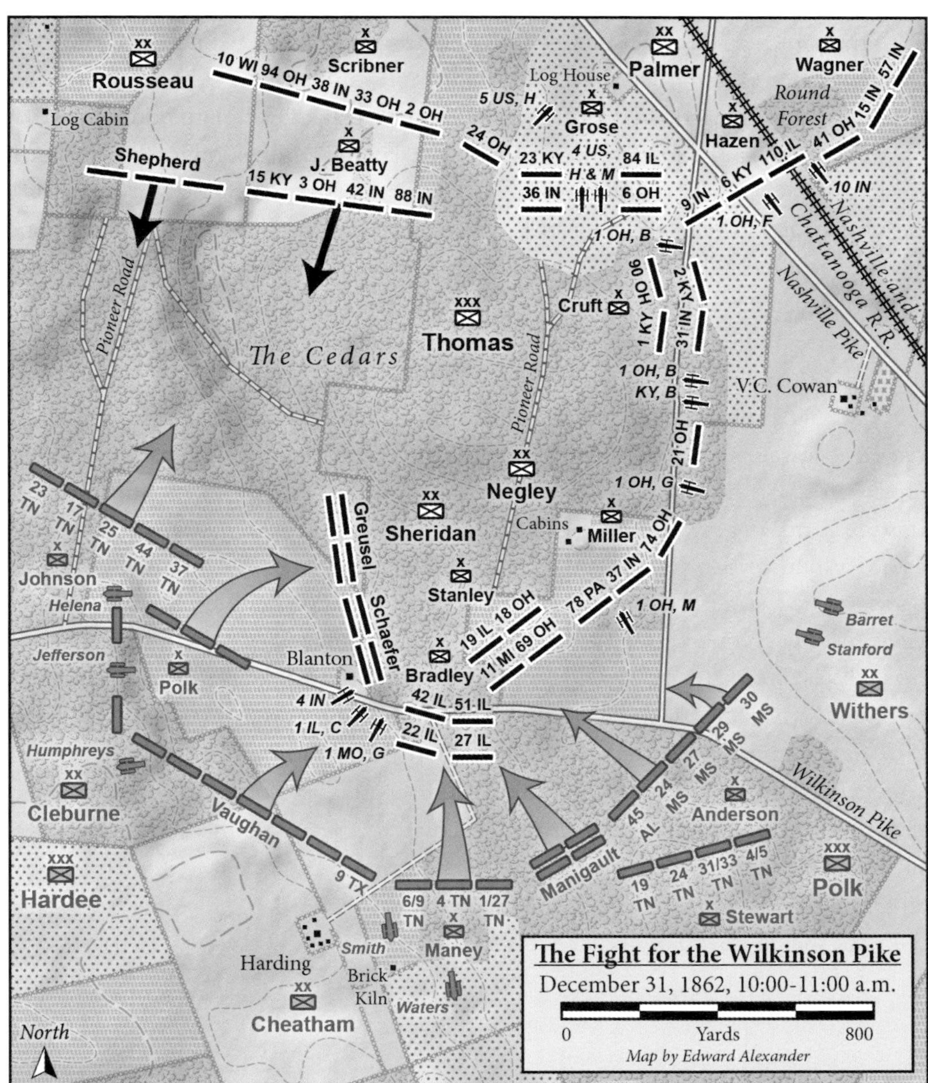

"Sending word quickly that a bayonet charge was to be made and for no one to fire without orders, the command 'Forward march!' was given with a loud voice," Stevenson recalled. "We moved as if on parade. A short distance to our front were the 88th Illinois and the 21st Michigan firing from behind the fences."

Roberts sent his adjutant to ask those regiments to throw down the fence so his brigade could charge over it. "But the battle raged so fiercely and the noise was so loud that the colonel did not understand the request," Stevenson noted, "and the adjutant thereupon rode to the fence and by motion and words got the men to level it, cease firing and lie down."[18] "Suddenly the grand form of Colonel Roberts could be seen riding in the rear of the regiment, telling the officers not to let a shot be fired; then, wheeling around the left wing, he rode in front of the regiment along the whole line with his cap in his hand, cheering the men to endless enthusiasm and shouted to them 'Don't fire a shot! Drive them with the bayonet!' The command 'Charge' was heard and with a loud hurrah the men ran for the enemy."[19]

Corporal William Austin of the 22nd Illinois recalled that "when we came out into the fields, the enemy opened upon us with artillery and rifles, shells, grape, and canister which began to tell on our ranks. At every step men fell and went to the rear; but our ranks readily closed up and forward we went, closing rapidly on the enemy in a bayonet charge. The 42nd drove away the enemy and captured a gun, but the 22nd was ordered back to a lane before they reached the enemy."[20]

"[W]hen we came within 30 rods of the Rebels, they broke and ran like a flock of frightened sheep," wrote Thomas Maxwell of the 42nd Illinois. "Seeing they were making the best time; we sent a shower of bullets after them which halted many. We kept on a half mile, loading and firing as we ran. The dead and dying strewed the ground. We had to leap over them." Stevenson proudly reported that "the Confederates ran with all their might to the woods and through it and the cornfield to their original position in the morning. The regiment pursued as far as the rail fence where Carpenter lost one of his guns which was still there. Soon it was observed that a large force of Confederate infantry was moving to get to the right and rear of the regiment whereupon General Sheridan ordered Colonel Roberts to fall back which he did in good order in quick step."[21]

*   *   *

The impetuous charge jammed the Confederate advance and bought the Federals sorely needed time to regroup. Roberts's men returned to their position

---

18 Stevenson, *Battle of Stone's River*, 56.

19 Ibid.

20 Diary of Corporal William M. Austin, Co. A, 22nd Illinois, Abraham Lincoln Presidential Library.

21 Private Thomas J. Maxwell, Co. C, 42nd Illinois, *Delaware Gazette*, Feb. 6, 1863, 1; Stevenson, *Battle of Stone's River*, 56-57.

on Sheridan's left but now faced southeasterly. The battered 36th Illinois, down to just 140 men and its ammunition exhausted, was ordered off the line and eventually fell back to the Nashville Pike before finding a supply of ammunition. Both Woodruff's and Carlin's brigades retreated north from the cedar glade, and Sheridan ordered Greusel, now commanding Sill's brigade with his right exposed, to disengage and fall back a few hundred yards to the new line being formed east of the Gresham House hospital.

The brigade did so under heavy fire. Lieutenant Colonel William McCreery of the 21st Michigan noted that the outbuildings of the Harding Farm threw his regiment into confusion during the retreat. "It was with much difficulty that I could compel the men to leave the cover they had taken behind the fences and buildings where they were delivering a well-directed fire," he wrote. Bush fixed prolongs and fired while retiring across the field, later reporting that one of his 6-pounder smoothbores was damaged while firing double charges of canister and a caisson was left behind after the horses had all been gunned down. Corporal Edgar Abbott of the 4th Indiana Battery was among the casualties. He had been dodging cannon balls throughout the battle when he flopped on the ground and struggled to get back on his feet. "I fell behind the wheel of the gun with a hole through my left thigh between the knee and the hip made by a Rebel bullet," he remembered. "A broken thigh was the result. My brother Bill and George Jackson saw my condition, took hold, and carried me back about 15 feet when my brother fell sprawling across me. I shall never forget the apparently foolish remark I made when he fell. I said, 'Bill, are you killed?' Bill was alive enough to answer, 'Not by a damned sight!' Our boys continued to fall back and the field was lost."[22]

Confederate success proved just as discombobulating. The 9th Texas, for example, marched well in front of the rest of Vaughan's Brigade, but lacking support on either flank hesitated in moving any farther. In addition, Wood's, Polk's, and Vaughan's brigades became entangled in the cedar glade; as they exited the glade, they came under Federal artillery fire and were forced to hunker down in place or fall back to the cover of the forest. Casualties for Wood and Vaughan were heavy, especially among their company officers. That complicated the task of reorganizing the regiments, as junior officers, suddenly thrust into command, grappled with the confusion endemic on a battlefield.

Many had fired off their full complement of cartridges and needed resupply to continue the attack. It took time for the ammunition wagons to be brought forward

22 *OR* 20/1:362; Abbott Article.

and new cartridges issued to the troops, though that at least gave the officers time to call roll and try to get their lines in some semblance of order. This relative "quiet" lasted between a half-hour and an hour, and by then Manigault had his brigade reformed with Maney's Tennesseans nearby. Vaughan moved slightly to the right to avoid having to attack through the cedar glade and formed on Maney's left, reuniting Cheatham's Division. Likewise, Cleburne's men, their cartridge boxes refilled and ranks rearranged, were ready to return to the fray. Far to the left of the line near Puckett Creek, McCown's Division—though worn down having faced action since dawn—was also ready to continue the drive. Intentionally or not, the reconstituted Confederate line would be quite powerful: three divisions supported by ample artillery.

Sheridan had his work cut out for him, though he also had an unlikely cheerleader in Corporal Joel McBride of the 45th Mississippi, who was captured after the scrap with Major Rosengarten of the Anderson Troop four days earlier at Triune. Sitting with fellow prisoners near McCook's headquarters, McBride could hardly restrain his joy at seeing the Yankees falling back in disarray. "In the midst of the battle that raged that morning," noted one veteran, "McBride would shout to his friends the enemy as they ran and dodged. 'What yer runnin' fer? Why don't you stand and fight like men?' He tried his best to rally Rosey's men until his fellow prisoner Captain Connor interposed saying, 'For God's sake Joe, don't try to rally the Yankees. Do anything to continue the demoralization and let's make our escape.' With all the disorder however, the guard kept their prisoners well in hand, escorting them to a place of safety."[23]

Chaplain Smith of the 75th Illinois described the scenes behind the lines. "Riderless horses fleeing from the smoke and fire, a pair drawing an artillery caisson on the gallop without a driver ran straight up against a small tree, one on either side tearing themselves loose by the shock and the caisson in a wreck at the foot of the tree," he wrote. "An ambulance, jolting and jouncing over stumps, logs, and knolls, the horses on a keen run and apparently without a driver. Then a constant scattered stream of wounded dribbling back and a few guns and accoutrements striding along, sometimes in small groups, but mostly single or in couples talking, gesticulating, glancing back at the fire and smoke and roar of musketry, but getting away from it all."[24]

23 Williams Article.

24 Smith, *Incidents and Reminiscences*, 11.

Chaplain Hiram Ashmore of the 25th Illinois rode up Gresham Lane with an ambulance trying to reach his regiment to pick up the severely wounded Colonel Williams. In in the direction of the battery, Ashmore could see four lines of Rebels and the embattled guns belching shell and canister at them, the enemy lines opening and closing because of the wounded "until they were seemingly but a few yards from the guns." The chaplain turned the ambulance toward where Colonel Williams lay, but "another line came and turned us back to the north side of Harding's cotton field when we were confronted by a division of Rebel cavalry turning us east on the Triune pike running into Murfreesboro." It was then he and his comrades spotted some men carrying General Sill's corpse. "A Rebel cavalry officer left his command a hundred yards distant and rode within 20 feet of General Sill's body," recalled Ashmore, "and with a drawn sword yelled 'Surrender you damned Yankees!' The words were scarcely out of his mouth until he and his horse were riddled with bullets."[25]

Near the Wilkinson Pike, portions of Willich's and Kirk's brigades formed into a ragged line through the efforts of Sgt. Maj. John Farquhar of the 89th Illinois. Farquhar reformed his regiment after discovering its command staff was scattered to the winds: Colonel Hotchkiss's horse had been shot down, Major Duncan Hall was missing, and adjutant Edward Bishop had suffered a ghastly face wound. Farquhar, a 30-year-old native of Scotland, "seeing that the day was lost unless something was done at once deployed his regiment and organized the stray and running troops into a new line." Once Farquhar had a line in place, he offered the command to several officers who flatly refused "and told the sergeant major to go ahead and finish what he commenced." For his actions, Farquhar would be commissioned a captain in February 1863 and received the Medal of Honor in 1902.[26]

Chaplain Smith witnessed other officers endeavoring to rally their men in those dismal moments of despair and ruin: "A well-mounted officer in a brilliant and glittering uniform was riding back and forth, swinging his flashing sword and yelling to the retreating men, 'Halt! Halt here and form a line! Halt there, I say! In the name of General Rosecrans, I command you to halt and form a line!' A few men were inclined to obey and a group would slow up and look around right and left and then towards the noise and smoke out of what they had escaped. Someone

---

25 Chaplain Hiram H. Ashmore, 25th Illinois, "Stone River: A Just Defense of the Men Who 'Straggled' From the Right of the Army," *National Tribune*, June 16, 1887, 3.

26 "Maj. Farquhar's Deeds," *Buffalo Evening News*, Jul. 28, 1912, 31.

broke out with 'another Bull Run, boys,' and instantly the officer on the horse heard the remark and firmly but decidedly said, 'I'll shoot the first man that repeats that.' He drew his pistol with his right hand to make his threat good. But I noticed there was no panic, no running or scrambling, but deliberately getting back out of the fight on a walk as if not knowing what to do or where to go."[27]

Among those survivors was the single remaining gun of Battery A, 1st Ohio Light—commanded by Lieutenant Belding, with perhaps 20 men. "A complete panic prevailed," averred one of Belding's veterans. "Teams, ambulances, horsemen, footmen, and attaches of the army mounted on horses and mules were rushing to the rear in the wildest confusion. The mules as well as their drivers had all seized the panic. It was like the rustling of the leaves before the tornado, so great was the confusion of the living mass pouring from the woods."

Serving as a provost guard in Sheridan's division, Otis Strong of the 44th Illinois related that the guards were "ordered to the rear with pointed bayonets, loaded rifles, and orders from General Rosecrans to bayonet or shoot every straggler that made his appearance. The battle raging with all its fury, back they would come and back they were forced into the fight. One poor fellow came back upon a full run and it became my duty to halt him, asking him at the same time if he was wounded. He shouted, 'Let me go, let me go! I am demoralized as hell!'"[28]

Johnson's division was out of the fight, its survivors streaming north toward the Nashville Pike while others headed for Nashville itself. Surgeon Solon Marks, busy treating battlefield casualties, was called from the operating table by a panicked orderly who reported that the hospital was about to be overrun by the Confederates. "As I stepped from among the buildings where I could look to the front, I confess that I was not only surprised but paralyzed," Marks noted. "Johnson's men were falling back as fast as their legs could carry them in the greatest possible confusion, followed by the enemy in perfect lines of battle and outflanking them at least a quarter of a mile. There was but a moment to consider what course to pursue. Any attempt to move our wounded would be worse than useless and humanity demanded that they should not be abandoned by their medical officers. Volunteers were called for to remain with the wounded, but as there was no response, I dismounted and told them that I would stay and that they

27 Smith, *Incidents and Reminiscences*, 12.

28 Davidson, *History of Battery A*, 64; Private Otis W. Strong, Co. D, 44th Illinois, *Adrian Daily Watchtower*, Feb. 14, 1863, 2.

were at liberty to leave or remain. To their credit, every surgeon returned to his duty and stood bravely at his post in the trying ordeal which followed."[29]

The Confederates advanced first along Gresham Lane, where they quickly punched through Davis's and Johnson's already battered lines. "Advancing through the pasture, the enemy was seen posted across an open field near one of their hospitals and only a few hundred yards of the pike," reported Lucius Polk. "My brigade was obliged to move across this open field with the enemy's artillery and infantry playing upon them. This they did most gallantly causing the enemy to fall back across the pike under a heavy undergrowth of cedars." Fatigue began to impact the men of McCown's Division, and McNair would be a casualty. McNair's Brigade pursued the remnant of Joseph Dodge's Union brigade for about half a mile before "arriving at another fence in front of a dense forest, I feared an ambuscade," Polk recalled, "and at the same time finding the men were out of ammunition, I ordered a halt and rested the men in the rear of a fence at the same time ordering up the ammunition train which arrived in due time and proceeded to replenish the cartridge boxes."

By this point, McNair was spent. Already in bad health, he turned over command of the brigade to Colonel Harper of the 1st Arkansas Mounted Rifles.[30]

Union hospitals were in the crosshairs as well. "I heard the whiz of bullets and stepped into the house and closed the door," surgeon Joseph Blount of the 25th Illinois reported from the Gresham House. "I had taken but two or three steps when I heard the pat of musket balls against the door and at the same instant also against the head of a man by my side. He fell dead at my feet. Other balls passed into and through the house wounding a number, but others were killed. The line of the enemy advanced up even with the house and were firing at our men while standing under the cover of our hospital," he continued. "I stepped out and remonstrated with General Liddell of Louisiana for such cowardly conduct. He gave me a fearful cursing and said if he could have his own way he would kill every one of us."

Liddell later explained he was enraged over news that his son Willie had been killed during the fighting that morning. "The third enemy line engaged us at the hospital," he penned in his postwar memoir. "Firing from the windows caused Colonel Govan to fire on all of the men mounted near the hospital enclosure. The enemy's line of battle at this hospital stretching far to the left, sustained our attack

---

29 Marks Article, 391-92.

30 OR 20/1:853, 945.

only a short time before giving way. Someone now told me that my son Willie was killed. I felt deeply distressed," he continued. "I knew that it was a fact of war, consoling myself with the reflection that he could not have fallen on a more honorable occasion."[31]

Federal prisoners swarmed around the Gresham House, and Liddell soon ordered them to the rear. "Many prisoners were brought to me," he wrote. "The prisoners seemed troubled and asked what they should do. I told them that no one would molest unarmed men. In marching to the rear, they would find the officer in charge of this business. But if they wished to escape and thought the thing practicable, I had no objection provided they promised never to fight us again. This pleased them. One man seized my hand saying, 'We agree, you are the man for me.' The hospital yard was full of them, whither they had gone to escape the fire of the line."[32]

Charles Dennis of the 101st Ohio was among those prisoners. "The scene within the hospital grounds was anything but cheerful, although the best possible care had been given the wounded, there was much that could have been done for their comfort, and many a poor chap died from lack of proper nursing," he recalled. "The grounds outside were covered with badly wounded men, some of them mangled horribly, waiting for room to be made in the operating rooms. Before they reached there many of them died. In a place screened off by brush, there was a row of more than a hundred dead that had died after being brought to the hospital."

Advancing Confederates soon captured the body of General Sill, finding him laid east of Gresham Lane "near a fence and 75 yards in the rear of the hospital." Soldiers stripped the body for souvenirs, a private in the 2nd Arkansas making off with the general's gloves before handing them over to his company commander.[33]

The collapse of McCook's positions south of the Wilkinson Pike posed an immediate danger to the corps ambulances gathered along the road. Wharton's triumphant troopers soon rode into sight, took one look at the train, and charged. "The road was literally packed with army vehicles of every description, all mingled in inextricable confusion, and the panic produced by this salute can be more easily imagined than described," wrote hospital steward Harvey Spencer of the 21st Michigan. "While the disorder was at its height, a sudden charge of the Confederate

---

31 Surgeon Joseph Blount, 25th Illinois, *Rockford Register*, Jan. 1863; Hughes, *Liddell's Record*, 109-10. It turned out that Willie Liddell was wounded and would survive the battle.

32 Hughes, *Liddell's Record*, 110.

33 Dennis Memoir; DeBruin Letter; Ashmore Article; *OR* 20/1:862.

cavalry was made on the straggling masses and in probably a space of five minutes, a solid mile of wagons and ambulances was in the enemy's possession. Our captors in my immediate vicinity were members of a Texan regiment. Long-haired, unshorn, and wild-looking while managing their horses as gracefully as Comanche Indians, they swept down upon the train and revolver in hand, each singled out a teamster and sharp and summary was the punishment of the unlucky driver who neglected or disobeyed their imperious commands to halt."

"One who had witnessed an army stampede is never anxious for a repetition of the sight," Spencer noted. "With the advent of the enemy began a scene of terror and confusion which almost defies description. Drivers cut their teams loose and galloped wildly in every direction in search of safety; others abandoned their entire outfits and escaped on foot. Some cooler or possessing more courage, endeavored to save their loads, but numbers of wagons were overturned by collisions with others or wrecked by running against stumps, logs, and trees. During the excitement, casualties were numerous: broken arms, legs, and heads were freely distributed, and many a chance shot from the combatants in front found a lodgment in a non-combatant in the rear. The ambulances were more easily managed than the wagons and after a mad scramble through the cedar thickets, among swamps and over stone ledges, they nearly all reached the Nashville Pike in safety, followed shortly by a portion of the wagon train."[34]

The Confederates captured hundreds of men and dozens of wagons, but resistance was widespread. Albert Foster of the 59th Illinois had been driving the regimental hospital wagon when he was halted by a Confederate trooper and "ordered … to drive his team off in the opposite direction. 'Certainly, certainly,' Foster said, but sprang from the wagon on the other side." Grabbing a musket a fleeing soldier had thrown upon the ground, Foster passed "rapidly to the rear and around the wagon he shot the Rebel from his horse, mounted it, and rejoined our cavalry. A few more heroic drivers would have saved many a government wagon from the torch."[35]

*　*　*

34 F. Henry Spencer, 21st Michigan, "The Rear at Stones River," *Philadelphia Weekly Times*, Dec. 29, 1883.

35 Lathrop, *History of the 59th Illinois*, 200.

Sheridan's new line stretched from the Wilkinson Pike on his left and curved west until terminating just east of the Gresham House, where Davis's and Johnson's divisions extended the line toward Puckett Creek. Manigault's Brigade made an attack against this line, but he enjoyed no more success on the second effort. The South Carolinian apparently attacked alone and paid dearly for the effort, lamenting, "Our reserves, still tardy in their movements (not appearing), reluctantly we were again compelled to withdraw." William Dennett wrote that his 24th Alabama "made a third charge. Changing direction to the right they advanced some 150 yards when they were ordered to lie down, the enemy being forced from his position by troops on the right, took position in the rear of his former one. The regiment was then ordered to support the troops on the right, the regiment moved forward and having nearly gained the line occupied by them found then falling back on confusion, passing through our ranks and breaking our line. We then fell back some 50 yards, rallied, and moved forward again."[36]

Manigault's repulse may have cheered Sheridan's men, but the swift collapse of Johnson and Davis on the right forced McCook to order Sheridan to fall back again to a stronger position north of the Wilkinson Pike. "They were closely pursued by the enemy whose columns were following the arc of a circle that would ultimately carry him in on my rear," Sheridan wrote. "This state of things would soon subject me to a fire in reverse." McCook, Davis, and Johnson rallied a scratch line of survivors north of the Wilkinson Pike on Sheridan's right, but it was a shaky proposition. The line included troops from seemingly every brigade in the right wing; for example, two regiments of Sill's old brigade, the 88th Illinois and 24th Wisconsin, took position on the right of the 81st Indiana of Woodruff's brigade. A few game troops from Willich's and Kirk's brigades fell in on the right of the line. McCook rode among the troops and, according to Lewis Day, "bravely encouraged the boys to hold the line at all hazards. He said he had sent for reinforcements and that we would soon drive the rascals back."

"Scarcely had he uttered his words of cheer, when a Rebel bullet struck his horse's shoulder, causing the blood to spurt over the general's lap and legs," Day added. "He was a large, fleshy man, slow of motion, but he dismounted as quickly as the lightest trooper."[37] Sheridan, he noted, assisted with rallying the survivors from Johnson's and Davis's divisions but was hardly surprised that they quickly fell back. "Davis and Carlin … endeavored to rally their men here but their efforts were

36 Smith, *Stones River: Confederate Army*, 677.

37 Sheridan, *Personal Memoirs*, 121; Day, *Story of the 101st Ohio*, 88.

practically unavailing. The calm and cool appearance of Carlin who at the time was smoking a stumpy pipe had some effect and was in strong contrast to the excited manner of Davis who seemed overpowered by the disaster that had befallen his command. But few could be rallied as the men were badly demoralized and most of them fell back beyond the Wilkinson Pike."

Wrote Carlin: "[H]ere were some rocks and some cavities in this ridge that I thought would enable my men to hold it. I fondly hoped that I should be able to stay there and retreat no farther. But we were closely followed. The Rebels advanced through the brush in close masses and their butternut clothing so harmonized in colors with the weeds and underbrush which were quite dark in hue that they approached very close to us before we could fire on them or even see them."[38]

Polk and Wood were the first to test this new line north of the Wilkinson Pike. "I did not proceed far when the enemy's batteries posted across a cornfield on the right of the pike commenced playing fearfully upon my ranks," Lucius Polk reported. "The battery was so placed by moving straight forward my line would have been enfiladed. To prevent this, my brigade was wheeled to the right. At this time, Captain Hotchkiss sending me word that he had three batteries that required supporting, I left two of my smallest regiments and moved the rest farther to the left for the purpose of trying to move the enemy's batteries."

Colonel Benjamin Hill of the 5th Tennessee, in Polk's Brigade, was among those to welcome the challenge, turning to his men with a smile on his face "that almost made one forget the bullets." As one comrade bragged, "When Ben Hill went into a fight, instead of 'Forward' he always said 'Come on boys! Recollect the mountains!'"[39]

William Bevens of the 1st Arkansas wrote that "our company color bearer William Mathews had been ill and this was his first fight. As we followed the fleeing Yanks, he said, 'Boys this is fun.' One of them answered, 'Stripes, don't be so quick, this is not over yet; you may get a furlough yet.' In 20 minutes, Mathews's arm was shot to pieces. George Thomas was in front of all the company. He had killed two men and was drawing down on the third when one, but a short distance away, shot him, wounding him in the arm. But George spotted the man who shot him and wanted to go on with one arm[;] however, he was taken off the field and sent to the hospital." S. L. Sanders of the 1st Arkansas took the colors from Mathews despite

---

38 Sheridan, *Personal Memoirs*, 122; Girardi and Hughes, *Carlin Memoirs*, 79.

39 *OR* 20/1:853; "5th Tennessee Infantry," *Confederate Veteran*, Mar. 1900, 101-02.

an arm wound from grapeshot. "Catching the flagstaff with the other hand, he heroically bore it throughout the fight, refusing to surrender it to another. Again, when the Confederate line was being pressed back by superior numbers, the colonel of the 1st Arkansas dashed up to Sanders and said, 'Give me the colors!' But Sanders refused saying, 'Colonel, I am the color bearer and will carry the colors wherever you order.'"[40]

Carlin soon saw a Confederate regiment marching on his position in textbook order that he could not help but admire. "Whoever the colonel or leading field officer of this regiment was a model soldier for a charge on the enemy," he noted. "The mounted field officer on the left flank of the leading division watched his men closely and called out, 'Steady, God damn you! Don't fire, God damn you! Now give 'em hell!' and they opened fire. My men gave one volley into this compact line and then backed from their cover."

William Hensley, carrying the colors of the 21st Illinois, remembered the smell of the attack most of all. "The Rebel balls skinned the cedars and such a smell as it did make, I could smell them for three weeks," he remembered. "Our battery pounded the Rebels terribly," Day would write, "but on they came, great columns of them still further to our right and rear. They were within easy musket range, but our ammunition was running low."[41]

Momentarily stymied, Polk ordered up the Helena Light Artillery to blast the Federals out of the woods. "The abolition infantry had ensconced themselves in a dense forest of timber and were awaiting the advance of our forces to mow them down as they pursued over an open field," recalled Thomas Key, the battery's commander. "This battery began shelling the woods and routed the abolitionists in front, but they rallied and renewed the attack and promptly we returned our guns upon them and they were hurled back in confusion, regiment rushing upon regiment, in disorder into the immense cedar thickets." Seeing Wood's Brigade fall back from the Wilkinson Pike, Cleburne ordered Bushrod Johnson to deploy Putnam Darden's Jefferson Flying Artillery to contend with the Federals. "We moved into the woods about midday, between the two fields on which the Federal

40 Sutherland, *Reminiscences of a Private*, 113-15; "S. L. Sanders," *Confederate Veteran*, Mar. 1910, 128.

41 Girardi and Hughes, *Carlin Memoirs*, 80; Hensley Autobiography; Day, *Story of the 101st Ohio*, 88.

hospitals were located, and opened fire on the enemy, who were then pursuing General Wood's brigade, and succeeded in driving them back," Darden reported.[42]

"[O]ur artillery replied with great spirit and we gave their infantry the best the range would allow," Day wrote. "The rascals in front of us were in no hurry to charge across the open cotton field and to tell the truth, we were not at all anxious to have them do so. Off to the west of our organized lines, we could see bodies of troops which we took to be Rebels. The fear of a rush by the enemy's cavalry caused considerable excitement but such a calamity was not added to our misfortunes." William Patterson of the 38th Illinois was on the receiving end of the Confederate artillery fire. "The 2nd Minnesota Battery returned the Rebel fire," he wrote, "but the Rebel shot and grape which they gave us without stint were arguments too persuasive to be disregarded and we again retreated."[43]

The right of the line was in the air; Johnson's division was in full rout; and most of Davis's division tramped along with them. It was time to leave. Bitterly disappointed, Carlin again ordered his men to fall back into the cedar forest. "Our retreat was beset by dangers of every hand and had to be conducted with great skill and caution," Day recalled. "It was against nature to go one step further without stopping to show our teeth. But we knew well and so did they that the right was crushed."

As soon as the Confederates saw the blue lines wavering, they surged forward, scooping up wounded prisoners. Colonel Charlton of the 45th Mississippi reported that "we engaged the enemy strongly posted behind a stone pile and cedar glade and drove him from his position to an open field, capturing some 60 or 70 prisoners." Pursuit quickly halted, as Wood's men had fired their last rounds in driving Carlin from the edge of the cedars; Wood reformed his line and marched the men back toward the Wilkinson Pike to meet up with the ammunition wagons.[44]

Sheridan's new position, particularly the positioning of his batteries giving them interlocking fields of fire, meant immense trouble for the Confederates. The infantrymen took cover behind the trees while Schaefer's brigade capitalized on the "natural and very favorable fortifications of huge and deeply cut rocks," one colonel noted. "The general course of this new position was at right angles with my

42 OR 20/1:855, 895.

43 Day, *Story of the 101st Ohio*, 88-89; Patterson Memoir.

44 Day, *Story of the 101st Ohio*, 90-91; OR 20/1:906.

original line," Sheridan reported. "It took the shape of an obtuse angle with my three batteries at the apex."

The 42nd Illinois, in Roberts's brigade, angled southeast with its left flank near the Wilkinson Pike; to its right, the 22nd Illinois extended the line. In the rear and facing to the southwest, Sheridan deployed 10 guns. Six were in Captain Charles Houghtaling's command and the most exposed; two were from Henry Hescock's Battery G of the 1st Missouri Light; the other two were from Bush's 4th Indiana Battery, deployed closest to the Wilkinson Pike. To the right of the gun line lay the 27th Illinois, and the 51st Illinois took a reserve position facing south along the pike, covering the brigade's rear.

Schaefer's brigade formed right of the 27th Illinois at the edge of the cedar swamp—the 2nd and 15th Missouri in front, and the 44th and 73rd Illinois in the rear. One battalion of the 73rd Illinois drifted to the west during the retreat and wound up fighting alongside Rousseau's division. The 21st Michigan, in Sill's brigade, supported two sections of Hescock's battery along the wood line.

When S.A.M. Wood's right flank appeared in the field on their front, the Federals let loose a storm of lead. "We could see the Rebels coming seven lines deep carrying a large black flag with a white star," remembered Lucius Gould of the 73rd Illinois. "They wore broad-brimmed hats and approached on the double quick, unaware of what awaited them. When within 50 yards from us, the order to fire came and as we leveled our guns at them, we could see them pull down those hat brims for protection. We fired, but those muskets kicked worse than an army mule. I set the butt of my gun against a cedar tree and it knocked the bark off my shoulder."

Leslie Mosely of the 21st Michigan likened "the sound of a volley of musketry to the sound imagined from a whole forest falling to earth nearly at once. After the first volley, the sounds of others are more disconnected, something like a storm approaching. It seemed strange to me that in such a storm of bullets no more are killed and wounded than really are."[45]

Manigault tried his luck twice against Sheridan's troops and had been swatted back with little to show for it but heavy casualties. Now that Maney's Brigade was at hand, the two commanders discussed how to coordinate their commands for a successful assault. "It was instantly arranged that Colonel Manigault should change

---

45 Sheridan, *Personal Memoirs*, 122; Private Lucius G. Gould, Co. I, 73rd Illinois, "Stone River," *National Tribune*, Mar. 1, 1917, 7; Musician Leslie Mosely, Co. C, 21st Michigan, *Hastings Reminder*, Apr. 6, 2013, 28.

his front to the right and engage the battery in the woods while I attacked the one in the open ground," Maney would write. The Tennessee brigadier lined up his three regiments with the 1st/27th on the right, the 4th Tennessee at center, and the 6th/9th on the left. Once he reached the ridge near the Harding farm's brick kiln, Maney intended to wheel the line right and strike north. He then directed the 6th/9th to continue marching directly ahead while the 4th Tennessee and 1st/27th headed for Houghtaling's guns. "These movements were executed with spirit and promptness," he reported, "but the enemy, seeing the approach of a fresh line, hastily withdrew his battery and its support from the ridge."[46]

Maney halted his men in the field and waited for Manigault to advance on their right. "The course of the 1st Tennessee took us through an old cotton field passing over the shattered remnants of a Confederate regiment that had been in the original front," recalled Samuel Seay. "We found ourselves with the four left companies in the brickyard separated from the others by a pond perhaps 30 yards in width. Immediately in our front," he continued,

> was the Wilkinson turnpike well fenced on each side with high rail fences. I was deliberating upon the disadvantage of climbing them under fire when within less than 200 yards of us, sharply diagonal to our right, came a volley of grape, canister, and shell from a battery perfectly masked in a natural cedar brake. The men in the left wing instantly laid down in the brickyard; the fire was simply furious. The position we occupied was one of the most perplexing and unfortunate in which it is possible to conceive a line to be placed. Subjected to a tremendous fire at an exceedingly close range the direction from which it came impressed the minds of the men with the belief that it was our own friends who did the shooting.[47]

Confusion reigned both in the ranks and with the officers. Colonel Hume Feild of the 1st Tennessee believed Houghtaling's guns were actually friendly cannon firing on his position by mistake and ordered his men to hold their fire. "Although this battery was playing havoc on us with grape and canister, we supposed it was our own battery and lay down without firing," wrote one officer. "Lieutenant Fred James, who was on General Cheatham's staff, rode rapidly up to within 30 yards of the battery to let them know we were Confederates. He whirled his horse and fell dead, shot through the head."

46 OR 20/1:734.

47 Seay article, 158-159.

Sam Watkins of the 1st Tennessee remembered events somewhat differently. "It was Christmas and John Barleycorn was general-in-chief," he wrote. "Our generals, colonels, and captains had kissed John a little too often. They couldn't see straight. They couldn't tell our own men from Yankees. We marched plumb into the Yankee lines with their flags flying. I called Lieutenant Colonel Frierson's attention to the Yankees and he remarked, 'Well, I don't know whether they are Yankees or not, but if they are, they will come out of there damned quick.' We were ordered forward to the attack and the Yankees were shooting our men down by scores. A universal cry was raised, 'You are firing on your own men! Cease firing! Cease firing!' I hallooed, the whole skirmish line hallooed, and kept on telling them that they were Yankees, but the order was to cease firing, you are firing on your own men. Oakley, the color bearer of the 4th Tennessee, ran right up in the midst of the Yankee line with his colors, begging his men to follow. I hallooed until I was hoarse. 'They are Yankees, they are Yankees, shoot, they are Yankees!'"[48]

Sheridan's division—anchored now behind trees and among the rock outcroppings, and with ample artillery support close at hand—had no doubts about whom they were firing at and blazed away with abandon. "Soon a magnificent column of the Confederates moved across the field west of Harding's house, making a right wheel," recalled Captain Stevenson. "Seldom has it been executed in a finer manner. There was no time to lose and Houghtaling sent shells in quick succession into the advancing line. Great gaps were visible where the screeching missiles went through it; but they were soon closed up and the column advanced. Sheltered by an intervening ridge, they were protected from our batteries and out of our sight. Again, there was a pause."[49]

"Soon an officer rode forward to our line to reconnoiter and ascertain whether we were Federal or Confederate," Stevenson continued. "As he came nearer, a few shots were fired and he fell dead from his horse. Still General Maney was in doubt whether we were friends or foes. Another officer approached our lines and when fired at, he wheeled his horse and escaped. Still, they were in doubt. Finally, the color bearer of the regiment still further to the right, Sergeant M. C. Hooks of the 9th Tennessee, climbed to the top of one of Harding's outhouses and there began to wave the Rebel flag. That was too much and Houghtaling, Talliaferro, and Flansberg all vied with each other in striking that hated emblem down. This

48 *ORS* 3:647; Watkins, *Company Aytch*, 84.

49 Stevenson, *Battle of Stone's River*, 60-61.

convinced Cheatham and Maney that the guns were those of the enemy and Turner's battery commenced to fire with terrible effect."[50]

Lieutenant William Turner, commanding Smith's Mississippi Battery, went into action firing Yankee artillery pieces captured from Parsons' Battery by the 1st Tennessee at Perryville. The battery consisted of two 12-pounder bronze Napoleons and two 12-pounder howitzers, making it one of the best-equipped batteries on the field, quite deadly at close range. Colonel James McMurry of the 4th Tennessee remembered that Turner's guns were "placed in a position by the brigade commander on an eminence, where it and all the infantry of the brigade opened a well-directed and destructive fire against the hostile battery and infantry, and after a heavy fire from us which continued some 15–20 minutes, we drove the battery and its support from their position." Turner reported that "the battery fired about 200 rounds and was engaged about 40 minutes and succeeded in silencing the enemy's battery as well as driving back their infantry."[51]

"An artillery duel ensued at the short range of 250 yards that has seldom been surpassed," Stevenson would write. "Tremendous branches of trees came tumbling down on our pieces; the shells burst continually among the cannons; every few seconds solid shot, missing the guns, hit the peaceful horses, quietly awaiting the guidance of their riders and brought them to the ground wounded in the most frightful manner. Here Colonel Roberts was again conspicuous. Being informed that the guns could not be worked by reason of falling timber, he quickly ran over and with his herculean strength helped to clear them of the encumbrances. The fire slackened for a moment, and the Rebels, believing the batteries silenced, commenced their attack."[52]

The Confederates charged Sheridan's position four times and were repulsed three times with heavy casualties. The first attack was by Maney's left-most regiment, shielded by a thin stretch of timber as it tried to close on Sheridan's line. "We were then ordered forward, bearing slightly to the right," wrote Major John Harris of the 6th/9th Tennessee. "After proceeding about 600 yards to the fence of a third field beyond which the enemy was strongly massed in the cedars with their batteries playing upon us continually, we were halted and fired one round at the enemy, they returning the fire, killing and wounding several of our men. We were then ordered by Colonel Charles Hurt to return to our former position and there

50 Ibid., 61-62.

51 OR 20/1:738, 742.

52 Stevenson, *Battle of Stone's River*, 62-63.

formed on a line with Smith's battery 100 yards in rear of our first line." Maney wrote that "about this time General Cheatham came in person to my line and Colonel Manigault reported his brigade reformed and again ready to advance. By order of the major general, we moved across the field in line together, bearing sharply to the right, General Cheatham accompanying us."[53]

"The crest occupied by the enemy was belching with fire and smoke and the Rebels were falling like leaves of autumn in a hurricane," Sam Watkins wrote. "The leaden hailstorm swept them off the field. General Cheatham came up and kept ordering "Go forward, go forward, forward," and his chief of staff James Porter was also trying to rally the brigade to the charge." Watkins kept his post on the skirmish line until he was struck twice through the arm, once by a shell fragment and then by a Minié ball. "The impression that General Frank Cheatham made upon my mind leading that charge on the Wilkinson turnpike I will never forget," he averred. "I saw either victory or death written on his face. When I saw him leading our brigade, I felt so sorry for him as he seemed so earnest and concerned and as he was passing me, I said, 'Well, General, if you are determined to die, I'll die with you.' Then it was that I saw the power of one man, born to command, over a multitude of men then almost routed and demoralized. He deserves a wreath of immortality."[54]

Manigault's two South Carolina regiments charged to within 120 yards of Houghtaling's battery and made a special target of the horses, eventually killing 80 of them. "The South Carolina regiments drove the gunners and supports from the battery, shot down the horses as they were endeavoring to retire the guns, and had succeeded in their undertaking when the Yankee reserve in turn advanced and drove them back," Manigault praised. Captain J. R. Nettles of the 10th South Carolina was struck down by seven bullets as his men charged the guns. D. H. Hannaford of Nettles' company remembered that "Nettles fell at the head of his company, literally shot to pieces. As Captain Nettles was falling, he shouted, 'Men, take that battery and bring its standard here to me before I die.' That was enough to make each of those men forget all else save bringing that standard to their fallen leader. They took that battery, going through a hail of leaden missiles, but enough of them survived to bring back that standard and receive that expression of commendation and triumph that death sealed on the face of their captain."

53 *OR* 20/1:735, 740.

54 Watkins, *Company Aytch*, 84-85.

Moving between Manigault's and Maney's brigades, C. Irvine Walker did his best to coordinate the attack. "I galloped back and found the two South Carolina regiments had gotten into a hornet's nest; the battery being supported by a heavy infantry force," he wrote. "I immediately ordered up the Alabama regiments of the brigade and they reached the South Carolinians just as the movement of the third brigade [J. Patton Anderson's] on our right had aided us."[55]

The third attack came within a whisker of breaking the Federal line, as Anderson's Mississippians struck Negley's division to put pressure on Sheridan's left. "The yell of Maney's and Manigault's men as they advanced the third time was but faint," Stevenson recalled. "…they had suffered and knew that noise did not scare the troops in front of them, but the Mississippians had not yet seen action and with full lungs they came on with a tremendous yell. But it availed them little. Hescock and Bush and the 42nd Illinois in their front caused fearful havoc and in ten minutes' time the column was in full retreat towards the breastworks in the rear. Through all this terrible fight in the midst of this frightful scene of death, General Sheridan could be seen riding continually closely watching his men. Again, there was a temporary lull and one had an opportunity to see what terrible havoc had been made. Death everywhere had reaped a great harvest and our poor wounded were asking for assistance. But very little aid could be rendered, as every man was needed to resist the enemy."

Stevenson also noted what he called a "peculiar incident" there, "showing the pluck and nerve of some of the men." It involved Lt. Col. Nathan H. Walworth of the 42nd Illinois, who praised his men for a "noble" stand as he walked behind his line. Corporal Alexander Smith of Company I approached Walworth and said, "Colonel, I come to return my gun to you, for I suppose I shall go on furlough now." As he took the gun, the colonel responded, "Why, what is it?" Wrote Stevenson: "Look,' he answered and as he moved his hand from his body the intestines followed it. 'To what hospital can I go," asked the wounded man. 'Go that way," said his commander pointing to the Blanton house."[56]

One the Confederate side, two soldiers—one a Tennessean, one an Arkansan—agreed to aid one another if either was wounded. "Pretty soon the Arkansas man called out to the Tennessean he was wounded and to take him off," it was reported. As they had agreed, "the Tennessean shouldered him and carried

<hr>

55 Tower, *A Carolinian Goes to War*, 57; *Recollections and Reminiscences, 1861-1865* (South Carolina Division, United Daughters of the Confederacy), Vol. 6, 1998, 14; Walker Papers.

56 Stevenson, *Battle of Stone's River*, 64-65.

him away to the rear. While going along, a cannon ball came and took the head off the wounded man but the bearer didn't observe it. When he arrived where the surgeon was, he laid him down and said, 'Doctor, here is a friend of mine; can't you do something for him?' The doctor in surprise wanted to know why he brought that dead man to him. The Tennessean turned and looked at him, and very coolly remarked, "Well, blast him, he told me he was only wounded."[57]

"Our regiment was ordered to support Captain Houghtaling's battery," remembered Captain James Jackson of the 22nd Illinois, "and though surrounded on all sides with three batteries playing on him while his horses and men fell all around, Houghtaling still held his ground. A regiment of the enemy's infantry had moved up with the evident intention of capturing the battery. But our regiment met them and gallantly repulsed them, but soon a whole brigade was hurled upon us. May God in mercy never let one look upon such a sight again."

The sight was equally appalling south of the pike. Major John Harris of the 6th/9th Tennessee reported that his regiment ground to a halt in the woods "being partially sheltered by the trees from the most terrific fire of shot and shell I ever saw, completely riddling the forest in every direction. We were again ordered forward amid the thunder of artillery and the crash of falling timber."[58]

From the other side of the field, Corporal William Austin of the 22nd Illinois remembered the oncoming enemy and he and his fellow Ilini were soon engaged. "Fast and thick rained the missiles of death upon our artillerists. Some could be seen working at the guns with mangled limbs, but none faltered for an instant but with shouts they continued to send the contents of their guns into the ranks of the desperate foe." By the time the battery ceased firing, claimed Austin, "every cartridge had been burnt, their caissons were empty, and their numbers sadly diminished." As far as he could tell, the infantry was doing all they could to hold the Confederates in check. "The roll of musketry nearly equaled the artillery and greatly exceeded it in rapidity," observed the corporal. "We all knew the dangers that surrounded us. We aimed our pieces coolly and random firing need not be indulged in for the foe was pressing close on to us and our aim was certain to find an object." Austin distinctly recalled glancing along friendly lines: "I could see men fall and

<hr>

57 "Only Wounded," *Macon Beacon*, Jul. 22, 1863, 1.

58 Captain James S. Jackson, Co. G, 22nd Illinois, *Salem Advocate*, Jan. 22, 1863; OR 20/1:740.

limp to the rear. My company thinned out fast until near half gone, but the rest kept their guns and did their duty like men."[59]

By this time the hour was approaching 11:00 a.m. After more than three hours of almost unceasing combat, Sheridan's men had been all but drained of their resolve. Ammunition was running low, and the batteries, which had done so much to hold back the Confederate advance, fell silent as their limbers were emptied. McCook's ammunition train was nowhere in sight. Realizing the division's batteries pointed in two directions, Lieutenant Moody "could see we were completely isolated and cut off," adding, "I thought of General [Benjamin] Prentiss at Shiloh and concluded a like fate awaited us"—referring to the desperate Union defense of the famed Hornet's Nest on April 6, 1862. "General Sheridan insisted that we hold this position as long as possible and that everything depended upon it."

Bush's 4th Indiana Battery fired 1,160 rounds that morning, with 23 casualties (six killed, 17 wounded) and two lost guns in the eventual retreat. Hescock's Missourians had been equally profligate in their ammunition expenditures, firing 1,112 rounds but drawing off all their guns, despite losing five men killed and 12 wounded. Although Houghtaling fired all his ammunition (1,154 rounds), with the battery's horses laying in heaps around the wreckage of his battery, he had no way to salvage his guns.[60]

The 1st/27th Tennessee's casualty count topped 80 during its occupation of the ground near the Harding's brick kiln. The coordinated assault, however, forced the defending Federals to shift their fire, giving Maney a breathing spell. Recounted Seay: "Promptly at the first lull, the riddle was solved to everyone as to whether it came from friend or foe by the intrepid command of our colonel shouting 'Forward First Tennessee Infantry!' Every man, with gun cocked and loaded, cartridge box open and at the front, instantly sprang forward. The fences which had disturbed the writer's imagination were no longer there. The furious cannonade had left no rail upon another. As we crossed the pike into the open field beyond, the Federal battery which had been sorely pressing us was endeavoring to escape over a road cut through the cedars."[61]

Once Captain Walker pushed ahead his three Alabama regiments, Manigault's men took a final crack at Sheridan's line. Colonel John Reid's 28th Alabama attacked in line, "the foe falling back until they gained the protection of a field

59 Austin Diary.

60 Moody Diary.

61 Seay Article, 159.

parallel with the Nolensville road and near their battery which filled the wood with shell, canister, and grape." The Federals offered an "obstinate resistance. The fire and shells and grape of the battery was making sad havoc, but at the command forward" Manigualt advanced the brigade. "On reaching the Nolensville road," continued Reid, "we found it impossible to advance across the open space without great slaughter and needless exposure to such considerable odds and the command was given and fell back under cover of the cedars, the regiment halting promptly and facing the enemy at the command."[62]

The fourth assault finally broke Roberts's hold on his position. "The enemy observed very soon that the firing had ceased and they charged upon the battery and the 22nd Illinois and drove the latter towards the pike," Stevenson recalled. "'Adjutant,' shouted Colonel Roberts, 'rally them on the north side of the pike and make a stand there. I'll rally the 42nd Illinois.' With these words he galloped towards that regiment still south of the pike. The 22nd responded to the order most gallantly; they rallied and took their position along the north side of the pike, being followed by the Rebels at a distance not greater than 50 feet at the most. Here again a terrible fire commenced. The all-pervading excitement, the fury displayed by some of the men, the loud commands of the officers trying to steady the troops in their firing, the general uproar combined to form a scene which it is impossible to describe. The excitement was so great, indeed, that many did not aim at the enemy, but loading with greatest speed, they brought their muskets to an aim and fired at the top of the trees. There was but one cry, 'For God's sake, get us ammunition!'"[63]

Added Stevenson: "After the 22nd and 42nd Illinois regiments had fallen back north of the Wilkinson Pike for some distance, they halted again, the enemy remaining nearer to the pike. General Sheridan then rode forward to Lieutenant Colonel Walworth and said in a very slow and determined manner, firmly biting a piece of cigar meanwhile, 'Colonel, when you cannot hold this point any longer and are out of ammunition, move the regiment in this direction (pointing northeast). This is about the only place for us to get out; they have nearly surrounded us.'"

Houghtaling would go down with a wound in the final moments, Stevenson later remembering that the captain was "carried away barely alive, the blood as it flowed from his wound leaving a track on the stones. Lieutenant R. C. M. Talliaferro [Battery G, 1st Missouri Light] who had never flinched even in the hottest fire was shot dead between his cannons. Houghtaling's men refused to

---

62 Smith, *Stones River: Confederate Army*, 678.

63 Stevenson, *Battle of Stone's River*, 66-67.

leave their guns and defended them with their revolvers, sabers, and ramrods till they were finally overpowered and many taken prisoners." Sergeant Chester Whitman was among the battery's few unharmed survivors. "We had some hopes of drawing off the battery by hand and saving it, but before it could be done, we were flanked both left and right and there was no possible way of saving it," he conceded. "Our boys stood up and fought like veterans and would have fought until they were all killed or disabled if we had a surplus supply of ammunition before we would have abandoned the battery."[64]

A tornado of bullets, shells, falling timbers, and shattered men marked the combat. The ground became so saturated with bodies, in fact, that the Illinoisans dubbed this patch of the ground the "Slaughter Pen." Colonel Fazilo Harrington of the 27th Illinois—remembered by one of his privates as "a very wicked man but a first-rate colonel"—hobbled back and forth behind his line encouraging his men in the desperate fight. He had already been struck once by a Minié ball that lodged in his thigh, but he refused to leave the field. According to one report: "While in the thickest of the fight, waving his sword and speaking words of cheer to his brave boys saying, 'Stand fast my brave boys, your guns are your only friends today.' He was again struck by a ball which passed through his face.'"

Surgeon Edward Bowman reported that Harrington was "wounded by a musket ball through his upper jaw, horribly mangling him and cutting his tongue about half off." The wound was ghastly as a steady stream of blood poured from his mouth, down his beard, and onto his chest. Harrington finally consented to being taken from the field. His men quickly missed his presence. "His familiar voice was missing," wrote William Fleming, "and the cry was 'Where is Colonel Harrington?' This caused sad feelings among the boys. But we had no time to mourn the loss of our brave officer as the Rebels were fast approaching us."[65]

Harrington was not the only officer to fall during Sheridan's final moments along the Wilkinson Pike. "Colonel Roberts, on reaching the 42nd Illinois, dashed in the rear of the line at a furious rate with his sword high in the air as though he would split the head of the first man whom he should see moving to the rear," Stevenson recalled. "Not a field officer could be seen on a horse; Roberts was not aware that every animal had been killed. Dashing again in the rear of the line, he

---

64 Ibid., 69-70; Whitman Letter. Two dozen of Houghtaling's men stood beside their guns until the bitter end and were captured.

65 "The Late Colonel F. A. Harrington," *Chicago Tribune*, Feb. 4, 1863, 2; Private William B. Fleming, Co. G, 27th Illinois, *Keithsburg Observer*, Feb. 12, 1863.

espied Lieutenant Colonel Walworth. As he rode towards him, his face brightened up with a smile that can never be forgotten, and when close to him he saluted with his sword, evidently as a token of his admiration for the gallant officers and men of his command." Roberts turned and galloped to the left cheering the men,

> but alas it was his last effort to drive the enemy. A few minutes later three bullets penetrated that grand form. The terrible shock unnerved his arm, the reins dropped from his hands, and he fell from his horse. A few men quickly ran to his help and he exclaimed with a husky voice, 'Boys, put me on my horse again!' The effort was made, but before it could be accomplished, a shudder passed through him and death had vanquished the bravest of the brave. The men in attendance carried him quickly towards the rear on the north side of the pike and, believing we would again regain the battlefield, placed the body near a large tree and covered it with brush to prevent its being disturbed.[66]

As the Confederates surged across the Wilkinson Pike, Houghtaling's four bronze Napoleons were captured by the 10th and 19th South Carolina. "This retreat soon became a rout," reported Colonel John Reid of the 28th Alabama. "They abandoned their guns and many readily gave themselves up and became captives. Some we found secreted in the crevices and rocks and in caves. Stopping long enough to collect 40 or more prisoners and placing them in charge of a lieutenant and sent to the rear, we resumed our rapid pursuit of the flying enemy."[67]

Seay witnessed the spectacle of Schaefer's well-trained Missourians pulling back through the cedars. "A gallant brigade of infantry which had been its support in the most perfect order and with hardly an attempt to return our fire emerged from the cedars and was double-quicking diagonally across our front but increasing its distance at every step," he wrote. "As we came into full view with no obstruction between us, the long-deferred fire from the Confederates became terrific. The retiring Federal infantry, being nearer to us, came in for most of our attention, though the battery which was trying to escape received its due notice, especially from the right wing. The work at this point was short and rapid and the Confederates fired cool and deliberately. In what appeared to be a few minutes, no foe remained in sight. The line closing to the right, marching by the right flank was aligned anew just back of the ground lately occupied by the enemy."[68]

66 Stevenson, *Battle of Stone's River*, 67-68.

67 Smith, *Stones River: Confederate Army*, 679.

68 Seay article, 159.

Roberts's brigade, now under the command of Colonel Luther Bradley of the 51st Illinois, split in two as it fell into the cedars. The 22nd and 42nd Illinois fled through Negley's division while the 27th and 51st Illinois scurried farther west, passing through Rousseau's advancing brigades. Schaefer's men also fired off their last rounds and pulled into the cedars under the cover of Rousseau's division.

Hescock managed to draw off his entire battery, but Bush lost two of his guns in the cedars. "My two rear pieces were captured by the enemy, after killing all the horses on them except one wheel horse on one and one wheel and two swing horses on the other," Bush reported, "the latter piece was stuck fast among the trees and the enemy within 40 yards of them." Noted Weber: "At the same time the enemy, as if multiplying himself on this spot, moved towards us with several batteries and a line of infantry six columns deep. What was to be done here but to retire slowly and cautiously until I reached the open field. I saw to my dismay that the enemy was surrounding us on every side and threatened my boys with destruction, the more so since the other regiments had already left the ground. With all dispatch, I gave the necessary orders and reached my brigade unscathed."[69]

Bowman set up shop in a sinkhole within the cedars and struggled to care for the dozens of casualties that inundated his makeshift field hospital. "The roar of cannon and musketry seemed to me to exceed Belmont tenfold," he wrote. "In a little time, our Colonel Fazilo Harrington came in. I dressed him and then began to dress the other wounded and was very busy when we heard yelling in our rear and firing, then heard the balls flying over and through us. The balls and shells were crashing frightfully through the cedars and exploding. It seemed as if escape was impossible. Nearly everybody laid down. One of my hospital men caught me by the arm and pulled me down saying "Doctor, you'll be killed if you don't lay down!" I thought so, too, by that time and lay down by Colonel Harrington. The Rebs charged upon us and fired a volley right into us, killing several of our wounded men although we had four red flags up to indicate the place as a hospital. They swept over, taking everything that could walk as prisoners."[70]

The withdrawal, Sheridan admitted, was particularly difficult for "wheeled carriages" because of the rocky ground and cedar growth. "Retiring sullenly under a heavy fire while the general line was reformed to my right and rear, my division was at length drawn through the cedars and debouched into the open space near the Murfreesboro Pike," he would write. "The division came out of the cedars with

69 *OR* 20/1:355; Weber Report.

70 Surgeon Edward Bowman, 27th Illinois, *Rock Island Weekly Union*, Feb. 4, 1863.

unbroken ranks, thinned only by its killed and wounded." Those ranks were frightfully thinned, as his division had lost 40 percent of its strength during its three-hour stand defending the Wilkinson Pike. Two of Sheridan's three brigade commanders, Sill and Roberts, numbered among the slain. Sill's brigade suffered 720 total casualties, Roberts' Illinoisans another 566, and Schaefer's brigade 398.

The men had not died in vain, though. Sheridan's primary objective was to stymie the Confederate assault long enough to buy time for Rosecrans to reorient the army, and that objective was accomplished. As Sheridan withdrew, Rousseau's division had waded into the cedars to his right, with Crittenden's corps not far behind. "In the remaining years of the war, though often engaged in the most severe contests, I never experienced in any of my commands so high a rate of casualties," Sheridan wrote. "Though our victory was dearly bought, yet the importance of gaining the day at any price was very great."[71]

The carnage was appalling. "Stretched before and behind us in every crevice in the rocks, the Federal wounded had crept for shelter," noted Seay. "Mangled masses of human forms, torn in every conceivable way, lay scattered in all directions." Not one of the horses that had drawn thee six pieces and their caissons, were standing. "When the command 'forward' was given," he added, "the writer passed between two pieces and two caissons, the twelve horses and six riders to which, the latter with whips still clutched in their hands, lay dead on each side."[72]

The retreat presented its own horrors. The Confederates, explained Private Arza Bartholomew of the 21st Michigan, "had us about as tight as need be. They drove us into a swamp, surrounded the swamp, and poured in shot and shell from both sides. It was awful to see the trees falling and horses running without riders. If you could just see the woods, you would say that a man could not get out alive for every tree had from one to 20 holes in it. I hope never to see such a time again."

John Frederick of the 44th Illinois, part of Schaefer's brigade, "saw what he could not believe possible" when he witnessed a man falling back into the cedars. "It was an artillery private sitting astride a cannon which he was attempting to save, drawn by one horse. The man had one leg shot off above the knee but not entirely severed, and the foot was dangling upon the ground as the owner moved solemnly along."[73]

71 Sheridan, *Personal Memoirs*, 125, 130-31.

72 Seay Article, 159.

73 Private Arza Bartholomew, Co. G, 21st Michigan, SRNBP; Philip S. Post, *Soldiers' and Patriots' Biographical Album* (Chicago, 1892), 226.

Negley in the Cedars

THE THUNDER OF approaching battle washing over the Federal army headquarters along the Nashville Pike spoke volumes on the condition of Alexander McCook's Right Wing.

"Battle was flowing along the line, communicating first with the center, then the left," recorded journalist William Bickham. "The enemy was pressing McCook swiftly and in disorder clean back upon the center. An aide from McCook advises that Rousseau had better be held in hand. What? Reserves so soon? 'Tell General McCook I will help him,' was the instant reply, and Rousseau marched into the cedar brakes. The battle is all against us. The plan of battle is crippled. The left wing cannot swing into Murfreesboro and cut them off. A third of the left wing is absolutely necessary to save the right from destruction. The general commanding comprehended the dire extent of the calamity and threw his own weighty sword in the scale of battle. Henceforth he consulted no one, asked no man's opinion, trusted in God, and relied upon himself."[1]

The 3rd Division in Crittenden's Left Wing, meanwhile, began execution of Rosecrans's orders to cross Stones River at McFadden's Ford and strike Bragg's right. Van Cleve's men moved out at 7:00 that morning, arriving at the ford a little before 8:00. Colonel Samuel Beatty's 1st Brigade crossed first and formed on the right, followed by Colonel Samuel Price's 3rd Brigade, which formed on the left. Sergeant Alfred Stambaugh of the 19th Ohio recalled hearing Rosecrans's order of

1 Bickham, *Rosecrans' Campaign*, 210-11.

the day read out loud and then "Major Charles Manderson, commanding our regiment, said, 'Boys, today the blow will be struck. Be cool, be brave, and aim low.'"

"Marching orders were then given," Stambaugh wrote. "After crossing a creek, skirmishers were deployed who soon [ran] up against the Rebels and now and then a shot was fired, the pickets advancing and we followed up slowly."[2]

It took time for both brigades to funnel across McFadden's Ford and deploy their regiments in line (1–2 hours), but in the process the men could hear the growing sounds of conflict to their right and rear. At Rosecrans's direction, Van Cleve initially retained Colonel James P. Fyffe's 2nd Brigade west of the river and halted his advance, but by 10:00 a.m., matters on the Union right had denigrated to the point that Van Cleve received orders to pull his entire division west of Stones River. "At this time one of Beatty's aides came riding up to our major and said, 'The Rebels have got in our rear, cross the creek as quick as possible,'" Stambaugh recalled. "We did so at a double quick we went through kiting. Oh heavens, what a sight! Thousands upon thousands of infantrymen double-quicking across the plain—artillery rolling with the swiftness of horses, while the musketry was roaring and shells bursting in every direction, killing horses and men, and knocking everything to pieces near them. We would double quick one way, then another, and came to a halt, front, and then start again for another position."

The confused men of Beatty and Fyffe's brigades soon found themselves moving toward the Nashville Pike to reinforce the army's endangered right flank.[3]

*　*　*

Deployed at the edge of the cedar brake north of the Wilkinson Pike on Sheridan's left, James Negley's two brigades listened with growing concern as the battle moved in their direction. Colonel Timothy Stanley's four regiments held the division's right and connected with George Roberts' brigade in Sheridan's division, while Colonel Miller's four regiments held the left and connected with Cruft's brigade in Palmer's division. It was good defensible ground with a clear field of fire to the front and (for the moment) secure flanks. A rough road that was cut through the cedars the previous day by Rosecrans's Pioneers lay directly behind Stanley's position, and McFadden Lane ran through Miller's position. Both offered a limited

---

2　Sergeant Alfred Stambaugh, Co. F, 19th Ohio, *Ohio Repository*, Feb. 28, 1863, 2.

3　Stambaugh Letter.

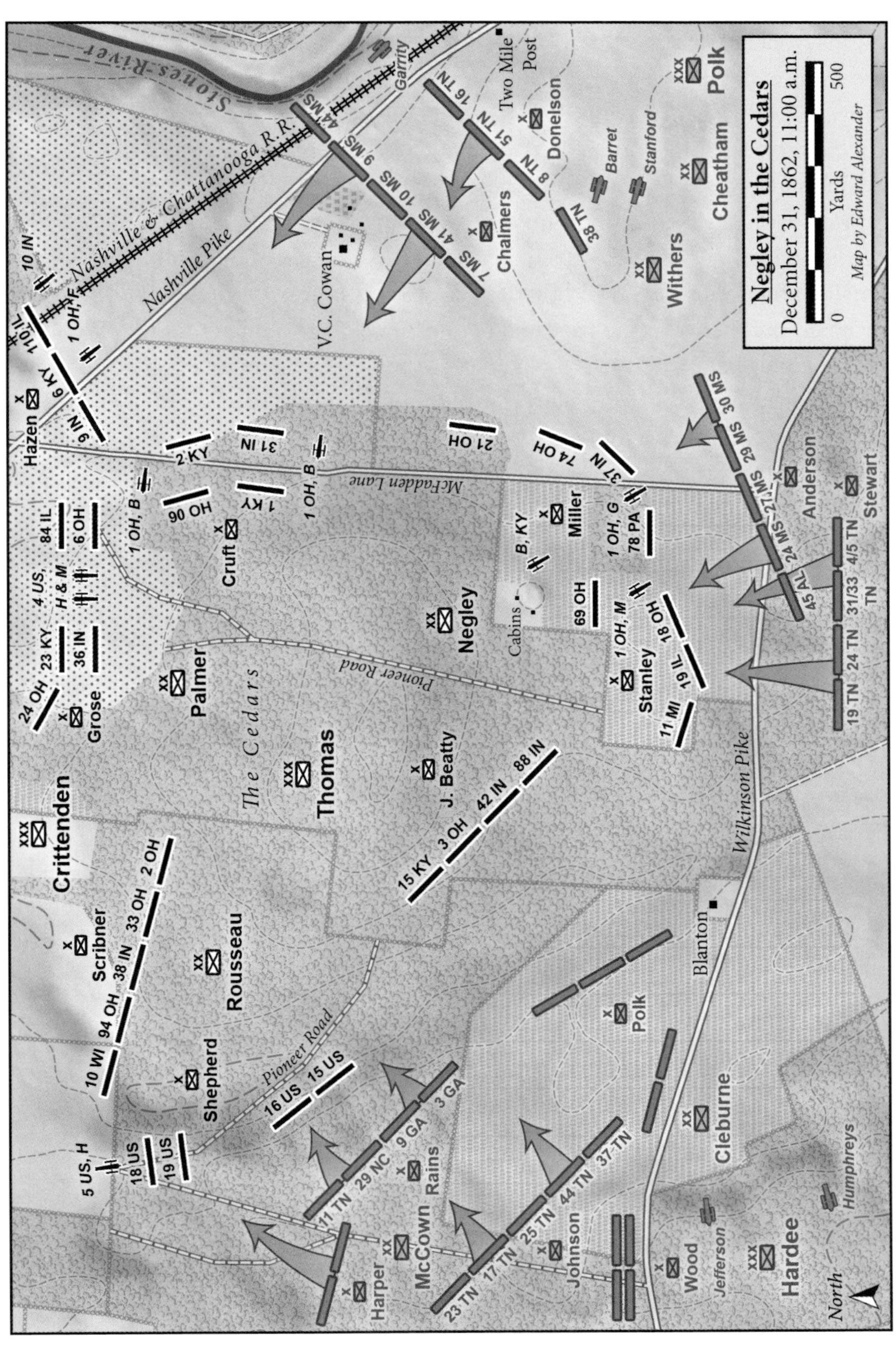
Negley in the Cedars
December 31, 1862, 11:00 a.m.
Map by Edward Alexander
0   Yards   500
Stones River
Nashville & Chattanooga R.R.
Nashville Pike
Garrity
Two Mile Post
Donelson
Barret
Stanford
Cheatham
Polk
16 TN
51 TN
8 TN
38 TN
44 MS
9 MS
10 MS
41 MS
7 MS
V.C. Cowan
Chalmers
Withers
29 MS
30 MS
27 MS
24 MS
45 AL
Anderson
Stewart
4/5 TN
31/33 TN
24 TN
19 TN
10 IN
1 OH, F
110 IL
6 KY
9 IN
Hazen
2 KY
31 IN
90 OH
1 KY
1 OH, B
Cruft
1 OH, B
21 OH
74 OH
37 IN
McFadden Lane
84 IL
6 OH
H & M
4 US,
36 IN
23 KY
24 OH
Grose
Palmer
Negley
B, KY
Miller
69 OH
1 OH, G
78 PA
1 OH, M
Stanley
18 OH
19 IL
11 MI
Cabins
Thomas
The Cedars
Pioneer Road
J. Beatty
3 OH
42 IN
88 IN
15 KY
Crittenden
Scribner
38 IN
33 OH
2 OH
94 OH
10 WI
Rousseau
Shepherd
Pioneer Road
16 US
15 US
Blanton
Polk
Cleburne
Wilkinson Pike
5 US, H
18 US
19 US
11 TN
29 NC
9 GA
3 GA
Harper
McCown
Rains
23 TN
17 TN
25 TN
44 TN
37 TN
Johnson
Wood
Jefferson
Humphreys
Hardee
North

means of resupply or retreat, if needed. Outside these narrow pathways, however, the forest floor was strewn with limestone boulders that would make any movement through the woods treacherous.

Stanley, the oldest brigade commander in Rosecrans's army at age 52, took position just east of the Blanton House, covering the Wilkinson Pike. The Ohioan arrayed his 1,822 men in line with two regiments up front, two in reserve: the 11th Michigan totaling 440 men on the right, with the 373 men of the 19th Illinois on the left. The four guns of Captain Frederick Schultz's Battery M of the 1st Ohio Light dropped trail between the frontline regiments, facing south across the Wilkinson Pike. Stanley kept his own 18th Ohio (446 men) in close reserve behind the guns, but he ran into trouble with the commander of his fourth and largest regiment, the 69th Ohio. Stanley was horrified to discover Colonel William Cassilly arrived on the field, in the words of one of his soldiers, "stupidly beastly drunk." "A man who will come to the field of battle, having the lives of so many in his keeping, in such a situation, no matter what his social position, is totally unfit for any command," Stanley chided in his official report. He had Cassilly arrested and sent to the rear, placing the shaken Ohioans (546 officers and men) under the command of the next senior officer present, Major Eli Hickcox.[4]

Miller's 2,181-man brigade took an adjacent line in the shape of a reversed L: the 555-man 78th Pennsylvania held the brigade right facing south across the Wilkinson Pike, with the 454 men of the 37th Indiana to its left facing south-southeast. Between the two regiments, Lieutenant Alexander Marshall deployed the six guns of Battery G, 1st Ohio Light. Following the edge of the woods, the 74th Ohio—the smallest regiment in the brigade, with 399 men under the redoubtable Colonel Granville Moody (the "Fighting Parson")—lay to the left of the 37th Indiana but faced east, and the brigade's largest regiment (the 611-man 21st Ohio) held the left. Three guns of Lieutenant Alban Ellsworth's 1st Kentucky Battery were positioned near the left flank by a log house.

---

4 OR 20/1:421. Colonel Cassilly was wounded in the left arm on the way to the rear and rode to Nashville in an ambulance. Colonel Stanley recommended his immediate dismissal, and an order was cut to that effect on Jan. 16, 1863, but Cassilly, "having stood fair as an officer and a gentleman in the army," was spared the humiliation and instead allowed to resign his commission.

Miller was a rising star in Rosecrans's army, and one of his subordinates later wrote "there was not perhaps in all the army a brigade having a commander in which it had greater confidence." Miller would soon show why.[5]

Negley's men spent the first few hours of the battle as spectators to the disaster on the right. As the roar of the battle "drew louder and louder, evidently directing itself somewhat at our rear, we began to choke in the throat, to think of home, and wondering if our turn would come soon," recalled Henry Haynie of the 19th Illinois. "The right was not so far off and we could see the enemy doubling up the boys in blue. We could hear the hoarse shriek of the shell, the swift rattle of musketry, the sound of buzzing bullets, the impact of solid shot, the chug when human forms were hit, the yells of pain, cries of agony, the fearful groans and encouraging words and the death gasps of which told of those who had reported to the God of Battles." Noting that his Buckeyes were starting to exhibit some nervousness, Lt. Col. Josiah Given of the 18th Ohio drilled the men in the manual of arms. Ira Gillaspie of the 11th Michigan had been warming himself over a large fire of cedar rails and drinking his morning cup of coffee when the call came to fall in. "We were but a moment getting into line and ready to meet the Rebels," he wrote. "Our colonel mounted his horse and addressed us. 'Now brave boys, be cool and calm and take good aim, shoot low and be sure of your men. Secrete yourselves and keep a good lookout for your colors and don't run until I do!'"[6]

While Sheridan's division occupied the attention of two Confederate divisions (Cheatham's and Cleburne's), General Withers threw in two of his brigades in an effort to crack Sheridan's and Negley's hold on the Wilkinson Pike. The job fell to J. Patton Anderson and James Chalmers. The two tough brigadiers would have as support the brigades of Brig. Gens. A. P. Stewart and Daniel Donelson from Cheatham's Division that Leonidas Polk had ordered forward. An old friend of Jefferson Davis, Anderson had assumed command of Edward Walthall's Brigade just a few days before. The Floridian had been part of Bragg's Gulf Coast command early in the war and led a brigade at Shiloh and a division at Perryville.

"Opposite there were three batteries strongly supported by infantry," Withers reported. "The capture of the batteries and rout of the supports was a necessity. Anderson was therefore directed to take the batteries at every cost." The combative Chalmers, meanwhile, had led his Mississippi "High Pressure" brigade in a rash

---

5 Wilson J. Vance, *Stone's River: Turning Point of the Civil War* (New York, 1914), 53.

6 Weber, *From Michigan to Murfreesboro*, 43; Haynie, *The 19th Illinois*, 180.

attack at Munfordville during the Kentucky Campaign earlier that year, and events were shaping up for a virtual repeat of that at Murfreesboro.[7]

Anderson's Brigade totaled about 1,800 men and occupied a line of rough breastworks south of the Wilkinson Pike. Positioned left to right were the 45th Alabama, 24th Mississippi, 30th Mississippi, and 29th Mississippi (whose right flank rested on the pike). Just beyond the 29th lay the 27th Mississippi, with Captain Overton W. Barret's Missouri Battery anchoring the brigade's right flank. The 2,094 Mississippians in Chalmers's Brigade lay to Anderson's east and behind a slight hill that concealed the men from the Federals. The 7th Mississippi held the left flank, with the 41st Mississippi at left center, the 9th/10th Mississippi at right center (its right resting on the Nashville Pike), and Blythe's Mississippi Infantry Battalion tucked between the Nashville Pike and Stones River on the right. That last regiment, which would be designated the 44th Mississippi in June 1863, went into the action "badly armed and equipped" with refuse arms, as its commander Major John C. Thompson later complained.[8]

At about 10:00 a.m., Chalmers received orders from Major Thomas Jack of Polk's staff to move his brigade forward in conjunction with Anderson's Brigade on his left. "When the order to charge was given, with a yell such as only Mississippians can give, they went over the hill and through the cornfield in front," wrote Captain Simon Mayer of the 10th Mississippi. "Notwithstanding the shower of shells and grapeshot and the leaden hail of bullets, they went onward until they reached Cowan's house where they were halted and again formed into line." The left-flank regiments, the 7th and 41st Mississippi, marched over gently sloping ground and bounded ahead of the rest of the line, which produced intense fire from Miller's left. "Before my regiments were properly in position, a most terrific fire was opened upon every part of the line by infantry and artillery," Miller would write.[9]

---

7 In this sector, Withers had operational command of two of his brigades (Anderson and Chalmers) and two from Cheatham's Division (Donelson and Stewart). Likewise, Cheatham had operational control of two of Withers' brigades (Loomis and Manigault).

8 The exact timing of the Confederate assault on Negley is difficult to pin down because of conflicting Confederate reports. Anderson's and Chalmers's assaults were intended to be made simultaneously, but accounts from the 21st Ohio, 74th Ohio, and Ellsworth's Kentucky battery reported opening fire against their left toward the Cowan House at the outset of their engagement. It is more likely than not that Chalmers attacked first, ahead of Anderson, and repulsed before Anderson was fully engaged.

9 *OR* 20/1:432; Mayer Letter.

Sergeant John Bolton of the 21st Ohio noted that Chalmers's men "moved at the double quick into the small open field," and then charged. "The Rebs came up two or three columns deep, screeching and yelping like nigger hounds," remembered Bolton's comrade Liberty Warner, who leveled his musket across the fence and "made them yell another tune. I was as cool as a cucumber and took steady aim at the cloud of flash and smoke."

"[T]his being the first heavy fire the regiment was ever under," wrote Jacob Adams, "the boys stood up under it in fine shape, and were greatly encouraged and enthused when Colonel Jim, as we called Colonel Neibling, went up and down the line repeating 'Give 'em hell by the acre boys.'" The fire rolled up and down the regimental line, which combined with Lieutenant Alban A. Ellsworth's canister fire tore great holes in Chalmers's formation.[10]

Miller's left came under fire from two Confederate batteries, focused on silencing Ellsworth's guns. One of those units, Captain James Garrity's Alabama Battery in Chalmers's Brigade, rolled forward with four guns and unlimbered on a section on a hill south of the Cowan House. "Here we were subject to a heavy crossfire of canister," Ellsworth noted. "I immediately ordered a return fire of canister, double shot, firing as rapidly as possible." Although Ellsworth's efforts did not silence the Confederate batteries, it stalled Chalmers's advance long enough for the rest of Miller's men to get in position.

After making room for his guns on a slight elevation of clear ground, Lieutenant Alexander Marshall of Battery G, 1st Ohio Light, ordered his caissons to the rear, wheeled his six guns to the left, and opened with canister on the advancing Confederates. The 7th Mississippi fixed bayonets and charged the right of the 21st Ohio line. "When about 30 yards distant, the order was given to fix bayonets," said Captain Silas Canfield of the 21st Ohio. "But about this time, they broke and fled, followed by a volley as a parting salute." Inspired by his men's steadiness under their first heavy fire, Neibling rode along saying, "My God boys! We gave 'em hell, didn't we?"[11]

The left of Chalmers's attack was faltering as the 74th Ohio entered the fray. Colonel Moody wheeled his regiment into line after a short prayer session and exhorted his troops, "Now men, resume your praying, fight for your God, your

---

10 John H. Bolton, Journal 1861-1863. MMS 1488. Center for Archival Collections, Bowling Green State University, 83; Liberty Warner, Papers. MS-624mf. CAC, BGSU. Feb. 10, 1863; Jacob Adams, *Diary of Jacob Adams, Private in Company F, 21st O.V.V.I.* (Columbus, 1930), 19.

11 OR 20/1:411, 413-414; Canfield, *History of the 21st Ohio*, 73.

country, your kind, aim low and give them Hail Columbia!" His two center companies opened fire and drowned out the end of his speech; his men later claimed he said, "give them hell," much to the pious colonel's chagrin.

After nearly a year in service, Ira Owens fired his first shots ever at the enemy that morning. "I was kneeling in a fence corner, loading and firing when we received orders to move to the left and make room for a battery," he said. "When I was just in the act of rising, I felt something hit me in the leg, which did not produce much pain at the time." A Mississippian's ball had struck his leg, and he soon hobbled to the rear seeking the regimental surgeon.[12]

To bring more fire into Chalmers's reeling and unsupported brigade, Miller advanced the 37th Indiana slightly forward of the 74th Ohio and wheeled it to the left. "At 10 a.m., we were ordered to advance up the eminence to our right, now become our front, and if possible, gain the woods but a few rods distant, and through the enemy," recalled Captain Hezekiah Shook of the 37th Indiana. "The enemy was within 80 yards of the knoll and opened a heavy fire upon us. Our line wavered, reeled, but steadied again." To support the Hoosiers, Moody advanced the 74th Ohio by swinging his sword over his head and shouting, "Come on, Christian brethren." The maneuver evidently worked.[13]

Combined fire from Miller's three regiments shut down the left of Chalmers's advance; Lt. Col. Williams of the 41st Mississippi soon went down with a wound, which put Captain Lewis Ball in command. "Not knowing Colonel Williams was wounded," Ball reported, "we advanced 50–75 yards and halted, seeking such protection as was afforded by the piling up of rails on the part of the enemy to protect their pickets."

The left flank of the 41st Mississippi halted about 50 yards from the 21st Ohio and took a hammering at such close range. The Federals were "securely located behind a natural defense of rock and also a fence between us which made our fire comparatively ineffectual," Ball explained. "The 7th Mississippi, failing to make the last advance, subjected us to a crossfire from the left and the direction of the enemy's line did the same from the right. Two batteries were pouring an incessant

---

12 Theodore W. Blackburn, *Letters From the Front: A Union 'Preacher' Regiment (74th Ohio) in the Civil War* (Dayton, 1981), 29; Owens, *Greene County in the War*, 33.

13 Hezekiah Shook, *Address delivered on the Occasion of the Second Annual Reunion of the 37th Indiana Volunteer Infantry, September 18, 1878*, Indiana Historical Society; George H. Puntenney, *History of the Thirty-Seventh Regiment of Indiana Infantry Volunteers* (Rushville, 1896), 34.

fire of grape and shell upon us; consequently, we were repulsed and fell back to our original line leaving many killed and wounded on the field."[14]

As the rest of Chalmers's line moved past the Cowan House, it plunged into a pocket of fire from two more Federal brigades: Cruft's four regiments on the left along the eastern edge of the cedar brake and Hazen's brigade then moving into position in what became known as the Round Forest. Cruft, a veteran of the Union debacle at Richmond, Kentucky, deployed his 1,207 men with two regiments in front, two in reserve, and split Lieutenant Norman Baldwin's Battery B of the 1st Ohio Light, placing three guns on each flank of his line. The 31st Indiana, supported by the 1st Kentucky, held the brigade's right close to Miller's left flank, and the 2nd Kentucky, supported by the 90th Ohio, anchored the left nearest to Hazen's brigade, with roughly 1,385 men.

As the action opened, Hazen's regiments were spread out. The 6th Kentucky, in line next to Cruft's 2nd Kentucky and supported by the 9th Indiana, was separated by about 200 yards from the 41st Ohio, which had its right flank on the Nashville Pike facing Murfreesboro; the untested 110th Illinois lay astride the railroad to the left rear of the Buckeyes. Captain Daniel Cockerill and the six guns of Battery F, 1st Ohio Light, dropped trail between the 6th Kentucky and 41st Ohio, enjoying an open field of fire to the Cowan House and beyond.

Hazen turned his brigade to face Chalmers's advance directly. "On they come steadily, firmly, in three lines of battle, connecting with their lines on our right and their left, the intervals between the battalions filled with artillery," recalled 1st Lt. Elias Ford of the 41st Ohio. "Cockerill's battery on the keen run took its position and wheeled into line on a crest just to the left of our regiment. Our line was formed and every officer and soldier at his post. On they came, banners flying, while the demonic yells of powdered whiskey rent the air and their officers urged them on, but not to victory. We withheld our fire until they were within 40 rods of us [220 yards], when [Lieutenant] Colonel [Aquila] Wiley, coolly but in stentorian tones, gave the order 'Fire by battalion! Battalion, ready, aim, fire!' We fired a volley into their ranks that halted them and told them we were ready."[15]

In Chalmers's center was the 9th/10th Mississippi, which enjoyed the burnt remains of the Cowan House and its outbuildings as cover as it moved forward, though that would change once it passed the house. "We moved forward across the open field at a run under a heavy fire of shell and canister from the enemy's battery

---

14 Smith, *Stones River: Confederate Army*, 662.

15 51st Lt. Elias A. Ford, Co. B, 41st Ohio, *Jeffersonian Democrat*, Feb. 6, 1863, 1.

which was placed near the skirt of woods on the right of the pike," recalled Colonel Thomas White of the 9th Mississippi. "The regiment halted at the picket fence between Cowan's House and the pike and opened fire upon the enemy who were retreating over the field in front of us. After keeping up this fire for a few minutes, I gave the order to cross the fence and press forward in pursuit."

Chalmers, however, quickly halted White's impetuous advance, directing White to move with his regiment toward the left to hold an exposed flank caused by the withdrawal of the 7th and 41st Mississippi. "I immediately moved to the west of the Cowan House where I found the guns of Ketchum's [Garrity's] battery hotly engaged with the infantry and artillery of the enemy which were posted in the wood," White wrote.[16]

Chalmers's men lived up to their reputation by applying "high pressure" to the Federals. Cruft recalled that "the enemy pushed toward us rapidly and charged my line in great force and in solid rank. The fight became very severe and obstinate. The enemy was driven back, although superior in numbers. His charge was made in two lines, with the appearance of a four-rank formation, and in most admirable order and discipline." Colonel Walter Whitaker of the 6th Kentucky, noticing that Chalmers's advance threatened his right, pulled back to a more advantageous position at the edge of the woods. "Three times the enemy advanced and as often they were driven back with great slaughter," the Kentuckian gloated.[17]

Despite the losses, Chalmers's men kept reforming and pushed closer to the Federal lines. Colonel John Osborn of the 31st Indiana noted that "a heavy force of the enemy appeared in our front, in an open field on a piece of rising ground, when they opened a severe fire upon our line, which was returned with a steady nerve by our men, which soon made them fall back. In a few moments they again returned to the crest of the field and attempted to charge our line, but the steady nerve of our boys and their deadly aim caused them again to retire."

Colonel Thomas Sedgwick of the 2nd Kentucky recalled that Chalmers's men "moved forward in splendid style until they reached the crest of the first hill in our front and there halted and delivered a well-directed volley full upon us. Captain [William E.] Standart's battery immediately on my right and my two regiments in

16 Smith, *Stones River: Confederate Army*, 660.

17 OR 20/1:527, 555.

front, simultaneously opened upon them, and with such effect that their front line gave way and fled to the rear."[18]

Blythe's 188 Mississippians likewise advanced between the Nashville Pike, the railroad, and Stones River before halting abreast of the Cowan House. Major Thompson reported that his men "poured into the enemy ranks a brisk and active fire," but the Magnolia State boys could advance no farther, as most of their fire from their shoddy guns could not reach Hazen's men in the woods to their front. Chalmers soon numbered among the casualties, "struck down by a fragment of a shell and borne senseless from the field," Withers reported. Captain Simon Mayer, already unhorsed by the Federals' intense artillery fire, discovered Chalmers lying senseless on the ground and conveyed him back to Murfreesboro. Apparently, no officer on Chalmers's staff thought to notify the next senior officer, Colonel White, that he now had command of the brigade. That would happen much later.[19]

*   *   *

The battle devolved into a slugfest. The Federals, snug behind their stone and fence defenses, eagerly peppered away at Chalmers's determined Mississippians, who scrambled to find cover in the open ground. Casualties mounted and the ground around the Cowan House was quickly became so littered with dead and wounded Mississippians that it became known as "Hell's Half-Acre." The 9th/10th Mississippi had 168 total casualties, the 41st Mississippi another 156, and the briefly engaged 7th Mississippi more than 100. Regardless of the carnage around him, Garrity's four guns continued to thunder away at both Miller's position to his left and Hazen's in the Round Forest to his right. With Chalmers's brigade in disarray, those guns were a tempting target for nearby Federal infantry.

Cruft recognized the opportunity. He had just finished performing a passage of the lines, a ticklish procedure when under fire that allowed him to rotate his frontline regiments to the rear where they could rest and replenish their ammunition boxes. Now he had the fresh 90th Ohio and 1st Kentucky up front with full cartridge boxes; turning to Colonel David Enyart, he ordered the 1st

18 Ibid., 533, 537-538.

19 Ibid., 1:756; "Brigadier General Chalmers," *Mobile Advertiser & Register*, Jan. 31, 1863, 2; Smith, *Stones River: Confederate Army*, 656, 663, 665. Blythe's Mississippi regiment suffered 52 casualties holding its position the remainder of the day, which indicates how heavy the fire was in this sector.

Kentucky forward. Enyart later reported that he was instructed "to move forward, and march over the 31st Indiana into the cornfield, 300 yards in front of them, where we were exposed to the fire of two pieces of artillery, supported by a regiment of infantry, about 100 yards distant. Our position here was in advance of that held by any other regiment in the army."

Enyart's men, Cruft noted approvingly, "made a gallant charge, and drove the enemy before it, rushing forward to the crest of the hill, clear beyond and to the right of the burnt house. The fire was so severe from the enemy's force at the burnt house, on the left, that the order to move up the 90th Ohio was countermanded; not, however, until many of the officers and men of this gallant regiment had pressed forward over the fence in line with the old 1st Kentucky."[20]

Fortunately for Garrity, the 9th/10th Mississippi arrived in time to provide support. "While here, a regiment of the enemy charged up the hill to take the battery but was repulsed in disorder by the fire of the artillery and from my regiment," White reported. "The enemy moved and attempted to take the battery and came within 40 or 50 yards of it when he was repulsed," Garrity recalled. The Alabamian saved his guns, but it came at a hefty cost, as the battery lost three men killed, 20 wounded, and 21 horses killed or disabled. Garrity himself was twice wounded, and one of his section commanders, Lieutenant Philip Bond, went down with three wounds.

After the repulse of the charge on Garrity's battery, White learned of Chalmers's wounding and looked around for the balance of the brigade; outside his own regiment, he could find no one. The Mississippians had lost more than 500 men in a little more than half an hour. The 7th and 41st Mississippi fell back to their original positions and waited for reinforcements while Blythe's Mississippians were pinned down near the Cowan House, unable to advance or retreat. As Withers made clear, upon the loss of Chalmers "this veteran brigade became disorganized and driven back."[21]

*   *   *

As Chalmers's men streamed back to their old entrenchments, Anderson's Brigade, comprised mostly of Mississippians, advanced across the Wilkinson Pike toward Stanley's and Miller's lines. Anderson had previously sent his left-flank

---

20 *OR* 20/1: 527, 536.

21 Ibid., 756; Smith, *Stones River: Confederate Army*, 660, 665.

regiments, the 45th Alabama and 24th Mississippi, forward to support one of Manigault's failed assaults on Sheridan, and now that he had reformed them, it was time to push the entire brigade forward. The line moved forward left to right: the 45th Alabama first, then the 24th Mississippi, followed in order by the 30th, 29th, and 27th Mississippi. Anderson sent his men forward with strict instructions to "preserve the touch of the elbow" during their attack and to swing toward the left, hoping to sweep Negley's men from their position.

Lieutenant Colonel Junius Scales of the 30th Mississippi considered the assault a "hopeless undertaking" but gamely led his men forward. "But a short distance was made before three men of Co. I were cut down," he wrote. "Every step from this time forth was marked by a terrific shower of grape, canister, and shell. Having to pass nearly 200 yards through thick woods, the line became somewhat disordered, but was promptly halted and reformed. Here again I received the order to take that battery at all hazards."[22]

Once Anderson's Mississippians crossed into the open cornfield, however, the advance crashed to a halt. John Roebuck of the 29th Mississippi recalled that "when we started across the field to make the charge, I thought those were the deepest middles between the corn rows that I had ever seen. The Yanks held their fire until we were within 30 yards of them and then they were ordered to fire. They were just mowing us down like weeds. We were ordered to fall down in order to escape their bullets, shells, and cannon balls. Then and there I changed my opinion about the middles—they were entirely too shallow."

Scales reported that "a large body of infantry in addition to the batteries on my flanks and front rained their leaden hail upon us. Men fell around on every side like autumn leaves and every foot of soil which we passed over seemed dyed with the life blood of someone. Still, no one faltered, but the whole line advanced boldly and swiftly to within 75 yards of the battery when the storm of death increased to such a fury that the regiment as if by instinct fell to the ground. I shouted 'forward' until I became hoarse but so deafening was the roar of artillery and musketry that nothing could be heard."

The neighboring 29th Mississippi, seeing Scales's men plunk to the ground, did likewise. "Having orders not to pass the 30th Mississippi, I ordered my command to lay down also," reported Colonel William Brantly. The explosion of a Federal

<hr>

22 OR 20/1:763; Smith, *Stones River: Confederate Army*, 671.

shell soon knocked him and his adjutant senseless, though, and "the regiment was repulsed with great loss."[23]

As the Confederate attack enveloped the position, the 11th Michigan found itself subjected to heavy fire both left and right. The regiment formed to the rear "under a galling fire and poured a well-directed fire into the advancing columns of the enemy and continued to load and fire with great coolness and bravery until the orders came to fall back," reported Colonel William Stoughton. Though in service since the outbreak of the war, the 18th Ohio had yet to take part in a large-scale engagement. "Now the moment had come for which we had been training for so many months," wrote Sergeant Launcelot Scott. "When the Rebels marched up to within 100 feet of us, we gave them such a well-aimed volley that they recoiled in confusion, but soon pluckily came to the attack again and then we played a deadly game of kill or be killed."

The Confederates targeted the gunners and horses of Battery M, and Captain Schultz fell wounded at the first fire. "When the Rebels got to within about 400 yards, we opened with canister in a lively manner," remembered gunner William Riniker. "It only seemed to check them for an instant and yelling like demons, they rushed up to the very muzzles of the guns."[24]

While Stanley's front-line regiments had their hands full battling wave after wave of Confederates, the ill-fated 69th Ohio—"much mortified at the conduct of their colonel and lieutenant colonel"—stood idly in the rear of the brigade waiting to be called upon like an errant schoolboy. The Ohioans took numerous casualties while waiting. Early on, Major Eli Hickcox's horse was shot from under him. He was so badly injured when the animal fell on him that he had little choice but to turn command over to his executive officer, Captain David Putnam. "The tops of the trees were falling and bombs bursting, grape, and canister plowing through the woods and the roar of musketry was dreadful," one lieutenant wrote. Captain James Hanna took in the nightmarish carnage: "riderless horses were galloping wildly over the field and shot and shell were now mowing our men down like weeds. Our condition was now truly a lamentable one as the enemy had a heavy force on our front and were closing in upon our right, having our division

23 Smith, *Stones River: Confederate Army*, 263, 760-61.

24 OR 20/1:426; Sergeant Launcelot L. Scott, Co. G, 18th Ohio, "Stone River," *National Tribune*, Apr. 23, 1903, 3; Account of Private William Riniker, Battery M, 1st Ohio Light Artillery, James Barnett Papers, WRHS.

surrounded. But we had no orders to retreat and should we receive such orders, we had no evidence that we could escape."[25]

On Miller's right, the 78th Pennsylvania held its fire until Anderson's Mississippians approached within 200 yards, then let loose. "The engagement here was fierce and bloody. I poured a terrific volley into their ranks, but as soon as one man was killed, another took his place," noted Colonel William Sirwell. "The enemy made a desperate charge, with heads down and bayonets glistening." The 37th Indiana, having advanced to receive Chalmers's attack, now pulled back in line with Sirwell's Pennsylvanians and opened fire on Anderson's advance. "The shells and balls were so thick that we could almost see them in the air," recalled Joshua Alfred of the 37th. "It was more like a thunderstorm than anything else only the balls hurt more than hail. The air was filled with bursting shells, bursting cannon balls roaring in the air, and cutting off whole tops of trees. It almost looked impossible for a man to get out alive."

Lieutenant Colonel William Ward of the 37th categorized the action as seesaw. "After a few volleys the command was given to charge which was promptly done and the Rebels driven back," he said. "They rallied and in turn drove us; we rallied and after a sharp encounter drove them again and held our position until our ammunition was exhausted."[26]

The 27th Mississippi was the last of Anderson's regiments to reach the open field and were the most exposed to Federal fire. They had jumped the gun earlier and marched into the field only to discover they were unsupported; the Mississippians promptly scampered back under cover before taking any losses. Now as they advanced in line while wheeling to the left with the rest of the brigade, the Mississippians observed Chalmers's 7th Mississippi retreating through the field to their right; they soon received heavy fire themselves. "A fierce engagement ensued," recalled Captain Andrew Jones.

Meanwhile, Colonel James Autry ordered his men to lie down "while he remained standing directing them where the enemy was," Anderson reported. "He then ordered us to take a battery which was pouring a murderous fire into our ranks when he was struck by a rifle ball and instantly killed." The commander's death, the

---

25 *OR* 20/1:430; "From the 69th Ohio," *Cadiz Sentinel*, Jan. 21, 1863, 3; 2nd Lt. William Larzalere, Co. F, 69th Ohio; *History and Biographical Encyclopedia of Butler County, Ohio* (Cincinnati, 1892), 249; Hanna Letter.

26 Gibson, *History of the 78th Pennsylvania*, 180; Private Joshua Alfred, Co. I, 37th Indiana, SRNBP; Lt. Col. William D. Ward, 37th Indiana, SRNBP.

general noted, brought their advance to a halt and "caused some confusion in the regiment until they were rallied and reformed."[27]

*   *   *

The combat was just as intense, if not as deadly, on the brigade's left, where the 45th Alabama and 24th Mississippi marched headlong into Stanley's two regiments and Battery M of the 1st Ohio Light. "For a moment these regiments appeared to reel and stagger before the weight of lead and iron that was hurled against them," Anderson wrote. Remembered Captain William Cunningham of the 24th Mississippi: "It was not long until we were in the midst of it and the fight became general. Our brigade charged two of their batteries not with bayonets but by advancing and shooting."[28]

The ground before the 19th Illinois "was thick strewn with dead and wounded," wrote Henry Haynie. "Struck horses, no longer neighing or whinnying, were agonizing in their frantic cries. Cannon balls cut down trees around and over us which, falling, crushed living and dead alike. 'Steady men, steady,' sang out Colonel Joseph Scott which the company officers repeated. Some in the ranks were shouting challenges to the fighters across that deadly field. 'Why don't you come over and take us into camp? Hey Johnny, step along this way a little quicker! Ah yes, Massa Reb, very well aimed but it never touched me.' We hugged Mother Earth, firing low in a determined effort to stay the onrushing tide of gray." In the bitter face-to-face fighting, the 460-man 24th Mississippi lost a quarter of its number; the 45th Alabama lost 84 men, and the 19th Illinois roughly 80.[29]

Battery G's gunners continued to pound round after round of canister into the advancing Confederates. Sergeant Clarence Riddle, commanding one of the pieces, wrote that they "when our guns were playing on them, we could see the canister sweep a space ten feet wide through their ranks, piling them up in winnows, but they would close up in a moment and press speedily upon us. It was a pretty tough fight. I went in with eight cannoneers and came out with but three. My horse was shot out from under me in the fore part of the fight, but it was no place to flinch

27 Smith, *Stones River: Confederate Army*, 669; OR 20/1:764.

28 OR 20/1:764; Captain William H. Cunningham, Co. I, 24th Mississippi, *Macon Beacon*, Feb. 4, 1863, 2.

29 Haynie, *The 19th Illinois*, 180-181; Adjutant W. W. Robinson, 24th Mississippi, *Mobile Advertiser & Register*, Jan. 17, 1863, 1.

and when the cannoneers were shot, I took their places. I acted in three men's places. The balls came thick and fast about my head and I could see men fall all around me and expected every moment to take my turn."[30]

Scales desperately tried to get his 30th Mississippi to move. "Asking several around me to aid in shouting, W. J. McGregor, an old man of Co. A, came forward and after shouting 'forward' at the top of his lungs in vain, he marched ahead of the line crying 'follow me boys, follow me!' He then marched among the officers shouting 'the colonel commands forward.' This was repeated by them but was lost amidst the clashing thunder around us. To lie there was death to the last man. But my order to retreat repeated again and again met with the same fate. Finally, by giving the order to individuals and causing them to give it in their turn, a retreat was effected."[31]

As elsewhere, dead and wounded men carpeted the ground: 62 killed and 139 wounded from the 30th Mississippi alone. The 29th Mississippi lost 34 killed and had 202 wounded, the second highest number of any Confederate regiment in the battle, and "all within a very short space of time and upon an area not greater than an acre of ground," Anderson noted. John Simmons of the 27th Mississippi recalled that "in the confusion and excitement, the men had fallen in every conceivable position, many on top and across their fellow comrades. Some had attempted to drag themselves and had died in the attempt. I believe I saw as much of the war as any man in it, but I never in all the war saw as many dead men of one single command in so small a space as I did there on the plains of Murfreesboro."[32]

The repulse of two determined Confederate assaults elated the Federals. Sergeant Robert Caldwell of the 21st Ohio wrote that the battle was "truly sublime, the fierce roar of the artillery and sharp rattle of musketry made an almost indescribable din. I had the pleasure of firing about 10 rounds and I flatter myself that I never pulled the trigger without first getting good sight." "[T]he battle," Miller noted, "continued with unabating fierceness on both sides until the 60 rounds of ammunition with which my men were supplied were nearly exhausted." The 37th Indiana ran out first and pulled out of line, heading back into the woods in search of the brigade's ordnance train. In the meantime, Miller reshuffled his line

---

30 Sergeant Clarence L. Riddle, Battery G, 1st Ohio Light Artillery, *Jeffersonian Democrat*, Jan. 23, 1863, 2.

31 Smith, *Stones River: Confederate Army*, 761.

32 OR 20/1:764; Private John W. Simmons, Co. E, 27th Mississippi, *Attala Ledger*, May 1897.

Brigadier General Alexander P. Stewart

Library of Congress

while Anderson regrouped his brigade as the two lines kept up an incessant long-range fire punctuated by artillery fire.[33]

A few minutes later, Colonel Hull led the 37th Indiana back into the fight with the disturbing intelligence that the ordnance wagons had fled to the Nashville Pike. The firing to Miller's right was a constant roar as Sheridan's ranks made their last stand against overwhelming odds. As Sheridan's men fired their last cartridges, however, they were forced to retreat under heavy fire from Cheatham's Division. With Sheridan's hold broken, Negley's situation became critical; to be sure, the general was in the middle of a Confederate nutcracker. Sheridan's retreat left Negley's right and rear exposed to an attack from the Wilkinson Pike. Coming into line in pursuit of Sheridan's division was Stewart's stalwart Tennessee brigade immediately behind Anderson's men. The 37th Indiana fired its last shots, then pulled back into the cedars a second time, leaving Miller with three regiments to hold the critical position.[34]

A. P. Stewart's Brigade witnessed the decimation of Anderson's command from Anderson's old breastworks only a few hundred yards away. Known by his nickname "Old Straight," Stewart had already gained a reputation as a dependable soldier and an outstanding combat leader. A fellow cadet in Rosecrans's Class of 1842 at West Point, Stewart resigned his commission just before the outbreak of the Mexican War to take a professorship in both mathematics and natural/ experimental philosophy at Cumberland (Tennessee) University. A Whig politically, he disagreed with secession but took up the cause of his native state and

---

33 Robert H. Caldwell, Papers, MS-623. CAC, BGSU; *OR* 20/1:432.

34 *OR* 20/1:432, 724.

first saw action at the battle of Belmont (Missouri) in November 1861. Stewart proved to be a gifted soldier, earning his brigadier's star, and leading this same brigade of infantry in Polk's Corps at Shiloh, where it struck the Hornet's Nest. Stewart's veterans were again in the thick of the fight at Perryville—universally considered a crack, cohesive unit under a trusted leader.[35]

Stewart's four regiments deployed with the 19th Tennessee on the brigade's left, the 31st/33rd Tennessee at left center, the 24th Tennessee at right center, and the 4th/5th Tennessee the right. Even hunkered down behind Anderson's breastworks, Stewart's men began to drop, as grapeshot and canister landed in their midst—the 19th Tennessee taking the worst of it. "The regiment halted for half an hour or more under a heavy fire from some unseen batteries in our front," reported Colonel Francis Walker. "At this point, while my men were lying behind the loose wall of rock, a shell struck the latter near the center of my left wing, wounding, by the fragments of shell and shattered rock, six of my men, all of whom were disabled and one of whom soon after died."[36]

By 11:00 a.m., Sheridan was pulling back, and Negley's men had reached the end of their tether, too. Nevertheless, at this critical moment, the Confederate front was also in disarray. Anderson's men were fought out, and Maney's and Manigault's brigades to Stewart's left had suffered heavily in their previous attempts to break the Union lock on the position. It fell to Stewart to break that lock and fervently pursue any retreat. The ground in front of them was hardly encouraging, littered with hundreds of dead and wounded from the previous failed attacks in this sector.

"The 29th and 30th Mississippi regiments fell back in disorder," Stewart recalled, "leaving a large number of dead and wounded in the open ground beyond the Wilkinson pike, over which they had charged. They were rallied in our rear chiefly by Major Luke Finlay, of my staff, and again sent forward. The brigade moved on from this position to the pike, where it was faced by the left flank and marched a short distance down the road, to bring its right under cover of the woods, when it moved again to the front."[37]

By shifting to the left, Stewart not only provided his men some cover, but he also avoided the ghastly spectacle of trying to march over Anderson's hecatomb

---

35 Ezra J. Warner, *Generals in Gray: Lives of the Confederate Commanders* (Baton Rouge, 1959), 293-94.

36 *OR* 20/1:728.

37 Ibid., 724.

north of the Wilkinson Pike. "It crossed the open ground intervening between the pike and the cedar forest beyond," he would write, "and advanced to the relief of the front line, which was giving way, and by a rapid fire repulsed the enemy, who fled in confusion to the dense cedar woods, leaving many dead and wounded behind." Stewart's men arrived in the nick of time, as Anderson's line was wavering badly under the blistering fire. Walker noted that "we could distinctly see by the action of the men in the front line that they were on the eve of being driven back if, indeed, they had not already entirely given away. Many were falling back and all seemed disorganized."[38]

The spectacle as the Tennesseans crossed the Wilkinson Pike was gut-wrenching. "Numbers of dead and wounded were lying about, both Confederates and Federals," Walker lamented. "Pushing forward, we crossed the field and entered the thick cedar woods in which the enemy had taken shelter. In the edge of this wood, we came up with three or four pieces of the battery which they had vainly endeavored to withdraw." Stewart's men may have been delighted to secure the prize, but Old Straight ordered them to keep driving into the woods. "We left them behind, and, pressing rapidly forward, drove the enemy before us," Walker added. "As we entered the woods, the enemy gave us a most galling fire but we moved steadily forward, driving them further into the thick wood."[39]

The Confederates, wrote Ira Gillaspie, "had driven back the right wing of our army clear back in the rear of us so as to give the Rebels a raking fire across on us, just mowing our men down. Colonel Stanley and General Negley seemed everywhere cheering and encouraging the men." As it approached 11:00 a.m., Sergeant Scott of the 18th Ohio crouched behind a dead horse from one of Sheridan's batteries, recalling, "The other horse received a ball and commenced plunging then he fell and balanced on the tongue. I lay ready to spring if he should roll towards me. Fortunately, he turned the other way and died, his blood pouring out on a dead cannoneer."[40]

By now, Negley's two brigades were down to their last rounds and nervously felt surrounded, eying the rear, where they heard the roar of musketry. The artillery horses, Negley recalled, "were nearly all killed or wounded and my ammunition train had been sent back to avoid capture. A heavy column of the enemy was marching directly to our rear through the cedars and communications with General

---

38 Ibid., 724, 728.

39 Ibid.

40 Weber, *From Michigan to Murfreesboro*, 43; Scott Memoir.

Brigadier General James S. Negley

Library of Congress

Rosecrans and Thomas … entirely cut off. It was manifestly impossible for my command to hold the position without eventually making a hopeless, fruitless sacrifice of the whole division." That said, Negley decided he had no choice but to retreat and cut his way through the swarming Confederates if necessary.[41]

His men believed they were winning the battle, however, and protested Negley's retreat order. "Boys you have pluck," the general reportedly said. "I believe you would be shot down before a man of you would retreat in disorder or retreat at all without an order," Gillaspie claimed. "Here General Rousseau rode up and said that a regiment was holding a point on our right was out of ammunition and he wanted somebody to take their place." The 11th Michigan marched to the right to assist Rousseau, but the greater danger lurked in Stanley's front, now being held by just two regiments and supported by the shaky 69th Ohio.

One of Negley's aides galloped up to Colonel Scott of the 19th Illinois under a storm of bullets. Explained Haynie: "'Colonel Scott, General Negley's compliments, and orders your battalion to hurry to the support of yonder guns,' pointing as he spoke to where Schultz's battery was feebly blasting away. No sooner were the words uttered than Colonel Scott, springing to his feet, sang out 'Attention Nineteenth! Dress on the left. Front! Forward, left oblique, march!' The sharp order was repeated along a regimental line and off we rushed. We presently found ourselves just behind all that was left of that battery." J. M. Tracy of the 19th reported that his regiment marched over the prone riflemen of both the 18th Ohio

41 OR 20/1:407-408.

and 27th Illinois "as coolly as though on dress parade while Scott rode at the head of the column amidst a storm of shot and shell."[42]

The Illinoisans found Schultz's men firing three cannons, but "nearly all the gunners were down and out and not a horse was fit for use," Haynie noted. "Those of the 19th who knew how to load and fire cannon sprang to the help of those surviving artillerymen. The order to fire followed quick and soon messages of destruction were hurled into soldiers not 200 yards away." The 31st/33rd Tennessee, with 379 men in its ranks, spied the slackening fire of the Ohioans and charged to capture the pieces. "We had advanced but a short distance until we came upon the battery which had been playing upon us all the time after leaving the breastworks and the infantry concealed in the woods," remembered Colonel Egbert Tansil. "One volley from our well-aimed pieces caused them to abandon two pieces of artillery which they were trying to get off and threw the enemy into confusion who commenced retreating immediately."[43]

Haynie wrote that "then came a piteous appeal from a wounded artillery officer not to let a single gun be captured, and several men of the regiment dragged the two pieces remaining on wheels into the woods to where we were now falling back. By this time, the enemy was so close that we could smell their burning powder and see into their exulting eyes." William Riniker of Battery M wrote that "the surface of the ground being uneven and rocky made the work of getting out the cedars very difficult. General Negley appeared on the scene and by his coolness and daring prevented a panic. The enemy already had possession of one gun when brave Corporal William Rettberg, while attempting to spike the second one, fell riddled with bullets. Before he expired, he was bayonetted several times."

"[W]ord came that we were surrounded and cut off and must cut our way out," Tracy remembered. "We faced about, formed column, and rushed into the cedar swamp with fixed bayonets. Fortunately, the Rebels had left us a little space to get out of and we rushed through and formed on the left of Sheridan."[44]

The arrival of Stewart's 1,635 Tennesseans posed an insurmountable problem for Negley, as he lacked the numerical strength or ammunition to hold them back. Confederate artillery fire only added to Negley's consternation. The rifled section

---

42 Weber, *From Michigan to Murfreesboro*, 43-44; Haynie, *The 19th Illinois*, 187; Private J. M. Tracy, Co. D, 19th Illinois, *Chicago Tribune*, Jan. 26, 1863, 2.

43 Haynie, *The 19th Illinois,* 188; OR 20/1:731.

44 Haynie, *The 19th Illinois*, 188; Riniker Letter; Tracy Letter. Battery M expended 750 rounds during the battle and lost only a single gun (captured).

of Stanford's Mississippi Battery from Stewart's Brigade rolled into the fields north of the Wilkinson Pike and opened fire, taking special aim at the little, red-daubed log house that lay right behind Miller's line. "Arriving in position in time to observe the enemy and the repulse of our forces at the same time, I threw a few well-directed shots into their ranks which caused them to retreat precipitately," reported Captain Thomas Stanford.

It was a grand spectacle. "Heavy clouds of white smoke rose from the fields and dense cedars," remembered gunner William Brown. "In the midst of those clouds we could see many quick flashes and white caps of smoke from the bursting shells. Now and then came the cheering of our men as they charged again and again on the lines of the Federals hidden in the thick cedar groves. With such a terrible anxiety did we stand by our horses and gaze on that sublime scene."[45]

In response to Stewart's advance, the 18th Ohio redeployed to the left to buttress Miller's embattled position. "When moving in that direction, a very considerable consternation was observed among our forces, many of the regiments moving to the rear," observed Lt. Col. Josiah Given. He continued:

> Observing that a regiment still held the position, I moved rapidly to its rear; that regiment was lying down, so that my men were enabled to remain in their rear and engage in the firing. By the combined efforts of the forces there, the enemy was driven from the woods, but very soon a piece of artillery was brought into position against us. I hastened to where our battery was, to ask that it might be brought to bear against the enemy's piece that was then doing fearful havoc among our ranks. I learned that for want of ammunition none of our pieces were available. In the midst of this terrible fire, I received your order to fall back, which I did, my men preserving perfect order.[46]

By this time the 11th Michigan had returned to Stanley's line. Negley rode up to the men and, according to Gillaspie, said, "'We are in a tight place and must retreat, but if you follow me, I will take you out. We are almost surrounded and we must cut our way out with fire, if necessary.' We commenced our retreat in perfect order, loading and firing as we went through the cedars."

The retreat through the cedars was remembered as a kaleidoscope of hellish scenes. Colonel William Stoughton of the 11th Michigan understated the case when he reported "some confusion was at first manifested. A large number of

---

45 OR 20/1:732; Dixon, *Civil War Travels of William A. Brown.*

46 OR 20/1:428.

regiments had fallen back here for protection and the enemy's artillery and infantry opened on us from all sides except to our left towards the Murfreesboro Pike." Daniel Rose of the 11th Michigan wrote that "several times we changed front to rear and charged back upon the advancing foe. The forest was thick with killed and wounded soldiers showing that that the fighting here had been desperate and the same ground had been fought over by friend and foe." And, Gillaspie noted, "the Rebels followed us so close in the rear that they were pouring a deadly fire into our ranks. We loaded, fixed bayonets, about-faced, and poured out a very destructive fire, sending many of the traitors to Mother Earth and putting the rest to a halt."[47]

As Stanley's men pulled back into the cedar forest, an unidentified staff officer galloped up to Colonel Sirwell and ordered the Pennsylvanians to retreat from their commanding hill position. Although incredulous, Sirwell promptly obeyed. Fortunately, Miller witnessed the blunder, but while riding back to the regiment to countermand the order, he received a severe neck wound. With blood pouring down his coat, the colonel ordered the 78th to fight its way back onto the hillock, as the Confederates were closing quickly. The wounded Miller attempted to change fronts and direct the balance of his brigade to the south to receive Stewart's assault. With the difficult movement almost complete, he received a belated order from Negley directing him to retire his brigade through the cedars. "The movement was executed in good order by the infantry, but it was impossible for the artillery to obey," Miller would note in his report.[48]

Marshall's Battery G lost a large number of horses and had two guns disabled. The lieutenant ordered the disabled pieces to the rear but ordered the remaining four guns to "fix prolonge and fire retiring." The retreat played out under a relentless fire, with Marshall later writing that his horse was "shot through the hips, neck, and forelegs before he had time to fall. I had four men killed, eight wounded, and 34 horses killed in 20 minutes time all by musketry. We lost five men killed, four guns, two caissons, and 46 horses lost. Thirty-two horses out of 36 were killed on the guns alone, the caissons being under cover of a thicket to the rear. We had a rather tough time in the battle before this place."[49]

---

47 Weber, *From Michigan to Murfreesboro*, 44; *OR* 20/1:426; Private Daniel D. Rose, Co. A, 11th Michigan, "Stones River," *National Tribune,* Nov. 13, 1884, 3.

48 *OR* 20/1:414.

49 Ibid., 432-433; Lieutenant Alexander Marshall, Battery G, 1st Ohio Light Artillery, *Cleveland Morning Leader,* Feb. 16, 1863, 1.

The 78th Pennsylvania accompanied the battery for a time, but so many horses had been shot down that Marshall was forced to abandon three pieces. "As we left the open fields, our eyes looked upon the most terrific scene of slaughter we were ever called upon to witness," wrote one soldier. "The artillery of the enemy was doing fearful execution. We saw one shell explode exactly in the line of the regiment to our left, killing at least three men."

Despite the incessant fire, a determined artilleryman attempted to recover one of the abandoned guns. "One of the last sights witnessed as we entered the cedar woods in our retreat was an artilleryman trying to haul his gun off the field with one horse, the other five being killed," recalled a member of the 78th Pennsylvania. "One wheel of the carriage had become fastened between two rocks, and the brave artilleryman was trying with a rail to pry it out."[50]

The dark woods filled with Federal troops streaming away from the Confederate divisions closing on three sides. The 37th Indiana managed to maintain order briefly but disintegrated once it became entangled in the cedars. "We were broken up by a regiment passing through our lines," Colonel Ward relayed. "We again collected our men when the 11st Michigan passed through our lines, causing some confusion." Rallying his regiment again, Colonel Hull marched his men out at the double-quick before he was struck down by a musket ball in his left hip, leaving more than 100 men casualties in the cedar forest. With the withdrawal of the 78th Pennsylvania and 37th Indiana, the 74th Ohio was also compelled to retreat. Battling Anderson's men, Lieutenant David Snodgrass of Company H clapped his hands and cheered his men on, saying, "Work away, my lads, we are gaining ground!" Within moments, he was wounded. The Ohioans were horrified when they looked behind them and saw yelping Confederates rapidly gaining their rear. They broke.[51]

Within the cedars, Colonel Moody attempted to rally his 74th Ohio, sometimes at gunpoint but with little success. "I rode on in search of further squads and as I neared a wooded region, nine or ten graybacks sprang out of the woods and opened fire on me," he would write. "My horse was soon crippled, stopped short, and stood still. I applied the spurs; he trembled and shrunk, and fell in agony on the ground, dead." Pulling himself from under the animal, the Ohioan grabbed his two pistols and hobbled toward the Nashville Pike. A few minutes later, an Irish private from his regiment rode up to the colonel on a captured horse. "Devil a bit; try again

---

50 *OR* 20/1:414, 432-433; Gibson, *History of the 78th Pennsylvania*, 53.

51 *OR* 20/1:437-439.

Colonel," he declared. "Try again, man or the devils will get ye, sure!" I tried again and the Patty almost lifted me into the saddle, and amidst the zipping bullets, which came thick and fast, I strode the saddle, and without waiting to find the stirrups, started for our lines."[52]

After taking part in the mauling of Chalmers's Brigade, the 21st Ohio pulled back to the edge of the cedar forest and fought until it witnessed the 74th Ohio's retreat. Orders soon arrived to fall back. As Samuel Linton of Company I headed into the woods, he became separated from his company and found himself surrounded by the enemy. "Soon there came a fire from the right, this said to me git, and for the first twenty rods I just wiggled my toes and flew," he wrote. "I found nothing in my way that I could not get over. The Rebs were helping me by their yells and cries of 'Halt you damn Yankee son of a bitch, run Yank, Bull Run, git thar damn you!' I knew they had just fired and if I could outrun them, I stood a good chance of getting out.[53]

Most of the 21st Ohio formed into column and marched from the field, but a few men stayed behind unintentionally. "My comrade John Shelly and I did not hear the order to about face and march to the rear we were so busily engaged in loading and firing that we were unconscious of our surroundings until we were ordered to surrender by a Rebel officer," Sergeant Bolton noted. "But both of us delivered a hurried shot at them and ran at the top of our speed through a volley of musket fire and succeeded in getting to our regiment with no marks or wounds, but our clothing was in different places pierced with musket balls."

The men who stayed together eluded most of the Confederate fire, but it was a close call. "How we got back through the cedars I can never tell, except that we walked—we didn't run," recalled Silas Canfield. "In falling back, the men of the regiment became badly scattered and mixed with other commands." During the confusion, an unfortunate private driving the regimental ambulance was captured and recaptured three times in an hour.[54]

Ellsworth's bloodied battery was the last unit of Miller's brigade to leave the field. "I noticed that our infantry and artillery were retiring at the same time that a heavy fire was being poured into our right, and almost into our rear," he reported. "Receiving no orders to retire, I made the change of position of the battery to the left and opened fire on the enemy. I soon found it impossible to do more without

---

52 Blackburn, *Letters from the Front*, 100.

53 Linton Memoir.

54 Bolton Diary, 83; Canfield, *History of the 21st Ohio*, 74.

losing the whole battery, and ordered it limbered to the rear, and retired into the cedar thicket." His gunners left one cannon and caisson on the field after expending 493 rounds of ammunition.

Clarence Marsh of Battery G attributed the escape of the batteries to reinforcements from Rousseau's division. "They gave it to us from three sides—right, rear, and front, and at one time they had Negley's division completely surrounded," he wrote. "I thought then that we would all be killed or taken prisoners. Never did bullets come thicker. Shells would come screaming through the air and they couldn't burst without killing some of us for they had us all in a huddle in a cedar wood. But we were soon reinforced from our left who made a hole for us to get out of."[55]

The shattered 29th Mississippi, now under the command of Lt. Col. James Morgan, attached itself to the left of Stewart's advance and managed to claim one of Battery G's 12-pounder Wiard rifles that had devastated the regiment only an hour before. Lieutenant Colonel Robert McKelvaine of the 24th Mississippi recalled that as his men entered the cedars, "General Patton Anderson dashed in front of my line and with his hat off called for the Mississippians to follow him." The 27th Mississippi charged into Miller's old position and discovered Ellsworth's battery attempting to withdraw—the withdrawal covered by a batch of Federals nested in a log cabin and firing through various openings in the structure. "We charged them," recalled Captain Jones, "and the whole party of 35–40 men including the officers was captured along with the battery and a stand of colors, a wagon and team, and an ambulance with mules, harness, etc. complete."[56]

Miller briefly rallied the brigade within the cedars. "He was like a lion in the toils," recalled Wilson Vance, his orderly. "While he never lost his head or forgot what he was doing, he raged and flashed through the cedars like a very god of war. His blood was up. He reluctantly gave the order to fall back, but in a moment a noble repentance seized upon him, and grasping a flag from a color sergeant, he sprang upon a rock, waved it over his head and called upon his men. 'Rally here men! If we cannot whip them, we can at least show them how men can die!'" The effect was electrical. From across the field came the shout, "There's John F, there's John F!" Miller pulled together a scratch line; the men dropped to their knees and

<hr>

55 OR 20/1:411-412; Private Clarence L. Marsh, Battery G, 1st Ohio Light Artillery, *Jeffersonian Democrat*, Feb. 6, 1863, 4.

56 Smith, *Stones River: Confederate Army*, 668-69. The 27th Mississippi captured a 6-pounder smoothbore from Ellsworth's battery.

opened fire. "The effect of this unexpected rally and sudden and heavy firing was to temporarily check the legions of Confederates. They did not know what to make of it and the low-hanging smoke was so thick they could not see."[57]

The tangle of the cedars justifiably disorganized many of the men who entered. Brigades and regiments fell apart; frightened men were found hiding behind trees or hiding down in sinkholes to save themselves from the wildly ricocheting bullets that struck down soldiers regardless of the color of their uniform. The 7th Mississippi moved into the cedars but immediately ran into a storm of fire and promptly lost Colonel William Bishop to a wound. "After driving the enemy from the field, we entered a dense cedar thicket where we again engaged the enemy who continued to fall back before us," reported Lt. Col. Benjamin Johns. "Upon taking command of the regiment, I found myself in another brigade which upon inquiring I found to be General [S.A.M.] Wood's. I therefore continued to act in concert with this brigade until it was withdrawn from the fight."[58]

The 9th/10th Mississippi remained under cover near the Cowan House, but observing the Federals retreating from the woods, Colonel White ordered his men to their feet in pursuit. "I moved my regiment to the left where the firing was loudest and passing through the cedar thicket into which the enemy was pouring a heavy fire of shell and grapeshot we captured and sent to the rear some half dozen prisoners whom I found attempting to conceal themselves among the rocks," he recalled. "I also found troops on the opposite side of the thicket firing at the enemy across an open field and joined in the fight. They seemed to be composed of parts of different commands and without any particular leader."[59]

The advancing Confederate line detained prisoners from Sheridan's and Negley's divisions by the hundreds throughout the forest. "Our regiment was obliged to retreat in perfect confusion," remembered Sidney Brewster of the 21st Ohio. "I couldn't bear the idea of being shot in the back so I took my position behind a cedar and resolved to give them the best I had. But it was all in vain. They were too many for us and it was too late to retreat by this time. The rest of the troops had got out of sight except a few of us that was playing Indian on them. I started to run but they were too close to us. The bullets whistled around us from every side. I jumped into a large hole which happened to be nearby. In a moment,

---

57 Vance, *Stones River*, 352.

58 Smith, *Stones River: Confederate Army*, 659-60.

59 Ibid.

Private Sidney Brewster,
Co. C, 21st Ohio Infantry

*Center for Archival Collections,
Bowling Green State University*

about 20 Rebels came up and demanded me to surrender, which I was obliged to do or die. I preferred to surrender."[60]

Exiting the woods under fire, Vance was riding at Miller's side when they spied one of Miller's orderlies, Nicholas Vail of the 19th Illinois, staggering between the lines apparently dazed. "Poor Nick had been shot right plumb in the crazy bone," Vance recalled. "His blood-drenched sleeve showed that he was wounded and his actions were those of a man demented. It seemed as if his elbow joint was shattered. He certainly was a wild man and extremely difficult to handle."

Vance dismounted and, "by dint of arguing with the crazy fellow and hard pushing, lifting, and shoving, finally had the sufferer in the saddle. I smote the little mare with the flat of a saber a resounding thwack across the rump which sent her careening forward after the vanishing bluecoats." When he turned around, he spotted the surging Confederates mere yards away howling for his surrender before sending "a storm of bullets about my ears, they were so close I could almost discern the color of their eyes." It was at this moment, he recalled that "began a mad chase for life. I ran as I never ran before,"

and it was not an easy matter to run at all. The low-hanging cedar boughs struck me and scratched my face while the little boulders tripped me up and the big ones placed

60 Private Sidney Brewster, Co. C, 21st Ohio Volunteer Infantry, MS-1066 Sidney Brewster Papers, CAC, BGSU.

themselves in my blind spot to be fallen over. To cap the climax and complete my embarrassment, the great cavalry saber which in my boyish ardor I had buckled on kept thrusting itself between my legs. It seemed that from one cause or another I tumbled down at every other step."

Flopping head over heels, clumsy "great cavalry saber" notwithstanding, the 17-year-old orderly dodged Southern lead and escaped the cedars. In 1897, he was awarded the Medal of Honor for saving Nicholas Vail's life.[61]

61 Vance, *Stones River*, 354-55.

Confederate High Tide

BY LATE MORNING on December 31, the mood at Braxton Bragg's headquarters on the Nashville Pike—just two miles southeast of Rosecrans's base of operations—bordered on jubilant. With his guns busily firing away at the Federals near the Round Forest, Corporal Benjamin Butt of Stanford's Mississippi Battery recalled a visit from Bragg and Leonidas Polk. "Bragg's hard, grim visage was wreathed in smiles as he announced to us that we had taken all the enemy's batteries on our left and that Hardee was driving them like sheep," Butt would write gleefully. Noted Colonel Urquhart on Bragg's staff: "Our attack had pivoted the Federals on their center, bending back their line as one half shuts a knife-blade. At 12 o'clock, we had a large part of the field with many prisoners, cannon, guns, ammunition, wagons, and the dead and wounded of both armies."[1]

Although McCook's Right Wing had been swept from the field and the Federal center was cracked, more than a third of Rosecrans's army had yet to be engaged. And, as historian Thomas L. Connelly astutely pointed out, though it "appeared that Bragg was on the verge of complete victory, [his] success was more illusory than genuine. He had gained the captured ground at an awful cost. Both Hardee's and Polk's corps were shattered." Fellow historian Stanley Horn proffered that "if [Carter] Stevenson's absent division could have been thrown into action at this

1 Butt Letter; Urquhart, *Battles & Leaders*, Vol. 3, 606.

juncture, it would probably have pulverized the Federal defense—a wishful thought that flashed through many Confederate minds that day."[2]

"The resistance of the enemy after the first surprise was most gallant and obstinate," Bragg conceded. "We succeeded in driving him from every position except the strong one held by his extreme left flank resting on Stones River. He was enabled to bring fresh troops at every point to resist our progress and he did so with a skill and judgment which has ever characterized this able commander." Indeed, the challenges of the ground and the potency of the Federal artillery forced Bragg's infantry into repeated costly charges against strongly defended positions that gutted the divisions.

According to Grady McWhiney, one of the general's biographers, Bragg realized soon after 10:00 a.m. "that the Confederate assault had lost much of its early drive." He also knew "several units were out of ammunition while others were intermingled and disorganized and nearly everyone who had been in action and was still alive was either wounded or exhausted. If the Federals were to be crushed," wrote McWhiney, "Bragg decided he must use Breckinridge's troops."[3]

John C. Breckinridge's four brigades in his 7,000-man division were holding the army's right flank east of Stones River. They were all veteran troops, some having first tasted combat at Shiloh. In addition, John Jackson's independent brigade, 874 officers and men, was also east of the river under Breckinridge's command. All told, these roughly 8,000 men represented Bragg's only ready reserve. To break the Federal line along the Nashville Pike, and specifically at the Round Forest, Bragg needed all of them on the other bank. The problem, however, was twofold and would take time to resolve. Not only were Breckinridge's troops on the wrong side of the river, but the former vice president-turned-general was loathe to part with them, convinced as he was that the Federals were moving to attack his position from the Lebanon Turnpike.

The root of Breckinridge's concern was Van Cleve's abortive effort against Bragg's right that morning. Van Cleve had moved two of his three brigades across the river about 8:00 a.m., deploying them into line, and his skirmishers and Breckinridge's even clashed briefly. Shortly after 10, Breckinridge messaged Bragg

---

2   Thomas Connelly, *Autumn of Glory: The Army of Tennessee, 1862-1865* (Baton Rouge, 1971), 56; Horn, *Army of Tennessee*, 202. Connelly disagreed with Horn's contention that Stevenson's Division would have tipped the balance, arguing that "how well Bragg would have done with Stevenson's help might be indicated by the poor use he made of the reinforcements he did have."

3   *OR* 20/1:665; McWhiney, *Braxton Bragg and Confederate Defeat*, 357-58.

that "the enemy are undoubtedly advancing upon me. The Lebanon road is unprotected, and I have no troops to fill out my line to it." Apparently, messages from both parties crossed, as about 10:30 a.m., Colonel J. Stoddard Johnston, a volunteer aide on Bragg's staff, arrived with an order directing Breckinridge to send one brigade west of the river to support Hardee's advance, seemingly ignoring what Breckinridge had just communicated.

Breckinridge, it seems, misunderstood Bragg's order, later reporting that the commander suggested he "move against the enemy instead of awaiting his attack. I preferred to fight on the ground I then occupied, but supposing that the object of the general was to create a diversion in favor of our left, my line, except Hanson's brigade, was put in motion in the direction from which the enemy was supposed to be advancing." The Kentuckian's interpretation of Bragg's order meant Adams's, Palmer's, and Preston's brigades advancing east of Stones River against what had been Van Cleve's early-morning position.[4]

Van Cleve, though, had hastily withdrawn his brigades across the river, leaving a single brigade (Colonel Price's) to cover McFadden's Ford from the western bank. This removed any immediate threat to Breckinridge, but for some reason his command did not proceed with any urgency, and when Colonel Johnston arrived with revised orders about 11:30 a.m., the men had advanced scarcely a half-mile. Johnston directed Breckinridge now to transfer two brigades west of the river to reinforce Polk's advance. That brought a fretful response from Breckinridge: "I am obeying your order, but my left is now engaged with the enemy, and if I advance my whole line farther forward and still retain communication with my left, it will take me clear away from the Lebanon road and expose my right and that road to a heavy force of the enemy advancing from [Dr.] Black's [residence]."[5]

Breckinridge directed Adams's and Jackson's brigades to start across Stones River, though the column had not gone far before it was halted again. Bragg reported he received what proved an errant report that "a heavy force of the enemy's infantry was advancing on the Lebanon road, about five miles in Breckinridge's front." Added Bragg: "General John Pegram, who had been sent to that road to cover the flank of the infantry with his cavalry brigade was ordered forward immediately to develop any such movement. The orders for the two

4 OR 20/1:665, 783.

5 Ibid., 665, 783. Dr. Black's residence stood at the intersection of the Lebanon Road and a road trace between Jefferson and Las Casas just north of the East Fork of Stones River, about 6½ miles north of Murfreesboro.

brigades from Breckinridge were countermanded, while dispositions were made, at his request, to reinforce him."

Whether Bragg had finally received Breckinridge's 10:10 a.m. dispatch reporting the enemy in his front or if it had been a separate communication from Pegram's troopers is uncertain. Regardless, the net impact was that Breckinridge's two brigades were halted, sitting for nearly two hours while the generals attempted to determine what was happening. It proved a crucial delay.[6]

Also interrupted was Breckinridge's advance east of the river, as he awaited reinforcements that Bragg had promised. "It is not certain that the enemy are advancing upon me in two lines," Breckinridge finally confessed in another message to Bragg at 12:50 p.m. "General Pegram promised to report the true condition of things. The two brigades you ordered to me might be held at the ford of the river, subject to further developments. If necessary, I could get them into position from that point before the enemy could reach me."

It was not until after 1:00 p.m. that Bragg and Breckinridge finally realized they were chasing phantoms when Pegram's cavalrymen reported there were no Federals east of the river. A bitter Breckinridge "regretted that sufficient care was not taken by the authors of the reports to discriminate rumor from fact," and Bragg was irate "that the only enemy in our immediate front was a small body of sharpshooters, and that there was no advance on the Lebanon road. These unfortunate misapprehensions on that part of the field (which, with proper precaution, could not have existed) withheld from active operations three fine brigades until the enemy had succeeded in checking our progress, had re-established his lines, and had collected many of his broken battalions."

The errors meant the reinforcements Hardee and Polk desperately needed to capitalize on their hard-won successes would not be in position to attack until nearly 2:00 p.m., giving the Federals two critical hours to solidify their new positions along the Nashville Pike. Meanwhile, both armies continued to wage a bitter fight for control of the cedar brake and the Round Forest.[7]

*　　*　　*

Rousseau's 1st Division in Thomas's corps departed the Nashville Pike about 9:00 a.m. that New Year's Eve. "Soon after taking our position in a low, level

---

6 OR 20/1:665, 783.

7 Ibid., 666, 783.

bottom covered with a dense forest of cedars, there was read at the head of every regiment the order of General Rosecrans encouraging the men to keep cool and aim low in the impending conflict," recalled Captain William W. Cockrum of the 42nd Indiana. Regarding his regiment, Cockrum also invoked a ghost of Hoosier state history during the Mexican War. "Our Colonel James Shanklin told us to remember Buena Vista and wipe out the foul stain cast on our state by that arch traitor Jeff Davis," remembered one soldier. "When the order was read," Cockrum offered, "the boys sent up a shout for General Rosecrans that seemed to echo more joyously from every tree in the forest, but the cheering sound had scarcely died away when the brigade was ordered off to the right to cover the retreat of General Johnson's division."[8]

"The regiment was then double-quicked for about one-half mile through a dense cedar forest to the point where General [sic] Beatty was ordered to place them in line and await the oncoming Rebel army," recalled one 42nd Indiana veteran. "As we were rushing through the cedars, birds were flying and rabbits running about as if addled by the terrific noise. The first man I saw of McCook's corps coming to us was General Richard Johnson. He called to General [sic] Beatty and told him not to fire on the first line of men as they were his, but that there was plenty of material to use our guns on not far behind them." After Johnson rode off, the Hoosiers could see no one following him but heard a cacophony of noise that meant brisk business was at hand.[9]

The cedars, of course, were no place to move an army. The Pioneer Corps cut some makeshift pathways through the woods the day before; however, as detailed in earlier chapters, the troops typically found themselves entangled once they left the road. The closely clustered trees were a navigational nightmare for men, horses, and artillery; the simple act of maintaining company and regimental alignment proved almost impossible on the thickly wooded and undulating ground. The absence of open space within the forest made the use of artillery particularly

---

8 Captain William W. Cockrum, Co. F, 42nd Indiana, *The Clarion*, Jan. 17, 1863, 2; unknown member of 42nd Indiana, *Proceedings of the Eighth Annual Session of the Survivors of the Battle of Stones River, Kokomo, Indiana, January 2, 1908*, 43. The Mexican War incident referenced by one soldier involved the 3rd Indiana Infantry, which broke and fled at the battle of Buena Vista after suffering heavy casualties; then-Colonel Jefferson Davis and his Mississippians covered the retreat. Buena Vista was also the battle in which then-Captain Braxton Bragg earned his notoriety.

9 *Proceedings Eighth Annual Session*, 43.

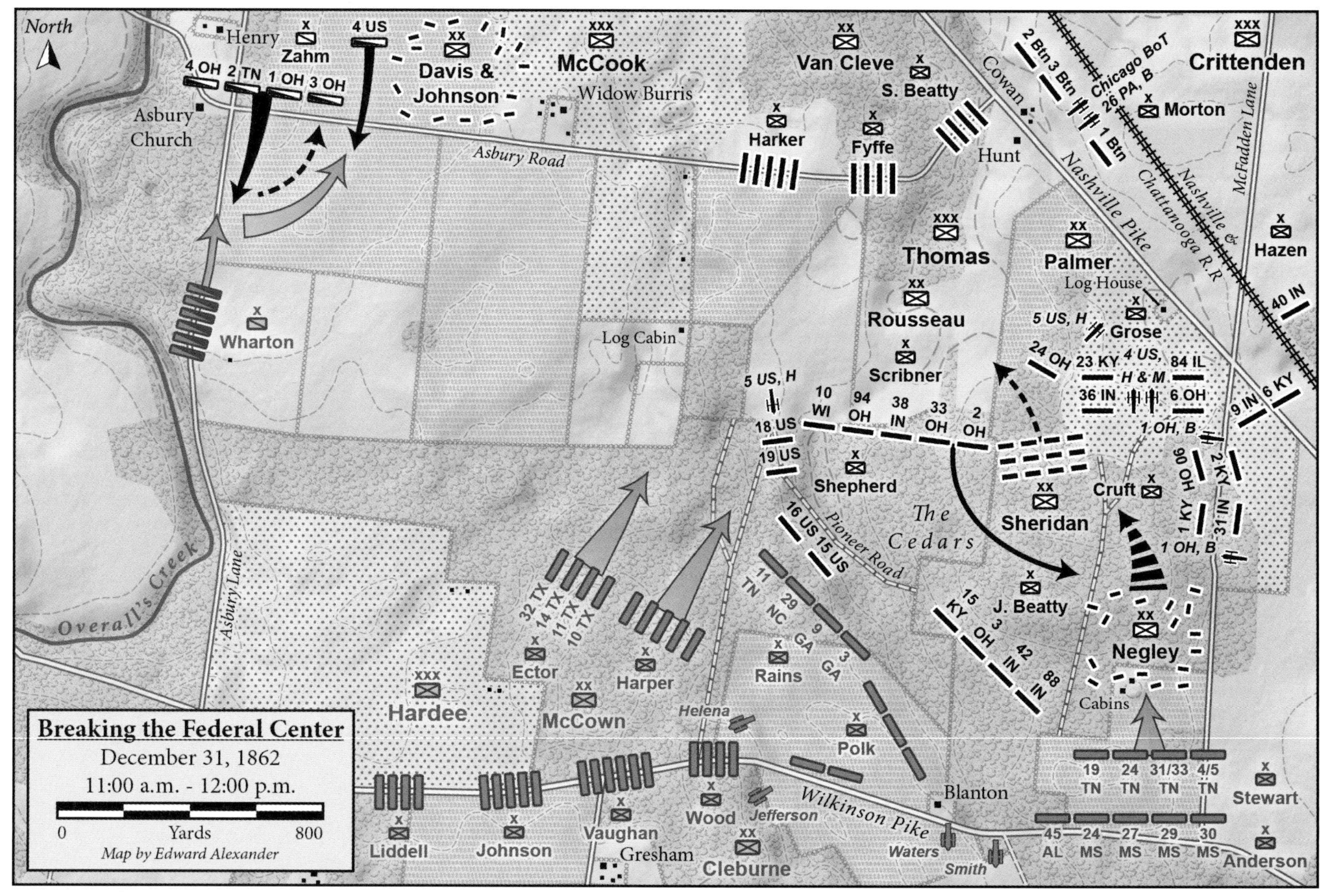
North
Henry
Zahm
4 US
4 OH 2 TN 1 OH 3 OH
Asbury Church
Davis & Johnson
McCook
Widow Burris
Asbury Road
Van Cleve
S. Beatty
Harker
Fyffe
Hunt
Cowan
2 Btn 3 Btn 1 Btn
Chicago BoT
26 PA, B
Morton
Crittenden
McFadden Lane
Nashville & Chattanooga R.R
Nashville Pike
Hazen
40 IN
9 IN 6 KY
Wharton
Asbury Lane
Overall's Creek
Log Cabin
Thomas
Rousseau
Scribner
Palmer
Log House
5 US, H
Grose
24 OH 23 KY 4 US 84 IL
H & M
36 IN 6 OH
1 OH, B
90 OH 2 KY 31 IN
1 KY
1 OH, B
5 US, H
18 US
10 WI 94 OH 38 IN 33 OH 2 OH
19 US
Shepherd
The Cedars
Cruft
Sheridan
16 US 15 US
Pioneer Road
32 TX 14 TX 11 TX 10 TX
Ector
Hardee
Harper
McCown
Helena
11 TN 29 NC 9 GA 3 GA
Rains
15 KY 3 OH 42 IN 88 IN
J. Beatty
Negley
Cabins
19 24 31/33 4/5
TN TN TN TN
Stewart
Polk
Wilkinson Pike
Blanton
Breaking the Federal Center
December 31, 1862
11:00 a.m. - 12:00 p.m.
0 Yards 800
Map by Edward Alexander
Liddell
Johnson
Vaughan
Gresham
Wood
Jefferson
Cleburne
Waters
Smith
45 24 27 29 30
AL MS MS MS MS
Anderson

perilous. If the Federals needed to retreat from this position, it would be hellish getting the cannons out.

With that known, Rousseau held back some of his batteries in open fields closer to the Nashville Pike, though it would not be much easier for the infantry to traverse this section of the field—covered with broken limestone outcroppings, slick with moss, and wet from days of rain. As his brigades filed into position, Rousseau pulled Colonel John Beatty aside and told the Ohioan to hold his position "until hell freezes over." The safety of the army depended on it, he stressed. The position had to be held by his men regardless of complications, difficulties, or cost.[10]"This ground was new and unknown to us all," Rousseau later reported. "The woods were almost impassable to infantry, and artillery was perfectly useless but the line was promptly formed."

Placing Beatty's brigade on the left, Rousseau instructed the colonel to push forward until he found the right flank of Stanley's brigade. Beatty deployed his veteran brigade with the 15th Kentucky on the right, Beatty's own 3rd Ohio at right center, the 42nd Indiana at left center, and the 88th Indiana on the left. Rousseau's 4th Brigade under Lieutenant Colonel Oliver Shepherd, featuring five Regular Army brigades, advanced into the cedars on Beatty's right—kept out of sight, however, by the thick foliage.

Rousseau kept the 1st Brigade, under Colonel Benjamin Scribner, a hundred yards or so behind Beatty's and Shepherd's brigades as a reserve. Scribner's brigade deployed from right to left with the 10th Wisconsin, 94th Ohio, 38th Indiana, 33rd Ohio, and 2nd Ohio. Within minutes, the 2nd and 33rd Ohio rushed to the left to plug a gap between Beatty's and Stanley's lines and were soon lost to sight, leaving just three of Scribner's regiments as Rousseau's reserve. In an attempt to cover as much ground as possible, Rousseau spaced the regiments roughly 75–100 yards apart once they deployed, which in the dense thickets meant the regiments went into action essentially alone, unable to see more than a few feet beyond either flank.[11]

Riding into battle in command of the 15th Kentucky of Beatty's brigade was 20-year-old Colonel James Brown Forman, mounted, as 1st Lt. Alfred Pirtle remembered, on "a splendid black charger which made him a prominent mark for the enemy." Forman, whom Rosecrans nicknamed "The Boy Colonel," apparently entertained few illusions of future grandeur. Turning to an officer friend on

10 Beatty, *Citizen-Soldier*, 201.

11 *OR* 20/1:377-378.

Rousseau's staff, he divined: "I will be killed in the fight. You have always wanted this horse. Now it is my desire that after this battle you should have him." His friend shrugged it off playfully, telling Forman that if that were how he felt, he would just as soon have the horse now. "I am in earnest," Forman replied. "I know what I'm talking about. I will be killed, you will be wounded, and the horse will also be wounded, and I want Major Allen to see that the horse is cared for and given to you." And with that gloomy exchange, Beatty's brigade with the 15th Kentucky on the right flank plunged into the cedars.[12]

December 31 would mark the first engagement for Shepherd's so-called "Regular Brigade" as a unit. Formed by Rosecrans a few days before the campaign began, the Regulars worked diligently to maintain their hard-won reputation for professionalism in an army of volunteers who looked askance at their rigid ways. Lieutenant Robert King of the 15th US bore no illusions about why the brigade was formed, referring to it as the "forlorn hope. We are attached to General Rousseau's division and our duty is to do the hard fighting."

The brigade consisted of various battalions from the 15th, 16th, 18th, and 19th US, and Rosecrans tried to secure a brigadier with a West Point pedigree to lead it, as majors or lieutenant colonels led these battalions. His top choice was Brig. Gen. Robert Granger, in command at Bowling Green, Kentucky, but Morgan's raid into Kentucky kept Granger occupied, and none of the colonels commanding the regiments from which the battalions were drawn was available, dropping the assignment into Shepherd's lap.

Shepherd, a graduate of West Point's Class of 1840 and thus two years Rosecrans's senior in the regular army, "set about organizing and training the brigade using the same methods that had honed the 18th Regulars the previous year—attention to detail, high standards, and tough discipline," according to historian Mark Johnson. The volunteers in Rosecrans's army respected the Regulars and worked hard to emulate their precision on drill, but they hardly admired them, at least not universally. The fact was that the Regulars, by the nature of their affiliation with the antebellum US Army, were considered a cut above by the army high command, giving rise to jealousies and charges of favoritism.

"Our volunteer neighbors used to make much sport of us because we were continually drilled no matter how inclement the weather," remembered Lieutenant Lewis Hosea of the 16th US. "Officers were instructed in tactics and army

12 "New Year's Eve on the Field of Battle," *Louisville Evening Post*, Dec. 31, 1915; Kirk C. Jenkins, *The Battles Rages Higher: The Union's Fifteenth Kentucky Infantry* (Lexington, 2003), 103.

regulations like schoolboys. Our enlisted men were about as good, and certainly no better, than the average volunteer." Marching under a distinctive blue flag with a gold star unique to the Regular Brigade, much was expected of these four regiments of veteran troops under disciplined and well-trained officers.[13]

Following the westernmost of the roads the Pioneers had cut through the cedars the day before, Major John King and the eight companies of the 15th US held the van in Shepherd's column of 1,562 officers and men. After a 15-minute, quarter-mile march into the woods, they filed to the right and assumed a battle line, followed by nine companies of the 16th US under Major Adam Slemmer, which deployed about a hundred yards left of the 15th. King deployed a single company of 45 men under Captain Henry Keteltas as skirmishers, ordering them to deploy about a hundred yards in front of his battalion. "The last part of the order the captain did not hear but at once deployed the whole command and set out in pursuit of the enemy," recalled 1st Lt. Roman Gray.

Keteltas's men advanced 800 yards farther, nearly reaching the Wilkinson Pike, before they started to observe scattered pockets of troops in the woods. "We saw on the left of our line a regiment of our troops that had been broken and were being rapidly driven in by the enemy and another body of troops nearer to us than the first numbering two companies and dressed in our uniforms moving leisurely down the left of our line," Gray noted. "They were laughing and holding their heads down and otherwise behaving very mysteriously. Captain Keteltas, supposing them to be our own troops, ordered the skirmishers to march by the right flank in order to let them pass."

The opposing body of troops advanced to within 50 yards, then opened fire on Keteltas's skirmishers. "Simultaneous with this firing appeared three dense straight lines of Rebel infantry in our front and extending to our left farther than I could see and flanking our whole position, advancing steadily with colors flying and filling the woods with their yells and hissing bullets," Gray detailed. "We returned the enemy's fire but could not succeed in checking their advance and commenced firing in retreat."[14]

13 Mark W. Johnson, *That Body of Brave Men: The U.S. Regular Infantry and the Civil War in the West* (Cambridge, 2003), 254-59; Lewis M. Hosea, "The Regular Brigade of the Army of the Cumberland," *Sketches of War History 1861-1865, Papers Prepared for the Commandery of the State of Ohio, Military Order of the Loyal Legion of the United States*, Vol. 5 (Cincinnati, 1903), 329-30.

14 1st Lt. Roman H. Gray, Co. E, 1st Battalion, 15th U.S., *Cleveland Plain Dealer*, Jan. 26, 1863, 2.

McCown's Division, refreshed and rearmed after crumbling the Union right flank in the morning, was advancing as part of the left flank of Hardee's attack against the Federal center. "The command was much exhausted," McCown reported. "Notwithstanding the exhausted condition of my men, having received orders from General Hardee, I prepared at once to advance." Hardee, his attention on the Nashville Pike, wanted McCown to push his men into position before Rosecrans had time to prepare a defense. While rearming near the Wilkinson Pike, McCown realigned his three brigades: He deployed Ector's Texans as the division's left flank; Colonel Robert W. Harper, now commanding McNair's Arkansans, took the center; and Brig. Gen. James Rains's relatively unbloodied brigade formed on the right, in the van for the advance. From right to left, the young Tennessee brigadier placed the 3rd Georgia Battalion, 9th Georgia Battalion, 29th North Carolina, and 11th Tennessee.[15]

McCown's men plunged into the woods north of the Wilkinson Pike and before long flanked Rousseau's position. Neither side realized it, though, because of the thick forest surrounding their position—that is until Captain Keteltas and his company stumbled into the 29th North Carolina pushing into the woods about 11:00 a.m. "The enemy in two or three lines of battle hurriedly advanced with a strong line of skirmishers in front," reported Captain Jesse Fulmer of the 15th US. "Our line of battle suffered somewhat by mistaking a body of Rebels dressed in our uniform for our troops."

Colonel Robert Vance of the 29th North Carolina reported that his regiment received a particularly hot reception. "The skirmishers fired one volley into us, which, being promptly returned, they retired rapidly across a cornfield and into a thicket of cedars, where the enemy were posted in strong force," he wrote. "This thicket of cedars was so dense that it formed in itself a natural breastwork and protection to the enemy posted therein. Here the struggle of the day took place. The enemy, sheltering themselves behind the trunks of the thickly standing trees and the large rocks, of which there were many, stubbornly contested the ground inch by inch. Our brave boys, cheered on and led by their field, staff, and company officers, advanced through a very tempest of leaden hail."[16]

---

15 OR 20/1:913, 939.

16 Ibid., 400, 938. Most accounts from the 15th US note that the Confederates advanced wearing what appeared to be Federal uniforms, which in turn induced them to hold their fire. More likely, the North Carolinians had been given cadet gray jackets that from a distance

The 9th Georgia advanced to support the North Carolinians, and the 11th Tennessee pushed around the Regulars' right flank. The 15th US put up a good fight but could not hold its ground for long, staying just long enough to fire a few rounds. Sergeant Frank Reed reported "it was discovered that we were vastly outnumbered and there were no troops immediately on our left[;] we were soon flanked and the order was given to fall back." Their departure was sped by Vance's North Carolinians, who, the colonel recalled, made a shout "which made the woods ring and another bayonet charge. This seemed more than the enemy could stand for they broke, followed closely by the brigade which succeeded in driving them clear through a dense cedar thicket." As happened throughout the fighting in this sector, the 15th felt isolated because of the woods' density, even though Slemmer's battalion had deployed a mere hundred yards to its left. "Major King saw the avalanche of Rebels that was following his skirmishers," Gray wrote, "and saw the desperate peril of his command who were now entirely without visible support and none too soon, he gave the order to fall back behind a high rail fence that was a little to the right and rear of where the command was lying."[17]

The fence—11 rails high, as one solider reported—proved the undoing of King's men, who stood briefly at the fence but were shot down in droves when they climbed it to continue the retreat. "In crossing this fence, the battalion was thrown into confusion," Reed explained. "Officers became separated from their men, and the men not seeing their leaders, became more and more perplexed, and by the time they could get a few of their men together, the Confederates were so close to us that they were compelled to fire and fall back."

Members of the neighboring 16th US could hear but not see the engagement taking place, and before long a company of skirmishers rushed in from the bush with the 3rd Georgia Battalion in hot pursuit. "Soon after entering the wood, we came upon a regiment and skirmishers, who had been engaged with the enemy," reported Colonel Marcus Stovall of the 3rd Georgia Battalion. "Passing the skirmishers, we found their line posted in a hollow. We delivered our fire at a distance of 150 yards or less, killing many." Slemmer's men took a knee and returned fire. "The command succeeded in checking their advance and the men

---

appeared dark blue. Regardless, the momentary confusion allowed Rains's Brigade to approach within close rifle range unimpeded.

17 Gray Letter; Sergeant Frank Reed, Co. H, 1st Battalion, 15th U.S., *Ohio Democrat*, Jan. 30, 1863, 2; *ORS* 20:650.

Major Adam J. Slemmer,
1st Battalion, 16th US Infantry

Library of Congress

behaved with the greatest possible coolness and aiming with accuracy," reported Captain Robert E. A. Crofton.[18]

The balance of Shepherd's brigade remained in column along the Pioneer-cut road: two battalions of the 18th US under Majors James Caldwell and Frederick Townsend; the single battalion of the 19th US under Major Stephen Carpenter; and Lieutenant Francis Guenther's Battery H of the 5th US Light Artillery. Once the firing began, Shepherd ordered King to take command of both the 15th and 16th battalions constituting the brigade's left while he took command of the balance.

Lieutenant Colonel Shepherd ordered the 19th US into line on the right and the two battalions of the 18th US on the left, but he had hardly commenced forming the lines when Rousseau apparently had second thoughts about sending Guenther's battery into the cedars. An order arrived directing the battery to exit the woods and deploy closer to the Nashville Pike, so Guenther promptly ordered his men to whip the horses to turn the guns around and make a run for the open fields—narrowly escaping capture before it had a chance to fire a round. "The cracking of musketry here was terrible," related gunner John Carroll. "Bullets came like hail around us and many a brave man on both sides fell here. Our battery came

18 Reed Letter; OR 20/1:401, 941.

out of there on a gallop and had we been three minutes later they would have had us."[19]

After Townsend deployed the 18th US into line, he turned to locate the artillery and did not see Guenther. Rousseau had ordered Shepherd to support the battery, but it was unclear to Townsend whether the battery was in his front or had retreated. Turning to his adjutant Frederick Phisterer, Townsend ordered the lieutenant to ride forward and find the rest of the brigade and (ideally) Guenther's guns.

Phisterer galloped through a blizzard of gunfire for several minutes along the pioneer road before finding Slemmer and the 16th US in their clash with Rains's Brigade. Slemmer informed Phisterer he had not seen Guenther's battery, indicating that those guns had likely retreated. Phisterer told Slemmer that the brigade's right wing would therefore retreat to support Guenther, meaning Slemmer's men would be isolated and in danger of capture. That realization compelled Slemmer to retire as well, a decision made easier by knowledge the 15th US on his left was already pulling back. "The battalion on our right having moved to the rear, it became necessary to fall back," Crofton wrote. "The men performed this movement with the same order and regularity as they would in an ordinary drill."

By then, Shepherd had placed his three battalions on the road leading out of the cedars. Phisterer rode back to rejoin his battalion as it exited the woods. His actions "unquestionably saved Slemmer's battalion and probably another from annihilation or capture," and in 1894 he would receive the Medal of Honor.[20]

*   *   *

Colonel Beatty pushed his brigade through the cedars until the open woods north of the Blanton House cornfield lay on his direct front, keeping him concealed "while the enemy, advancing through the open woods, is fully exposed," he wrote. "To my right and left the cedar thicket was so dense as to render it impossible to see the length of a regiment." It was nearly 11 that morning when Beatty's men were fully in position. The soldiers of the 42nd Indiana received orders to "throw up such temporary breastworks as they could make from fallen trees and then lie down

---

19 *OR* 20/1:394; Private John Carroll, Battery H, 5th US Light Artillery, *Cleveland Morning Leader*, Jan. 16, 1863, 2.

20 Beyer, *Deeds of Valor*, 129-30.

for the advance of the Rebels," remembered Captain Spillard Horrall. There seemed to be a misunderstanding that General Johnson's troops would deploy on Beatty's flank and help defend the position, so Horrall's troops were "cautioned against firing into them should they be compelled to retire upon us for support." Skirmishers, however, soon spotted approaching troops "acting very unlike Federals, "as one soldier recounted, "and after some hesitancy, we gave them the contents of our muskets."[21]

It was S.A.M. Wood's Brigade, just resupplied with ammunition along the Wilkinson Pike and now hot on the trail of the scattered survivors of Davis's and Johnson's divisions. Wood's men marched into the forest expecting no serious resistance. "The Rebels, four columns deep and flushed with success, came rushing down upon our brigade which was now only one column deep," Cockrum remembered. "But the boys, true to their purpose, steadily and rapidly poured back upon them a deadly volley with most fearful and telling effect." Sergeant Gilbert McWhirk of the 3rd Ohio noted that "we were scarcely in line when the enemy appeared in front and the firing on the right became terrific. Our skirmishers kept up a lively fire and my company was ordered by Colonel [Orris] Lawson to advance through the timber. We thought the whole line was to advance and kept on and came near being surrounded."[22]

No surprise, units stumbling into one another would continue. The 88th Indiana on Beatty's left had a sharp scrap with the 19th Tennessee, arrayed on A. P. Stewart's left flank, which was pursuing Stanley's and Miller's brigades north from their positions near the Wilkinson Pike. "Some 200 yards into the woods, the enemy appeared in great force rather to my left," reported Colonel Walker of the 19th Tennessee. "They here poured in upon me a most effective and murderous fire. This we returned with all the vigor and rapidity possible, gradually moving forward, swinging, according to orders, a little from left to right. This constant and severe fire continued for near an hour." By sliding to the right, Walker's men soon lost sight of the 88th Indiana and continued moving toward the Nashville Pike.[23]

Wood's advance sputtered to a halt in front of Beatty's left three regiments, but all was not well for the Federals on the right. "Our brigade got into the same kind of

---

21 Beatty, *Citizen-Soldier*, 201; Spillard F. Horrall, *History of the Forty-Second Indiana Volunteer Infantry* (Chicago, 1892), 167; Tent No. 1, Co. E, 42nd Indiana, *The Clarion*, Jan. 31, 1863, 1.

22 Cockrum Letter; Sergeant Gilbert B. McWhirk, Co. G, 3rd Ohio, *Ohio State Journal*, Jan. 16, 1863, 2.

23 *OR* 20/1:729.

Colonel John Beatty

Larry M. Strayer Collection

position that it held at Perryville, that is, one on the extreme right wing of the army with the 15th Kentucky on the right of the brigade," remembered adjutant William McDowell. "With instructions to hold the enemy until the artillery could be gotten out of the thicket, we again met the enemy and stopped for a while his triumphant charges."

Repulsed in their first crack at this line, Wood's men began to work their way around Beatty's flank and found the isolated 15th Kentucky. Thick brush and hastily constructed fieldworks helped shield the Federals from much of Wood's fire, and the Confederates took heavy losses, but they smelled blood in the water. Pushing farther to their left, the Confederates soon found the flank and swept in to capture the Federals.

Colonel Forman rode back and forth behind the lines of his 15th Kentucky encouraging his men to keep up their fire. His horse had already taken a bullet in the hind leg, and within a moment Forman's prophecy from the previous night was fulfilled. Pierced by a Minié ball, the young Kentuckian quickly expired, having been in action less than 10 minutes when he was hit. Command fell apart with Forman's death, as Major Henry Kalfus, overwhelmed by the Confederate fire now striking his regiment from three directions, panicked and ordered a precipitate retreat. "With no effective direction from the surviving field officers to maintain discipline and fold the line back on the rest of the brigade, the men of the 15th began cutting their way out of the cedars," explained historian Kirk Jenkins.

"Holding our position a little too long," McDowell noted, "we had to fight both front, flank, and rear to get back to the position in the center for the enemy had passed around our right and were enveloping us before we knew it." It was a confusing, ferocious, and bloody scramble to get out of the cedars, and the 15th Kentucky lost a third of its numbers in the process.[24]

With the 15th Kentucky gone, the 3rd Ohio's right flank now hung in the air. The 33rd Alabama soon found it and opened fire. The Confederates, Horrall recalled, "were still rapidly moving through the woods in order to gain our right and rear, so as to completely cut off the command and that result could have been nothing short of the capture of the whole brigade." His brigade imperiled, Beatty decided to anchor his line on the left-flank regiment, the 88th Indiana, and reorient his three regiments to face west. It was done under fire with parade-ground precision. The 33rd Alabama, moving forward on Wood's left arrived just in time to see the 3rd Ohio redeploy, mistaking the movement for a retreat.[25]

"The regiments changed front under a terrible fire of the enemy with as much apparent coolness as if on drill in the open field," wrote a member of the 42nd Indiana. "I noticed the line officers of one regiment command 'support arms' as the companies were successively aligned and then again, they let into the Rebels with a desperation only exceeded by the patriotic zeal they felt for a bleeding country." Horrall proudly noted that "Captain William Cockrum of Co. F on reaching the new line placed himself at the head of the company in the front rank and gave the command 'right dress' which was followed by every company commander. Such coolness under heavy fire as evinced by the officers aligning the ranks is unusual, very unusual. Discipline did it. Then the fighting began in earnest."[26]

Beatty's maneuver allowed his three regiments to open fire on Rains's right, which stumbled into them in the woods after driving back the Regulars. "The lines of the Federals and Confederates were at no time more than 70–100 yards apart," Horrall noted. The lines shifted from flank to flank as pockets of Confederates from both Wood's and Rains's brigades threatened both of Beatty's flanks. "The slaughter went on, our regiment frequently changing front upon the first and tenth companies in an orderly manner," Cockrum recalled.

24 Jenkins, *The Battle Rages Higher*, 107-08.

25 Horrall, *History of the 42nd Indiana*, 168. Beatty's specific order was "change front forward on the first company, by company, right half wheel, march!" It essentially moved his brigade's line of battle from facing south to facing west. The 75- to 100-yard spacing Beatty maintained between the regiments when they initially deployed into the cedars allowed him the maneuvering room to reorient his battle line without entangling the regiments.

26 Horrall, *History of the 42nd Indiana*, 168; J. Q. Juniper Wiggins, *Nashville Daily Union*, Jan. 20, 1863, 2.

Remembered another Federal: "We had to change front several times to avoid being flanked. Back and forth through those cedars we fought for hours. Occasionally when we were ordered to lie down for a few minutes, we could have the opportunity to listen to the roar of battle. The cannons kept up their regular beating like the ticking of a clock. They made the air vibrate like they were the great heart throbs of nature itself. Now and then they sound like great anvils underground and fancy would conjure up visions of the infernal regions, with grim monsters at work forging chains and fetters for the lost."[27]

The fighting in the close quarters of the cedars lasted nearly an hour and proved more intense than anything Beatty's men experienced at Perryville. "It is terrible to hear the singing of a bullet and follow its course as it flies on its way, and then hear that keen whistle of the little piece of lead suddenly terminate in a dull crash as the ball leaps through the brain of some friend beside you," lamented Lieutenant Franklin Embree of the 42nd Indiana in a vivid and palpably emotional letter home to his sister. "There is no man, when the first wave of a battle such as this surges upon him, who does not involuntarily and mentally appeal to God for protection." Embee continued:

But the man soon begins to fire at his foe and this animates him; he will soon in the earnestness of purpose forget that there is danger. His heart throbs wildly, the lifeblood hurries like a racehorse through his veins, and every nerve is fully excited. The arm of the weak man become engorged with almost a giant's strength. His brain is all alive; thought is quick and active and he is ten times fuller of life than before. He seems so full of life that it is hard for him to realize that death is so near.

I noticed one case where the ball came obliquely from the left and front and passed several feet in front of me. It seemed that I could hear it singing almost from the time it left its bed in the Rebel's gun and as it swiftly came, I knew where it was going by the sound. This happened when we were not very hotly engaged and when our men were not firing else, I could not have heard the singing of the bullet. We were all kneeling among some brush. Suddenly I heard the same ball go crash and I knew by the sound that it had burst a human skull. I barely had time to look around to my right than I saw Sergeant Chauncey Glassmith quivering and dying. Every one of us could not refrain from casting a glance at the dying man who lay there trembling in every limb and blood spurting from his nostrils and the wound in his forehead. In the heat of action such seems to not affect one much, but it is awful indeed.[28]

<hr>

27 Horrall, *History of the 42nd Indiana*, 168; Cockrum Letter; Tent No. 1 Letter.

28 1st Lt. Franklin D. Embree, Co. E, 42nd Indiana, SRNBP.

In the middle of the intense engagement, Horrall, serving as Beatty's ordnance officer, managed to bring forward a wagonload of ammunition; while under fire he threw out box after box behind the lines of the regiments so they could continue to fight. "He had an axman with him and in many places had to cut the road for the wagon in the thick cedar woods," noted one witness. "Just as the wagon was in the rear of our regiment, I saw a shell burst near it and a fragment tore off half of the canvas cover. Yet the driver and the ordnance sergeant stuck to their posts and drove steadily ahead, delivering ammunition. Had it not been for the timely arrival of ammunition, our brigade would have had to retreat with empty guns."[29]

*   *   *

Along the Nashville Pike, Donelson and the five Tennessee regiments of his brigade marched in support of Chalmers's attack and witnessed the slaughter of the Mississippians near the Cowan House. "When we arrived at the position formerly occupied by General Chalmers's brigade, we were ordered to halt and lie down behind the little fortification formed by his brigade of logs and rails," recalled Lt. Col. John Anderson of the 8th Tennessee. "We remained in this position about 20 minutes under a perfect storm or shot and shell, and it soon became apparent to everyone that Chalmers' brigade was giving way for it was with great difficulty that I could keep his men running over my men. They came running back in squads and companies and I am perfectly satisfied that at least two-thirds of the regiment that had formerly occupied the position we were in had returned."[30]

At 61, Donelson was the oldest commanding officer in either army on the field at Stones River. He graduated fifth in the West Point Class of 1825, his path to success in life considerably eased because he was raised by his uncle, General Andrew Jackson, who was elected president three years later in 1828. Donelson served multiple terms in the Tennessee legislature and upon the outbreak of hostilities was appointed adjutant general of Tennessee. A new fortification on the Cumberland River, soon to gain infamy as the site of a major Confederate defeat, was named in his honor. Donelson, however, was not there; he had taken command of a brigade of Tennesseans and would see action in both western Virginia and Perryville.

29 *Proceedings of the Eighth Annual,* 44.

30 *OR* 20/1:714.

It was at the latter battle in Kentucky that Donelson made an implacable enemy of one of his key subordinates. Few officers were more poignantly named than Colonel John Savage of the 16th Tennessee. An old-school Southerner, the hot-headed Savage was a master at poker, faro, and the art of dueling. He was also an attorney of noted ability and a wealthy land speculator who both distrusted and hated the planter class that dominated Tennessee politics. A man of intense, frothing hatred for his numerous enemies and fierce devotion to his men, Savage described himself as a Rebel but no secessionist, claiming secession was the "invention of John C. Calhoun's sophistry and speculative theories."

Savage had little use for Southern politicians such as Calhoun, Tennessee Governor Isham Harris, and even his own brigade commander, blaming them for the war that he considered an unmitigated disaster to the South. Savage was a competent and experienced self-taught soldier who had served honorably first in the Seminole War and then the Mexican War, suffering a serious wound in the latter. His current bitter animosity with Donelson stemmed from the commander's orders at Perryville that cost Savage's regiment 199 casualties in roughly 30 minutes of combat. "When he saw the terrible execution among his men, he dropped down at the foot of a tree and cried like a child," noted one writer. Once the tears stopped, however, Savage indignantly blamed Donelson, Cheatham, and Bragg for the decimation of his regiment and refused to let it go. Donelson and Savage had not spoken to each other since Perryville.[31]

The contentious mood was not restricted only to Donelson and Savage that morning. Lieutenant William Otey recalled that Leonidas Polk had sent his aide-de-camp Lieutenant William Richmond to Colonel Sidney Stanton of the newly organized 84th Tennessee, one of Donelson's regiments, with orders for Stanton's men to pull down a rail fence that Polk felt would obstruct the movement of troops. "Some words passed that led to blows and though the bullets were flying thick and fast, here was seen the ludicrous spectacle of two officers engaged in a personal fight on the battlefield," Otey recalled. "Stanton had got Richmond's thumb in his mouth while Richmond was gnawing away at Stanton's ear. Finally wiser counsel prevailed, and the interference of friends parted the belligerents and they at once resumed their respective posts of duty."[32]

---

31 John H. Savage, *The Life of John H. Savage: Citizen, Soldier, Lawyer, Congressman* (Nashville, 1903), 138-39; "Col. John H. Savage Dead," *Southern Standard*, Apr. 14, 1904.

32 "Organizing a Signal Corps," 1st Lt. William Mercer Otey, *Confederate Veteran*, Dec. 1899, 550.

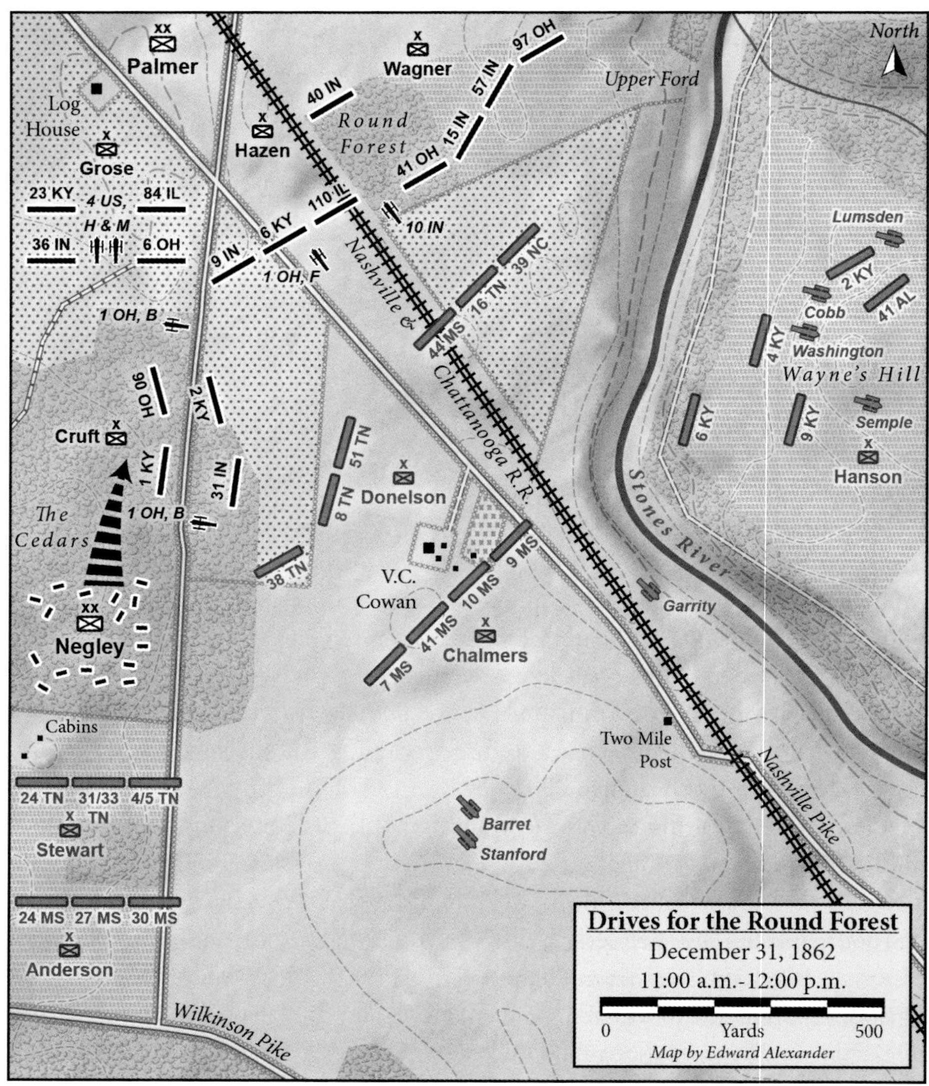

Regardless of the internal tensions wracking the brigade, Donelson received orders from Polk to march to the succor of Chalmers's battered Mississippians that he noted were "under a shower of shot and shell of almost every description." The Tennessean arrayed his regiments with Savage's 407-man 16th Tennessee on the right, tucked between Stones River and the Nashville Pike; the 51st Tennessee with 293 men at right center and west of the Nashville Pike; the 474-man 8th Tennessee, the brigade's biggest regiment, at left center; and the 282-man 38th Tennessee on the left. Donelson elected to leave the 84th Tennessee behind to support Captain

William Carnes's Battery due to its small size (roughly 200 men) and inexperience. In all, Donelson led 1,456 officers and men into the maelstrom.

The advance, as described by Dr. Joseph Cross, was "like an ocean wave upon a rocky shore. Colonel Savage on the right was raging to and fro across the [Nashville and Chattanooga] railroad and the Nashville Pike, stretching his regiment out from the river to Cowan's home and thus holding a large space of ground under a tremendous hail of shot and shell." The 51st Tennessee moved forward less than 200 yards when a Federal shell exploded above the color guard, killing one, wounding two, and knocking the colors to the ground. Donelson's brigade split apart at the Cowan House, with Savage's men marching unimpeded toward the Round Forest while the left three regiments bogged down in the carnage at the house. "We found the Cowan house and yard filled with men of Chalmers's brigade in great confusion," noted Colonel John Chester of the 51st Tennessee. "Owing to this confusion, my regiment became somewhat scattered." Three of Chester's rightmost companies drifted to the east and ended up fighting with Savage's regiment.

The 8th Tennessee bogged down, too. "The regiment was thrown into some confusion, caused by the house and some picket fence and a portion of Chalmers' men that had remained behind the house, causing some four of the companies on the right of the regiment to pass around and through the best way they could," Anderson reported. "At this juncture the enemy in our front opened a terrible fire upon us with small arms, at a distance of about 75 or 100 yards. Such a fire I do not suppose men were ever before subjected to."

Colonel William Moore, riding upon a small black horse captured by his men at Perryville, was endeavoring to rally the men when the horse was struck down. Word quickly spread within the regiment that Moore also had been killed, though that was inaccurate. "Colonel Moore extricated his legs quickly from beneath his horse, drew his sword and went on with my company," recalled Sergeant John D. McLane.[33]

*　　*　　*

Cruft's men barely had time to recover from its clash with Chalmers's Mississippians when they detected the advance in their direction of Donelson's

---

33 Dr. Joseph Cross, *Holston Journal*, Feb. 19, 1863, 3; *OR* 20/1:714-715, 718; Sergeant John D. McLane, Co. K, 8th Tennessee, *Confederate Veteran*, June 1901, 268.

troops. "My regiment advanced over an open field and under a very terrific fire," recalled Colonel John Carter of the 38th Tennessee. "The enemy was strongly posted in a dense cedar thicket and well supported by artillery. At first, he seemed unwilling to yield his ground." Sergeant William Buskey of the 1st Kentucky (US) agreed. "This was a close fight, the Rebels being but a few yards from us," he wrote. "The Rebels hurried reinforcements to the point in overwhelming numbers and proudly did they advance, the flags of half a dozen regiments fluttering above the corn stalks, the men passing in our front as orderly as on dress parade although we were mowing down scores of them at every volley."[34]

"[W]e poured volley after volley from our trusty rifles into the foe," recorded Corporal Charles Reck of the 90th Ohio. "Our brave boys hewed gaps in their lines that still advanced, but these were closed up as if nothing had happened. When they were about 100 yards from us, their lines broke off from the center and filed to our right and left. We were flanked! We were under a crossfire and the order given to fall back. But our brave boys did not hear the order. They still held their places under the most murderous and withering fire, while their commanders were mowed down by scores. Our colonel seeing the situation, ordered us back. We fell back scatteringly."[35]

Matters reached a crisis point for Donelson at the Cowan House. The Tennesseans had been caught flat-footed in the open, pummeled in front and on both flanks by incessant Federal artillery fire and raked by repeated volleys of musketry. It was death to fall back and death to move forward, as the Tennesseans fell by the score. Anderson, among those believing Moore was dead or at least incapacitated, took command of the 8th Tennessee and determined that the only way out of the mess was to drive the Federals from his front and gain the cover of the woods. He directed the men to fix bayonets and ordered a charge, recalling that "[t]he gallant 8th responded with a shout and leaped forward like men bent on conquering or dying in the attempt."

The regiment surged ahead of the 38th and 51st Tennessee to close in on Cruft's increasingly nervous Federals. Anderson was surprised to find Moore again in front, encouraging the men. His earlier fears about Moore's status quickly became reality, however. "He had just reached the regiment again when he fell dead, shot through the heart with a Minié ball," Anderson recalled. "The enemy in

---

34 *OR* 20/1:718; Buskey Letter.

35 Corporal Charles J.E. Reck, Co. G, 90th Ohio, *Weekly Lancaster Gazette*, Jan. 22, 1863, 2.

our front contested stubbornly and those on our right and left continued to pour a deadly fire into us."[36]

At an especially lethal range of 250 yards, all six guns of Battery B of the 1st Ohio Light blasted away at Donelson's supporting artillery. "We were in the edge of the cedars," wrote Lieutenant Eben Sturges. "We gave them about half an hour of shrapnel and Schenkl shell fire. The action became very hot and I changed shrapnel for canister at the same time advancing my pieces by hand a few rods in order to get a better range. Their battery returned the same kind of ammunition (canister) and it seemed to shower." Thomas Potter noted that the Rebels "made charge after charge up to within 30 yards of the muzzles of our guns in solid columns despite shot, shell, and canister that tore great gaps in their ranks. But their ranks were quickly closed up again and a perfect storm of musketry hit them. Never did I see men face the music like this. When so close to our guns they pulled their hats over their eyes so that they could not see the flash of our pieces and moved up as steadily as if they were on the parade ground."[37]

By now, Negley was streaming through the woods in Cruft's rear, and it was clear the Indianan could not maintain his position much longer with his right flank uncovered. The din in the woods was indescribable. "In all my four-and-a-half years of service in the war I never elsewhere heard such a roar of artillery as was made by our guns and all of the active Rebel artillery responding," remembered Lieutenant John Brown of the 31st Indiana. "The whole region was thick with grapeshot, canister, shells fragments and rifle bullets."[38]

As Anderson's men closed in, Cruft was left with few options but a retreat toward the Nashville Pike. "We commenced retiring on our reserve, but it was not there," Buskey recalled. "Now we found our regiment almost isolated from the rest of the command and the horrible truth flashed upon me: a rout complete." Cruft complained that "our own troops impeded my retreat. Cannon, caissons, artillery wagons, and bodies of men in wild retreat filled the road and woods to my rear, precluding everything like a proper and orderly retreat. The enemy's fire was on three sides of my position. Seeing my little brigade failing rapidly without hope or further ability to hold on, I withdrew it in as good order as practicable."

36 OR 20/1:715.

37 Horn, *Battle of Stones River*, 15; Private Thomas C. Potter, Battery B, 1st Ohio Volunteer Light Artillery, *Blue & Gray Magazine*, 2004, 24-25.

38 2nd Lt. John W. Brown, Co. E, 31st Indiana, "At Stone River," *National Tribune*, Sept. 29, 1910, 7.

Cruft handled the retreat deftly and even managed to salvage all of Battery B's guns before Donelson's men surged into the cedars, though it would be a close shave that cost him a quarter of his brigade. The Buckeye gunners had fought almost to the last round and rolled back with only 16 shells total for their six pieces.[39]

Donelson was not alone in this fight, as some of Chalmers's battered survivors reformed to help, including the 7th and 41st Mississippi. Captain Ball of the 41st Mississippi struggled to convince his troops to renew the attack when he observed the 8th Tennessee marching past and "the commander of which called on us to rally to the assistance of the troops on our right. I rallied a portion of the regiment but many of which were so completely exhausted they did not advance." Regardless, Ball marched forward with the willing, the men soon finding themselves back in the body-strewn fields around the Cowan House under a torrent of fire. "We were receiving a galling fire from the artillery," he noted, "but after all had succeeded in crossing the fence and flanking the enemy on our left, I succeeded in directing the attention of the left wing to them and a heavy volley was poured into their lines which caused them to give way."[40]

"The enemy's first line gave way before my men and their second was brought forward, but could not stand the impetuosity of our charge, and they gave way," Anderson reported. Added Private Lancelot C. Ewbank of the 31st Indiana: "As we were retreating through the cedar swamp we continued to load and fire on the graybacks as they pursued us. We gave them a fighting retreat for about a quarter mile through the cedars."

The 38th Tennessee and 51st Tennessee soon surged into the woods beside Anderson, and the triumphant Tennesseans, spotting the mass of retreating Federals to their left, waded in with the Rebel yell. "I captured at this point about 400 prisoners belonging to the artillery and infantry," Anderson reported. Colonel John Chester of the 51st Tennessee swerved to the left and drove toward Cruft's position but took heavy fire from enemy artillery. "We continued to follow and fire on them for a long distance through the woods, taking three cannon and several hundred prisoners sending 153 of them to the rear at one time," he wrote.[41]

Donelson broke Cruft's line at the cost of the wholesale sacrifice of the 8th Tennessee; the regiment lost 306 of 474 men who charged, including 30 out of 37

39 Buskey Letter; *OR* 20/1:527-528.

40 Smith, *Stones River: Confederate Army*, 662.

41 *OR* 20/1:715, 720; Diary of Private Lancelot C. Ewbank, Co. I, 31st Indiana, SRNBP.

officers. Moore was killed, as were seven of ten captains. The Norris Creek Guards (Co. D) lost 11 of their 12 commissioned and non-commissioned officers and were led off the field by a corporal (no regiment at Stones River would lose that many killed and wounded). One of those captains, recalled Captain Carnes, was under arrest at the time of the attack but went into the ranks as a private and was killed. "I think there were but 26 men in that regiment who escaped without any bullet marks on their clothes or person," he noted. The 38th Tennessee, moving on the left flank of the 8th Tennessee, lost 85 of 282 men; the 51st Tennessee 86 of 293.[42]

*　　*　　*

William Babcock Hazen's brigade waited for the 16th Tennessee on Donelson's right in a small four-acre patch of elevated woods nestled between the Nashville Pike and the Nashville & Chattanooga. Historians would later refer to this ground as the Round Forest, but at the time of the battle it was a nameless tract of trees. It proved to be the key to the Federal position at Stones River, a position as unbending as the man commanding its defense. Colonel Hazen, a 32-year-old native of Vermont, graduated 28th of 34 cadets in West Point's Class of 1855 and spent the prewar years on infantry assignments out West. Hazen was wounded during an 1859 fight with Comanches in Texas while with the 8th Infantry and spent more than a year on sick leave. Tapped by Governor William Dennison to lead the 41st Ohio when it formed in the summer of 1861, Hazen arrived in camp in what was compared to a thunderclap. "Every minute detail of the daily routine and life from sunrise to the putting out of lights at night was specified and prescribed with the precision of a disciplinarian," recalled one veteran. "The men began to wonder if two days' work was not crowded into a twelve-hour program."

Hazen was an energetic worker, a relentless stickler for detail, and a merciless driver of men. "It was a tremendous pace the colonel set in this business so entirely new to the recruits—too fast for some to endure and they, good men but unable to keep up, were left behind, dropping out one after another," noted another veteran. Hazen drove his officers even harder than his enlisted men, putting the "most work where there was the most responsibility." No detail was too small to escape his notice, one soldier commenting that "the work of instruction never ceased in any command of Colonel Hazen's."

<hr>

42 "Eighth Tennessee at Murfreesboro," *Confederate Veteran*, Aug. 1901, 355-56.

Hazen's unstinting labors helped the 41st Ohio earn a reputation as one of the best-disciplined regiments in the Army of the Cumberland, and few could match its spit-and-polish manner or precision on the drill field, even the vaunted Regulars. After proving the regiment could fight as well as it drilled on the second day at Shiloh, Don Carlos Buell bumped Hazen to brigade command, where he quickly infused the other regiments of his command with his same brand of strict discipline. The men would need every ounce of that discipline to endure the trials they would face over the next five hours in the Round Forest.[43]

Savage reported that as he advanced toward the Round Forest, his regiment split along the railroad, with two companies moving on its right and the other eight to the left. The 10th Indiana Battery pelted Savage's advancing line with shells on his right while Captain Daniel Cockerill's Battery F, 1st Ohio Light, fired salvo after salvo of canister at nearly point-blank range directly on his front. "A cannon ball knocked down a soldier near my horse which so frightened the horse that it made desperate attempts to throw me which caused the regiment to halt to see the result," Savage admitted. "Unable to quiet the animal, I dismounted and sent it to the rear and went on foot for the balance of the battle."[44]

Hazen deployed his men in two ranks—the front line had the 41st Ohio on the left and the 6th Kentucky on the right. The 9th Indiana and 110th Illinois aligned a few paces behind them in support, the gently sloping ground offering them a clear field of fire over the heads of the front-line regiments. Beyond Hazen's left and a few hundred yards to the rear lay Colonel George D. Wagner's 2nd Brigade in Wood's 1st Division. "The enemy had by this time taken position around the burnt [Cowan] house and the action at my position became terrific," Hazen recalled. "The efforts of the enemy to force back my front and cross the cottonfield were persistent and were prevented only by the most unflinching determination on the part of the 41st Ohio and 110th Illinois to hold their ground to the last."[45]

"The enemy came on in fine style to the attack of this position," recalled the regimental historians of the 41st Ohio. "The fire of the regiment was held until the enemy was within easy range and then let go with tremendous effect. The enemy was staggered, struggled forward a few yards further, but could make no more headway." Federal artillery showered the Tennesseans with canister shot. "The advance was made under a heavy cannonade, and the line of battle and direction

---

43 Kimberly, *The 41st Ohio*, 9-12.

44 Savage, *Life of John H. Savage*, 139.

45 Kimberly, *The 41st Ohio*, 40; OR 20/1:544.

Sergeant Andrew M. Chandler, Co. F, 44th Mississippi (left) and his slave Silas Chandler.

Library of Congress

maintained, although serious obstructions impeded the march," Savage would write. Under withering fire, the left companies of the 16th Tennessee closed through an open field to within 150 yards. "At this moment it seemed to me that I was without the expected support on my left, and that the line had divided and gone off in that direction," he added. "My men shot the horses and gunners of the battery in front, but I could not advance without being outflanked and struck by the enemy on my right; I therefore ordered them to halt and fire."[46]

Savage discovered the 44th Mississippi lying prone about 150 yards from Hazen's line and moved his command to that regiment's right, going to ground soon as well. In a few minutes, he received unexpected but welcome support from the 39th North Carolina under Colonel David Coleman, arriving behind the 16th

46 OR 20/1:717.

Tennessee's line. Savage promptly had the North Carolinians bulk up his right flank. "We were marched to the right of the center division unattached to any brigade and on our approach to a fence, the Yanks shelled on us our and wounded several," wrote Captain Alfred W. Bell of the 39th. Coleman was leveled as the regiment went into line and command devolved to Bell, who would write: "We pitched in our little regiment and the 16th Tennessee with not many more men than we had. The Yankees played on us with two batteries."[47]

The 41st Ohio had exhausted about half its ammunition repulsing Chalmers's charge, and as the slugfest with Savage continued, its supply ran further short. Hazen's efforts to obtain a fresh hoard came to naught, and a new crisis arose when the 16th Tennessee seemed on the verge of a charge. Hazen turned to his reserve regiment, the 110th Illinois, and directed Colonel Thomas Casey to have his rookies fix bayonets. "I replied that we had no bayonets and received the answer that we should club muskets if attacked," Casey recalled. Hazen ordered Lt. Col. Aquilla Wiley to have his Ohioans of the 41st fix bayonets but soon ordered Colonel William Blake's 9th Indiana forward to relieve the Ohioans. "The Indianans had come to the war with a feeling that some taint was on them because an Indiana regiment in the Mexican War met with harsh censure on its conduct," recalled one veteran. "The 9th Indiana, from the day it took the field, was set to prove that the men from its state would fight."[48]

Carrying 60 rounds of ammunition, the Hoosiers double-quicked from their reserve position. Blake "brought his regiment up marching by the flank a few paces in the rear of the 41st Ohio which was then engaged and under severe artillery fire," recorded one Buckeye, who would be appalled by "this magnificent but useless bravado when a shell flying waist high exploded at the point where the fours were wheeling to take place in the line. Strange to say, the missile took but four men, two before it and two behind, and caused not an instant's pause in the movement." The shell "mangled them desperately and set fire to their clothes," recalled Captain Dyer McConnell of the 9th Indiana. "The left companies marched past those struggling wretches, opening ranks as they passed, and closing them again and then as the respective companies came on the line and the markers stepped out, inverted their guns, and the line was dressed as if on parade."

---

47 Captain Alfred W. Bell Papers, Co. B, 39th North Carolina, Book, Manuscript and Special Collections Library, Duke University. The 39th North Carolina would be assigned to Brig. Gen. J. Patton Anderson's Brigade for the remainder of the battle.

48 OR 20/1:551; Kimberly, *The 41st Ohio*, 40.

The right of Blake's line rested on the Nashville Pike and the left stretched to the railroad; "with a shout that inspired confidence in all," the Hoosiers relieved the Buckeyes. "They had proved that they could be as steady in a fight as men cut out of stone," noted one impressed Ohioan. The Buckeyes reciprocated, Hazen noted proudly, retiring "with its thinned ranks in perfect order as if on parade. A few discharges from the fresh regiments sufficed to check the enemy who drew out of range."[49]

Federal artillery took a beating from both close-range musketry and the converging fire of several Confederate batteries. Cockerill's Battery F lost 16 horses in short order, the captain unhorsed and wounded in the process, and lost one of the limbers struck by a shell. Two of the battery's guns had their axles shivered when struck by solid shot. "[T]he very air was full of metal," Cockerill recalled. "The Rebels were getting fearfully close to us but the brave 9th Indiana stood their ground and held them from charging us. The enemy artillery was playing havoc with us and literally tore up the ground and logs around us."

A momentary panic arose when the gunners reported that the limbers were getting empty, and Cockerill, looking to the rear, discovered his caissons were nowhere in sight. Confusion in orders pressed the lieutenant commanding the caissons to move them farther north than Cockerill desired; now the battery risked capture due to lack of ammunition. Private James Blair gallantly rode back and brought forward an armful of shells. "I left [them] at the gun and started back to the caissons and saw a short distance in front of me two men carrying a wounded comrade on a stretcher," he wrote. "The next moment a cannon ball passed near me and struck both men, tearing them to pieces without touching the man on the stretcher."[50]

Once the 41st Ohio cleared out of the way, Blake and the 9th Indiana got their first clear view of the Confederate force they faced. "The Rebels occupied the burnt house with one battery and their infantry, partially covered by the outhouses and a stockade fence extending to the pike," the colonel recalled. "I at once opened

---

49 Kimberly, *The 41st Ohio*, 40-41; Captain Dyer B. McConnell, Co. K, 9th Indiana, "The Ninth Indiana," *National Tribune,* Nov. 11, 1886, 2; William B. Hazen, *A Narrative of Military Service* (Boston, 1885), 73. The 110th Illinois went into action "poorly armed" in Casey's estimation, being armed with a mix of smoothbores and rifled muskets "of various calibers and manufacture ranging from 1812 to 1856." The regiment did not even receive shoulder straps for their cartridge boxes until mid-December.

50 Captain Daniel T. Cockerill and Private James F. Blair, Battery F, 1st Ohio Light Artillery, James Barnett Papers, WRHS.

fire upon them and but a short time intervened until their artillery limbered up and retired in confusion to the rifle pits on the ridge where they went to battery and opened fire. After three-quarters of an hour, the fire from the infantry in our front slackened and many of them ran to the rear in disorder." The 16th Tennessee, 44th Mississippi, and 39th North Carolina all went to ground and continued to pepper the Federal line with long-range musketry, but with the cotton field ahead of them carpeted with the dead and dying, the Confederates refused to venture into the field again.[51]

Thomas Wood, Crittenden's 1st Division commander, was wounded in the heel during the morning fighting, and General Hascall, commanding Wood's 1st Brigade, took the initiative at this crisis moment. Realizing Hazen needed help, he ordered Colonel Samuel McKee's 3rd Kentucky in his brigade to deploy on Hazen's right. The Kentuckians would proceed into a maelstrom of lead, though, losing 10 of 14 company officers in quick succession. Within moments McKee, too, fell dead from his horse. Major Daniel Collier took command but would be struck once in the leg and in the chest, and adjutant William Bullitt's horse was killed beneath him. With the 3rd Kentucky in serious trouble now, too, Hascall sent Captain William H. Squires's 26th Ohio and Lieutenant George Estep's 8th Indiana Battery as reinforcements. "No sooner had the 26th got into position than they became hotly engaged," Hascall reported, "and the numerous dead and wounded that were immediately brought to the rear told how desperate the contest was."[52]

"The Rebels made two or three most determined attacks on different parts of the line, thinking to break it, as they had broken others before during the morning, but they could not do it," wrote Captain John James of the 26th Ohio. "Forming in the edge of the woods, they advanced boldly about half across the open field but the fire was too much for them, and they fell back to repeat the attempt on some other part with better success."[53]

Federal stragglers in their front created confusion for the 26th Ohio. "While we were firing here, a cry was raised in the ranks that we were firing on our own men, that another line was in front of us and we were firing into their rear," James

---

51 *OR* 20/1:552.

52 Ibid., 468. General Wood supposedly refused to have his wounded heel dressed and remained on the field for the rest of the day. The wound was serious enough to sideline him for the remaining two days of the battle and he did not return to action until February 15, 1863.

53 James Letter.

recalled. "This created great doubt and hesitation for a time and partly suspended our fire. Determined to ascertain the truth of the matter if it could be ascertained, I went down to ask the major, leaving Lieutenant Foster in command of the company. Major Squires, who sent the adjutant to General Hascall for information, said the General knew of no forces of ours there and if they were our men, they had no business to be there, and his answer to me was to pour it into them."[54]

Estep's battery quickly turned the fortunes of battle in the Federals' favor. "The enemy in three lines made three desperate charges and were as often repulsed by my battery," the lieutenant reported. "I expended 70 rounds of canister and was compelled four or five times to double-charge the pieces in order to drive the enemy; this beginning at a range of 90 yards and increasing as the enemy became confused and retired. I also fired from this position 106 rounds of shrapnel and solid shot, at a range of about 800 yards, at the lines of the enemy advancing on our right."[55]

Confederate casualties mounted rapidly; eventually Savage would lose 207 of the 407 men he led into the fight. "In a few moments my acting lieutenant colonel Lucius Savage fell by my side, supposed mortally wounded, and my acting major Captain James Womack had his right arm badly broken," Savage reported. The contest with Hazen's line, Womack remembered, was "most severe. At this time, the enemy advanced a few paces, emerging from the cedars and keeping up an incessant fire. The space between the two lines was now an unobstructed plain of about 100 yards, we were lying down and shooting and they were standing."[56]

"There were batteries to the right and left of the railroad which literally swept the ground," observed Savage. "The left companies, being very near and without any protection, sustained a heavy loss. Thirty men were left dead upon the spot where they halted dressed in perfect line of battle."[57]

"All that morning I was oppressed with a dark foreboding that evil awaited me, and sure enough it came about 11 o'clock," recalled John Nichols, orderly sergeant of the 16th Tennessee. According him, his company suffered so heavily at Perryville that it could only muster 23 for service at Stones River battle, only six of whom would escape unhurt. In the current combat, "My right and left file were

---

54 Ibid.

55 *OR* 20/1:717.

56 Ibid.; James J. Womack, *The Civil War Diary of Capt. J. J. Womack* (McMinnville, 1961), 78.

57 *OR* 20/1:717.

both killed before I was wounded. Our men were falling so fast I saw that we must be reinforced or be defeated." Nichols continued:

> Just then I received a one-ounce Minie ball in my right hip which completely paralyzed my right leg. For some minutes I lay on the ground watching the maneuvering of the enemy, but fully realizing the great danger to which I was exposed, I determined to try to leave the field. I arose, but immediately fell to the ground. I summoned all of my strength and it seemed to concentrate in my left leg, so I did a first-rate job of hopping for about one-fourth of a mile where I took shelter behind an oak tree near a pond of water. Tip, tip, tip went an occasional ball into that pond but I felt much safer there than I did on the field.[58]

In the Federal ranks, the soldiers felt both relief and delight. Aquilla Wiley, now out of the range of enemy fire, marched his 41st Ohio back about 50 yards behind the railroad embankment and began dispensing ammunition to his drained Buckeyes. "Just as we lay down, proud of what we had done," recalled Lieutenant Elias Ford, "Colonel Wiley waved his hat while a glow of earnestness and enthusiasm tinged his cheek and shouted, 'Soldiers of the 41st Ohio! You're the bravest set of men God ever let live! If we get close upon the enemy and are ordered to charge, I want you to charge as though you were the very demons of hell.'"

For a brief period the fight at the Round Forest had devolved into an artillery engagement, which in turn gave the infantry a brief respite. Hazen's men held their ground against Donelson—the second attack of the day on the position—and for the first time in the battle, the Confederates had been stymied.

As the Union Right Wing and Negley's battered division fell back to safety behind the Nashville Pike, the focal point of the battle shifted west, where Rousseau's division found itself locked in a swirling fight with a pair of Confederate divisions in the cedar thickets.[59]

---

58 "Experiences in the Battle of Murfreesboro," Orderly Sergeant John H. Nichols, Co. F, 16th Tennessee, *Confederate Veteran*, Apr. 1902, 162-63.

59 Ford Letter; Corporal Charles P. Bail, Co. B, 41st Ohio, *Jeffersonian Democrat*, Jan. 23, 1863, 1.

Breakwater Before the Torrent: The Fight to Hold the Nashville Pike

CAPTAIN GATES P. THRUSTON was in charge of the 76 wagons constituting General McCook's ordnance train. After witnessing the damage inflicted to the rest of the train along the Wilkinson Pike, Gates was determined to move the vehicles out of danger. Thruston had 75 soldiers and a pair of orderlies with him, but lacking "special orders, just what to do was something of a problem," he remembered. "I decided to direct my train toward the center of the infantry line, keeping well to the front. At the very start a detachment of Confederate cavalry charged wildly upon the train, attacking and endeavoring to stampede our teamsters and animals, but with the aid of the plucky train guards and some help from Captain Henry Pease of General Jefferson Davis's staff, we repulsed the attack and moved on. It was a toilsome struggle to guide and push our unwieldy trains through byways, ravines, and fences, and to cut our way through the cedar thickets."[1]

<hr>

1 Gates P. Thruston, "Personal Recollections of the Battle in the Rear at Stone's River, Tennessee," *Sketches of War History, 1861-1865*, in *Papers Prepared for the Commandery of the State of Ohio, Military Order of the Loyal Legion of the United States*, Vol. 6 (Cincinnati, 1908), 225.

John A. Wharton's intrepid Rebel cavalry pushed more than two miles into the Federal rear near the Wilkinson Pike, where the swaying white canvas tops of Thruston's wagons attracted the Confederate general's attention. Colonel John T. Cox formed his 1st Confederate troopers, as well as three Tennessee battalions, for a charge while Captain Benjamin F. White's Tennessee Battery dropped shells amid the fleeing Federals. "The enemy's immense wagon trains, guarded by a heavy force of cavalry could be seen moving near and in the rear of the enemy in the direction of the Nashville Pike," Wharton noted. "I determined to move across the country, give the cavalry battle, and attempt to capture the train."

Thus far, the battle had been a lark for Wharton's troopers, who had gathered as many as 1,500 prisoners and two pieces of artillery while losing roughly only 20 killed or wounded. The men were exultant but hungry. "General Wharton complimented the regiment for its dash and gallantry, but his compliments fell on empty stomachs for we had eaten no supper or breakfast and the morning exercise had generated a taste for something more substantial than compliments from the general commanding," recalled Lieutenant William R. Friend of the 8th Texas.[2]

Thruston saw them coming. "In my anxiety for its safety," he would write, "I already reported the importance of the train to every cavalry officer within reach and appealed for protection." Colonel Lewis Zahm answered the call, lining up his 1st and 3rd Ohio Cavalry for a charge. Although Confederate artillery fire quickly broke his formations, mortally wounding Major David A. B. Moore of the 1st Ohio in the process, Zahm responded adeptly. "I now fell back, formed a new line, received the enemy's charge, repulsed them, and made many of the Rebels bite the dust," he reported.

After repelling two thrusts by Wharton, Zahm withdrew to an open lot, hoping that the move of his brigade between Wharton's advance and Thruston's wagons would shield the train. "The enemy's cavalry was working round our right all the time, and the infantry and artillery following us closely in our rear and to our left," he recalled. "They had cavalry enough to spare to strike, or to take position, whenever required." Corporal Edward Burlingame of the 1st Ohio put it more succinctly: "We were like a drove and still harder pressed, the foe riding down on us and with their revolvers firing on us as they came. As we were compelled to go through fences, we lost our formation and became mixed up. This kept getting

2 *OR* 20/1:967.

worse. We were nearing the pike, our line of communication to the rear, and the sight of the long line of wagons must have given the Rebels encouragement."[3]

The ammunition train, now stretched along Asbury Lane, continued its scramble north toward the perceived safety of the Nashville Pike. Zahm deployed three battalions of the 3rd Ohio as direct protection for the lumbering train, then sent the shaky troopers of the 2nd East Tennessee to guard his right and the 1st and 4th Ohio the left. "A heavy body of cavalry was drawn up near and parallel to the pike, facing me, and a considerable body was drawn up nearer me to give battle," Wharton wrote. "The battery was placed in position. [Colonel Henry M.] Ashby's 2nd Tennessee Cavalry and [Captain] L. T. Hardy's company formed in front of the enemy. [Colonel] Harrison's command [8th Texas] formed on his right flank. The battery opened with considerable effect. It was ordered to cease firing and Ashby and Hardy ordered to charge, which they promptly did."[4]

Zahm's men were unprepared for the charge. "When the crisis came a few moments later, they were not in position to successfully withstand the shock," Thruston conceded. The East Tennesseans were the first to bolt—"running like sheep," Zahm acidly reported—but the Ohioans did not fare much better. Confederate shells landing within the ranks of the 4th Ohio made them skittish, and Wharton's charge moments later sent them scampering off the field "at a pretty lively gait." Thruston reported that Confederate artillery "opened fire furiously upon the 4th Ohio Cavalry and threw the regiment into some confusion. Soon . . . his entire command charged down upon us like a tempest, his troopers yelling like a lot of devils. They first struck the 4th Ohio which could make but little resistance." Major John Pugh of that regiment reported apologetically that his men were soon "driven away from the train by shells from the enemy's guns and by his cavalry. The panic now became so general that our regiment in leaving the field got scattered."[5]

Colonel Minor Millikin, the 1st Ohio's spirited young commander, had thirsted for a moment like this since he first donned a blue uniform a year earlier. "The very acme of Colonel Millikin's ambition had been to have the regiment make a saber charge and now the supreme opportunity had arrived," noted one of his subordinates, Lieutenant William Curry. Regarded by many as the finest swords-man in Rosecrans's army, Millikin was an early convert to General Stanley's

3 Thruston, *Personal Recollections*, 227; OR 20/1:636; *History of Washington County, Ohio* (1881), 188.

4 *OR* 20/1:637, 967.

5 Ibid., 637, 644-645; Thruston, *Personal Recollections*, 228.

The Charge of the 1st Ohio Cavalry at Stones River,
as drawn by Sergeant Nathan Finegan of Co. D a few days after the battle.

William L. Curry, Four Years in the Saddle: History of the First Regiment Ohio Volunteer Cavalry
(Columbus: Champlin Printing Co., 1898)

emphasis on saber drill. Perturbed at the lack of direction from Zahm, the colonel impetuously decided to take matters into his own hands and unsheathed his new saber, a Christmas gift from his father. "He must act at once or his regiment would be stampeded and driven from the field as they were being pushed and crushed by an overwhelming force of the enemy flushed with victory," Curry recalled. "No officer of the brigade seemed to grasp the situation; no orders were given by the brigade commander." Millikin sent word to Lt. Col. Douglas Murray of the 3rd Ohio of his intentions and asked for support, but he did not wait for it before charging into the approaching Confederates.[6]

"He wheeled his regiment by fours to the rear, giving the command 'Draw saber!'" Curry recalled. "There was no time to tighten girths or to look after the condition of revolvers but tightening the reins on his noble bay Archie and raising in his stirrups, gave the command 'Charge!' which was repeated to the right and left along the line." Captain Martin Buck, who led Company H in the charge, recalled how "[W]e were yet moving at a rapid pace while not more than 100 yards from us

6 Curry, *Four Years in the Saddle*, 83.

was a long line of Rebel cavalry popping away at us as though they didn't care if they hit somebody. But now the command 'Charge' was given, and the boys went in with a yell, the Colonel leading. After charging and driving their first line several hundred yards," he added, "we came to another line to our right, drawn up at nearly right angles, which gave us a crossfire as we passed them, but being on rather lower ground than they were, I think they must have shot over us, particularly Co. H, as we were on the right and nearest to them."[7]

Wharton dispatched the 2nd Georgia to charge the train. The Georgians, however, lacked sidearms and were practically defenseless against Millikin's saber-wielding Buckeyes once they had fired the single round from their Enfield rifles. They tumbled in retreat, although that allowed Wharton to swarm around the Buckeyes' flanks with the 8th Texas, armed to the teeth with revolvers, shotguns, and carbines. Harrison prepared his Rangers for a counterattack, having observed Millikin's charging troopers from afar. "[Harrison] exclaimed, 'Now boys, we will have some fun'," recalled Lieutenant James Blackburn of the 8th Texas. "There is a regiment out there preparing to charge us, armed with sabers. Let them come up nearly close enough to strike and then feed them on buckshot.'"[8]

Lieutenant Frank Batchelor of the 8th Texas wrote that "as we rose over the hill, an exciting scene presented itself. The poor Georgians who, being unable to load in the face of the advancing foe, had turned and with heads smartly stretching forward like turkeys in a drive, were kicking their horses for dear life while Mr. Yankee had drawn his shining sword and was bending forward in hot pursuit making the air whiz with saber cuts." Harrison's Texans waded into the fight. "[We] charged them and drove them back and run them in every direction," recalled Ranger Dunbar Affleck. "I had eight shots and killed two Yankees, one of them I am certain I killed, shooting him in the back with 16 buckshot at ten steps, the other I shot in the body somewhere with my pistol."

"[A]s the Texans stood their ground the Yankees ran up to within a few steps and halted suddenly, giving our boys the chance they were wishing for," Blackburn recalled. "One volley from the shotguns into their ranks scattered these saber men into useless fragments of a force. Many of them surrendered and our boys quizzed

7 Captain Martin Buck, Co. H, 1st Ohio Volunteer Cavalry, *Highland Weekly News*, Feb. 12, 1863, 1. The author's great-great-great grandfather was one of the men Buck commanded during this charge.

8 *OR* 20/1:967; Blackburn Article.

them with merciless questions. 'Why did you stop?' 'Are your sabers long ranged weapons?' 'How far can you kill a man with those things?'"[9]

"They now began to close in around us when all saw at a glance that we had to cut our way out or be taken prisoners," Buck noted. "All except those who had already surrendered, now took the chances of being shot in the back rather than surrender as prisoners of war. Your humble servant was among the latter, and by the good use of spurs and pistols, escaped without even a scratch." Millikin, too, saw the danger and ordered a retreat but remained engaged in the fight. "Single-handed and alone, surrounded by Rebel cavalrymen with his father's gift in his hand, his splendid swordsmanship came into play," wrote Alexander McClurg, a friend. "He cut down and disabled three of his assailants. Unheeding the shout of his adjutant William Scott who lay wounded on the ground near him, 'For God's sake, Colonel, surrender or they'll kill you!' Millikin acting on his resolve that 'I will never surrender to a Rebel' had nearly extricated himself from the melee when a pistol shot struck him." According to one account, "the ball, supposed to be a from a carbine, entered the neck and severed the jugular vein."[10]

"The Colonel, overanxious to distinguish himself in this war, probably acted in this affair without proper discretion," Buck admitted. "But he was nevertheless a brave man and exhibited more coolness and presence of mind than any other cavalry commander on the ground." Millikin's death left command of the regiment with Captain Valentine Cupp, who gathered the survivors and trotted them north along Asbury Lane, grumbling that it was "very unfortunate for us that the regiment had not been removed to the rear long before." The rout of Zahm's brigade "was not very creditable," Cupp declared—a gross understatement. "I was with the three regiments that skedaddled and among the last to leave the field. I tried hard to rally them but the panic was so great that I could not do it. Matters looked pretty blue now."[11]

---

9 Blackburn Article; Rugeley, *Batchelor-Turner Letters*, 42; Robert A. Williams and Ralph A. Wooster, eds., "With Terry's Texas Rangers: Letters of Dunbar Affleck," *Civil War History*, Sept. 1963, 312.

10 Buck Letter; Alexander C. McClurg, "An American Soldier: Minor Millikin," *Military Essays and Recollections*, in *Papers Read Before the Commandery of the State of Illinois, Military Order of the Loyal Legion of the United States*, Vol. 2 (Chicago, 1894), 370-71; *History of Butler County*, 221. Private John Bowers of the 8th Texas Cavalry, Co. K, is credited with shooting Colonel Millikin.

11 Buck Letter; Captain Valentine Cupp, Co. F, 1st Ohio Volunteer Cavalry, *Weekly Lancaster Gazette*, Jan. 29, 1863, 2; OR 20/1:637.

The failure of Millikin's valiant, though ill-conceived, charge bought only a moment's respite for Thruston's ordnance train. "There was no staying the Confederates," he observed. "They outnumbered and outflanked us and to tell the melancholy truth, our defending cavalry retired in confusion to the rear and left the ammunition train to its fate—high and dry in a cornfield." Wharton quickly took advantage of the situation. "The wagon train, consisting of several hundred wagons, many pieces of artillery, and about 1,000 infantry who were either guarding the wagons or were fugitives from the field, was ours," Thruston reported. "The trains were turned round and started back on the pike toward Murfreesboro."

Sergeant Austin Miller of the 101st Ohio was among those captured. "As the secesh cavalry bore in sight, the stars and bars fluttering in the wind, they came on, firing, cursing, yelling like a set of fiends let loose from pandemonium," the Ohioan recounted a few days later. "Our cavalry was falling on every side until at length coming up with the rear of the train with their cocked revolvers pointed in the driver's faces, ordered our teams to about face."[12]

"As may be imagined, our teamsters, the train guards, and the ordnance officer were not left far behind in the general stampede," Thruston acknowledged. "We fired one volley from behind the protection of our wagons and then hunted cover in the rear of a friendly fence and in the nearest thicket. Our teamsters outran the cavalry and most of them never reappeared. The Confederates began to collect and lead away our teams and wagons, and our condition seemed desperate, indeed hopeless. Happily, this state of affairs did not last long."[13]

*　　*　　*

The triumphant Confederates thundered down Asbury Lane, taking prisoners by the bushel, but they would also range too far. Despite the chaos threatening to engulf them, two 3rd Ohio battalions kept together. Major James Paramore reported that his men "did not break their lines nor join in that stampede but received the galling fire of the enemy with the firmness of heroes. The enemy, seeing our determination and bold resistance, turned and left us, and pursued the broken columns of our cavalry that had fled. We then wheeled and charged upon their rear with terrible effect scattering their columns in worse confusion, if

---

12 Thruston, *Personal Recollections*, 228; OR 20/1:967; Sergeant Austin W. Miller, Co. H, 101st Ohio, *Tiffin Weekly Tribune*, Jan.16, 1863, 2.

13 Thruston, *Personal Recollections*, 228.

possible, than they had just routed the balance of our brigade, killing a number of men and horses and taking some 10 or 12 prisoners, and releasing a large number of our brigade that they had captured."[14]

Wharton's troopers, recalled Sergeant Coleman Watts of the 7th Pennsylvania Cavalry, barreled ahead "with as motley a crowd of ragamuffins as I ever beheld. They passed one wagon when the 3rd Ohio, with Colonel Zahm and Lieutenant Colonel Murray at their head, went for them and in less than five minutes there was such a lot of dirty gray and cinnamon color lying on the road and flying in a retrograde movement as would have made the hearts of the loyal North think the rebellion was squelched." Noted 3rd Ohio orderly sergeant Wordon Welcher: "[W]e were so often mixed up that we could not tell friends from foes except by the butternuts' coats, and they even came at us in the coats of our slain comrades. How any of us escaped with our lives seems now, to look upon it, one of the great mysteries."[15]

Since eight that morning, Captain Elmer Otis had hovered west of Rosecrans's headquarters with six companies of the 4th US Cavalry on the Army of the Cumberland's right flank, keeping an eye out for roving bands of Confederate cavalry. Two-thirds of his 300 troopers were new recruits, though not in the traditional sense. The men who joined Otis's command in Nashville enlisted directly from their volunteer regiments, as many had seen months of infantry service and wished to try their hand perched atop a saddle in combat. The men received roughly five days of training. As such, they were green cavalrymen but not green soldiers, and they were fortunate to serve under accomplished officers such as Otis and Captain Eli Long. The Regulars had yet to find many Confederates, but the woods were filled with "stragglers who on our approach endeavored to escape," wrote one trooper. "Some took courage and the remnants of two regiments were rallied by their colonels."[16]

"Learning from some men of General Davis's division the position of the enemy's cavalry," Otis reported, "I made a turn to the right, moving about one-quarter of a mile, and discovered the enemy." Turning his command to the west, he rode in squarely on Wharton's rear, finding an unguarded artillery battery

---

14 *OR* 20/1:643.

15 Sergeant Coleman H. Watts, Co. M, 7th Pennsylvania Volunteer Cavalry, "Lovejoy Station," *National Tribune*, Dec. 3, 1891, 4; Orderly Sergeant Wordon W. Welcher, Co. F, 3rd Ohio Volunteer Cavalry, *Lorain County News*, Jan. 28, 1863, 2.

16 Regular, 4th US Cavalry, *Lancaster Daily Express*, Jan. 28, 1863.

in the open. The surprise arrival of Otis's troopers was a rude shock for Wharton. "I was informed that a heavy cavalry force immediately in my rear was about to charge my battery, which, being unable to keep up with the cavalry in a charge, was some distance behind," he reported. "My arrival was most opportune. About 300 of the enemy's cavalry, not over 400 yards distant, were bearing down upon the battery with a speed that evinced a determination to take it at all hazards. A few men, with Colonel Smith, were promptly formed, and the battery unlimbered and ordered to fire upon the approaching enemy. Several shells were exploded in their ranks."[17]

"I came out of a piece of timber I was in," Otis recalled, "and, getting over the fence rapidly, charged the enemy with my entire command, completely routing them, with the exception of two pieces of artillery." Rapid fire from those two guns caught the Regulars by surprise. Lacking the strength to take them, Otis rallied his men out of range and sought another target, but he then noticed "about 300 of the volunteer cavalrymen on my right.… I rode over to them and asked them to charge the artillery with me and the few men I had rallied to take the pieces."[18]

Otis's supplication was fruitless, so he returned his attention north. Opportunity knocked when he came upon a flock of Wharton's troopers swarming a collection of Federal ordnance wagons. "Quickly moving round by the right in a half circle, we neared an open field on the opposite side of which we beheld a brigade of Rebel cavalry," recorded one trooper. "We dared not stop to count numbers. Our commander gave the word, 'Front, into line, charge!' And such a charge. Our column, small in number, closed up and in good order we advanced. On we came, yelling like so many savages and scattered them like chaff. When we neared them, they broke. We recaptured 300 of [General] Johnson's men and brought back with us 170 Texas Rangers and Ashby's cavalry."[19]

Otis's two swift strikes, combined with a counterattack by the 3rd Ohio Cavalry farther north on Asbury Lane, sucked the wind from Wharton's attack. He withdrew his troopers down the lane, abandoning the train. "The command that had captured the wagons, thinking that they had driven the entire force of the enemy's cavalry across Overall's Creek, and apprehending danger only from that quarter, were prepared to meet it only from that direction," Wharton acknowledged. "Owing to this and to my being detailed to defend the battery, we

17 *OR* 20/1:649, 967.

18 Ibid., 649.

19 4th US Cavalry Letter.

were able only to bring off a portion of the wagons, five or six pieces of artillery, about 400 prisoners, 327 beef cattle, and a goodly number of mules cut from the wagons."[20]

Watching from the nearby cedars, Thurston could not believe his luck. "I hastened to appeal to the commander to aid our train guard in saving the train," he wrote. "He at once covered our front and held the enemy in check until our badly wrecked train, with its disabled wagons and scattered animals was reorganized and put in moving order. We repaired and patched up the breaks." Everyone, even officers and stragglers, helped and nearly every wagon was recovered. "The train guards and volunteers mounted the leaders," he continued, "and we were soon moving towards Murfreesboro pike and the left of our army at double quick speed. The enemy, still bent on destroying our train, followed us like sleuth hounds."

Rallying squads of volunteers as drivers, Thruston soon had his lumbering wagons moving again on the Nashville Pike, where Federal reinforcements continued heading toward the front lines. McCook's ordnance train was finally safe.[21]

By 9:00 a.m., the trickle of stragglers from McCook's wing had turned into a flood, all running for the perceived safety of the Nashville Pike. Surgeon William Mills of the 18th Ohio was stunned by the spectacle. "God knows that I never before saw anything like it," he wrote. "I had not the least conception of what the word skedaddle meant. It means horrors beyond description. Just imagine a thousand wagons, ambulances, and the like, mixed up with a thousand panic-stricken soldiers, throwing away their arms and accoutrements, running like mad; wagons breaking down or getting jammed into each other, with the enemy hotly pursuing with cavalry and infantry, sending a continuous shower of bullets after the running miscreants, killing, wounding, and capturing them with impunity, and you have a faint idea of what I saw Wednesday morning."[22]

Thomas's provost guards, the 9th Michigan under Lt. Col. John Parkhurst, rounded up stragglers and herded them back into the ranks. Parkhurst could not hide his disgust. "I noticed many stragglers crossing the fields from the … right wing of the army and sent out force to bring them in until I had 100–200 collected," he wrote. "I discovered several cavalrymen approaching with great speed from the direction of the front and very soon discovered that a large cavalry force with

<hr>

20 *OR* 20/1:967.

21 Thruston, *Personal Recollections*, 228-29.

22 Assistant Surgeon William W. Mills, 18th Ohio, *Gallipolis Journal*, Jan. 30, 1863, 2.

infantry and a long transportation train were in the most rapid retreat, throwing away their arms and accoutrements, many without hats or caps, and apparently in the most frightful state of mind crying 'We are all lost.'"[23]

"Before many had passed me, I drew my regiment up in line of battle across the road extending on either side and ordered my men to fix bayonets and take a position of guard against cavalry," Parkhurst continued. "This was done with celerity and much difficulty. I succeeded in checking their course and ordered every man to face about. Within half an hour I had collected about 1,000 cavalrymen, seven pieces of artillery, and nearly two regiments of infantry, among them a brigadier general. From the reports made by these troops, I did not know but the enemy were in pursuit in force and consequently I organized the force I had collected and formed them in line of battle on the crest of the hill on the other side of Overall's Creek, planting the artillery on the left and center."[24]

General Stanley soon appeared with a portion of the army's reserve cavalry and waded into the debris of battle choking the pike. "About three miles from the right of McCook's corps we first met stragglers—first a few dozen, then a hundred, and finally not less than 5,000," he observed. "These shameless scoundrels had thrown away their guns, their ammunition, their blankets, and overcoats, had stripped themselves of everything impeding flight, and were off for Nashville as fast as their cowardly legs could carry them. I never saw a more shameful thing than this runaway."[25]

Farther north on the Nashville Pike, near Stewart's Creek, Colonel Moses B. Walker's brigade in George Thomas's corps met the torrent of fleeing stragglers as it marched toward the sound of the guns. "There is always a drifting away of more or less stragglers from a line of troops under fire," observed Samuel McNeil of the 31st Ohio, "but the wreckage of an entire division which had been swept from the Union right that morning by an overwhelming force of Confederates was a real surprise to us as we marched with ranks well closed." McNeil and other marching Buckeyes and Hoosiers looked on as many of the severely wounded were helped along by stronger comrades. Most of them, thought McNeil, "appeared to be overcome by the awful disaster of the early morning, but some were terror-stricken and seemed to think of nothing except their own personal safety. We offered some

---

23 OR 20/1:652.

24 Ibid., 652-653. It is unclear which brigadier Parkhurst collected in his dragnet; one name offered by Colonel William Carlin was William Woodruff.

25 Stanley, *Personal Memoirs*, 126.

advice to the latter class and one of my comrades suggested to one of the stragglers that he ought to stop for dinner at a sand pit. But in spite of our kidding, if we had expressed our honest opinions, we were not encouraged." Jokes aside, McNeil could see "the tide of battle was against our comrades on the battle line."

The marching reinforcements peppered the stragglers with questions. "How is it going now at the front?" they shouted.

"One bright boy with a shattered arm," recorded a Buckeye, "replied as follows: 'They drove our men back to the Nashville Pike this morning, but I'll bet a brass watch that before Bragg gets through with this job, he will want Rosecrans' men to stop killing Rebels.'"

His optimistic reply was the exception, recorded McNeil. The consensus among the exhausted soldiers was that the Confederates "were having everything their own way. We had been in active service at the front more than a year, and we really thought that ours was a regiment of seasoned veterans, but the anxiety of both the officers and soldiers was perceptible as our column approached the battlefield."[26]

McNeil also described how the men stripped themselves for combat. "During the last two miles of our march towards Stones River, cards were thrown aside as undesirable property, and at one place the Nashville Pike was so nearly covered with the little pasteboards that one could imagine the cards had snowed down," he recalled after the war. "I have serious doubts about there having been one deck of cards left in the pocket of a soldier belonging to the brigade when we arrived at the front; kings, queens, and spots were at a discount," he added poetically, "but the pocket Bibles and testaments held their own as they have in times of peace and times of war for many centuries."[27]

Captain Thruston, meanwhile, breathed a deep sigh of relief as he led McCook's ammunition train to a safe point behind the lines near Stones River. "Soon after the train was parked," he recalled, "General Rosecrans with staff and escort appeared on the main road not far away and I happened to meet Captain Thomson, one of his aides[,] who congratulated me on my escape, remarking that he heard I was captured with my train. 'No,' I replied, 'my ammunition train is safe.' He said the General was greatly worried about the loss of that train and hastened to inform him of its safety. In a short time, General Rosecrans with Captain Thomson

26 McNeil, Samuel A. *Personal Recollections of Service in the Army of the Cumberland and Sherman's Army* (Richwood, 1910), 2.

27 Ibid., 3-4.

and his military retinue came trotting toward me and the General called out to me, 'Are you the officer who says that McCook's ammunition train is saved?' I replied, 'yes sir' with a salute. 'How do you know it?' he asked. 'I had charge of it, sir,' I said. 'Where is it?' he asked and riding with him a few yards around a cedar thicket, I pointed to the train."

"It really looked fairly well considering the wear and tear of the day," Thruston continued. "'How did you manage to get it away over here?' I replied, 'Well General, we did some sharp fighting but a great deal more running.' He seemed delighted and asking me my name and rank, he slapped me on the shoulder and remarked in a voice loud enough for all to hear, 'Captain, consider yourself a major from today!' It was a promotion on the field in true Napoleonic style."[28]

*　　*　　*

As midday approached, control of the Nashville Pike became the principal objective for both armies. With his battle lines in disarray and battle plan in shambles, Rosecrans's entire focus now centered on holding the pike regardless of cost. He eventually employed nearly his entire army to secure this objective, centering his defense along a low ridge running between the pike and the railroad, where battery after battery took position facing the broad open fields to the west. Rosecrans would hunker down in defensive positions that afternoon to protect his supply line and fight for time, hoping to wear down Bragg's troops so he could launch a counteroffensive on his own timeline. Retaining the open road to Nashville would permit Rosecrans to draw reinforcements and supplies in numbers far beyond Bragg's means to interdict or counter them, which would ensure the ultimate success of the Federal effort at Murfreesboro.

Conversely, Confederate control of the pike signaled the potential death knell of Rosecrans's army. If Bragg could take and hold the Nashville Pike, he could sever Rosecrans's supply line and pin him at the bend of Stones River. So situated, Rosecrans's options would be bleak. He could attempt to force a breakout in the face of concentrated Confederate artillery batteries commanding the river plain, or he could attempt a highly dangerous river crossing at one of several nearby fords in the face of an enemy present on both sides of the river. If this second option were successful, Rosecrans would be stuck east of the river with Bragg between him and his base at Nashville. That said, since time was Bragg's greatest enemy, he would

28 Thruston, *Personal Recollections*, 231.

gamble all to seize the pike that afternoon regardless of cost. The challenge for both sides lay in the deployment of their available manpower to decide the issue.

The Union right wing had been broken, however, and was streaming toward the Nashville Pike, where Rosecrans's staff fanned out desperately trying to aid McCook and his subordinates in rallying the survivors. Rousseau's brigades had disappeared into the cedars on Negley's right about 10:00 that morning, and the storm of noise and smoke was the only evidence that they, too, were now fully engaged with the Confederates. Thomas's two divisions in the center, fighting in concert with Sheridan's division, had bought perhaps 90 minutes of time, but Negley's division now poured out of the cedars, likewise rushing for the Nashville Pike. Rousseau was certainly not far behind.

Palmer's division in Crittenden's corps still held the left center. Hazen's brigade, locked in the death struggle with Donelson, held the Round Forest, but Cruft's brigade to his right began retreating from the cedars as the flight of Negley's brigades exposed his right flank. On the far left, Crittenden halted his crossing of Stones River and sent brigades from both Van Cleve's and Wood's divisions west toward the Nashville Pike, where Rosecrans could dispatch them as needed to counter the onrushing Confederate tide.

At no place on the battlefield was the confusion and terror more prevalent than for the thousands of men battling within the cedar forest where Rousseau's struggle to hold the Federal right had quickly turned desperate. Beatty's and Shepherd's brigades made a reputable fight of it, but they were like two rocks with a Confederate ocean breaking upon and all around them. With the retreat of Sheridan's division and then Negley's on his left, Rousseau faced both Pat Cleburne's and John McCown's divisions alone on his front and right while Cheatham's and Withers' divisions moved into the cedars on his left. That Rousseau could not see what was coming his way only increased the difficulty.

And unfortunately, the battered survivors of Johnson's and Davis's divisions proved no help at all. "General McCook's troops, in a good deal of confusion, retired through our lines and around our right under a most terrific fire," Rousseau reported. "The enemy, in pursuit, furiously assailed our front, and, greatly outflanking us, passed around to our right and rear. By General Thomas' direction, I had already ordered the artillery to the open field in the rear. Seeing that my command was outflanked on the right, I sent orders to the brigade commanders to retire at once also to this field."[29]

---

29 *OR* 20/1:378.

The order arrived not a moment too soon, as already the leakage of men from Rousseau's lines had accelerated. Alfred Pirtle, Rousseau's divisional ordnance officer, observed the withdrawal of his division from the cedars. "Across the cotton fields, a few men straggled leisurely to the rear," he wrote. "An ambulance trotted out of the cedars with wounded men, then a squad of soldiers moved rather briskly away from the men. I saw the number of sound men growing larger very rapidly. I was mortified to see a color guard with their regimental flags falling back and then the swarm grew apace so that I thought I was in the midst of another Bull Run."

Pirtle spied Rousseau himself debouching from the woods attended by only a single orderly: "I spurred my horse toward him and turned so as to face my wagons. 'General, shall I post the battery where my wagons are? It is the best position on the field.' Rousseau replied, 'Do it instantly. Tell [Lieutenant George] Van Pelt I will get him infantry support,' and away he went to look for troops. I galloped over to the cotton patch and delivered my order to Lieutenant Van Pelt. He looked at the spot, nodded affirmatively, and rode away to direct the foremost piece of the battery."[30]

Colonels Scribner and Shepherd both received Rousseau's order to retreat; Colonel Beatty did not and quickly found himself alone. "Neither Rousseau nor Loomis' battery could be found," Beatty wrote. "I sent a staff officer to the right and ascertained that Scribner's and Shepherd's brigades were gone. I concluded that the contingency had arisen to which General Rousseau referred to; that is to say that hell has frozen over and I about faced my brigade and marched to the rear where the guns appeared to be hammering away with redoubled fury."

As Beatty's men reached the edge of the cedars, they stumbled into a line of Federals under William Grose poised to plunge into the woods. Colonel Grose, commanding the reserve brigade in Palmer's division, had taken a defensive position on Hazen's right earlier that morning. The Indianan arrayed his five regiments (1,768 men) in three lines, all facing southwest. The front line consisted of Grose's two most senior regiments: the 6th Ohio held the left; the 36th Indiana, Grose's old command, the right. The 84th Illinois supported the Buckeyes, and the 23rd Kentucky supported the Hoosiers. Grose deployed the veteran 24th Ohio as a general reserve. His line had substantial artillery support: Lieutenant Charles

---

30 1st Lt. Alfred Pirtle, Co. H, 10th Ohio, "Donelson's Charge at Stone River," *Southern Bivouac*, Sept. 1886, 769.

Parsons's eight guns constituting Batteries H and M of the 4th US Light, the largest battery on the field.[31]

Spotting the wave of Federals retreating from the cedars, Grose ordered his frontline regiments (roughly 800 men) forward as support. The 36th Indiana, believing the Regular Brigade was directly on its front, entered the woods without a skirmish line. What they did not know was that Rains's Brigade, following Beatty's withdrawal through the woods, had advanced on their position. After moving about 40 yards into the woods, the Hoosiers detected movement in the trees. First Lieutenant Zene C. Bohrer recalled that "we could not see them until they were within 20 yards of our regiment. We saw them and supposed to be Johnson's men as many were dressed in U.S. overcoats; consequently, we were ordered not to fire upon our own men. The Rebels hallowed out 'Don't fire on your own men' then they opened fire, and a most terrific fire was poured out upon us." Captain Pyrrhus Woodward explained that "concealed from the view of my men by the thick undergrowth of cedars, the first indication we had of his presence was a volley from his muskets which riddled our ranks."[32]

The 11th Tennessee struck the Hoosiers ferociously and with precision, targeting the officers first. "Our men displayed as much coolness as veterans, sighted their guns as well, and with as much deliberation as if they were shooting at game," noted one Tennessee officer. Within moments, Major Isaac Kinley, commanding the 36th, went down with a fractured left thigh, and each mounted officer in the regiment but one had his horse shot from beneath them. "We gave them three heavy volleys and then we were forced to retreat," Bohrer recalled. "They were nearly all around us and would have captured all of us had we remained two minutes longer. They came up in two distinct columns and our men fell thick and fast when they opened on us. The regiment was completely cut to pieces."

Finding the Hoosiers' left flank exposed, Colonel Vance of the 29th North Carolina took advantage. "This arrival was opportune for one or two moments of firing drove the Yankee regiment away and thus saved the 11th Tennessee from being cut to pieces," he reported. The 36th Indiana was struck hard by Rains's assault and then rattled when the retreating 15th US passed through his left wing,

---

31 Beatty, *Citizen-Soldier*, 202; *OR* 20/1:560.

32 1st Lt. Zene C. Bohrer, Co., E, 36th Indiana, Linda Bohrer Anderson Collection; *OR* 20/1:567.

Brigadier General James Rains

Library of Congress

so Woodward concluded his "position could not be held." Leaving nearly 100 dead and wounded behind him, he ordered a withdrawal.[33]

The Hoosiers, however, had drawn blood—Vance describing the fight as a "hard one" and "the struggle of the day." When Rains rode up to compliment the Tar Heels, declaring, "I will bet my black horse on the Twenty-Ninth," a line of Federals, Vance recalled, "arose almost in our faces and fired. Struck in the heart by a Minié ball, Rains was killed instantly. As the young Tennessean fell to the ground, his horse bolted into the Federal lines. Captain William McCauley of the 11th Tennessee witnessed his commander's final moments, writing, "I saw General Rains fall from his horse mortally wounded and as I turned to tell one of my men that General Rains had fallen, a Minie ball penetrated three of my ribs and paralyzed my right leg."[34]

Pursuing the Hoosiers into the open field beyond, Rains's men ran into a blizzard of fire. "The enemy arrayed in three lines on a slope beyond his batteries and the fire was terrible, shells bursting, canister rattling, and musket and Minie balls striking around incessantly, killed and wounded men and horses continually," wrote Vance, who had assumed brigade command. The 29th North Carolina's color-bearer gamely advanced to the front and waved his banner to encourage the men; within moments, though, 13 bullets shredded the flag. Another soldier noted

33 Report of Co. F, 11th Tennessee, *ORS* 66:613; *OR* 20/1:567; Report of Colonel Robert B. Vance, 29th North Carolina, *ORS* 3:651.

34 Clark, *Histories of the Several Regiments*, 489; Reminiscences of Captain William H. McCauley, Co. C, 11th Tennessee, http://www.scvcamp260.50megs.com/custom2.html, accessed Aug. 21, 2003; *OR* 20/1:938.

that "Colonel Vance's horse was killed in this fire, the shell going through the body near the left stirrup leather. Sixty of the 29th North Carolina were killed and wounded in a few minutes."

Colonel George Gordon of the 11th Tennessee fell from his horse severely wounded, and his Tennesseans likewise suffered heavily during their brief time in the field. "The men stood in their places amid this storm of shell and shell and grape and canister until it was ascertained that their ammunition was exhausted," Vance claimed. The men were exhausted, too, and did not stay long at news of Rains's death, "running like wildfire along the whole line produced a temporary confusion which induced the senior colonel of the brigade to order the command to fall back."[35]

As the two left regiments of Rains's line clashed with the 36th Indiana in the woods, the 3rd and 9th Georgia battalions on the right continued to advance alone, disrupting the brigade's alignment. Almost out of the woods, the Georgians came upon Colonel Nicholas Anderson's 6th Ohio at the edge of the cedars, the Nashville Pike just 200 yards away. "A sudden halt, a hurried alignment such as a body of old troops makes almost instinctively, and then I noticed that our field officers had dismounted and were commanding on foot," recalled Corporal Ebenezer Hannaford of the 6th Ohio. "Great numbers of stragglers, fugitives, and wounded men were falling back in disorder from the battle which was now raging close at hand. In a few moments, a terrible fire was opened on us scarce 100 yards distant from a Rebel line apparently four ranks deep. A dreadful carnage ensued."[36]

The Georgians, totaling roughly 430 men under the overall command of Lt. Col. Marcus Stovall, plunged into the fight. Casualties quickly mounted. Adjutant Albert Williams of the 6th Ohio was among the first struck down, and Anderson suffered a leg wound. Confederate riflemen singled out the regimental color guard and fired, dropping six men in a heap (though the colors were retrieved by 6th Ohio Corporal William Thorp). Silhouetted against the sunshine of the open field beyond, the Ohioans made easy targets.

"It was terribly earnest work," Hannaford recalled. "The regiment fought desperately, giving volley for volley and cheer for cheer until within 20 minutes one-third of its number lay dead or wounded at its feet. A score of gory corpses—brave men but a half hour before—marked the line where the 6th had

---

35 *ORS* 3:651; Clark, *Histories of the Several Regiments*, 489; OR 20/1:938.

36 OR 20/1:570; Hannaford, *The Story of a Regiment*, 395; Hannaford, in the Ranks article, 813.

fought and five score more were suffering there or wending their painful way toward the rear in search of the surgeon."

Hannaford was one of them, struck by a rifle ball in the neck and right shoulder. "I remember no acute sensation of pain, not even any distinct shock, only an instantaneous consciousness of having been struck," he acknowledged. "Then my breath came hard and labored with a croup-like sound and with a dull aching feeling in my right shoulder, my arm fell powerless at my side and my Enfield dropped from my grasp. I threw my left hand up to my throat and withdrew it covered with warm, bright-red blood. I turned and staggered away to the rear."[37]

The Georgians suffered, too. "Captain Meredith Kendrick had been disabled from a severe wound in the thigh and was lying with his head against a tree, pale from the loss of blood," wrote Joseph Hutcherson of the 3rd Georgia. "W. D. Clark, a private from Co. C, seeing his captain struck down, went to him and offered to take him to the rear. Kendrick declined the proffered assistance when Clark, looking toward the enemy with a view to resuming his fire, was struck in the jugular vein and fell dead at Captain Kendrick's feet. Within a few feet, the writer was wounded in the left arm." Adjutant B. M. Turner, worried that his men were wavering under fire, rode forward "waving his hat and telling the men to follow him." The horse fell dead under him, but Turner escaped injury.[38]

Turner need not have worried, as Anderson already was contemplating breaking the fight with either a charge or a retreat. The withdrawal of the 36th Indiana and all Federal troops on his right left his Buckeyes dangerously exposed. "Finding myself hotly pressed, I had determined on a charge," Anderson recounted, "and the order was already given to fix bayonets when I saw my regiment flanked almost completely on both sides by two Rebel regiments. I gave the order to fall back firing."

The 6th Ohio would be cut to pieces, with more than 100 casualties in the short engagement, but the regiment's stand bought critical moments for Rousseau to finish extracting his command from the cedars and to arrange a warm welcome of artillery for the surging Confederates. By the time Stovall led his 3rd Georgia out of the cedars, Rains's left wing was already retiring. "We filed out of the woods in order to the top of the hill where we first fired upon the enemy," Stovall noted.

---

37 OR 20/1:570; Hannaford, *The Story of a Regiment*, 395-396; Hannaford, In the Ranks article, 813-14.

38 Private Joseph Hutcherson, Co. E, 3rd Battalion, Georgia Infantry, "More About Gen. James E. Rains," *Confederate Veteran*, Aug. 1908, 391.

"Finding myself entirely alone with 300 men, it was deemed imprudent to make an unsupported attack upon the enemy."[39]

Stovall soon had plenty of company, as Anderson's, Donelson's, Stewart's, and Maney's brigades converged at the wood line and finished driving Negley and Cruft out of the woods. Grose had prepared for this eventuality, placing Lieutenant Parson's battery, supported by the 84th Illinois on the left and the 23rd Kentucky on the right. Advancing from its reserve position, the 24th Ohio would deploy slightly forward and to the right of the Kentuckians. Once the 6th Ohio and 36th Indiana cleared his front, Parsons's gunners opened fire. "When he had arrived within 300 yards we opened upon his first line with an enfilade fire of canister," he reported. The canister blasts slammed the brakes on the Confederates; a subsequent attack that Parsons labeled as "feeble" was repulsed just as quickly, and the lieutenant soon turned his guns to the left to confront other Confederates exiting the cedars.[40]

Recognizing the confusion in front as Grose's two regiments fell back, the 84th Illinois lay down, only to find itself under crossfire from one of Donelson's regiments advancing west of the Nashville Pike and from A. P. Stewart's line in the cedars. "A regiment of the enemy had taken position lying down and we could see a heavy force coming upon the brigade on the right," recalled Louis Simmons of the 84th Illinois. "We were partly protected by a low ledge of rocks and the boys fired as fast as they could load and with the help of the batteries drove the enemy back into the woods. Our regiment opened a brisk fire upon them which told upon the regiment across the Pike but upon the heavy force menacing our right it had no apparent effect."

Recalled Sergeant John McCabe of the 84th Illinois: "I could not get my gun to go off. I laid on my back picking powder in the tube of my gun in order to get it to shoot. In ten or fifteen minutes, we were ordered to our feet and forward. I saw Charley Roberts fall wounded, so I ran and got hold of his gun and then I was all right."[41]

---

39 Surgeon R.B. Garner, 3rd Battalion, Georgia Infantry, *Atlanta Intelligencer*, Jan. 20, 1863, 2; OR 20/1:570, 941.

40 OR 20/1:524.

41 Private Louis A. Simmons, Co. A, 84th Illinois, *Macomb Weekly Journal*, Jan. 30, 1863, 2; Louis A. Simmons, *The History of the 84th Regt. Ill. Vols.* (Macomb, 1866), 30; Sergeant John McCabe, Co. A, 84th Illinois, *Daily Rushville Citizen*, Dec. 31, 1907, 1.

Fighting about 50 paces back in support of the 6th Ohio, the 24th Ohio took heavy casualties from converging Confederate fire, and once Anderson's 6th Ohio retreated, the 24th followed course, establishing a new position 150 yards back in the cotton field. "On they came like a tornado that would destroy everything in its path," reported Captain Armistead T. M. Cockerill. It was "a terrible encounter. Encouraged by their success in driving the forces upon our right, they charged upon a battery lying upon our right when almost simultaneously our forces lying in their front opened upon them with a tremendous fire from our infantry and artillery, mowing them down almost by ranks, causing dismay and confusion when they broke and fled in disorder to the cover of woods from which they had just emerged."[42]

Parsons and his infantry support slugged it for about half an hour at a range of roughly 100 yards before Grose ordered them to fall back to the railroad. The 84th Illinois was the first to peel back. "The enemy, in spite of our exertions, continued to advance and was gradually turning our left flank which seemed to be entirely unsupported or covered," Simmons wrote. The regiment fell back a hundred yards to a ledge of rocks then went to ground again. "The enemy was pouring in upon us a most galling fire as we lay in this position, the balls falling like hail in a heavy storm." The regimental color guards were all killed or wounded, and the flagstaff was hit nine times, the colors shredded.[43]

The 24th Ohio, left of Parsons's gunners, also helped support Hazen's position in the Round Forest, but the survivors of Donelson's Brigade made that a particularly hot assignment. "We commenced firing on the enemy through a cotton field into a neck of woods which extended across our front and join a cornfield which was occupied by the Rebel artillery and infantry," remembered Corporal James Orton. "We held this ground about 30 minutes then fell back about ten rods, with the left wing of our regiment on one side of the pike and the right wing on the other. The Rebels appeared on both flanks and front leaving us in one corner of a triangle exposed to a murderous crossfire on all sides."

Orton fired 30 rounds before he was shot through the thigh. "The ball entered the inside of my left leg about an inch below the groin and coming out on the

42 OR 20/1:572.

43 Simmons, *History of the 84th Illinois,* 30-31.

opposite side just above the hip bone, providentially missing the bones and arteries. I now have the bullet in my pocket; it is an old-fashioned round ounce ball."[44]

Nearly 90 members of the 24th Ohio fell in short order, and the regimental command structure was wrecked. "We had remained in this position but a few minutes, exposed to a severe crossfire of the enemy, when Colonel Frederick Jones was mortally wounded and carried from the field," Cockerill noted. Within moments of taking command, Major Henry Terry was also mortally wounded, struck in the head by a shell fragment, leaving the command to the senior officer present, Captain Enoch Weller. "We remained in this position amid the most terrible shower of ball and shell when we were ordered to fall back to the turnpike," Cockerill lamented.[45]

Rousseau, Thomas, and even Rosecrans all played a part in reforming the Federal line along the pike, and many of the regiments, once reformed, were sent back toward the cedars. "As we were marching towards the Nashville Pike, some officer halted us and asked Beatty to take the brigade back and aid the 2nd Kentucky battery in bringing off their guns," recalled a 42nd Indiana veteran. That officer happened to be Rosecrans. "He said to the colonel to go back into the cedars in another place for just 20 minutes and then he would relieve us so that we might get our dinner," noted Sergeant Frank Carlisle. "We about-faced and filed down into the woods and laid down. In a few minutes, the 38th Indiana [in Scribner's brigade] came running back over our entire line and it proved to be Hardee's Rebels were making a desperate charge on our line."

One soldier stated "the artillery company was there and went back with us. General [sic] Beatty put his men in line just in front of where the battery was. All the horses were dead or disabled, being shot down as the battery was trying to get to the rear. Our line was immediately attacked and here we had the most severe engagement of that day. The Kentucky boys worked with a will and determination to get their guns loose from the dead horses. After holding the position for 25 or 30 minutes, we were outflanked and had to retreat, but we brought off four of the battery's guns with us." Carlisle reported that "those 20 minutes cost our regiment about 150 of our men and ten from my own company.[46]

---

44 Corporal James R. Orton, Co. C, 24th Ohio, *Sandusky Register*, Jan. 20, 1863, 2.

45 *OR* 20/1:572.

46 *Proceedings of the Eighth Reunion*, 44-45; Autobiography of Sergeant Francis M. Carlisle, Co. D, 42nd Indiana, Paul Barnett Collection.

Likewise, Colonel Stanley's brigade had no sooner marched out of the cedars than it was ordered back in. The 18th Ohio had retreated into the open field when Rousseau rode up and ordered them to charge the woods again, offering to lead the effort. Colonel Josiah Given complied, even though the "men were already breathless with fatigue." Corporal Nicholas Karns recalled that "as we were making the charge with fixed bayonets down through the open, General Rousseau was riding in front of the colors and during the progress of the charge called out 'Come on boys, I can see the whites of their eyes!' A cheeky member of the 18th Ohio's color guard bellowed to Rousseau, 'General, if you want us to go, get out of the way with your damned old horse!' At this General Rousseau turned in his saddle and looking down on the man said, 'You're a soldier made of the stuff for me,' and wheeling his horse he rode back through the lines."

The Federals plunged 50 yards into the cedars, formed a line, and hunkered down to await the Confederates' approach. "We approached the close woods," Given noted, "but slowly yet in perfect order notwithstanding the enemy met us with a withering fire from the cover of the woods."[47]

Given spied the Confederates chasing another Federal regiment and ordered his men to lie down and hold their fire. "The first line passed over my men, closely followed by the enemy," he reported. "My men, observing well the caution I had given, poured a well-directed fire into the enemy which checked them." Launcelot Scott found the body of a dead Confederate and rolled it into position as a ready-made breastwork. "With the enemy to the right and front and soon to the left pouring in a deadly fire," he wrote, "it was something that human endurance would not stand and we gave way. It seemed to me that all of the bushes around me were cut off by the enemy's balls."

One veteran remembered that the "11th Michigan with the 19th Illinois charged into the cedars and delivered two or three terrible volleys right into the very faces of the enemy. It completely staggered them for a few moments." Given reported that "we held them at bay for 20 minutes but seeing that I was unsupported and standing against a much stronger force and that some 50 of my command had already fallen, I ordered to the retreat, returning to the same place from which I had started under General Rousseau's order."[48]

---

47 Corporal Nicholas H. Karns, Co. B, 18th Ohio, "An Incident of Stone River," *National Tribune*, Oct. 4, 1906, 5; OR 20/1:428.

48 OR 20/1:429; "Stone River" Brief Notes on One of the Great Battles of the Civil War,"; St. Jo., 11th Michigan, *Detroit Free Press*, Jan. 16, 1863, 4.

Private Owen E. Moore, Co. B, 3rd Ohio, killed in action on December 31, 1862.

Larry M. Strayer Collection

Sergeant Henry Breidenthal of the 3rd Ohio remembered that his regiment "formed in line, threw out skirmishers, and lay down where we kept up a lively fire upon the enemy's skirmishers who were posted in large numbers behind rocks and trees, harassing us with a galling fire. It was here that we sustained our greatest loss in killed and wounded. We did not remain here long unsupported but were ordered to fall back which we accomplished in tolerably good order until we came to the open field. In the act of forming our regiment into line, another regiment rushed through our partially shattered column, throwing us into considerable confusion."

"[B]eing outflanked, the Rebels had a crossfire on us," admitted Sergeant Gilbert McWhirk of the 3rd Ohio, "and as the mass poured out into the open field, a perfect storm of bullets swept us and the entire division broke in confusion in spite of the efforts of General Rousseau and other to rally them."[49]

"For a time—I cannot even guess how long—the line stood bravely to the work; but the regiments on our left get into disorder, and finally become panic-stricken," Colonel Beatty would later report. "The fright spreads, and my brigade sweeps by me to the open field in our rear. I hasten to the colors, stop them, and endeavor to rally the men." The field was by this time filled with troops running for their lives, "and the enemy's fire is most deadly," continued the officer. "My brigade, however, begins to steady itself on the colors, when my horse is shot under me, and I fall heavily to the ground. Before I have time to recover my feet,

---

49 McWhirk Letter; Sergeant Henry Breidenthal, Co. A, 3rd Ohio, *Ohio State Journal*, Jan. 24, 1863, 2.

my troops, with thousands of others, sweep in disorder to the rear, and I am left standing alone."[50]

Scott reported that the Confederates plowed the field with artillery fire, adding that "I dropped just in time to save myself from a shell, it passed on and took a shoulder from a man in front. We were double quicking towards one of our batteries and the cannoneers waved their hands for us to get out of the way as quick as possible. A line of Rebels was just issuing from the woods and when we got near the battery we dropped and it opened on the enemy with terrible effect."[51]

*   *   *

As Grose's men pulled back, Thomas realized he needed time to complete the reformation of the Federal line on the Nashville Pike, determining that the Regular Brigade would have to purchase that time with blood. It was high noon. "General Thomas went up to Colonel Shepherd," Lieutenant Freeman remembered, "and pointing to the cedars on the right from which were streaming the broken remnant of the army, he said, 'Colonel Shepherd, put your brigade in there and for God's sake keep those devils back for 20 minutes,' We formed right front into line and scarcely had the men cleared our front than the Rebels were with a yell upon us."

The resulting struggle would be incredibly violent and short, with Major Slemmer suffering a severe leg wound almost immediately. Lieutenant Edgar Kellogg of the 16th US noted that "the Rebel lines were only twelve rods from us and I saw a mounted Rebel officer riding up and down the lines in front of me cheering and urging on his men. I pointed him out to three or four of my men and his horse was soon without a rider."[52]

Opined Sergeant Allen Barrows of the 18th US: "[W]e were made a breastwork to hold the Rebels in check until a line of batteries could be formed and we did it against a charging column four lines deep who rose, advanced, fired, and laid down to load alternately." The Confederates, Captain Henry Haymond of the 18th US reported, "had the advantage of position and in standing beneath the shadow of the pines enveloped in smoke while we stood at the edge of the timber in bold relief

50 Beatty, *Citizen-Soldier*, 202-03.

51 Scott Memoir.

52 Reed Letter; Henry B. Freeman, "Eighteenth U.S. Infantry from Camp Thomas to Murfreesboro and the Regular Brigade at Stone River," *MOLLUS* Minnesota, Vol. 3, 128; 1st Lt. Edgar R. Kellogg, Co. F, 1st Battalion, 16th U.S., *Norwalk Reflector*, Jan. 27, 1863, 2.

against the light. They fired very low and their shots told fearfully upon us. I was kept busy urging my men to load rapidly and fire low when suddenly I felt a sudden sharp pain in my right knee and a momentary fainting came over me. I knew that I was hit."[53]

After 20 minutes, the Regulars were ordered to retreat. "Ere our brigade was fairly in position, the volunteers who were on our right gave way, as we had done before, being forced to yield the ground on account of vastly superior numbers," said Sergeant Frank Reed of the 15th US. "We had gone but four or five rods when the enemy again came towering down upon us like the rolling thunder of heaven, engulfing us on the right and in front-making an attempt at extrication, almost certain death; and so, it proved to be, for scarcely a man came out without having been wounded or having the marks of a bullet in his clothing." Captain James Biddle of the 16th US noted that "our retreat commenced in good order but on reaching the open ground the men could not stand the heavy fire to which they were exposed and but broke and ran to the shelter of our batteries."[54]

The open field grew carpeted with blue coats as hundreds of retreating Regulars went down killed or wounded. Freeman heard the cries of one and stopped to see that it was Captain Henry Douglass of the 18th US. Noticing Douglass was about to be captured, historian Mark Johnson wrote, Freeman "left his battalion and ran through a storm of bullets, picked Douglass up, and carried him to safety," later receiving a Medal of Honor.

Private J. L. B. Harden of the 19th US went down with a leg wound between the two lines. "I concluded the best thing for me was to lie down and did so," he would write. "The Rebels came up and halted within three or four rods of us and I heard one Reb say, 'We have given those Yanks hell.' I confess I felt like I had got a bad dose of something."[55]

The 18th US took fearful losses in particular, as Caldwell's battalion lost 145 of 288 men and Townsend's 139 of 298. "When the retreat was ordered, we immediately scattered and rallied on the colors again in five minutes time behind the battery which was about 60 rods from the edge of the woods where we fought," noted one 18th US soldier. "Had we retired in good order under this fire, we would

---

53 Sergeant Allen C. Barrows, Co. B, 2nd Battalion, 18th U.S., *Cleveland Morning Leader*, Jan. 13, 1863, 1; Henry Haymond Papers, Pearce Civil War Collections, Navarro College.

54 Reed Letter; Memoir of Captain James Biddle, Co. B, 2nd Battalion, 16th U.S., SRNBP.

55 Johnson, *That Body of Brave Men*, 295; Harden, J. L. B. "Battle of Stone River," *National Tribune*, Mar. 9, 1893, 4.

have suffered much more severely than we did." Corporal Robert Kennedy remembered that "in falling back, we tried to rally between the railroad and the cedars but Sergeant Fleagle fell mortally wounded and the captain said, 'For God's sake men, get back of the railroad or we will all be killed.'" Captain Haymond of the 18th US gloomily concluded that "it was necessary for a sacrifice to be made to save the army, and we made it."[56]

Major Stephen D. Carpenter, commanding the 19th US, was killed during the retreat. "Suddenly, above the din and roar of battle," wrote Joseph Prentice, "I heard the major call out 'Scatter and run boys!' and was about to join the rest in the rush to a place of safety when I heard a horse bearing down on me like mad." It was Carpenter's horse, and Prentice secured permission to find his commander. "Back I went at the top of my speed and as soon as I entered the clearing, the enemy's sharpshooters opened a brisk fire on me. Still, I was bound to find the major if possible and knowing about where he fell, rushed to the spot. Bullets ploughed up little puffs of dust at my feet and whistled around my head. Glancing round, I saw him lying face downward upon the dust and rushed to his assistance. But, poor fellow, he was past need of human assistance! Nevertheless, I picked him up and carried him to the rear, my ears filled with the mournful dirge of bullets that threatened me at every step." Prentice would receive a Medal of Honor in 1894 for his actions.[57]

"For a few moments, the contest was doubtful," recalled Captain Archer Gay of the 31st Tennessee, in A. P. Stewart's Brigade. "A shout passed down the line that could be heard above the din of battle; onward is the command until we reached the plantation where we came to a halt and had the satisfaction of seeing the enemy retreat across the field." The Tennesseans' elation was short-lived, as once the Regulars retreated across the Nashville Pike, the Confederates were confronted with an array of Federal guns backed by masses of infantry that had been reformed by Rosecrans and Thomas. Freeman was astonished at the rapid change. "But a short half hour before, all had been dismay and confusion," he wrote, "and now order reigned supreme and the eye fell upon dark lines of infantry with their glistening muskets while on the knoll behind were the unfired guns,

56 Unknown member of 18th US, *Toledo Blade*, Jan. 31, 1863, 2; Memoir of Corporal Robert Kennedy, Co. C, 2nd Battalion, 18th US, SRNBP; Haymond Letter.

57 Beyer, *Deeds of Valor*, 127-28.

double-shotted with canister, the cannoneers in place and all prepared to meet the enemy in a deadly grapple on the result of which hung victory or defeat."[58]

Two brigades from McCown's Division now moved into view. Colonel Robert Harper's Arkansas brigade (formerly led by Evander McNair) and Ector's Texans on his left managed to navigate through the cedars, barely encountering any Federals until they neared the edge of the woods to discover the Regulars in full retreat. On their front, the Arkansans could see the Nashville Pike defended by an array of Federal batteries on a slight rise of ground east of the pike. "No time was to be lost as the enemy had evidently made this their last stand point and had opened on us with artillery and musketry," Harper recalled. McCown ordered a charge by Harper and Ector toward the pike. "This order was immediately repeated to the command and," reported Colonel Harper, "flushed with success and buoyant with hope, they rushed forward to accomplish more brilliant results. The growth through which the right was compelled to pass rendered it impossible to keep an unbroken line.[59]

The Union batteries enjoyed plenty of infantry support, as Scribner reformed his brigade just behind them mere minutes before the charge. Guenther's six-gun Battery H of the 5th US Light and Lieutenant George Van Pelt's Battery A of the 1st Michigan Light opened on the Confederates as soon as the Regulars cleared their front. "We had scarcely double quicked into position before the ball opened in the woods we had just left," wrote Sergeant Tobias Ross of the 2nd Ohio, "and in a short time regiments came rushing from the woods, in more or less disorder. The 15th U.S. Regulars came out in complete disorder and made directly for where we were lying flat on our faces, the Rebels close in their rear and cutting them down at every step. They immediately charged for [Captain Cyrus] Loomis' battery, but our colonel shouted, 'Up boys and let them have it!' We instantly jumped to our feet and poured a well-directed fire into their close ranks, which brought them to a halt. They were within 100 yards of us, and you may imagine the effect of our fire."

As they exited the cedars, Colonel Henry Bunn of the 4th Arkansas recalled a whirlwind of fire. "Our advance was steady until we arrived in full view of the enemy's guns," he noted. "At this juncture, a battery on our left, one to our front, one to the right of front, and one on the right poured upon us a most murderous

58 Captain Archer T. Gay, Co. E, 31st Tennessee, SRNBP; Freeman Article, 128-29.

59 OR 20/1:947.

fire of grape and canister shot. The farthest could not have been more than 400 yards distant, the nearest not more than 100 yards."[60]

"The Rebels followed with three extended lines and in perfect order they advanced," Freeman wrote. "It was a moment in which the blood rushed upon the heart when from our line burst forth a flash of flame and smoke and roar. In a few minutes, all was still, the smoke cleared away and we saw the field before us bare of life, as if swept by a hurricane." Charging toward Guenther's battery, Harper's Arkansans met the storm directly. Captain Lavender of the 4th Arkansas remarked that "the whole railroad bank exploded and such a storm of grape and bullets I have never before or since seen or heard. The earth seemed to be in perfect commotion as if a heavy earthquake was on. It seemed as if heaven and earth had broken loose." The Federal infantry wavered in spots, but this seemed only to make "their artillerists renew their energies and pour a continuous fire of grape and canister shot when many of my command were less than 100 yards from the enemy's guns," observed Lt. Col. James Williamson of the 2nd Arkansas Mounted Rifles.[61]

"[T]hey knew it was a fearful thing to attack a battery in an open field, but they nevertheless attempted it," Haymond wrote. "They advanced boldly with columns doubled upon the center, their long gray lines stretching from one side of the field to the other and when within fair range of the six heavy guns of Guenther's battery, each loaded with 96 canister shot, thundered over the plain. I could distinctly see wide deep gaps out of their ranks, but still they advanced. They were playing a deep game, but if successful, the day was theirs."[62]

Going to ground, the Arkansans continued the bitter slugfest. With heavy punishment on his right from Van Pelt's Michigan battery—which was firing volley after volley of double-shotted canister rounds—and his ranks rapidly decimated, Harper sent for reinforcements. Major Leander Ramsaur of the 1st Arkansas Mounted Rifles went down with a wound, as did Major James Franklin of the 30th Arkansas. Captain William Cotter of the 30th Arkansas noted that "the enemy began to pour in grape at such a murderous rate that it appeared little less than suicide to advance farther. Still, some few, nothing daunted, determined to go on, and some did go to within 100 yards of the enemy's stronghold. Among the rest

60 Sergeant Tobias Ross, Co. B, 2nd Ohio, *Cincinnati Daily Commercial*, Jan. 29, 1863, 4; OR 20/1:952.

61 Freeman Article; Worley, *War Memoirs of Captain John W. Lavender*, 42-43; OR 20/1:950.

62 Haymond Letter.

was our gallant flag-bearer, whose hand was shot off and he was compelled to abandon his colors."[63]

All but three officers of the 2nd Arkansas fell during the charge. "Every field and staff officer of my regiment except myself was wounded and all of them were wounded within 15 feet of me," Williamson recalled. "My horse was struck with a piece of shell within a foot of my leg and of the seven captains in my regiment, all were killed or wounded. It seemed that the commanders expected our brigade and a Texas brigade to rout the entire Federal army."[64]

It proved an impossible task. "Our ranks had been thinned during the day and the troops were fatigued and worn out," Bunn offered. "To advance and take the battery in front would have placed us in a position to be raked without any means of defense and without any support on our right." Sergeant Coke Witten of the 1st Arkansas Mounted Rifles wrote that "they had six masked batteries and they turned them all loose with grape and canister and I never heard the like before in my life. They were like ten thousand peals of thunder. We had to give back."

Robert H. Dacus, Witten's fellow 1st Rifles trooper, agreed. "Our only show was to reform our broken lines and to charge or fall back," he wrote, "and as it was utterly impossible to form under such a fire as we were being subjected to with half our men behind us either dead or wounded and those of us who were there worn out with fatigue, our officers ordered us to fall back behind the cedar brake." Conceded Harper: "After ten or twelve minutes of the severest fighting it has even been my lot to witness, we were compelled to fall back with heavy loss."[65]

As the Arkansans faded from the Nashville Pike, orderly sergeant William Garner of the 30th Arkansas noticed the body of his company commander and close friend, Captain John Thomas, lying nearby. "I was wounded and ordered to the rear and examined the captain who was lying cold and stiff in a puddle of his own frozen blood," Garner grieved. "The ball entered one side of the neck and came out the other, severing the arteries. It seems he had a presentiment that he would be killed." The 18th US's Captain Haymond believed that "no troops in the

---

63 OR 20/1:954. The 2nd Ohio retrieved the colors of the 30th Arkansas from the field, but credit for the capture properly belongs to Battery H, 5th US Light.

64 Lt. Col. James Williamson, 2nd Arkansas Mounted Rifles, SRNBP.

65 Witten Letter; *OR* 20/1:949, 952; Robert H. Dacus, *Reminiscences of Company H, First Arkansas Mounted Rifles* (Dayton, 1972).

world could stand such slaughter. Foiled in his attempt to take our battery," he proudly noted, "the enemy turned his attention to the troops upon our left."[66]

*   *   *

Matt Ector's brigade of Texans soon crossed swords with another Federal unit that refused to give ground: the Chicago Board of Trade Battery, supported, by the Pioneer Brigade. Ector's men had drifted away from Harper during the march through the cedars, and debouched from the woods essentially alone facing a line of roaring Federal batteries. "The enemy were in ambuscade in this cedar brake on the left of my command," Ector reported. "They had a very formidable battery planted about 250 yards in a northeast direction from us; one nearly in a north direction about the same distance off, and the third one in a field a quarter of a mile northwest of us. All these batteries turned loose upon us. About the same time their infantry, whose position had been ascertained by my skirmishers, unmasked themselves and opened fire. The 14th and 15th Texas Regiments were soon in a desperate struggle; the regiments on the right of them were equally exposed to their artillery."[67]

Ector's men had already taken one Federal battery that morning (Edgarton's), and eagerly sensed an opportunity to repeat the remarkable feat. "The usual Texas yell was raised and our line moved off in a charge," remembered Lt. Col. Joseph Bounds of the 11th Texas. "We soon reached the line of skirmishers that was nearly equal to our line and fired on them, killing and wounding a great many." Bounds advanced his regiment to within 80 yards of the Chicago Board of Trade Battery but could go no farther and found that the balance of the brigade had fallen back. "I halted and ordered them to lie down until the other regiments arrived in line," he wrote. "The grape and canister and bombs were flying like autumn leaves … before a tornado." Lieutenant J. T. Tunnell of the 14th Texas concurred, claiming the "artillery opened on us and cut the timber off over our heads and it seemed that the heavens and the earth were coming together. Our men sheltered themselves as best they could behind trees, ledges of rocks, etc. Their front line of battle seemed to

66 Haymond Letter; Garner Letter.

67 OR 20/1:935.

take fresh courage and began to advance upon is, walking a few steps, then firing and falling down to reload."[68]

It marked the first time the Chicago Board of Trade Battery had been under fire. "We had gone about 300 yards when zip went a shell just over our heads, then another, then a shot, then two or three together, until the whole air seemed filled with these deadly missiles," remembered gunner Charles Maple, who left a fine account of the fighting. "We laughed at first," he recalled,

but in a few moments, we were ordered to take a position and it was not long before we sobered down and nary a laugh. Suddenly a howl was heard from the Rebs, and as the roar dies away, the howling increases. The Rebel howl is similar to that of a wolf. At this juncture our battery is ordered to commence firing with this injunction from Captain Stokes, "Hold your fire, boys, until you see the whites of their eyes and then give it to them!" For one hour our boys poured in the shell and canister so fast that the forward course of the Rebs was checked. The enemy began to waver, and our boys began to work faster and pour in the shot so fast that they are compelled to fall back. General Rosecrans, who was just behind the battery, was cheering and urging the boys.[69]

Ector's brigade alignment fell apart during the advance. The 14th and 15th Texas on the left wound up fighting on their own, while the 10th and 11th Texas stumbled through the undergrowth on the brigade's right. The Texans realized they would need assistance to break the Union line. "I immediately sent Major F. M. Spencer to Colonel Harper, who was in command of the brigade on my right to move his brigade up to my assistance," Ector recalled. "I hastened to the left of my command. My men had driven back one line of their infantry upon the second line; still them was a third line. The cedars were falling and being trimmed by bombs, canister, and iron hail, which seemed to fill the air. My men had not yielded an inch, but, sheltering themselves behind the rocks, would lie down and load, rise to their knees, fire into the closed blue line not over 60 yards from them."[70]

---

68 Gammage, *The Camp, The Bivouac, and the Battlefield*, 63. Gammage survived the heavy artillery fire and the war, only to die in Mobile, Alabama, in 1865 on his way home to Cherokee County, Texas.

69 Lt. Col. Joseph M. Bounds, 11th Texas Cavalry, *Dallas Daily Herald*, Mar. 11, 1863, 1; Tunnell Article.

70 Private Charles H. Maple, Chicago Board of Trade Battery, *Fulton County Ledger*, Jan. 27, 1863, 1.

Colonel Julius A. Andrews of the dismounted 32nd (15th) Texas Cavalry arrived asking where the balance of the brigade was; Ector did not know. "I remarked to him that it was impossible for my regiment and Colonel [John L.] Camp's to contend against a brigade of infantry and artillery, too, as our regiments were comparatively small," reported Andrews, who had only 300 men left. "Believing it to be impossible to bring my entire brigade to bear with full force, and that an attempt to do it would be attended with great sacrifice of life," Ector conceded, "I ordered them to fall back." He had little choice but to retreat, lacking the strength to move the Federals and, as Lewis Jones of the 10th Texas noted, the "cannonading from so many cannons all at once appeared to completely demoralize the men." After eight hours of fighting, the Texans were worn out—finished charging Yankee guns.[71]

At Ector's direction, Andrews ordered his command "to give back, but the booming of cannon and musketry was so terrific at the time that it was impossible for my voice to be heard. The men who heard the command obeyed it, which was discovered by the men up and down the line and also by the left of Colonel Camp's regiment which caused both regiments to fall back in as good order as possible under the circumstances." W. T. Coker of the 10th Texas and a comrade fighting at his side were so caught up firing away that they scarcely noticed they had been left behind. "When we discovered the mistake," Coker wrote, "we made the run of our lives thinking we would certainly be killed but we escaped without a scratch."[72]

Beatty's brigade soon reformed under Rosecrans's supervision behind the line of batteries adjacent to the railroad. "Rosecrans rode up to us in his everlasting old black conical hat which looked as if it, like us, could not withstand the outside pressure and had caved in," remembered Sergeant Breidenthal of the 3rd Ohio. "His old blue overcoat hanging somehow on his shoulders, his face all scratched up by the brushes with a stump cigar about two inches long, unlighted, between his fingers and himself generally as cool as cucumber. We were drawn up in line and received him with a military salute accompanied by three rousing cheers for 'Rosecrans and victory.' He said, 'Soldiers, I thank you. No honor to me. I pay honor to you.'"

Rosecrans grasped Beatty's hand, Breidenthal added, and exclaimed: "'Why Colonel Beatty, how do you do? I thank God, I see you here.' Turning to us, he said, 'Boys I am glad to see you all. You have done nobly and I hope by the blessing of

71 OR 20/1:928.

72 Ibid., 928, 935; Jones Article.

God we will today strike this infernal rebellion a crushing blow.' He then gave us a very plain little lesson. 'Did you see that little affair a while ago on the right? Why it was the easiest thing in the world. We reserved our fire until we could see the buttons on their coats, then let loose upon them and then we up and at them with the bayonet and they skedaddled. Why boys, it was just as easy as rolling off a log. That is the way to do it. Now, am I understood?' Aye, aye was the lively response and as he rode off, we gave three cheers for the hero of Rich Mountain, Iuka, Corinth, and today."[73]

Against a seemingly endless fire from Union guns, John McCown's battered division held on grimly at the edge of the cedars. McCown had come closest to reaching the Nashville Pike, but Federal resistance, particularly in the form of artillery fire, had been too much to overcome.

Surgeon Washington Gammage of the 4th Arkansas (McNair's/Harper's Brigade) never forgot the intensity of that iron rain. "The shells went whizzing through the air just over our heads and every man fell to the ground until they passed by and burst into a thousand pieces," he recalled in a short book published the following year. He observed a general riding the lines offering encouragement: "Keep cool, my men- do not get excited. If they charge you, hold your fire until you see the whites of their eyes and then give it to them. Aim low, be sure you do not pull trigger too quick and pick your man before you fire." The barrage continued unceasingly: "Boom, boom, boom went the Federal cannon again and a half dozen 12-lb shells came gracefully curving through the air and burst, some in front, some in the rear, and some just over the column of men. Eighteen were wounded and one man was killed," reported the surgeon, "but the wounded were quietly carried away and the dead laid to one side, and all was still."[74]

---

73 OR 20/1:935; Yeary, *Reminiscences*, 144.

74 Gammage, *The Camp, The Bivouac, and the Battlefield*, 63. Gammage survived the heavy artillery fire and the war, only to die in Mobile, Alabama, in 1865 on his way home to Cherokee County, Texas. How he perished and his final resting spot is unknown.

Miracle at the Three-Mile Marker

PAT CLEBURNE'S DIVISION moved north from the Wilkinson Pike in pursuit of Alexander McCook about 11:30 a.m. The hard-fighting Irishman's command constituted the left flank of the Army of Tennessee. Its ammunition now replenished, Cleburne pushed his men in the wake of John McCown's Division, targeting a strike on the Nashville Pike. John Wharton's Rebel troopers galloped ahead on the left, chasing McCook's ordnance train while shielding Cleburne's flank.

Thus far the battle had gone Cleburne's way. Despite the ferocity of the fighting, the popular general had avoided getting wounded, as he had in his two previous battles in Kentucky at Richmond and Perryville. Corps commander William Hardee considered Cleburne his top subordinate, and he justified that regard by demonstrating tenacity and smarts at Murfreesboro. "His eyes were a clear steel-gray in color, cold and abstracted usually, but beamed genially in seasons of social intercourse and blazed fiercely in moments of excitement," Hardee wrote after the war. "He was modest as a woman, simple in his tastes and habits, and utterly regardless of personal comfort was always mindful of the comfort and welfare of his troops."[1]

---

1   William J. Hardee, "Biographical Sketch of Major General Patrick R. Cleburne," *Southern Historical Society Papers*, 52 vols. (Richmond, 1876-1959), Vol. 31, 151-65.

Brigadier General Patrick R. Cleburne

Library of Congress

Cleburne moved his command north through the Smith Farm's cotton field and then into a narrow branch of the cedar forest; the forest was roughly only 200 yards wide near Asbury Lane but gradually widened as it stretched to the east. Lucius Polk's Brigade on the right moved ahead of the rest of the division and plunged into the thicker part of the woods as S.A.M. Wood's Brigade followed on Polk's left. Again, the challenges of moving formations of men through the thick woods north of the Wilkinson Pike disheveled Cleburne's arrangements; as the men advanced, a gap of several hundred yards developed between Wood's line and the adjacent brigade, Bushrod Johnson's. On the far left, Liddell's Arkansans advanced close to Asbury Lane, with Lieutenant Harvey Shannon's Warren Light Artillery keeping pace—the only Confederate troops in this sector supported by a long arm.

During the advance, Lycurgus Sallee of the 1st Arkansas would witness an extraordinary sight while racing forward to catch his advancing regiment. "As I paused to look for my flag," he wrote with disbelief, "two good looking young men from Ector's brigade dropped out of line, dashed their guns to the ground, knocked the blood from each other's noses and not over five seconds later picked up their guns and ran to their places."[2]

Waiting ahead of Cleburne were three Union brigades in Crittenden's Left Wing that had been hurriedly shifted from the McFadden's Ford crossing of Stones River to positions in the Widow Burris's corn and cotton fields. Colonel Harker's 3rd Brigade in Wood's 1st Division arrived first at 11:00 a.m., taking a position covering Rousseau's far right and rear. While still in line near Stones River, Wood

____

2 Yeary, *Reminiscences*, 661.

had begun facing two of his three brigades westward when Rosecrans and his headquarters escort appeared. After briefly discussing the perilous situation with Wood, Rosecrans galloped "across Harker's left and wheeled to the right to ride up the front line of battle," recalled William Bickham. "He gave Harker's orders in person as Harker was already moving in column by the right flank at the double quick. There was serious business at hand, but the gallant fellow seemed desirous to show the Chief how compactly he could move his noble brigade under fire."

As the men marched, a torrent of shells from Confederate batteries on Wayne's Hill landed within the compact body of men. The shells "danced around their heels, whizzed over their heads, bounded under their horses, and a few wicked missiles sped through the midst of them," Bickham noted with awe. "Every man, save the leader, ducked his head clean to the saddle bow. One shot gutted a gap through Harker's column; the hideous rent was visible an instant then it was healed but the column was shorn of four men. It was not even shaken."[3]

The contingent moved swiftly across the Nashville Pike and along Asbury Road, then turned south about two miles from the river. Harker formed his five regiments, roughly 1,700 officers and men, in the open fields, with the edge of the cedars a half-mile in front. Arriving hard on Harker's heels was Fyffe's brigade of roughly 1,300 men; Colonel Samuel Beatty's brigade, also from Van Cleve's division, arrived a few minutes later. Fyffe's men fell in on Harker's left and deployed into two lines, with the 44th Indiana in front on the right supported by the inexperienced 86th Indiana, while Fyffe's own 59th Ohio, supported by the 13th Ohio, held the left. The six guns of Captain George R. Swallow's 7th Indiana Battery galloped into position on Fyffe's right rear.[4]

Beatty deployed on Fyffe's left, the 1,216 men of his brigade in two lines atop a rock-strewn cedar ridge: the 19th Ohio on the right with the 79th Indiana in support, and the 9th Kentucky on the left supported by the 11th Kentucky. Rosecrans supervised Beatty's deployment and must have smiled when he saw the

---

3 Bickham, *Rosecrans' Campaign*, 213. During the battle, neither Asbury Road nor Asbury Lane were known as such. To avoid any confusion, Asbury Road runs east and west just north of the present park boundary, whereas Asbury Lane runs north to south a mile west of the park boundary, the two roads intersecting at Asbury Church. The shell Bickham described exploded in the ranks of Company B of the 65th Ohio.

4 The strength of Fyffe's brigade was erroneously stated as 798 men in Rosecrans's official report, but this figure likely represented the number remaining in the ranks at the end of the battle. Based on figures provided by the regimental commanders, Fyffe went into action on December 31, 1862, with about 1,300 officers and men.

flags of the 19th Ohio pass. The 19th served in Rosecrans's army in the western Virginia campaign of 1861 and saw its first fight at Rich Mountain that July. In that engagement, Rosecrans had three Indiana regiments charge a Confederate encampment; when those regiments wavered, he reluctantly sent in the 19th Ohio. Previously derided by Rosecrans as a "band box regiment,' the Buckeyes felt they had something to prove and promptly delivered two devastating volleys that broke the Confederate line, winning the battle and Rosecrans's everlasting respect.

Now at Stones River, the old "band box regiment" stepped into the breach at another critical juncture. "At this moment," recalled Sergeant Alfred Stambaugh, "General Rosecrans came riding up at full gallop and alone, not an aide with him, and said to Major [Charles] Manderson, 'Form a junction with that brigade in the woods quick, quick.' We immediately started for the new position and he quaintly said, 'Hurry, and you give them hell.'"[5]

Confusion reigned. "It was difficult to tell in which direction we were worst needed," wrote Marcus Woodcock of the 9th Kentucky (US), a private at the time. "We started down off the pike in the direction of the skirt of woods and just as we started, we saw our lines give way in utter confusion. General Rosecrans rode among us with his sword gleaming above his head and tears streaming down his cheeks saying, '[B]oys, you must drive them!" Rosecrans, Crittenden, Van Cleve, and their respective staffs and escorts rode alongside to guide the Left Wing into line.

Numerous accounts describe Rosecrans's disheveled appearance at this time; what the troops learned later was that Rosecrans missed death by inches moments earlier while riding near the Nashville Pike. "A flight of Mine balls slitted through the troop and one of them struck Garesche's black horse in the nose," Bickham noted. "The spirited animal flung his head scornfully at the sting, scattering blood upon his rider. A drop of blood, fiercely flung away by the wounded horse crimsoned the cheek of Rosecrans and an hour later gave rise to apprehensions who fancied it was his own blood and spread the report that he was wounded." It was Rosecrans's first narrow escape of the day, but it would not be his last.[6]

The 86th Indiana, in Fyffe's brigade, marched into action ruffled by a command change that had occurred that morning. The regiment began the day under the command of Colonel Orville Hamilton, but Van Cleve—warned of Hamilton's inexperience and inability to handle his regiment under fire by

---

5 Stambaugh Letter.

6 Noe, *A Southern Boy in Blue*, 122-23; Bickham, *Rosecrans' Campaign*, 216-17.

Hamilton's own subordinates—ordered the Hoosier colonel to maneuver his regiment prior to going into action. "After several attempts, Hamilton signally failed[,] whereupon he was relieved of his sword and his command," explained the regimental historians.

Lieutenant Colonel George Dick, a well-regarded veteran, took command. Hamilton, utterly humiliated but determined to do his duty, grabbed a rifle and cartridge box and accompanied the regiment into the fight, behaving with conspicuous bravery through the rest of the engagement as an enlisted man.[7]

"By the time our five regiments got over to the right, our whole army seemed to be in the greatest consternation," remembered Captain Orlow Smith of the 65th Ohio. "Regiment after regiment broke before the enemy and the day seemed almost lost to us. Our brigade moved rapidly amid the bursting of the enemy's shells and met them coming down on us with all the fury of demons." Sergeant Christian Lenker of the 19th Ohio noted that "at a distance the cedars seemed to vomit from their confines masses of defeated, disorganized men while their recesses sent forth the sound of the clash and clatter of arms and shouts of angry men in conflict as if emanating from the denizens of the infernal regions."[8]

Colonel Benjamin Grider of the 9th Kentucky complained that McCook's men went "in every possible direction except towards the enemy. Throughout this we had to pass and by keeping our men well up and resorting occasionally to the sword or bayonet we did so. We had to wait a moment till our retreating troops cleared out front, and in doing which they tried to pass through our ranks. It was difficult to prevent them but I stood on my horse in front of my regiment with a drawn sword and had to strike them back. We got them to pass around us." Colonel Frederick Knefler of the 79th Indiana agreed with Grider, writing that "this was a terrible initiation for troops who had never been under fire. There was no use talking as no human voice could be heard above that tumult. I trusted in God and the valor of Hoosiers."[9]

7 OR 20/1:597; James A. Barnes, James R. Carnahan, and Thomas H. B. McCain, *The Eighty-Sixth Regiment Indiana Volunteer Infantry: A Narrative of Its Services in the Civil War of 1861-1865* (Crawfordsville, 1895), 99-100.

8 Captain Orlow Smith, Co. G, 65th Ohio, *Ashland Times*, Jan. 22, 1863, 1; Michael Barton, *The Civil War Memoir of Sergeant Christian Lenker, 19th Ohio Volunteers* (2014), 108.

9 Benjamin C. Grider Papers, SC2679, Folklife and Manuscripts Archives, Western Kentucky University; Letter from Colonel Frederick Knefler, 79th Indiana, Indiana Historical Society.

Beatty reported that "it was with the utmost difficulty that the line established was maintained. The enemy was rapidly approaching in three heavy columns and fire had to be reserved on account of our own troops, who were in front of the line." Jason Hurd of the 19th Ohio remembered that the 74th Illinois in Post's brigade was the last regiment to clear the field, fighting to the last. "In a few minutes, they passed through our lines but a few of them, bolder than the rest, still remained in our front having lingered behind to get better shots at the enemy," he stated. "But in a moment, they were past us and the enemy burst into view. Elated with success, they were advancing in heavy mass with a solid front, cheering and waving their flags and pouring upon us a deadly fire."[10]

The flock of fleeing bluecoats finally cleared Beatty's front as Polk's Brigade debouched from the woods a short distance ahead. "I discovered the enemy again prepared to make a stand, having taken a strong position on a cedar hill with rock so placed by nature as to afford great protection," Polk reported. His men opened fire on Beatty's line, but the Federals did not respond until Polk advanced within 100 yards, then opened fire, dropping Confederates by the dozens. "From every musket leaps a missile of death and the Confederate line wavered," Manderson observed. Within moments, the major's horse went down, which tossed the Buckeye to the ground, breaking his spectacles and leaving the near-sighted commander practically blind. Manderson directed an orderly to return to the regimental wagons to retrieve his other pair.

After the war, 2nd Lt. William S. S. Erb of Company A would joke about what occurred next, writing: "In a remarkably short time when within hailing distance, [the orderly] commenced shouting for those in charge to 'throw off the regimental chest' and that 'Manderson has lost his glasses and the battle must stop!' The glasses were soon found and he was off with the speed of a Kansas cyclone." Despite the urgency, the frightened orderly apparently could not stomach heading back into battle with the new pair and instead rode a horse back to Nashville. It was somehow five days before Manderson received his glasses.[11]

Polk's men surged forward hoping to break the Union line by a show of force—"keeping up the scare," as Nathan Bedford Forrest once famously said. It did not work. "Being desperate, they drew near and endeavored to press us back as they had all others who came in their way," Hurd asserted. "A short distance in

---

10 *OR* 20/1:584; Memoir of Orderly Sergeant Jason Hurd, Co. D, 19th Ohio, SRNBP.

11 William S. S. Erb, *Extracts from the Battles of the 19th Ohio* (Washington, 1893), 17-18; Charles F. Manderson, *The Twin Seven-Shooters* (New York, 1902), 16.

front we could see their flag bearers standing behind a tree and shaking their Rebel sheet almost in our faces." Beatty's men fought valiantly under Rosecrans's personal supervision, the general riding back and forth behind the front lines, impressing the men with his courage. "He was right in the jaws of death strengthening us with his presence and encouraging words," Erb noted. "He said, 'I know you boys; you are the 19th Ohio. You helped to whip this army at Shiloh and I can trust you here, only keep cool and fire low!' Each word he spoke was worth a thousand men as every man would have been glad to die right there rather than he should see them falter."[12]

*　*　*

With Polk's line beginning to precipitate rearward, Rosecrans decided it was time to counterattack and ordered Beatty to lead it. "Spurring up to the very heels of Beatty's men until his steed almost trampled them, he shouted cheerily 'Now let the whole line charge! Shoot low! Be sure! Then charge home,'" Bickham recalled. "The loud and distinct voice of Colonel Beatty was now heard above the din of battle and ringing in clear and even tones was heard the command to charge bayonets," explained Woodcock, who noted that the charge "rather astonished the shattered lines of the chivalry and caused them to break and flee without even resisting our charge. When the Rebels seemed to be almost entirely gone, we had the opportunity to try our skill at an occasional one as he would jump up from behind a rock or tree and run off."

"[T]he enemy in this place made a most obstinate stand," admitted Polk, whose brigade incurred heavy losses in the brief clash The 1st Arkansas suffered particularly, losing Lt. Col. Donelson McGregor, who sustained a mortal thigh wound. "Especially hard hit were the company commanders with one killed and four wounded, but the carnage among the lieutenants and noncoms was hardly less severe," noted historian John Hammock.[13]

As Beatty's brigade peppered away at Polk's men, ammunition began to run low and Beatty ordered a passage of the lines. His men reportedly accomplished the movement in "fine order under the very heavy fire of the enemy." Sergeant Lenker recalled that the 79th Indiana, eager for the trial, was "a new regiment of fine, tall

---

12 Hurd Memoir; Erb, *Extracts*, 16-17.

13 Bickham, *Rosecrans' Campaign*, 219; Noe, *A Southern Boy in Blue*, 123-24; OR 20/1:854; Hammock, *With Honor Untarnished*, 79.

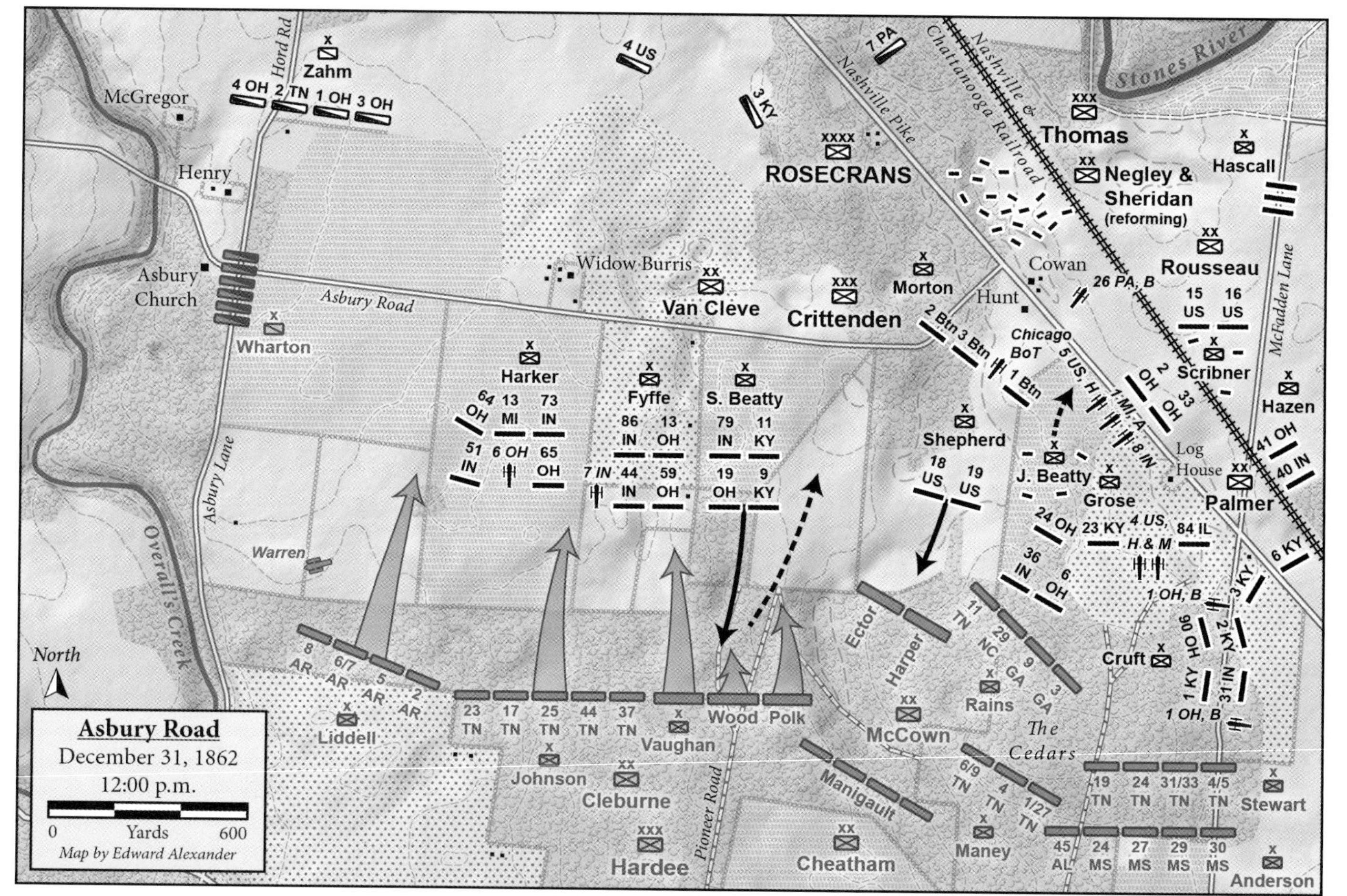

Hord Rd
Zahm
4 US
7 PA
Nashville & Chattanooga Railroad
Stones River
Thomas
4 OH 2 TN 1 OH 3 OH
McGregor
3 KY
Nashville Pike
Hascall
Negley & Sheridan (reforming)
Henry
ROSECRANS
Cowan
Rousseau
McFadden Lane
26 PA, B
15 16 US US
Asbury Church
Widow Burris
Van Cleve
Crittenden
Morton
Hunt
Scribner
2 OH 33 OH
Asbury Road
Wharton
2 Btn 3 Btn
1 Btn
Chicago BoT
5 US, H
Hazen
Harker
Fyffe
S. Beatty
Shepherd
1 MI, A
8 IN
41 OH
40 IN
64 OH
13 MI
73 IN
86 IN
13 OH
79 IN
11 KY
18 19 US US
J. Beatty
Grose
Log House
Palmer
51 IN
6 OH
65 OH
7 IN
44 IN
59 OH
19 OH
9 KY
24 OH
23 KY
4 US, H & M
84 IL
6 KY
Asbury Lane
36 IN
6 OH
1 OH, B
3 KY
Overall's Creek
Warren
Ector
Harper
11 TN
29 NC
9 GA
3 GA
Cruft
90 OH
2 KY
1 KY
NI 31
1 OH, B
North
8 AR
6/7 AR
5 AR
2 AR
Liddell
23 TN
17 TN
25 TN
44 TN
37 TN
Vaughan
Wood
Polk
Rains
McCown
The Cedars
Asbury Road
December 31, 1862
12:00 p.m.
Johnson
Cleburne
Pioneer Road
Manigault
6/9 TN
4 TN
1/27 TN
19 TN
24 TN
31/33 TN
4/5 TN
Stewart
0 Yards 600
Map by Edward Alexander
Hardee
Cheatham
Maney
45 AL
24 MS
27 MS
29 MS
30 MS
Anderson

young men. They were armed with an old Belgian rifle having a large bore and long sword bayonet and when their line opened fire, it made a tremendous noise and did heavy execution in the enemy's ranks." Another member of the 19th Ohio believed the Hoosiers used mountain howitzers in their attack, and "when they opened, it sounds as though the thundering heavens above had opened." Colonel Knefler noted that "such a storm as broke loose at that moment as we faced each other in the open field as it rained lead and iron. Men were falling in all directions dead and wounded. It was terrible beyond description."[14]

Rosecrans, who accompanied this counterattack, ordered the Hoosiers and the 11th Kentucky to fix bayonets and continue the push. "They advanced rapidly, the enemy retreating," Beatty reported. "An uninterrupted fire was kept up and the enemy compelled to take refuge behind his works which could not be assailed for want of artillery which could not advance in that direction owing to the very rough and uneven nature of the ground."[15]

At this juncture, Fyffe arrived on Beatty's right, halting at a fence line marking the southern boundary of the Burris fields. The 44th Indiana and 59th Ohio leveled portions of the fence and continued south cautiously, firing occasionally at Polk's line. Fyffe was right to hesitate; Cleburne's Division was on the move, heading toward an imminent collision with Harker, and already Liddell's and Bushrod Johnson's brigades threatened Fyffe's right flank. Beatty was walking into a trap. "I sent three different messengers by my aides calling Colonel Harker's attention to my exposed flank and at length reported in person to General Van Cleve," Fyffe recalled.

Van Cleve, overwhelmed by the changing fortunes of his division, was not much help. The generally indecisive 53-year-old commander from Minneapolis received an order from Rosecrans to "press hard" and enjoined Fyffe to do the same, promising to try to round up support for the Ohioan. "At the same time, I was notified by a messenger from Colonel Harker that the enemy were in force on my right, in a wood, and were planting a battery there," Van Cleve noted. "I immediately sent a message to Colonel Harker to press the enemy hard, as I had no reserve to protect my right; to Captain Swallow not to suffer the battery to be captured; to Colonel Beatty to send two regiments if they could possibly be spared, to the support of Colonel Fyffe, and a fourth to General Crittenden, to inform him

14 Barton, *Memoir of Christian Lenker*, 113; Justice, 19th Ohio, *Zanesville Daily Courier*, Feb. 24, 1863, 2; Knefler Letter.

15 OR 20/1:584, 594.

of my critical situation." Sitting atop his favorite horse, Bessie, Van Cleve was struck by a bullet that passed through his knee and lodged in his horse's shoulder—a wound that eventually disabled the general. Rosey's bold strike south from Asbury Road now teetered on the precipice of disaster.[16]

Unaware of the jeopardy he faced, Beatty continued his advance alone for about three-quarters of a mile into the Smith cotton field, approaching the Wilkinson Pike, when the shattered remnant of a Federal brigade materialized out of the woods to his left. It was, Woodcock would write, "the most shocking and mangled sight of any body of troops I ever saw in my life. A large number of the wounded were borne off by their comrades while many others who had received flesh wounds about the body, arms, and head were bringing themselves off." Major Erasmus Mottley of the 11th Kentucky reported that his advance "was interrupted by about four regiments of scattered troops rushing through my line."[17]

The brief intermission gave Polk time to rally his brigade, and Cleburne, aware that the woods to his right were swarming with Confederates who had just broken Negley's line, directed Wood's Brigade to charge past Beatty's exposed right and strike Fyffe's position at the edge of the woods, aiming to bag the whole lot. It was several minutes before Beatty saw Cleburne's line on the move and realized his peril. The brigade had outrun its support, as Fyffe's men lingered at the edge of the woods several hundred yards to Beatty's right rear, their commander unwilling to advance with his own right in the air. Beatty's frontline gamely opened fire in what Woodcock called "one of the most magnificent shooting scenes that was presented in that day's battle," but it quickly became evident that Beatty would have to retire before the brigade was surrounded.[18]

Fyffe's skirmishers tumbled back to the main line once S.A.M. Wood's line materialized on their front, reporting that a heavy force was advancing and already threatened Fyffe's right. The 44th Indiana, veterans of Fort Donelson and Shiloh, promptly dropped to the ground, allowing the Confederates to advance within 100 yards before opening fire. "[W]e had fired but three rounds from our guns when a great blunder was discovered," wrote Corporal George W. Squier. "We were

---

16 Ibid., 574, 597. Van Cleve, Rosecrans's oldest divisional commander, graduated from West Point in 1831, long before most of his soldiers were born. He had been out of the army for more than 20 years before returning as colonel of the 2nd Minnesota in 1861. He was promoted to brigadier general after the battle of Mill Springs.

17 Noe, *A Southern Boy in Blue*, 124; OR 20/1:592.

18 Noe, *A Southern Boy in Blue*, 124; OR 20/1:592.

flanked on our right and in few minutes, we would have been prisoners." As Lieutenant Marvin Butler wrote, it was not a surprise. "We had hardly touched the ground when the Rebel yell was responded to by a heavy volley of musketry from the front, and canister, grape, and musketry from the right," he noted. "We were in a slaughter pen and while our line was steady and cool, firing low and as rapidly as possible, it was evident that we could not hold the position many minutes. We pressed the ground hard and I am quite sure my impression could have been seen for some time thereafter."

The 44th did not stay put for long; indeed, Squier confessed, "for the first time the 44th was panic-stricken and became perfectly unmanageable. Away they ran, the officers vainly endeavoring to rally at the fence where lay the 13th Ohio as our reserve. Colonel Williams sees that he no longer commands the 44th and in his agony he cries, 'Oh heavens! Can it be?'"[19]

To blunt the Confederate advance, Fyffe attempted to order the 86th Indiana from his second line to deploy to the right of the 44th Indiana. Before the order reached the 86th, however, "the enemy appeared coming through the woods," Fyffe wrote. "Seeing the force would have to fall back, I galloped to the 7th Indiana Battery and ordered it to open fire to the right of my flank into the woods for the purpose of checking and confusing the outflanking force and to save my brigade from the effects of a crossfire." Swallow deployed his four 10-pounder Parrott rifles in the Burris cotton field and opened fire. "I immediately ordered the battery into position, and the firing to commence with shell to our right and front, where the enemy's infantry was rapidly advancing upon us," he reported. "They soon entered the field, when I ordered the battery to open upon them with canister, at the same time ordering the caissons to the rear."[20]

"The enemy came up in magnificent order four lines deep and his opening fire was like the opening jaws of hell," declared the regimental historians of the 86th Indiana. "It was a duel to the death, at every step men fell like wheat before the sickle." Major John Cameron's 3rd Confederate struck Fyffe's line first and, in the confusion, both 86th Indiana color-bearers went down, leaving their flags upon the ground, scooped up promptly by Sergeant John Lovin of the 3rd Confederate. "I deployed my regiment on the right of the fourth company and opened fire on the

---

19 Julie A. Doyle, John David Smith, and Richard M. McMurry, eds., *This Wilderness of War: The Civil War Letters of George W. Squier, Hoosier Volunteer* (Knoxville, 1998), 36; Marvin B. Butler, *My Story of the Civil War and the Underground Railroad* (Huntington, 1914), 265-66.

20 OR 20/1:579, 597.

enemy's line posted behind a fence and with the aid of 50 stragglers, I charged the fence, driving the enemy and capturing their colors with about 30 prisoners," Cameron recalled. Adjutant Erasmus Thomas of the 86th Indiana described the Confederate assault as "the ugliest sight I ever saw. They fight wonderfully."[21]

Cleburne's Division split as it marched north, creating a gap of several hundred yards between Wood's left and Bushrod Johnson's right. Fortunately, the gap coincided with the one between Fyffe's and Harker's lines and was soon filled by Colonel Alfred Vaughan, leading the Fourth (Smith's) Brigade in Cheatham's Division. The dense cedars split Cheatham's pursuit of the Federals, and Vaughan, on the division's far left, found himself alone until he wandered into the rear of Cleburne's advance.

Vaughan's arrival was both timely and opportune. "General Wood desired my support to save him from being flanked on the right," the colonel noted. "Accordingly, I moved forward and engaged this force, driving him across the open field and dirt road into the only remaining field between us and the Nashville Pike." Cleburne gave Vaughan due credit for making his push at such a critical point, as Fyffe's and Beatty's men responded defiantly. "The enemy were stubborn, being principally old tried troops and regulars and his loss was awful, ours heavy," granted Captain Alfred Fielder of the 12th Tennessee.[22]

The 59th Ohio in Fyffe's brigade, advancing smartly with a new set of colors, busily traded volleys with Polk's line when Lt. Col. William Howard, lacking the numbers to contest a brigade, ordered them to fall back to the fence and rally on the reserves. "We poured volley after volley into the advancing ranks of the enemy and held them in check until Major Granville Frambes upon the right informed me that we were being flanked on that wing," Howard wrote.

The withdrawal, however, left the 13th Ohio alone to face both Polk's and Wood's troops. Colonel Joseph Hawkins of the 13th Ohio spotted the front-line regiments falling back in disarray and ordered his men to lie down behind the fence and ready themselves for the trial. He had scarcely uttered the words when a Confederate bullet ripped through his heart and, remembered one of his shocked subordinates, "he breathed but twice after the fatal wound and received another wound in his neck after he fell." Color-bearer Odin Wood went down at almost the same time. "The Rebels immediately doubled on our right flank and advanced in

---

21 Barnes, *The 86th Indiana*, 103; Catherine Merrill, *The Soldier of Indiana in the War for the Union*, 2 vols. (Indianapolis, 1869), Vol. 1, 174.

22 OR 20/1:744; Franklin, *Civil War Diaries of Captain Alfred Fielder*.

our front in three lines of battle," remembered Captain Elhanan Mast. "This placed us under a direct and also a crossfire along the whole length of our regiment. We were forced to fall back but doing so cost us dear."[23]

With Hawkins's death, Major Dwight Jarvis took command as the sole surviving field officer. "I held the position until the enemy completely outflanked us and was then compelled to fall back in disorder to the line of reserves," he wrote. William Hast noted that "unfortunately several of the companies did not hear the order and consequently kept their position until they could not get back to their command as they were completely surrounded before they were aware of their danger. Seeing there was no chance for escape, we broke our guns and surrendered."

In the brief fight, the 13th lost its colors and had 29 men killed, 74 wounded, and 69 captured, including Mast. "I was struck on the back of the head with a piece of shell, but the cranium proved too solid for a mere portion of a charge but it knocked me down," Mast wrote. He awoke surrounded by Confederates eager for souvenirs: "The first thing I knew my hat was taken from my head; I merely turned over and asked the intruder to give me my hat. The only answer I received was his old sun-burned hat thrown at my side. My next visitor took my sword and the third demanded the scabbard and belt."[24]

The Federal rout exposed the right of Beatty's second line to enfilade fire from Wood's surging Confederates, the 19th Ohio taking the brunt of it. "I sent word twice to Colonel Beatty that the enemy had flanked our position in great force but received no orders," Manderson noted. "The regiment was suffering most terribly from the fire, and, seeing the enemy within 50 yards of our right and in position to destroy us, I ordered a change of front to the right and rear." Fyffe's fleeing brigade blundered into Manderson's line. The Buckeyes were thrown into temporary disorder but, Manderson would write, "gathered in an instant, formed an excellent line in good position, and fired with such precision, that, with the aid of a battery of artillery in our rear and left, we held the ground and drove the foe from the open field in our front." Wood's men belched forth a "a perfect hailstorm of bullets," recalled Sergeant Stambaugh. "The ground blubbered under my feet like hot mush in a pot. The men fell dead and wounded all around me and it did appear to me as if

23 *OR* 20/1:605; 2nd Lt. Joseph Coe, Co. D, 13th Ohio, *Marysville Tribune,* Jan. 28, 1863, 2; Captain Elhanan M. Mast, Co. H, 13th Ohio, *Urbana Union,* Jan. 21, 1863, 2.

24 *OR* 20/1:603; Private William H. Hast, Co. I, 13th Ohio, *Cadiz Sentinel,* Feb. 18, 1863, 1; Mast Letter.

my life was suspended upon the point of a needle." With their ammunition exhausted, the Buckeyes fell back toward the Nashville Pike.[25]

The sight of Van Cleve's fleeing division was too much for Swallow and his Hoosier gunners. "I saw part of the brigade falling back in disorder and the enemy advancing across the field toward the battery, with a yell," he recalled. "I ordered the battery to limber to the rear and retire as rapidly as possible, which was done in not the best order." Squier called it "a perfect stampede—men running for dear life, disengaging haversacks, cartridge boxes, canteens, overcoats, and guns, everything that could impede their progress." Observed Lieutenant Butler: "[O]ur whole line was soon in full retreat up the slope and over the hill with the Rebels crowding in on either flank. The ridge was covered with our retreating troops in disorder and confusion. A panic seemed inevitable and Rosecrans rode through from left to right giving the order, 'Form behind the turnpike, boys!' This gave them all one purpose and they seemed to act in concert."[26]

Thomas McCain of the 86th Indiana fell behind during the retreat. "Nearly every step I took across that field I saw a man fall near me," he recalled. "An exclamation of 'Oh, I am killed!' and all would be over with those who came in contact with the fatal shot. Their groans and shrieks are still ringing in my ears. Such a scene I never witnessed before and hope never again to witness a similar one." Moments later, McCain was captured along with more than 100 members of his regiment.[27]

While the sides contested for control of the Burris fields and woods, Confederate Generals Johnson and Liddell moved their brigades north and spotted Harker's Federals awaiting. Harker deployed his brigade in three lines: the first had the 51st Indiana on the right, the 65th Ohio the left, and the 6th Ohio Battery the interval between, slightly retired; the second consisted of the 64th Ohio in support of the 51st Indiana, and the 73rd Indiana in support of the 65th Ohio; and the 13th Michigan formed the rear, mainly a reserve force tasked with guarding the caissons. Harker's men understood the stakes. "Our brigade was sent as a kind of forlorn

25 *OR* 20/1:594; Stambaugh Letter.

26 *OR* 20/1:579; Doyle, *This Wilderness of War*; Butler, *My Story of the Civil War*, 267.

27 Richard K. Rue and Geraldine M., eds., *In Song and Sorrow: The Daily Journal of Thomas Hart Benton McCain of the Eighty-Sixth Indiana Volunteer Infantry* (1998), 45.

hope to prevent the turning of our right flank," recalled Wilbur Hinman of the 65th Ohio, "and upon that movement hung the fortunes of the day."[28]

Colonel Streight ordered three companies of skirmishers from his 51st Indiana to protect the brigade's right; they soon ran into Cleburne's advance and opened fire. "We were fired upon by a large force of the enemy concealed in the standing corn to my front and right," Streight reported. "I at once ordered the whole line forward at a double-quick. My skirmishers came in sight of the enemy in a moment, when our well-directed fire soon put them to flight. We had a fair chance at them while they were retreating some 400 yards, and large numbers of them were killed and wounded."

No sooner had Harker become engaged on his right than "a staff officer from the command upon my left [Fyffe] reported a strong force of the enemy in his front," the colonel reported. "I replied that my right was in danger, and that a strong force and battery was in front."[29]

The trouble in front emanated from Bushrod Johnson's Tennesseans, just beginning to materialize in the woods ahead. Johnson's Brigade advanced from left to right with the 23rd Tennessee, 17th Tennessee, 44th Tennessee, 25th Tennessee, and 37th Tennessee. Captain William Harder of the 23rd Tennessee noted that the unusual Federal movements created confusion about their identity. "Some distance in front could be seen in the thick cedars men that appeared to be Confederate, sometimes advancing, and then moving to the right as if desirous of uncovering our line," he wrote. "We were in doubt of who they were. They advanced to within about a hundred yards of our line and then with folded colors lay down amongst the stones and cedars."

Ordered to determine who these men were, Harder moved forward along a derelict wagon trace. "There were many of them in brown clothing and I was taken off guard when within 40 yards they rose up and fired at me a heavy volley, missing me but killing and wounding 16 men in the road behind. I called to our regiment and returned to the line under a galling fire."[30]

Johnson's regiments on the right found themselves in an unexpectedly hot fight; the balance of the brigade to their left, hidden by the tangled forest, was hardly scratched. "After a few rounds it was found that a heavy force was flanking our right, where we were unsupported," Johnson wrote. "I consequently moved

28 Wilbur F. Hinman Papers, 1862–1865. MS 3862, WRHS.

29 *OR* 20/1:502, 507.

30 Harder Memoirs.

my command to the rear in good order. Major Joseph McReynolds, the last field officer on duty with the 37th Tennessee, was here mortally wounded, and Captain Charles Jarnagin assumed command of the regiment."[31]

"We suddenly found them in line at a short distance, and immediately commenced firing," said Major Horatio Whitbeck of the 65th Ohio. "The enemy, though in brigade front, three columns deep, staggered, concealed himself as far as possible, and did not venture to advance under our fire." Hinman wrote that the reality of battle "far exceeds anything I ever conceived. The roar of artillery and musketry was deafening while every moment it seemed a score of balls were hissing as near my head as they could come without striking. Many of our gallant boys were soon stretched upon the ground killed or wounded, and how our hearts ached to hear the groans of the suffering ones without being able to do anything for their relief. Never was I so moved as when I saw those of my own company with whom I have associated every day for 14 months mangled and bleeding by my side."[32]

Fyffe's abrupt retreat exposed Harker's left to Vaughan's and Wood's advance. "The line of the enemy on our left advancing completely outflanked us, and we were suffering under a raking crossfire," Whitbeck reported. Recognizing the danger, Streight requested that the 6th Ohio Battery roll forward to enfilade the Confederate line. "The battery was promptly on the ground, but not too soon, for by the time it was in position the enemy had engaged the troops to my left," Streight wrote. "Captain [Cullen] Bradley opened a most terrific fire, their dead were literally piled in heaps by the terrific fire from the battery. Nothing else could have saved our troops to my left from total destruction."

The Hoosiers had their hands full, though, popping away at Liddell's skirmishers concealed in a cornfield. "A well-directed fire sent them scurrying through the corn like the shoats at Gadara," asserted Sgt. Maj. William Ross Hartpence of the 51st Indiana. "We had a fine chance at them as they were skedaddling down those long furrows."[33]

Liddell ordered the Warren Light Artillery into position about 500 yards from Harker's right and opened fire on the 6th Ohio Battery. "The firing of the battery was remarkably good, compelling the enemy to change his position several times," recalled Lieutenant Shannon, "and that of one of his guns as often as six times, when he abandoned the field." Harker responded quickly, moving his battery to the

<hr>

31 *OR* 20/1: 879.

32 Ibid., 514; Hinman Papers.

33 *OR* 20/1:508, 514; Hartpence, *History of the Fifty-First Indiana*, 107.

crest of a small hill and shifting the entire brigade to the right. Bradley directed a single section of two guns to trade shots with the Mississippians while the remaining four guns concentrated on Johnson's line, expending 150 rounds of case shot and canister. "We poured in a heavy and destructive enfilading fire of canister upon the infantry, dozens of them dropping at every discharge," recalled Daniel Hoover of the 6th Ohio Battery.

Adjutant Alfred Wade of the 73rd Indiana noted that Shannon's shells often fell short "but bouncing as they struck the ground, they were a dangerous thing to men. One 10-lb shell struck the ploughed ground in the cornfield and made a tremendous bounce of 30-40 feet, struck the ground, then jammed square through one of the Ohio regiments."[34]

Liddell arrayed the 8th Arkansas on the left, the 6th/7th Arkansas at left center, the 5th Arkansas at right center, and the 2nd Arkansas on the right. Harker's new position, however, allowed him to pummel Liddell's line as it approached, with the 51st Indiana especially effective. "A very closely contested fight here took place, the enemy holding their position until [we] approached within 25 steps of their line," recalled Colonel Daniel Govan of the 2nd Arkansas. Lieutenant Colonel John Murray of the neighboring 5th Arkansas agreed, noting that "the enemy made a most determined stand, fighting until our men got in 20 or 30 steps of them, but they could not withstand the impetuosity of our troops, and soon broke and fled in disorder."

It was not long before Fyffe's men streamed to the rear, which exposed Harker's left to both Bushrod Johnson's line and enfilade fire from Vaughan's and Wood's position. Liddell's charging line completed the hat trick. "The need of haste is urgent and every instant of delay increases the imminence of their peril," Hinman admitted.[35]

"My command was in a most precarious position," Harker conceded. After a fight lasting roughly 20 minutes, the colonel ordered the battery, then the front-line regiments to fall back. "Quickly the sections are limbered up and go whirling back nearly the line of the fence behind which the infantry rallied," Hinman noted. "[Lieutenant Aaron] Baldwin's section does not in the confusion receive the order

34 OR 20/1:872; Wade, op. cit.; Private Daniel Hoover, 6th Ohio Battery, *Summit County Beacon*, January 22, 1863, 2.

35 OR 20/1:861, 866; Hinman, *Story of the Sherman Brigade*, 349. The 51st Indiana lost four men killed and 25 wounded on December 31. The 65th Ohio lost a total of 173 killed, wounded, or missing.

to fall back and so intent are the men upon their work that they are ignorant of the movement to the rear. The section receives the galling fire of both infantry and artillery. Two horses are killed by a cannon ball and a driver has his arm torn off. Just in time, the dead and wounded horses are cut loose and the section dashes to the rear."[36]

It took Harker three attempts to get the 65th Ohio to disengage. One soldier recalled that "we held our position until the enemy had come within ten steps and their right forming around us when we fell back. I expected every minute to get a chuck in my back, but luck was on my side." The 65th lost more than 150 men, nearly half the regiment, during this brief engagement. Streight ordered his Hoosiers to gather their wounded and then fall back, but Harker neglected to tell him where to rally, so Streight continued all the way to the Nashville Pike. Liddell's alert Arkansans redoubled their fire, Govan claiming that Harker's line "gave way in confusion and fled across the field, exposed to a murderous fire from my regiment as their dead were thick on the ground."[37]

This dropped the onus of battle to Harker's second line, the 73rd Indiana and 64th Ohio. Once the 65th Ohio cleared their front, the Hoosiers leapt to their feet and opened fire to cover the withdrawal. "The Rebels were seen flushed with success pressing on in pursuit but a word of caution from the officers and every man resumed his position until the word was given, when they rose and poured a deadly volley into the Rebel ranks," recalled Alfred Wade, the regiment's adjutant. Recounted Colonel Gilbert Hathaway: "Twelve rounds were fired with great spirit and effect, when it was seen that the enemy was retreating in disorder, taking an oblique direction to the left. I ordered an advance, and well, indeed, was it obeyed-pressing forward on the double-quick; the ground recently occupied by the 65th Ohio was attained, the enemy still fleeing before us."[38]

Harker tapped the 64th Ohio to cover the withdrawal of his guns, although Lt. Col. Alexander McIlvain apparently misunderstood the order. "The direction was indicated to the commanding officer, but, unfortunately, he moved too far to the right," Harker reported, which exposed the 73rd Indiana's left, "permitting the enemy to advance much farther than could have been done had my design been carried out." As Ulysses Greene of the 64th Ohio recalled: "[A]ll was going well with us when the Rebels with one giant effort broke the lines on our left and they

36 *OR* 20/1:502, 508; Hinman, *Story of the Sherman Brigade*, 349.

37 Corporal John Sowash, Co. F, 65th Ohio, *Holmes County Farmer*, Feb. 12, 1863, 3.

38 *OR* 20/1:510; *ORS* 18:65; Wade Diary.

precipitated themselves onto our unfortunate brigade. Torrents of bullets poured into our fast-thinning ranks while scores fell at every discharge. The carnage was frightful, and unable longer to stem the fire that was now poured upon us, we broke and fled before the enemy."[39]

Swooping in after the Buckeyes' retreat, Liddell's veterans opened a devastating enfilade fire on the 73rd Indiana, which had not received Harker's directive to withdraw. Wade saw a solid Confederate line less than a hundred feet from his left swing broadside preparing to open fire. He attempted to alert Hathaway, but the colonel believed instead that he was being reinforced. By then, it was too late. "Their right wing was in position behind the fence scarce 50 feet from our left and already their terrible crossfire was mowing us down," Wade related. "All this time my attention had been directed to the extreme left of our regiment. When looking toward the right I saw the 64th Ohio and our right on the full retreat[;] immediately thereafter the left gave way unable to stand the terrible fire." Hathaway belatedly saw the peril, and "in a somewhat disordered state" the Hoosiers withdrew, leaving a third of its 290 men on the field as casualties.[40]

Harker rallied his line behind a fence just north of Asbury Road. All he could gather were the survivors of the 65th Ohio, the 6th Ohio Battery, and the as-yet-unbloodied 13th Michigan—a scratch line of perhaps 600 muskets. Liddell's and Johnson's men hardly gave the Federals a moment to settle at their new position before renewing the attack. Hinman confessed that "our hearts nearly sank within us as we saw the long dark lines advancing bold and defiant, flaunting their banners of treason mockingly toward us. Our boys loaded and fired with all their might at 150 yards distance. We were partially protected by the fence but a perfect hailstorm of bullets rattled against the rails and trees around us while many found their way between the rails and took fatal effect."

Charles Nickerson of the 65th Ohio marveled at the bravery of one of the charging Confederate color-bearers. "He would run ahead of his regiment, get behind a tree, then wave the flag and cheer them on," he wrote. "We shot these colors down three times but I saw the flag over the top of my gun again."[41]

Johnson's line attacked Harker cautiously. "Under cover of the fence and rocks our men took deliberate aim and poured upon the enemy a destructive fire, which was returned with spirit," the general reported. Colonel Watt Floyd of the

<hr>

39 OR 20/1:503; Private Ulysses Greene, Co. K, 64th Ohio, *Bucyrus Journal*, Feb. 6, 1863, 3.

40 OR 20/1:503, 510; Wade Diary.

41 Hinman Papers; Nickerson Letter.

17th Tennessee wrote that the "battery was playing heavily upon us, but the well-directed fire of our boys soon drove the gunners from their pieces and stopped the trouble from that quarter." The Tennesseans charged forward and, taking cover among some sinks and basins, opened fire 75 yards out. "Never have I seen such cool, deliberate aim taken in battle," Floyd gloated. "The enemy stood the fire well, and returned it briskly, but with little effect."[42]

Johnson's fire broke the 65th Ohio, leaving behind the 6th Ohio Battery, then taking a beating from both Shannon's rifled cannons and Putnam Darden's Jefferson Flying Artillery. "While Lieutenant Baldwin was limbering his section," Hoover remembered, "a solid shot struck the lead horse on the head, killing it instantly and covering George Chitty with blood but doing him no injury." Bradley reported that this second stand at the fence lasted only five minutes, during which his guns fired a dozen rounds. "I was again compelled to retire my battery and abandon two pieces of the battery, one of which I had spiked," he reported. "Two of the guns have lost eleven of their twelve horses and the four other guns of the battery dash away," Hinman added, "but the Rebels are close at hand and there is no chance to attach the prolongs, and the two pieces are abandoned."[43]

This left Colonel Shoemaker's 13th Michigan alone against portions of two Confederate brigades. Spread along a snake rail fence, Shoemaker kept his men under cover until the Rebels approached just yards away. "I knew that my regiment could be depended upon, as we had not as yet been in the fight at all," he wrote. "My men were excited but fresh and cool so that every shot told. The advance of the Confederates was checked at once and they retreated to the fence between the woods and the open fields which they lined with their men and which became at once a line of fire blazing at my little regiment."

Captain Valentine McGehee of the 2nd Arkansas noted that "we were whipping two regiments back when we suddenly came up to a regiment of Yankees, ambushed behind a fence. It seems to me only a providential occurrence that kept them from killing every man in our regiment."[44]

The shooting match continued for half an hour until Liddell's men lapped around his open right flank, compelling Shoemaker to order a retreat. Once the Federals rose from their cover, Johnson recalled, "a volley was discharged upon them with remarkable effect, and our men rapidly advanced to the cedars,

---

42 *OR* 20/1:879, 884.

43 Ibid., 1:479; Hoover Letter; Hinman, *Story of the Sherman Brigade*, 350.

44 Shoemaker Narrative; McGehee Diary.

capturing the fine battery of Parrott guns against which they had been fighting." The last volley proved especially devastating, and the wrecked Federal position was shrouded in bodies. "Many were lying side along the ledge in the position they assumed to await our approach, while others had fallen as they turned to retreat," Johnson would write, to which Floyd concurred, insisting that "along the edge of the cedar glade was the greatest destruction of Yankees I have seen on any battlefield."[45]

Shoemaker rallied his regiment a few hundred yards north and, seeing the enemy wandering idly around the old position, resolved to charge. "The blood of my men was now up, every man moved forward with a will and as if actuated by a common impulse," he noted. "As we advanced, every man shouted and yelled to the top of their bent as if confident of success. As we emerged from the thicket, our men poured a volley of musketry into the ranks of the Confederates who were engaged in examining our dead and wounded."

The surprise foray forced the Rebels to scatter and flee, giving Shoemaker the opportunity to collect 58 prisoners and the two guns Bradley had abandoned. From there, Shoemaker headed to the Nashville Pike with his prizes in tow, the Confederates following cautiously. Harker in particular was thrilled, crowing that "they completely routed the enemy. For this act of gallantry Colonel Shoemaker and his gallant regiment are deserving of much praise."[46]

As Harker's men fell back toward the pike, they came across some surprising support: Colonel Luther Bradley leading survivors of the 27th and 51st Illinois from Sheridan's division. Unable to find Sheridan or ammunition after retiring from the cedars, Bradley was heading up the pike when Rosecrans, then conferring with General McCook, saw them. "Who commands these troops?" Rosecrans queried. "I do," Bradley replied. "Send your regiments quickly into yonder thicket and stop the advance of the Rebels," Rosecrans countered. "Quick, quick, lose not a moment, colonel. This battle must be won."

Bradley's men had only about three rounds of ammunition per man, but he gamely told Rosecrans, "[W]e will drive them with the bayonet." According to Edward Tabler of the 51st Illinois, one of Rosecrans's staff officers directed Bradley's men into position, stressing, "Make a stand here and hold this pike, you

45 OR 20/1 879, 884.

46 Ibid., 1:503.

must hold this pike come what will. When your ammunition is exhausted, hold it with the point of the bayonet."[47]

Lieutenant Moody of the 51st Illinois wrote that the initial venture of Bradley's line into the field was daunting. "We advanced to the edge of the thicket and endeavored to hold a position there but we didn't have half a chance as the fire was so hot from the unseen enemy that we had to fall back to the pike," he wrote. "General McCook then came up furious and said the pike had to be held as the safety of the whole army depended upon it." Chastened, Bradley wheeled his men about and, after a short advance, ordered them to lie down and wait for Harker's men to clear their front. William Ranson of the 27th Illinois noted that the men in the ranks "became impatient and yelled out Charge! The whole length of the two regiments scaled the hill, yelling at the top of our voices, firing and loading as we went. The enemy soon became confused and began to break ranks and scatter before us. On we went, not forgetting to keep up the yell." Moody noted that "both regiments charged into the thicket with a shout and a yell that ought to have been heard all over the Southern Confederacy. It was really the most brilliant thing I saw the whole day."[48]

The unordered and uncontrolled charge miraculously turned the tide for the Federals. Hinman admired the spectacle with unbounded joy as Bradley's men "charged bayonets upon the surprised Rebels with a cheer that seemed to rend the skies. The Secesh broke and ran in the wildest confusion, throwing away guns, cartridge boxes, and whatever else impeded them in their flight. Cheer after cheer went up from the brave 'Suckers' as they pursued the flying enemy across the fields. The fate of the day was decided—the right wing was saved."

The steam had been taken out of the Confederates' drive, "but I wished for spoils," confessed Private John McBride of the 51st Illinois. "I ran on about 20 rods and found eight of them hidden in a cave in the rocks. When I came up, one of them was going to shoot me but I stepped behind an oak tree and was going to fire when they threw up their hands and they were mine." The Illinoisans discovered among the prisoners some men from the 13th Tennessee, a regiment the 27th Illinois had fought before at Belmont in November 1861. Blowing the bugle to

---

47 Stevenson, *Battle of Stone's River*, 99-100; Major William A. Schmitt, 27th Illinois, *Weekly Quincy Whig & Republican*, Jan. 24, 1863, 2; Private Edward L. Tabler, Co. K, 51st Illinois, *Grundy County Herald*, Feb. 4, 1863, 2.

48 Moody Diary; Private William H. Ranson, Co. K, 27th Illinois, *Jacksonville Herald*, Jan. 29, 1863, 2.

sound the rally, Bradley corralled his excited troops and, with nearly 200 Confederate prisoners in tow, retired to safety beyond the Nashville Pike.[49]

49 Private John McBride, Co. D, 51st Illinois, www.51stillinois.org/mcbrideletters.html, retrieved Jan. 12, 2023; OR 20/1:371; Hinman Papers. Rosecrans was so complimentary of Bradley's Illinoisans that Major William Schmitt of the 27th Illinois observed, "he would rather be major of the 27th than president of the United States."

* * *

Although Cleburne's assault had shown success, Shoemaker's and Bradley's determined counterattacks had temporarily disorganized his division. S.A.M. Wood's brigade—1,100-men strong when the day began but now down to 500—found itself out of ammunition, so Cleburne sent it to the rear to resupply. Hardee would keep Wood's men along the Wilkinson Pike protecting the ordnance wagons for the balance of the day. In the meantime, the wounded received care and dozens of Federal prisoners were gathered into squads and sent to the rear. It took time for Cleburne's officers to gather their scattered troops, call the men into line, reform ranks, and reconstitute the regiments. With most of the division short of ammunition, ordnance officers scrambled to the rear to bring forward a resupply.

Liddell was concerned his own left flank was in the air. "Finding myself alone at this point, with no support on my right or left," he reported, "I halted my command in the woods near the fence and threw forward a line of skirmishers to reconnoiter and develop the enemy, not then visible from our position." Cleburne's men spent nearly an hour reforming in the fields north of Asbury Road, granting Rosecrans precious time to rally his army into a dominant position along the Nashville Pike, blessed by abundant Federal artillery.[50]

Cleburne moved his men again about 1:30 p.m., shifting their advance to the left, in order right to left as follows: Polk, Vaughan, Johnson, and Liddell. The disorganized Federal retreat was evident. "The turnpike road at this time was filled with trains of wagons moving in the direction of Nashville," wrote Liddell, "and I ordered the battery to fire upon that part of the train to the right of the cavalry, which caused the train to break in confusion and seek shelter behind the embankment of the railroad."[51] According to Cleburne, Liddell's struggle with the Federals was "the most obstinately contested and, to the enemy, most destructive fight which had yet occurred." The enemy line in the woods did not give way until Liddell "was within 25 paces." Liddell galloped off to reconnoiter new positions, giving temporary command of the brigade to Colonel Govan.

Colonel John H. Kelly's 8th Arkansas held the extreme left of the entire Confederate line and came under fire from portions of McCook's reformed line.

---

50 *OR* 20/1:857. Liddell's men obtained a full supply of 40 rounds of ammunition along the Wilkinson Pike before making this attack. They consumed nearly all of it driving back Harker's brigade, which gives some indication of the ferocity of the fighting.

51 Ibid.

The Warren Light Artillery soon rolled into position and commenced counterbattery fire.[52] Meanwhile, the balance of Cleburne's line advanced. "Johnson's, Vaughan's, and Polk's brigades moved rapidly in pursuit, obliquing to the left as they advanced," the general reported. Throughout the day, Hardee ordered Cleburne to maintain the push and not allow the Federals time to rally or reform, but as his division moved across these fields, no time was lost correcting alignment or distances.

Cohesion inevitably fell apart. "The line had not advanced a quarter of a mile when a fresh line of the enemy was discovered in open fields supported by numerous and well-served batteries," Cleburne wrote. "My line advanced steadily, pouring in a deadly fire, and drove the enemy across a small dirt road. That portion of his line opposite Johnson rallied behind a fence on the far side of the dirt road, but was driven from there also, when his whole line disappeared in the cedar woods, which here border the Nashville pike, and [we] were close behind him. He fled back in the woods, leaving the ground in front of Johnson's brigade thickly covered with dead and wounded."[53]

On the right, Cleburne discovered the wreckage of McCown's Division, which had previously tested the Federal defenses along Nashville Pike. "Their officers were endeavoring to rally and carry them forward," recalled Colonel John Fulton of the 44th Tennessee. "At this moment we reached and passed them, passing a small house, and, crossing two fences, we entered a cedar thicket, which was the strongest natural position we encountered through the day, it being one of large ledges of rock of very rugged formation, protected by a heavy growth of cedar." Captain Jarnagin of the 37th Tennessee noted that his men pursued the Federals "all the time pouring heavy volleys of musketry into them. We pressed upon them, taking possession of the crevices in a ledge of rocks the enemy had just occupied. We then poured buck and ball into them heavy. They had commenced running and scattering at a terrible rate."[54]

Stephen Tanner of the 9th Texas was "spellbound" at what he saw as his regiment approached Nashville Pike. "The smoke from hours of fighting in the cedars made a midnight darkness at 2 p.m.," he wrote. "The blaze from their guns made a wall of fire that revealed the faces of the men and was reflected by their

52 OR 20/1:847, 857.

53 Ibid., 1:847.

54 Ibid., 1:892, 893. Jarnagin's mention of buck and ball ammunition indicates his regiment used smoothbore muskets.

glazed cap bills as far as I could see up and down the Union lines. The fire from their guns plainly showed their grim faces and slouched hats while taking deadly aim at the foe. It seemed to me to be a field of glory. We had been fighting from sunrise almost constantly and I had emptied my 40-round cartridge box and picked up a fine Union gun and used it until it choked and I couldn't press the load down, and in my effort ran the gun rod into my hand bringing the blood freely. Then I pounded it against the fence to force the load home but failed as it stopped about one third of the way. I poked the muzzle through the fence over my head, crouched down under the gun and pulled the trigger, thinking if you want to burst, burst."[55]

"Our brigade was told by Colonel Vaughan that we could only carry our point by driving this force across Nashville Pike which would force those threatening our flank to retire also," wrote one veteran of the 154th Tennessee. "Our brigade readily responded to the order of the colonel to move forward, the gallant Major [John W.] Dawson of the 154th Tennessee, seizing the broken staff with the colors of his regiment carried them on his horse at the head of his command. The brigade on our left not carrying out our alignment and our boys moved forward so quickly as to cause us soon to be entirely unsupported, fighting a force in our front and on our right flank alone. Here we succeeded in driving them from two of their guns and almost up to the Nashville Pike when, on account of our solitary position the evident certainty of our being flanked, we were forced to retire."

Major John Johnson of the 29th Tennessee reported that "the firing was so heavy that after a short while, seeing that they were too strong for our greatly reduced brigade, orders were given to fall back." Vaughan's men got as close to the Nashville Pike as any Confederate force, as Cleburne's Division unknowingly marched into the jaws of a Federal meatgrinder, a position that had already torn the life out of McCown's advance on the pike a short time before.[56]

*   *   *

Anchored west of the Nashville Pike, the three battalions of the Union Pioneer Brigade hunkered down in support of a deadly nest of 24 guns of artillery, including six guns from the Chicago Board of Trade Battery and six from Battery B of the

---

55 Tanner Autobiography.

56 C, 154th Tennessee Infantry, *Memphis Daily Appeal,* Jan. 29, 1863, 1; *OR* 20/1:748. Dawson ended the war as a lieutenant colonel and was with General Joseph Johnson's army that surrendered at Durham Station, NC, on April 26, 1865.

26th Pennsylvania Light arrayed in the open ground where today the battlefield's visitor's center is located. Six more guns from Battery H of the 5th US covered the Pioneers' left flank, and six Parrott rifles of the Coldwater Light Artillery, parked atop the ridge in the middle of what is now the park's national cemetery, had range over a wide swath of the field.

Moving north along the pike, the six-gun 7th Indiana Battery supported Van Cleve's two retiring brigades (Beatty's and Fyffe's) while Moses Walker's newly arriving brigade went into position on Van Cleve's right at the Three-Mile Marker near Rosecrans's headquarters—adding the six guns of Captain Josiah Church's Michigan battery to the already formidable array of guns. Next in line was Harker's brigade with the four remaining guns of the 6th Ohio Battery, still recovering from its drubbing on the Burris Farm but eager for another go at the Confederates. Beyond Harker's right, two of the rallied divisions from McCook's wing, now resupplied with ammunition, took their places in line. East of the railroad, two more Federal batteries covered the rear, including Battery B of the 1st Ohio Light (Cruft's brigade) and four guns from the 5th Indiana Battery.

It was the strongest concentration of artillery by either army yet at Stones River: Rosecrans had 50 guns total covering a half-mile stretch of the Nashville Pike. To contest this incredible array of firepower, Cleburne had merely the four guns of the Warren Light Artillery on his left flank and the determination of his infantrymen. It would not be enough.

Federal officers had used the previous hour profitably, rallying thousands of men into a patchwork line that proved much stouter than expected. Adjutant Wade, separated from his 73rd Indiana during the wild retreat, found barely 100 survivors boldly marching over the railroad back to the pike. "They came to front stout-hearted and determined to breast another lead storm, if need be," he applauded. "I regret much that we fell back in disorder,"

> but we immediately rallied and came to the front again ready, if not eager to engage the overwhelming force of the enemy. Our proud old banner still waved over us pierced by eight bullets. Every man of our color guard was either killed or wounded but a hundred brave hearts gathered around that noble flag who would spill their last drop of blood before it should be trailed in the dust by Rebel hands.[57]

57 Wade Diary.

"At this critical moment the enemy met my thinned ranks with another fresh line of battle, supported by a heavier and closer artillery fire than I had yet encountered," Cleburne divulged. In their eagerness of pursuit, Cleburne's three brigades lost alignment and struck the Federal salient piecemeal—a crucial mistake. As Vaughan's men emerged into the field on the right, they came under a debilitating barrage beyond their right. "My right flank so severely enfiladed that I was compelled to retire them after again driving the enemy from one of his batteries, which on that account I was unable to bring off," he wrote.

Detached from the brigade during the approach, Colonel William Young's 9th Texas found itself too far forward. The short fight at the pike was in one Texan's estimation "the bloodiest struggle of the day. The enemy was stronger at this point than anywhere else on the field and fiercely contended for the position. Directly in front of us was a wide area of clear land and across this it was necessary to advance under the sweeping fire of six batteries, but with doubtless hearts and step as proud of though on parade, the men sprang forward at the word and marched on to the face of death. The enemy poured in a perfect hail of iron through their ranks."[58]

Few things are more contagious than panic, and Vaughan's rapid withdrawal, however justified, spread panic throughout Cleburne's divisional line, with Johnson's Brigade next to catch the fever. The former University of Nashville professor had just managed to align his Tennesseans for the next big push when alarm gripped the line. Confederate troops to his right were seen retiring, Johnson lamented, and worse "it was reported that our right was flanked by a heavy force." Colonel Fulton reported that "the troops on our right were found suddenly to have broken and given back in confusion without any apparent cause." Fulton's own lieutenant colonel galloped up and proclaimed: "[W]e were under a heavy crossfire and must retire. The men, witnessing the flight on our right fell back in disorder."

Jarnagin heard the same cry. "I could not see the danger," he noted, "so I got on a very high rock in order that I might make some discovery. I soon saw that Colonel John Fulton and others were trying to rally their regiments but failing. I waited until the enemy were about to close on us, and I gave the command to fall back."

"This was more than our men could stand," Cleburne reported. "Vaughan's brigade was driven back in great confusion. Polk's and Johnson's followed. As our broken ranks went back over the fields before the fire of this fresh line, the enemy opened fire on our right flank from several batteries which they had concentrated

58 *OR* 20/1:744-745, 750.

on an eminence near the railroad, inflicting a heavier loss on Polk's brigade than it had suffered in all the previous fighting of the day." Within moments, Federal fire struck a number of officers, and the color-bearer of the 25th Tennessee fell along with the colors, which were lost. Floyd, on the left of the line, described the disintegration of the entire position. "I saw the brigade on the right of yours had fallen back considerably, and that the right wing of the brigade was falling back also," he wrote. "I turned to the left, and found it giving back, too. I immediately ordered my command to fall back to the fence. No one seemed disposed to stop and support me, and I ordered my men to fall back as rapidly as possible."[59]

Liddell's Arkansans were appalled by the rout of their division mates. An enraged Lt. Col. John Murray of the 5th Arkansas: "Johnson's Tennesseans "gave way and fled in a disorderly and disgraceful manner, the men running through our ranks perfectly panic-stricken . . . compelling us to fall back with them." Lieutenant Colonel George Baucum of the 8th Arkansas tried in vain to halt the Tennesseans.

Johnson's withdrawal left the Arkansans isolated with few good options. "I was at first at a loss what course to pursue," Govan recalled. "Our success had been all that we wished, and we had not met with a single repulse." Govan, however, was down to his last few rounds of ammunition (the wagons having not yet arrived), and he lacked the strength to storm the Federal position on his front. He had no real option left but to order a retreat. The Federal artillery drew blood even in the retreat, wounding Colonel Samuel Smith of the 6th/7th Arkansas, leaving Lieutenant Colonel Feaster Cameron in command. Colonel Kelly of the 8th Arkansas also went down. "We fell back to a stronger position across the open fields and into the woods in rear, where we reformed our line and awaited the advance of the enemy that was never made and closed the fighting on our part for the day," recalled Major William Douglass.[60]

Cleburne's collapse was as sudden as it was unexpected. "At the moment in which I felt the utmost confidence in the success of our arms I was almost run over by our retreating troops," recalled General Johnson. "The retreat was made without order. The lines were broken and men of different regiments, brigades, and divisions were scattered all over the fields." The stakes were high. "Our men were in sight of the Nashville pike; some have said they were on it. The enemy's right was doubled back upon their center. Had we held this position the line of

59 Ibid., 1:849, 892-893.

60 Ibid., 1:857, 861, 866, 868.

communication of the enemy would have been cut. We could have flanked them and enfiladed their whole line, which was no doubt in disorder."[61]

Stephen Tanner fell behind in the retreat and offered insight into the condition of Cleburne's men. "Looking back, not a man of our command could be seen. I said, 'Lewis [a comrade], they are all gone.' He looked up and retreated on the double quick. I made the effort but my breath was gone, my liver gorged and very painful and I could not double quick. The bullets seemed to come in showers. I felt my exposed position and got mad and said aloud, 'Kill me, plague on you, if you want to!' I walked back in the direction I thought our men had retreated and found them half a mile back. But I was done up for the present and when the men moved, I had to remain with my heels on a log." Tanner's statement could be applied to most of Bragg's army: the men had fought magnificently but were drained.[62]

Cleburne scrambled to reform his command along Asbury Road, fully expecting the Federals to counterattack. He rallied his troops on the edge of the opposite woods 400 yards behind "the scene of disaster," though Cleburne admitted some of his men could not be stopped until they reached the Wilkinson pike. "I reformed my division as rapidly as possible," he continued, "Polk's brigade on the right, Johnson's in the center, and Liddell's on the left. A fresh supply of ammunition was served out, and I waited in momentary expectation for an advance of the enemy in overwhelming force. He never advanced a foot, and the question presented itself, ought I to again advance?" Cleburne took note that he was in possession of about three miles of ground conquered from the enemy, large numbers of captured Federals, guns, and small arms. He knew that if he was repulsed again, he might "lose all these and cause the demoralization and destruction of my division." The division leader reported his situation to General Hardee, who ordered him hold the ground he had won, rest and reorganize his division, and await further orders. The command may have given Cleburne some relief. "Pushing my pickets well forward," he added, "I bivouacked in line of battle on the same line which the division rallied on after the repulse."[63]

Rosecrans had won this first round for control of the Nashville Pike. The battle was approaching a crescendo at the Round Forest—perhaps the entire battlefield's most critical piece of ground.

61 Ibid., 1:879.

62 Tanner Autobiography.

63 *OR* 20/1, 848-849.

17

Bragg's Last
Thrusts of the Day

WITH THE CRISIS finally averted on his right, General Rosecrans and his headquarters staff galloped toward a hillock near the Nashville and Chattanooga Railroad and behind the Round Forest to observe the fighting. Across Stones River, three Confederate batteries in Breckinridge's Division had a fine view of the Federals from atop Wayne's Hill; the cavalcade of horsemen could indicate only a general and his coterie, so the gunners let fly a volley of shells at them. "They were galloping through a tumult of the iron missiles," recalled William Bickham. "Apparently unconscious of personal hazard, General Rosecrans moved about unscathed, calm, and absorbed by the intensity of his own thought with inflexible purpose. An unexploded shell whizzed close by and the head of Garesche vanished with it. Sickening gouts of his blood were spattered upon his comrades who turned in horror from the ghastly spectacle. The mutilated form of the hero careened gently over the saddle and fell upon the field."

Missing death by inches, Rosecrans "seemed not to observe it," Bickham opined. More shells fell into their midst, knocking down three more members of the escort and wounding another of his staff. "General, do you think it right to expose yourself so much?" asked his aide, Frank Bond. Rosecrans responded by galloping up to the 97th Ohio, then positioned on ground along the pike, and reminding the men to shoot low: "[G]ive them a blizzard at their shins, and then charge with the cold steel." When Bond mentioned Garesche's death, "it seemed to occur to Rosecrans as a half-remembered dream. "I am very sorry. We cannot help it," he said.[1]

About 2:00 p.m., Rosecrans learned that a body of Confederate cavalry was actively engaged against Samuel Price's brigade, tasked with guarding McFadden's Ford. With all his attention focused on salvaging the line along the Nashville Pike, the last thing Rosecrans needed was to have his left turned. He summoned Price by courier and used the opportunity to bolster the perhaps uneasy colonel. When Price arrived, he was met with a curt hello: "Colonel Price, you command here, do you?" Price replied that he did. "Well sir, will you hold this ford?" Price replied, "I will try, General." Rosecrans asked again, "Will you hold this ford?" Price said, "I will die in the attempt." Rosecrans snapped, "That won't do sir; will you hold this ford? Look me in the eyes and tell me if you will hold this position." Divining the object of this rigid inquiry, Price answered with great emphasis, "I will!" To which Rosecrans replied, "That will do, sir" and rode off.[2]

The security of the Federal line depended on holding the Round Forest, and by 2 o'clock thousands of bluecoats held the position, along with a substantial array of artillery. In a way, Rosecrans could thank the Confederates' morning successes for collapsing the Federal line upon itself. Negley's and Sheridan's men, protected by Rosecrans's powerful artillery line, rallied behind the railroad embankment, dodging occasional shells from Confederate guns on Wayne's Hill but safe from any roving Confederate cavalry or infantry. This gave the men time to regroup and reorganize, and after drawing a resupply of ammunition from the ordnance wagons, these divisions returned to the battle. Both had suffered heavily in the morning's fighting but proved their fighting mettle, and as shown by Bradley's recent charge across the Nashville Pike, they still maintained a fair degree of combat efficiency.

This gave Rosecrans a decided advantage in the final hours of daylight. For the first time in the battle, Federal commanders could draw upon ready reserves to hold the line. William Hazen's brigade still held the center of the line at the Round Forest, not having budged since repulsing the first two attacks that morning. To Hazen's right, Hascall's and Grose's brigades faced southwest covering the

---

1 Bickham, *Rosecrans' Campaign*, 277-79. Garesche's death occurred in what is today the open field between the south end of the national cemetery and the northern fringes of the Round Forest.

2 "Some Famous Fighters: Interesting Anecdotes Concerning the Great Generals of the War," *National Tribune*, Oct. 5, 1882, 7.

Nashville Pike. On Hazen's left, Wagner's brigade advanced and covered the ground between the Round Forest and Stones River. With Negley's and Sheridan's men close at hand, eight brigades now held this crucial sector. Rosecrans could hardly have accumulated more men in the area.

Although the Round Forest held thousands of Federals, what it did not have was a general officer tasked with coordinating its defense. It is curious that Crittenden and Rosecrans neglected to appoint a commander to hold such a vital piece of ground. In theory, this job should have fallen to either John Palmer or Thomas Wood, whose divisions contributed two brigades to the area's defense. In the absence of specific directions, however, one of Wood's brigade commanders—the rather feisty Regular, Hascall—readily assumed the job knowing the high stakes involved. "I found that along the entire line to the right and left of the railroad, which had not yet been carried by the enemy I was the only general officer present, and was, therefore, in command, and responsible for the conduct of affairs," Hascall would write. "To have lost this position would have been to lose everything, as our left would then have been turned, and utter rout or capture inevitable."[3]

The Round Forest was in effect the hinge upon which the entire Federal position swung. As the day progressed, it turned into a salient with Confederates on three sides. Breckinridge's batteries on Wayne's Hill shelled the forest from the left front; Donelson's intrepid survivors, huddled at the far end of the cotton field, kept up a desultory fire in front; and portions of Cheatham's and Withers' divisions fired at the position from the edge of the cedars to the right. If the Federal defenders of the Round Forest failed to hold the ground, the entire line along the Nashville Pike would be flanked, and the army risked certain collapse. At some point during the fighting that afternoon, Palmer rode up to Hazen and said, "Hazen, you'll have to fall back," to which Hazen replied, "I'd like to know where in hell I'll fall back to."[4]

* * *

The command mix-up involving Breckinridge, Bragg, and the phantom Federals beyond the Confederate right resolved about 1:00 p.m., finally freeing up John Jackson's independent brigade and that of Daniel Adams to cross Stones River. Jackson crossed at the double quick with his 874 men and reported to

3 OR 20/1:470.

4 Hazen, *A Narrative of Military Service*, 80.

Leonidas Polk, who wrote that he directed Jackson to take his brigade and "dislodge the enemy from his position in the Round Forest. Unfortunately, the opportune moment for putting in these detachments had passed. The time lost between Donelson's attack and the coming up of these detachments in succession enabled the enemy to recover his self-possession, to mass a number of heavy batteries, and concentrate a strong infantry force on the position, and thus make a successful attack very difficult." Though justified to point this out, Polk compounded the timing error by ordering these reinforcements to charge piecemeal, which made the resulting attacks against the Round Forest essentially light thrusts of a rapier instead of the crushing blow of a broadsword.[5]

Jackson and his men were discouraged to see the countless bodies of dead and wounded Confederates fronting their objective. Jackson aligned his force from right to left: the 8th Mississippi, 5th Mississippi, 2nd Battalion of Georgia Sharpshooters, and 5th Georgia. A two-gun section of Lumsden's (Alabama) Battery, deployed on a rise, had directions to open fire on the Round Forest as Jackson's men stepped off. Rather than following in Chalmers' and Donelson's bloody footsteps, Jackson diverted his march to the left of the Cowan House, which would effectively shield his men from most Federal artillery fire during the approach. Shifting to the right after entering the cedar brake beyond the Cowan House, they soon came upon A. P. Stewart's men busily firing away at the Federals across the Nashville Pike.

As Jackson approached, Hazen advanced the 6th Kentucky to the right of the 9th Indiana. While firing their last rounds of ammunition, the men of the 3rd Kentucky in Hascall's brigade discovered many of their guns were now so fouled they were impossible to load, so Hascall had the regiment fall back behind the railroad and replaced by the 58th Indiana. "I then threw forward the right of the 6th Ohio which was on the right of the 26th Ohio," Hascall reported, "so that its line of battle was more nearly perpendicular to the railroad, and so that its fire would sweep the front of the 26th Ohio and 58th Indiana." He then ordered the 8th Indiana Battery to redeploy to the right to support the 6th Ohio and brought forward the 97th Ohio to further strengthen the right.

Spotting Rosecrans nearby, Hascall rode over to request additional support. "He rode to the front with me," Hascall noted, "approved the disposition I had made, spoke a few words of encouragement to the men, cautioning them to hold their fire till the enemy got well up, and had no sooner retired than the enemy

5 OR 20/1:690.

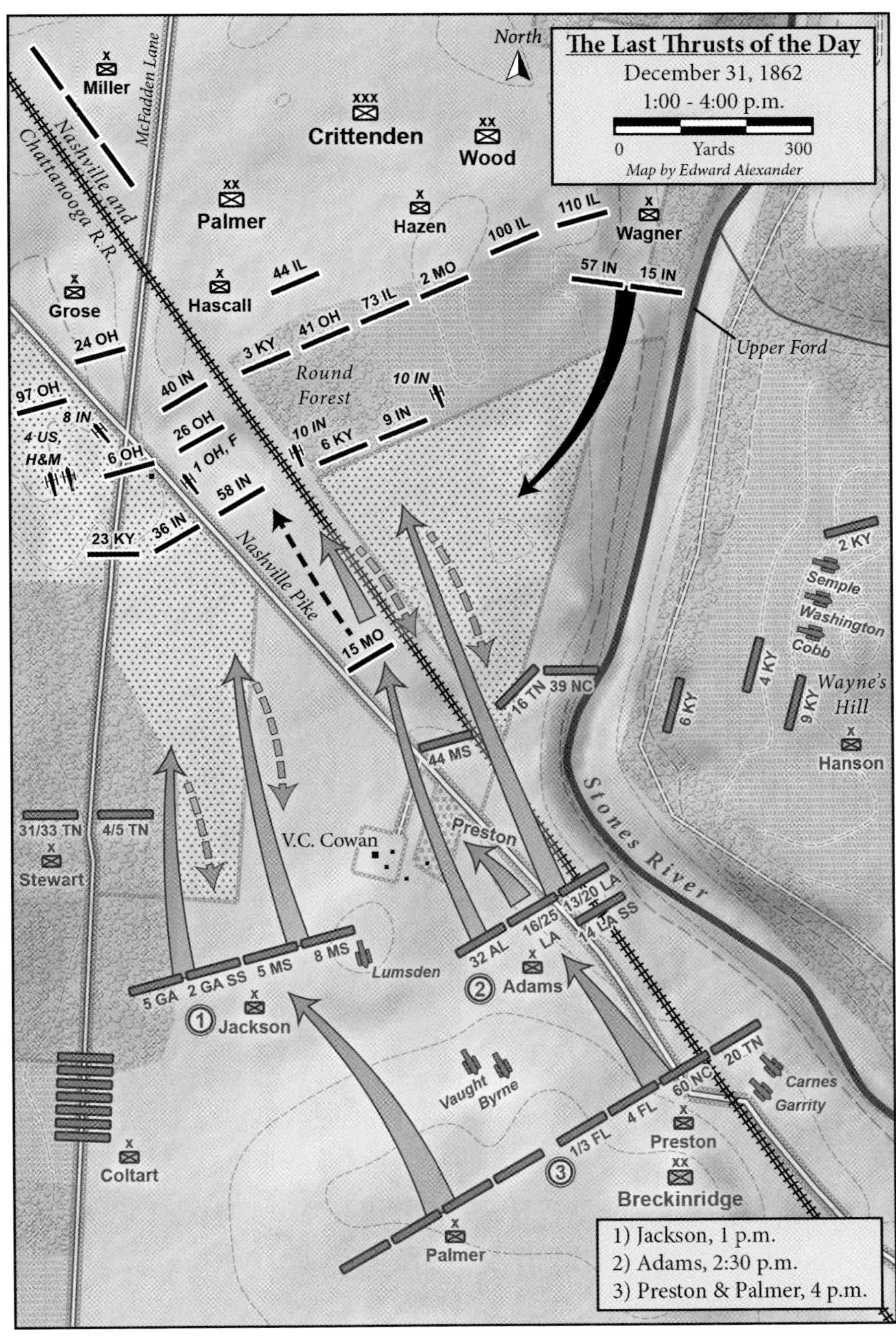
North
The Last Thrusts of the Day
December 31, 1862
1:00 - 4:00 p.m.
0   Yards   300
Map by Edward Alexander
Miller
Nashville and Chattanooga R.R.
McFadden Lane
Crittenden
Wood
Palmer
Hazen
100 IL
110 IL
Wagner
Grose
Hascall
44 IL
2 MO
57 IN
15 IN
24 OH
73 IL
Upper Ford
3 KY
41 OH
Round
Forest
40 IN
97 OH
8 IN
10 IN
4 US,
H&M
26 OH
10 IN
9 IN
6 OH
1 OH, F
6 KY
58 IN
2 KY
23 KY
36 IN
Nashville Pike
Semple
Washington
Cobb
15 MO
4 KY
16 TN
39 NC
6 KY
9 KY
Wayne's
Hill
44 MS
Stones River
Hanson
31/33 TN
4/5 TN
V.C. Cowan
Preston
Stewart
13/20 LA
16/25 LA
14 LA SS
5 GA
2 GA SS
5 MS
8 MS
32 AL
x LA
Lumsden
2 Adams
1 Jackson
Vaught
Byrne
20 TN
60 NC
Carnes
Garrity
4 FL
Preston
Coltart
1/3 FL
3 Preston
Breckinridge
Palmer
1) Jackson, 1 p.m.
2) Adams, 2:30 p.m.
3) Preston & Palmer, 4 p.m.

emerged from the woods and over the hill, and were moving upon us in splendid style and in immense force."[6]

About 2:00 p.m., Jackson aligned his regiments again and ordered a charge out of the cedars. His men advanced with "great coolness and courage" but without much success, as each one of his three regimental commanders went down with wounds, two of those mortal. The Georgia sharpshooters advanced a bit farther than the rest of the line, targeting any Federals artillerists they could make out in the smoke and confusion. Stopped on their initial advance, Jackson's men recoiled and reformed at the edge of the cedars but had no better results on the second attempt.

The 58th Indiana quickly found itself under heavy fire. "The Rebels had now advanced to the edge of a thick woods in our front not more than a hundred yards distant across an open field," wrote John Hight, the regiment's chaplain. "They were sheltered behind trees from which they poured a galling fire of musketry. The men were lying flat on the ground and were loading and firing at will. Twice the enemy left the woods in our front and started on a charge across the open field, but they could not stand against the shower of lead that was poured into their ranks."[7]

Hazen noted that Jackson's unsupported assault was a bloodbath, with 307 Confederate casualties. He also noted that it "was resisted much more easily than the previous ones there now being a large force of our artillery bearing upon this point," and Corporal George Leavitt of the 9th Indiana acknowledged that "it was too horrid for human eye to look upon, men shot in every conceivable form imaginable. I took particular notice of the work of our artillery as their aim must have been very deliberate." One of Jackson's men seemingly got through the fight without a scratch, but discovered a hole in his shoe, one in his haversack, and a third through the back of his coat. Bullets tore off his vest pocket, cut his coat, and his pocket Bible stopped yet another. What Jackson's attack lacked in numbers, however, was more than made up for in courage. Yet despite the gallant effort, Rosecrans's line remained set.[8]

Jackson's line had hardly retired into the cedars when Adams reported to Polk with his brigade. His 1,634-man brigade of Louisianans and Alabamians was considered one of the army's crack units—and certainly among its most colorful, as

---

6 Ibid., 468-469.

7 Ibid., 838-839; John J. Hight, *History of the 58th Regiment of Indiana Volunteer Infantry* (Princeton, 1895), 117.

8 OR 20/1:545, 839; Smith, *Stones River: Confederate Army*, 336; Corporal George P. Leavitt, Co. E, 9th Indiana, *Steuben Republican*, Jan. 31, 1863, 2.

Adams's Louisiana regiments featured several companies of Germans and New Orleans dock workers of every race, color, and creed. When Adams asked Polk for orders, the "Fighting Bishop" pointed to a Federal battery a mile ahead between the pike and river and declared, "Look at yonder battery. Take it, and the day is won!"

Adams decided a head-on approach was best and deployed his cosmopolitan 13th/20th Louisiana on the right, the consolidated 16th/25th Louisiana at center, and the 32nd Alabama on the left. Austin's sharpshooter battalion fell in behind the 13th/20th Louisiana as support while the 5th Company of the Washington Light Artillery remained behind near the river crossing. Colonel Henry Maury turned to his 32nd Alabama and told the men, "Alabamians, we must not let the Louisiana boys get ahead of us today."[9]

Making a rare battlefield appearance, Bragg rode up as Adams's men were about to begin their assault. Bragg knew these fellow Louisianans from the beginning of the war, and the embattled chief remained a popular figure with them. "Loud cheers greeted him as he passed rapidly along the line and hastily checked his horse in front of the colors," recalled Captain John Ellis of the 16th/25th Louisiana. The excited general turned toward the cheering men, pulled off his cap, and waved it "as if for silence," continued Ellis. "I shall never forget Bragg as I saw him then with his pale emaciated face slightly flushed with the ardor of battle, his fierce eyes supernaturally large and full of light, his thin lip compressed and his form compact yet attenuated." He continued:

The words came short and clear. "Louisianans, the enemy's right has been routed and we are steadily driving it back. He still stands firm in the center. He must be defeated there. It remains for you to do this and the victory is ours.". . . The most deafening cheers greeted the general as he rode rapidly away, then we began to advance. Every heart was full of enthusiasm and each man seemed to feel that no task was beyond our accomplishment.[10]

Adams's men stepped off about 2:30 p.m., marching toward the Cowan House in column of companies, their arms at right shoulder shift for 200 yards, as Federal shells occasionally dropped into the ranks. One soldier, Calvin Hennegan of the 16th/25th Louisiana, stepped out of ranks to kill a frightened rabbit. "Hennegan,

9 Stevenson, *Battle of Stone's River*, 111; Adjutant John L. Chandler, 32nd Alabama, "A Charge at Stones River," *Philadelphia Weekly Times*, Jul. 2, 1887, 1.

10 Ellis Memoir.

why in the devil did you do that," barked Ellis, to which the private replied, "Captain, the Yanks is too far and I want to be a-killin' what I shoot at."

The brigade deployed into line of battle in the open fields south of the Cowan House, but as it approached the house grounds and fences, Adams reported that the layout presented "such serious obstacles as preventing my continuing to advance in line of battle." He reformed his two Louisiana regiments into a column of companies and marched them neatly through an open gateway before they resumed a line of battle, all while facing long-range Federal fire. The 32nd Alabama now stood left of the pike, the 16th/25th Louisiana between the pike and the railroad, and the 13th/20th Louisiana held the land between the railroad and Stones River. The Round Forest stood just 200 yards ahead; unfortunately, Hardee's famed antebellum book of tactics did not have a neat maneuver to get around that obstacle: it would have to be taken at the point of the bayonet in the teeth of a blizzard of iron and lead.[11]

One Federal unit that Adams's men would shove out of the way during their advance was the 15th Missouri of Colonel Schaefer's brigade in Sheridan's division. After resupplying their ammunition, the Missourians followed in the wake of Jackson's repulse and set up a skirmish line across the pike and railroad near the Cowan House. "In order to shelter ourselves," Weber reported, "we occupied the railroad track on both sides of which the ground was rising some four or five feet, from which place, by an incessant fire, the ever-advancing regiments of the enemy were mowed down. About an hour we maintained this position, until I perceived that the enemy, at a distance of half a mile, planted a piece of artillery on the same track, whilst the infantry moved toward us in great numbers to fall in our back. Without delay, I gave the order to take up the former battle line. A deadly fire was sent after them until our ammunition was again exhausted."

Sheridan, however, would soon lose his third brigade commander of the day. As Weber's men fell back toward the Round Forest, Schaefer "rode forward to give the regiment some orders [and] was hit by an enemy's bullet and fell to the ground dead." Lieutenant Colonel Bernard Laiboldt of the 2nd Missouri assumed brigade command.[12]

Adams's line took canister both in front from Battery F of the 1st Ohio Light and from the six guns of the 8th Indiana Battery on its left front. "As the men approached the brow of the hills," Adams reported, "they came fully in view and

11 *OR* 20/1:793; Ellis Memoir.

12 Weber Report; Stevenson, *Battle of Stone's River*, 109-10.

range of the enemy's guns and were checked by a terrible fire from his artillery, posted on the second elevation, about 150 or 200 yards distant." Colonel Maury's Alabamians opened fire, but he called for a quick halt once he realized it was a waste of ammunition; instead, he ordered his men forward.

"At this moment we were exposed not only to the sweeping fire in front," Maury recalled, "but to a withering fire of musketry and grape from the cedar brake on our left, not more than 200 yards distant, and also a severe fire from the right, under which my men fell rapidly." Confederate artillery fire detonated one of Battery F's limbers and shivered the axles of two guns, forcing Captain Cockerill to withdraw the battery.[13]

Adams's daring assault elicited widespread admiration from the Federals. Chaplain Hight wrote that "we could see their men falling like leaves, but the broken ranks were filled and they held their ground with a heroism worthy of a better cause." Another Federal commented that "Adams' men fell by the hundred, yet still they moved on with irresistible force. It was a magnificent brigade."

Moving "through a shower of grape, shell, and canister our brave little band worked steadily across an open field while men were falling at every step," recalled the 32nd Alabama's Lieutenant J. Morgan Smith. "Both sides turned loose with their rifles and such as fire can scarcely be imagined much less described." The regiment's color-bearer went down as the Alabamians approached the Federal line. Maury was also wounded after securing the colors, which were then taken up by Lieutenant Jules Keith, who promptly handed them off to adjutant John Chandler and was mortally wounded soon thereafter. "A ball struck Keith in the breast and Lieutenant Tatum and myself ran to his assistance," recalled Captain Benjamin Smoot. The men were trying to get him off the field when another bullet struck his head. "He turned towards me and remarked with his dying breath, 'Tell my wife how I died.'"[14]

The din of battle proved awe-inspiring. "If you can imagine yourself in something like a very heavy thunderstorm with hail and heavy wind, keen flashes of lightning and hard claps of thunder," remembered Corporal Gilbert Stormont of the 58th Indiana, "you can form some faint idea of the noise at that time on the battlefield." Adams's men made some headway, and the 16th/25th Louisiana

13 *OR* 20/1:800.

14 Hight, *History of the 58th Indiana*, 117; Stevenson, *Battle of Stone's River*, 111-12; 1st Lt. J. Morgan Smith, Co. F, 32nd Alabama, SRNBP; Captain Benjamin H. Smoot, Co. C, 32nd Alabama, *Mobile Weekly Advertiser*, Jan. 17, 1863, 2.

reported it nabbed two of Battery F's guns left behind after the caisson explosion. "The regiment with wild cheers swept forward and the battery was reached and two guns were captured," Ellis recalled. "Then we were halted and at 70 yards distance the deadliest fire of musketry I ever saw was opened upon us from an unseen foe. Every instant someone was struck down but the survivors fought on."[15]

Although an unsuspecting Adams implored his men to resume the charge, the brigade was charging directly into a Federal beartrap. Stones River curved away from the brigade's right as Adams advanced, which opened a widening gap between the river and the 13th/20th Louisiana's right flank. Wagner, commanding a brigade on Hazen's left, sensed an opportunity and rushed his Hoosiers forward to seize it. Wrote Adams: "They continued to advance until the enemy opened with a battery from a cedar thicket on my left, and what appeared to be a brigade of infantry, and at the same time they commenced moving down the river in force, apparently to get in rear of my command."[16]

Wagner had thus far spent the battle guarding Harker's crossing and dodging the rain of shells thrown at them from the Confederate gunners atop Wayne's Hill. "Our losses were heavy and the worst of it was we could not strike back as we were not within musketry range of the Rebels," said adjutant Edwin Nicar of the 15th Indiana. Adams's assault left the Confederate right flank dangling temptingly on Wagner's front. He quickly formed the 440-man 15th Indiana into line and, supported by the 57th Indiana, moved into the cotton field. "The cotton had been imperfectly picked and the bolls with their loads of fleecy whiteness gave us fair concealment from the advancing Rebels," Nicar noted.[17]

Colonel Randall Gibson of the 13th/20th Louisiana recognized the trap and hastily called a halt. "Ascending the elevated position, I discovered the enemy moving troops rapidly up the river, on our right, and placing them also in ambush in the cornfield on our front," he wrote. "The line of battle on the rail track, as the line of battle along the riverbank, was at right angles to our advancing line, and the enemy reserved his fire until the command was flanked. So soon as I discovered the

---

15 Corporal Gilbert Stormont, Co. B, 58th Indiana, *Princeton Clarion Leader*, Jan. 31, 1863, 2; Ellis Memoir. Confederate and Federal account differ as to the number of guns involved, with the Confederates claiming two and the Federals just one. The 9th Indiana recovered the cannon after repulsing Adams's assault.

16 OR 20/1:793.

17 Nicar Article.

Colonel Randall L. Gibson,
13th/20th Louisiana Infantry

Library of Congress

disposition of the enemy, I rode across the railroad and informed General Adams. It was, however, too late to accomplish a timely change in our position."[18]

While Gibson galloped off to persuade Adams to suspend the attack, the brigade continued pushing forward. Nicar recalled the "splendid appearance presented by them as they marched to the attack, the stars and bars flung to the breeze, mounted officers and company officers all in place, their lines presenting a solid front and all determined to emulate the success achieved by their comrades on the right. Before reaching our position, the Rebels had to cross the railroad and the deep cut somewhat deranged their formation. Just as they emerged from the cut, we sprang to our feet and the command came 'Ready! Aim! Fire!' Our Springfields responded in a hail of death and after a minute or two of firing at will, the order came 'Fix bayonets! Forward! Double quick! March!' We went at them with a right good will."

"[T]hey came up within a few rods of us and we gave them heavy volleys of musketry and our battery just mowed them with grape and canister," noted James Jones of the 57th Indiana. "They turned their course and went back as fast as they came."[19]

18 *OR* 20/1:795.

19 Nicar Article; Private James H. Jones, Co. E, 57th Indiana, Indiana Historical Society. The 57th Indiana picked up the abandoned colors of the 5th Georgia of Jackson's Brigade during this counterattack.

Wagner's charge struck the Louisianans hard. Captain John McGrath of the 13th/20th acknowledged that the Federals "instantly raised up and poured a deadly volley into our surprised ranks. We were knocked into confusion and fell back to a fence." Gibson redeployed his regiment to face this threat to his flank, but the convergence of Federal fire from several points created considerable mayhem. "The first fire we received was from the riverbank, and directed upon the infirmary corps of the regiment, posted considerably in our rear," he reported. "The right of the regiment stood firm for a few minutes, but under the combined fires gave way. The men naturally faced the direction in which the severest fire came, and this caused some confusion."[20]

As the 15th Indiana waded into the Louisianans, Nicar remembered that he "became so excited that I didn't know what I was doing, but I was later told that I ran up and down the lines with my sword drawn shouting at the top of my voice, 'Give them Hail Columbia!'" The charge "which was executed in a most brilliant style" broke Adams's line and netted nearly 200 prisoners, so many that Colonel Gustavus Wood could not keep them all under guard. "A portion of the prisoners escaped while on the way to the rear. We delivered over to the provost-marshal 170," Wood reported.[21]

Gibson's withdrawal exposed the flank of the 16th/25th Louisiana. "As we neared the enemy's position we were met by a storm of missiles from small arms," reported Major Francis Zacharie. "When we finally halted, I noticed that some of our men were being wounded in the rear and being struck on the back myself and turning to the direction of the fire, I discovered that the regiment of the enemy was in our rear while we were being engaged in the front and on the left by a large body of the enemy." Colonel Stuart Fisk would be mortally wounded, and within moments of assuming command, Zacharie received Adams's order to withdraw. "I attempted to withdraw my right, which was most exposed, by a flank movement," he wrote. The line fell apart; the three companies on the left mistakenly marched left, not right, throwing the entire line into disorder, leading him to admit later: "I attempted to rally the regiment several times, but, being unhorsed during the engagement, found it difficult to do so until we had retreated nearly a quarter of a mile."[22]

20 *OR* 20/1:795, 803.

21 Nicar Article. Most of the prisoners taken were from the 13th/20th Louisiana.

22 *OR* 20/1:801.

Major John Austin's 126-man battalion of sharpshooters rushed forward to try to cover the retreat. "I found the enemy directly in my front and opened fire upon him with a staggering effect," he noted proudly. "His attention had been drawn just previous to this to the brigade, which was falling back, and the rapidity of my movement caused a confusion in his ranks." Austin's effort cost him 15 casualties but took the steam out of Wagner's charge. George Banks, color-sergeant of the 15th Indiana, reported that the regiment's colors were "pierced by 52 small balls and one cannon ball, the shaft was badly shattered, while I had two bullet holes in my hat, one in my blouse, my canteen shot off, and my haversack shot through. I escaped without a scratch." That was more than could be said for the regiment, which suffered 188 casualties during the fighting that day.[23]

Adams's assault came within 50 yards of the Round Forest, yet the brigade could go no farther and was almost destroyed. "Had not the timely order of retreat been given, none of us would now be left to tell the tale," confessed Lieutenant Smith. Adams received a nasty wound that broke his arm and forced him to turn brigade command over to Gibson. Adams privately wrote his wife a few weeks later that he was at a loss to understand why his brigade was slaughtered. "Two brigades had previously attempted jointly to take this same battery but had been repulsed with great loss," he wrote. "How or why General Polk … expected me to take it I cannot imagine for it consisted of 20–30 pieces of artillery posted in a cedar thicket and supported by 6,000–8,000 troops with the whole Federal army nearby to reinforce if necessary. I cannot help regarding the order as a very imprudent and unwise one."

The gallant effort cost Adams a third of his men, and other than giving the Federal line a brief scare, it had accomplished nothing but deepen the morass of bodies in front of the Round Forest.[24]

Captain Jerome Cox of the 10th Indiana Battery waxed ecstatically at Adams's decisive repulse. "I mowed 'em, I more than mowed them," he shouted to Wagner. "I guess them fellows don't want my battery as bad they did." Wagner responded, "Oh, you're excited?" Cox replied, "No sir, I'm mad, mad, mad." When Wagner asked him why he was mad, Cox smirked: "Why, to see all those cowards running without firing a gun, whole thousands of them running like damned cowards. If I had ammunition, I could keep all the Rebels back that could come before me."

---

23 Ibid., 795, 803; Color Sergeant George L. Banks, Co. C, 15th Indiana, S.1536 Civil War Flags, Rare Books and Manuscripts, Indiana State Library.

24 Morgan Smith Letter; Smith, *Stones River: Confederate Army*, 351; OR 20/1:793.

The Hoosiers had fired 1,600 rounds of ammunition—exhausting their stocks completely, which enraged Cox "at the thought of being compelled to remain silent at the next Rebel onset. The captain repeatedly declared that the enemy should never have his battery as long as he was able to fire a gun and if surrendered at all, it must be after he was dead." The 58th Indiana was surprised to see some of Adams's men give up. "When the firing was hottest, they fell upon the ground and when the Rebel force fell back these men skipped across to our lines and surrendered," recalled one Hoosier. "One of these deserters came to our regiment carrying an old blanket that had once been white as a flag of truce."[25]

Adams's defeat left members of his proud brigade crestfallen at the horrible losses. "It was with terrible anguish that I saw men falling and writhing on the ground and yet I was powerless to aid them," Ellis confessed. "General Adams said to the boys near him, 'Boys, we fell back but damn it we are not whipped!'" The retreat itself revealed its own horrors. "A constant stream of shells flew over and around us," Ellis noted. "One burst a few feet from me and it killed six men, the skull of one of those miserable men was blown off with the quivering brain still attached. It flew several paces and fell upon the body of one of his comrades who was lying down."

Gibson's Louisianans discovered the blood-stained colors of the 16th Tennessee on the ravaged grounds in front of the Round Forest and carried them back during the retreat. One Federal later stated that "the assault of Adams' brigade was, without doubt, the most daring, courageous, and best-executed attack which the Confederates made on our line between the pike and river." It was also not Bragg's last attempt to take the Round Forest.[26]

* * *

From 2:30–3:00 p.m., Breckinridge crossed Stones River at the head of two more of his brigades. "We had to wade the river which was two to three feet deep," recalled Lieutenant Spencer Talley of the 28th Tennessee. "We made no halt but plunged right through it and soon after crossing our pants were frozen and rattled like rawhide." Breckinridge's meeting with Bragg and Polk probably was equally as

25 *Annals of the 57th Regiment Indiana Volunteers*, 159; Hight, *History of the 58th Indiana*, 118.

26 Stevenson, *Battle of Stone's River*, 111; Ellis Memoir. Adams's Brigade had 82 killed, 344 wounded, and 118 captured (544 total) during its assault on the Round Forest, roughly one-third of the brigade.

Federal line holds the Nashville Pike on the afternoon of December 31, 1862.

chilly, given what had transpired between Bragg and Breckinridge regarding the Asa Lewis execution on December 26. The former vice president found Bragg and Polk watching Jackson's and Adams's bloody repulses from a hillock overlooking the river crossing. "I arrived in time to see at a distance the brigades of Jackson and Adams recoiling from a very hot fire of the enemy," Breckinridge recalled. "I was directed by General Polk to form my line, with its right resting on the river and its left extending across the open field, crossing the Nashville turnpike almost at a right angle."[27]

Breckinridge marched his men into an open field behind Chalmers' old breastworks and deployed his two brigades. General William Preston's 1,640-man brigade took the right; the 20th Tennessee on the far right, their sleeves brushing the banks of Stones River. The newly formed 60th North Carolina took right center, the 4th Florida left center, and the 1st/3rd Florida the left. Colonel Joseph Palmer's 1,446-man brigade, consisting of the 18th, 26th, 28th, 32nd, and 45th Tennessee regiments, formed on Preston's left.

27 Talley Memoir, *OR* 20/1:783. Neither Palmer nor any of his subordinates left a record of what order the brigade was formed in for this attack.

With roughly 3,000 men, Breckinridge's attack would be the largest yet launched against the Round Forest. The Kentuckian ordered his two brigades to approach the Round Forest line abreast with Palmer's Brigade wheeling to the right to hit the Federal flank once Preston was warmly engaged.

Preston, a Mexican War veteran and former US minister to Spain, had served on his brother-in-law Albert Sidney Johnston's staff until Shiloh, then bounced between a series of brigade commands before he was placed in charge of this new brigade in early December. The brigade was fighting as a unit for the first time at Murfreesboro. He had before him a daunting task: four Confederate brigades had made this same approach in attacking the Round Forest. "This field had been the theater of a bloody conflict during the early part of the day," noted Captain Tod Carter of the 20th Tennessee, "and fragments of shells, torn and trampled ground, broken vehicles, and other debris of battle indicate a hard-fought field. The enemy in heavy force hovered darkly around the skirts of a scrubby growth of timber just across this field. Their sharpshooters, thick as locusts, were concealed in the grass, behind trees and fences, and in the clefts of the rocks along the bank of the river."[28]

The parade of mauled men they met heading back to the hospitals was anything but encouraging. "One man walking with his arm shot off enquired what regiment as our beautiful flag passed him," remembered Washington Ives of the 4th Florida. "A little soldier was in one of the ambulances and appeared to be hit in four or five places, his back broken, but he bore it like a man except as the wagon would jolt, he'd groan. As we formed in line of battle, there was a dead Confederate lying on his back with a cannon ball hole through his breast which I could stick my head in." One wounded man from Adams's brigade hailed the 60th North Carolina but nevertheless exclaimed that "it was useless to go any further for all hell couldn't dislodge the bluecoats from their strongly fortified position."[29]

It was approaching 4:00 p.m. Hascall could see Breckinridge's attack forming in the dim distance and rotated his front-line regiments. The 58th Indiana and 26th Ohio moved behind the railroad, their places taken by the 40th Indiana of Wagner's brigade and the 23rd Kentucky of Grose's. The 8th Indiana Battery also fell back. Captain James of the 26th Ohio observed Rosecrans as his regiment filled their cartridge boxes. "He has changed very much since I saw him in Columbus in June 1861," he observed,

28 Captain Theodorick Carter, Co. H, 20th Tennessee, *Chattanooga Daily Rebel*, Jan. 15, 1863, 1.

29 Jim R. Cabaniss, *Civil War Journal and Letters of Washington Ives, 4th Florida, C.S.A.*, 34; Clark, *Histories of the Several Regiments*, 477.

Colonel William B. Hazen,
defender of the Round Forest.

Library of Congress

He now appears to have gained greatly in size and weight, appearance which was probably increased by being on horseback and wearing a large cavalry overcoat. He bore a much sterner expression of countenance. He inquired which regiment this was and found fault with its being left in such as exposed position while replenishing ammunition, directing it to be faced about so as to take advantage of a little undulation in the ground as a shelter. "The most exposed place in the field," said he. "Right where my adjutant general was killed."[30]

A few minutes later, the 26th Ohio moved east of the railroad into line with the 57th Indiana, 100th Illinois, and Estep's battery, all tasked with holding the Federal left from any Confederate attempt to attack the Round Forest from Harker's crossing. The enemy atop Wayne's Hill gave Estep's gunners plenty of work. "The Rebel battery engaged with ours was on the top of a bare hill about a half mile off and was most effectively served. We could see them plainly against the sky with a heavy column of infantry near them as supports," James said. "We laid there till 5 with nothing to do, nothing we could do, but lie there and take it."[31]

* * *

Breckinridge's men had no sooner stepped off than Federal artillery opened on them, prompting the general to send for additional artillery support. His adjutant, Colonel Theodore O'Hara, brought forward both the 5th Company of the

30 James Letter.

31 Ibid.

Washington Light Artillery under Lieutenant William Vaught and Captain Edward Byrne's Kentucky horse artillery. Both unlimbered in the open fields south of the Cowan House and opened long-range fire in support of the attack. Major Henry Leaming's 40th Indiana could see the Confederates heading toward them. "The order was given that no one should fire and our boys laid flat and motionless," he recalled. "As the line advanced, the fire from three of their batteries was directed on us. The limbs from the trees overhead were cut off by their shells, wounding and bruising quite a number of our boys." As Hazen later observed: "[T]he battle had hushed and the dreadful splendor of this advance can only be conceived. He advanced steadily and, as it seemed, certainly to victory."[32]

"The brigade moved forward in solid column," wrote Tod Carter. "Staff officers galloped backwards and forwards, up and down the line giving orders, field officers giving commands as the colors fluttered wildly in the wind. They reached the crest of a long swell and saw the woods and fields bristling with bluecoats and Yankee bayonets. Down went blankets and knapsacks and giving the old-fashioned Tennessee yell, they closed in." When the soldiers in Carter's 20th Tennessee reached the picket fence near the Cowan House, they simply tore a hole through it and surged forward. William J. McMurray, one of those soldiers, professed that "we moved as if driven by a whirlwind and passed across the turnpike leaving the railroad cut to our left."[33]

The confusion at the Cowan House split the brigade's alignment, and as the 20th Tennessee swept past the house, it found itself approaching the Round Forest alone. "After an advance of half a mile we encountered the enemy, strongly posted among the rocks and heavy growth of timber on the river bluff," recalled Major Fred Claybrooke. "Here the firing was very heavy, and we lost many men." The air, Carter noted, "screamed with hissing shot and bursting shells! The field was thickly strewn with killed and wounded, Southern and Yankee, laying side by side in ghastly confusion."

The 20th Tennessee marched directly at the 40th Indiana. "We observed a brigade of the enemy moving toward us in order, with the evident intention of attacking us," Leaming recalled. "On nearing the ruins of the burned brick building in our front, one regiment was detached from the brigade and bore down upon us. I allowed them to gain a point within easy range of musketry fire, and directed the

32 OR 20/1:545; Merrill, *The Soldier of Indiana*, 159-160.

33 "Concerning the 20th Tennessee," William J. McMurray, *Confederate Veteran*, 6:123; Carter Letter.

regiment to open upon them, which they did with great briskness, and with such effect as to repulse the enemy handsomely."[34]

"[T]he firing by this time had turned into a regular roar of both artillery and small arms," wrote Captain James Cooper of the 20th Tennessee, "and as we rose on a little hill, it was so heavy that the line was ordered to lie down. We lay there close to the ground in an old cotton patch for a few moments[,] then with the regular old Tennessee yell, we rose to our feet and started for the Yanks. A large proportion of our men had been wounded by this time, for they were falling at every step. We had done all men could do and had to fall back."

The 20th Tennessee's casualty count would be 67, and among the first to fall was Colonel Thomas Smith, struck in the arm and breast. "We were in danger of being surrounded; were in very small force and had no support," Claybrooke wrote. "Under these circumstances I ordered the men to fall back 200 yards, and at this place we remained until night, when we were ordered to rejoin our brigade, which had taken position under cover of a thick cedar woods on our left." The Tennesseans managed to capture 25 Federals but fell back rather worse for wear.[35]

The 1st/3rd Florida on the far left of the line moved past the Cowan House into the cedars without much strain, but a nest of trouble met the 60th North Carolina and 4th Florida. According to Preston, his men had "great difficulty in pressing through the ruins and strong enclosures of the farmhouse, and, retarded by these obstacles and by a fire from the enemy's sharpshooters in front, and a very fierce cannonade, partially enfilading their lines."

The green 60th North Carolina split apart at the picket fence, four of the companies angling toward the Nashville Pike intending to join the 20th Tennessee. Weldon Scales likened the approach march to being in front of a firing squad. "My company encountered the fence around the garden," he wrote. "The fence was made of posts, pickets, and cross pieces of solid cedar. We had to beat and tear down this fence using our muskets for clubs and thus we were delayed awhile." Colonel Joseph McDowell reported that "during our march through the cotton-field we were subjected to a most terrific fire of grape and shell and musketry, losing at this point about 28 in killed and wounded." Washington Ives of

---

34 *OR* 20/1:498, 822; Carter Letter.

35 "Service with the 20th Tennessee Regiment," James L. Cooper, *Confederate Veteran*, 33:58; *OR* 20/1:822.

the 4th Florida, meanwhile, complained that the North Carolinians "ran like sheep leaving us under the hottest kind of fire from sharpshooters."[36]

Colonel Wylde Bowen reported that his 4th Florida started milling about in confusion and quickly lost 55 men. "The only man killed in my company had his throat cut at my right side and as he fell on my feet, the blood spurted a stream a large as two forefingers," a horrified Ives recalled. "He could not speak but grabbed at the wound and tried to rise up." To stand still was to be slaughtered; safety lay in moving forward. Preston rode forward at this critical moment, seized the colors of the 4th Florida and, relayed one observer, "sinking the spurs deep into the sides of his horse, cried out in tones sounding above the crash of battle, 'Follow me, my brave men.' The act and the words were electrical, and with a shout the men sprang forward as if freshly reinforced."[37]

Bowen reported that his Floridians "rushed forward to grapple in a hand-to-hand fight with the enemy's sharpshooters, but they fled precipitately to an adjacent wood, leaving several wounded and the killed to fall into our hands." Noted Preston: "[T]he enemy turned upon the wood a heavy fire from many pieces of artillery, across a field 400 or 500 yards distant, and, though we lost some valuable lives, the brigade maintained its position with firmness in the edge of the wood."[38]

The 1st/3rd Florida would suffer the least, swiftly marching into the cedars to fall in on A. P. Stewart's right. "We didn't fire a gun but every other regiment in our brigade got into it pretty deep and suffered severely," said William Rodgers of the 1st Florida. "We had eight men wounded by shells and grape but none killed." The 4th Florida and 60th North Carolina soon plunked down beside the 1st Florida, sheltering themselves behind the rocks and steeling themselves for the hard task they faced. It was as far as Preston's men would go, however. Breckinridge and Hardee met in the woods and, after an examination of the grounds followed by a short conference, Breckinridge wrote "it was deemed reckless to attack with the force present."

Preston expressed relief that the attack was suspended before the bloodbath worsened, confessing in a letter a few weeks later, "I lost a tenth of my command in the engagement and if I had hammered away like Adams would probably have lost

36 OR 20/1:812, 819; "A Partial Record of the Ancestry, Life and War Experiences of Weldon C. Scales," Southern Historical Collection, University of North Carolina at Chapel Hill.

37 OR 20/1:816; Clark, *Histories of the Several Regiments*, 478.

38 OR 20/1:812.

half." His brigade had 155 casualties during its brief offensive, the 20th Tennessee and 4th Florida suffering worst of all.[39]

As Preston's men suffered, Palmer advanced with his brigade toward the cedars west of the Cowan House. Corporal William McKay of the 18th Tennessee noted that the brigade proceeded steadily under "a heavy fire of artillery with grape, canister, and bombshells wounding a number of our regiment," And a 26th Tennessee soldier wrote that "we advanced for nearly a mile through an open field; no murmuring was heard, no faltering seen, officers in position and men in ranks in the face of a dreadful fire. Our loss was slight."

After reaching the edge of the cedars, however, Palmer observed Union skirmishers retiring across the Nashville Pike and taking cover behind the railroad embankment. Deciding it would be a mistake to charge alone against the Round Forest, Palmer ordered his men to hug the ground and opened a desultory long-range fire on the Federals.[40]

Breckinridge's order to suspend the attack soon reached him. "[W]hen we reached Withers' division, the firing had nearly ceased," Spencer Talley recalled. The sun had been down for some bit and darkness was fast coming on us, so much so that it made the sheets of fire from the enemy's cannon look hideous and dazzling." The cannon's blazing light revealed a hideous sight lurking in the forest shadows as Breckinridge's men found hundreds of dead and wounded men covering the ground.[41]

Bragg's last and strongest effort against the Round Forest, it turned out, ended as one grand fizzle.

*   *   *

Two miles north on the Nashville Pike, Joseph Wheeler's cavalry made one last effort as nighttime neared to break the Federal grasp on the vital roadway. After riding from Nolensville, Wheeler arrived on the field with his brigade about midday and immediately received an order from Bragg to push around the Federal right

---

39 William D. Rodgers, 1st Florida, SRNBP; *OR* 20/1:783-784, 812; General William Preston, Mrs. Mason Barret Collection of William Preston Johnson Papers, Tulane University; Carter Letter.

40 "The Gallant Color Guard," *Confederate Veteran*, 34:245; Hardshell, 26th Tennessee, *Athens Post*, Feb. 27, 1863, 1.

41 Talley Memoir.

and strike at Rosecrans's rear again. Wheeler gathered not only the roughly 1,100 troopers of his brigade but also Brig. Gen. Abraham Buford's 631 Kentuckians and rode north along the banks of Overall's Creek aiming for the Nashville Pike crossing. Buford's men rode along the northern bank of Overall's Creek while Wheeler's brigade traversed the southern bank. The exact location of the Federal right flank was unknown, and Wheeler did not have a firm understanding of the force in his front, but his cavalrymen had run roughshod over any Yankee opposition for two days straight and he had no reason to believe this would be any different.[42]

Wheeler would have been wise to be wary, as by this late in the afternoon Rosecrans's rear was no longer a ripe target. Lieutenant Colonel John Parkhurst of the 9th Michigan, General Thomas's provost guards, spent a taxing day gathering as many as 5,000 stragglers and sending them back to the front, but by late afternoon, order had been restored. One of Garesche's last dispatches that morning directed General Stanley to return to the army from La Vergne with whatever cavalry forces he could gather and reinforce the Federal right. Riding down the Nashville Pike, Stanley brought forward Colonel Robert Minty's brigade as well as the Anderson Troop and the 1st Middle Tennessee (US) from the reserve, about 1,000 troopers in all. Upon arrival, Minty deployed a skirmish line to protect the road, now swarming with Federals. Before long, he spotted Wheeler's cavalry approaching.

A portion of the Confederate cavalry dismounted and approached the Federal skirmishers on foot, briefly leading Stanley to believe he was facing infantry. The Federal skirmish line opened fire, but Wheeler's men swarmed around its exposed flanks. "They drove back the 4th Michigan to the line of the 1st Tennessee skirmishers and then attacked the 7th Pennsylvania with great fury but met with determined resistance," Minty reported. "I went forward to the dismounted skirmishers and endeavored to move them to the right to strengthen the 7th Pennsylvania, but the right of the line showed itself from behind the fence and the whole of the enemy's fire was directed upon it, turning it completely around."

"A heavy mounted force now attacked," he added, "and drove back the battalion of the 7th and the detachment of the Anderson Troop, thus uncovering the flank of my dismounted line." At this point, Minty noted, the Anderson Troop bolted from the field, "leaving the battalion of the 7th Pennsylvania and the

---

42 OR 20/1:959.

dismounted men almost entirely unsupported and leaving them no alternative but to retreat."[43]

Wheeler's troopers felt jubilant and pushed ahead, not suspecting that a larger force waited for the Rebel line to close. "The Confederate cavalry followed us onto the open ground, showing three strong lines of mounted men, any one of which outnumbered my command," Minty would write. As Wheeler's troopers closed the range, Minty's line delivered a torrent of fire.

"Eager to win new honors, we rushed upon the enemy and were received with a volley which emptied many a saddle," recalled one Confederate. Colonel William Allen of the 1st Alabama Cavalry sustained a disabling wound when a shot struck his saber and shattered in his hand, and Lt. Col. James Webb of the 51st Alabama Partisan Rangers was struck in the head by a shell fragment, the regiment losing 11 men total. Although the Confederate line was temporarily stymied, the contest was far from decided.

Stanley conferred briefly with Minty, telling him, "you look after those fellows in front and I will take care of this force," pointing to a force approaching Minty's left. "Stanley took two companies from the left of the 4th Michigan," Minty noted, "and was about to charge when, suddenly halting, he said to the officer in command, "wait here and I will bring you assistance." Stanley called on the shaky Anderson Troop to join him in the charge and was incensed when the Pennsylvanians resisted his petition; according to Minty, he bellowed, "The man who does not follow me is a damned coward," then wheeled his horse and "dashed back to the two companies of the 4th Michigan. The Pennsylvanians followed and with a raging cheer this little band of heroes charged home into the center of the Rebels and drove it from the field."[44]

Stanley, it seems, chose his company well. The 4th Michigan Cavalry entered the combat armed with Colt's revolving rifles. Although the troopers outgunned their opponents, the general relied on the saber to finish the job. "We got within 600 yards of the Rebel front and immediately charged them," Stanley wrote. "They hesitated a moment and then broke into squads but not until our men had ridden over their formation and knocked over a number of them." The impetuosity of the charge netted the Anderson Troop the colors of the 3rd Tennessee Cavalry Battalion and Medals of Honor for two: John G. Bourke of Company E and John

---

43 Ibid., 624; "The Saber Brigade," *National Tribune*, Aug. 11, 1892, 3.

44 Dashing Operations article; Vindex, *Mobile Advertiser & Register*, Jan. 27, 1863, 2; Saber Brigade article.

Tweedale of Company B. Sergeant Henry Potter of the 4th Michigan wrote that "we made two charges upon the Rebel cavalry and Captain Frank Mix had a splendid horse shot under him, our quartermaster sergeant was wounded, and I had three or four narrow escapes. I did not think of getting killed at all but expected to be wounded."

It was a ferocious fight, but also a short one. "The gloom of the evening was still brightened by the flash of cannon and the ceaseless barrage of rifles seemed to gleam like a swarm of fireflies," remembered one trooper. Minty ordered his line forward "but the Confederates, not wanting to receive us, broke and left the field on the gallop." Stanley's focus on the saber showed its value here; the Confederates, armed with single shot weapons, struggled to reload while in the saddle and once they fired off their single round, were essentially defenseless against Federal steel. "In the midst of it all, Wheeler dashed about unconcerned for personal safety" but saw the effort was futile and ordered his men to retreat.[45]

Buford's brigade had no more success than Wheeler. His brigade consisting of the 3rd, 5th, and 6th Kentucky Cavalry regiments was a recent addition to the army, representing one of the few concrete fruits of the summer's Kentucky Campaign. Recruited during Bragg's invasion, the troopers followed the army into Tennessee but went into action at Murfreesboro poorly armed. The 3rd Kentucky carried the .54-caliber Columbus carbine, "a weapon short of range, loosely constructed, unreliable in almost every respect and a cause of uneasiness in battle." Buford—an 1841 graduate of West Point and cousin of the soon-to-be-famous Union cavalry general, John—was "a man of enormous proportions and his strength and endurance equaled his size. He was a born fighter and so rigid a disciplinarian that he could not always resist the temptation to command in civil life."

His brigade's small numbers barely made a dent on the Federal line north of Overall's Creek. Buford reported that his Kentuckians ran into a Federal force "consisting of artillery, cavalry, and infantry, escorting a large wagon train, the enemy occupying quite a strong position on a hill near Miller's." Deploying a company as skirmishers with the rest of the brigade in battle line, Buford had hardly stepped off before Wheeler ordered him to withdraw. Buford would lose four men in the skirmish and promptly paroled 30 prisoners before turning their horses

<hr>

45 Stanley, *Personal Memoirs*, 127; Dashing Operations article; Sergeant Henry A. Potter, Co. B, 4th Michigan Volunteer Cavalry, Richard Baumgartner Collection.

south. The threat to the Federal right proved illusory. As the sun set, Rosecrans maintained control of the Nashville Pike on both of his flanks.[46]

* * *

"Time passes slowly when a man has nothing to do but lie still under battery fire," penned John James of the 26th Ohio. "If we had known more of how the day was going, or had anything to do, or had any responsibility, we might have felt differently. As it were, we only looked for night. At last, at twenty minutes past 5 o'clock, by my new Waltham watch, the sun went down and soon after we were moved to another position where we lay about an hour longer before it got dark and the firing entirely ceased. Then we got up and moved about and gathered in groups to talk over the events of the day, and I tell you, it was a luxury to do so. We were stiff and tired and cold and it was a great treat to be free to move about as we pleased once more and to stretch ourselves."

Marcus Woodcock's 9th Kentucky, meanwhile, was far enough from the front lines that the men risked a fire. "We are now trying to forget the terrible scenes of the day by taking a nap," he noted. "I lay down and was soon asleep and, strange to say, had pleasant dreams."[47]

For the Confederates, surgeon Joseph Cross remembered: "The two armies lie opposite each other like two wild beasts exhausted with the rage of battle, eyeing each other ferociously and ready to spring upon each other's throat." While riding behind the lines to offer aid to the wounded, Cross was appalled at what he saw: "Here were sights to sicken the bravest heart. A foot shot off at the ankle, a fine model for a sculptor. Here is an officer's hand severed from the wrist, the glove still upon it and the sword in its grasp. Here is an entire brain, perfectly isolated and showing no sign of violence as if carefully taken from the skull that enclosed it by the hands of a skillful surgeon. Here is a corpse sitting upon the ground with its back to a tree holding before its face the likeness of a good-looking old lady, probably the dead man's mother. Here is a poor fellow who has crawled into the corner of the fence to read his sister's letter and expired in the act of its perusal. Many others present the melancholy contrast of scattered cards, obscene pictures,

46 *OR* 20/1:970; *History and Genealogy of the Buford Family in America*, SRNBP.

47 James Letter; Noe, *A Southern Boy in Blue*, 128.

and filthy ballad books. One lies upon his face literally biting the ground, his rigid fingers fastened firmly into the gory sod."[48]

Lieutenant Thomas Shipman of the 60th North Carolina gazed with horror at the sights surrounding his position in the cedars. "This thicket was a horrible and sickening sight to look upon as this ground had also been fought upon and was covered in places by the dead enemy as well as many of our own soldiers," he recalled. "In the stampede of the Federals, it was impossible for them to pull their heavy artillery through the thicket. A number of their cannons were left, each of which had six or eight horses attached lying with their throats cut, to prevent their falling into our hands." The equine tragedy impacted many others on both sides. "I can never forget the pitiful sight of those horses lying there kicking and dying," Scales grieved. "They were as fine a lot of horses as I ever saw—big, fat, splendid fellows."[49]

Major Luke Finlay of the 4th Tennessee found a college roommate among the dead Federals near the Wilkinson Pike. "The contest being over, I rode back to the spot and saw his manly form lying there," Finlay wrote. "I asked his wounded comrades who he was, and they gave me his name and said had he not fallen, you would not be here." It was Colonel George W. Roberts, another of Sheridan's three brigade commanders to be killed in battle that day. Finlay attended Yale with Roberts before the war, but he did not tell that to his brigade commander, Stewart. "[S]uch a soldier deserves proper marks of respect," the major confided to the general, who replied, "Well, you may bury him there. I will send a detail of men to aid you."

"We returned to where he lay, dug a grave, wrapped him in his oil cloth, and buried him where he fell," Finlay added. "Earth to earth, ashes to ashes, dust to dust."[50]

Captain Ellis of the 16th/25th Louisiana found a wounded Federal soldier rendered maniacal from his wound. "His face was as besmeared with dirt and blood and his hair was stiff with congealed gore," Ellis noted. "I never saw a more hideous sight. Yet I had but a man to deal with. We washed his head and face with water from a canteen and examined the wound. A Minie ball had struck him just between and a little above the eyes and had nearly buried itself but yet could be

---

48 Cross Letter.

49 Reminiscences of Lieutenant Thomas J. Shipman, Co. D, 60th North Carolina, SRNBP.

50 Pirtle article; Shiloh Battlefield Commission. *Ohio at Shiloh* (Washington Courthouse, 1903), 208-209.

plainly seen and felt in the wound. Our efforts to extract it failed. We spread a few blankets, laid the poor fellow on them, tied his feet so he could not get up, and left him in charge of the infirmary corps. I no longer hated that man and these dead men who lay stark and stiff gazing with deathly intensity toward the moon."[51]

On the Federal side of the line, stretcher-bearers took advantage of the cover of night to retrieve the hundreds of wounded men lying between the lines. Lieutenant Samuel Maxey of the 110th Illinois led a company of pickets into the body-strewn cotton field in front of the Round Forest and encountered one of the wounded. "After posting my pickets and directing them to fall back at daylight without further orders, I returned to my command," he wrote. "As I went back all alone in the dense stillness of the night amidst the groans and cries of the wounded, I heard one fellow crying bitterly. 'Do come,' he said, 'for my poor mother's, nay wife and child's sake, and help me.' This impelled me to go to him. He told me he belonged to a Kentucky regiment and was shot through the hips and could not stand. He had lain in the mud until he was nearly chilled to the death. While we were talking, I heard the voices of men and one said 'Let's go up here and get this fellow. We have passed him two or three times.' I called out, 'Are you hospital men?' They said yes and I said, 'then come and get this man at once.'"[52]

Stephen Tanner of the 9th Texas explored the battlefield in the final moments of daylight. "I saw the dead in rows behind the fences and such large, fine-looking Union men," he wrote. "It seemed impossible that we scrawny Southerners could beat such men at a game of killing. One Union soldier attracted my special attention, lying on his back dead with a testament closed and lying upon his breast, the work, no doubt, of a ghoul searching for money. I stopped and looked at him, so healthy and strong in appearance, and a face that was truly handsome."[53]

*　　*　　*

The sights in Murfreesboro compared with the horrors of the battlefield. Sergeant Major Samuel Bird of the 35th Illinois had been wounded and captured during his brigade's fight in the cedar glade south of the Harding House. Now tramping painfully into town, he had a chance to see his opponents up close. "They

<hr>

51 Ellis Memoir.

52 "On Stone River Field," Second Lieutenant Samuel T. Maxey, Co. B, 110th Illinois, *National Tribune*, Apr. 6, 1899, 3.

53 Tanner Autobiography.

were in high glee," he wrote. "I was suffering from my wound and extreme thirst and each time I reached for a dead Rebel's canteen I invariably found whiskey tinctured with gunpowder. In addition to this, the rank and file of the Rebel army were terribly exasperated that that day of all others, owing to the fact that on the morrow the Emancipation Proclamation was to take effect. We were taunted and sneered at as 'nigger-loving Yankee sons of bitches' at almost every step of that three-mile tramp into town and when we reached there found the streets lined with female Rebels who had turned out en masse to make wry faces and spit on the Lincoln soldiers which they repeatedly did."[54]

As the battle raged, the mother of Captain William P. Campbell of the 1st Arkansas Mounted Rifles frantically looked through town seeking news of her son. "I came into town on Wednesday morning," she wrote. "The muskets and cannons roared as no one on earth can describe and can I ever tell you my heart was aching? After some inquiry and search I found where General Smith's commissary was camped and went there to inquire for General McCown's division, McNair's brigade. One of William's men came from the field and said Captain Campbell was wounded and brought off. I said, 'Can you tell me where he is?' to which he replied, 'He is not dangerously wounded and is in the old [Soule Female] Academy.' I went into three rooms looking at all the wounded soldiers, perhaps 150 men, then into another room where I found William badly wounded in the leg about halfway between the ankle and knee. The bone was much fractured; it was awful and is still horrid. I was afraid for two days that his life was in danger and thought his leg would have to be amputated."[55]

Captain Campbell was one of the lucky ones; most of the wounded men at Stones River could look only to the overwhelmed surgeons for care and comfort. James Ellis of the 4th Arkansas, wounded in McNair's opening charge on the right, now found himself in a hospital in town. "So many wounded soldiers were there that received no attention," he wrote. Regarding his own wound, Ellis heard one surgeon state, "Don't fool with him now, in the morning we will take that arm off." Ellis found that unacceptable, later writing: "In the morning, I was not there, for soon after dark I crept out, took up an empty bucket, put my blanket over my wounded arm, and passed the guards as if I were going to the pump out on the

---

54 Sergeant Major Samuel W. Bird, 35th Illinois, "Stone River: Comrade Bird Says the Rebels Drank Whisky and Gunpowder," *National Tribune,* Jul. 22, 1886, 3.

55 Letter from Grandmother Campbell, File of Captain William P. Campbell, Co. B, 1st Arkansas Mounted Rifles, SRNBP.

street. With much difficulty I reached the depot and left on the first train going southward. I had relatives of my mother at Shelbyville to which place I made my painful weary way. They received me as if I had been their own son."[56]

The hospitals of Murfreesboro were overwhelmed with the wounded and dying. A local woman recalled being called on to work as a nurse at the Soule hospital. "The large assembly hall that had once known only young, bright faces and girlish laughter was now filled with wounded and dying men and the sounds heard were groans and curses," she noted. "They had been placed on pallets on the floor, that being the best that could be done for them in a hurry. Every woman that could leave home at all was there doing what she could for our own soldiers. One poor fellow I remember so distinctly had one side of his face torn off and was suffering so intensely and begging to be taken to a private house. A neighbor of my mother's was waiting on him especially when he was seized with convulsions and died in a few moments. The whole town was a hospital, the people all mourners, and the place one vast cemetery."[57]

Food for the wounded ran short at the Smith House hospital, located west of where Willich's brigade had been overrun in the morning. "All the chickens in the neighborhood had been killed," remembered John Rennard of the 15th Ohio. "The doctors were troubled about it and Mr. Smith, who owned the premises, suggested they get robins. Doctor William Park [49th Ohio] laughed and said there would be nothing left of the robin when shot by one of our guns. Mr. Smith then suggested that if the attendants would go out after night with a lantern into the second growth cedars where they roosted and tap them with clubs, they could get numbers of them. This was tried and the first party came back with half a bushel basket full and the next with a two-bushel bag and a basket full. They usually served them with hulled barley and they were fine eating."[58]

The soldiers of the 28th Tennessee in Palmer's Brigade, still soaked from crossing Stones River a few hours earlier, appreciated the thoughtfulness of their young commanding officer Preston Cunningham, who sent them a barrel of whiskey. One officer for each company headed back to get the company ration. "Having gathered a dozen or more canteens, I started for the barrel which was

56 Private James W. Ellis, Co. E, 4th Arkansas, "Gratitude of Veterans," *Confederate Veteran*, Dec. 1909, 581.

57 M. E. Robinson, "Stone River: A Southern Woman's Memories of the Battle," *National Tribune*, Feb. 15, 1906, 3.

58 Cope, *The 15th Ohio*, 248.

300–400 yards away," wrote Lieutenant Talley. "When I got there, I found the barrel sitting on its end with the head out and a crowd around it with the same mission as myself. When my time came to fill up, I would take the canteen in each hand and sink them in the liquor and they would say good, good, till they were full. Then I would take two more and do likewise until all were full. With these full canteens swinging around my neck, I started back and found that it was all I could do to walk, bending over the barrel and inhaling the fumes had made me drunk. When I got there, I said, 'Boys, here is your liquor.' It made me drunk without tasting it. With the hot fires they had now burning and the big drink of liquor they had taken, put them in full plight for sleeping and resting which they greatly enjoyed till the bugle notes sounded warning us of the near approach of daylight."[59]

It was a gloomy camp behind the Nashville Pike that night. The 15th Kentucky, a hard-luck regiment if there ever was one, was "orphaned" again. The loss of Colonel James Forman in the fight that day cut to the core, and a few hardy souls of the regiment were determined to do something about it. "His men formed a small squad after the night had fallen and with great caution and silence, made their way into the intense darkness of the forest and after some efforts, found his body and slowly brought it into our lines with much labor," recalled Alfred Pirtle. "I shall never forget how martial he looked, all accoutered as was his wont, as he lay like a marble statue in the bottom of an army wagon in which the beams of a lone candle strove to dispel the shadows."

Corporal Thomas Dornblaser of the 7th Pennsylvania Cavalry called it "blue Wednesday" and wearily went out on vidette duty after being in the saddle all day. "We sat on our horses weary and hungry," he noted, "and with heavy eyelids and distended pupils, we strained the optic nerve to penetrate the thickening fog to catch the outline of the victor and antagonist of tomorrow. The eyelids would drop in spite of all we could do. By beating the skull with the fist and pinching the ears, we managed to keep sufficiently wakeful to halt the grand rounds."[60]

Before the troops bedded down for the night, company commanders in both armies commenced calling the roll. Companies that had once been led by captains now had lieutenants, sergeants, or even corporals in command. "The evening roll call was a very sad one," recalled Charles Cunningham of the 5th Wisconsin Battery. "As the names were being called, someone would answer 'Killed'

---

59 Talley Memoir.

60 Pirtle article; Thomas F. Dornblaser. *Sabre Strokes of the Pennsylvania Dragoons in the War of 1861-1865* (Baltimore, 1998), 103.

'Wounded' 'Captured' and 'Unknown.' It made a feeling of sorrow pass over the soul. I know it was with a tremulous voice that I answered for Dave Welty. I thought of the night before and of my messmate Dave as I lay beside Clark Baker, whose cheeks were streaked with the powder and smoke of the morning's battle."[61]

Louis Simmons of the 84th Illinois recalled how "tears coursed down the cheeks of our brave colonel when he counted only 113 guns in the stacks, and not a few cheeks that had not blanched in battle were moistened with manly tears. Each survivor had lost comrades and friends, and several found near and dear kinsmen and brothers missing." Launcelot Scott of the 18th Ohio felt "almost helpless that night as I lay down on my bed of cedar boughs tired and half-starved. I could have no bright anticipation of victory on the morrow. Nothing but my faith in Rosey and Negley kept me from despairing."[62]

The mood in the Confederate camps ranged from subdued to jubilant. "We employed ourselves talking over the events of the day and deploring the loss of our comrades and speaking perhaps harshly of those who were absent and as we thought unjustifiably," wrote Captain Taylor Beattie of the 1st Louisiana Regulars. Edward Carruth of the 7th Mississippi lamented that it was "truly a day of dark distress. The day after the fight at Murfreesboro, so many of my friends were killed or lying around wounded, many of them mortally. My old friend Captain McDowell was killed. I went and hunted up his body, and helped to bury him. Oh, what a noble man! Who has not lost a friend? I have lost many in the cruel war. My only brother at Corinth and friend after friend ever since."[63]

"There was great rejoicing in the army and throughout the South on the result on the first day's fight as well there might be," recalled Captain William Pickett of Hardee's staff. There was wide belief Bragg's army had won the battle. Bragg certainly thought so, and it would be hard to argue with his logic. Rosecrans's lines had been driven back nearly three miles; in the process, the Confederates had captured dozens of cannons, numerous battle flags, and several thousand Federal prisoners now crowded around the Rutherford County Courthouse awaiting transportation to Chattanooga. Late that night, in fact, Bragg dispatched a message to General Samuel Cooper in Richmond all but proclaiming victory. "We assailed the enemy at 7 o'clock this morning, and after ten hours' hard fighting have driven him from every position except his extreme left, which he has successfully resisted

61 Cunningham article.

62 Simmons, *History of the 84th Illinois*, 32; Scott Memoir.

63 Beattie Diary; Letters of Edward B. Carruth, 7th Mississippi, Ron Skellie Collection.

us," it read. "With the exception of this point, we occupy the whole field. We captured 4,000 prisoners, including two brigadier generals, 31 pieces of artillery, and some 200 wagons and teams. Our loss is heavy; that of the enemy much greater."[64]

All told, the Army of Tennessee lost roughly 8,000 men, mostly killed or wounded; few Confederates had been captured. The losses on the Federal side ran to more than 12,000 killed, wounded, or missing with as many as 4,000 prisoners.

The absence of so many familiar faces made abundantly clear how bloody the day's work had been. "As the darkness of night came on the stars by the million came out and appeared to quietly gaze on the dead and groaning thousands," lamented Sergeant Samuel Stallard of the 15th Indiana. "I could not help thinking of the harmony that existed among the heavenly bodies and feel myself reproached for the work I had helped to do. The still clearness of the night, the low whispering of the men, and the groans of the wounded rendered everyone sad and melancholy. Thus ended the year 1862."[65]

64 Colonel William D. Pickett, "Reminiscences of Murfreesboro," *Confederate Veteran*, 16:451; OR 20/1:662.

65 Samuel T. Stallard Papers, 15th Indiana, Indiana Historical Society.

18

The Waiting Hours

THE SUN WAS setting on December 31, 1862, when Colonel John C. Starkweather's veteran Union brigade in George Thomas's corps reached the field. The brigade arrived with more than then it set out with, supplemented by hundreds of stragglers picked up along the Nashville Pike. These men were no strangers to the carnage of battle, having been put through the wringer just three months before at Perryville. Thus, far, however, Stones River had taken that carnage to another level entirely. Sergeant John Otto of the 21st Wisconsin recalled how "an indescribable scene met our ears as the night did not allow us to see it distinctly. The dead and wounded were many, some groaning, some praying, some swearing and cussing the damned Yankees." Adjutant Michael Fitch, also of the 21st, remembered that "the two armies lay facing each other like two worn-out gladiators, tired, muddy, and bloody."[1]

Rumors of massive Confederate reinforcements from Virginia spread like wildfire through the Union lines, deepening the gloom. "We had gained no material advantage and with no hopes or prospects of reinforcements for us made up a gloomy night," remembered Quartermaster Lewis Zecher of the 79th Pennsylvania. Captain Wilberforce Nevin of the 79th also felt the overwhelming gloom of the field, writing: "There on that dismal night, a frosty bleak December night without blankets, without coffee or meat, without a solitary fire as we dared

1 Gould, *Memoirs of a Dutch Mudsill*, 83-84; Fitch, *Echoes of the Civil War*, 105.

not make them, our men threw themselves on the bare frozen ground and slept waiting for the coming of the morning uncheered by a single ray of hope."[2]

Rosecrans's army had suffered through "the devil's own day," but nightfall found the army in a strong compact formation. After dark, a 200-wagon provision and ammunition train rolled across the Overall's Creek bridge. A quick survey of ammunition showed that the army had sufficient supplies for another engagement; food, however, was scarce because of the havoc Wheeler caused in the Federal rear in the days preceding the battle. Thousands of stragglers from the army had fled to Nashville, and several thousand more returned sheepishly to the ranks that evening after being caught by the provost guard's dragnet across the Nashville Pike.

The rest of the men, though rattled and battered by the day's reverses, kept their places in line, grimly determined to see this through. Morale varied from unit to unit, but overall, as Colonel John Beatty noted, the men were "despairing but not despondent, weary and hungry but still hopeful lay on its arms ready to renew the conflict on the morrow." Sheridan concurred, noting that the losses suffered by his division was "naturally disheartening" but maintaining that "the men had been made veterans by the fortunes and misfortunes of the day and as they went into their new places still confident of final success, it was plain to see that they felt a self-confidence inspired by the part they had already played."[3]

On the far right, General Stanley's cavalrymen patrolled the Nashville Pike to the Overall's Creek crossing beyond. Moving south, Negley's two brigades held the ground parallel to the pike with five artillery batteries in support—Colonel Stanley's men on the right and Miller's on the left. McCook's wing continued the line behind a set of breastworks thrown up during the evening. In Davis's 1st Division, Post's 1st Brigade formed on the right, supported by Woodruff's 3rd Brigade, with Carlin's 2nd Brigade next in line. On their left was Sheridan, with Schaefer's 2nd Brigade (now commanded by Lt. Col. Bernard Laiboldt) supported by Sill's old brigade (now under Colonel Greusel) on the right, and Colonel Luther P. Bradley (commanding Roberts's 3rd Brigade) holding the left. The few survivors of Richard Johnson's division were sandwiched between Walker's and Starkweather's brigades on Sheridan's left.

Closer to the Nashville Pike, John Beatty's men held Starkweather's left, ahead of the Pioneer Brigade; the line turned from facing west to south, with Scribner's

---

2 Quartermaster Lewis Zecher, 79th Pennsylvania, *Lancaster Inquirer*, Jan. 14, 1863, 2; Captain W. Wilberforce Nevin, Co. G, 79th Pennsylvania, *Lancaster Daily Express*, Mar. 3, 1863, 2.

3 Beatty, *Citizen-Soldier*, 204.

men holding the critical junction at the McFadden Lane crossing. To Scribner's left, stretching toward Stones River, was Harker's brigade, supported by four artillery batteries as well as Milo Hascall's old brigade, now under Colonel Buell of the 58th Indiana. Wagner's men took position to Harker's left, and Hazen to Wagner's left, with Cruft's and Grose's brigades, supported by Samuel Price's brigade, guarding McFadden's Ford. The balance of the army lay safely tucked within this pocket. The vexing question for Rosecrans remained: What should he do next?

About eleven that evening, Rosecrans summoned a council of his senior commanders to his headquarters in the Daniel Cabin along the Nashville Pike to discuss the situation and plans for the next day. "The glimmering light of the smoldering fire concealed the sad, careworn faces of that group," Negley remembered. General Wood, injured in the fighting, was present, and though he hobbled into the cabin with a crutch, when Rosecrans offered him a chair, he refused to sit. The army's position was discussed first, with one recommendation to give up the Round Forest and draw the line back 250 yards, and then conduct a general withdrawal before dawn. Because the Confederates surrounded the salient on three sides, however, this was believed untenable.

Rosecrans then asked the key question: "Shall we fight it out here, or withdraw to an advantageous position covering our depots at Nashville?" Accounts differ widely on which generals advocated either course. Rosecrans indicated that McCook and Stanley backed a retreat, and that Thomas and Crittenden pledged their support but offered no opinion. (Crittenden later claimed that he and Thomas wanted to stay and fight.) Rosecrans reviewed the army's casualty figures, then asked his chief medical director, Eben Swift, whether he had sufficient means to transport the wounded back to Nashville—assured by Swift he could manage. Rosecrans seemed to be leaning toward a withdrawal, but before deciding, he and Stanley left to survey the ground in the immediate rear, traveling beyond Overall's Creek.[4]

The ride took two hours. Whatever they saw or discussed convinced Rosecrans to stay and fight it out, but neither general ever revealed the reasons behind the decision. On his return, Rosecrans directed a long line of fires to be lit extending far beyond the army's right to give the illusion his command was larger

---

4 *Third Reunion*, 36; Cleaves, *Rock of Chickamauga*, 131; Stanley, *Personal Memoirs*, 127-28; Lamers, *Edge of Glory*, 235. In Rosecrans's version, neither Thomas nor Crittenden gave an opinion; McCook suggested the army retreat to Nashville.

and less concentrated than it actually was—the same trick he had used the night before to try to fool Bragg on his army's location. He would add a new wrinkle by having his men represent phantom reinforcements, tapping Colonel Stanley's brigade on the extreme right for the assignment.

"We marched away up the Nashville Pike beyond the right of the army. The night was still and of that murky condition when voices may be heard [at] a great distance," recalled Daniel Rose of the 11th Michigan, part of Stanley's command carrying out Rosecrans's strategy. "Upon arriving," continued Rose,

> each soldier in the detail became a brigadier general, colonel, or some active officer and each worked very industriously for half an hour or more maneuvering and commanding in a loud voice his imaginary battalions into comfortable and secure positions for the night. When this was done, each resigned his high rank, was a private again, and went at work very assiduously building campfires of the fine cedar rails then found in abundance. When all the fences which could be found were converted into blazing, crackling campfires, the detail returned to their respective commands and at midnight all was quiet.[5]

Sheridan saw Rosecrans and Stanley returning from their late-night ride but had no idea what information they had attained. Dame Rumor filled the void. "It was rumored that while the party was looking for a new position…," Sheridan wrote, "the enemy's troops [were discovered] moving toward our right and rear, the head of his columns being conducted in the darkness by the aid of torches and that no alternative was left but to hold the lines we then occupied." Sheridan later learned the truth, but the story that Rosecrans was convinced the Confederates had cut off his retreat to Nashville colors much postwar literature.

It was about 1:00 a.m. on January 1, 1863, when Rosecrans and Stanley returned to headquarters. The two warmed themselves by a fire. "Rosecrans was very silent," Sheridan explained, "and after dismounting and as we crouched about the smoldering embers to warm ourselves.

"General, what are you going to do?" inquired Sheridan.

"By God's help, I am going to beat the enemy right here," Rosecrans shot back.

The army commander walked inside the cabin to inform his subordinates of his decision. "Well, gentlemen, we shall not retreat, but fight it out here and to the front," he affirmed. "Go at once to your posts and hold your commands ready to

---

5 Rose Article.

receive any attack from the enemy. We shall not attempt to attack him until the arrival of our ammunition which I have ordered up from Nashville." On hearing Rosecrans's decision, "grand old General Thomas's face glowed with delight while General McCook and Crittenden were pleased," noted Captain Alexander Stevenson. "As each one of the corps commanders took the hand of the general commanding in bidding him good night, they gave him a soldier's warm grasp and said, 'We will stand by you, General, to the last.'"[6]

Like King Henry V in Shakespeare's immortal play, Rosecrans wandered through his army's camps throughout the night. Alexis Cope of the 15th Ohio saw the general twice, in fact. "The night was very cold, all had lost their blankets and overcoats and fires were forbidden," he wrote. "A group of shivering men, in violation of the order, had made a small fire between two rocks and were trying to warm themselves when General Rosecrans came by on foot. He said, 'My men you must not do that. Just a short while ago some men farther along the line made a little fire and the Rebels threw a shell into their midst and killed or wounded some of them. Better bear the cold.' The men put out the fire very promptly."

Sometime later, Rosecrans passed the camp again, alone and still wearing his sky-blue army overcoat stained with the blood of his deceased chief of staff. "His face was drawn, his jaw set, and we heard him say more than once, 'Bragg's a good dog, but Hold Fast's a better,'" Cope wrote. "His presence inspired confidence. He gave us to understand that there was to be no retreat, but that we would fight it out where we were. We got the impression that we were receiving large reinforcements, and stragglers coming in reported seeing the campfires of several thousand new troops coming to our help."[7]

*   *   *

Three miles south at Confederate headquarters, Braxton Bragg had long since retired for the night. It was widely believed within the army's high command that Rosecrans would retreat during the night and the dawn would find the Confederates in possession of the field. "We were masters of the field," asserted one of Bragg's confident staff officers. Bragg gave no thought of retreating, nor did

6 Sheridan, *Personal Memoirs*, 127-28; Stanley, *Personal Memoirs*, 127; Lamers, *Edge of Glory*, 235; Stevenson, *Battle of Stone's River*, 119-21.

7 Cope, *The 15th Ohio*, 338.

he issue any orders modifying the position of his army, though he did direct that the public buildings of Murfreesboro be used as hospitals for the wounded.

The Confederate line stretched for nearly a mile east to west, generally facing north. Pegram's cavalry brigade held the far right beyond the eastern bank of Stones River protecting the Lebanon Pike approach to Murfreesboro. Hanson's Kentuckians still held Wayne's Hill supported by assorted artillery batteries, and Palmer's Brigade crossed the river during the night and set up in support behind the hill, but those were the only Confederate forces beyond the eastern bank. Chalmers's Mississippians, now under the command of Colonel Thomas White of the 9th/10th Mississippi, continued to hold their breastworks south of the Cowan House, with five artillery batteries arrayed nearby. General Anderson's battered brigade lay far to the rear in reserve. The Cowan House itself was occupied by skirmishers from the 84th Tennessee in Donelson's Brigade.[8]

The main Confederate line stretched through the edge of the cedar forest behind a row of hastily constructed breastworks. Brigades from both Withers's Division and Breckinridge's Division held the right. Daniel Adams's old brigade, now under Randall Gibson, held the right, followed by Preston's brigade to their left, supported by Jackson. Loomis's Alabamians, now under Colonel John Coltart, were to Preston's left, supported by Donelson's Tennesseans. Stewart's Brigade lay to Coltart's left, and Maney's fellow Tennesseans were posted to Stewart's left, supported by Manigault's Brigade.

McCown's Division was next, with Rains's Brigade (now under Colonel Vance) on the right, McNair's Brigade (now under Colonel Harper) at center, and Ector's Texans on the left, supported by Vaughan's Brigade from Cleburne's Division. Cleburne held the army's extreme left, with Lucius Polk's Brigade on the right, Johnson's at center, and Liddell's on the left. While several batteries camped nearby to support the position, the tangled cedars meant only two batteries were posted on the front line. Wheeler's, Wharton's, and Buford's cavalry brigades bivouacked beyond the army's far left.

An unpleasant surprise greeted Bragg and his officers when they discovered Rosecrans was still on the field at dawn. Bragg ordered his skirmish lines to press forward to "feel the enemy and report any change in his position. It was soon reported that no change had occurred, except the withdrawal of the enemy from the advanced position occupied by his left flank." Colonel White sent Captain Osborne West's 9th Battalion of Mississippi Sharpshooters to occupy the Round

8 Urquhart, *Battles & Leaders*, Vol. 3, 607.

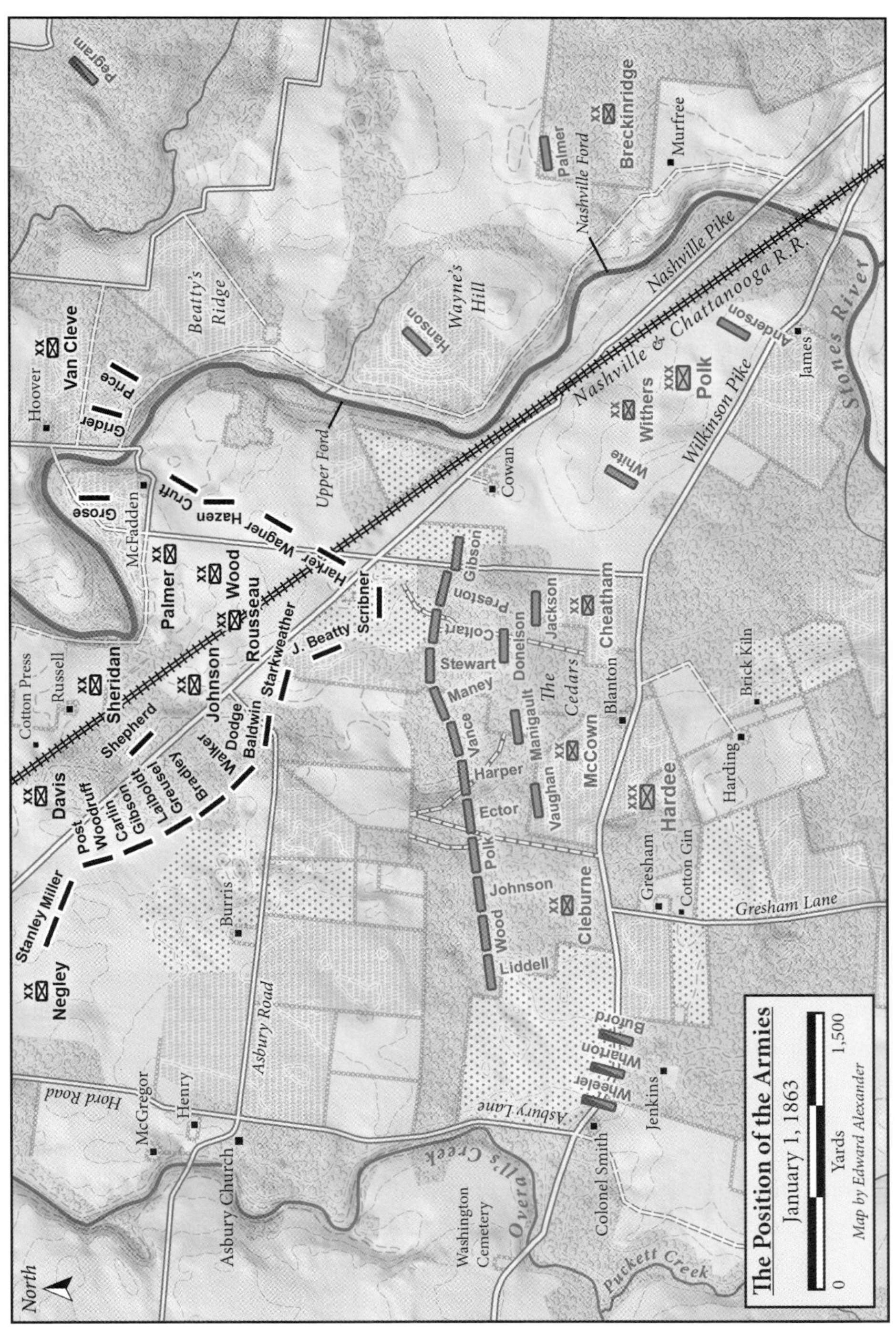

North
Pegram
Hoover
Van Cleve
Price
Grider
Beatty's Ridge
Wayne's Hill
Hanson
Nashville Ford
Palmer
Breckinridge
Murfree
Nashville Pike
Nashville & Chattanooga R.R.
Anderson
Stones River
James
Withers
Polk
White
Wilkinson Pike
Cowan
Grose
McFadden
Cruft
Hazen
Wagner
Harker
Upper Ford
Palmer
Wood
Rousseau
Scribner
Starkweather
J. Beatty
Gibson
Preston
Jackson
Cheatham
Blanton
Donelson
Coltart
Stewart
Maney
Brick Kiln
Sheridan
Shepherd
Johnson
Russell
Cotton Press
Bradley
Greusel
Laiboldt
Gibson
Carlin
Woodruff
Post
Davis
Walker
Dodge
Baldwin
Vance
The Cedars
Manigault
Vaughan
McCown
Harper
Harding
Ector
Hardee
Polk
Gresham
Cotton Gin
Stanley
Miller
Negley
Burris
Johnson
Wood
Cleburne
Liddell
Gresham Lane
Asbury Road
Hord Road
McGregor
Henry
Buford
Wharton
Wheeler
Asbury Lane
Ils Creek
Overa
Washington Cemetery
Asbury Church
Colonel Smith
Jenkins
Puckett Creek
The Position of the Armies
January 1, 1863
Yards
0
1,500
Map by Edward Alexander

Forest. "The command advanced in good order and drove the enemy from the woods capturing one surgeon and four men besides inflicting other losses on the enemy in killed and wounded," West reported. The Round Forest was an appalling scene of carnage soon to be known as "Hell's Half-Acre."

"This shortened our line considerably, and gave us possession of the entire battlefield," wrote Bragg. "It was soon ascertained that the enemy was still in very heavy force all along our front, occupying a position strong by nature and improved by such work as could be done at night and by his reserves." The enemy showed no disposition to attack, so Bragg ordered his men to scour the field for abandoned weapons. William Hutson of the 60th North Carolina—a "daring fellow conspicuous for his cool bravery under fire"—brought in 35 guns, more than enough to rearm his entire company.[9]

Bragg suspected Rosecrans had maintained a show of force at Murfreesboro to cover an impending retreat. In the early morning, he ordered Wheeler to take most of the army's cavalry (Wharton's, Buford's, and his own brigade) north of the Federal position to slash at any enemy traffic along the Nashville Pike. It took an hour or two to get the approximately 2,500 troopers in the saddle and moving west along the Wilkinson Pike. Riding six miles out to Wilkinson's Crossroads, the column turned north for Stewardsboro. After a brief brush with a Federal detachment guarding the Stewart's Creek bridge, Wheeler sidestepped north and arrived in the vicinity of the Nashville Pike near La Vergne in the early afternoon. Hundreds of Federal wagons filled the road, all heading north.

Earlier that morning, Rosecrans ordered the empty ordnance and commissary wagons gathered and sent north; dozens of ambulances joined the column accompanied by hundreds of walking wounded destined for the hospitals at Nashville. Colonel Zahm guarded the train with the 3rd Ohio Cavalry and a portion of the Anderson Troop, perhaps 500 troopers in all guarding a train nearly 10 miles long. Sensing an opportunity, Wheeler split his column, taking his brigade farther south while directing Wharton to lead his brigade and Buford's against the wagons lumbering along the pike about a mile south of La Vergne.

Wharton deployed two guns from White's Tennessee Battery into a field overlooking the crowded road and opened fire on the Federal wagons. After dismounting a portion of his force of roughly 1,500 troopers, the Confederates plunged against the train with reckless abandon. "We captured about 100 wagons,

---

9 OR 20/1:667; Smith, *Stones River: Confederate Army*, 657, 664; Clark, *Histories of the Several Regiments*, 480.

150 prisoners, 300 mules, and one piece of artillery," Wharton reported. "The remaining wagons, with the quartermaster's commissary, and ordnance stores contained in them, were burned."

What Wharton did not know was that the 391-man 1st Michigan Engineers and Mechanics was camped nearby, assigned to repair the railroad bridge over Stewart's Creek. The sound of Wharton's guns spurred the Wolverines into action. "Company, fall in! Fall in!" sounded throughout the camp," remembered Private William Clark of Company K. "Each company took its assigned position with directions to change points of defense whenever ordered."

Colonel William Innes had the foresight to have his men construct rough breastworks of trees and brush earlier that morning and confidently awaited Wharton. "Along a ridge at right angles to the road, a long line of cavalry was drawn up, preparing to charge upon us," Clark recalled. "As they appeared fairly upon the highest point, some eighty rods off, a heavy volley was fired upon them. They turned and retreated down out of sight and commenced firing upon us with artillery and sharpshooters." Noted Innes: "The enemy attacked us with great fury, making seven distinct charges upon us, attacking us on every side, mounted and on foot, dashing forward in a gallant and determined manner, but were again and again severely repulsed by my gallant regiment. During the interval between their cavalry charges their artillery were throwing shot and shell, some of them causing considerable damage."[10]

The troopers fell back, redeployed, then tried to strike the engineers on the flank. Innes's alert men caught them flat-footed. "Coming up in good order as fallen treetops, stumps, and obstructions would permit, they were allowed to gain a close distance before they were assailed by a volley so well-directed that a rapid retreat ensued," Clark wrote. "Mule teams and horses had broken loose and ran about, and several teamsters ventured pretty close to the enemy's position after them without injury." Wharton rolled his artillery to within 400 yards of Innes's works and opened fire while rallying his troopers for another charge. Wharton spread his command around such to strike Innes's position from the north, east, and south. The 1st Confederate, 14th Alabama Battalion, and Smith's 4th Tennessee charged the breastworks a third and then a fourth time. "Forming behind the woods, they charged up handsomely along the road and through the woods on the southwest corner," Clark noted.

10 OR 20/1:651, 968; Private William L. Clark, Co. K, 1st Michigan Engineers & Mechanics, *Marshall Statesman*, Jan. 21, 1863, 2.

In that last attack, Wharton's men tried to jump their horses over the breastworks only to be repulsed with heavy losses. "The main force came plunging up on the left of the company, discharging their pieces and wheeling to the left when they found our defenses so good that they could not gallop their horses over them," Clark recalled. "They were an excellent mark for every musket, rifle, and revolver loaded in the company and many were killed or wounded." As Wharton conceded: "The charge was repeated four times, but the enemy was so strongly posted that it was found impossible to dislodge him."[11]

While Wharton hammered at La Vergne, Wheeler's 1,000 troopers encountered difficulty trying to get at the Federal wagons farther south. Zahm's flankers discovered Wheeler's movement before Wheeler could close the range, so Zahm deployed in a line of battle west of the pike and ordered the waggoneers to trot ahead to La Vergne. This was "almost equivalent to telling the drivers to run their teams into the ditch, cut the traces, mount a horse or a mule and get away," adjutant Josiah Reiff of the Anderson Troop noted laconically. "After leaving the woods, the rebels quickly formed into line and indeed looked formidable."

Light skirmishing broke out, but Wheeler's aim was the wagons, not the escort, so he deftly moved farther north, forcing Zahm to disengage and gallop in that direction to guard the train. Wheeler's men won the race and were already opening fire on the teamsters by the time the Federal cavalry arrived. "It is immaterial in attacking a train whether they kill any men or even horses," Reiff explained. "The first idea is to present a show of force and the fears of the teamsters produce a panic. The wagons become blocked up two or three abreast across the road, each driver endeavoring to get ahead. If they do not immediately become disentangled, they abandon their charge."[12]

Reiff stood at the rear of the train watching the confusion when Wheeler's troopers struck again. "The train was going along at a trot," he noted, "when the yell of the stragglers and Negroes was the Rebels are coming! This startled the teamsters again."

"The enemy was among us in a moment," recalled M. B. Colton. "As we were doing what we could to prevent a general stampede of the train, several of us were captured. We were rushed rapidly through the woods and were soon out of gunshot. We found they had with them about 150 prisoners, most of them infantry." Zahm complained that Reiff and his comrades "scampered off in most

---

11 Clark Letter; *OR* 20/1:968.

12 *OR* 20/1:634, 964; Kirk, *History of the 15th Pennsylvania Cavalry*, 97-98.

every direction and did not stand up to the work at all." The colonel met the panicked Pennsylvanians, along with the recently recruited 2nd Tennessee (US), falling back from the train and charged ahead with his 3rd Ohio. The fight for the train lasted an hour. "They were well posted on an eminence behind houses, a train of wagons parked, and fences," recalled Colonel Webb of the 51st Alabama Partisan Rangers "The contest for the time was very warm."[13]

Despite the panic, Zahm claimed he was able to recover nearly all of the wagons, even though the teamsters charged with driving them to Nashville had scattered. "Such skedaddling you never heard of," wrote one artillerist. The stampede barreled into Rosecrans's Provost Guard, the 10th Ohio, commanded by Lt. Col. Joseph Burke, who was guarding Stewart's Creek along with several detachments of cavalry. "Cavalrymen with jaded horses, artillery and infantry soldiers, breathless and holding on to wagons, came streaming down the road and pouring through the woods on their way toward the bridge," Burke wrote. "In vain did my small guard stationed on the road try to check this panic. Officers drew their revolvers, but the fugitives heeded them not. The fugitives crowded in thousands, and at one time pressed closely up to the bayonets of my men. I ordered the battalion to load, and determined to fire if the crowd did not move back; seeing which, many took flight back toward the front." Using a detachment from the 4th US Cavalry to drive the stragglers, Burke's dragnet eventually corralled nearly 4,000 men.[14]

Burke no sooner quelled the panic than a courier from Innes arrived asking for reinforcements. After sending four companies of cavalry and two guns from Battery D of the 1st Ohio Artillery toward La Vergne, Burke awaited developments. Another civilian courier from La Vergne arrived within an hour with dire news that the reinforcements were falling back, prompting Burke to gather his Ohioans and march to Innes's relief. "I met the section of artillery returning, as well as part of the cavalry," he recalled. "I ordered them to fall in behind me and sent in a strong support of infantry to the guns. The scene on the road was indescribable. Teamsters had abandoned their wagons and came back mounted on their mules and horses; wagons were packed across the road, and many capsized on the side of the pike; horses ran wild through the woods, and, although men were allowed by me to pass as wagon guards, there were none at their

---

13 Kirk, *History of the 15th Pennsylvania Cavalry*, 97, 121-22; OR 20/1:634, 655.

14 Kirk, *History of the 15th Pennsylvania Cavalry*, 98; Pork & Beans, Battery H, 5th US Light Artillery, *Toledo Daily Commercial*, Jan. 16, 1863, 2; OR 20/1:634, 655.

posts. They had left the road and were bivouacking in small parties in the woods, evidently careless of the fate of the trains."[15]

However grim the view might have been to Burke, Wharton's bloodied troopers were essentially fought out. About 5:00 p.m., Wharton demanded Innes's surrender. "The enemy sent in two flags of truce, demanding an immediate surrender of our position, which I peremptorily refused," Innes noted. A second flag of truce soon arrived, Isaac Roseberry remembered, asking for permission to retrieve the dead and wounded. "Colonel Innes told them they could have all they could find out of the range of our guns, but if they came in range, we should fire on them," Roseberry wrote. "So, on the head of that they skedaddled leaving about 50 dead outside of our stockade. The sun is now down and ends this New Year's dance for it was a dance I assure you."[16]

Wharton admitted that his losses were "very considerable," and his troopers were clearly drained after a 20-mile ride in the wake of five days of constant activity. As Wharton's men slipped away toward Murfreesboro, Burke's reinforcing column arrived on the field. Other than capturing a few wagons and a few hundred prisoners who were promptly paroled, Wheeler's strike on Federal communications netted few tangible benefits. The fight at La Vergne cost Innes's engineers 16 casualties, but the intrepid little command held its ground. Zahm conducted the remainder of the wagon train unmolested into Nashville that evening.[17]

*   *   *

Meanwhile on the battlefield, Rosecrans dusted off his previous day's battle plan by ordering General Crittenden to cross Stones River at McFadden's Ford with Van Cleve's division (now under Samuel Beatty) and assume a defensive position atop a ridge about half a mile southeast of the ford. Colonel Samuel Price's command crossed before daybreak and formed in a double line perpendicular to the river. The 51st Ohio took the right flank near the river, the 8th Kentucky the center, and the 35th Indiana the left. As support for the 51st Ohio, Price deployed the 21st Kentucky; for the 35th Indiana, it would be the 99th Ohio. A heavy

---

15 OR 20/1:655-656.

16 Diary of Private Isaac Roseberry, Co. D, 1st Michigan Engineers & Mechanics, Stuart A. Rose Manuscript, Archives, and Rare Book Library, Emory University.

17 OR 20/1:651.

skirmish line pushed forward and "had not advanced far before a spirited fire was opened between them and the enemy's line of skirmishers," reported Colonel Richard McLain of the 51st Ohio. "In a few minutes I received orders to halt the line of skirmishers and not bring on an engagement." The brightening skies revealed Confederate batteries atop Wayne's Hill about 1,200 yards away. Lieutenant Cortland Livingston's 3rd Wisconsin Battery quickly rolled across McFadden's Ford to provide artillery support.[18]

James Fyffe's brigade finished crossing the river by mid-morning and slid into position in an open field on Price's left; the 13th Ohio and 44th Indiana assumed the front line, with the 59th Ohio and 86th Indiana as support. "Small parties of the enemy's cavalry and infantry were occasionally seen, and at length a strong line was distinctly visible through the openings in the wood," Beatty reported. A few shells from Livingston's guns drove them off.

Throughout the day, Federal reinforcements continued to arrive. Beatty's old brigade, now under Colonel Benjamin Grider, crossed in the early afternoon, and before sunset Grose arrived at the ford with his brigade. These Federals used the rolling topography admirably to conceal their numbers. Pegram's small cavalry brigade (two regiments) patrolled the Confederate army's extreme right, and his troopers were among those contesting Crittenden's skirmishers, but he apparently did not report this to Bragg. Neither Bragg nor Breckinridge seemed to notice the Federal division now east of Stones River, even though the advance represented a threat that could not be ignored. Guns placed atop this ridge would flank and enfilade Polk's position, and with just two brigades of infantry east of the river to combat them, this lodgment opened the door for a possible thrust into Murfreesboro itself that could cut Bragg off from his railroad.[19]

Both armies spent January 1 mostly watching, waiting, and building breastworks. "I directed my men to throw up a breastwork upon our front, which they very soon did, constructing it of loose rocks and logs gathered together for that purpose," reported Colonel Walker, commanding one of Thomas's brigades. "So well was this work constructed, and with such rapidity, that by 10 o'clock we had a strong line of defenses, which were continued by other troops on our right, who evinced equal energy, skill, and industry."

18 Ibid., 575, 614.

19 Ibid., 575. Bragg stated in his report that he did not learn the Federals had crossed Stones River until Friday morning, when it was determined by a personal reconnaissance by his staff.

Daylight brought an opportunity for the men to warm themselves at a fire and cook what rations could be found—much-appreciated relief after so many days of hectic activity. "We drew one day's rations of hardtack, bacon, and coffee," Cope recalled. "The conflict of the preceding day had been so fierce and deadly that it seemed both armies were loath to renew it."[20]

Lieutenant Chesley Mosman of the 59th Illinois attested that "nothing happened of any importance. All we did was to lay concealed and watch the Rebel skirmishers. Sometimes when we could see the Rebels, we would see the glistening of the gun in his hands." Skirmishing continued nearly without break all day, and occasionally the artillery of both armies would throw a few shells into the opposing lines. Williamson Ward of the 39th Indiana remembered several cannon balls that came "uncomfortably close to us as we were lying on the ground. One struck a stack of guns, knocking them to pieces while another struck the heel of one of the boys, knocking off the heel of his shoe and laming him quite seriously." Sergeant Otto acidly noted the Confederates inviting "us in their usual hospitable way to a superb dinner of shot and shell, or grape, and canister, of bullets and bayonets, all finely garnished with an enticing view of Libby prison. Added to that empty haversacks, a couple ears of corn, and a handful of coffee beans for the enjoyment of a craving stomach and happiness seemed complete."[21]

"On Thursday morning instead of following up the enemy as the boys thought they would, we fell upon that drill commonly known by West Pointers as ditch digging," observed one disgusted Confederate. "A ditch was dug in front of our line of battle which sufficed our day's work. Occasionally through the day there was a little cannonading and picket fighting." John Street of the 9th Texas noted "our troops have been busily engaged building breast works of rocks and logs and now have a line of breast works all along our lines; bullet proof but would prove but little protection from bombs and cannon balls."

When they were not busy digging, the Confederates kept busy gathering abandoned weapons and equipment, assisting the wounded, and burying the dead. "Details buried our dead in ditches dug some two feet deep and putting them in side by side, wrapped in their blankets if they had any with their hats over their faces," wrote W. E. Mathews Preston of the 33rd Alabama. "We did not carry them far, often burying them singly or two or three together near where they fell and there were many who in expressing the fact that a man had been killed would say

---

20 OR 20/1:443; Cope, *The 15th Ohio*, 239.

21 Gates, *The Rough Side of War*, 39; Ward Diary, 84.

that 'he hit the dirt.' We exchanged our cedar canteens on the battlefield with the cloth-covered, oval-shaped Yankee canteens and those who had not picked up a U.S. blanket, a good black hat, blue overcoat, or shelter tent could usually buy such cheap if needed from men who had more than one."[22]

George Morris of the 81st Indiana also performed this sad task of battlefield burial. "The fatigue party came around with picks and shovels and gathered up the Union dead in one row and the Secesh dead in another," he wrote. "When they got a good pile together, they would dig trenches and put in the Union soldiers with a board at the head and a name on it if known. If the dead were not thick, they would bury them singly always putting the name up if known. We laid the dead Rebels in rows on the flat of their backs with no covering over them. I saw one boy not more than 14 years old, neatly dressed, lying as naturally as if he had fallen asleep. His features were as calm and tranquil as if slumbering on his mother's knee with his left arm thrown under his head. Had I met him in the wood in time of peace, I should have thought some poor tired boy had laid down to sleep, but a little purple stream oozing from his breast explained it all."[23]

The memories of the dead haunted the living. Colonel Dodge of the 30th Indiana remembered that morning he was "just beginning to comprehend the terrible losses we sustained yesterday. In the excitement of battle, you have no time to deplore the loss of a friend. Your best friend may be killed by your side, and you pay no more attention to it than if his existence was a matter of the most utter indifference to you. It is afterward that you miss them."[24]

*   *   *

The uncertainty surrounding Federal intentions continued to worry Bragg, and by late morning he ordered Hardee to stage a reconnaissance to test the rumors that Rosecrans was retreating. Hardee assigned the job to Cleburne, directing the Irishman to "ascertain the true state of affairs in our front." Cleburne directed Liddell to move his brigade along with Lieutenant Harvey Shannon's Warren Light Artillery north to the vicinity of the Burris Farm along Asbury Road. Liddell's advance started a skirmish, one shot dangerously wounding Lt. Col. Feaster

---

22 Dixie, *Fayetteville Observer*, Jan. 15, 1863, 1; Street Letters; Preston Letter.

23 Corporal George W. Morris, Co. H, 81st Indiana, *New Albany Daily Ledger*, Jan. 21, 1863, 2.

24 Colonel Joseph B. Dodge, 30th Indiana, "What I Saw at Stones River," *Northern Indianian*, March 11, 1875, 1.

Cameron commanding the 6th/7th Arkansas. "The enemy's skirmishers appeared before the entire front of our right wing, their heavy columns not far behind but they seemed afraid to risk an engagement," noted Captain Inskeep of the 17th Ohio.

While infantry on both sides peppered away at each other, Shannon moved his battery to within 800 yards of Overall's Creek and opened fire on the Federal traffic moving along the Nashville Pike. This fire "greatly disturbed the enemy's trains" but did little to divulge the Federal position. Captain Valentine McGehee of the 2nd Arkansas agreed, noting that "nothing satisfactory resulted, only a little artillery duel ensued." Hardee, in fact, complained to Cleburne that he could not hear his guns. That, combined with a request from Liddell for support on his right, prompted Cleburne to order forward S.A.M. Wood's Brigade.[25]

Wood received his orders about 2:00 that afternoon and dutifully moved north until he, too, crossed Asbury Road—only to find himself alone, as Liddell had inexplicably fallen back and Wood now dangerously exposed. Corporal William Austin of the 22nd Illinois saw Wood's men "stealing along our front towards a cluster of buildings for the purpose of standing picket. The word was passed up and down the line not to fire but wait for orders and let the enemy get close. When they were within 200 yards of us, a battery commenced shelling them and the infantry sent a shower of bullets at them. They stood this kind of work a little while and then they began to hide and run back to their lines."[26]

The hot reception surprised Wood. "As soon as we had shown ourselves in the field, a terrific fire of shell, grape, shot, and Minie balls fell around us," he wrote in his after-action report. The gunners of Captain Josiah Church's 4th Michigan Battery blasted at Wood's men advancing infantry. "Church placed his guns in the most commanding positions, and, whenever the opportunity offered, the most destructive fire I ever witnessed from artillery was poured upon the Rebel masses as they thickened upon the margin of the opposite woods," recalled Colonel Walker. "I watched the progress and observed the effect of my own shot and saw the Rebel masses torn down and scattered before it like leaves before a storm." Wood's right-flank regiments, the 3rd Confederate and 45th Mississippi, drove the Federals from a group of outhouses on the Burris farm while "the enemy poured a

---

25 *OR* 20/1:849; Inskeep Diary; McGehee Diary.

26 Austin Letter.

perfect hailstorm of canister and grape upon us," recorded Lieutenant Colonel Richard Charlton of the 45th Mississippi.[27]

Wood soon saw a brigade of Federals moving around his left flank—it proved to be Colonel William Gibson leading the 1,300 survivors of Willich's old brigade in Johnson's division. All afternoon, these men had been marching circularly to and from Overall's Creek. "We did this a number of times for the purpose of giving the Rebels the impression that we were receiving reinforcements," Cope recalled. "We were a nervous lot although we made a bluff of seeming as brave as ever. When we were making one of these marches, a single musket ball from the enemy's lines came singing over our heads and every man in line ducked his head as it passed, which caused a general laugh." In a bit of supremely fortuitous timing, Rosecrans directed Gibson to reconnoiter toward Asbury Lane to gauge Bragg's intentions just as Wood's men approached the Federal lines near the Burris Farm.[28]

With an aroused Federal line on his front and a brigade sweeping by on his left, Wood recognized the perils of his position and sought orders to retire before matters worsened. As he galloped toward Cleburne to explain what he faced, Wood encountered Captain D. G. White of Hardee's staff, who ordered the Alabamian to fall back. The recall arrived too late for some of Wood's men, however. Spotting a portion of Wood's command skulking in the rocks, Bradley sent out a patrol from the 27th Illinois to capture them. Bradley's men scooped up two lieutenants and 117 men, among them F. M. Martin of the 45th Mississippi. "The right of our regiment got cut off from the main line and pressed up to some cribs where we were subjected to an artillery fire of shot and shell, after which they sent out a detachment which whipped around and captured us," Martin wrote. "We were within 300 yards of Rosecrans' headquarters and the Yanks were terribly excited." However excited the Federals might have been, they clearly were showing plenty of fight. "It was now clear the enemy was still in force in my front, and I so reported it," Cleburne later stated laconically.[29]

Unaware of what had occurred in the fields on his left, Gibson continued his reconnaissance. His men reached Cleburne's extreme left flank, with Gibson reporting that he reached the woods south of Asbury Road "unobserved" before

---

27 OR 20/1:443, 907.

28 Cope, *The 15th Ohio*, 239-40.

29 OR 20/1:371, 849, 899; Yeary, *Reminiscences*, 465. Captain William Wiles reported that the army captured 56 members of the 3rd Confederate and 94 of the 45th Mississippi during the battle. Most were captured on January 1.

running into cavalry videttes and sharpshooters. He "discovered the enemy massing his infantry under the cover of these woods with the apparent design of attacking our extreme right."

Another member of Gibson's command noted that "we discovered immense bodies of the enemy's infantry and artillery approaching, preceded by cavalry which made one dash upon us and were handsomely repulsed." What Gibson likely saw was Wood's Brigade returning from its own brief but bloody reconnaissance; Cleburne had no intention of striking the Federal line again regardless of how ominous matters appeared to Gibson. Regardless, the Ohioan prudently headed back to Union lines under moderate shellfire from enemy artillery, losing just one man wounded. He then reported to Rosecrans that Bragg was preparing to strike the Union right near the Nashville Pike. This erroneous report set off a series of movements on the Federal side, including the recall of the Regular Brigade, which had been sent toward Stewart's Creek earlier that afternoon in response to Wheeler's attack on the supply train near La Vergne.[30]

As the armies settled in for the night, Colonel Dodge received a welcome dinner invitation from fellow brigade commander Colonel Walker, who conveyed that he had "nothing but fresh beef to eat." Walker's cook, continued Dodge,

> had told him that he had got some somewhere. I thought it strange that he should have the beef but told him that as I had nothing but hard tack and coffee we might mess together for once, a proposition which he promptly accepted. The savory smell that was arising from four or five great big, fine-looking round steaks that were broiling on a bed of coals, was simply delicious, and in a few moments the cook handed each of us one of them on a large cedar chip that served as a plate, a piece of hard bread, and a tin cup full of coffee, and we had a glorious feast.

By the time the men had eaten the second steak, the two officers began to wonder where the cook could possibly have found cattle surrounded by an army of hungry soldiers. "After a good deal of coaxing and a promise of immunity from harm," explained Dodge, "the cook acknowledged that he had cut it out of the ham of a dead horse that had been killed the day before: but it was good any way, and we had had a splendid supper."[31]

---

30 OR 20/1:306; Cope, *The 15th Ohio*, 240.

31 Dodge, "What I Saw."

While Dodge and Walker dined on horsemeat, others considered the desperation of their plight and considered withdrawal. Captain Alexander Stevenson of the 42nd Illinois relayed an intriguing story in his history of the battle concerning the shaky Federal morale that night. One division commander "grew faint hearted and was inclined to retreat to Nashville." The unnamed general spoke with one of his brigade commanders and said "this army is whipped. The Rebels are between us and Nashville and the only thing to do now is to cut our way through. Someone has to take the lead and I want you to do it tomorrow." The unnamed brigade commander disagreed, stating that the army would whip the Confederates and then challenged the general, asking him if he had discussed his proposed course of action with Rosecrans. He had not but ordered his subordinate to be ready to cut his way to Nashville tomorrow. The brigade commander went to another brigade commander within the division and learned that the division commander had given him those same orders. When asked what he was going to do, the brigade commander responded, "[I]f he orders me to desert the balance of this army and run away to Nashville, I'll arrest him as a traitor and march him under guard to General Rosecrans' headquarters."[32]

The sun set that night with few changes in the position of either army. Augustus McDonnell of the 1st Florida gazed over the field with melancholy. "I am sad tonight," he confessed in his diary. "While I write, the reverberations of distant cannon break upon my ear and denote in deep toned language the fearful carnage of yesterday. The battlefield is still strewn with the enemy's dead, their bland eyes and distorted features show in what agony they died. Among this beautiful forest wreck are the graves of the noble dead. They have passed from earth, but their memories are embalmed in the hearts of a grateful people, and when the springtime comes, the daisy and violet will spring up and spread their sweet fragrance over their moldering forms. The blue bird will warble his song of love, and the gentle zephyrs chant a requiem to the heroes of the past."[33]

Bragg watched the sun set with the fulsome praise of General Joe Johnston ringing in his ears. Telegraphing from Jackson, Mississippi, where he kept close watch on the developments at Vicksburg, Johnston messaged, "I congratulate you on your glorious termination of last year." Bragg's dispatch proclaiming victory at Murfreesboro caused exaltation in Richmond, already bursting with enthusiasm

---

32 Stevenson, *Battle of Stone's River*, 125-26. It is unfortunate Stevenson did not provide specifics about who the actors were in this episode. It may have been Richard Johnson.

33 McDonnell Letters.

Second Lieutenant Augustus O. McDonnell,
Co. K, 1st Florida

William Griffing Collection

over the recent successes of Confederate arms. "A dispatch from Bragg which put us almost beside ourselves with joy and caused even enemies to pause and shake hands in the streets," recorded War Department clerk John B. Jones. "Yesterday he attacked Rosecrans' army near Murfreesboro and gained a great victory. He says he drove him from all his positions except on the extreme left and after ten hours' fighting occupied the whole of the field. We had, as trophies, 31 guns, two generals, 4,000 prisoners, and 200 wagons. This is a western dispatch, it is true, but it has Bragg's name on it and he does not willingly exaggerate."[34]

Bragg's apparent victory completed a trifecta of recent Confederate triumphs: Fredericksburg, Chickasaw Bayou, and now Murfreesboro. The *Weekly Mississippian* called it "a happy termination of the old year 1862 and ushers in the new year under more cheering auspices." Those seeking concrete proof of this exulted when several trainloads of Federal prisoners soon arrived in Chattanooga.

The initial reports by Bragg fed widespread reports in the press that Rosecrans was retreating to Nashville. "As the clouds clear away, we become more and more convinced of the completeness of the victory," opined the *Chattanooga Daily Rebel*. "Rosecrans will fall back upon the defenses of Nashville. Whether he can remain in that city with an army routed and demoralized, his communication cut off, and with the promise of a sudden rise in the Cumberland is a matter which time or General Braxton Bragg may decide." The correspondent for the *Mobile Register* asserted that

---

34 OR 20/2:475; Jones, *A Rebel War Clerk's Diary*, 144-45.

"the enemy being cut off from supplies must either retreat tomorrow or make a desperate fight."[35]

Wheeler's and Wharton's commands rode back into the army's lines well after midnight January 2 "greatly exhausted from long continued service with but little rest or food," Bragg reported. Their boasts of success along the Nashville Pike only reinforced Bragg's perception that Rosecrans's army was on the cusp of retreat. "This faulty intelligence from Wheeler helped Bragg form the decision to firmly hold his position and gave him the impression only a little more pressure would cause Rosecrans to rapidly withdraw," argued historian Dennis Belcher. The men and horses, having been in action now for nearly a week straight with barely a spare moment, desperately needed time to rest and refit. Bragg's shortage of cavalry, however, gave him no luxury to grant the hard-riding troopers more than a few hours respite before they were called into service again. Shortly after daylight, Wharton's men rode off to the army's right to reinforce Pegram's undermanned brigade in guarding the Lebanon Road approach to Murfreesboro, and Wheeler was ordered to prepare to stage another raid on Rosecrans's supply line.[36]

*   *   *

"Friday morning was raw and chilly but the clouds soon dispersed and the sun glowed pleasantly," was William Bickham's description of January 2, 1863. For the Federals, though, the day would be one of watchful waiting and, unfortunately, gnawing hunger. The rations issued at Nashville ran out, with the men scrounging or begging what they could from their comrades. Many soldiers reported that they were subsisting on corn cobs or their last bits of fried pork and hardtack. In the Federal center, an officer's magnificent horse lay dead just outside of the lines. Aware of his men's suffering, Rousseau rode along the lines, saying, "Boys, there is a good fat horse lying up here that was killed this morning." His hungry men took the hint, and a daring few stole into the field to cut horse steaks from the corpse.

"General Rosecrans still persisted in his scheme of wheeling into Murfreesboro with his left and directed his attention chiefly to the position

---

35 "The news from Murfreesboro," *Weekly Mississippian*, Jan. 7, 1863, 2; "The Situation," *Chattanooga Daily Rebel*, Jan. 4, 1863, 2; "Letter from Middle Tennessee," *Mobile Advertiser & Register*, Jan. 9, 1863, 1.

36 Dennis W. Belcher, *The Cavalries at Stones River: An Analytical History* (Jefferson, 2017), 229-30.

occupied by Beatty," Bickham noted. The wagons that ran Wheeler's gauntlet yesterday were not the prelude to a general retreat as Wheeler had reported. They were sent back to Nashville to collect a supply of ammunition and provisions to continue the battle. Rosecrans expected the first detachment of wagons to rejoin his army late Friday or early Saturday morning along with reinforcements from the Nashville garrison. Once they arrived, he intended to assume the offensive, with Beatty's division the vanguard of that assault.[37]

At dawn the Confederate skirmishers again pushed into the fields to ascertain any changes in the Federal position. They discovered that the 51st Indiana of Harker's brigade had reoccupied the Round Forest with skirmishers; this time, however, the Confederates had ample artillery in place to contest control of this patch of woods. During the night, four batteries from Cheatham's Division (Carnes's, Scott's, Smith's, and Stanford's) rolled into position a little to the north of the Cowan House on a slight rise of ground within 400 yards of the Federal lines. Carnes's guns held the far right near Stones River, Stanford's Battery to Carnes's left, Turner's Mississippians just to the right of the railroad, and Scott's Tennesseans to the railroad's left. Captain Felix Robertson's six-gun battery, recovered from its roughing up on the night of December 30, took position just north of the Cowan House.

"[T]he spot on which the battery was placed had on the first day of the battle been the scene of a desperate conflict," recalled Lieutenant Lucius Marshall of Carnes's Battery. "The place was horrible; the horses shied and snorted as they picked their way among the prostrate bodies in the early morning darkness." The five batteries totaling 22 guns represented the largest concentration of Confederate artillery thus far in the battle. With White's Mississippians in support, the Confederates let loose an intense artillery barrage at daylight. "We all opened simultaneously to clear our front of the enemy's sharpshooters, who had reoccupied the woods along our front during the night," Marshall reported.[38]

The intensity of the Confederate fire alarmed the Federals, and the 51st Indiana's skirmishers bolted back to the brigade lines, followed by White's men, who then reoccupied the Round Forest. Three Confederate batteries on Wayne's Hill added their contribution to the din. "At sunrise on the morning of January 2, we were saluted with a shower of solid balls from the enemy's batteries, falling in too close a vicinity to be agreeable," reported Lieutenant Alanson Stevens of

37 Bickham, *Rosecrans' Campaign*, 306-07.

38 OR 20/1:581, 722; Smith, *Stones River: Confederate Army*, 500.

Independent Battery B, Pennsylvania Light Artillery (also known as Muehler's Battery or Stevens' Battery). Alfred Wade of the 73rd Indiana wrote that "they opened a terrific fire upon us and for half an hour the scene was grand beyond description. The Rebels had obtained accurate range and the famous Washington battery from New Orleans played upon us with round shot and shell until the air was perfectly alive with death-dealing missiles. Soon a caisson with six frightened horses attached dashed back to the rear all the riders having been disabled. The wildest confusion reigned."[39]

For the Confederate artillery, it marked a rare contribution to the battle. "We had a lively time during the day shelling the enemy's sharpshooters from the woods and engaging a line of batteries in front," boasted Corporal Butt of Stanford's Battery. "At times, the fire of the enemy was tremendous but being just behind the crest of the hill we suffered but little."

"I amused myself by crawling out among our sharpshooters with an opera glass and taking observations," wrote John Magee of Stanford's Battery. "I was fired on several times, pretty close places sometimes." Long-range Confederate fire from Wayne's Hill pummeled both the 10th Indiana and 8th Indiana; neither battery could return fire at such a range. "I was forced to retire my battery, leaving for the time being two pieces on the field," recalled George Estep. "Some of the horses of one of the limbers were severely wounded and became so badly frightened by the bursting of the enemy's shell that the drivers were unable to control them; they ran to the rear in spite of every effort made to bring them to the piece." Captain Robertson's gunners had a direct fire on Battery B of the 1st Ohio, which also quickly retired from the field.[40]

The retirement of these batteries allowed the Confederate gunners to concentrate their fire on the 6th Ohio Battery and its support, the 13th Michigan. "When the cannonade commenced, the men were ordered to lay down on their arms and in this trying position they were obliged to remain while the balls and shells were flying not over and around them, but within their ranks, killing and wounding their comrades, scattering their blood and brains over the survivors in every direction," recalled Colonel Shoemaker. "This was a most trying ordeal and the severest test of courage and discipline." Captain James Stokes's Chicago Board of Trade Battery, located 250 yards in the rear of Harker's line, mistakenly opened

39 *OR* 20/1:471, 581; Wade Diary.

40 Butt Letter; Diary of John Euclid Magee, Stanford's Mississippi Battery, *ORS* 3: 643; *OR* 20/1:476.

fire with canister, the rounds wreaking havoc not within the Confederate ranks but within the 6th Ohio Battery and the 13th Michigan. "The 13th had been cut up considerably by the enemy's fire and when our own battery opened on us, it was more than they could stand," Wade noted. "They broke and ran, reforming again however and taking position in the rear of us who were protected somewhat from the enemy's fire by the trees."

Stokes quickly halted the firing, but the damage had been done. According to Shoemaker, Captain Cullen Bradley of the 6th Ohio Battery was incensed enough to say "he would prefer charges against the commander of the offending battery, but if he ever did so they were suppressed for the good of the service." Bradley was right to be indignant. In addition to opening a hole in the Union line, the Chicagoans' error wounded four of his men and killed four horses.[41]

After half an hour, however, the Confederates received an order to cease fire and fall back 50 yards to the cover of a nearby crest. Relative quiet, punctuated by the skirmishers popping away at each other, again prevailed in the Federal center. Bragg displayed no intention of following up on this small success with a full-bore infantry attack; a dozen Federal batteries covered the ground and any foray into the open field would end disastrously. Battered but triumphant, the 6th Ohio Battery held its ground, As the gunners rolled their guns back by hand, they were "lustily cheered by us for their brave work" Wade noted.

The Confederate gunners made a good showing and certainly created discomfort for their opponents—Charles Maple of the Chicago Board of Trade Battery calling it "the sharpest artillery practice I ever witnessed." In the end, the noisy 40-minute engagement did little to budge the Federal line, but the increase in activity all along the line presaged matters coming to a head. Colonel Dodge noted that the enemy "are extremely active and evidently trying to find a weak point. Bragg means business now and will get up a fight that will count before night."[42]

*   *   *

With the armies at a stalemate, Bragg needed to find a way to break the impasse if he were to complete his victory. In reconsidering his options, Bragg could not rule out retreat. President Davis had given him permission to do so a few weeks earlier when he said to "fight if you can and fall back beyond the Tennessee." Good

---

41 Shoemaker Memoir; Wade Diary.

42 Maple Letter; Wade Diary; Dodge, "What I Saw."

ground on the banks of the Elk or Duck rivers would be only a day's march to the south. Those lines offered several defensive options that would ultimately allow Bragg to keep control of his vital railroad connection with Chattanooga.

Bragg, however, resisted retreat for three reasons: logistics; the potential negative impact on the army's morale; and the impact on his standing with the Confederate government. If Bragg retreated south to the Highland Rim, he would be unable to supply his army with needed forage and foodstuffs from the area, and, worse, the railroad lacked the rolling stock to make up for the deficiency. Time was of the essence, as prolonged close contact with Rosecrans's army would rapidly deplete the Murfreesboro region of forage, forcing a departure to find a new source of sustenance. Second, morale in the ranks remained high after Wednesday's success, and the men firmly believed they had whipped the Yankees; to order a retreat now after such a victory would stir bad memories of the retreat after the Pyrrhic victory at Perryville. Army morale in turn might buckle under the strain. Finally, Bragg had boxed himself in when he sent his telegram to the government on New Year's Eve in which he all but proclaimed victory. To fall back now would risk humiliation and removal from command. All of these reasons meant Bragg would stay at Murfreesboro, and he needed this battle decided quickly.

To stay, however, meant to fight. Bragg remained convinced that all he needed to do was persuade Rosecrans to retreat. After the hefty casualties of Wednesday, Bragg had fewer than 25,000 men holding the line against Rosecrans, who had roughly 30,000. But the only reliable way his infantry could get at Rosecrans was to attack his right or center along the Nashville Pike, which meant running the gauntlet of Federal batteries again. Cleburne's and McCown's experiences on the afternoon of December 31 showed the prospects of this being successful were slim to none.

His cavalry arm, its effectiveness seriously degraded by the constant activity over the past week, lacked the strength to interdict Rosecrans's supply line. Only a few hundred reinforcements had joined the army since Wednesday, and Bragg had no substantial reserves left to call on; he had to rely on what he had on hand. The general knew that Rosecrans could call upon thousands of reinforcements from Nashville, and eventually the weight of numbers alone, combined with Bragg's steadily worsening supply situation, would force the Confederates to retreat if Rosecrans maintained his position. Again, time would not be a Confederate ally.

"God fights on the side with the best artillery," Napoleon once pronounced, and the Federal artillery arm had repeatedly demonstrated its primacy at Stones River. Nevertheless, as the morning's engagement indicated, the Confederate guns also packed a powerful punch. If he commanded superior ground and could concentrate a powerful contingent of batteries, could Bragg perhaps use his artillery to blast the Federals away? About a half mile north of Wayne's Hill, a high ridge on Stones River's east bank offered the highest ground on the battlefield, and as Colonel George Brent noted in his journal, the ridge "commanded the entire field of battle." By redeploying a substantial portion of his army's artillery batteries to that ridge, he could enfilade Rosecrans's lines and perhaps force the issue of retreat.

Plenty of firepower was available; as a matter of fact, Bragg had more guns than he had gunners after the hefty battlefield captures on Wednesday. Three batteries sat atop nearby Wayne's Hill, and seven batteries were posted in the open fields around the Cowan House. Another eight supported Cleburne's and McCown's divisions farther to the left, though five of those batteries were parked along the Wilkinson Pike, as it was inadvisable to try to move them through the thick cedar forests. It was simply a matter of selecting batteries for the assignment, then moving them to the river's east bank.[43]

Breckinridge, however, suspected that the Federals already occupied the desired ridge. Two members of his staff would recall observing a Federal force east of Stones River on January 1. While passing over the open fields between Hanson's and Palmer's brigades early that morning, Major James Wilson "discovered that the enemy had during the night brought across the river and planted a battery of artillery about 1,500 yards in front of the line we now occupied. I was now convinced that a considerable force of the enemy had been thrown on this side of the river."

Lieutenant Colonel John Buckner concurred, noting that a Federal rifled piece fired on Palmer's Brigade as it marched into position nearby about 10:00 Thursday morning. "This disclosed the fact that the enemy had thrown a body of troops across the river and the movement was evidently intended to protect the point against which his left flank was then resting," he wrote. It defies belief to think that both of these staff officers had seen these Federals east of the river on Thursday and not informed Breckinridge. That neither Breckinridge nor Pegram made any report to Bragg about the force is similarly perplexing.[44]

Regardless, on Friday morning, Captain William Bramblett, commanding a company of pickets from the 4th Kentucky, crawled within a hundred yards of the

---

43 Diary of Colonel George Brent, Braxton Bragg Papers, Western Reserve Historical Society.

44 Reports from Lt. Col. John A. Buckner and Major James Wilson, John C. Breckinridge Papers, Manuscript Department, New York Historical Society.

Federal lines to observe dispositions. The fact that Rosecrans had so little artillery east of the river convinced the captain that the Union commander was baiting a trap. A second captain soon confirmed Bramblett's observation; two members of Breckinridge's staff accompanied a detachment from the Washington Light Artillery forward to test the Federal line and quickly became convinced there was power behind the skirmish line.

The reports compelled Breckinridge to make a personal reconnaissance of the ground. He initially rode toward Stones River accompanied by Polk and Hardee, but those generals returned to headquarters, leaving Breckinridge to complete the excursion with three members of his staff (including his son, Cabell) and Captain William Pickett, Hardee's inspector general. The Kentuckian ordered two companies of skirmishers from Hanson's Brigade to push forward and flesh out the Federals. "The reconnaissance showed there were no troops of any kind in sight though the hill was of sufficient prominence to hide from view a considerable force," Pickett recalled. "The fact that a picket line was in front was prima facie evidence of such a force being ready to defend it."[45]

But the army needed more than prima facie evidence. It needed solid proof. Lieutenant Colonel John Buckner on Breckinridge's staff proposed to drive away the Federals with a strong combat patrol consisting of troops from the 18th and 45th Tennessee in Palmer's Brigade. Such a move would reveal the Yankees' strength or prove merely a skirmish line was there. Major Rice Graves, Breckinridge's chief of artillery, accompanied two sections of the Washington Light Artillery with the patrol. As they rolled through Hanson's Kentuckians, the burly Palmer called to Graves, "Why are you taking that battery so far in front?" Graves called back, "These boys will go anywhere."

By 11:00 a.m., Palmer reported they had encountered a "very heavy line of Federal skirmishers." The Federals of Price's and Fyffe's brigades were posted 400–500 yards in front of the ridge while some of the men took cover behind a few scattered log cabins at the edge of the woods. "We remained a couple of hours doing some fancy practice," recalled Lieutenant William Vaught of the Washington Light Artillery.[46]

With his battery atop the ridge, Lieutenant Livingston had his hands full trying to fend off the Confederate artillery all morning. His Badgers had dodged shells

---

45 OR 20/1:784-785; Pickett Article, 452.

46 OR 20/1:805; "Memories of Major Rice E. Graves," Lieutenant Joseph Chalaron, Washington Light Artillery, *Daviess County Historical Quarterly*, Vol. 3, No. 1 (1985), 3.

fired from Wayne's Hill since 9:00 a.m., and now he had Vaught's Louisianans firing into his right flank. Another battery soon started to fire on his left. "We found it very dangerous to remain there," he reported. One gunner remembered that "we had a splendid time to note the different sounds produced by the different kinds of shot in their swift passage through the air—the screaming whiz of the shell, the sharp twang of solid shot, and the zip of the bullets. By hugging the ground close, the enemy's shots passed over our heads."[47]

Confederate artillery shells shivered the flagstaff of the 8th Kentucky and killed or wounded about a dozen Federals. "Our advanced position made us an especial target for their artillery while the skirmish balls kept up that ominous singing," wrote Captain Thomas Wright of the 8th Kentucky. The skirmishers surged back and forth throughout the afternoon with neither side gaining a decided advantage. Pummeled by multiple batteries, Colonel Beatty ordered Livingston to withdraw from the ridge, much to the consternation of his infantry. "About 1 p.m. the Rebel artillery commenced throwing shells among us, greatly to our annoyance," reported Lt. Col. James Evans of the 21st Kentucky. "At this time our artillery was withdrawn to the opposite side of the river, to the astonishment of all. It seems that our little brigade had been forgotten, or was left there all alone to be sacrificed, in order to draw the enemy on, which latter turned out to be the case."[48]

Before noon, Bragg learned from his chief of staff George Brent that the Federals had indeed crossed the river. Brent and Captain Robertson, sent by Bragg to scout the best ground on which to place his artillery, stumbled across a firefight between Breckinridge's skirmishers and Beatty's men. "Reconnaissance by several staff officers soon developed the fact that a division had quietly crossed unopposed and established themselves on and under cover of an eminence from which Lieutenant General Polk's line was both commanded and enfiladed," Bragg noted. The ridge commanded the area around the Round Forest that constituted the center of Bragg's line now held by three brigades. "The dislodgment of this force or the withdrawal of Polk's line was an evident necessity" Bragg declared. "The latter involved consequences not to be entertained."

If Federal possession of that ridge continued, Polk's position would become untenable, leaving him no option but to fall back. Polk's retirement would also require Hardee to abandon the cedars, thus leaving the entire Confederate position

---

47 *OR* 20/1:582, 613; Jericho, 3rd Wisconsin Battery, *Wisconsin State Journal,* Jan. 26, 1863, 2.

48 Thomas L. Wright, *History of the Eighth Regiment Kentucky Vol. Inf. During Its Three Years Campaigns* (St. Joseph, 1880), 128; *OR* 20/1:613.

at Murfreesboro in tatters. In Bragg's view, taking the ridge was a must or the army at Murfreesboro was finished.[49]

Breckinridge received Bragg's summons at about noon. Riding back to the river's west bank, he met Bragg in camp beneath a large sycamore tree. What happened at this conference is open to debate. "Prefacing his orders with the remark that as his division had not been much engaged in the battle of Wednesday, Bragg's orders to Breckinridge were that a vigorous attack on the position just reconnoitered should be carried, held, and strongly fortified having in view the positions for four field batteries," Pickett claimed.

Accounts differ from there. Reportedly, Breckinridge protested, claiming that McFadden's Heights commanded the ridge he was being tasked to secure and the attack would result in the destruction of his command. The Kentuckian then picked up a stick and began laying out the dispositions of his command and the Federals. "Sir, my information is different," countered a testy Bragg. "I have given the order to attack the enemy in your front and expect it to be obeyed." The stunned former vice president, "shocked but helpless" stood in mute silence as Bragg explained the remainder of the assault plan. "Considerable time was occupied in their discussion, but General Bragg remained firm and ordered Breckinridge to proceed," Stevenson would write.[50]

Neither Breckinridge nor Pickett make any mention of a protest in their accounts of this conference. "My impression is that General Bragg had already determined to make the attack as he at once commenced explaining the order of attack," Pickett recalled. Breckinridge would attack with his entire division while Wharton's and Pegram's cavalry, roughly 2,000 troopers, would cover Breckinridge's right. Bragg also assigned 10 guns under the Robertson's command as additional artillery support.

Bragg indicated the attack would commence at 4:00 p.m., late enough in the day to prevent a Federal counterattack but giving the Confederates "ample time to

---

49 OR 20/1:667-668.

50 Pickett article, 452; William C. Davis, *Breckinridge: Statesman, Soldier, Symbol* (Lexington, 2010), 340; Stevenson, *Battle of Stone's River,* 131. The historical basis for the story of Breckinridge's dramatic protest comes from the pen of Colonel Theodore O'Hara, a member of Breckinridge's staff and former editor of the *Mobile Register.* Bragg and O'Hara shared a long dislike because the former had dismissed O'Hara from the army early in the war, describing him as "a drunken loafer from Mobile." O'Hara returned the favor by leaking reports critical of Bragg to his old friends in the newspaper business until he was again booted from the army in March 1863.

fortify," Pickett noted. "Breckinridge began at once to make the necessary preparations for carrying out the battle." Breckinridge reported simply that Bragg gave him "an order to form my division in two lines and take the crest with the infantry. After doing this I was to bring up the artillery and establish it on the crest, so as at once to hold it and enfilade the enemy's lines on the other side of the river."[51]

The key premise of Breckinridge's supposed protest was that McFadden's Heights commanded the ridge he was directed to seize (what we will call here "Beatty's Ridge"). That, one historian argued, made his attack "senseless" and "an insane order." But was it?[52]

First, according to the US Geological Survey, Beatty's Ridge (the objective) is 586 feet above sea level, but the highest point of McFadden's Heights is 554 feet—or 32 feet shorter.

Second, Bragg's detractors have repeatedly argued about the folly of sending Breckinridge's Division against a position defended by 58 Federal guns. None of those batteries commanded Beatty's Ridge. Instead, they swept the cornfield in the river plain north of Beatty's Ridge—a key point, as we will soon see.

Most of these batteries, however, were not in position until late in the afternoon January 2. "It has been stated that Generals Bragg and Breckinridge knew of this massing of artillery," Pickett later wrote. "I feel sure this statement is not correct and am further of the opinion that the attack would not have been made had this fact been known."

Bragg's proposed attack was not a tactical absurdity, but a tactical imperative. The ridge represented the highest ground on the battlefield, and its control was crucial to the army's continued presence at Murfreesboro.[53]

Victory or defeat hung in the balance.

---

51 Pickett Article, 452; *OR* 20/1:785.

52 Davis, *The Orphan Brigade*, 159, 160.

53 Pickett Article, 453.

Beacons of the Grave:
Breckinridge's Doomed Assault

IT WAS NOW past 2:00 p.m. on January 2. John C. Breckinridge had less than two hours to prepare his division for the assault. Two of his brigades—Adams's (now led by Colonel Randall Gibson) and Preston's—had to make a hasty two-mile march from their positions west of Stones River to the northern slope of Wayne's Hill. The soldiers, though, did not suspect they were being sent back into combat. "Colonel William Miller of the 1st Florida rode along our lines and told us to fall in as we were going to move from there and were to be relieved by another brigade," wrote one soldier. "We did so with cheerful hearts as that had been quite a warm place for us. We left there and were going back as all thought to the rear for a rest as we had not slept for three days and two nights. We marched on for about two and a half miles towards the right of our line of battle and there we found our division in line, facing the enemy, and waiting for us."[1]

As Preston approached at the head of his column, Breckinridge pulled the brigadier aside, telling him the "attack is made against my judgment and by the special orders of General Bragg. Of course, we all must try to do our duty and fight the best we can. If it should result in disaster and I be among the slain, I want you to do justice to my memory and tell the people that I believed this attack to be very

---

1 P.S.S., *Macon Beacon*, Feb. 25, 1863, 2.

Major General John C. Breckinridge

Library of Congress

unwise and tried to prevent it." With those gloomy words, Breckinridge rode off and Preston began to form his men.[2]

Bragg had few reinforcements for Breckinridge, but in the early afternoon he sent him Brig. Gen. Gideon Pillow, newly arrived on the field. The 56-year-old Pillow was a former law partner of President James Polk who in 1846-48 fought as a brigadier in Polk's war with Mexico, where he was wounded twice. When the Civil War began, Pillow sided with the South and was commissioned the senior general of Tennessee's provisional army, and served as Leonidas Polk's second in command at Belmont, Missouri, in November 1861.

Pillow briefly held the reins at Fort Donelson in February 1862, but with Confederate surrender near the morning of February 16 he controversially handed command over to Brig. Gen. Simon Buckner and fled the fort along with Maj. Gen. John Floyd. Pillow's behavior at Fort Donelson understandably ruined his reputation, and the now-untrusted Tennessean bounced from assignment to assignment in the Western Theater until his appearance at Murfreesboro on January 2. He had begged Bragg for a command and a chance to redeem himself, so Bragg sent him to Breckinridge, who would place him at the head of Colonel Joseph Palmer's Second Brigade. "A liar, intriguer, and almost wholly incompetent, Pillow could only claim high connections in Richmond," offered historian William Davis. "Breckinridge did not attempt to conceal his displeasure at this change in his command."[3]

<hr>

2 Stevenson, *Battle of Stone's River*, 132.

3 Warner, *Generals in Gray*, 241; Davis, *Breckinridge*, 342.

Breckinridge arrayed his four brigades, totaling roughly 5,600 men, in two lines under the cover of woods on the northern slopes of Wayne's Hill. The front line consisted of Pillow's brigade (roughly 1,400 men) on the right and Hanson's 1,800-man Orphan Brigade on the left. Deployed in a single line, Pillow's command featured, from right to left, the 18th Tennessee, 26th Tennessee, 28th Tennessee, and 45th Tennessee, and the Orphan Brigade formed in two lines, with the 2nd Kentucky on the left nearest Stones River, the 4th Kentucky at center, and the 41st Alabama on the right. The 6th Kentucky supported the 2nd Kentucky, and the 9th Kentucky remained on Wayne's Hill supporting Cobb's Kentucky Battery.

Breckinridge's second line featured the commands rushed east of the river that morning: Gibson's and Preston's brigades. Gibson's force, roughly 900 men, arrived first and filed into line about 150 yards behind Hanson, with the 13th/20th Louisiana on the right and the 16th/25th Louisiana the left. About 300 men from the 32nd Alabama and 14th Louisiana Sharpshooters, meanwhile, stayed behind to support a section of Lumden's Battery on Stones River's eastern bank.

Preston's 1,500-man brigade arrived shortly thereafter and assumed a supporting position about 300 yards behind Pillow. Preston placed the brigade on a single line—from right to left, the 20th Tennessee, 60th North Carolina, 4th Florida, and 1st/3rd Florida. Minus skirmishers and units left behind as artillery support, Breckinridge's assault force totaled about 4,700 men.[4]

The time constraint inevitably amplified the confusion. Bragg informed Breckinridge that Wharton's and Pegram's cavalry were "to protect my right and cooperate in the attack," but Wharton would insist he never received orders regarding an attack, and though Pegram apparently did receive orders, he failed to move. Apparently, Breckinridge also did not notify Pillow that the cavalry would support his right.

There was trouble, too, with the artillery. Captain Felix Robertson arrived with his battery's six guns as well as four belonging to Lumsden's Battery. Robertson's understanding of Bragg's order was "to wait until the infantry had crowned the crest, and then to rush up and occupy it," though Breckinridge clearly felt differently. "He supposed it was to be made by a combination of both arms, while I was positive the general's orders were that infantry alone should take the hill," Robertson recalled. "General Breckinridge then desired me to form my batteries in

4 The makeup of Breckinridge's assault brigades was (approximately) as follows: Pillow (1,400), Hanson (1,200), Preston (1,500), and Gibson (perhaps 600). Another way to visualize the attack was 2,600 infantry in the first wave and 2,100 in the second. The various artillery batteries attached to the advance added perhaps 400–500 men to the overall count.

the space between his two lines of infantry and advance. This I declined to do, stating as a reason the danger both of confusion and loss from such an arrangement. He then desired me to form and advance behind his second line of infantry." Robertson refused to comply with that also.

Breckinridge believed Robertson was subject to his orders. Robertson, however, insisted that he reported directly to Bragg, and Breckinridge eventually tired of arguing with the captain, leaving him to do as he wished and instead ordering Major Rice Graves, his chief of artillery, to accompany the assault with the division's batteries. Accordingly, Wright's Tennessee Battery fell in behind Preston's line, Anderson's Georgia Battery in the center, and the Washington Light Artillery behind their fellow Louisianans of Gibson's brigade.[5]

The Federals on Beatty's Ridge readily spotted Breckinridge's preparations. As Lt. Col. Richard McLain of the 51st Ohio wrote, "[W]e could distinctly see in the distance large bodies of infantry forming in our front and moving to our left, accompanied by artillery and cavalry." McLain sent couriers to apprise General Thomas Crittenden and Colonel Samuel Beatty of these movements, and then more after that once Breckinridge's men moved out. "They advanced to within between 600 and 800 yards of our front and halted and commenced throwing down a line of fence running parallel to our line," he wrote. "I immediately directed Adjutant William Nicholas to report the fact, and he informed Major Lyne Starling of the enemy's movements, as well as the brigade and division commanders that the enemy were in the act of attacking us." Beatty instructed Price "to let his first line fall back behind the crest of the hill but before he could receive them the enemy was advancing across the field at a charge."[6]

By the time McLain sent this last report about 3:30 p.m., abundant Federal reinforcements were already close. West of Stones River, Cruft's brigade of about 800 men remained in position along McFadden's Heights supporting George Swallow's six-gun 7th Indiana Battery. Lieutenant Charles Parsons and the eight guns of Batteries H and M, 4th US Light, lay right of Swallow's guns along the ridge. Battery F, 1st Ohio Light, now under Lieutenant Norval Osburn's command, held Parsons' right with another five guns.

---

5 *OR* 20/1:759-760, 785-786. The four guns of Captain Edward Byrne's Kentucky battery would also be attached to Robertson's special command, giving Robertson 14 guns in total. With 10 12-pounder Napoleons, two 3-inch Parrott Rifles, and two 12-pounder howitzers, Robertson's command packed quite a punch.

6 Stevenson, *Battle of Stone's River*, 132; *OR* 20/1:577, 615.

Negley's division received orders about 1:00 p.m. to march to McFadden's Ford to support Beatty. His two brigades accompanied by the three divisional batteries arrived about 2:30, taking position a few hundred yards to Cruft's left rear. The 1,400 men of Colonel Miller's brigade went into position on the left while Colonel Stanley's brigade of approximately 1,300 men took the right. Negley brought only six guns to McFadden's Heights. A Parrott rifle belonging to Lieutenant Alban A. Ellsworth's Battery B, 1st Kentucky Light, went into position alongside the two surviving guns of Lieutenant Alexander Marshall's Battery G, 1st Ohio—all three assuming a place on Swallow's left. Captain Frederick Schultz's Battery M, 1st Ohio, went left of Marshall with three guns, giving the Federals 25 guns on McFadden Heights, supported by approximately 3,500 infantrymen.[7]

The Federal forces defending Beatty's Ridge across the river were also substantial, totaling about 2,800 infantrymen. Colonel Price's 1,800-man brigade held the right of the ridge, its front line consisting of, from right to left, the 51st Ohio, the 8th Kentucky, and the 35th Indiana. On the second line, the 99th Ohio supported the 51st Ohio and the 21st Kentucky supported both the 8th Kentucky and the 35th Indiana. Roughly 1,000 men in Fyffe's brigade held the left, with the 44th Indiana on the right and the 13th Ohio the left. The 79th Indiana from Grider's brigade lay tucked between the 44th Indiana and 35th Indiana. The 59th Ohio held a supporting position behind the 44th Indiana and 13th Ohio, and the 86th Indiana deployed to the left of the 59th Ohio, positioned to provide cover for the front line.

Colonel Benjamin Grider, now commanding Samuel Beatty's old brigade of about 1,100 men, positioned his three remaining regiments in a single line a few hundred yards behind Price and Fyffe—from right to left, the 19th Ohio, the 9th Kentucky, and the 11th Kentucky. Grose moved his roughly 1,000-man brigade across McFadden's Ford in the early afternoon and took a position near the ford guarding the left rear of Beatty's line. The Ohioan arrayed his brigade in three lines, with the 23rd Kentucky in front about 200 yards behind the 59th Ohio of Fyffe's brigade. The 24th Ohio assumed a position 300 yards to the rear of the Kentuckians, and the 36th Indiana set up to the Ohioans' left rear.

Meanwhile, the 6th Ohio and 84th Illinois took reserve positions at the river crossing, and the 3rd Wisconsin Battery—the only Federal artillery east of Stones River—unlimbered on the river bluff slightly to those regiments' left rear. Grose took the precaution of ordering his men to construct rough field fortifications from

---

7 OR 20/1:408, 412, 415, 433, 528, 579.

logs, brush, and stone. Grider's and Grose's brigades meant that 2,100 Federals were in supporting positions a few hundred yards behind Beatty's Ridge, giving Beatty about 4,900 men east of the river, almost the same number as in Breckinridge's assault column.[8]

*   *   *

Breckinridge made the effort to explain the assault plan directly to each of his brigade commanders. Lieutenant Colonel John Buckner of Breckinridge's staff recalled that "the plan of attack … was for the artillery to move in the rear of the second line and as soon as the hill was cleared of the enemy to take position on the crest and hold it." Once forming his brigades into line, Breckinridge rode in front atop his white charger to address the men. "He made a short but eloquent speech," recalled one veteran. "He said, 'When I give the command 'Forward' I do not wish to see a man falter. All I want you to do is follow me and do as I command you to.' We then gave him three cheers. He replaced his hat, turned his horse's head to the front, drew his sword and gave the command 'Forward, men!'"

Hanson rode to his command, then turned to Colonel Joseph Lewis of the 6th Kentucky. "Colonel, the order is to load, fix bayonets, and march through this brushwood," he said. "Then charge at the double quick to within a hundred yards of the enemy, deliver fire, and go at him with the bayonet." Ed Porter Thompson remembered that at Hanson's remarks, "the men nerved themselves for the struggle knowing that the decisive moment had come. Then came the loading, then the order to carry arms and march, and they stepped off in line of battle. With low, cautionary commands the officers exerted themselves to preserve formation, the brushwood was passed, the line was dressed, the pieces brought to a charge bayonet and then the order was heard along the line, 'Forward! Double quick! March!'"[9]

Breckinridge's serried ranks presented a breathtaking scene of martial beauty. "Legions of Rebels were forming in squads, companies, and regiments, and soon came pouring down the hill," remembered Lieutenant Butler of the 44th Indiana. "Their batteries wheeled in line and concurrently with their heavy column began the movement. How symmetrically they moved, as if inspired by one motive and one mind! They moved forward like an irresistible tidal wave with magnificent

---

8   Ibid., 561-562.

9   Buckner, Breckinridge Papers; Thompson, *History of the Orphan Brigade*, 179; P.S.S. Letter.

daring as if to victory." Another Federal said "the scene presented to my mind one of those sublime spectacles of the pomp of war which form the bright, delusive side of the picture in which horror, misery, and death sadly predominated."[10]

Breckinridge accompanied the second line, and once they exited the woods he saw the Orphan Brigade sweeping toward Price's position. "The front line was at a full charge and Hanson's brigade on the left was more in view as it passed up over a rise in the field," recalled Captain William Pickett, accompanying Breckinridge. "It presented a fine sight as at right shoulder shift with arms glistening in the sunlight giving rousing cheers, they double quicked up the slope. General Breckinridge could not restrain his enthusiasm exclaiming as he pointed to the left, 'Look at old Hanson!'"[11]

*　　*　　*

To draw enemy fire away from Breckinridge's assault, Bragg ordered Polk to have every battery in his corps fire in unison at the Federal positions beginning at 4:00 p.m., using a single round launched by Stanford's Mississippi Battery as the signal. After firing that round, Stanford's gunners received a bucketload of Federal iron in response. "They turned all their batteries on me, producing a concentration of shot and shell such as I never before witnessed," Stanford reported. William Brown, one of Stanford's gunners, noted that "the cannon balls and shells were as thick as I ever heard Minie balls. We went in at a trot, and each team took position behind its respective gun. The riders dismounted and got as close to the ground as convenient." For Stanford in particular, the attempt to draw Federal fire was poor. "During the few moments we were under fire," Brown noted, "two of my squad and three or four of our horses were wounded. The shells seemed to explode amongst us every second, and there was not an instant when shots did not hiss by."[12]

About 3:30, Rosecrans rode across Stones River to a spot near the 3rd Wisconsin Battery and watched Breckinridge's advance open. "They marched in splendid military style and advanced as coolly and gracefully as if on dress parade," wrote Chaplain James Morrow of the 99th Ohio. "Thorough discipline was

10 Butler, *My Story of the Civil War*, 274-75; Wright, *History of the 8th Kentucky*, 128.

11 Pickett Article, 453.

12 OR 20/1:732-733; Brown Memoir.

indicated in all their movements." Beatty and Fyffe consulted near the ford when word reached them that the attack had begun; both galloped ahead immediately. Fyffe ordered the 86th Indiana forward and instructed the men to fortify their position with rails. "The main column of the attack moved diagonally across in front of the wood, striking toward a wooded height on the bank of the river," he noted. When the Confederates moved within 200 yards of his line, McLain acknowledged that "they set up a most hideous yell and charged upon us in two lines of battle, closed in mass, while their skirmishers rallied to their left."[13]

Pillow's and Hanson's lines surged toward the Federals but converged as they approached the Union line, forcing regiments to halt briefly in the field to prevent collision. "When thus halted, they would lie down in order to shield themselves from the enemy infantry fire in front who had by this time opened a lively fusillade from behind their temporary works," recalled Lieutenant Lot Young of the 4th Kentucky. As the 2nd Kentucky advanced, the men found a pond directly in their path. The seasoned unit, however, maneuvered deftly around the obstacle, "closed ranks on the opposite side, sprang forward up the hill a few paces and delivered fire."

After getting off those single shots, the Confederates charged the Federal skirmish line with fixed bayonets and a hearty chorus of Rebel yells. Hanson's men would find themselves obstructed by a fence in the field, which gave the Federals time to fire a second, then third volley. Ed Porter Thompson recalled that soon "we were bearing down upon them in full career and could not be checked."[14]

In their push, Hanson's Kentuckians aimed for the 51st Ohio. Guarding the crest of Beatty's Ridge, the Buckeyes lay flat on the ground with bayonets fixed awaiting the word to rise and fire; McLain hoped that by lying down, the enemy's first volley would pass harmlessly overhead. His regiment waited until Hanson's men were only 60 yards away "so that we could plainly see their breasts" before firing. "Don't rise until you can see their hats, then rise and fire," McLain implored.

"When their first line was almost to the top of the hill, they raised the Rebel yell—yeep, yeep, yeep!" recalled Sergeant Samuel Welch of the 51st. "When we saw their hats, we rose and fired a volley simultaneously with a volley from their front

13 Chaplain James Morrow, 99th Ohio, *Lima Weekly Gazette*, Jan. 28, 1863, 1-2; OR 20/1:599, 615.

14 Reminiscences of Lot Dudley Young, 4th Kentucky, Western Historical Manuscript Collection–Columbia, University of Missouri; Thompson, *History of the Orphan Brigade*, 179; Butler, *My Story of the Civil War*, 276.

line. In that single volley, 24 of the 51st Ohio fell dead and 21 fell mortally wounded. When the shock of this double volley was over, it seemed to me that both lines were annihilated."[15] (Confederate casualties in the exchange were not reported.)

Soon, the 8th Kentucky added to the storm of lead crashing into Hanson's assault. "Our sturdy mountain boys received the anxiously awaited order 'fire by file, fire,'" recalled Captain Thomas Wright. "A blaze of fire and smoke ran along down our ranks, every man taking deliberate aim. This effect of this murderous fire became visible to all our men and infused them with fresh courage." Captain John Banton, commanding the 8th Kentucky's skirmishers, was killed almost instantly, however.[16]

As Breckinridge's men crossed the field, Theodore O'Hara on Breckinridge's staff spotted Fyffe's brigade threatening Pillow's right and ordered Graves to dispatch a battery to protect the flank. Graves sent Captain Elisha Eldridge Wright's Tennessee Battery, then following Preston's Brigade on the right, which went into action in an open cornfield where it could target both Fyffe's line and the 3rd Wisconsin Battery. "As we were advancing at a gallop in the field, before taking our first position, the off-lead horse in one of our 6-pounder gun teams was struck in the head with a ball and fell dead," recalled Lieutenant John Mebane. "Before the team could be halted, the carriage was rushed against the horse and the pole broken, which caused the piece not to be in action in our first position at all."[17]

Fyffe's and Price's volleys ripped gaping holes in the Confederate lines. The rolling nature of the ground presented further difficulties in the advance. Alignment in Pillow's command quickly fell apart as the 26th Tennessee, veterans of Fort Donelson, surged ahead of their brigade mates. "The impetuosity and eagerness of the 26th threw the column into the form of a rainbow," one report claimed. "On rising a slight elevation, the enemy poured a deadly volley into their ranks but quick and steady, the 26th moved on returning the fire with deadly aim." The daring Tennesseans, unfortunately, advanced without their brigade commander, as Pillow sought safety behind a tree, refusing to enter the open field.

15 P.S.S. Letter; *OR* 20/1:615; Sergeant Samuel Welch, Co. E, 51st Ohio, "Battle of Stone River," *National Tribune*, May 12, 1904, 2.

16 Wright, *History of the 8th Kentucky*, 128-29.

17 *OR* 20/1:608, 824.

Graves found him there moments later, but it was not until Breckinridge ordered Pillow to enter the fight that the general could be induced to advance.[18]

The portion of the line held by the 79th Indiana and 35th Indiana was Pillow's prime target. "The enemy fired not a single shot till they got within ten rods when they gave the Rebel yell which was followed by volley after volley of musketry," Butler recalled. "The regiment to our right [79th Indiana] jumped to their feet as the Rebels gave their yell and I believe that one-half of them fell to the ground as if cut down by a scythe." Colonel Knefler of the 79th Indiana noted that his men lay on the ground and held their fire until the Confederates were within 50 yards "when it was ordered to rise up and commenced firing with very destructive effect on the enemy."[19]

"I considered it to best to let them advance to within 30-40 paces of my line before I opened my fire," recalled Colonel Bernard Mullen of the 35th Indiana. "When their right flank was immediately opposite my line, I gave the order to rise and fire. A plunging volley staggered the advancing columns and before the enemy could recover his surprise, my regiment had reloaded and commenced a well-aimed and telling fire." The Federals, though, began dodging shells from Breckinridge's artillery, taking a heavy toll that forced Mullen to seek reinforcements. Turning to Colonel Peter Swaine of the 99th Ohio, Mullen implored the Buckeyes to advance. Lacking direct orders from Price, however, Swaine refused.[20]

Staggered by the heavy volleys from Price's line, Hanson had his men slip left, seeking a way around the flank; they quickly found it. Within roughly 10 minutes, both Hanson's and Pillow's brigades surged against both of Price's flanks. "Seeing to oppose them further would only end in the slaughter of my men," wrote Price, who ordered his front line to retire and uncovered his second line featuring the 21st Kentucky and 99th Ohio. His regimental commanders remembered the withdrawal differently, reporting that it was done on their own authority. Major Green Broaddus of the 8th Kentucky insisted that the 51st Ohio's retirement exposed his regiment's flanks and prompted him to retreat as well. "The enemy was not more than 40 steps in our front when we received the order to fall back, leaving

18 Hardshell Letter; Smith, *Stones River: Confederate Army*, 552-53. Graves drew up charges and specifications against Pillow for conduct unbecoming an officer, but Hardee suppressed the effort. Regardless, Pillow's days as a field commander were finished.

19 Butler, *My Story of the Civil War*, 275-76; OR 20/1:590.

20 *OR* 20/1:611.

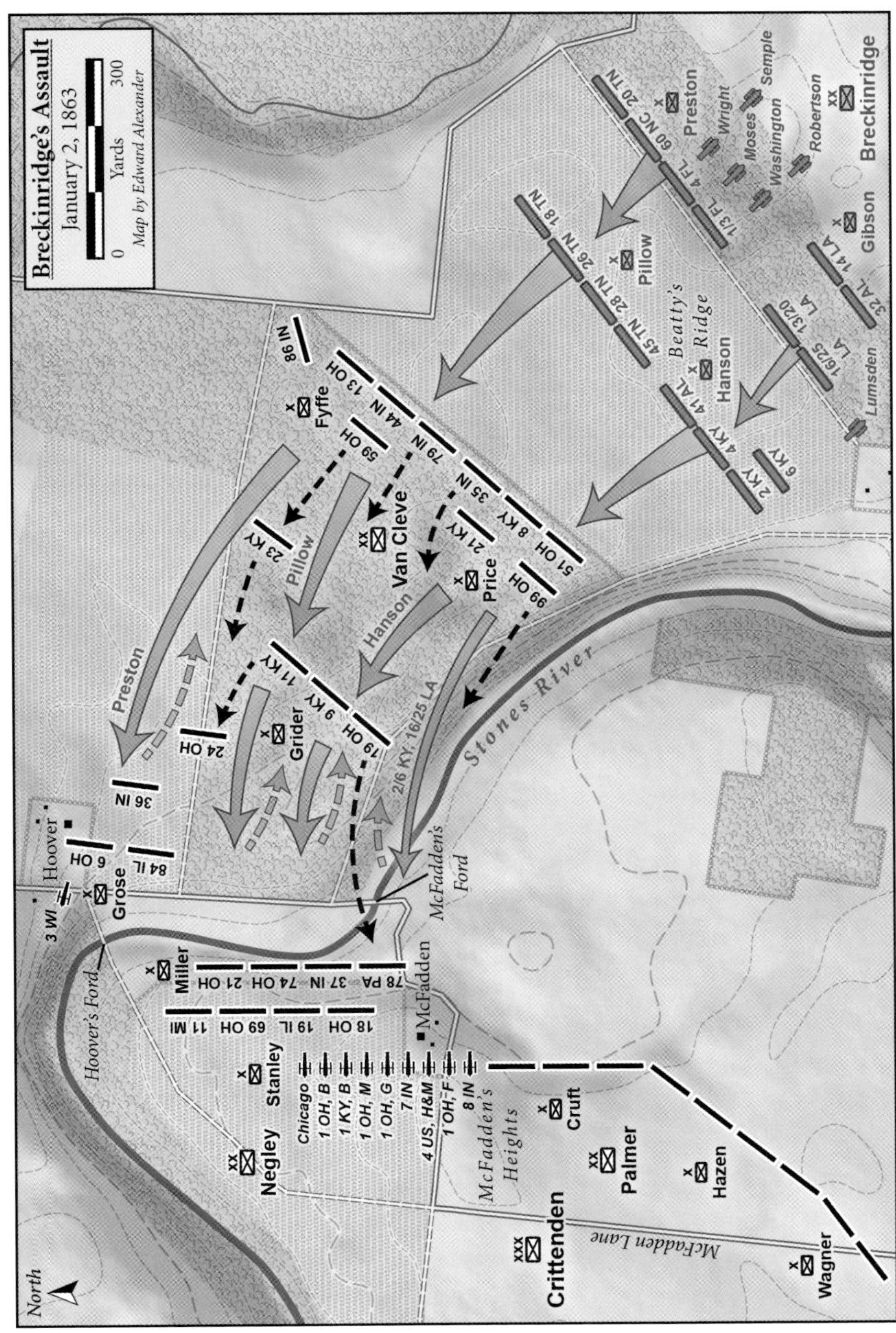
Breckinridge's Assault
January 2, 1863
Map by Edward Alexander
Yards
0   300
North
Breckinridge
Gibson
Robertson
Washington
Moses
Semple
Wright
Preston
Pillow
Beatty's Ridge
Hanson
Lumsden
32 AL 14 AL
16/25 13/20
2 KY 4 KY
6 KY
45 TN 28 TN 26 TN 18 TN
13 FL 4 FL 60 NC 20 TN
86 IN
Fyffe
13 OH
59 OH
44 IN
79 IN
35 IN
8 KY
51 OH
99 OH
Price
21 KY
Van Cleve
Pillow
Hanson
Preston
23 KY
11 KY
24 OH
9 KY
79 OH
Grider
2/6 KY: 16/25 LA
36 IN
84 IL
6 OH
Hoover
3 WI
Grose
Hoover's Ford
McFadden's Ford
Stones River
McFadden
Miller
78 PA 37 IN 74 OH 21 OH
18 OH 19 IL 69 OH 11 MI
Stanley
Chicago
1 OH, B
1 KY, B
1 OH, M
1 OH, G
7 IN
4 US. H&M
1 OH, F
8 IN
Negley
McFadden's Heights
Cruft
Palmer
Hazen
McFadden Lane
Crittenden
Wagner

many of our brave comrades cut down by the leaden messengers of death," recalled Thomas Wright of the 8th Kentucky.[21]

Price's plan to have the second line replace the first in action proved impossible. "The 35th Indiana was in the advance of us hence we dared not shoot or we should shoot them," explained Samuel Bolton of the 99th Ohio. "So, the Rebels got on to us and we could not do anything." Lieutenant Colonel James Evans's 21st Kentucky watched the fight in front of them with intense scrutiny until someone noticed Hanson's line sweeping around the brigade's right "until they completely flanked us. I at once ordered my men to rise and fall back," he reported. Major William Dowden of the 21st Kentucky, who told Chaplain Thomas Gunn before the battle that he desired an honorable wound in the thigh, would get part of his wish in the subsequent retreat, forced to spend the rest of his life crippled.[22]

The 99th Ohio quickly buckled. Lieutenant Colonel John Cummins saw "a solid column of the enemy within 50 yards of me firing a perfect stream of bullets and charging bayonets. How I escaped so well appears miraculous." According to one officer, the line fell back "like fallen leaves before a wintry wind." Morrow affirmed that "we did not retreat until the enemy was within 30 or 40 yards of us. It would have been a little less than murder to have not done so." Confederate infantryman Gervis Grainger of the 6th Kentucky claimed Price's line fled "like blackbirds. Then came forth a deadly volley into the ranks of the flying enemy. It was terrific! The ground for a hundred yards was covered with the fallen."[23]

Among them was Samuel Mullet of the 51st Ohio. "Within ten minutes I had been shot, the ball passing between the two bones of my leg and came out the opposite side," he wrote. "We retreated some 20 feet then everything grew dark and I dropped helplessly to the ground." Milton Romig of the 51st Ohio asked: "Who the devil wouldn't run with 10,000 yelling, whooping savages coming double quick against 3,000? I felt a pale determined calmness and shot 30 rounds on the

21 Ibid., 608-609; Wright, *History of the 8th Kentucky*, 129.

22 OR 20/1:608-609, 613; Private Samuel H. Bolton, Co. D, 99th Ohio, *Church Advocate*, Feb. 5, 1863, 5.

23 James L. McDonough, "The Last Day at Stones River: Experiences of a Yank and a Reb," *Tennessee Historical Quarterly*, Volume XL, Spring 1981; McCray, *A Shouting of Orders*, 66; Morrow Letter; Gervis D. Grainger, *Four Years with the Boys in Gray* (Franklin, 1902), 14.

retreat with as sure [an] aim as ever I pulled trigger. Somehow, I thought I would not be hit and didn't care a damn just then."[24]

Some soldiers were struck repeatedly in the ferocious firefight. Captain John Crowe of the 35th Indiana was hit three times, but John Lowe of the 35th had it worst, somehow surviving five strikes in just 20 minutes: once in the side by a piece of a shell, two slight wounds to his extremities, a bullet in the hip, and another that fractured his skull. Another of the fallen was John Purvis of the 51st Ohio. In the tumult of battle, he did not hear the order to retreat and continued firing at the onrushing Confederates. "Just as I had brought my gun up to fire the sixth time, a ball struck me on the top of my head, knocking me over on my back, but the wound was not deep and I quickly sprung to my feet, discharged my musket, and loaded again," he wrote. "But the blood streamed over my face and into my eyes so that I could not see. Then I turned around to go behind a tree a short distance off, carrying my gun with me. But no sooner had I reached the tree than a ball entered my left leg just above the ankle. This brought me down to my knees, and just as I fell another rifle ball struck me in the lower part of my bowels, and a buck shot hit me on the left knee but this last did not go very deep. Thus, I was wounded in four places and I then thought the wound in my bowels was mortal. I was glad to lie down by the tree, faint from the loss of blood which flowed freely from my head and leg."[25]

Beatty ordered Grider to move the divisional reserve forward and sustain the line. "Undaunted by the terrible and desperate state of affairs," Grider's line advanced with the 19th Ohio on the right, the 9th Kentucky at center, and the 11th Kentucky the left. Stumbling roughly a hundred yards through a thick undergrowth of briars that disrupted any hope of maintaining alignment, the three regiments slammed into Breckinridge's assault with a deafening crash. "We met our troops retreating in great confusion," wrote Lt. Col. George Cram of the 9th Kentucky. "Nothing could be more discouraging to my men than the aspect of affairs at that time, but they never faltered." Grider's men opened their ranks to allow Price's men to pass through, then closed them again—all under unrelenting fire.[26]

24 "Civil War Days Recalled," *Newcomerstown News*, Dec. 13, 1972, 1; Private Milton A. Romig, Co. B, 51st Ohio, SRNBP.

25 Post, *Soldiers and Patriots*, 262; Sergeant John H. Purvis, Co. B, 51st Ohio, *Tuscarawas Advocate*, Feb. 6, 1863, 2.

26 OR 20/1:591; Noe, *A Southern Boy in Blue*, 132.

Their first volley struck the Confederates like a thunderbolt. Marcus Woodcock of the 9th Kentucky claimed "their first column almost entirely disappeared, the few that were left standing going off at the double quick towards our right flank. Oh, but their balls did fearful execution in our ranks, the more so on account of our inexperience as every man kept on his feet and offered a fair mark for the enemy." It was a brief but bloody stand-up fight in the open; Rebel officers galloping back and forth on their horses "as if they knew not the principle of fear," Woodcock observed.

"[T]hey came like an avalanche of desperation, irresistible as fate," recalled one soldier in the 19th Ohio. At times, it became a hand-to-hand fight. "We fought for minutes that seemed like hours with bayonet and clubbed musket, with deep cursing and loud yells, with hot rage and bold defiance," wrote Major Charles Manderson of the 19th Ohio. Casualties quickly mounted: the 9th Kentucky lost its major, adjutant, and a half-dozen company officers. Noted Colonel Cram: "The enemy gave way after the fourth or fifth round, the colors of the regiment in front of us having fallen no less than three times."[27]

Grider believed he had halted the Confederate attack. Turning to Beatty, he said, "Colonel, we have them checked, give us some artillery and we will whip them." Replied Beatty, "You shall have it." Kentuckian Woodcock discovered his gun barrel was bent and could not be fired, but he yelled and cheered on his comrades as they fought. "Some of the men were on one knee," he noted, "others nearly flat upon the ground, while others were standing up, but all were doing their utmost as if the fate of the day depended upon the exertions of a single arm."

A few of Price's survivors rallied with Grider. Sergeant Charles Gentsch of the 51st Ohio dropped behind a log and commenced firing until he saw Lt. Col. Reuben May of the 8th Kentucky ride up to the line, still atop his fine black horse. "The Rebels were firing grape and shrapnel and one of these struck the horse, killing him instantly," Gentsch recalled. "The horse went down on his front knees with his hips well elevated and apparently never moved. Colonel May was not thrown but gained his feet and never looked back at the poor animal. He ran directly past me as though he had not been mounted at all."[28]

---

27 OR 20/1:587, 591; Noe, *A Southern Boy in Blue*, 132; Erb, *Extracts from the Battles of the 19th Ohio*, 30; Manderson, *Twin Seven-Shooters*, 19.

28 OR 20/1:577; Noe, *A Southern Boy in Blue*, 132; Orderly Sergeant Charles Gentsch, Co. K, 51st Ohio, SRNBP.

Hanson's Kentuckians probed Grider's ranks and soon discovered a weak point beyond the 19th Ohio's right flank. In their advance, Grider's men had angled to the left, opening a 200-yard gap along the river that the Orphan Brigade quickly exploited, pummeling the vulnerable 19th. Manderson ordered a retreat by file, starting on the right. "We fired one round and our line too was compelled to give way to the overwhelmingly superior force of the enemy," conceded Alfred Stambaugh of the 19th Ohio. "Every man then started for himself and the Rebels for us all. I stopped twice to see if they were still coming—they did come by thousands."[29]

Grider tried to rally the 19th Ohio behind the 9th Kentucky's line, but Manderson advised, "[W]e are flanked on our right and had better fall back and rally at the foot of the hill if we can." Hanson's Orphans unleashed a raking fire on the two Federal Kentucky regiments, and Grider, realizing his whole line had been flanked, ordered the 9th and 11th Kentucky to break contact and retreat. "The order to retreat rang along the line, but all seemed to think that it had been given by someone who did not have authority," Woodcock noted. During the retreat—made "in the greatest disorder"—the 28th Tennessee captured one of the 9th Kentucky's flags.

Major Erasmus Mottley of the 11th Kentucky never received Grider's retreat order; however, seeing the right of the line collapsing, he ordered his men back. "The storm of missiles was terrific and for a few moments no men could have stood under it," reported Manderson, who would have 25 of his men captured while falling back. "Attempts were made to rally the men at several points," Beatty noted, "but it was impossible from the heavy fire and the close proximity of the enemy. Most of them were therefore forced across the river where many of them rallied and returned with the first supporting troops."[30]

Price's and Grider's collapse exposed Fyffe's right flank, compelling Fyffe to order his men to turn right and fire into the advancing Confederates' flank. Butler's 44th Indiana stayed low and was fortunate to miss the bulk of the enemy fire, which the lieutenant recalled came "rushing through the air as countless swarms of mad bees. As we sprang to our feet, it seemed to be that I could have caught my hands full of balls by holding them over my head." Reported Lt. Col. William Howard of the 59th Ohio: "We were about wheeling to give him a flank fire when we discovered emerging from the woods the same number of his columns moving

---

29 Stambaugh Letter.

30 OR 20/1:577, 588, 595; Noe, *A Southern Boy in Blue*, 133-34.

with his right upon our left." It was Breckinridge's second line of Preston's and Gibson's brigades racing toward Beatty's Ridge.

Caught in the middle, Fyffe could order his men only to fall back toward the river. "I was exhorting the boys to fire low, keep cool, and did not hear the order to retreat," wrote George Squier of the 44th Indiana. "When by chance I looked around, I found that Co. D was alone and said, "Boys, fire your loads out and run!" I told the men to follow the colors and away we went pell-mell over the field."[31] An exploding shell would frighten Fyffe's horse, which bucked and then dragged the colonel for some time, leaving him badly bruised and disabled on the field. It also left the brigade without a leader, though at the moment that did not matter. With thousands of howling Confederates on their tail, Fyffe's men needed no guidance to the river.

Also joining the retreat was the 13th Ohio. Although these Buckeyes were not even scratched by infantry fire, several shells from Wright's Tennessee Battery in their midst spurred a 300-yard scramble to safety. For the 44th Indiana, meanwhile, Colonel William Williams was captured during the retreat, but fellow Hoosier George Casper narrowly escaped. As the regimental historian wrote, Casper was "closely pursued by a Rebel who repeatedly ordered him to halt and surrender or he would shoot. Not heeding the demand, the Rebel fired, wounding Casper in the hand. At that, he turned upon his adversary and thrust him through with his bayonet, killing him on the spot. He then continued his retreat."[32]

The retreat presented numerous scenes of horror. "The smoke rolled up in great clouds and covered the sun," Butler wrote. "The air was full of invisible messengers of death, gravel, stones, and sand were flying in all directions from the ground as it was being plowed with balls, grape, canister, and bursting shells. I could see scores of the enemy falling, dragging a shattered limb, holding a torn arm, covering some ghastly wound about the head and face, all struggling to escape the deadly peril." George Squier "saw a man leap in the air and fall heavily to the ground dead. Still another man claps his hand upon his breast, turns quickly half the way around and falls to rise no more. One to my left fell with the loss of his head, the effect of a shot from one of our own guns."[33]

Another Federal confronted by an impassioned Confederate soldier was Corporal Edward Hockensmith. The Rebel demanded Hockensmith surrender

---

31 Butler, *My Story of the Civil War*, 275; Doyle, *This Wilderness of War*, 41.

32 *OR* 20/1:577, 605; Rerick, *The 44th Indiana*, 82.

33 Butler, *My Story of the Civil War*, 277; Doyle, *This Wilderness of War*, 41.

with the regimental flag he carried. "Myself I will surrender, but my colors never," was the reply, and the Kentuckian chucked the flag into the river, quickly secured by another soldier in the regiment then fleeing across the water. Corporal Jacob Reep of the 19th Ohio and two others were struck down while on a small island as they crossed Stones River. Lieutenant Phil Reefy, carrying his regiment's flag, thrust it underwater into the roots of a sycamore tree to hide it from the pursuing Confederates before he leapt to the opposite shore. Reep rolled over to cover the protruding staff with his body when members of the 26th Tennessee opened fire from the bank of the river. "Two of their men came to the island where we were and posting themselves behind the tree spoken of, fired at random," he wrote. "They were ugly and insolent in their talk to us, ordering us to get up and go to the rear of the line which we insisted was impossible."[34]

After retreating to their left, Fyffe's men rallied along a fence on the river bluffs, near a building on the Hoover Farm where Grose's brigade was positioned. From here, they helped pour flanking fire at Breckinridge's men, though the effort fell short. "The enemy, by his terrible discharges of musketry and artillery and the weight of his columns, bore down and threw disorder into our lines," recalled Colonel Howard. "We succeeded in again rallying our line at a fence in our rear, but all in vain for no human power of our strength could withstand such a force."[35]

As the Federals retreated, Lieutenant Cortland Livingston of the 3rd Wisconsin Battery realized his position on the river bluff was in danger of collapsing. "The enemy advanced steadily, driving in our pickets," he wrote. "Our fire was very effective, but their ranks closed up immediately." Another member of the battery noted that the Confederates "were making things lively for us and to stop them with our small command was like stopping the flow of the Mississippi with bull rushes." Matters seemed so hopeless that Livingston ordered the battery to retire across McFadden's Ford. "When the last section reached the ford, one regiment of the enemy was within 100 yards of it and poured a galling fire into us. Many of our horses were shot dead in the river, but our brave boys cleared them from the teams, and everything was got across." Livingston's rapid retreat caught Breckinridge's attention, and he reported that the Badgers "took time by the forelock in crossing the stream."[36]

---

34 *OR* 20/1:609; Memoir of Corporal Jacob A. Reep, Co. G, 19th Ohio, SRNBP.

35 *OR* 20/1:606.

36 Ibid., 582-583, 786; *History of the Services of the Third Wisconsin Light Artillery* (Berlin, 1902), 16.

"In the madness of pursuit all order and discipline were forgotten," recalled Ed Porter Thompson, and Colonel Lewis noted that "on account of the want of space to maneuver and the considerable change in direction that had to be made to face the enemy, some confusion occurred and no line of battle was kept, and there was great danger from the fire of our own men." Because Hanson's Kentuckians began to bunch along the riverbank, they presented the Federals an inviting target. "Cooper [a comrade] was loading his gun when a round shot struck his gun, carrying it out of his hand, the gun, at the same time, cutting a man in two and the round shot doing the same," one soldier wrote. "Just then I saw a Yankee aiming at me. I threw up my gun and cut down at him and Cooper says I killed him. I think I must have, too, for I took as good an aim as if I was shooting at a mark. However, he paid me for it as I fell at the same time pierced by a Minie ball. It struck me through the arm into the side; a flesh wound. Cooper and I walked off the field as big as major generals."

Some 6th Kentucky soldiers resorted to sheltering behind stout trees but "had scarcely done so when bullets were cutting the bark from them at every cardinal point of the compass," Thompson recalled. "The air was literally burdened with flying projectiles. It seemed impossible for a man to live a minute in such a horrid hail of shot and shell. It was one of those appalling storms in which humanity sometimes finds itself without the hope of escape."[37]

*   *   *

Thomas Leonidas Crittenden was riding with his staff along the Nashville Pike when Breckinridge commenced his attack. The general paused at McFadden's Heights and observed the action atop Beatty's Ridge with growing concern: Beatty's division was on the run. Did this foreshadow another Federal disaster? Turning to Captain John Mendenhall, his chief of artillery, Crittenden implored, "[Y]ou must cover my men with your cannon!" Mendenhall swiftly went to work assembling a grand battery for the mission. He ordered Swallow's and Parson's batteries to open fire and then sought assistance from other nearby batteries.

The first available he found was George Estep's 8th Indiana Battery, and Estep's six guns were soon en route to McFadden Heights, unlimbering on Parsons's right. Mendenhall next appealed for assistance from Captain James

<hr>

37 OR 20/1:833; Thompson, *History of the Orphan Brigade*, 180-81; P.S.S Letter; Henry D. Jamison, *Letters and Recollections of a Confederate Soldier 1860-1865* (1964), 158.

Major General Thomas L. Crittenden

Library of Congress

Morton, commanding the Pioneer Brigade. Morton offered the six guns of the Chicago Board of Trade Battery, which rushed immediately to McFadden's Heights. Mendenhall followed by having the six guns of Lieutenant Alanson Stevens's Battery B, 26th Pennsylvania Light, redirect their fire toward the left, and he then obtained the services of three guns in Captain Standart's Battery B, 1st Ohio, for the effort on McFadden's Heights. As he prepared to return to the heights, Mendenhall came upon the six guns of Captain Cullen Bradley's 6th Ohio Battery, already firing opposite Beatty's Ridge, and had them continue their efforts against Breckinridge's advance.

In all, Mendenhall added 15 guns to the 25 already deployed on McFadden's Heights, and by redirecting the fire of 12 guns in two batteries, it meant 52 guns were now firing at Breckinridge's ranks surging toward Stones River (not to discount the additional six in the 3rd Wisconsin Battery, redeployed from its position on the Hoover Farm).[38]

Within minutes of occupying Beatty's Ridge, Breckinridge had his divisional artillery firing on the Federal guns west of Stones River. Before long, Confederate gunners hammered at the three batteries on the northern side of the heights (Chicago Board of Trade Battery; Battery B, 1st Ohio; and Battery B, 1st Kentucky). The Washington Light Artillery also targeted the left of the Federal line on McFadden's Heights and landed shells with deadly accuracy, while Cobb's Kentucky Battery atop Wayne's Hill lobbed in a few shells for good measure.

---

38 OR 20/1:451, 455-456. The six guns of the 3rd Wisconsin battery, while firing from the east side of the river, are included in Mendenhall's often-reported total of 58 guns.

Lieutenant Marshall, commanding Battery G of the 1st Ohio, reported that he "observed the enemy moving in masses through the open country and on the opposite side of the river and driving back our forces. We commenced shelling them as fast as possible while receiving a crossfire from the enemy's artillery." A corporal of his battery was killed by a 6-pound solid shot that also killed two horses; Marshall's own horse had its ear shot off by another shell, which then killed the team's lead horse.[39]

The convergence of Confederate artillery proved too much for Captain Schultz's Battery M of the 1st Ohio, which briefly opened fire before the torrent of shells forced him to retire. Swallow reported being fired upon from three directions, and after a short fight he ordered his 7th Indiana to attach ropes to the guns and fire retiring. When one gun became disabled and started for the rear, the other drivers mistakenly followed, going 40 yards before Swallow could halt them. Once Swallow began to retire, Marshall followed and the batteries reformed about 40 yards below the crest of McFadden's Heights, safely out of sight of the adept Confederate gunners atop Beatty's Ridge. This left Parsons atop the heights with his four rifled pieces, the four howitzers being held on the reverse slope for close-range work. "The batteries around me were silenced far too soon," he complained, "for when my rifled ammunition was exhausted, I found that some scoundrel had led off my caissons, and I was left only with the howitzers to reply to the enemy's concentrated artillery fire."

The retirement of a dozen cannons combined with Parsons's ammunition outage at such a critical moment set the stage, however, for Negley's infantrymen to make their most vital contribution to the battle.[40]

*   *   *

Bragg's orders to Breckinridge had been to drive the Federals off Beatty's Ridge, then hunker down and wait for the artillery to arrive. It is clear Breckinridge and his brigade commanders understood the objective, but they lost control of their men once Beatty's lines broke. The men were following a sound military stratagem: once an enemy is running, keep him on the run. Sergeant Dan Turney of the 2nd Kentucky said "the race was too exciting and our boys too impetuous. We

39 *OR* 20/1:415; Marshall Letter.

40 *OR* 20/1:415, 525, 579.

could not hold but must pursue and sped recklessly on regardless of his own safety's fate."

Lieutenant Colonel John Buckner offered that "after the enemy cleared the hill it became necessary for them to advance and drive the enemy across the river. The timber between the hill and the river afforded him excellent protection and the hill could not have been held with artillery until this was done." Ed Porter Thompson offered that "heedless alike of those who were falling now and of the sure destruction awaiting them at the front, they rushed on firing as fast as they could and cheered amid the carnage and the din that perhaps now, they were dealing the finishing blow to what had been begun on Wednesday." Necessary or not, overrunning the objective would prove to be the fatal error of Breckinridge's attack.[41]

By now, the Washington Light Artillery had run out of long-range ammunition, with Lieutenant Vaught frantically calling for the limbers to be brought forward. Robertson's 10-gun battery was nowhere to be found. This brief suspension gave the Chicago Board of Trade Battery time to gallop into position atop McFadden's Heights and open fire. Parsons noted appreciatively that Swallow's battery moved back into position on his left about the same time, adding 11 guns to the growing number firing at Breckinridge's charging division. "If ever shell and shot came in heaps, it did at this time," remembered Board of Trade gunner Charles Maple. "Right in the face of two batteries we charged up in full view and took our position and for two hours we engaged them."

The Federal gunners split their fire. Captain Stokes reported that two rifled pieces focused on the guns atop Beatty's Ridge while his 6-pounder field guns fired canister and case shot into the Confederate infantry. "The battery opened a destructive fire of shell on the Rebel battery, so destructive to our troops, completely silencing and destroying it, so that several of its pieces were captured by our advancing infantry," Stokes crowed.[42]

With careful aim at their opponents across the river, the Federal guns fired slowly but with crippling effect. "It now appeared that the ground we had won was commanded by the enemy's battery who were within easy range on better ground upon the other side of the river," Breckinridge reported. "I do not know how many guns he had, but he had enough to sweep the whole position." Added the regimental historian of the 60th North Carolina: "[T]o say the fire was terrific but

41 Buckner, Breckinridge Papers; Turney Diary; Thompson, *History of the Orphan Brigade*, 180.

42 *OR* 20/1:251; Maple Letter.

mildly expresses it. How any escaped has ever been a matter of wonder. Nothing but a Divine Providence could carry men through such an ordeal."

Hanson had hardly crossed Beatty's Ridge when a shell fragment severed the femoral artery just above one his knees. Pickett came across Breckinridge holding his hand firmly over Hanson's wound. Captain Charles Helm, Hanson's brother-in-law, rode up with an ambulance, tears streaming down his face as they loaded the mortally wounded Kentuckian and raced off to the surgeons. "It was a sight indelibly impressed on my memory and all this under the fiercest fire of artillery that can be conceived," Pickett remembered.[43]

Amid this hail of fire, the second line of the Confederate assault reached the crest of Beatty's Ridge and took cover, Preston's men on the right and Gibson's on the left. "Balls whistling around us thick and loud, we were ordered to lie down," wrote Major John Lesley of the 4th Florida. The men stayed for perhaps ten minutes before Gibson rode forward to consult with Hanson and saw the general shot down before they could speak. "I determined not to engage the second line until the first gave way," Gibson recalled, "but General Hanson had hardly fallen when his line began to show symptoms of yielding."

Gibson deployed the 13th/20th Louisiana to the right and the 16th/25th Louisiana angled left toward Stones River, while under heavy Federal artillery fire. Gibson's horse was shot from under him, so he led the rest of the attack on foot. "The woods were full of troops, apparently in great confusion," he wrote. "The 13th Louisiana went into action in perfect order and succeeded in driving the enemy a considerable distance into the woods." Losses quickly mounted, among them Major Charles Guillet commanding the 13th regiment, as well as 14 of 28 officers. "Its position was such that in falling back we had to leave nearly all the wounded in the woods. In several instances those who were bearing the wounded off we shot as soon as they entered the cleared field," he noted.[44]

Preston's Brigade promptly followed suit. The commander bellowed, "Up and to the charge!" and, as Major Lesley wrote, the line rushed forward "with such impetuosity as to throw the enemy for a moment into confusion." Observed Colonel William Miller of the 1st/3rd Florida: "As we moved on through the woods, the ground gradually descended and our left rested on the river whose high banks were covered by the enemy who poured a galling fire upon us from the opposite side. Further forward the river by a sudden bend appeared in our front

---

43 OR 20/1:786; Clark, *Histories of the Several Regiments*, 480; Pickett Article, 454.

44 OR 20/1:798, 818.

and we found ourselves exposed to a deadly fire from the hills that overlooked us left and front."

The 86th Indiana, now squarely on the right flank of the surging mass, marveled at the impact of the Federal artillery. "The opening roar was terrific and the crash of the iron storm through the thick-set ranks was overwhelming," one veteran noted. "It was madness to face it, yet the Rebel columns closed up and pressed on. Their line seemed to shrivel in the fire that met it." William McMurray of the 20th Tennessee likened it to "the lighting and heard the thunderbolts of a tornado at the same time the stars of destruction were sweeping everything from the earth."[45]

Colonel Lewis of the 6th Kentucky reported that men from every regiment of the Orphan Brigade took position behind a picket fence in the middle of the field and began firing at the Federals. Spotting a number of Yankees hunkered down behind the riverbank and displaying a white flag, Lewis ordered the firing to cease and eventually sent more than a hundred Federal prisoners to the rear. As he tried to get his disorganized men into line, his men shuddered under a sudden blaze of cannon fire. "The very earth trembled as with an exploded mine and a mass of iron hail was hurled upon them," one soldier wrote. "The artillery bellowed forth such thunders that the men were stunned and could not distinguish sounds There were falling timbers, crashing arms, the whirring of missiles of every description, the bursting of the dreadful shells, the groans of the wounded, the shouts of the officers mingled into one horrid din that beggars description."[46]

Lieutenant Young of the 4th Kentucky witnessed a shell burst amid the ranks of his regiment's Company E. "The shell exploded right in the middle of the company, almost tearing it to pieces.," he wrote. "When I recovered from the shock, the sight was appalling as some 10-20 men were hurled in every direction." Tod Carter of the 20th Tennessee said "their artillery opened upon us a most terrific fire and our forces melted away like night shadows before the break of morning. For an hour the demons of hell seemed to have met in wild, blood-drunken revelry."[47]

It was the Federal artillery that broke the back of Breckinridge's assault, and his brigades soon staggered under the barrage. Lieutenant Hannibal Paine of the 26th

<hr>

45 Ibid., 815, 818. Barnes, *The 86th Indiana*, 113; William J. McMurray, *History of the Twentieth Tennessee Regiment Volunteer Infantry, C.S.A.* (Nashville, 1904), 238.

46 *OR* 20/1:833; Thompson, *History of the Orphan Brigade*, 180-81.

47 Young Reminiscences; Carter Letter.

Tennessee acknowledged that "we had to march back for half a mile through an open cornfield and many were so much exhausted that they could not go faster than a slow walk. The enemy all the while were pouring in a murderous fire of shells, canister, shot, and Minie balls upon us. I really thought your humble servant would go up a spout."

The Tennesseans found themselves in the middle of a horrific crossfire. Colonel John Lillard's horse was shot beneath him; Lt. Col. James Bottles went down with a wound; and the colors were repeatedly struck. The regiment would incur 104 casualties, more than a third of those who joined the attack. Lieutenant Spencer Talley of the 28th Tennessee took a musket ball in his rib cage, his life saved no doubt by a thick blanket roll he carried over his shoulder. "The ball felled me to the ground, knocked the breath out of me, and I felt that I was dangerously hurt," he wrote. "I could feel the blood running down my side but could not tell whether the ball was lodged in me or if it passed through." He walked back to the field hospital, where a surgeon found the ball "mashed flat against my rib. I reckon I was the happiest one in the army."[48]

The Federal shellfire left heavy casualties among Breckinridge's regimental commanders That included Colonel Palmer, who had been knocked from brigade command by Pillow's arrival and assumed command of the 18th Tennessee, receiving three wounds during the assault, and Colonel Miller of the 1st/3rd Florida, who had his thumb shot off. In the Orphan Brigade, Major James Hewitt of the 2nd Kentucky was hit by a shell fragment, as was Lt. Col. Martin Stansel of the 41st Alabama. The 28th Tennessee lost its young commander, Colonel Preston Cunningham. "After he was shot, he took from his pocket several articles including a comb, pocketknife, and pocketbook," Major John Bransford wrote to Preston's father. "Your son was shot early in the action and while on horseback. His conduct was all you have desired, and his last request was that he might be buried decently."[49]

The right of the Confederate advance encountered unexpected opposition from Grose's brigade, supporting the left rear of Beatty's original line. The 23rd Kentucky under Major Thomas Hamrick was posted behind a fence just to Fyffe's left rear, but when Fyffe retired, the 59th Ohio barreled directly through Hamrick's lines. In the midst of the confusion this created, Hamrick tried to reorient his lines

48 1st Lt. L. L. Hannibal Paine, Co. E, 26th Tennessee, SRNBP; Hardshell Letter; Talley Memoir.

49 "Gallant Preston D. Cunningham" *Confederate Veteran*, June 1902, 268.

to hit the Confederate flank as it surged past him, yet "had no sooner done so than a battery opened on my left with grape at the same time a fire of small arms was opened upon my left and rear, placing me in a crossfire." When Hamrick ordered a retreat, some of his men shouted that they were surrounded, and the orderly retreat turned into a rout. "They fell back in confusion," confessed the Kentuckian.

Hamrick's continued withdrawal through the ranks of the 24th Ohio, now under Captain Enoch Weller, threw that regiment into confusion. "The enemy was now rushing wildly and madly on and were near flanking our position," recalled Captain Armistead Cockerill. Weller tried to reorient his line to fire upon the Confederates but would be killed outright almost immediately. Cockerill, the regiment's fourth commander at Stones River, took command and, under increasing pressure on his left flank, ordered the regiment to fall back to the brigade's left, continuing to fire in the process.[50]

Grose shifted the 36th Indiana to cover the retreat. The Hoosiers, now arrayed along the axis of Breckinridge's advance, poured a devastating flank fire into the Confederate columns as they surged toward Stones River. It was not enough to hold back the onslaught, but after shoving aside the 36th Indiana, the Confederates ran squarely into Grose's two reserve regiments entrenched on the Hoover Farm: the 84th Illinois and the 6th Ohio.

With his 84th Illinois nearest the Confederate advance, Louis Simmons held a ringside spot to the chaos of retreat. "Each man seemed to be looking out only for himself and making every possible effort to get out of range," he wrote. "Out of the woods pursuing them came the brigades of the enemy in most splendid lines of battle." At 300 yards range the 84th's commander, Colonel Louis H. Waters, ordered his men to rise and fire. "Both these regiments saluted them with a terrible fire and by this time all of my regiments were engaged," Grose reported. Noted Simmons: "At our first volley the enemy wavered and soon began to fall back. The 84th Illinois and 6th Ohio now sprang over their breastworks with a yell that was heard three miles and charged on the enemy." Waters no sooner mounted the breastworks than a bullet passed through his hat.[51]

Frank Lavender's 20th Tennessee, on Preston's right flank, suffered the most from these volleys. "As soon as we were unmasked, the front line of Yankees poured a volley into the 20th that made them stagger and waver like a drunken man," recalled William McMurray. Added Claybrooke, "For a time, the conflict

50 *OR* 20/1:569.

51 Simmons, *History of the 84th Illinois*, 34; *OR* 20/1:562.

was desperate." The Tennesseans managed to close within 40 yards, firing their Enfield rifles with deadly precision. "While lying as flat as I could in a fence corner, a Federal shot at me and knocked off a piece of rail across my back," McMurray wrote. "I returned the fire with a good rest on the rail for my gun. Another one shot at me and tore off a large portion of the rail against my left breast and by this time I had fired three shots, then the order was given to charge. The regiment did not take time to climb the fence but caught the fence about the third rail from the bottom and the fence, line, and all went over together."[52]

*   *   *

Thousands of Beatty's men streamed northward over Stones River in what was shaping up as an utter rout. Watching the tragic turn of events, Colonel John F. Miller and his fellow Union brigade commanders grew angry at not being ordered to assist their comrades. "Miller sent his staff officers and orderlies to scour the field and ask permission to cross the stream," wrote headquarters orderly Wilson Vance. The orderlies tried to work up the chain of command, but neither Negley nor Thomas could be found. While waiting, Miller abruptly realized that it was his duty, as the senior officer present, to make this decision independently before it was too late. "He was surrounded by a group of regimental commanders who alternately studied the field and his face … [when] he turned to the officers around him saying quietly, I will charge them." Colonel Joseph Scott of the 19th Illinois offered Miller his complete support before digging in his spurs and galloping back to his regiment, as did the other commanders.[53]

Miller later revealed his thinking at that critical moment. Banking that the surging Confederates were "already intoxicated with the spirit of victory," Miller decided to "meet this movement of the enemy by a countercharge[,] regarding that as the only way possible of averting a great disaster."

"The ridge of ground immediately behind the line being sufficiently high to mask the movement of troops in our rear behind the ridge," he continued, "the fact that there was no support to our line could not be well known to the enemy then on low ground on the east bank of the river. Supposing that the audacity of an advance of our line would take the enemy by surprise and cause him to suspect that strong support was advancing behind our line, I ordered the advance of my line." The

---

52 OR 20/1:822; McMurray, *History of the 20th Tennessee*, 239.

53 Vance, *Stones River*, 70.

cards Miller threw down were ultimately a bluff. In this case, though, the bluff did the trick.[54]

From their vantage point above McFadden's Ford, the heartrending sight of comrades in full flight convinced a few Federal soldiers that the proper place for them was in the rear and they bolted. "I asked is it any wonder that men talked of running, even to saying, 'I'll run if you do,' a few did go," recalled Samuel Linton of the 21st Ohio. "But there was one man, Sergeant Michael Rice, who did more to hold the boys in line at this time than all the officers we had, and he did it by very few words. 'We can check them, and anyone who runs now is a damn coward.' At this, all hug the ground the harder and kept quiet."[55]

Before long, the Confederates neared the river, prompting Lt. Col. James Neibling of the 21st Ohio to order his regiment to open fire. "We commenced to pour a withering fire into their advancing ranks which caused them to fall back," wrote Lieutenant Robert Dilworth. As his brigade opened its ranks, allowing some of Beatty's men to flee, Miller and his staff splashed into Stones River and, while coolly observing the enemy heading for his position, scouted the ground for his own attack. Suddenly, an orderly arrived to report that "only Major General John Palmer could be found and from him came, instead of the desired permission, a positive prohibition—an order not to cross." Grimly taking stock of the situation, Miller replied, "It's too late now," and immediately raised his sword, bellowing, "Charge!"[56]

Colonel Timothy Stanley galloped back to his line and, as Daniel Rose noted, shouted to the 11th Michigan, "Up my Michiganders and at 'em. We did not wait for a second invitation or command. The double quick became a rush and a run." The Federals plunged into the water with a yell, though the brigade lines swiftly commingled. "I don't believe I ever felt better in my life than I did just then," claimed Launcelot Scott of the 18th Ohio.

Bullets, however, zipped into the ice-cold water and into the concentrated ranks, taking a heavy toll, including those injured and killed by friendly fire. "I reached the bank all right and had fired once and was loading when a man at my left placed his gun on top of the bank, which was about breast high, and dropped his

---

54 John Franklin Miller, *U.S. Army Generals' Reports of Civil War Service, 1864-1887*, Volume X, Record Group 94, National Archives, 20-21.

55 Linton Memoir.

56 Vance article; 1st Lt. Robert S. Dilworth, Co. I, 21st Ohio, *Pittsburgh Commercial Gazette*, Nov. 16, 1896.

head to sight his gun, when a ball from the rear struck him in the back of the head, and his brains went over and beyond his gun," wrote a horrified Samuel Linton. "In crossing the river, the ranks were necessarily broken but it did not stop our progress or slacken our speed," Rose confirmed.[57]

Recovering from their initial panic, some steadfast Confederates took position behind a rail fence near the bank and opened fire. "At this fence, the Rebels rallied, and as our men ascended the bank, they were greeted by a storm of bullets, which for the moment checked their advance," recalled Ira Owens of the 74th Ohio. Yet the Federal assault proved too determined to be halted; following a few well-directed volleys, the Confederates fled. "The colors of the 78th Pennsylvania and 19th Illinois were the first to cross the river, the men followed in as good order as possible," Miller reported. "Taking cover behind a rail fence on the left bank, the men poured a heavy fire into the ranks of the retreating force." Miller would ignore a second order from Palmer not to cross the river. Noticing the 21st Ohio closing in on his left in "splendid style," in fact, he urged the men forward to fully exploit their charge.[58]

J. M. Tracy of the 19th Illinois was one of the first men across the river. "Colonel Joseph Scott rushed in without stopping and Adjutant Bangs was beside him urging on the men," he remembered. "Scott put his cap on his sword and shouted "Forward!" I rushed out with one or two others from the cover and went ahead to Scott. I received a shot in the hand but fought on. Scott soon fell wounded in the leg, then we fought for revenge. We ran forward and drove the Rebels in perfect terror before us. The Rebels fought with the courage of desperation—even their wounded fought, and we had to kill them for even with a bayonet at their breasts they would not surrender."

Woodcock's 9th Kentucky recrossed as well. "The enemy seemed disposed to contest our right of recrossing the river and answered us with a severe fire of musketry," he would write. "Their officers advanced to the brink of the stream cheering and hollering, 'Come on boys, damn them! We have got the run of 'em!' Into the river our brave boys plunged, cheered by the cry of fresh troops who were coming onto the field by thousands and waded across."[59]

---

57 Rose article; Scott Memoir; Linton Memoir.

58 Owens, *Greene County in the War*, 37; OR 20/1:434. The charge of the 19th Illinois inspired the popular George Root song "Who'll Save the Left?"

59 Tracy Letter; Noe, *A Southern Blue in Blue*, 135.

The turnabout in the fortunes of battle was remarkably swift. Chaplain Thomas Gunn of the 21st Kentucky said "when I comprehended the turn which affairs had now taken, I leaped to my feet and standing on the brow of that river bluff cried with a yell that would have done credit to an Indian, 'Rally men, they are running! Rally, rally!'" The effect was electric. Captain Wright of the 8th Kentucky wrote that "before the water had ceased to squirt from our boot legs, the greater part of the command that remained alive reentered the river, this time the pursuers."[60]

Although Breckinridge's men were indeed pushed back quickly, the Federals encountered fierce resistance from the center of Preston's line. "At length the line began to yield on our left and then our right," noted Colonel Wylde Bowen of the 4th Florida. "The men still continued to fire with that deliberate accuracy that characterizes the Florida woodsman. The accidents of the ground which my command occupied afforded a partial protection and I determined to hold it as long as possible." The Floridians, in fact, would use nearly all 40 rounds of their ammunition before Bowen acceded to a full retreat. With the Federals now on both their flanks, that proved a perilous enterprise, but Bowen and his men reached Beatty's Ridge intact and rallied around Captain Wright's newly arrived guns.[61]

Belatedly arriving atop Beatty's Ridge with four of his 18 guns, Captain Robertson acquiesced that the Confederates' fortunes were rapidly deteriorating. "The enemy's fire had brought the artillery of General Breckinridge's division to a halt and had overturned two pieces; the others had begun firing obliquely to the right, but for a time I thought they were firing into their own men," he reported. "I waited some time for the infantry to clear the crest, so that I could order [my] battery up to its place but saw unmistakable evidence of a retrograde movement." Colonel George St. Leger Grenfell of Bragg's staff happened to be riding by; Robertson asked him to send word to Bragg that he believed Breckinridge's men would not be able to hold Beatty's Ridge before bringing his own six-gun battery into action.[62]

While trying to rally his 4th Kentucky on Beatty's Ridge, Colonel Robert Trabue learned that he now had command of the entire brigade. He hoped to rally a defense around the newly arrived batteries, but it was not to be. "Exposed to the fire of seemingly all his artillery and a large portion of his infantry in unassailable

<hr>

60 Gunn Journal; Wright, *History of the 8th Kentucky*, 130.

61 *OR* 20/1:817.

62 Ibid., 760-761.

positions as well as to the flanking fire from the right, it was deemed prudent to withdraw," he wrote.

Colonel Lewis tried to rally the 2nd and 6th Kentucky near Semple's Battery, where the 2nd Kentucky's color-bearer bravely waved his flag. A Federal shot soon struck both the flagstaff and the color-bearer, who plunged to the ground. An officer rushed to lift the flag but had no sooner reached it than an angry soldier rushed over demanding the honor. "That's our flag! It belongs to the 2nd Kentucky sir and I'll carry it!"[63]

Trabue sat calmly on his horse amid the storm of shells, rallying the troops, when he spotted a Federal bugle lying on the ground. After ordering one of the men to pick up the instrument, he accosted a soldier then running back to the ridge. "Halt sir, don't run! You're in just as much danger running as you would be in a walk." The man stopped, turned to the colonel, and said, "I know that, but then you see we get away so much quicker!"[64]

"When we reached the top of the hill our men were in full retreat," reported Lieutenant Mebane of Wright's Battery. "We opened on the enemy with spherical case and canister and continued to fire with effect until the enemy had charged within 75 yards of our pieces." Captain Wright would be mortally wounded by a bullet, at which point Major Graves stepped in and directed the battery to "limber to the rear." It was too late, however, as Miller had already caught sight of Wright's guns and ordered the 78th Pennsylvania to take them. With a whoop, the Pennsylvanians advanced, shooting down horses and gunners. Graves was soon wounded in both the head and the knee, and the Tennesseans abandoned two of their guns. Wright's infantry support would waver, then break for the rear, with the 4th Florida losing three color-bearers.[65]

The surging Federals swarmed the battery. James Thorne, a 16-year-old Tennessee recruit in the 78th Pennsylvania, jubilantly climbed astride one of the cannons, patting it as he exclaimed to his company commander, "Here it is Captain!" Captain Wright of the 8th Kentucky noted that "a few brave Rebels were trying to drag off the piece having thrown down their arms for that purpose and the boys succeeded in capturing three of them. The spirit of Bragg's army was broken. As one of the drunken prisoners expressed it, 'We are whooped for our rations and whisky's about out!'" Groaned Mebane: "[H]ad our battery gone to the rear when

---

63 Ibid., 827; Thompson, *History of the Orphan Brigade*, 200.

64 Thompson, *History of the Orphan Brigade*, 203.

65 *OR* 20/1:817, 824.

the other batteries of the division did, we would have saved our guns; but being under the immediate supervision of the chief of artillery, we did not move without orders from him."[66]

A smaller Federal force consisting of the right five companies of the 18th Ohio from Stanley's brigade, the 31st Indiana from Cruft's brigade, and the 32nd Indiana from Gibson's brigade advanced along the western bank of Stones River to drive off the few Confederates who had made it across the river. The force took cover among the buildings of the McFadden Farm, using the fences as cover before opening fire. "Seeing that our fire brought the enemy to a halt and that our forces were advancing, I ordered my men forward across the stream," reported Lt. Col. Josiah Given of the 18th Ohio. The Confederates made their presence known beyond his right, which prompted Given to redirect the charge in that direction. Palmer then sent in the 31st Indiana, and soon both regiments resumed the advance. But because the Hoosiers moved hesitantly, Given was forced to sound a retreat to maintain alignment with them. "They are flanking us from the woods on the right," one man shouted, which caused "some of the men to fall back hastily." Palmer soon rallied the line, however, and led them both in a bayonet charge.[67]

Gervis Grainger of the 6th Kentucky was one of the Rebels creating so much trouble for Given and his regiment. The Kentuckian had crossed west of Stones River and had kept busy plugging away at some Federals using a riverside cabin as a makeshift fort when the artillery commenced. "Such a dense cloud of smoke enveloped the troops that scarcely a man was discernable. The fact did not dawn upon me that the Kentucky brigade was almost annihilated," wrote Grainger, who turned his focus back to the Federals on his front and fired roughly 30 rounds before the sounds of a brass band to his right captured his attention. "I saw a line five or six columns deep advancing to cross," he wrote. "In the direction I had left our men, not one was to be seen. Our army had retreated leaving me alone to fight the Federals single-handed." After delivering a few more rounds towards the charging Federals, Grainger plunged back into the river and raced back to the Confederate lines amid continued enemy fire.

66 Ronald S. Gancas, *The Gallant Seventy-Eighth: Colonel William Sirwell and the Pennsylvania Seventy-Eighth: Stones River to Pickett's Mill* (Plum Baro, 1997), 121-2; Wright, *History of the 8th Kentucky*, 130. Soldiers from the 9th Kentucky and 19th Ohio also claimed they were the first to reach the guns, as did men in nearly every regiment in Miller's, Stanley's, and Price's brigades. It is possible they are all right because the Federals lines were completely commingled in this charge.

67 *OR* 20/1:429.

Elsewhere, Corporal Daniel Bevis of the 19th Ohio, who was captured during his regiment's retreat, turned the tables on his captors. "As soon as our men came in sight, I took my hat and gave three cheers and then took the guns from the Rebels telling them that the tide had changed and they were now my prisoners," he recalled. "I gave the prisoners in charge of some of our men, picked up my gun, and commenced pouring it into them as fast as I could load."[68]

On Beatty's Ridge, the Federal advance continued into the cornfield beyond, where Sergeant John Bolton of the 21st Ohio noticed a Confederate banner on the ground. "I picked up the flag and saw it belonged to the 26th Tennessee Regiment and intended to bring it with me but at once comprehended that it was impossible to use my musket and carry the flag with me, so I hurriedly threw it down by the side of the dead Rebel where I found it." The flag would soon be picked up by William Davis of the 78th Pennsylvania, who handed it to Colonel Sirwell.

An elaborate story of how the flag was captured eventually evolved. In it, the 56-year-old Davis chased the Confederate standard bearer and shot him, and Corporal William Hughes of Company B then bayoneted the wounded man, allowing the pair to seize the flag from him. Given to a 78th Pennsylvania officer, it was delivered to Rosecrans. According to historian Ronald Gancas, the officer claimed the prize had an "electric effect upon our men. Almost instantly soldiers sprang to their feet and cheered for the Union."[69]

Colonel Miller's counterattack put the spurs to a retreat that threatened to degenerate into a rout. "Some rushed back precipitately, while others walked away with deliberation and some even slowly and doggedly as though they scorned the danger or had become indifferent to life," recalled Ed Porter Thompson. Added Clifton Breckinridge: "[T]he men, finding they were in a vortex of fire and had captured a red-hot iron, threw down what they had taken and as quickly as possible returned to the point from which they had started. Had our men only delayed a short time longer they would have been utterly annihilated."

Recognizing the peril, Colonel Gibson wheeled his two Louisiana regiments toward the rear, trying to use the river bluffs to shield his men as much as possible from the Federal fire. "It was a matter of doubt whether this could be

---

68 Grainger, *Four Years*, 15; Corporal Daniel Bevis, Co. E, 19th Ohio, *Zanesville Daily Courier*, Jan. 20, 1863, 2.

69 United States Army, Ohio Infantry Regiment, 21st. MS 562, Box 13, Folder 2. CAC, BGSU; Gancas, *The Gallant Seventy-Eighth*, 122. The Pennsylvanians also claimed the capture of a guidon from the 4th Florida.

accomplished successfully," he confessed. "Scarcely anyone could enter the open field to our right and rear without being shot down either by the infantry or by the batteries of the enemy."[70]

The Federal counterattack also bought time for Price's and Fyffe's brigades to rally. Chaplain Morrow recalled in particular the pluck of the regiment's color-sergeant Moore E. Thorne. "After reforming on the riverbank, an officer of another regiment asked Thorne where he belonged," Morrow wrote. "The 99th Ohio was the reply. Then fall in here said the officer. 'No, damned if I will. I will wave this flag over the 99th Ohio or I will wave it nowhere. Men of the 99th Ohio, rally around your own flag and follow me,' shouted Thorne."

Colonel Howard of the 59th Ohio recalled how "my command seemed aroused to a sudden sense of duty and dashed in to rally what he could for a grand stand." John Purvis of the 51st Ohio, lying wounded near the banks of the river, cheered the Confederates on their retreat. "All who could escape did so and back they fled in wild confusion, throwing away their guns and everything else they carried and uttering bitter curses in their flight," he wrote. "It did my heart good to see them run, closely pursued by our men. I raised up on my knees and hurrahed with all my strength for the old flag."[71]

Positioned beyond the Confederate right, Pegram's and Wharton's troopers watched the spectacle but did little to assist. Wharton later claimed he had no knowledge an attack was to be made but gamely accompanied Pegram's guns with a few companies of Texas Rangers. Pegram, fearful of hitting Confederate troops, refused to open fire, prompting Wharton to take over the battery himself. Preston soon arrived and seconded Pegram's objection, informing the cavalrymen that the division was retreating. Once Preston's men cleared the guns, Wharton sprang into action. "We opened fire upon a heavy column of the enemy advancing from their extreme left to turn Breckinridge's right," he wrote. "The fire was so effective (the range not being over 500 yards) as to shoot down their standard and throw them into confusion." Once he saw Breckinridge's line falling back, he rode back to his command and ordered the men to dismount and help cover the retreat.[72]

*   *   *

70 Thompson, *History of the Orphan Brigade*, 182; "Breckinridge's Losses at Murfreesboro," *Confederate Veteran*, Feb. 1908, 73; OR 20/1:799.

71 OR 20/1:606; Morrow Letter; Purvis Letter.

72 OR 20/1:969.

Sunset brought a quick halt to the Federal pursuit. "The Rebel batteries poured in grape and canister but shot too high," Tracy recalled. "We formed in line to make a charge, but it was so dark that we had to discontinue the fight. We took our positions, stacked arms, and went back to get blankets out of the knapsacks of the dead Rebels. The ground was heaped with the Rebel dead and as we looked over the field by the light of torches for our fallen comrades, the scene was terrible."

Captain Henry Clay, grandson of the famed Kentucky senator, witnessed the end of the engagement from beyond the Confederate right. "As our infantry fell back much disordered," he wrote, "they rallied at their old position but our command soon began to receive attention and under a sharp fire the command, guns and all were withdrawn. The Yankees' three cheers sounded hatefully in my ears after they realized that the attack had failed and would not be renewed."[73]

Accounts differ as to how disorganized the Confederate retreat became. Breckinridge reported that his men "fell back in some disorder but without the slightest appearance of panic." Sergeant William Rodgers of the 1st Florida suggested much the same: "I never felt the least frightened until we were ordered back then I was so badly scared my back itched the whole time." Robertson, however, disagreed. According to the artillerist, he tried to form a line in the middle of the cornfield, "supposing it would be good to rally the broken division [emphasis added], but the hope proved utterly fallacious. Except about 150 fugitives collected in a ravine to my right," he continued, "I saw no body of troops, and fearing an advance of the enemy, under cover of the darkness I moved to the rear again and established a new line along another skirt of timber."[74]

With the sun now setting, Robertson's guns reached the northern slope of Wayne's Hill. "The contagion of flight had spread to the artillery," he admitted,

> and it was with great difficulty that several pieces of artillery were brought away, owing to the drivers being frightened. In more than one instance I found it necessary to cock my revolver and level it in order to bring men to a realizing sense of their duty. I am clearly of the opinion that if there had been no artillery on that field, the enemy would have gone into Murfreesboro easily that evening. I have never seen troops so completely broken in my military experience.

73 Tracy Letter; "On the Right at Murfreesboro," Captain Henry B. Clay, Pegram's Cavalry Brigade, *Confederate Veteran*, Vol. 21 (1913), 589.

74 OR 20/1:76, 786; Rodgers Letter.

Robertson also reported the color-bearer of the 6th Kentucky courageously tried to hold the line, halting frequently with his stand of colors to face the enemy and call for the men of the 6th Kentucky to rally. The brave unnamed soldier "did not receive much attention," though he "lingered as long as there was any infantry on the field, and then passed to the rear, calling out, 'Here's your 6th Kentucky.'"[75]

Thousands of Federal reinforcements flowed toward McFadden's Ford. General Davis offered a brigade but arrived with his division, and McCook sent Gibson's brigade. Breckinridge's collapse led Bragg to order J. Patton Anderson's Mississippians, shot up after their assault on the cedars, to pull out of line and race east of Stones River. They arrived at dark and skirmished briefly, but with darkness now enveloping the battlefield, that skirmishing puttered out quickly.

More worrisome for Anderson was that, other than Robertson's artillery, Breckinridge's command was nowhere to be found. "General Anderson reported through me to his division commander General Withers that he could find no line support and there were no Confederate forces save his own picket line in front," recalled staff officer Captain Edward Sykes. The shrieks and groans of thousands of freshly wounded men echoed over the battlefield, punctuated by the creaking, and crashing of wagons and ambulances as they splashed back and forth across Stones River bearing the victims to the hospitals. A cheer echoed from one end of the Union line to another as a Federal officer rode along the Nashville Pike waving the captured flag of the 26th Tennessee and proclaiming victory on the left.[76]

The entire affair was over in less than an hour, the combatants back where they had started. This action "left our line of battle firmly established on the east side of the river from which the Confederates could be enfiladed and nearer than Murfreesboro than the enemy," observed Captain Ephraim Otis of Van Cleve's staff. "Another hour of daylight would have placed the Union army in Murfreesboro and left Bragg cut off from his supplies." The tide now decisively favored Rosecrans. With the ridge secure, Rosecrans could fortify the position and cross reinforcements to resume the drive against Murfreesboro at his leisure.[77]

The survivors of Price's brigade returned to their former positions, appalled at the carnage. "[I]f there is any satisfaction in getting even with the enemy," Samuel

<hr>

75 OR 20/1:761, 786.

76 Major Edward T. Sykes, "General Braxton Bragg: A Cursory Sketch of His Campaigns," *Southern Historical Society Papers*, Vol. 11 (1883), 473.

77 Captain Ephraim A. Otis, "The Murfreesboro Campaign," *Papers of the Military Historical Society of Massachusetts*, Vol. 7 (Wilmington, 1989), 316.

Welch wrote, "I will say that I found 30 dead Rebels in front of where we fired our first volley when I returned an hour afterwards. Our dead were lying where they fell, our knapsacks undisturbed." Overall, the Federal triumph east of Stones River came at a heavy cost: Beatty's division had nearly 1,100 men killed, wounded, or missing; Grose lost about 100; and Negley lost roughly 250 in the counterattack. All told, that meant about 1,500 casualties added to the roughly 12,000 the Federal army suffered during the fighting December 31—a rate of 1-in-3 now dead, wounded, or missing for Rosecrans's command.[78]

Breckinridge's assault was an unmitigated disaster for Bragg's army. Casualty estimates in his division range from 1,300 to 1,800—figures Breckinridge and Bragg would argue about vociferously for months. Regardless of the exact figure, the losses totaled roughly one-third of the Kentuckian's command—a percentage that held true for the balance of the army, which had suffered more than 10,000 casualties spread across three days of fighting, the infantry bearing the large bulk of the loss. John C. F. Jenkins, a member of Breckinridge's escort, "rode over the battlefield after it was all over and it was enough to make one's blood run cold. It was the most awful and painful sight that I ever beheld. I was anxious at first to see a battle," he admitted, "but it is now my earnest wish that if I live a hundred years more, I may never behold such a scene again."[79]

Lot Young of the 4th Kentucky spoke for many when he called Breckinridge's attack a "terrible blunder and a useless sacrifice, a wicked and useless sacrifice." General Hanson lay dying in the back of a ambulance with a bloody tourniquet applied to his mangled leg as it hauled him back to Murfreesboro. "General Breckinridge rode up and a few hurried but pathetic words passed between him and his wounded brigadier and then he dashed away to look after his lines," wrote surgeon John Scott of the 2nd Kentucky. "Hanson did not utter a groan or speak a complaining word." The former vice president rode amongst his troops calling on them to reform, but the wreckage sustained by his division provoked an emotional outburst. "He was raging like a wounded lion as he passed the different commands from right to left," recalled Ed Porter Thompson. "Tears broke from his eyes when he beheld the little remnant of his old brigade, his personal friends, and his countrymen: "My poor Orphan Brigade torn to pieces," was all he could say.[80]

---

78 Memoir of Sgt. Samuel Welch, Co. E, 51st Ohio, SRNBP. Brigade losses (k/w/c) for Beatty's division include Grider (337), Fyffe (about 170), and Price (583).

79 Private John C. F. Jenkins, Breckinridge Guards, Special Collections, LSU.

80 Thompson, *History of the Orphan Brigade*, 183, 200.

The Staggering Toll of Victory

THE MISERIES SUFFERED by the men in both armies only worsened when a driving cold rain began to fall shortly after sunset.

"The night was a hard one for us as we had nothing to eat, the rain poured down all night, no fires were allowed, mud ankle deep, and on all sides lay the dead and a great many of the wounded whose piteous cries and moans were heart rendering to hear," recalled a member of the 3rd Wisconsin Battery. "It was the dark side of the picture of war." Johnny Green of the Confederate 9th Kentucky readily agreed, calling it a "night of sleet and discouragement. With meager rations, loaded guns, and a quick eye, we went out on picket duty that night to watch lest the enemy, encouraged by our repulse, should attempt to overpower us." An unexpected reprieve at least changed the mood of Wilbur Hinman of the 65th Ohio. "[O]ur rations were completely exhausted," he recalled. "While working on the entrenchments at night, we received the welcome intelligence that a supply train had arrived from Nashville," allowing the Buckeyes to appease "our ravenous appetites with crackers and raw bacon, thankful to be able to do even that."[1]

General Breckinridge's disaster prompted soul-searching within the Army of Tennessee's high command. Corps and division commanders would meet that night at Braxton Bragg's headquarters north of town to determine the next steps.

---

1 Jericho Letter; Hinman, *Story of the Sherman Brigade*, 356; Kirwan, *Johnny Green*, 69.

When intelligence from Anderson that the Confederate line east of the river could not be found contradicted what Breckinridge reported, Bragg called for Captain Edward Sykes, one of Anderson's staff officers, to appear in person for verification. Sykes, "besmeared with mud and tired from exposure and loss of sleep," met Bragg in a well-furnished parlor, the commander surrounded by his key subordinates. "I felt decidedly out of place in this galaxy of generals," he admitted, "but on entering the room I was somewhat relieved when General Withers rising introduced me as the officer who had penciled the dispatch about which the council of war had assembled."

After questioning Sykes, and satisfied with the accuracy of the report, Bragg turned to Breckinridge, who conceded the error and confirmed his brigades had reformed far to the rear of where they had been ordered. "The darkness of night and the density of undergrowth having prevented him from accurately discerning and forming where directed was sufficient palliation for the error committed," Sykes offered as an explanation, though Bragg's response to what he no doubt considered Breckinridge's latest failure was apparently never recorded.[2]

Breckinridge's battered division was in no condition to protect Murfreesboro unaided. If Rosecrans chose to build on the evening's success by pushing toward Murfreesboro the following day, additional troops would be needed to hold the line. Before the night's conference, Bragg ordered Hardee to pull both McCown's and Cleburne's divisions from the line's left and return them to the positions they originally held east of Stones River on December 29. This left only Polk's Corps, roughly 7,000 men, defending the army's left. It did, however, simplify the army's command problem, as all of Hardee's men were now on the right (east of the river) and Polk's two divisions west.

The incessant rain created another concern, as a rising Stones River would undoubtedly hamper the army's ability to move troops across the river, although Bragg made no moves to remedy that possibility. With papers captured from McCook's headquarters wagon brought to his headquarters that night, Bragg deduced that Rosecrans' army on the field numbered about 70,000 men—odds that apparently produced a consensus that the army should retire. Hardee later made as much clear, telling Liddell that "all the officers [at the conference] agreed to retreat," despite admitting he "had only concurred without advising."[3]

---

2 Sykes Article, 473-74.

3 Hughes, *Liddell's Record*, 116.

The division commanders departed the conference about 10:00 p.m., and Polk and Hardee reportedly returned to their respective headquarters an hour later. The generals may well have recommended retreat, but a specific note by Polk (discussed below) mentions his fears of failing "in [a] meditated attack." That phrasing begs the question: Did Bragg intend to attack Rosecrans's new line on Beatty's Ridge with Cleburne's and McCown's divisions Saturday morning? Was he hoping to retrieve victory by repeating the success of his December 31 dawn assault with the same troops who had proved so successful? If so, it might explain what subsequently occurred.[4]

About 9:00 p.m. Friday, Wheeler's cavalry began a scouting venture around the Federal army, intending also to interdict communications along the Nashville Pike. A dispatch from Wheeler about midnight alerted Bragg that the Federals "were advancing on our right wing," leading Bragg to send Colonel Urquhart of his staff to inform Hardee at his Ready House headquarters in downtown Murfreesboro. Hardee in turn rode to deliver the news of the advance to Breckinridge and then returned to consult with Bragg again, while Urquhart rode to Polk's headquarters to detail him about the purported Federal activity.

Just before midnight, Anderson alerted General Withers that wide gaps existed on both Confederate flanks (apparently as much as 800 yards on the left), meaning their position east of Stones River was dangerously exposed. After consulting with Cheatham on the condition of the army, they agreed "this army should be promptly put in retreat" and, in a note to Polk sent at 12:15 a.m. January 3, expressed their conviction that only three brigades "are at all reliable and even some of these are more or less demoralized from having some brigade commanders who do not possess the confidence of their commands." The note further stated: "[W]e do fear great disaster from the condition of things now existing and think it should be averted if possible."[5]

It is unclear whether Polk spoke with Urquhart before receiving his division commanders' note at 1:30 that morning. If he did, he learned via Wheeler's dispatch that the Federals were moving against the right and that Anderson's Brigade stood ominously threatened, with Breckinridge's shaky survivors the only

4 Colonel David Urquhart to Braxton Bragg, June 12, 1863, Bragg Papers, WRHS.

5 OR 20/1:700; Urquhart Letter. In their note to Polk, Cheatham and Withers intended "three brigades" to read "three divisions." The erroneous language, which took several months to correct, implied that if combat was renewed, the Army of Tennessee could not rely on 17 of its 20 brigades.

support near at hand. On reading the Cheatham–Withers note, combined with the other intelligence he received, Polk grasped the peril. He forwarded the note to Bragg along with his own comments: "I am compelled to add that after seeing the effect of the operations today added to that produced by the troops by the battle of the 31st, I very much fear the consequences of another engagement at this time with the enemy's army. We could perhaps get off with some safety and take some credit if the affair is well managed. Should we fail in the meditated attack, the consequences might be very disastrous."

Bragg received the dispatch while in bed and reportedly read only half the note before replying, "[S]ay to the general we shall maintain our position at every hazard." The blunt reply did not sit well with Polk, who by 3:00 a.m. had reached out to Hardee, forwarding him the Cheatham–Withers note. "I think the decision of the general unwise and am compelled to add, in a high degree," confessed Polk. "I think it is due to you to let you know the views of myself and my two division commanders especially as we all believe the conflict will be renewed in the morning."

Polk had little choice but to order his men to be ready for fighting at dawn, though he feared the likely outcome.[6]

*   *   *

Pat Cleburne's Division went into position east of Stones River in the early morning hours of January 3, and to seek shelter from the driving rain, Liddell rode to Bragg's headquarters, surprised to find him awake. The note from Cheatham and Withers clearly was on Bragg's mind; he held no special regard for Cheatham, but Withers was one of his closest allies, whom he trusted deeply. Bragg's deepest fears about his own army had been aroused.

"I inquired out his instructions and our hopes," Liddell recalled. "He was thoughtful and hesitating, and finally gave me to understand that the troops were exhausted with such continued fighting" and that it would be necessary to withdraw. Liddell attempted to argue the point, but Bragg emphasized Wheeler's report about the extensive "reinforcements" Rosecrans had received. Liddell, stationed on the army's far left until only recently, scoffed at the idea and urged his commander to continue the fight. "I would rather bury my bones here than give up this field and our previous successes," he declared. "You have Rosecrans in a close

6 OR 20/1:700–701.

place. You have only to push him to extremities." Bragg sighed and shook his head sadly. "General, I know that you will fight it out, but others will not. It has now become a matter of imperative necessity to withdraw. It must be done at once." The decision had been made: the Army of Tennessee would retreat after all.[7]

Matters were hardly settled in the Federal camps. Despite the apparent victory on the left, Rosecrans worried that Bragg might assault his right and center again. Colonel Moses Walker's brigade had ventured from its entrenchments while Breckinridge's attack was underway January 2 and met with a sharp response. Additional reconnaissance during the evening showed the Confederates still in force all along the front. Again, Rosecrans resorted to one of his favorite tricks. "Deeming it possible that the enemy might attack our right and center," Bickham wrote, the general ordered a long line of campfires be lit extending the right "and left it for the serious contemplation of the enemy." Rosecrans also assigned three staff officers with stentorian voices to ride along to give the impression of arriving reinforcements. As Captain Alexander Stevenson noted: "A loud voice could be heard calling out, 'Fourteenth Division, halt!' and immediately afterwards other voices could be heard in the stillness of the night giving the necessary orders by which the imaginary regiments were to take their respective camping grounds and companies to stack arms and break ranks."[8]

It is likely Wheeler witnessed these flambeaux and phony reinforcements before sending his erroneous report that Bragg's right would be assailed by a large number of freshly arrived Federal troops. Actually, rather than extend his right flank, Rosecrans had significantly contracted it. Davis's three brigades of McCook's corps now occupied the front line along Beatty's Ridge: Post's on the right, Carlin's in the center, and Woodruff's the left, all hunkered down behind rough breastworks and supported by the remaining guns of the division's artillery. To their left rear were the three brigades of Wood's division now under Milo Hascall: Colonel George Buell's (formerly Hascall's) on the right, Harker's on the left, and Wagner's in support.

Colonel Samuel Beatty's three brigades recrossed Stones River, meanwhile, and assumed reserve positions around the Hoover Farm. Negley's and Palmer's divisions occupied McFadden's Heights, supporting the still smoking gunline that Mendenhall assembled to repulse Breckinridge. Although arrayed for defense, the line was no doubt designed with a potential future offensive in mind. Growing

---

7 Hughes, *Liddell's Record*, 114-15.

8 Bickham, *Rosecrans' Campaign*, 317-18; Stevenson, *Battle of Stone's River*, 144.

more confident at the prospects of victory, Rosecrans "rubbed his hands complacently and repeated, "We shall beat them!"[9]

As the generals consulted, argued, fretted, and worried, the men of both armies commenced the grim work of recovering the casualties. In their onerous searches for the dead and wounded, men sadly learned that in many cases Kentuckians had been fighting Kentuckians—yes, brother versus brother. Colonel Samuel Price recalled meeting his mortally wounded Confederate cousin Kidder Woodson of the 2nd Kentucky on the field. "An inquiry was made in a feeble voice by a man lying nearby if that was Colonel Woodson Price of Lexington," Price recalled. "I at once dismounted and removing the blanket from the face of the prostrate man discovered by the light of my lantern the familiar features of my relative."

Lieutenant Edward Breene of the 35th Indiana was among those to find fellow Irishmen he knew from the old country in the ranks of the wounded. "Many who had been friends from boyhood fired upon each other and killed each other, and lay side by side in death," he wrote. And a sergeant of the 35th Indiana found himself deposited in a field hospital with a severe wound, discovering that the wounded Confederate at his side was his brother whom he had not seen in years.[10]

Ambulance after ambulance conveyed casualties to hospitals set up around the McFadden Farm. The surgeons plied their trade, giving each man a brief examination, rendering judgment on whether it was worth the time to operate, and while they busily hacked and sawed away all night, the grisly remnants piled up outside. "It has been a glorious field for the surgeon," wrote Dr. William Johnson of the 18th Ohio. "I have performed a large number of operations of almost every kind from the amputation of a little finger to trephining the skull. This city is one vast hospital full of misery and suffering."

Robert McEwen of the 19th Ohio wrote he "saw nearly a cord of amputated legs, arms, and feet, interspersed with slices of human flesh lacerated and torn by shells and cannon balls. Every few minutes men would arrive with a wounded man on a stretcher and dump him down as if he were a mere log of wood," adding, "Such is war." Thomas Wright of the 8th Kentucky reached one hospital carrying a stretcher bearing a lieutenant. "On our arrival at the house, we soon became very

---

9 Bickham, *Rosecrans' Campaign*, 317-18.

10 "Some Famous Fighters: Well-Told Anecdotes of the Great Generals of the War," *National Tribune*, Oct. 12, 1882, 7; Lieutenant Edward G. Breene, Co. G, 35th Indiana, *Dayton Empire*, Jan. 27, 1863, 1. Private Richard Kidder Woodson died of his wound on January 22 in Nashville and is listed on the Confederate Roll of Honor for his heroism.

sick at the sight and smell of so much human blood," he recalled. "For 19 days with scarcely an average of four hours rest per day, we busied in amputating limbs, dressing wounds, writing letters, and washing and burying the dead," Noted Chaplain Thomas Gunn of the 21st Kentucky:"All who died in the hospital were washed clean as to face and hands, dressed as neatly as possible, wrapped in their blankets, and buried with a head mark with name and date strictly kept."[11]

Where the surgeons stopped, the chaplains often took over. When Father Jeremiah Trecy, for instance, found Captain J. S. Ryan of the 13th/20th Louisiana on the field, after establishing that Ryan was Catholic, he mollified him, "Well, my poor fellow, I am a priest and I suppose during the past night lying here in this mud, you have made as good a preparation as ever made in your life. I will hear your confession." The Confederate, however, was having none of it until Trecy offered him a drink from his canteen, which held sustenance other than water. In addition to the good draught of whiskey, Ryan finally was convinced Trecy was indeed a man of the cloth when the priest placed his stole around his neck. "The soldier actually shed tears and after hearing his confession, the captain said, "I wish I were sitting by that tree," pointing to one about 50 yards away. "I will help you," Trecy responded, lifting the man up and helping him hobble to the tree. As they neared it, however, three bullets zinged by the men—two plunking into the bark mere inches from Trecy's head. According to Civil War journalist David Power Coyngham, an Irish Catholic himself, Ryan groused: "Oh, the damned rascals, what are they shooting at you for? The priest immediately got on his saddle and fled over the crest, followed by a volley."[12]

*　　*　　*

Under orders to hold his position, Polk decided possession of the Round Forest was a must. Federal pickets from the 42nd Indiana of John Beatty's brigade now occupied the grounds, and at daybreak on January 3, Polk sent in a detachment to clear them out. The force consisted of the 19th Alabama, 25th Alabama, and Yancey's 17th Battalion Alabama Sharpshooters from Colonel John Coltart's Brigade and the 9th/10th Mississippi of Colonel Thomas White's Brigade.

---

11 William Parker Johnson Papers, Mahn Center for Archives and Special Collections, Alden Library, Ohio University; Wright, *History of the 8th Kentucky*, 133; Private Robert S. McEwen, Co. A, 19th Ohio, *Ohio State Journal*, Jan. 13, 1863, 2; Gunn Journal.

12 Coyngham, *The Soldiers of the Cross*.

Lieutenant Colonel James Shanklin of the 42nd Indiana, commanding the Federal skirmishers, suspected trouble was coming. Throughout the night, he heard the sounds of Confederate artillerymen arranging their guns within speaking distance of his position and reported his concerns up the chain of command, requesting reinforcements. General Thomas received the report, responding, "Tell Lieutenant Colonel Shanklin to hold that position at all hazards," but did nothing more.[13]

At first light, a barrage of canister fired by Captain William Scott's Tennessee Battery roused those Hoosiers who had bothered to try and sleep; the Mississippians and Alabama sharpshooters advanced as soon as the cannons ceased firing. "The regiments charged at a run with bayonets fixed and drove out the enemy who fled precipitately," Colonel White reported. In a short but vicious fight, the Hoosiers were overwhelmed and fell back with heavy casualties. "Our loss in that 30-minute time was almost equal to that of the seven hours of the first day," lamented Captain Spillard Horrall.

Among the 10 Federals captured was Shanklin, who later confessed to his wife that "the truth of the matter is I felt so utterly worn out and my feet were so very sore that I was almost indifferent whether I was taken or shot." He noted that the Confederates were so pleased at his capture that they gathered around him rather than chase after the rest of his men. Coltart and White quickly set about fortifying the position under orders from Polk to "hold the position at all hazards."[14]

Saturday dawned under a gray, leaden sky, the cold rain unrepentant. After the brief clash at the Round Forest, both armies settled for desultory skirmishing, continuing to shiver in the rain. It was "wretchedly disagreeable," Hinman grumbled. "The armies did little to disturb each other although a continual fire was kept up along the picket lines." Several of the Ohioan's Confederate counterparts echoed his displeasure. John Magee of Stanford's Battery wrote that the troops slept in the open air all night and woke up "out of humor. It rained all day, hardly any fighting, only heavy skirmishing. Our battery lay all day doing nothing." Liddell rode into his brigade's soggy encampment that morning in a foul temper, too. "Some of my men familiarly called out to me, 'What's up now, General?'" Liddell would write. "Ask General Bragg," was the impatient reply. "They saw the hidden

---

13 Horrall, *History of the 42nd Indiana*, 173.

14 Smith, *Stones River: Confederate Army*, 657; Horrall, *History of the 42nd Indiana*, 173; Kenneth P. McCutchan, *Dearest Lizzie: The Civil War as Seen Through the Eyes of Lieutenant Colonel James Maynard Shanklin* (Evansville, 1988), 263; OR 20/2:480.

meaning," he noted, "and said, 'Well boys, retreat again. All our hard fighting thrown away as usual.'"[15]

An early Confederate reconnaissance on their right Saturday morning showed that Rosecrans's men spent the overnight hours fortifying Beatty's Ridge. "The enemy has entrenched on the hill carried last night so strongly that it is beyond our power to reoccupy it," recorded George Brent, Bragg's chief of staff. Inevitably, the bad news spread quickly and many of Bragg's soldiers could scarcely believe the rumors the army was retreating. "[T]his seemed to be electric shock to the army," wrote one soldier. "Instead of that mirth and glee which had but a few moments previous pervaded the army, you could hear the mutterings of who had won a bright victory." Offered Corporal Benjamin Butt of Stanford's Mississippi Battery: "[T]here was at least one good reason for our retrograde movement. Our troops have been out for a week, exposed to the rain and the cold with but a single blanket each and for the most part without fires. Human nature could not hold out much longer under such exposure."

Sergeant John Street of the 9th Texas conceded it was a bitter pill but wrote his wife that "it is unanimous opinion that to retreat would be the best thing to do. It is generally believed that the enemy has been heavily reinforced. We all, soldiers and officers of the army, have the utmost confidence in Bragg." Not all soldiers were so understanding. "With victory on our side, we cannot divine this movement," commented a displeased Chaplain Robert Bunting of the 8th Texas Cavalry. "It was a matter of great surprise to all when on Saturday night our army moved from its position. The abandonment of Murfreesboro loses to us the moral effect of our victory."[16]

About 10:00 a.m., Bragg summoned Polk and Hardee to communicate his decision to withdraw; by noon, orders came to transport away those wounded who could be moved and to empty the town of army stores, prisoners, and captured artillery pieces. Polk's and Hardee's corps were to depart after sunset, the army's cavalry covering the retreat.

Bragg offered that his primary reason for retreating was the condition of his troops, beyond exhausted after fighting the battle and sleeping outdoors for nearly a week, exposed to the elements with scarcely a fire. "The necessary consequence was the great exhaustion of officers and men, many having to be sent to the

---

15 Brent Diary; Magee Diary; Hinman, *Story of the Sherman Brigade*, 356; Hughes, *Liddell's Record*, 115-16.

16 Dixie, *Fayetteville Observer*, Jan. 15, 1863, 1; Butt Letter; Street Papers.; Bunting Letter.

hospitals in the rear, and more still were beginning to straggle from their commands, an evil from which we had so far suffered but little," he would write. "Common prudence and the safety of my army, upon which even the safety of our cause depended, left no doubt on my mind as to the necessity of my withdrawal from so unequal a contest." In the meantime, the men would remain in defensive positions awaiting any potential offensive moves by Rosecrans, the sharpshooters ordered to keep up a warm fire on the Federals.[17]

Rosecrans was not going anywhere. "The field of battle was a morass," Bickham yielded. "The camps were a wretched muck of water and slop. Military operations upon an important scale were impracticable. The plowed fields being impassable by artillery, no advance could be made profitably and besides, the ammunition train did not arrive until 10 o'clock." General Spears' brigade, roughly 1,500 men, accompanied the train and briefly assumed a place within McCook's lines. Later that afternoon, he continued farther south to Thomas's line along the Nashville Pike. Rosecrans evidently was content to await the arrival of more ammunition, supplies, reinforcements, and for the rain to cease before continuing the drive into Murfreesboro. With time on his side, Rosecrans felt no reason to rush matters.[18]

Federal reinforcements were indeed heading toward Rosecrans, although that would prove far from routine. That morning in Nashville, Colonel Dan McCook headed south with 95 wagons loaded with ammunition and hospital stores. To escort the train, he assembled six companies of the 60th Illinois, Companies A and D of the 10th Michigan, five companies composing the left wing of his own 52nd Ohio, and the 6th Tennessee—roughly 1,000 men as well as teamsters. The wagons, however, had proceeded only about seven miles along the Nashville Pike, reaching Cox's Hill, when a detachment of Wheeler's cavalry, supported by a battery, struck and cut the train in half. "About 2 p.m.," Wheeler reported, "we attacked a large ordnance train at Cox's Hill, heavily guarded by cavalry and infantry, and succeeded in driving off the cavalry guards and in breaking down and upsetting a large number of wagons."

Climbing the wooded slope of Cox's Hill right of the pike, the 60th Illinois and two companies of the 10th Michigan opened fire on the Rebel cavalry, while the

17 OR 20/1:669.

18 Bickham, *Rosecrans' Campaign*, 319.

Ohioans and Tennesseans confronted the attackers directly.[19] "Wheeler's cavalry attacked us," recalled Sergeant Samuel Harper of the 52nd Ohio, "and before the battalion could be concentrated, they cut a wide swath through the moving train." McCook, he noted, dove right into the fight for the train, having what was described as "a beautiful fight" with Major Clarence J. Prentice of Dortch's 2nd Battalion of Kentucky Cavalry. "I looked up to see how Colonel Dan was faring and saw him and a Confederate officer riding in a circle firing rapidly at each other with their Colt revolvers," Harper relayed. "Finally, the Confederate officer fell from his horse. Colonel Dan rode on to form the arriving companies and Colonel Dan soon had his men in hand and drove Wheeler off."

To McCook's dismay, he would learn that the Confederate officer he gunned down happened to be the son of Louisville Journal editor George D. Prentice, a family friend. "He was grieved beyond measure that he had shot the son of the old friend of his family and himself," Harper revealed. "However, he had young Prentice cared for and used his influence to have him sent home."[20]

Wheeler was left to concede that "the enemy's infantry being in such force (treble our numbers) we were prevented from destroying the train," acknowledging that by the time Abraham Buford's cavalry arrived on the scene it was too late to render any assistance. By 3:00 p.m., Wheeler and his men were on their way back toward Murfreesboro.

*　　*　　*

As expected, the pouring rain had Stones River's water level on the rise. Crittenden was so alarmed that by midday he gathered his division commanders and decided to pull back all troops east of the river. Waiting until late afternoon, the men slipped across the river on timbers laid at McFadden's Ford. This rearward movement did not escape Confederate notice, though, and led to rumors that the Federal army was retreating to Nashville. But Rosecrans, resolved to maintain his position, gave the Confederates notice of his intentions as dusk approached. "A heavy and constant picket firing had been kept up on our right and center, and extending to our left, which at last became so annoying that in the afternoon I directed the corps commanders to clear their fronts," he recalled. The Confederates occupying the Round Forest, however, proved to be a particularly

19 *OR* 20/1:959.

20 "McCook-Prentice Duel," *Neodesha Register*, March 3, 1905, 6; *OR* 20/1:959.

active and troublesome set. Having annoyed Rousseau's lines throughout the day, Thomas decided "to dislodge them and their supports."[21]

"Pap" handed the assignment to Rousseau, who tapped John Beatty's brigade to carry it out. The plan was for Lieutenant Guenther's Battery H, 5th U.S. Light, to pound the Round Forest to keep the Confederates pinned down, while Beatty led forward his 3rd Ohio and the 88th Indiana to grab control of the woods. To support the attack, Spears added the 85th Illinois as well as the 1st and 2nd East Tennessee regiments to his brigade.

By now, though, the 1st Louisiana Regulars and the 39th Alabama had moved in for their turn guarding the position, with Captain Douglas West of the 1st Louisiana reporting that the men formed at the forward edge of the woods or "took shelter in a very shallow but wet ditch where they lay in the steady rain all day." West reported that his men were nervous they would be unable to return fire "owing to the dampness of their guns … and that they would fall easy prey to the enemy." When West reported that to Lt. Col. Frederick Farrar, who had just rejoined the regiment from leave that afternoon, Farrar told the anxious captain to go to the rear to bring forward support. Although the Confederates knew the army was pulling out that night, Polk's orders remained in force: Hold the position at all hazards.[22]

About 6:00 p.m., a dozen Federal guns began shelling the woods as Beatty formed his attack column. The 3rd Ohio would advance with its right on the Nashville Pike, the 88th Indiana to the left near the railroad embankment. A detachment of five men from each company—given, inappropriately it seems, the cynical label of "forlorn hope"—was sent 50 yards ahead of the main line. "We formed in line in front of the column and ordered forward by Beatty's encouraging command: 'Forward, advance like men!'" recalled Sergeant Henry Breidenthal of the 3rd Ohio. "When within a short distance from the woods, the Rebel advance opened on us and we returned it, fell down, loaded our pieces and waited until the regiment got within supporting distance, then got up, fired, and made for the trees yelling like Indians." The bugle sounded the charge, and the two regiments surged with fixed bayonets into the pitch-dark woods.[23]

It was a quick and brutal clash. Sergeant Isaac Wark of the 1st Louisiana wrote that the Ohioans were "not discovered until within about 30 feet of us," and Beatty

---

21 OR 20/2:294, Ibid., 1:196.

22 Smith, *Stones River: Confederate Army*, 652.

23 Breidenthal Letter.

recalled that the "Rebels opened a heavy fire, but in the darkness, shot too high. The blaze of their guns revealed their exact position to us." The Federals leapt over the breastworks of cut logs standing only a few feet in height and waded into the Confederate defenders. "So impetuous was our charge that we surprised and captured the outposts, drove the next line from the works, and then held them in the face of a galling fire for half an hour," declared Sergeant Gilbert McWhirk of the 3rd Ohio.[24]

Colonel George Humphrey of the 88th Indiana broke into a hand-to-hand scuffle with one of the Confederates, taking a bayonet thrust in his shoulder but reportedly knocking "one down with his sword and another with his fist." Farrar would be mortally wounded by a shell fragment. That, combined with the men's concerns about misfiring guns, threw the regiment "into considerable confusion at a very important moment," West allowed. Within moments, the Confederate line broke for the rear. "Those that were able to," Wark offered, "got up and dusted or, in military parlance, fell back to the regiments that were supporting us. When they saw us coming back, they immediately broke and ran back to the breastworks with the exception of the 19th Alabama." While granting that "the Rebels fought stubbornly," Lieutenant William Pickering of the 3rd Ohio was not hesitant to crow, "we were too much for them."[25]

The rapid retreat of the 1st Louisiana and 39th Alabama prompted mayhem in Colonel Coltart's ranks. Lieutenant Colonel Samuel McSpadden of the 19th Alabama would complain that the other regiments of the brigade (save the 25th Alabama) had abandoned him, leaving him to hold the right of the line alone until reinforcements from White's Brigade arrived. With the 7th and 41st Mississippi now on hand, McSpadden wheeled his right wing and "using the railroad as protection I was soon enabled to relieve my left wing."

Lieutenant Colonel Benjamin Johns of the 7th Mississippi argued that in the darkness his regiment blundered into friendly fire, which prompted him to order the men back under cover until the mess could be sorted out. White also advanced the 9th/10th Mississippi to hold the left of the line, but without any true success. A "rigorous attack was made on us," reported Colonel James Walker of the 10th

24 Wark Letter; Beatty, *Citizen-Soldier*, 209; McWhirk Letter.

25 Private Albert L. Henry, Co. H, 88th Indiana, SRNBP; Smith *Stones River: Confederate Army*, 652; First Lieutenant William B. Pickering, Co. C, 3rd Ohio, *Athens Messenger*, Jan. 15, 1863, 3.

Mississippi. "After an engagement of some 30 minutes finding the enemy in superior force, I retired the regiment back and joined the brigade."[26]

The engagement failed to show either army at its best. Nighttime attacks were always difficult to execute, and it was evident the men on both sides were physically and mentally exhausted. Sergeant Breidenthal recalled the duress suffered by one comrade who was "so terror-stricken as not to be able to reload his rifle which he discharged into the air and fell back prone on his back. Some of the boys thought him dead but upon examination found him half alive. Captain Swayze, learning this," continued Breidenthal, "took his gun away from him and gave it to one who needed one. A short time later, this man was seen to crawl away and that was last seen of him for several days."[27] Sergeant Wark was disgusted by the behavior of the officers of his 1st Louisiana, "as cowardly a set of men as could be found. They were all drunk during the fight and with one or two exceptions could not be seen during any of the heavy fighting."[28]

Further confusion ensued when Federal shells began to drop among Beatty's ranks, forcing the colonel to ride back to Guenther and request that he elevate his fire. Beatty quickly turned his focus to Spears' Tennesseans, then advancing to his support "without any definite instruction." The raw troops, he recalled, became "either excited or alarmed at the terrible racket in the woods, [and] delivered scattering shots in our rear." Beatty admonished the Tennesseans to cease firing and move to the left; one regiment complied, but the other continued to blaze away for a period before Beatty finally convinced them "that in firing they are more likely to injure foes than friends."[29]

By this time, his own regiments had depleted their supply of ammunition, and as the Confederates abandoned the position, the firing slackened to a stop. The hour-long scrap raised such a cacophony that men in both armies scrambled back into ranks thinking a general engagement had broken out. "It caused us to arouse suddenly from our cozy beds of weeds and cornstalks and stand in line for two hours," noted Captain Wright of the 8th Kentucky. "We were not very anxious for a renewal of the fight and as the firing ceased were not displeased to resume our peaceful if not luxurious couches."

---

26 Smith, *Stones River: Confederate Army*, 646, 659, 661.

27 Breidenthal Letter.

28 Wark Letter.

29 Beatty, *Citizen-Soldier*, 210.

Despite heavy casualties in his ranks, Beatty took satisfaction that a critical patch of ground was now under Union control, and he had possession of 70 Confederate prisoners. The Federals had won the final battle for the Round Forest, a chaotic scrap in the dark that would conclude the Battle of Stones River.[30]

*   *   *

It was well after dark before the Army of Tennessee began its formal retreat. The rain continued to fall, and as the hundreds of wagons, artillery pieces, limbers, and ambulances rolled along, their wheels cut deep ruts in the roadbed, producing "shoe-top deep" mud, in the words of one soldier. The army's two corps followed separate paths. Hardee's Corps departed first, abandoning its position east of Stones River and following the Sulphur Spring Road to the Lebanon Pike. After a short hike into town, the head of the column turned southeast on the Manchester Pike, heading toward Manchester.

Polk's Corps departed about midnight, crossing Stones River on the Wilkinson and Nashville pikes before entering the town, then angling southwest on the Shelbyville Pike. The 1st Tennessee waded the river fully dressed. "The water was up to our waists and the rain furnished enough more to justify our claim to an orthodox immersion," wrote Samuel Seay. "In this uncomfortable condition, we set out on the march of some 25 miles." Wharton's and Pegram's cavalrymen stayed behind to cover the army's retreat; Wheeler's and Buford's commands would join them in the overnight hours.[31]

The march was one more hardship to bear after an excruciating week of action. "All was quiet as no one spoke scarcely above a whisper," John Street recalled. "Notwithstanding we had borne so much hardship and privations for the last week, I heard not a murmur from anyone. All were satisfied that Bragg knew what he was doing and were willing to do his bidding satisfied that all would work out right in the end." Reflecting on the horrors of the night retreat, Thomas Colman of the 11th Texas would write: "As we retreated off the battlefield, it was 1 o'clock in the night and raining very hard. It made me feel bad to see the dead Yankees as they lay thick upon the ground and in every shape you could imagine or think of their bodies mutilated and torn by the hogs. Their looks were ghastly as we passed

---

30 Ibid.; Wright, *History of the 8th Kentucky*, 134.

31 Seay Article.

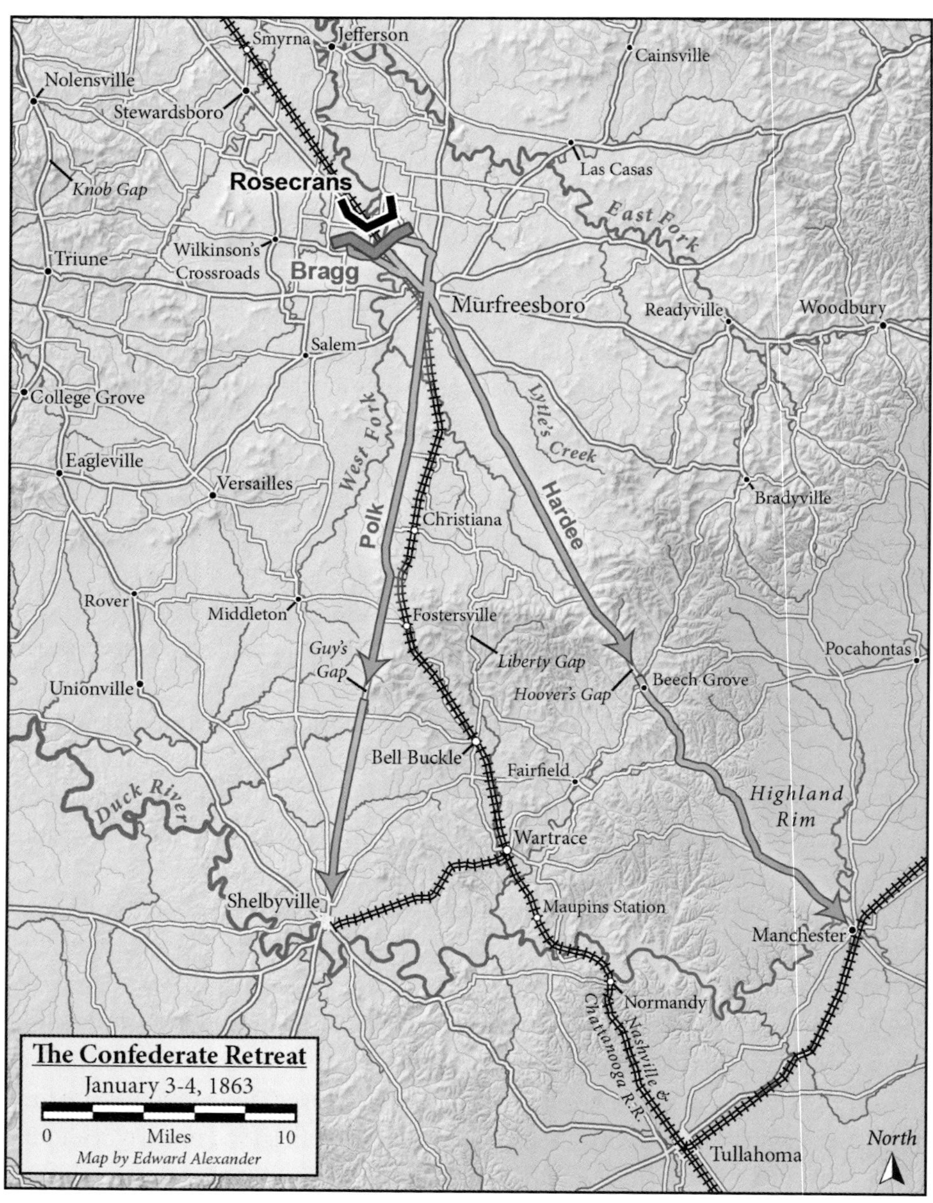

through them as it looked as if every one of them was making faces at you or looking at you."

"[I]t was raining all the time and the creeks were up, the mud awful," noted John Magee of Stanford's Battery. "My God-what suffering! Cold and chilly, no sleep for four or five nights, march through mud and water, some without any shoes, some sick, while behind on the bloody field thousands were moaning out the little life left in them while the rain still poured down."[32]

*   *   *

The rain finally ended just before dawn, and a short time later the sun burned brightly that Sunday morning. Suspecting the Confederates had retreated, General Palmer slipped his division across Stones River and indeed found that the Confederate lines were vacant. The good news rapidly made the rounds, though plenty of skepticism remained. "Few believed it while others argued that some hired spy had probably brought the news to draw us out of our position that the battle might be continued a few miles south of Murfreesboro," wrote Stevenson. He added that cavalry pickets soon reported "no enemy in sight and parties sent to the town confirmed the report that General Bragg had retreated. What shouts arose on every side!" The news traveled from one regiment to another as cheers rose along the column. "The men began to shout and hurrah with all the power of their lungs," continued Stevenson. "Some hugged each other and danced while others wept for joy."[33]

Federal pursuit was tepid at best. Writing to Cheatham, Wharton reported that "at 2:30 this afternoon the enemy was advancing on Murfreesboro very slowly and with great caution. You need feel no uneasiness and your command can rest in perfect security." As a matter of fact, Federal cavalry would not begin its pursuit south of Murfreesboro until January 5, skirmishing warmly with enemy cavalry at Lytle's Creek on the Manchester Pike and then lightly on the Shelbyville Pike. Other than capturing a few stragglers, Colonel Lewis Zahm reported that "the enemy had entirely disappeared."[34]

General Stanley was on the field early Sunday morning and remembered the grim carnage spread around him. "The dead lay strewn upon the ground by hundreds, the blue and the gray equally mingled," he wrote. "Most men die on their backs. A heavy frost had fallen the night before and the bearded men lay with their upturned whiskers whitened with hoar frost whilst the boys with clean fresh faces looked like the boys of a farmer's household not yet wakened from their morning's

32 Street Papers; Colman Letter; Magee Diary.

33 Stevenson, *Battle of Stone's River*, 148.

34 OR 20/2:483, Ibid., 1:618, 638.

sleep. And there were so many of these boys, it seemed that they formed one-half of death's harvest strewn like sheaves of wheat upon the ground."

Writing to his wife, surgeon William Johnson of the 18th Ohio noted that "war has its glories but it also has its ten thousand horrors and human tortures that would sicken any feeling heart. This city is one vast hospital full of misery and suffering. I have often wished to see a big battle but I pray God that I may never again witness such scenes as I have had to for the last two weeks."[35]

Captain William Robinson of the 77th Pennsylvania was among those who recorded the heart-wrenching scenes he witnessed. "Men had died while vainly striving with weakened hands to draw tightly the strings about the opened veins, their eager eyes still turned away towards our lines, looking for the help that never came," he wrote. "Some had crawled some distance then propped themselves into a sitting posture and with brave calmness greeted death's approach." William White of the 13th Ohio grieved that he personally buried 18 Federals and three Confederates in the following days, including a dear friend. "I went out to the Rebel breastworks and carried in four cartridge boxes, tore the sides out of them, and made a sort of coffin for Nelson," he wrote. "I did this so he can be handily taken up should his remains be sent for. We buried all of them in one grave though he can be taken up just as well as though he had been buried by himself. I could not see where he had been hurt, only a little scratch on the side of the neck, and where the Rebels ran a bayonet through his foot. I cut his name on a board then burnt it on so as to make it plain."[36]

*   *   *

The carnage at Murfreesboro was staggering. Rosecrans reported 1,730 men killed, 7,802 wounded, and 3,717 missing—a total of 13,249 from the roughly 43,400 engaged. Bragg, on the other hand, lost 1,294 men killed, 7,945 men wounded, and 1,027 missing—a total of 10,266 from the 37,712 engaged. The number of men reported missing in both armies is confusing; thousands of those captured were also listed as wounded, so it is likely many of those were double counted.

35 Stanley, *Personal Memoirs*, 128-29; Johnson Letter.

36 Robinson Letter; Private William H. White, Co. F, 13th Ohio, *Marysville Tribune*, Jan. 21, 1863, 2.

Rosecrans also reported that his army captured 3,694 men during the campaign, 2,667 more than Bragg reported. Likewise, Bragg reported that he captured 6,273 Federals at Murfreesboro, 2,556 men more than Rosecrans reported. Final reported casualty figures showed that the two armies lost a grand total of 23,515 casualties, making it the second costliest engagement of the Civil War to that point. In fact, if the figures for missing were truly closer to the higher figures both commanders reported, Stones River had been the costliest engagement of the war yet fought, topping two-day Shiloh (23,746 casualties) and one-day Antietam (22,717 casualties).

Stones River's purported time atop this cataract of horrors would last scarcely four months, however, before it would be eclipsed by the 1863 battles of Chancellorsville in May (30,500), Gettysburg in July (51,118), and by these same two armies again at Chickamauga in September (34,624). The first two engagements of Grant's Overland Campaign in May 1864 would also surpass Stones River, ultimately relegating the engagement to the sixth bloodiest of the war. "It was another one of those indecisive but fierce and deadly battles which illustrate the whole history of our Civil War," noted Union Captain Ephraim A. Otis. "The army that holds the battlefield and buries the dead may safely claim that it has won the victory."[37]

As the Federals moved in to occupy Murfreesboro, they found roughly 1,700 Confederates had been left behind, most of them sick or wounded. They needed to be cared for, fed, and housed. "Every house within ten miles of the rear of our army was made a hospital of, and to many of them large numbers of tents were added," noted Surgeon William Mills. "At one hospital alone, there was said to be 1,700 wounded and dead soldiers. The medical force was entirely inadequate to the task of attending to those men as they should have been attended to. Yet all was done that could be done to add to their comfort and save their lives. As it is, a single hospital may contain men from a hundred regiments, and many Rebel soldiers mixed up with our own men. Thousands of the Rebel wounded fell into our hands and are now receiving the same attention from us that our own wounded do."[38]

Surgeon George Coatsworth of the 88th Illinois literally worked himself to death attending to the wounded men of Sheridan's division. "Dr. Coatsworth was in the midst binding up the broken wounds and cheering the spirits of the mangled soldiers," observed one biographer. "The doctor was on the very edge of the battle,

37 Otis Article.

38 Mills Letter.

his ears appalled every now and then by hideous death yells, his heart smitten by beseeching eyes appealing to him so long as his strength lasted. All that time without food or rest, Dr. Coatsworth continued his almost superhuman efforts, drawn by the relief of one poor soul only to put his hands upon some other, in an endless succession of shattered and mutilated bodies. So, he worked until his strong frame gave way and he sank, utterly exhausted." Coatsworth took sick, developed pneumonia, and died on January 9, 1863—"in the noblest way a man can die: at his post in the laborious and faithful performance of his duty."[39]

* * *

Leonidas Polk's Corps arrived in Shelbyville on Sunday afternoon and went into camp near the Duck River. "Heard all kinds of rumors about the enemy, but one thing is certain," admitted artillerist Magee. "They have Murfreesboro." As he approached Tullahoma, Bragg came across a bedraggled Tennessean and inquired whether he "belong[ed] to Bragg's army." According to Colonel Urquhardt, the man replied, "Bragg's army? He's got none. He shot half of them in Kentucky and the other got killed up at Murfreesboro. The general laughed and rode on."

If the story was true, Bragg's laughter proved short-lived. The retreat from Murfreesboro landed him in hot water with both Richmond and the men of his army. Bragg's congratulatory message to his army, written at Winchester, Tennessee, on January 8, rang hollow. "Your gallant deeds have won the admiration of your general, your government and your country," it began. "Your achievements have been unparalleled. In retiring to a stronger position without molestation from a superior force, you have left him a barren field on which to bury his hosts of slain and recuperate his shattered ranks." Bragg suggested that he intended to send the army's cavalry to harass Rosecrans's supply lines "until we goad him to another advance only to meet a signal defeat. The proudest reflection of your general's life is to be known as the commander of an army so brave and invincible as you have proven. To share their trials and to stand or fall with them will be the crown of his ambition."[40]

The first reports of Bragg's retreat reached Richmond from Colonel Benjamin Ewell in Chattanooga, who telegraphed Secretary of War Seddon on January 4 that "Bragg has retreated from Murfreesboro and was by last accounts at Shelbyville."

39 Barnet, *Martyrs and Heroes of Illinois*, 226-27.

40 Magee Diary; Urquhart, *Battles & Leaders*, 3:609; Bunting Letter.

The following day Ewell reported the arrival in Chattanooga of "about 4,000 Federal prisoners, 5,000 stand of small arms, and 24 cannon brass and steel" and that Bragg "retreated from Murfreesboro in perfect order." Bragg sent his own dispatch from Tullahoma on January 5, stating that "unable to dislodge the enemy from his entrenchments and hearing of reinforcements to him, I withdrew from his front night before last. He has not followed."[41]

This news leaked quickly to the public. "During the day, an absurd rumor was invented to the effect that Bragg had been beaten," wrote war department clerk John Jones in Richmond. "It is to be feared that too many of Bragg's men were ordered to reinforce Pemberton. If that blunder should prove disastrous, the authorities here will have a hornet's nest about their ears." On January 6, the rumors became fact. "We are all down again," Jones wrote. "Bragg has retreated from Murfreesboro. I do not know how to reconcile Bragg's first dispatches and particularly the one saying he had the whole field and would follow the enemy with the last one announcing his withdrawal and retirement from the field. Eight thousand men were taken from Bragg a few days before the battle. It was not done at the suggestion of General Johnston for I have seen an extract of a letter from General Johnston to Senator Louis T. Wigfall deprecating the detachment of troops from Bragg and expressing grave apprehensions of the probable consequences."[42]

The retreat from Murfreesboro was a particularly bitter pill for Southerners to swallow. "Our army has fallen back to the hills and there among the hills they intend to make a stand and Bragg says he will fight Rosecrans again," wrote poet and diarist Lucy Virginia French. "Whether he will or not there is no telling." Bragg, continued the perceptive observer of the war in central Tennessee,

seems to be very unpopular with both soldiers and people. Old Mr. Spurlock gave free utterance in regard to him as a general. He says our position at Murfreesboro was badly chosen and blames Bragg that he did not renew the fight on Thursday January 1 before the enemy was reorganized. He says he doubts if Bragg knew what was going on in his front that day as he always saw him a half mile back of his rear line. While the battle was going on

41 *OR* 20/2:484.

42 Jones, *A Rebel War Clerk's Diary*, 147-48; "From Our Army in Tennessee," *Richmond Whig*, Jan. 7, 1863, 2.

and the men were beginning to see how it was managed, Mr. Spurlock said that Colonel John Savage remarked to him, "This may be good generalship, but if it is, I can't see it."[43]

Most of the army could not see it either. Recriminations and complaints about Bragg grew cacophonous. Captain Irving Buck on Cleburne's staff was unequivocal insisting that "giving up of Murfreesboro had a depressing effect upon the army. As at Perryville, the troops felt they had won a victory, the fruits of which had been lost from no fault of theirs and the retreat caused deep dissatisfaction which extended to many officers of high rank. The murmurs were not long in reaching General Bragg."

One officer wrote "every Tennessean is bitter beyond expression. Some swear he is a fool. I think he has been blessed with very little sense and no genius. It is useless to disguise the fact that Bragg's career as commanding general has eventuated in a disaster and disgraceful failure. He is almost universally hated by all our troops, especially the Tennesseans." And William Bryant of the 3rd Florida lamented that "could General Bragg have held Murfreesboro, it would have done wonders for him. As it is, it is unfortunate occurring so soon after the Kentucky campaign as the moral effect on the troops and the people is bad."[44]

Press reaction varied, most riding the line between questioning the results and outright criticism. The *Montgomery Weekly Advertiser* conceded that Bragg may have won a victory in Tennessee but also claimed that if not for Bragg's bumbling during the earlier Kentucky campaign, Stones River "would very likely never have been fought. Had the plan of General Beauregard been followed, it is more probable that the enemy would have been driven out of Tennessee and through Kentucky last fall." The generally anti-Bragg *Chattanooga Daily Rebel* cautioned the public against letting criticism descend into "personal abuse. General Bragg, it must be owned, is not popular as he unfortunately alienated many of his subordinates within the rank and file of his army who entertain neither confidence nor affection for him."[45]

The Western Confederate newspapers, though disappointed with the result of the battle, by and large accepted Bragg's explanation for his action. The *Mobile*

43 Journal of Lucy Virginia French, SRNBP. French, who lived near McMinnville, Tennessee, kept a detailed diary from February 1862 through June 26, 1865.

44 Buck, *Cleburne and His Command*, 124; Arch Frederic Blakey, ed., *Rose Cottage Chronicles: Civil War Letters of the Bryant-Stephens Families of North Florida* (Gainesville, 1988), 188; "A Rich Intercepted Letter from One of Bragg's Officers," *Nashville Daily Union*, Jan. 30, 1863, 2.

45 "The Battle of Murfreesboro," *Montgomery Weekly Advertiser*, Jan. 14, 1863, 1; "Criticism," *Chattanooga Daily Rebel*, Jan. 9, 1863, 2.

Advertiser & Register opined that "if General Bragg is open to censure at all, it is for fighting the enemy in such unequal force, but every man knows that if he retired without fighting the present drizzle of criticism would have turned into a storm of abuse. The humblest private in that army is worthy of more praise and honor than the author of the most learned and superb criticisms on what they failed to accomplish." The *Savannah News* agreed, declaring that "General Bragg has failed to do in Tennessee what our generals have failed to do in every general battle that has been fought since the commencement of the war. He has failed to utterly destroy or capture an army nearly three times as large as his own. For this he is given a bad name and must succumb to the prejudice or ignorance which his critics assume to be public opinion."[46]

Jones Withers was the first in the army to publicly raise his voice in Bragg's defense, stating in a letter on January 17 that the retreat was suggested by "two division and sustained by a corps commander" (Withers did not offer that he was one of them) and "was rejected by the General commanding. On the morning of the 3rd, [Bragg] ascertained that all the corps and division commanders concurred in the opinion that the army should be withdrawn. Suppose the general had adhered to his first determination, and disaster had been the result, what would have been his proposition then? If this movement did not command the approbation of every brigade, division, and corps commander then present with the army, I have yet to hear of the exception."

Another officer argued that "the fight at Murfreesboro was a brilliant victory to our arms and we secured in it fruits in arms, transportation, and prisoners. A second victory was achieved in the retreat." He reminded readers of the army's state of exhaustion, Stones River's rising waters, and the late reinforcements Rosecrans received. "Was it not wise to avoid a conflict between troops such as ours then were and fresh men?" he argued. "Anything more than the slaughter of numbers of our men and final retreat was out of the question, and our total dispersion was entirely in the range of possibilities. The event the enemy would have cheerfully bought with the lives of 5,000 of their soldiers. General Bragg was the last to consent to the proposition for a retreat; let the more active of General Bragg's enemies say, if they dare, who proposed this retreat from Murfreesboro."[47]

46 "Murfreesboro," *Mobile Advertiser & Register*, Jan. 10, 1863, 2; "General Bragg," *Mobile Advertiser & Register*, Jan. 16, 1863, 2.

47 Letter from Major General Jones Withers, *Mobile Advertiser & Register*, Jan. 18, 1863, 2; Letter from Luck, *Mobile Advertiser & Register*, Jan. 27, 1863, 2.

All the same, an unsigned article in the *Chattanooga Daily Rebel* stung Bragg to the core, charging that he retreated from Murfreesboro against the advice of his generals. This latest perfidy convinced Bragg that his reputation was being destroyed from within by unscrupulous staff officers. He shared the article with members of his staff on January 10, saying that if the accusations were true, he would resign his command. Then he asked his staff whether they believed he had lost the confidence of the army and, if so, he would retire. "The staff met and compared opinions and the conclusion was that under existing circumstances, the general interests concerned that General Bragg should at once be relieved," recorded George Brent. The following day Bragg drafted a letter requesting his corps and division commanders to put in writing that they had counseled Bragg unanimously to retreat from Murfreesboro. That question was straightforward enough, but the commander added a last line that implied a secondary issue: "I shall retire without regret if I find that I have lost the good opinion of my generals upon whom I have ever relied as upon a foundation of rock."[48]

With that statement, Bragg undoubtedly was asking his generals if they had lost their confidence in him; at least that was how most of the generals interpreted it. Hardee responded first, agreeing that he had advised Bragg to retire from Murfreesboro and stating "frankness compels me to say that the general officers, whose judgments you have invoked, are unanimous in the opinion that a change of command of this army is necessary. In this opinion I concur." Breckinridge's brigadiers agreed with their chief that Bragg did not "possess the confidence of the army" as did Cleburne and his brigadiers.

General Polk, who was away from the army for personal reasons until January 20, did not reply until January 30 when he expressed confusion on what exactly Bragg was asking. By then, Bragg had hotly reiterated to his subordinates that the note contained only one avenue of inquiry and that it had been "grossly and intentionally misrepresented for my injury." Bragg remained in command following a visit by Jefferson Davis in late January Purportedly out of trouble with Richmond, he submitted his after-action report of the battle in late February, principally criticizing Breckinridge for his actions on December 31 and for the poor execution of the attack on January 2.

Bragg's comments so incensed Breckinridge that he demanded a formal court of inquiry. He never got one, and the in-fighting would continue until Breckinridge was reassigned to Mississippi in the spring. The widespread dissension within the

48 Brent Journal; *OR* 20/1:699.

officer corps that this episode laid bare became the hallmark the Army of Tennessee for the remainder of the war.[49]

*   *   *

The battle led to recrimination and fault-finding within the Army of the Cumberland, too. General McCook came in for some measure of criticism, but many in the army settled on General Richard W. Johnson as the villain of the affair, blaming him for the disaster that befell the right on December 31. The hue and cry against Johnson spread throughout the army but reached its heights within his own division, some men going as far as to call Johnson a traitor. Colonel Charles Anderson of the 93rd Ohio, in Baldwin's brigade, wrote to his wife that it would have been better for all concerned if General Sill had been retained in command of the division instead of Johnson. "If he had stayed in it and the other changes had not been made, not only would both commands have fared better but I really believe we should have had for the whole army the most overwhelming, crushing, and exterminating victory in the war. For we were surprised and with Sill, that was an utter impossibility."[50]

Another Buckeye wrote to a legislator back home that Johnson's whereabouts during the battle were a complete mystery. "Johnson was God knows where," he wrote. "I have not yet found a single man of the Second Division who saw him that morning until nearly 12 o'clock when the division had been driven back some three miles to near the Nashville Pike, then for the first time he was seen. He was a fugitive from his division and the earnest prayers of the men and officers of the division upon that memorable morning was that he might never get off the field alive. We are taught to be mere machines to be handled by these skillful and watchful Generals at their pleasure. The commanding General of our division, however, was only capable of taking care of himself, and his division shifted for itself."

James Martin of the 6th Ohio complained in a letter to his mother that Johnson's "incredible negligence or treason" caused the Federal disaster, averring that "if we had as good generals as the Southerners, the war would be over." One soldier from the 15th Ohio blamed newspaper men for screening "the officers who did the blundering and who are to blame for the disasters that befell the army. But

49 OR 20/1:700-701.

50 Colonel Charles Anderson, 93rd Ohio, David T. Dixon Collection.

this is all we can expect from these hired pimps who exist here by the sufferance of these same officers and who get their bread by writing of the heroic deeds of the same starry gentry."[51]

Rosecrans became the new shining star of the Northern press as William Bickham's widely copied laudatory reporting in the *Cincinnati Commercial* ensured that the general's heroism during the battle received ample notice. "Have we found our leader?" asked the *Toledo Blade*. "His name is in the columns of every paper and upon the lips of every patriot. He has been more uniformly successful than any of our generals as he never loses a battle." The *New York Daily Tribune* lauded the victory with "no one can read the description of our correspondent that in its course our army was at one time upon the very brink of utter destruction, and that the presence of mind, coolness, judicious and prompt use of what remained of means of resistance by the commander-in-chief alone saved the day and ensured our ultimate success." The editor further opined that Rosecrans "possesses the qualities of a great captain in a higher degree than any other of our generals has had capacity or opportunity to exhibit."[52]

Enhancing Rosecrans's bona fides were numerous soldiers' accounts that attested to his courage and sagacity under fire. Some soldiers, however, privately expressed doubts about Rosecrans' capacity for high command. "He failed to produce an impression as one who grasped the whole situation with the hand of a master," observed the regimental historians of the 41st Ohio. "After this came the usual supply of stories about the battle and, true or false, they had their effect on the army's estimate of its commander. Somewhere there had been a lack of vigilance to which the 41st was accustomed."[53]

Was Stones River really a Federal victory? Northern politicians, press, and historians certainly viewed it that way. The legislatures of both Ohio and Indiana passed resolutions thanking Rosecrans and his army for their battlefield accomplishments at the battle. The Union army claimed the field, but the Confederates obtained more of the spoils of war. Most of the Federals delighted in their victory, but many struggled to see it as any vindication of Federal superiority.

51 Unknown Ohio officer, *Ohio State Journal*, Feb. 11, 1863, pg. 1; Private Jacques Martin, Co. I, 6th Ohio, SRNBP; Unknown soldier of 15th Ohio, *Belmont Chronicle*, Feb. 19, 1863, 1.

52 "Have We Found Our Leader," *Toledo Blade*, Jan. 9, 1863, 2; "The Battles Before Murfreesboro-Gen. Rosecrans," *New York Tribune*, Jan. 9, 1863, 4.

53 Kimberly, *The 41st Ohio*, 44.

Lieutenant John Cummins of the 99th Ohio complained to his wife that "our brigade and division was very badly mangled. I am willing to fight every day but I don't like to be sacrificed by incompetent men. We made but little of the fight. It was a dearly bought victory." One soldier of the 13th Ohio conceded that in the fight "both sides were badly used up though our papers will claim it as a victory. The real truth is we have nothing to exult over." Colonel Grider of the 9th Kentucky agreed, stating that "the victory was only left to the side on the field for neither had anything to boast of. We held out the longest and hence were victorious and this is the only claim to victory we have."[54]

A common perception of Stones River is that it represented meaningless carnage, one historian summing it up as "few Civil War battles ever cost more or meant less." While true that the battle did not return large swathes of territory to Union military control, this assessment overlooks the battle's significance in the overall trajectory of the war. A third defeat following Fredericksburg and Chickasaw Bayou might have proved fatal to the Union cause, potentially opening the door further to intervention by England. The political importance of the timely victory to the Lincoln administration cannot be overstated. "It was known by President Lincoln that the Emancipation Proclamation amounted to nothing unless it was enforced by force of arms at the sword's point," wrote Captain Milton Bell of the 86th Indiana. "On that day Lincoln was anxious for a victory as we had lost at Vicksburg and Fredericksburg."[55]

Lincoln concurred with Bell's assessment, writing Rosecrans a heartfelt letter in August 1863 in which he said, "I can never forget, whilst I remember anything, that about the end of last year and the beginning of this, you gave us a hard-earned victory which, had there been a defeat instead, the nation could scarcely have lived over."

Stones River represented yet another step on the bloody continuum of the war in the West. These two armies would contest for control of Middle Tennessee for the next six months before Rosecrans's maneuvering in the Tullahoma Campaign finally drove Bragg's army out of Tennessee. The primary objective of the Federal army since mid-1862 had been to gain control of the critical railroad junction at Chattanooga, and this aim would consume both armies for the balance of 1863. As

---

54 McCray, *A Shouting of Orders*, 74; "From the 13th Ohio, *Cadiz Sentinel*, Jan. 21, 1863, 3; Grider Letter.

55 *Proceedings of the Eighth Annual*, 7.

such, Stones River marked both the end of the beginning of the war, and the beginning of the end of the war.[56]

The commanding generals of both armies had nothing but praise for their enlisted men. "Above all, the sturdy rank and file showed invincible fighting courage and stamina, worthy of a great and free nation, requiring only good officers, discipline, and instructions to make them equal, if not superior, to any troops in ancient or modern times," boasted Rosecrans. Bragg, who was rarely noted for eloquent expression, outdid Rosecrans in praising his men. "No encomium is too high, no honor too great for such a soldiery," he declared. "In the absence of the instruction and discipline of old armies, and of the confidence which long association produces between veterans," he continued,

> we have had in a great measure to trust to the individuality and self-reliance of the private soldier. Without the incentive or the motive which controls the officer, who hopes to live in history; without the hope of reward and actuated only by a sense of duty and of patriotism, he has, in this great contest, justly judged that the cause was his own, and gone into it with a determination to conquer or die; to be free or not to be at all. However much credit and glory may be given the leaders in our struggle, history will yet award the main honor where it is due: to the private soldier, who, without hope of reward, and with no other incentive than a consciousness of rectitude, has encountered all the hardships and suffered all the privations.[57]

The fighting at Stones River turned the soldiers of both armies into hardened veterans. The campaign tested their fortitude and endurance far beyond anything they had yet experienced. Marching, fighting, and living for days under conditions marked by frequent rain, abundant mud, and bitter cold, forced them to discover reserves of inner strength they had no inkling they possessed. It was the first time under fire for thousands on both sides. Mistakes were made that cost some their reputations and others their lives. The fighting was intense, personal, and bloody, and those who survived were forever marked by the experience.

One thing the soldiers of both armies now knew was that they had underestimated their opponents at their own peril. After the bloodbaths at Shiloh, Perryville, and Stones River, any thoughts doubting the courage, skill, or tenacity of their opponents had been replaced by a healthy respect for one's adversary.

56 Otis Article.

57 OR 20/1:199, 670-671.

Unfortunately, with the advent of these veteran armies, the war in the West would only grow bloodier in the coming two years.

Brigadier General William Hazen, promoted for his critical actions in holding the Round Forest, believed that the men of his brigade deserved a permanent monument to commemorate their heroism at Stones River. On the last weekend of March 1863, a detail of 25 men under the command of Lieutenant Edward Crebbin of the 9th Indiana in Hazen's command returned to the Stones River battlefield from its encampment at Readyville, Tennessee, tasked with erecting a monument to their fallen comrades. "We took spades, picks, guns, accouterments, haversacks, and canteens and took passage in two government wagons," recalled Henry Warner of the 41st Ohio.

The detachment arrived at the shattered remnant of the Round Forest and set to their work of commemoration. "The enclosure is 94 feet long and 19 feet wide and parallel to the railroad. At the east end lies Anthony Douse of Battery F of the 1st Ohio Light Artillery—his head is to the south," Warner continued. "Those of the 41st are at the east end with their heads to the east. Next to them is the 6th Kentucky, then the 9th Indiana, and lastly the 110th Illinois. The fence consists of cedar posts set close together four-and-a-half feet high. In the center of the enclosure stands a cedar 40 feet high. Beside it, we built a pyramid of 65 12-lb shot and a stile over the side of the fence next to the pike, filled the mound for each grave, and at the head of each, planted a cedar."[58]

Later that summer, a limestone masonry monument described as a "quadrangular pyramidal shaft ten feet square and eleven feet in height" was erected, with an inscription carved the following year by stonemasons from the 115th Ohio commemorating the names of the 17 officers of Hazen's brigade who fell during the battle. The south face of the monument reads as follows: "Hazen's Brigade/To the memory of its soldiers who fell at Stones River, Dec. 31st 1862/Their faces towards Heaven, their feet to the foe."

Interestingly, in 1985, when the National Park Service commenced restoration work on the monument, nine relics were discovered buried within its interior. A virtual time capsule of the battle, the relics included three rifled cannon shells, three cannon balls, two rifle barrels, and a cedar staff—likely placed inside by Hazen's men.

*　　*　　*

58 Private Henry J. Warner, Co. G, 41st Ohio, *Jeffersonian Democrat*, May 15, 1863, 2.

Six months after the carnage, Private Henry J. Warner of the 41st Ohio returned to the scene where so much blood had been spilled. The scene was still haunting. "When at leisure, I wandered over the field. Shells of various descriptions lay scattered harmlessly about and here and there a pile of rails marked the abode of death," he observed. "I could not stay the trembling tear when so forcibly reminded of my departed comrade Joel Strong who shared with me our blankets and pillow and who breathed his last amid the roar of battle. 'Tell my friends that I die for my country and trusting in my God,' he said. I hope to never again be called to witness such soul-sickening scenes as I was obliged to view at night upon that awful field."[59]

59 Ibid.

Postscript:
The Case for Preservation

"To appreciate history, we must evoke our imaginations, and this is best achieved through direct contact with the things that remain from past days." — Senator John Heinz[1]

MURFREESBORO REMAINED IN Federal hands for the rest of the war. The grounds along Stones River would once more thunder with the clash of arms in December 1864 during Confederate General John Bell Hood's invasion of Tennessee, but as the armies moved south after the initial battle, Murfreesboro's importance as a Federal supply depot diminished. By the end of the conflict, it had reverted to a backwater community.

Like so many other Southern towns whose names were attached to the horrible carnage marked by the collisions of the armies, Murfreesboro was left to pick up the pieces and get on with the business of living. Families returned to the battlefield and planted corn and cotton, raised cattle and hogs, married, had children, and died. Farmers frequently plowed up bullets, shell fragments, buttons, bones, and other reminders of the men and the armies.

The thousands of Federal soldiers who died here and at nearby battlefields were buried in a national cemetery between the Nashville and Chattanooga Railroad and Nashville Pike atop the ground defended by Rosecrans's men during the fierce fighting the afternoon of December 31. Initial work on the cemetery began in 1864 as hundreds of Federal dead from Franklin, Cowan, Columbia, Shelbyville, and Tullahoma were disinterred, conveyed to Murfreesboro, and reburied. The identities of thousands of these men were lost during the transfer.

---

1   Francis H. Kennedy, *The Civil War Battlefield Guide* (Houghton Mifflin, 1998), 201.

In 1867, local citizens moved more than 2,000 Confederate dead from a mass grave south of town into the Confederate Cemetery. Within a few years, the graveyard fell into such disrepair that the city of Murfreesboro purchased a plot in Evergreen Cemetery and reinterred the Southern dead there. The process took nearly a decade, and the wooden markers that once noted the final resting places deteriorated. Most of the names of those buried there are now lost.

As the 19th century drew to a close, Civil War veterans began to lobby for the creation of national battlefields to commemorate those sacred grounds. Following establishment of the Chickamauga & Chattanooga National Battlefield Park in 1895, a private organization called the Stones River Battlefield and Park Association sought to preserve the battlefield in Murfreesboro in a similar manner while lobbying Congress to designate it a national military park. Initial efforts centered around erecting wooden signs pointing out important battlefield locations while securing options to purchase up to 6,000 acres of battlefield land.

The location of the railroad east of the national cemetery made it a popular stopping place for veterans, and what was now the Nashville, St. Louis, and Chattanooga Railroad capitalized on this by using imagery depicting the battle in their advertising and also by purchasing six acres of land along the rail bed to commemorate the battle. The railroad even erected a highly visible 31-foot obelisk in 1906 to mark the location of the Federal artillery line on January 2 above McFadden's Ford on what was known as McFadden Heights.

Despite these efforts, Congress refused to take action, partly because of the continued opposition of Chickamauga & Chattanooga National Military Park commissioner Charles H. Grosvenor, a veteran of the 18th Ohio who had fought at Stones River. Grosvenor argued that "more than 50 years have elapsed since the battle of Stones River and the marks, locations, earthworks, and whatever else there was entirely obliterated."

A study from the 1926 passage of the Act for the Study and Investigation of Battlefields, however, led to the recommendation that established Stones River National Military Park on March 3, 1927. Although more than 3,100 acres had been identified as core battlefield, the War Department lacked funding to purchase it all and focused on what it considered the most crucial tracts, aiming to add subsequent tracks if funding became available.

The first acquisition of 325 acres encompassed the core of today's battlefield, bordered by the railroad to the north, the Wilkinson/Manson Pike to the south, McFadden's Lane to the east, and west toward the Blanton House. Two small tracts marking the headquarters locations of Bragg and Rosecrans were also added, and by 1934 the park totaled 344 acres. Work began in July 1930 to revert the field to its wartime appearance, which included the destruction and removal of postwar agricultural structures and homes. New roads spanned the park, and four public access gates were opened along the old Nashville Pike to accommodate visitors. A wire fence marked the perimeter of the park and served to prevent the encroachment of wandering livestock.

Four trailside exhibits detailing the movements of the armies were erected to help portray the story of the battle, and during the busier summer season, a hired guide would help visitors navigate the grounds or find an ancestor's grave in the cemetery. The park was officially dedicated July 15, 1932—a torrid 100-degree day on which General Benjamin F. Cheatham Jr., son of the Confederate division commander who had fought at Stones River, provided the keynote address.

Administrative responsibility for Stones River transferred from the War Department to the Department of the Interior and the National Park Service in August 1933. Stones River remained a rarely visited "backwater" national park for much of its early existence, but the outbreak of hostilities in Europe combined with a rapid increase in the size of the U.S. Army led many visitors to stop at the park while visiting their relatives in the army.

In July 1941, the Murfreesboro Daily News-Journal reported that, "so far this month 1,000 people have visited the park which is a record figure except during the recent army maneuvers which saw as high as 1,700 visitors in one weekend." The assistant superintendent reported that "people are mostly interested in the number of casualties in the battle" and that "every few days we have someone from the northern states visit the park and ask to see grandpa's grave."[2]

In the mid-1950s, National Park Service Director Conrad Wirth secured congressional support for a widespread program of revitalization for all of the national parks known as Mission 66. "This ambitious, multi-million-dollar project involved improving roads, expanding park facilities, and repairing existing infrastructure," explained park historians. In 1960, as part of the national centennial commemorations of the Civil War, the park was enlarged by six acres and renamed Stones River National Battlefield Park. Mission 66 work began in Murfreesboro in 1962 with construction of a new visitor's center and parking lot, which opened in time for the battle's 101st anniversary in 1963.

"Where once stood an ancient white frame house with one room for the park staff and several rooms for the superintendent and his family now stands an interesting three-façade visitor's center," boasted the Nashville Banner. The new

2 "Visitors Increase at Park," *Murfreesboro Daily News-Journal*, July 24, 1941, 1

visitor center also offered a 60-seat auditorium, lobby, and a museum where park historians explained the story of the battle and its significance in the Civil War. Workers also updated the landscaping and built a new single loop road through the park, in addition to constructing three residences for park personnel and a new shop and utility building for park maintenance. A dedication ceremony on April 11, 1964, marked the park's rebirth "as a reminder of the United States' struggle to maturity as a great nation." The Mission 66 improvements led to a 45-percent increase in visitors in 1964 and remain features of the battlefield today.[3]

It was also in the early 1960s that the core battlefield suffered its first major loss with the construction of Interstate 24, which runs directly through the ground contested by Sheridan's and Cheatham's divisions on the morning of December 31. The park's holdings grew slowly in the latter half of the 20th century and early 21st century with the donation of a portion of Fort Rosecrans in 1992 along with 74 acres secured by the American Battlefield Trust through five separate acquisitions.

The introduction of the interstate led to rampant commercial growth west along Tennessee 96, and by the early 21st century the southern half of the field seemed irretrievably lost to development. Dozens of hotels, restaurants, stores, and malls sprang up along the Wilkinson Pike in the early 2000s. This sprawling growth trend continues for Murfreesboro as we approach the battle's 162nd anniversary with the publication of this book.

Prospects for battlefield preservation at Murfreesboro appear dire. Only a thin few scattered pockets of undeveloped land exist south of the Wilkinson Turnpike—sectors quickly being turned into apartments, townhouses, or commercial enterprises. The site of where the battle began, near the intersection of Gresham Lane and Franklin Road, is lined with a proliferation of gas stations, nail salons, and fast-food restaurants.

An undeveloped lot of land along Agripark Drive that roughly follows the line occupied by Union Brig. Gen. Edward Kirk's 2nd Brigade in Richard Johnson's 2nd Division has been turned into an unofficial residence for Murfreesboro's homeless population. The site of the ferocious battle between Union Colonel Philemon P. Baldwin's brigade and St. John Richardson Liddell's Arkansans is today a residential neighborhood. Interstate 24 cuts right through where the Union brigades commanded by William Carlin, William Woodruff, and Joshua Sill fought

---

3 "Stones River Battlefield Facelifting Includes New Headquarters, Museum," *Nashville Banner*, December 17, 1963, 28; "Renewed Battlefield Called Reminder," *The Tennessean*, April 12, 1964, 2.

against Cheatham's Division, while the urban sprawl that is Medical Center Parkway sits atop the ground where Phil Sheridan's men fought and died during those crucial hours the morning of December 31. One wonders what General Sill would think of folks sipping their morning lattes on the very ground where he and so many of his comrades gave their lives.

Following the battle's progress north, a large neighborhood has been built west of the park proper where the wreckage of McCook's Right Wing retreated with the Confederates in pursuit on December 31. The same neighborhood sits atop ground fought on by Charles Harker's, James Fyffe's, and Samuel Beatty's Federal brigades and the Confederate commands of Liddell, Alfred Vaughan, S.A.M. Wood, and Bushrod Johnson at the crucial midpoint of the first day's fighting.

Asbury Lane broadly follows the retreat route of McCook's wing and where the major cavalry fighting of December 31 occurred. Thankfully, the national battlefield has preserved the majority of the cedar forest, the Round Forest, and the grounds held by the Federals to maintain control of the Nashville Pike. Just beyond the park boundaries lies the site of the bloody ground where hundreds of Mississippians of J. Patton Anderson's Brigade went down assaulting James Negley's division. Today this land is a residential neighborhood and a medical center. Crossing Stones River, the site of the Breckinridge's assault and the Kentuckians' lament, is one neighborhood after another, the last undeveloped land ploughed up in 2021. Perhaps we are fortunate that Wayne's Hill became part of a golf course, which should remain greenspace for at least the foreseeable future.

It would be reasonable to think all opportunity for preservation is lost at Stones River. That might not be the case. Consider the remarkable changes that have been made in nearby Franklin, Tennessee, where a hard-fought and long-term effort by dedicated preservationists has resulted in stunning changes for the better in the past 20 years. Previously, the epicenter of the fighting at Franklin was marked by a Pizza Hut and concrete. Today the Pizza Hut is long gone and interpretive signage and greenspace mark some of the most hallowed ground in Tennessee.

Opportunity still exists to preserve portions of the field at Stones River west and north of the park itself, but it will take determined efforts by local preservationists teaming with national partners to raise sufficient funding to secure these tracts. The real estate market in Murfreesboro has been booming for years, and the appetite for land to build new homes and businesses appears insatiable. Unless action is taken within the next few years, these few remaining open tracts of battlefield land will be eyed as potential sites for development and lost forever.

Order of Battle

Army of the Cumberland
Maj. Gen. William Starke Rosecrans

Right Wing
Maj. Gen. Alexander McDowell McCook

First (former 9th) Division
Brig. Gen. Jefferson Columbus Davis

First (former 30th) Brigade
Col. Phillip Sidney Post
59th Illinois, 74th Illinois, 75th Illinois, 22nd Indiana,
5th Wisconsin Light Artillery Battery

Second (former 31st) Brigade
Col. William Passmore Carlin
21st Illinois, 38th Illinois, 101st Ohio, 15th Wisconsin,
2nd Minnesota Light Artillery Battery

Third (former 32nd) Brigade
Col. William E. Woodruff
25th Illinois, 35th Illinois, 81st Indiana,
8th Wisconsin Light Artillery Battery

Second Division
Brig. Gen. Richard W. Johnson

First (former 6th) Brigade
Brig. Gen. August Willich/Col. William Wallace/
Col. William H. Gibson
89th Illinois, 32nd Indiana, 39th Indiana, 15th Ohio,
49th Ohio, Battery A, 1st Ohio Light Artillery

Second (former 5th) Brigade
Brig. Edward Needles Kirk/
Col. Joseph B. Dodge
34th Illinois, 79th Illinois, 29th Indiana, 30th Indiana,
77th Pennsylvania, Battery E, 1st Ohio Light Artillery

Third (former 4th) Brigade
Col. Philemon Prindle Baldwin
6th Indiana, 5th Kentucky, 1st Ohio, 93rd Ohio,
5th Indiana Light Artillery Battery

Third (former 11th) Division
Brig. Gen. Philip Henry Sheridan

First Brigade
Brig. Gen. Joshua Woodrow Sill/
Col. Nicholas Greusel, Jr.
36th Illinois, 88th Illinois, 21st Michigan, 24th
Wisconsin, 4th Indiana Light Artillery Battery

Second (former 35th) Brigade
Col. Frederick Schaefer/
Lt. Col. Bernard Laiboldt
44th Illinois, 73rd Illinois, 2nd Missouri, 15th
Missouri, Battery G, 1st Missouri
Light Artillery Battery

Third Brigade
Col. George Williamson Roberts/
Col. Luther Prentice Bradley
22nd Illinois, 27th Illinois, 42nd Illinois, 51st Illinois,
Battery C, 1st Illinois Light Artillery Battery

Center Corps
Maj. Gen. George Henry Thomas

First (former 3rd) Division
Maj. Gen. Lovell Harrison Rousseau

First (former 9th) Brigade
Col. Benjamin Franklin Scribner
38th Indiana, 2nd Ohio, 33rd Ohio, 94th Ohio,
10th Wisconsin

Second (former 17th) Brigade
Col. John Beatty
42nd Indiana, 88th Indiana, 15th Kentucky, 3rd Ohio,
Battery A, 1st Michigan Light Artillery

Third (former 28th) Brigade
Col. John Converse Starkweather
24th Illinois, 79th Pennsylvania, 1st Wisconsin,
21st Wisconsin, Battery A, Kentucky Light Artillery

Fourth Brigade "Regular Brigade"
Lt. Col. Oliver Lathrop Shepherd
15th U.S. Infantry, 16th U.S. Infantry, 18th U.S.
Infantry, 19th U.S. Infantry, Battery H,
5th U.S. Light Artillery

Second (former 8th) Division
Brig. Gen. James Scott Negley

Second (former 29th) Brigade
Col. Timothy Robbins Stanley
19th Illinois, 11th Michigan, 18th Ohio, 69th Ohio,
Battery M, 1st Ohio Volunteer Light Artillery

Third (former 7th) Brigade
Col. John Franklin Miller
37th Indiana, 21st Ohio, 74th Ohio, 78th
Pennsylvania, Battery B, Kentucky Volunteer Light
Artillery, Battery G, 1st Ohio Volunteer Light Artillery

First Brigade, Third Division
Col. Moses B. Walker
82nd Indiana, 17th Ohio, 31st Ohio, 38th Ohio,
Battery D, 1st Michigan Volunteer Light Artillery

Spears' Provisional Brigade
Brig. Gen. James Gallant Spears
85th Illinois, 14th Michigan, 1st Tennessee, 2nd
Tennessee, 3rd Tennessee Cavalry,
10th Wisconsin Volunteer Light Artillery Battery

McCook's Provisional Brigade
Col. Daniel McCook
60th Illinois, 10th Michigan, 52nd Ohio,
6th Tennessee

Left Wing
Maj. Gen. Thomas Leonidas Crittenden

First (former 6th) Division
Brig. Gen. Thomas John Wood /
Brig. Gen. Milo Smith Hascall

First (former 15th) Brigade
Brig. Gen. Milo Smith Hascall/
Col. George Pearson Buell
100th Illinois, 58th Indiana, 3rd Kentucky, 26th Ohio,
8th Indiana Light Artillery Battery

Second (former 21st) Brigade
Col. George Day Wagner
15th Indiana, 40th Indiana, 57th Indiana, 97th Ohio,
10th Indiana Light Artillery Battery

Third (former 20th) Brigade
Col. Charles Garrison Harker
51st Indiana, 73rd Indiana, 13th Michigan, 64th Ohio,
65th Ohio, 6th Ohio Light Artillery Battery

Second (former 4th) Division
Brig. Gen. John McAuley Palmer

First (former 22nd) Brigade
Brig. Gen. Charles Cruft
31st Indiana, 1st Kentucky, 2nd Kentucky, 90th Ohio

Second (former 19th) Brigade
Col. William Babcock Hazen
110th Illinois, 9th Indiana, 6th Kentucky, 41st Ohio

Third (former 10th) Brigade
Col. William Grose
84th Illinois, 36th Indiana, 23rd Kentucky,
6th Ohio, 24th Ohio

Divisional Artillery
Battery B, 1st Ohio Volunteer Light Artillery, Battery
F, 1st Ohio Volunteer Light Artillery, Batteries H and
M, 4th U.S. Light Artillery

Third (former 5th) Division
Brig. Gen. Horatio Phillips Van Cleve/
Col. Samuel Beatty

First Brigade
Col. Samuel Beatty/Col. Benjamin C. Grider
79th Indiana, 9th Kentucky, 11th Kentucky,
19th Ohio

Second (former 14th) Brigade
Col. James Perry Fyffe
44th Indiana, 86th Indiana, 13th Ohio, 59th Ohio

Third (former 23rd) Brigade
Col. Samuel Woodson Price
35th Indiana, 8th Kentucky, 21st Kentucky, 51st
Ohio, 99th Ohio

Divisional Artillery
7th Indiana Volunteer Light Artillery Battery, Battery
B, (26th) Pennsylvania Volunteer Light Artillery, 3rd
Wisconsin Volunteer Light Artillery Battery

Cavalry Corps, Army of the Cumberland
Brig. Gen. David Sloane Stanley

Cavalry Division
Col. John Kennett

First Brigade
Col. Robert Horatio George Minty
3rd Kentucky, 4th Michigan, 7th Pennsylvania

Second Brigade
Col. Lewis Zahm
1st Ohio, 3rd Ohio, 4th Ohio

Reserve and Unattached Cavalry
15th Pennsylvania, 1st Middle Tennessee, 2nd
Tennessee, 4th U.S. Cavalry

Divisional Artillery
Battery D, 1st Ohio Volunteer Light Artillery

Pioneers and Mechanics
1st Michigan Engineers and Mechanics

Pioneer Brigade
Capt. James St. Clair Morton
1st Battalion, 2nd Battalion, 3rd Battalion,
Chicago Board of Trade Battery

Army of Tennessee
Gen. Braxton Bragg

Polk's Corps
Lt. Gen. Leonidas Polk

Cheatham's Division
Maj. Gen. Benjamin Franklin Cheatham

Donelson's Brigade
Brig. Gen. Daniel Smith Donelson
8th Tennessee, 16th Tennessee, 38th Tennessee,
51st Tennessee, 84th Tennessee,
Carnes' Tennessee Battery

Stewart's Brigade
Brig. Gen. Alexander Peter Stewart
4th/5th Tennessee, 19th Tennessee, 24th Tennessee,
31st/33rd Tennessee, Stanford's Mississippi Battery

Maney's Brigade
Brig. Gen. George Maney
1st/27th Tennessee, 4th Tennessee,
6th/9th Tennessee, Maney's Tennessee
Sharpshooters, Smith's Mississippi Battery

Smith's Brigade
Col. Alfred Jefferson Vaughan, Jr.
12th/47th Tennessee, 13th Tennessee, 29th Tennesse,
154th Tennessee, Allin's Tennessee Sharpshooters,
9th Texas, Scott's Tennessee Battery

Withers' Division
Maj. Gen. Jones Mitchell Withers

Deas's Brigade
Col. John Quincy Loomis/Col. John Gordon Coltart
19th Alabama, 22nd Alabama, 25th Alabama,
26th Alabama, 39th Alabama,
17th Battalion Alabama Sharpshooters,
1st Louisiana Regulars, Robertson's
(Alabama and Florida) Battery

Chalmers' Brigade
Brig. Gen. James Ronald Chalmers/
Col. Thomas W. White
7th Mississippi, 9th/10th Mississippi, 41st Mississippi,
44th Mississippi, 9th Battalion Mississippi
Sharpshooters, Garrity's Alabama Artillery Battery

Walthall's Brigade
Brig. Gen. James Patton Anderson
45th Alabama, 24th Mississippi, 27th Mississippi,
29th Mississippi, 30th Mississippi, 37th Mississippi,
39th North Carolina, Barret's Missouri Battery

Anderson's Brigade
Col. Arthur Middleton Manigault
24th Alabama, 28th Alabama, 34th Alabama,
10th/19th South Carolina, Waters' Alabama Battery

Hardee's Corps
Lt. Gen. William J. Hardee

Breckinridge's Division
Maj. Gen. John Cabell Breckinridge

Adams' Brigade
Brig. Gen. Daniel Weisiger Adams/
Col. Randall Lee Gibson
32nd Alabama, 13th/20th Louisiana,
16th/25th Louisiana, 14th
Battalion Louisiana Sharpshooters,
5th Company, Washington Light Artillery

Palmer's/Pillow's Brigade
Col. Joseph Benjamin Palmer/
Brig. Gen. Gideon Johnson Pillow
18th Tennessee, 26th Tennessee, 28th Tennessee,
45th Tennessee, Moses' Georgia Battery

Preston's Brigade
Brig. Gen. William Preston
1st/3rd Florida, 4th Florida, 60th North Carolina,
20th Tennessee, Wright's Tennessee Battery

Hanson's "Orphan" Brigade
Brig. Gen. Roger Weightman Hanson/
Col. Robert P. Trabue
41st Alabama, 2nd Kentucky, 4th Kentucky,
6th Kentucky, 9th Kentucky,
Cobb's Kentucky Battery

Jackson's Independent Brigade
Brig. Gen. John King Jackson
5th Georgia, 5th Mississippi, 8th Mississippi,
2nd Battalion Georgia Sharpshooters, Pritchard's
Georgia Battery, Lumsden's Alabama Battery

Cleburne's Division
Maj. Gen. Patrick Ronayne Cleburne

Polk's Brigade
Brig. Gen. Lucius Eugene Polk
1st Arkansas, 13th/15th Arkansas, 5th Confederate,
2nd Tennessee, 35th Tennessee,
Helena (Arkansas) Battery

Liddell's Brigade
Brig. Gen. St. John Richardson Liddell
2nd Arkansas, 5th Arkansas, 6th/7th Arkansas,
8th Arkansas, Warren (Mississippi) Light Artillery

Johnson's Brigade
Brig. Gen. Bushrod Rust Johnson
17th Tennessee, 23rd Tennessee, 25th Tennessee,
37th Tennessee, 44th Tennessee,
Jefferson (Mississippi) Flying Artillery

Wood's Brigade
Brig. Gen. Sterling Alexander Martin Wood
16th Alabama, 33rd Alabama, 3rd Confederate,
45th Mississippi, 15th Battalion
Mississippi Sharpshooters, Semple's Alabama Battery

McCown's Division
Maj. Gen. John Porter McCown

Ector's Brigade (dismounted cavalry)
Brig. Gen. Matthew Duncan Ector
10th Texas, 11th Texas, 14th Texas, 15th Texas,
Douglas' Texas Battery

Rains's Brigade
Brig. Gen. James Edwards Rains/
Col. Robert Brank Vance
3rd Battalion Georgia, 9th Battalion Georgia,
29th North Carolina, 11th Tennessee, Eufala Alabama
Light Artillery

McNair's Brigade
Brig. Gen. Evander McNair/
Col. Robert Withers Harper
1st Arkansas Mounted Rifles, 2nd Arkansas Mounted
Rifles 4th Arkansas, 30th Arkansas,
4th Battalion Arkansas, Humphrey's Arkansas Battery

Wheeler's Cavalry Division
Brig. Gen. Joseph Wheeler

Wheeler's Brigade
Brig. Gen. Joseph Wheeler
1st Alabama, 3rd Alabama, 51st Alabama Partisan
Rangers, 8th Confederate, 1st Tennessee, Douglass'
Battalion, Tennessee Cavalry, Holman's
Battalion, Tennessee Cavalry, McCann's Detachment,
Tennessee Cavalry, Wiggins' Arkansas Battery

Buford's Brigade
Brig. Gen. Abraham Buford
3rd Kentucky, 5th Kentucky, 6th Kentucky

Pegram's Brigade
Brig. Gen. John Pegram
1st Georgia, 1st Louisiana

Wharton's Brigade
Brig. Gen. John Austin Wharton
14th Battalion Alabama, 1st Confederate,
3rd Confederate, 2nd Georgia, 3rd Georgia,
4th Tennessee (Smith), 4th Tennessee (Murray),
Davis's Battalion, Tennessee Cavalry, 8th Texas,
White's Horse Artillery Battery

Cavalry Division Artillery
Byrne's Kentucky Horse Artillery
Gibson's Georgia Battery

Bibliography

Newspapers

Adrian [MI] *Daily Watchtower*
Ashland [VA] *Times*
Athens [GA] *Messenger*
Athens [GA] *Post*
Atlanta Intelligencer
Attala [MS] *Ledger*
Austin [TX] *American-Statesman*
Belmont [OH] *Chronicle*
Bucyrus [OH] *Journal*
Buffalo Evening News
Cadiz [OH] *Republican*
Cadiz [OH] *Sentinel*
Charleston [SC] *Mercury*
Chattanooga Daily Gazette
Chattanooga Daily Rebel
Chicago Tribune
Church Advocate [PA]
Cincinnati Daily Commercial
Cleveland Daily Herald
Cleveland Morning Leader
Cleveland Plain Dealer
Confederate Veteran
Daily Milwaukee News
Daily Pittsburgh Gazette
Daily Rushville [IN] *Citizen*
Daily St. Louis Republican
Daily Selma [AL] *Reporter*

Daily State Sentinel [IN]
Dallas Daily Herald
Dawson's [IN] *Daily Times and Union*
Dayton [OH] *Empire*
Dayton [OH] *Journal*
Delaware [OH] *Gazette*
Detroit Free Press
Eaton [OH] *Weekly Register*
Evansville [IN] *Daily Journal*
Fayetteville [NC] *Observer*
Fremont [OH] *Journal*
Fulton County [IL] *Ledger*
Gallipolis [OH] *Journal*
Galveston [TX] *Daily News*
Grant County [MN] *Herald*
Grundy County [TN] *Herald*
Hastings [MI] *Reminder*
Highland [OH] *Weekly News*
Holmes County [OH] *Farmer*
Holston [TN] *Journal*
Howard [IN] *Tribune*
Ironton [OH] *Register*
Jacksonville [FL] *Herald*
Jacksonville [AL] *Republican*
Jeffersonian [PA] *Democrat*
Keithsburg [IL] *Observer*
Knoxville [TN] *Daily Register*
Lancaster [PA] *Daily Express*
Lancaster [PA] *Inquirer*
Lima [OH] *Weekly Gazette*
Lincoln [NC] *Herald*
Lorain County [OH] *News*
Los Angeles Herald
Louisville Daily Journal
Louisville Evening Post
Macomb [IL] *Weekly Journal*
Macon [MS] *Beacon*
Madison County [OH] *Democrat*
Madison [IN] *Daily Evening Courier*
Marshall [MI] *Statesman*

Marysville [OH] *Tribune*

McArthur [OH] *Democrat*

Memphis Daily Appeal

Mobile [MS] *Advertiser & Register*

Mobile [MS] *Daily Register*

Mobile [MS] *Evening News*

Mobile [MS] *Weekly Advertiser*

Montgomery [AL] *Daily Mail*

Montgomery [ALI] *Weekly Advertiser*

Morgan County [OH] *Herald*

Murfreesboro [TN] *Rebel Banner*

Nashville Daily Union

Natchez [MS] *Daily Courier*

National Tribune [DC]

Neodesha [KS] *Register*

New Albany [IN] *Daily Ledger*

Newcomerstown [IN] *News*

New Orleans Daily Picayune

New Orleans Times-Picayune

New York Tribune

Northern Indianan

Norwalk [OH] *Reflector*

Ohio Democrat

Ohio Repository

Ohio State Journal

Ottawa [IL] *Republican*

Ottawa [OH] *Telegram*

Philadelphia Weekly Times

Pittsburgh Commercial Gazette

Pomeroy [OH] *Leader*

Portsmouth [OH] *Daily Times*

Pottsville [PA] *Miners' Journal*

Princeton [IN] *Clarion-Leader*

Richmond [VA] *Dispatch*

Richmond [VA] *Enquirer*

Richmond [VA] *Whig*

Rockford [IL] *Register*

Rock Island [IL] *Weekly Union*

Rock River [IL] *Democrat*

Salem [IL] *Advocate*

Sandusky [OH] *Register*

Scioto [OH] *Gazette*

Semi-Weekly Wisconsin

Shreveport [LA] *Weekly News*

Southern Confederacy [GA]

Southern Standard [TN]

Springfield [MA] *Republic*

St. Louis Globe-Democrat

Sterling [IL] *Republican Gazette*

Steuben [IN] *Republican*

Summit County [OH] *Beacon*

The Clarion [MS]

The Tennessean

Tiffin [OH] *Weekly Tribune*

Toledo [OH] *Blade*

Toledo [OH] *Daily Commercial*

Troy [AL] *Messenger*

Tuscarawas [OH] *Advocate*

Union County Star and Lewisburg [PA] *Chronicle*

Urbana [OH] *Union*

Valley Spirit [PA]

Weekly Carroll County [IL] *Mirror*

Weekly Lancaster [OH] *Gazette*

Weekly Mississippian

Weekly Pioneer & Democrat [MN]

Weekly Quincy [IL] *Whig & Republican*

Western Reserve [OH] *Chronicle*

Whiteside [IL] *Sentinel*

Winchester [TN] *Daily Bulletin*

Wisconsin Pinery

Wisconsin State Journal

Wyandot [OH] *Pioneer*

Zanesville [OH] *Daily Courier*

Manuscripts, Letters, Diaries, and Related Materials

Alabama Department of Archives & History, Montgomery
George Knox Miller, Monograph of the 8th Confederate Cavalry Regiment

Linda Bohrer Anderson Collection
Zene C. Bohrer Letter

Arkansas Historical Association, Fayetteville
Valentine M. McGehee Diary

Paul Barnett Collection
Francis M. Carlisle Autobiography

Richard A. Baumgartner Collection
Francis M. Allhands Letter
Ambrose Doss Letter
William A. Hubbard Letter
Henry A. Potter Letter
W. E. Matthews Preston Letter
Henry Watson Letter

Bowling Green State University, Bowling Green, Ohio
John H. Bolton Journal
Sidney Brewster Papers
Robert H. Caldwell Papers
William J. Sullivan Collection
Liberty Warner Papers

Archives, Chicago Public Library, Chicago
Nathaniel B. McCutcheon Letter

David T. Dixon Collection
Charles Anderson Papers
Abraham Songer Reminiscences

Duke University, Durham, North Carolina
Alfred W. Bell Papers
John Buie Papers
Brigadier General John K. Jackson Letter in Charles Colcock Jones Papers

Emory University, Atlanta, Georgia
Isaac Roseberry, Diary

Filson Historical Society, Louisville, Kentucky
Squire Helm Bush Diary
Lewis Conrad Diehl Memoirs
Alfred Pirtle Papers

Robert Grenier Collection
Alfred D. French, Memoir

Rutherford B. Hayes Presidential Library, Fremont, Ohio
Private Charles B. Dennis Memoir
Samuel A. Linton Memoir

Illinois State Historical Library, Springfield
George Gresham Sinclair Letters

Indiana Historical Society, Indianapolis
Edgar Abbott Recollections
James H. Jones Letter
Frederick Knefler Letter
Samuel T. Stallard Papers
Williamson D. Ward Diary

Indiana State Library, Indianapolis
George L. Banks Papers

Abraham Lincoln Presidential Library, Springfield, Illinois
William M. Austin Diary
Gillett Family Papers

Louisiana State University, Baton Rouge
John C. F. Jenkins Letter

Lyon College, Batesville, Arkansas
Frank Desha Denton Papers

Daniel A. Masters Collection
   Sergeant George R. Bradshaw, Co. F, 74th Illinois Letter
   Enoch J. Wall, Co. F, 2nd Arkansas Letter

Navarro College, Corsicana, Texas
   Henry Haymond Papers
   William McGregor Papers

New York Historical Society, New York
   John C. Breckinridge Papers

Ohio University, Athens, Ohio
   William Parker Johnson Papers

Ross County Historical Society, Chillicothe, Ohio
   Sill Family Papers

Anthony Rushing Collection
   Coke Witten Letter

Judd Shull Collection
   Joseph W. Coe Letter

Ron Skellie Collection
   Edward B. Carruth Letters

State Historical Library of Wisconsin, Madison
   Eugene E. Comstock Collection
   Alvah Philbrook Collection
   Quiner Scrapbooks

Stones River National Battlefield Park Regimental Files, Murfreesboro, Tennessee
   John S. Alexander, 21st Illinois
   Joshua Alfred, Co. I, 37th Indiana
   Josiah D. Austin, Co. G, 74th Illinois
   Arza Bartholomew, Co. G, 21st Michigan
   James Biddle, Co. B, 2nd Battalion, 16th US
   Alpheus S. Bloomfield, Battery A, 1st Ohio Light Artillery
   Frederick N. Boyer, Co. H, 59th Illinois

Joseph Buckley, Co. H, 89th Illinois

History and Genealogy of the Buford Family in America

William P. Campbell, Co. B, 1st Arkansas Mounted Rifles

William H. Doll, Co. C, 6th Indiana

Noah W. Downs, Co. D, 39th Indiana

Oscar Easley, Co. F, 84th Illinois

Ezekiel John Ellis, Co. F, 16th/25th Louisiana

Thomas Benton Ellis, Co. C, 3rd Florida

Franklin D. Embree, Co. E, 42nd Indiana

Lancelot C. Ewbank, Co. I, 31st Indiana

Lucy Virginia French, Journal

Kaufman Funk, Co. K, 30th Indiana

William A. Garner, Co. C, 30th Arkansas

Archer T. Gay, Co. E, 31st Tennessee

Charles Gentsch, Co. K, 51st Ohio

Daniel Griffin, 38th Indiana

Thomas M. Gunn, 21st Kentucky

Albert L. Henry, Co. H, 88th Indiana

John M. Hook, Co. G, 6th Indiana

Jason Hurd, Co. D, 19th Ohio

Robert Kennedy, Co. C, 2nd Battalion, 18th US

Sophronius S. Landt, Co. D, 10th Wisconsin

Elbridge G. Littlejohn, Co. G, 10th Texas Cavalry

Jacques Martin, Co. I, 6th Ohio

Simon Mayer, 10th Mississippi

Alexander McGowin, Co. D, 16th Alabama

Charles H. Nickerson, Co. E, 65th Ohio

Edward P. Norman, Co. C, 28th Alabama

L. L. Hannibal Paine, Co. E, 26th Tennessee

Thomas Prickett, Co. E, 9th Indiana

Jacob A. Reep, Co. G, 19th Ohio

William D. Rodgers, 1st Florida

Milton A. Romig, Co. B, 51st Ohio

Launcelot Scott, 18th Ohio

Thomas J. Shipman, Co. D, 60th North Carolina

David C. Shotts, Co. A, 18th Ohio

J. Morgan Smith, Co. F, 32nd Alabama

John A. Snodgrass, Co. H, 22nd Indiana

Silas Stevens, Chicago Board of Trade Battery

William Tomlinson, Battery A, 1st Ohio Light Artillery
Dan E. Turney, Co. G, 2nd Kentucky (CSA)
Henry A. Vincent, Battery E, 1st Ohio Light Artillery
Cornelius Irvine Walker, 10th South Carolina
William D. Ward, 37th Indiana
Isaac F. Wark, Co. E, 1st Louisiana Regulars
James C. Watson, Co. I, 25th Illinois
Clement C. Webb, Co. E, 13th Michigan
James K. Weir, Co. B, 25th Illinois
Samuel Welch, Co. E, 51st Ohio
James Durham West, Co. L, 13th Tennessee
James Williamson, 2nd Arkansas Mounted Rifles
Aurelius M. Willoughby, Co. H, 39th Indiana
John H. Wingert, Co. C, 34th Illinois
Noah W. Yoder, 51st Ohio

Larry M. Strayer Collection
Alexander Varian Letters

Tennessee State Library and Archives, Nashville
Robert F. Bunting Letters
William Henry Harder Memoir

Tulane University, New Orleans
William Preston Johnston Papers

United States Army Military History Institute, Carlisle, Pennsylvania
Civil War Times Illustrated Collection
Lewis Leigh Collection

University of Missouri, Columbia
Colman-Hayter Family Papers
William E. Patterson Memoirs
Lot Dudley Young Reminiscences

University of North Carolina, Chapel Hill
Taylor Beattie Papers
Samuel Henry Lockett Papers
Weldon C. Scales Papers
John Kennedy Street Papers

Virginia Polytechnic Institute and University, Blacksburg, Virginia
William W. Hensley Autobiography

Western Kentucky University, Bowling Green, Kentucky
Benjamin C. Grider Papers

Western Reserve Historical Society, Cleveland, Ohio
James Barnett Papers
Braxton Bragg Papers
Wilbur Hinman Papers
John D. Inskeep Diary

Government Publications

U.S. Army Generals' Reports of Civil War Service, 1864-1887. Record Group 94, National Archives

The War of the Rebellion: A Compilation of the Official Records of the Union and Confederate Armies, 128 vols. Washington, DC, 1880-1901.

Personal Narratives and Unit Histories

Adams, Jacob. *Diary of Jacob Adams, Private in Company F, 21st O.V.V.I.* Columbus, OH: F. J. Heer, 1930.

Ager, Waldemar. *Colonel Heg and His Boys: A Norwegian Regiment in the American Civil War.* Northfield, MN: The Norwegian-American Historical Association, 2000.

Aldrich, C. Knight. *Quest for a Star: The Civil War Letters and Diaries of Colonel Francis T. Sherman of the 88th Illinois.* Knoxville, TN: The University of Tennessee Press, 1999.

Andreas, A. T. *History of Chicago From the Earliest Period to the Present Time.* Chicago: The A. T. Andreas Co., 1885.

Annals of the Fifty-Seventh Regiment Indiana Volunteers: Marches, Battles, and Incidents of Army Life. Dayton, OH: W. J. Shuey, 1868.

Anderson, Dean C., ed. *Alexander Campbell Pepper: Memoirs of the Civil War.* n.p., 1987.

Andrews, J. Cutler. *The South Reports the Civil War.* Princeton, NJ: Princeton University Press, 1970.

Arlikas, Thomas M. *Cadet Gray and Butternut Brown.* Gettysburg, PA: Thomas Publications, 2006.

Barnes, James A., James R. Carnahan and Thomas Hart Benton McCain. *The Eighty-Sixth Regiment Indiana Volunteer Infantry: A Narrative of Its Services in the Civil War of 1861-1865.* Crawfordsville, IN: The Journal Company, 1895.

Barnhill, Floyd R. and Calvin L. Collier. *The Fighting Fifth: Pat Cleburne's Cutting Edge: The Fifth Arkansas Infantry Regiment, C.S.A.* Jonesboro, AR: Floyd R. Barnhill, n.d.

Barnet, James, ed. *The Martyrs and Heroes of Illinois in the Great Rebellion*. Chicago: J. Barnet, Book, and Job Printer, 1866.

Barton, Michael. *The Civil War Memoir of Sergeant Christian Lenker, 19th Ohio Volunteers*. Bloomington, IN: Xlibris, 2014.

Baumgartner, Richard A., ed. *The Bully Boys: In Camp and Combat With the 2nd Ohio Volunteer Infantry Regiment, 1861-1864*. Huntingdon, WV: Blue Acorn Press, 2011.

Beatty, John. *The Citizen-Soldier: Memoirs of a Civil War Volunteer*. Cincinnati: Wilstach, Baldwin, and Co., 1879.

Belcher, Dennis W. *The Cavalries at Stones River: An Analytical History*. Jefferson, NC: McFarland & Co., 2017.

Bennett, L. G. and William Haigh. *History of the Thirty-Sixth Regiment, Illinois Volunteers During the War of the Rebellion*. Aurora, IL: Knickerbocker and Hodder, 1876.

Beyer, W. F. and O. P. Keydel. *Deeds of Valor*. Detroit: The Perrien-Keydel Co., 1907.

Bickham, William D. *Rosecrans' Campaign With the Fourteenth Army Corps of the Army of the Cumberland*. Cincinnati: Moore, Wilstach, Keys, & Co., 1863.

Bishop, Judson Wade. *The Story of a Regiment, Being a Narrative of the Service of the Second Regiment, Minnesota Veteran Volunteer Infantry in the Civil War of 1861-65*. St Paul, MN: Published by the Surviving Members of the Regiment, 1890.

Blackburn, Theodore W. *Letters From the Front: A Union 'Preacher' Regiment (74th Ohio) in the Civil War*. Dayton, OH: Morningside Bookshop, 1981.

Blair, William A. *A Politician Goes to War: The Civil War Letters of John White Geary*. University Park, PA: The Pennsylvania State University Press, 1995.

Blakey, Arch Frederic, ed. *Rose Cottage Chronicles: Civil War Letters of the Bryant-Stephens Families of North Florida*. Gainesville, FL: The University Press of Florida, 1988.

Blegen, Theodore, ed. *The Civil War Letters of Hans Christian Heg, 15th Wisconsin Infantry*. Northfield, MN: Norwegian American Historical Association, 1936.

Briant, Charles C. *History of the Sixth Regiment Indiana Volunteer Infantry of Both the Three Months' and Three Years' Services*. Indianapolis: William B. Burford, 1891.

Buck, Irving A. *Cleburne and His Command*. Wilmington, NC: Broadfoot Publishing Co., 1991.

Butler, Jay Caldwell. *Letters Home: Jay Caldwell Butler, Captain, 101st Ohio Volunteer Infantry*. Binghamton: n.p., 1930.

Butler, Marvin B. *My Story of the Civil War and the Underground Railroad*. Huntington, IN: The United Brethren Publishing Establishment, 1914.

Cabaniss, Jim R. *Civil War Journal and Letters of Washington Ives, 4th Florida, C.S.A.* n.p., n.d.

Canfield, Silas S. *History of the 21st Regiment Ohio Volunteer Infantry in the War of the Rebellion*. Toledo, OH: Vrooman, Anderson, and Bateman, 1893.

Charles, W. T. *Recollections of Christmas During the War*. n.p., 1959.

Cist, Henry M. *The Army of the Cumberland*. Edison, NJ: Castle Books, 2002.

Clark, Walter, ed. *Histories of the Several Regiments and Battalions From North Carolina in the Great War 1861-65*. Goldsboro, NC: Nash Brothers, 1901.

Cleaves, Freeman. *Rock of Chickamauga: The Life of General George H. Thomas*. Norman, OK: The University of Oklahoma Press, 1948.

Collier, Calvin L. *First In–First Out: The Capitol Guards, Ark. Brigade*. Little Rock, AR: Pioneer Press, n.d.

Cope, Alexis, *The Fifteenth Ohio Volunteers and Its Campaigns*. Columbus, OH: Alexis Cope, 1916.

Coyngham, David Power. *The Soldiers of the Cross: Heroism of the Cross or Nuns and Priests on the Battlefield*. South Bend, IN: University of Notre Dame Archives, 1870.

Cozzens, Peter. *The Darkest Days of the War: The Battles of Iuka and Corinth*. Chapel Hill, NC: The University of North Carolina Press, 1997.

——. *No Better Place to Die*, Urbana, IL: The University of Illinois Press, 1990.

Cummings, Charles M. *Yankee Quaker, Confederate General: The Curious Career of Bushrod Rust Johnson*. Rutherford, NJ: Fairleigh Dickinson University Press, 1971.

Curry, William L. *Four Years in the Saddle: History of the First Regiment Ohio Volunteer Cavalry*. Columbus, OH: W. L. Curry, 1898.

Dacus, Robert H. *Reminiscences of Company H, First Arkansas Mounted Rifles*. Dayton, OH: Morningside Bookshop, 1972.

Daniel, Larry J. *Battle of Stones River: The Forgotten Conflict Between the Confederate Army of Tennessee and Union Army of the Cumberland*. Baton Rouge: The Louisiana State University Press, 2012.

——. *Cannoneers in Gray: The Field Artillery of the Army of Tennessee, 1861-1865*. Tuscaloosa, AL: The University of Alabama Press, 1984.

——. *Soldiering in the Army of Tennessee*. Chapel Hill, NC: The University of North Carolina Press, 1991.

Davis, William C. *Breckinridge: Statesman, Soldier, Symbol*. Lexington, KY: The University Press of Kentucky, 2010.

——. ed. *Diary of a Confederate Soldier: John S. Jackman of the Orphan Brigade*. Columbia, SC: The University of South Carolina Press, 1990.

——. *Lincoln's Men: How President Lincoln Became Father to an Army and a Nation*. New York: Simon & Schuster, 1999.

——. *The Orphan Brigade: The Kentucky Confederates Who Couldn't Go Home*. Garden City, NY: Doubleday & Co., 1980.

Day, Lewis W. *Story of the 101st Regiment, Ohio Volunteer Infantry*. Cleveland: W. M. Bayne Printing Co., 1894.

DeWees, Joseph W., ed. *Joshua DeWees: His Civil War Diary*. n.p., 1991.

Dixon, David T. *The Lost Gettysburg Address: Charles Anderson's Civil War Odyssey*. Santa Barbara, CA: B-List History, 2015.

——. *Radical Warrior: August Willich's Journey From German Revolutionary to Union General*. Knoxville, TN: The University of Tennessee Press, 2020.

Dodge, William Sumner. *A Waif of the War, or a History of the 75th Illinois Infantry, Embracing the Entire Campaigns of the Army of the Cumberland*. Chicago: Church and Goodman, 1866.

Dornblaser, Thomas F. *Sabre Strokes of the Pennsylvania Dragoons in the War of 1861-1865*. Baltimore: Gateway Press, 1998.

Doyle, Julie A., John David Smith and Richard M. McMurry, eds. *This Wilderness of War: The Civil War Letters of George W. Squier, Hoosier Volunteer*. Knoxville, TN: The University of Tennessee Press, 1998.

Driskell, Steven. *History of the 25th Alabama Infantry Regiment, 1861-65*. n.p., n.d.

Duke, Basil Wilson. *Morgan's Cavalry*. New York: The Neale Publishing Company, 1906.

Elliott, Sam Davis. *Soldier of Tennessee: General Alexander P. Stewart and the Civil War in the West*. Baton Rouge, LA: The Louisiana State University, 1999.

Erb, William S. S. *Extracts From the Battles of the 19th Ohio*. Washington, DC: Judd and Detwiler, 1893.

Fisher, Horace Cecil. *A Staff Officer's Story: The Personal Experiences of Horace Newton Fisher in the Civil War*. Boston: Thomas Todd Co., 1960.

Fitch, John. *Annals of the Army of the Cumberland*. Mechanicsburg, PA: Stackpole Books, 2003.

Fitch, Michael H. *Echoes of the Civil War as I Hear Them*. New York: R. F. Fenno & Company, 1905.

Fleming, James R. *Band of Brothers: Company C, 9th Tennessee Infantry*. Shippensburg, PA: White Mane Publishing, 1996.

Francis, Charles Lewis. *Narrative of a Private Soldier in the Volunteer Army of the United States During the Period Covered by the Great War of the Rebellion of 1861*. Brooklyn: William Jenkins & Co., 1879.

Franklin, Ann York, comp. *The Civil War Diaries of Captain Alfred Tyler Fielder, 12th Tennessee Regiment Infantry, Company B, 1861-1865*. n.p., 1996.

Fry, James B. *Operations of the Army Under Buell From June 10th to October 30, 1862, and the "Buell Commission."* New York: D. Van Nostrand, 1884.

Gammage, Washington Lafayette. *The Camp, the Bivouac, and the Battlefield*. Little Rock, AR: Arkansas Southern Press, 1958.

Gancas, Ronald S. *The Gallant Seventy-Eighth: Colonel William Sirwell and the Pennsylvania Seventy-Eighth: Stones River to Pickett's Mill*. Plum Boro: Mark V Enterprises, 1997.

Garrett, Jill K., trans. *Confederate Diary of Robert D. Smith*. Columbia, TN: Captain James Madison Sparkman Chapter, United Daughters of the Confederacy, n.d.

Gates, Arnold, ed. *The Rough Side of War: The Civil War Journal of Chesley A. Mosman, 1st Lieutenant, Company D, 59th Illinois Volunteer Infantry Regiment*. Garden City, NY: The Basin Publishing Co., 1987.

Gibson, Joseph Thompson. *History of the Seventy-Eighth Pennsylvania Volunteer Infantry*. Pittsburgh: Press of the Pittsburgh Print Co., 1905.

Giles, L. B. *Terry's Texas Rangers*. Austin, TX: The Pemberton Press, 1967.

Girardi, Robert I., ed. *Campaigning With Uncle Billy: The Civil War Memoirs of Sergeant Lyman S. Widney, 34th Illinois Volunteer Infantry*. Bloomington, IN: Trafford Publishing, 2008 [formerly Victoria, British Columbia].

Girardi, Robert I. and Nathaniel Cheairs Hughes, eds. *The Memoirs of Brigadier General William Passmore Carlin, U.S.A.* Lincoln, NE: The University of Nebraska Press, 1999.

Goodwin, Doris Kearns. *Team of Rivals: The Political Genius of Abraham Lincoln*. New York: Simon & Schuster, 2005.

Gould, David and James B. Kennedy. *Memoirs of a Dutch Mudsill: The War Memories of John Henry Otto, Captain, Company D, 21st Regiment Wisconsin Volunteer Infantry*. Kent, OH: Kent State University Press, 2004.

Granger, Gervais D. *Four Years With the Boys in Gray*. Franklin, KY: The Favorite Office, 1902.

Greiner, Henry C. *General Sheridan as I Knew Him: Playmate, Comrade, Friend*. Chicago: J. S. Hyland & Co., 1908.

Grose, William. *The Story of the Marches, Battles, and Incidents of the 36th Regiment, Indiana Volunteer Infantry*. New Castle, IN: The Courier Company Press, 1891.

Hallock, Judith Lee, ed. *The Civil War Letters of Joshua K. Callaway*. Athens, GA: The University of Georgia Press, 1997.

Hammock, John C. *With Honor Untarnished: The Story of the First Arkansas Regiment, Confederate States Army*. Little Rock, AR: Pioneer Press, 1961.

Hannaford, Ebenezer. *The Story of a Regiment: A History of the Campaigns and Associations in the Field of the Sixth Regiment, Ohio Volunteer Infantry*. Cincinnati: Hannaford, 1868.

Hartpence, William Ross. *History of the Fifty-First Indiana, Veteran Volunteer Infantry: A Narrative of Its Organization, Marches, Battles, and Other Experiences in Camp and Prison From 1861 to 1866*. Cincinnati: The Robert Clarke Co., 1894.

Haynie, John Henry. *The Nineteenth Illinois: A Memoir of a Regiment of Volunteer Infantry Famous in the Civil War of Fifty Years Ago for Its Drill, Bravery, and Distinguished Services*. Chicago: M. A. Donohue and Co., 1912.

Hazen, William B. *A Narrative of Military Service*. Boston: Ticknor and Co., 1885.

Head, Thomas A. *Campaigns and Battles of the Sixteenth Regiment, Tennessee Volunteers in the War Between the States*. Nashville: Cumberland Presbyterian Publishing House, 1885.

Hebert, Walter H. *Fighting Joe Hooker*. Lincoln, NE: The University of Nebraska Press, 1999.

Herr, George W. *Nine Campaigns in Nine States, et al*. San Francisco: The Bancroft Company, 1890.

Hess, Earl J. *The Rifle Musket in Civil War Combat: Reality and Myth*. Lawrence, KS: The University Press of Kansas, 2008.

Hewitt, Janet., ed. *Supplement to the Official Records of the Union and Confederate Armies*. Volumes 3, 18, 20, and 66. Wilmington, NC: Broadfoot Publishing Co., 1994.

Hight, John J. *History of the 58th Regiment of Indiana Volunteer Infantry*. Princeton: Press of the Clarion, 1895.

Hinman, Wilbur F. *The Story of the Sherman Brigade*. Self-published, 1897.

History and Biographical Encyclopedia of Butler County, Ohio. Cincinnati: Western Publishing Co., 1892.

History of the Services of the Third Wisconsin Light Artillery. Berlin, WI: Courant Press, 1902.

History of Washington County, Ohio. Cleveland: H. Z. Williams & Bro., 1881.

History of the Seventy-Third Indiana Volunteers. Washington, DC: Carnahan Press, 1909.

Holm, David D. *History of the Fifth Indiana Battery*. n.p., n.d.

Horn, Stanley F. *The Army of Tennessee*. Wilmington, NC: Broadfoot Publishing Co., 1987.

——. *The Battle of Stones River*. Harrisburg, PA: Historical Times Inc., 1972.

Horrall, Spillard F. *History of the Forty-Second Indiana Volunteer Infantry*. Chicago: Donohue and Henneberry, 1892.

Hughes, Nathaniel Cheairs, ed. *Liddell's Record*. Baton Rouge, LA: The Louisiana State University Press, 1985.

——. *The Pride of the Confederate Artillery: The Washington Artillery in the Army of Tennessee*. Baton Rouge, LA: The Louisiana State University Press, 1997.

Jamison, Henry D. *Letters and Recollections of a Confederate Soldier 1860-1865*. n.p., 1964.

Jenkins, Kirk C. *The Battles Rages Higher: The Union's Fifteenth Kentucky Infantry*. Lexington, KY: The University Press of Kentucky, 2003.

Johnson, Mark W. *That Body of Brave Men: The U.S. Regular Infantry and the Civil War in the West*. Cambridge, MA: Da Capo Press, 2003.

Johnson, Richard W. *A Soldier's Reminiscences in Peace and War*. Philadelphia: J. B. Lippincott Co., 1886.

Johnston, Robert U. et al., eds. *Battles and Leaders of the Civil War, Volume III: The Tide Shifts*. Secaucus, NJ: Castle Books, n.d.

Johnston, William Preston. *The Life of Gen. Albert Sidney Johnston*. New York: D. Appleton & Co., 1879.

Jones, Adoniram J. *A Private of the Cumberland.* n.p., n.d.

Jones, John Beauchamp. *A Rebel War Clerk's Diary.* Edited by Earl Schenk Miers. New York: Sagamore Press, Inc., 1958.

Kimerly, Robert L. and Ephraim S. Holloway. *The Forty-First Ohio Veteran Volunteer Infantry in the War of the Rebellion, 1861-1865.* Cleveland: W. R. Smellie, 1897.

Kinard, Jeff. *Lafayette of the South: Prince Camille de Polignac and the American Civil War.* College Station, TX: The Texas A&M University Press, 2001.

Kirk, Charles H. *History of the Fifteenth Pennsylvania Volunteer Cavalry, Which Was Recruited and Known as the Anderson Cavalry in the Rebellion of 1861-1865.* Philadelphia: 1906.

Kirwan, A. D., ed. *Johnny Green of the Orphan Brigade: The Journal of a Confederate Soldier.* Lexington, KY: The University of Kentucky Press, 1956.

Lamers, William M. *The Edge of Glory: A Biography of General William S. Rosecrans, U.S.A.* Baton Rouge, LA: The Louisiana State University Press, 1961.

Lathrop, David. *The History of the Fifty-Ninth Regiment Illinois Volunteers.* Indianapolis: Hall & Hutchinson, 1865.

Longacre, Edward G. *A Soldier to the Last: Major General Joseph Wheeler in Blue and Gray.* Washington, DC: Potomac Books Inc., 2007.

Lowry, Thomas P. *The Story the Soldiers Wouldn't Tell: Sex in the Civil War.* Mechanicsburg, PA: Stackpole Books, 1994.

Manderson, Charles F. *The Twin Seven-Shooters.* New York: F. Tennyson Neely, 1902.

Mann, Richard F. *The Buckeye Vanguard: History of the 49th Ohio Veteran Volunteer Infantry, 1861-1865.* Milford, OH: Little Miami Publishing Co., 2010.

Marshall, Randolph V. *A Historical Sketch of the Twenty-Second Regiment Indiana Volunteers.* Madison, IN: Courley Co., 1884.

Masur, Louis P. *Lincoln's Hundred Days: The Emancipation Proclamation and the War for the Union.* Cambridge, MA: Harvard University Press, 2012.

McCray, Kevin B. *A Shouting of Orders: A History of the 99th Ohio Volunteer Infantry Regiment.* Bloomington, IN: Xlibris, Kevin McCray, 2003.

McCutchan, Kenneth P. *Dearest Lizzie: The Civil War as Seen Through the Eyes of Lieutenant Colonel James Maynard Shanklin.* Evansville, IN: Friends of Willard Library Press, 1988.

McDonough, James Lee. *Stones River: Bloody Winter in Tennessee.* Knoxville, TN: The University of Tennessee Press, 1980.

McElroy, John. *Si Klegg: Thru The Stone River Campaign and in Winter Quarters at Murfreesboro.* Washington, DC: The National Tribune Co., 1910.

McNeil, Samuel A. *Personal Recollections of Service in the Army of the Cumberland and Sherman's Army.* Richwood, OH: S. A. McNeil, n.d.

McWhiney, Grady. *Braxton Bragg and Confederate Defeat. Volume I.* Tuscaloosa, AL: The University of Alabama Press, 1969.

Merrill, Catherine. *The Soldier of Indiana in the War for the Union. Volume I.* Indianapolis: Merrill & Co., 1869.

Mitchell, John Lendrum. *In Memoriam: John Lendrum Mitchell.* Milwaukee, 1906.

Morris, George W. *History of the 81st Regiment of Indiana Volunteer Infantry in the Great War of the Rebellion, 1861 to 1865...A Regimental Roster, Prison Life, Adventures, Etc.* Louisville, KY: Franklin, 1901.

Noe, Kenneth W., ed. *A Southern Boy in Blue: The Memoir of Marcus Woodcock, 9th Kentucky Infantry, U.S.A.* Knoxville, TN: The University of Tennessee Press, 1996.

———. *Perryville: This Grand Havoc of Battle*. Lexington, KY: The University of Kentucky Press, 2001.

Owen, Mark E. *A Narrative of the Campaigns of the 39th Alabama Volunteer Infantry, Deas' Brigade, Army of Tennessee, Confederate States Army (1862-1865)*. n.p., n.d.

Owens, Ira S. *Greene County in the War, Being a History of the Seventy-Fourth Regiment, With Sketches…* Xenia, OH: Torchlight Job Rooms, 1872.

Palmer, John McAuley. *Personal Recollections of John M. Palmer—The Story of an Earnest Life*. Cincinnati: Robert Clarke Co., 1901.

Parks, Joseph H. *General Leonidas Polk, C.S.A. The Fighting Bishop*. Baton Rouge. LA: The Louisiana State University Press, 1962.

Payne, Edwin W. *History of the Thirty-Fourth Regiment of Illinois Volunteer Infantry*. Clinton, IL: Allen Printing Co., 1902.

Pennsylvania Shiloh Battlefield Commission. *The Seventy-Seventh Pennsylvania at Shiloh, History of the Regiment*. Harrisburg, PA: Harrisburg Publishing Co., 1908.

Post, Philip S. *Soldiers' and Patriots' Biographical Album*. Chicago: Union Veteran Publishing Co., 1892.

Powell, David A. and Eric J. Wittenberg. *Tullahoma: The Forgotten Campaign That Changed the Course of the Civil War, June 23–July 4, 1863*. El Dorado Hill, CA: Savas Beatie, 2020.

Proceedings of the Eighth Annual Session of the Survivors of the Battle of Stones River. Kokomo, Indiana, January 2, 1908.

Prokopowicz, Gerald J. *All for the Regiment: The Army of the Ohio, 1861-1862*. Chapel Hill, NC: The University of North Carolina Press, 2001.

Puntenney, George H. *History of the Thirty-Seventh Regiment of Indiana Infantry Volunteers*. Rushville, IN: 1896.

Quaife, Milo M. *From the Cannon's Mouth: The Civil War Letters of Alpheus S. Williams*. Detroit: Wayne State University Press, 1959.

———— *Recollections and Reminiscences, 1861-1865*, South Carolina Division, United Daughters of the Confederacy, Volume 6, 1998.

———— *Record of the 94th Regiment, Ohio Volunteer Infantry in the War of the Rebellion*. Cincinnati: Ohio Valley Press, 1895.

Reinhart, Joseph R. *A History of the 6th Kentucky Volunteer Infantry U.S.: The Boys Who Feared No Noise*. Louisville, KY: Beargrass Press, 2000.

———, ed. *August Willich's Gallant Dutchmen: Civil War Letters From the 32nd Indiana Infantry*. Kent, OH: Kent State University Press, 2006.

———— *Report of the Proceedings of the 15th Annual Re-Union of the Eighth Indiana Veteran Cavalry*. Noblesville, Indiana, 1898.

Robertson, Brian K. *Things Grew Beautifully Worse: The Wartime Experiences of Captain John O'Brien, 30th Arkansas Infantry, C.S.A.* Little Rock, AR: Butler Center for Arkansas Studies, 2001.

Rue, Richard K. & Rue, Geraldine M., eds. *In Song and Sorrow: The Daily Journal of Thomas Hart Benton McCain of the Eighty-Sixth Indiana Volunteer Infantry*. Self-published, 1998.

Rugeley, Helen J. H., ed., *Batchelor-Turner Letters, 1861-1864: Written by Two of Terry's Texas Rangers*. Austin, TX: The Steck Co., 1961.

Sauers, Richard A. *Advance the Colors! Pennsylvania Civil War Battle Flags*. Harrisburg, PA: Capitol Preservation Committee, 1987.

Savage, John H. *The Life of John H. Savage: Citizen, Soldier, Lawyer, Congressman.* Nashville: John H. Savage, 1903.

Seitz, Don C. *Braxton Bragg: General of the Confederacy.* Columbia, SC: The State Company, 1924.

Sheridan, Philip H. *Personal Memoirs of P. H. Sheridan, General, United States Army.* New York: Da Capo Press, 1992.

Shiloh Battlefield Commission. *Ohio at Shiloh.* Washington Courthouse, OH: T. J. Lindsey, 1903.

Shook, Hezekiah. *Address delivered on the occasion of the second annual reunion of the 37th Indiana Volunteer Infantry. September 18, 1878.* Indiana Historical Society.

Simmons, Louis A. *The History of the 84th Regt. Ill. Vols.* Macomb., IL: Hampton Brothers, 1866.

Smith, Lanny K. *The Stones River Campaign: 26 December 1862–5 January 1863. Army of Tennessee.* Lanny Smith, 2010.

———. *The Stones River Campaign: 26 December 1862–5 January 1863. The Union Army.* Lanny Smith, 2008.

Smith, William Hutchinson. *Incidents and Reminiscence of the Civil War.* Lee County Genealogical Society, Florida, 2002.

______ *Society of the Seventy-Fourth Illinois Volunteer Infantry: Reunion Proceedings and History of the Regiment.* Rockford, IL: W. P. Lamb, 1903.

Spence, John C. *A Diary of the Civil War.* Murfreesboro, TN: Rutherford Co. Historical Society, 1993.

Spruill, Matt and Lee Spruill. *Decisions at Stones River.* Knoxville, TN: The University of Tennessee Press, 2018.

———. *Winter Lightning: A Guide to the Battle of Stones River.* Knoxville, TN: The University of Tennessee Press, 2007.

Stanley, David S. *Personal Memoirs of Major-General D. S. Stanley, U.S.A.* Cambridge, MA: Harvard University Press, 1917.

Stevenson, Alexander F. *The Battle of Stone's River Near Murfreesboro, Tenn. December 30, 1862, to January 3, 1863.* Boston: James R. Good, 1884.

Strong, Elijah M. *Marches of Battery E, 1st O.V.L.A.* Delta, OH: Atlas Printing Co., 1892.

Sutherland, Daniel E., ed. *Reminiscences of a Private: William E. Bevens of the 1st Arkansas Infantry, C.S.A.* Fayetteville, AR: The University of Arkansas Press, 1992.

Tanner, E. Russell. *The Stephen Jennings Tanner Autobiography and Genealogy.* n.p., 1970.

Taylor, Lenette S. *The Supply for Tomorrow Must Not Fail: The Civil War of Captain Simon Perkins, Jr., a Union Quartermaster.* Kent, OH: Kent State University Press, 2004.

______ *The Annals of the War, Written by Leading Participants North and South.* Philadelphia: The Times Publishing Company, 1879.

______ *Third Reunion of the Society of the Army of the Cumberland at Indianapolis, Indiana, December 15–16, 1869.* Cincinnati: Robert Clarke & Co., 1870.

Thompson, Ed Porter. *History of the Orphan Brigade.* Dayton, OH: Morningside Books, 1991.

Tower, R. Lockwood, ed. *A Carolinian Goes to War: The Civil War Narrative of Arthur Middleton Manigault.* Columbia, SC: The University of South Carolina Press, 1992.

Vallandigham, Clement L. *Speeches, Arguments, and Letters.* New York: J. Walter and Company, 1864.

Vance, Wilson J. *Stone's River: Turning Point of the Civil War.* New York: The Neale Publishing Co., 1914.

Walker, Cornelius Irvine. *Rolls and Historical Sketch of the Tenth Regiment So. Ca. Volunteers in the Army of the Confederate States*. Charleston, SC: Walker, Evans, and Cogswell, 1881.

Warner, Ezra J. *Generals in Blue: Lives of the Union Commanders*. Baton Rouge, LA: The Louisiana State University Press, 1964.

———. *Generals in Gray: Lives of the Confederate Commanders*. Baton Rouge, LA: The Louisiana State University Press, 1959.

Watson, William. *Life in the Confederate Army: Being the Observations and Experiences of an Alien in the South During the American Civil War*. New York: Scribner & Welford, 1885.

Watkins, Sam R. *Company Aytch, or a Sideshow of the Big Show: A Memoir of the Civil War*. Nashville: Turner Publishing Co., 2011.

Weber, Daniel B., ed. *From Michigan to Murfreesboro: The Diary of Ira Gillaspie of the Eleventh Michigan Infantry*. Mount Pleasant, MI: Central Michigan University Press, 1965.

Wheeler, Richard. *Lee's Terrible Swift Sword: From Antietam to Chancellorsville: An Eyewitness History*. Edison, NJ: Castle Books, 1992.

Wiley, Bell Irvin. *The Life of Johnny Reb: The Common Soldier of the Confederacy*. Baton Rouge, LA: The Louisiana State University Press, 1943.

Williams, John A. B. *Leaves From a Trooper's Diary*. Philadelphia: Self-published, 1869.

Williams, T. Harry. *P. G. T. Beauregard: Napoleon in Gray*. Baton Rouge, LA: The Louisiana University Press, 1954.

Williamson, David. *The Third Battalion Mississippi Infantry and the 45th Mississippi Regiment: A Civil War History*. Jefferson, NC: McFarland & Company, Inc., 2004.

Willis, James. *Arkansas Confederates in the Western Theater*. Dayton, OH: Morningside Books, 1998.

Wilson, Suzanne Colton. *Column South With the Fifteenth Pennsylvania Cavalry*. Flagstaff, AZ: J. F. Colton and Co., 1960.

Womack, James J. *The Civil War Diary of Capt. J. J. Womack*. McMinnville, TN: Womack Publishing Co., 1961.

Woodruff, George H. *History of the One Hundredth; or Will County Regiment. Fifteen Years Ago: or the Patriotism of Will County, Designed to Preserve the Names and Memory of Will County Soldiers*. Joliet, IL: James Goodspeed, 1876.

Woodworth, Steven E. *Jefferson Davis and His Generals: The Failure of Confederate Command in the West*. Lawrence, KS: The University Press of Kansas, 1990.

Worley, Ted R., ed. *The War Memoirs of Captain John W. Lavender, C.S.A. They Never Came Back: The Story of Co. F, Fourth Arkansas Infantry, C.S.A.; Originally Known as the Montgomery Hunters, as Told by Their Commanding Officer*. Pine Bluff, AR: W. M. Hacket and D. R. Perdue, 1956.

Wright, Thomas L. *History of the Eighth Regiment Kentucky Vol. Inf. During Its Three Years Campaigns*. St. Joseph, MO: St. Joseph Steam Printing Co., 1880.

Yeary, Mamie. *Reminiscences of the Boys in Gray, 1861-65*. Dallas, TX: Wilkinson Printing Co., 1912.

Zorick, Robert J. *Study of the Union and Confederate Reactions to the Emancipation Proclamation*. Missoula, MT: The University of Montana Press, 1964.

Magazines, Journals, and Periodicals

Blackburn, James K. P. "Reminiscences of the Terry Rangers." *Southwestern Historical Quarterly*, Vol. 22, 1918-1919.

Calkins, Emerson R. "Recollections of the Battle of Stones River." *National Tribune Repository*, Vol. 1, No. 4, 1907.

Chalaron, Joseph. "Memories of Major Rice E. Graves." *Daviess County Historical Quarterly*, Vol. 3, No. 1, 1985.

Dodge, Joseph B. "What I Saw at Stone River." *Northern Indianian*, February 25, 1875.

——. "What I Saw at Stone River." *Northern Indianian*, March 11, 1875.

Douglas, Albert. "General Joshua Woodrow Sill." *Ohio History Journal*, Vol. 31, No. 2, April 1922.

Hannaford, Ebenezer. "In the Ranks at Stones River." *Harper's Magazine*, Vol. 27, 1863.

Hardee, William J. "Biographical Sketch of Major General Patrick R. Cleburne." *Southern Historical Society Papers*, Vol. 31, n.d.

Hay, John. "Life in the White House in the Time of Lincoln." *Century Magazine*, November 1890.

Jackman, John S. "Battle of Murfreesboro." *Southern Bivouac*, March 1885.

McDonough, James L. "The Last Day at Stones River: Experiences of a Yank and a Reb." *Tennessee Historical Quarterly, Volume XL,* Spring 1981.

McDowell, William P. *Southern Bivouac*, 1886.

Pirtle, Alfred. "Donelson's Charge at Stone River." *Southern Bivouac*, September 1886.

Potter, Thomas C. *Blue & Gray Magazine,* Holiday 2004.

Rogers, William J. "William J. Rogers Memorandum Book." *The West Tennessee Historical Society Papers, No. IX,* McCowat-Mercer Press, 1955.

Seay, Samuel. "A Private at Stone River." *Southern Bivouac*, August 1885.

Shoemaker, Michael. "Narrative of Colonel Michael Shoemaker." 1878 Annual Meeting of the Pioneer Society of Michigan, Lansing.

Stewart, Robert B. "The Battle of Stone River, as Seen by One Who Was There." *Blue and Gray*, Vol. 5, 1895.

Sykes, Edward T. "General Braxton Bragg: A Cursory Sketch of His Campaigns." *Southern Historical Society Papers*, Vol. 11, 1883.

Vance, Wilson. "A Man and a Boy at Stone River." *Blue and Gray*, Vol. 3, 1893.

Williams, Robert A. and Ralph A. Wooster, eds. "With Terry's Texas Rangers: Letters of Dunbar Affleck." *Civil War History*, September 1963.

Military Order of the Loyal Legion of the United States Papers

Castle, Henry A. "Sheridan with the Army of the Cumberland." *MOLLUS Washington, D.C.*, Vol. 3.

Freeman, Henry B. "Eighteenth U.S. Infantry From Camp Thomas to Murfreesboro and the Regular Brigade at Stone River." *MOLLUS Minnesota*, Vol. 3.

——. "Some Battle Recollections of Stone's River." *MOLLUS Illinois*, Vol. 3.

Hosea, Lewis. "The Regular Brigade of the Army of the Cumberland." *MOLLUS Ohio*, Vol. 5.

Kendall, Henry M. "The Battle of Stone River." *MOLLUS Washington, DC*, Vol. 3.

Kniffen, Gilbert C. "Army of the Cumberland and the Battle of Stones River." *MOLLUS Washington, DC*, Vol. 3.

Marks, Solon. "Experiences at the Battle of Stone River." *MOLLUS Wisconsin*, Vol. 2.

McClurg, Alexander C. "An American Soldier: Minor Milliken." *MOLLUS Illinois*, Vol. 2.

Otis, Ephraim A. "The Murfreesboro Campaign." *MOLLUS Massachusetts*, Vol. 7.

Pirtle, Alfred. "Stone River Sketches," *MOLLUS Ohio*, Vol. 6.

Thruston, Gates P. "Personal Recollections of the Battle in the Rear at Stone's River, Tennessee." *MOLLUS Ohio*, Vol. 6.

Woodard, James H. "General A. McD. McCook at Stones River." *MOLLUS California/Oregon*, Vol. 1.

Websites

Diary of First Lieutenant James Bragg, Co. F, 40th Indiana, https://sparedshared22.wordpress.com/2021/05/26/an-awful-neglected-army-the-partial-1862-diary-of-lt-james-bragg-co-f-40th-indiana-infantry/.

Burks, John C. *The Handbook of Texas Online*, http://tshaonline.org/handbook/entries/burks-john-c.

Biography of Colonel John S. Fulton, from Notes of Sergeant G. W. D. Porter, Co. B, 44th Tennessee, http://www.tennessee-scv.org/4455/fulton.html.

Harding, Cody J. "Crossed Hatchets and Detached Service: The Creation of the Pioneer Brigade." https://www.libertyrifles.org/research/unit-histories/pioneer-brigade.

Letters of George Waterman Jackson, 4th Indiana Battery, https://sparedcreative21.art.blog/2020/02/08/1863-george-waterman-jackson-to-james-hall-smith.

Letters of Private John McBride, Co. D, 51st Illinois, https://51stillinois.org/mcbrideletters.html.

Reminiscences of Captain William H. McCauley, Co. C, 11th Tennessee, http://scvcamp260.50megs.com/custom2.html.

Diary of First Lieutenant Otis Moody, Co. K, 51st Illinois, https://51stillinois.org/moody_st_river.html.

Captain William Austin Munger, Co. G, 100th Illinois, https://sparedshared22.wordpress.com/2021/07/28/1863-william-austin-munger-to-elisabeth-patrick-gookin/

Pitts, Jim. "Inspection Report of the 36th Mississippi Dated April 21, 1862, at Rienzi, Mississippi." www.westerntheatercivilwar.com/post/inspection-report-36th-mississippi-infantry-regiment-1862.

Diary of Sergeant Thomas Jefferson Talbott, Co. G, 31st Ohio, https://sparedshared22.wordpress.com/2021/10/09/1861-64-the-civil-war-diaries-of-thomas-jefferson-talbot-co-g-31st-ovi/.

Index

Acknowledgments

OVER THE COURSE of 20 years of research I've met countless folks who shared my passion for telling the story of the Battle of Stones River. Many of them shared letters, diaries, and stories of their ancestors who fought there. They include: Linda Bohrer Anderson, Paul Barnett, Hunter Brooks, M. Chris Bryan, Bob Bundy, Steve Charles, Glenn Davis, David T. Dixon, Robert Grenier, Stan Hutson, Charles Koberg, Marilyn Levinson, Dick Mann, Joseph C. Meyer, Brad Quinlin, Anthony Rushing, Judd Shull, Ron Skellie, Rob Tong, and Bob Van Dorn. Special thanks to Paul Eilbes, Tom Parsons, Phil Spaugy, Gary Milligan, and Lee White for providing valuable feedback on the manuscript.

Thanks and a tip of the kepi to David A. Powell for not only writing the Foreword but for discussing the project with me throughout the process. Likewise, thanks to my publisher Theodore P. Savas for suggesting the project and championing it along the way and to his production supervisor Veronica Kane and all the staff of Savas Beatie. Kudos to Edward Alexander for the superb job he did in creating the maps that illustrate this volume, and to my editor Chris Howland for his work polishing the manuscript into its final form.

Larry Strayer and I have worked together on several book projects over the past few years and this one was no different. A hearty thanks for your advice, guidance, and friendship over the years.

I also owe a special thanks to Dennis Keesee for graciously permitting me to utilize the Stones River files of the late Rick Baumgartner. Rick's superb research skills uncovered many obscure sources, many of which were used in this manuscript.

Another historian who deserves special mention is Lanny K. Smith. Lanny's discovery and subsequent publication of the complete regimental and brigade reports from Jones Withers' Division within the Braxton Bragg Papers made a tremendous contribution to expanding our understanding of the battle. Lanny readily provided support for this project, and his own superb two-volume campaign study served as a constant resource.

This book couldn't have been written without the guidance and help of Jim Lewis, park historian at Stones River. Jim graciously supported this project from day one. His knowledge of the battlefield and the combatants is second to none, and his passion for ensuring that the Stones River story is told proved a constant source of inspiration.

Above all, thanks to my beloved wife Amy who has supported my writing endeavors with the patience of Job. Writing is very much a solitary activity and Amy's unremitting efforts to keep the household going while I disappeared into the 19th century made possible the book before you.

About the Author

Daniel A. Masters is a graduate of the University of Toledo with a BA in communications. Perhaps best known for his popular blog Dan Masters' Civil War Chronicles, his work focuses on the war in the Western Theater from the perspective of the men in the ranks. He is the author of many articles in various journals and magazines and ten books on the Civil War. His 2017 book *Sherman's Praetorian Guard: Civil War Letters of John McIntyre Lemmon, 72nd Ohio Volunteer Infantry* won a local history publication award from Bowling Green State University. His most recent work, a collaboration with Larry M. Strayer entitled *Echoes of Battle: Annals of Ohio's Soldiers in the Civil War*, was released in 2022.

Dan is a supply chain manager for a metals manufacturing company. He, his wife Amy, and five of his six children live and work in Perrysburg, Ohio.